Political Research
Methods and Practical Skills

Sandra Halperin and

Oliver Heath

OXFORD
UNIVERSITY PRESS

OXFORD
UNIVERSITY PRESS

Great Clarendon Street, Oxford OX2 6DP

Oxford University Press is a department of the University of Oxford.
It furthers the University's objective of excellence in research, scholarship,
and education by publishing worldwide in

Oxford New York

Auckland   Cape Town   Dar es Salaam   Hong Kong   Karachi
Kuala Lumpur   Madrid   Melbourne   Mexico City   Nairobi
New Delhi   Shanghai   Taipei   Toronto

With offices in

Argentina   Austria   Brazil   Chile   Czech Republic   France   Greece
Guatemala   Hungary   Italy   Japan   Poland   Portugal   Singapore
South Korea   Switzerland   Thailand   Turkey   Ukraine   Vietnam

Oxford is a registered trade mark of Oxford University Press in the
UK and in certain other countries

Published in the United States
by Oxford University Press Inc., New York

© Oxford University Press, 2012

The moral rights of the authors have been asserted
Database right Oxford University Press (maker)

British Library Cataloguing in Publication Data

Data available

Library of Congress Cataloging in Publication Data

Data available

Typeset by TNQ Books and Journals Pvt. Ltd.
Printed in Great Britain
on acid-free paper by
Ashford Colour Press Ltd., Gosport, Hampshire.

ISBN 978-0-19-955841-4

10 9 8 7 6 5

Political Research: Methods and Practical Skills

Contents

Detailed contents

Preface

Students devote a lot of time and effort to working on undergraduate, MA, and PhD theses, and there is a large number of texts available which can help with various aspects of this task. Some texts are devoted to the various debates and controversies relating to the philosophy of the social sciences, others to specific aspects of the research process, or to different research methods and approaches. But sometimes the various aspects of research that are the focus of different texts can seem disconnected, not only from each other, but from the process of pursuing knowledge about the political world. What we have tried to do is to incorporate all these different aspects of research within a single text and to discuss, step by step, how all of them relate to the research process. We begin with (1) an overview of key issues in the philosophy of social science (the problems of what we can know and how we can know it, in politics and in general). We then present (2) a 'nuts and bolts' or 'how to' of research design: *how to* find and formulate a research question; *how to* engage with literature to develop a rationale for both the question and the approach that the researcher proposes to take in answering it; *how to* construct a theoretical framework and define concepts that provide help in answering the question. Then, in the final part of the book, we examine (3) different methods of data collection and analysis that can be used to answer research questions, the principles and procedures that guide the employment of each, and the variety of considerations and decisions that researchers must confront when using different methods.

Our aim is to provide students with an understanding of the perspectives, assumptions, logic, and methods that contribute to political research, as well as an accessible step-by-step approach to designing and completing the different phases of a research project. We hope that this will help you to learn how to read analytically and think systematically about issues, problems, puzzles, and questions relating to the political world; and how to design and conduct independent research.

This book is based in large part on our experience of teaching at undergraduate and graduate levels. We would like to thank our students, whose questions, queries, and problems have informed many aspects of this book, and who have offered comments and criticisms on early drafts. We would also like to express our thanks to Patten Smith from Ipsos Mori, Rob Johns, David Sanders, Paul Whiteley, and the late Eric Tanenbaum from the University of Essex, George Gaskell, Sally Stares, and Jouni Kuha from the Methodology Institute at the London School of Economics, and our colleagues in the Department of Politics and International Relations at Royal Holloway, University of London. In particular, we would like to thank Didem Buhari Gulmez and Baris Gulmez for their help with the online resources for this text. Finally, we would like to thank our editor Kirsty Reade, and all the team at OUP who worked on this book, for their support, and the anonymous reviewers for their valuable feedback.

Political Research

This book has been written for undergraduate and graduate students of politics, with two main purposes in mind. The first is to provide you with the analytic skills and resources to evaluate research findings in political research. The second is to provide you with the practical skills you need to carry out your own independent research. Our aim is to offer practical advice on how to be critical and rigorous, both in how you evaluate the research of others and how you do your own research. These twin goals are important for getting the most out of your study of politics.

The study of politics can often be complicated, confusing, and controversial. In studying politics, we are frequently confronted with opposing ideas and arguments about a wide variety of different political phenomena. Is multiculturalism doomed to failure? Has globalisation undermined national sovereignty? Is there a crisis of democracy and participation? Is conflict an inevitable consequence of religious, ethnic, and social difference? The answers to these questions, whether provided by academics, politicians, or journalists can be inconsistent and contradictory. This can make it difficult to know what to believe or who to trust.

Making sense of conflicting arguments and interpretations can seem like a daunting, if not futile, task. But a solid training in research skills can help us to distinguish between arguments that are relatively sound and robust, and those that are unsubstantiated or rely on misleading or faulty inference. These skills are therefore crucial for helping us to make sense of the world. They help us to evaluate the merits of different arguments and the research of others, and to make our own arguments strong and convincing. Learning research skills is an active process that engages you in developing the ability to investigate the world around you and discover things for yourself. Pursuing research that enables you to find your own answers to questions, rather than just relying on what is said or has been written by others, can be exciting and challenging. It can lead you into new and surprising terrain.

These skills are at the core of political research. And understanding them and being able to use them transforms you from being a passive recipient of knowledge into an active protagonist. As students of politics, you are not only acquiring knowledge about the world of politics, you also are joined to a research community. Through engagement with research and writing in our field, and the independent thought and research you pursue in your own research projects, dissertations, or theses, you contribute to knowledge about the political world. But these skills also have wider relevance. They enable you to solve puzzles, find creative solutions to problems, and hone your analytical skills. Research skills can be applied to answering questions in many different fields, and are a genuinely transferable skill that you can use in whatever you do. We hope that through this book, and by engaging seriously with the principles and practices of political research, you will not only be more informed or knowledgeable about political affairs, but also become engaged, yourself, in a search for solutions to important problems of a public, political, or collective nature.

This book then, is about how, through systematic inquiry, to ask and answer questions about the political world. The ways in which we do this, the methods or methodology that we use, allow us to connect abstract ideas and concepts about the way the political world works to evidence of what actually happens. Methods for pursuing systematic inquiry also encompass the system of values, beliefs, principles, and rules that guide analysis within a given discipline. Perhaps because of this association of methods with specific traditions of inquiry, students often view the study of methods as a kind of imposition—a set of rules and constraints designed to mould research into conformity with the conventions of a given field of study. This is unfortunate and misleading. Methods are not constraining: they are enabling. They are embedded in the ways that we normally think and reason about things. Research methods build upon our natural ability to think and reason; they enable us to hone the skills we already possess into instruments of analysis, so that you are better able to evaluate an argument and make one of our own; to figure out what makes the most sense among competing accounts or interpretations, and to make up our mind about what is true and what isn't.

Research methods are essentially about how to make arguments. All of us already *know* how to make arguments. We make them every day. We come up with well-reasoned arguments why others should believe what we believe, or why our way of doing something is better than other ways. And to make our arguments convincing we sometimes illustrate them with examples. What social science research requires you to do is to apply the skills of reasoning and argumentation you use in everyday life to larger questions of political life, and to hone these skills by thinking about what sort of evidence or examples you need to really support your argument. We have all learned to be wary about the use of anecdotal evidence. The friend of a friend who saw or heard something is not a reliable source, and we will therefore often discount what people say if it is based on unreliable evidence. Research skills simply build on these intuitive everyday skills that we employ all the time. They are an organic and creative aspect of thinking and problem-solving. Moreover, they are intrinsically linked to the substantive concerns of our field. In our view, devising a research strategy that enables you to investigate or demonstrate an argument, hunch, or hypothesis is one of the really creative aspects of doing political research. It is the aspect of research that perhaps provides the greatest scope for independent thinking and creativity. Methods help you to build upon or synthesize the work of others, to connect up the work of different writers and thinkers with each other, or link together separate areas of study or studies of a single issue, in a way that generates fresh insights, that expands, extends, refines our knowledge of a political problem, puzzle, issue, system, process, structure, issue, or event.

Our approach to political research consists of three basic positions. *First*, we encourage pluralism in methodological approaches to political research. Politics is a multi-method field of study. The authors of this text reflect this pluralism. One of us pursues qualitative and exploratory historical-comparative work; the other quantitative and comparative work. *Second*, we believe that research should be *problem*-driven, rather than method-driven. A research design or method of data collection only makes sense in so far as it is a way of investigating some problem. The value of any design or method can only be determined in relation to a research question; and the choice of which to use should always be driven by the research question that is to be investigated (see, for background and debate on this issue, Laitin 2005 and Shapiro 2005a, 2005b). *Third*, we believe research should have relevance to important political questions and policy issues. For research to be worth pursuing, we have to be interested in the question, and interested in the answer.

Issues in political research

This book, then, is concerned with how to formulate questions that are significant and how to develop meaningful and persuasive answers to them. A *significant question* is one that is 'directly relevant to solving real-world problems and to furthering the goals of a specific scientific literature' (King, Keohane, and Verba 1994: 18). There is not always agreement about what constitutes a *meaningful and plausible answer* to a research question. But we can all agree that our answers should help to generate valid and reliable knowledge about the questions that they address. This requires that answers be developed through a process of inquiry that, at every step, is both self-aware and critical, and that researchers make clear and transparent how their conclusions were reached.

Which research practices and methods enable political researchers to offer credible answers to important questions? What constitutes good research? These questions have generated considerable debate.

Agreement on these questions is difficult to achieve, in part, because politics is such a diverse discipline. It struggles to even agree on a name. The study of politics is carried on in Departments of Politics, or Government, or Political Science or, in the U.K., Departments of Politics and International Relations, to name just a few. The array of names reflects a variety of views about what constitutes the discipline. The growing tendency for sub-fields of political research, such as International Relations, to become institutionalised as almost separate fields of inquiry, further fragments the field of study. Other divisions exist within the discipline, as well. There is a tendency to define empirical issues and the study of the 'real world', and normative issues and the study of political 'ideas and values', as involving separate research areas and traditions of inquiry. And even among those who study 'real world' problems scholars are divided about what constitutes empirical knowledge, and how this knowledge can be arrived at. Although these divisions are the source of lively debate and disagreement within the discipline, they should not be overstated. Ultimately many of these oppositions are not as profound as they are often presented as being, and there is still more that unites the discipline than divides it. Below we discuss some of these controversies in more detail.

Politics and International Relations

In recent years there has been a tendency for Politics and International Relations to become regarded as separate areas of study, with different professional associations, journals, degree schemes, and even, in some universities, different departments. The establishment of these sub-fields institutionalized a division of the political world into processes and structures that are internal to states (local, domestic, or national politics), and those that are external to them (interactions and relations among states). However, like many in our field, we have come to question whether, within the general study of politics, it is analytically productive to treat domestic and international processes, systems, events, and issues as definably separate. Increasingly, scholars in our field are recognizing that this analytical division tends to obfuscate fundamental interdependencies of interstate and domestic systems. Politics and International Relations are both concerned with the nature of states, and with political systems, development, conflict, ideology, social movements, geopolitics, nationalism, political participation, and political philosophy. Moreover, all aspects of politics are affected by governments, public administration and public policy, elections and voter behaviour, political parties, political culture, mass publics and electorates, interest groups, and public opinion; as well as by the interactions among states, the workings of the international system as a whole, international political economy, international organizations, and international law.

Researchers have increasingly come to appreciate the extent to which political processes operate across levels or at multiple scales. Relations across levels or political scales encompass sets of interactions that have hitherto not been the central focus of conventional approaches: the interaction of societies, not just with their own governments, but with other societies and governments, and with international organizations. International Relations theorists recognize that states have to answer to groups within their societies and that consequently a consideration of domestic relations is necessary to an explanation of outcomes in international relations. With a growing awareness of structural linkages between societies and the multiple channels that connect societies has come a tendency not to assume the sufficiency of any one scale of analysis to an understanding of political outcomes. Consequently, this book addresses the study of Politics and of International Relations as a single area of inquiry; and we address ourselves, as well, to students of all sub-fields of political research, including Political Theory (classical political philosophy and contemporary theoretical perspectives), Public Policy (the process by which governments make public decisions), Public Administration (the ways that government polices are implemented), and Public Law (the role of law and courts in the political process).

Empirical vs normative research

Political research has also tended to define a sharp distinction between 'empirical' and 'normative' research and theory. Empirical research addresses events and political phenomena that we observe in the real world; questions about what *is* (empirical questions); normative—or theoretical—research addresses ideas and thoughts and questions about what should or *ought to be* (normative questions). However, this distinction between the study of events and the study of ideas is also something of a false distinction. Empirical research is always grounded in ideas and theories; normative research is never entirely divorced from reality either, and embodies 'empirical' claims about the character of human and natural realities (Smith 2004: 86).

As John Gerring and Joshua Yesnowitz argue, empirical study of social phenomena 'is meaningless if it has no normative import; and it is misleading if its normative content is present, but ambiguous', if we don't know how it matters (Gerring and Yesnowitz 2006: 104). Indeed, the justification for why a research question is interesting or relevant or meaningful is essentially a normative one. But at the same time normative arguments that propose or justify one value system over another will lack relevance if they make no attempt to relate to the facts of actual practice or public life. As Steve Buckler (2010: 156) points out, normative theory is concerned both about the world as it is and as we might think it ought to be. In sum, good social science is both empirically grounded 'and relevant to human concerns' (Gerring and Yesnowitz 2006: 133). Normative theorizing 'must deal in facts' and empirical work 'must deal in values' (2006: 108). While we must be sensitive to the difference between normative and empirical questions and statements, we must also recognize that they are not independent of each other, and that there are costs in keeping them separate.

Recent discussions about the theory of deliberative democracy illustrate these points. Early research on the subject by scholars like Jürgen Habermas and John Rawls debated the normative justifications of deliberative democracy, interpretations and necessary components of the theory, but failed to take account of the sheer complexity of contemporary societies (Elstub, 2010: 291). However, recent research has tried to engage more seriously with the empirical realities of this social complexity (see Baber and Bartlett, 2005, O'Flynn 2006, Parkinson 2006). As Chapter 3 will endeavour to show, theory and evidence inform each other. Seeing either one as entirely divorced from the other generates either fantasy or mindless empiricism.

Questions of method continually arise in so-called normative research, and these are sometimes more analogous to those in empirical work than is always recognized. Normative theorists are concerned to convince others by means of drawing logical inferences and presenting the logical development of their ideas. They want to persuade others that the conclusions they reach are reasonable and plausible. An argument for any conclusion needs to be evaluated in the light of the kind and nature of its premises, the strength of the inferential links to the conclusion from these premises, and its possible criticisms or refutations. Does it make unrealistic assumptions about human behaviour; and if so, on what basis can this be established? The association of theory and the empirical world is continually being tested, and investigation into the relationship between ideas and practice is to be encouraged rather than resisted. The link between theory and evidence can be conceived in different ways. Empirical researchers may use theory in order to try and understand or explain or describe social and political reality; whereas normative researchers may use theory to challenge political reality (Thompson 2008). But in either case it is important to describe the nature of reality in the first place in order to be able to challenge it or explain it, or do both.

Positivism vs interpretivism

However, studying 'political reality' is far from straightforward, and there is substantial disagreement about how the empirical world can be analysed. Debates over methodology and the respective strengths of different methods are often conflated with issues relating to different ontological and epistemological positions within the discipline. These positions—which we return to later—are about the nature of knowledge in the social world, and what is knowable. However, we argue that many of these different positions are also overstated when it comes to analysing the social world in practice.

Many researchers have pointed to the tendency to cast positivist and interpretivist approaches as 'two grand traditions in social science epistemology' and to exaggerate the differences between them (Pollins 2007: 93). *Positivism* maintains that scientific knowledge of the social world is limited to what can be observed; and that we can explain and predict social phenomena by discovering empirical regularities, formulating law-like generalizations, and establishing causal relationships. Interpretivism maintains that knowledge of the social world can be gained through interpreting the meanings which give people reasons for acting, and that we can, in this way, *understand* human behaviour, but we cannot *explain* or *predict* it on the basis of law-like generalizations and establishing the existence of causal relationships.

Positivism and interpretivism have different ontological and epistemological commitments—different views with regard to the nature of the social world and how we can have knowledge of it. However, researchers working in both traditions generally follow the same methodological conventions; and while researchers may be interested in different types of questions, 'practical investigation of these questions often leads them to similar methodological tasks' (Finnemore and Sikkink 2001: 395). Both are concerned to show the relations between premises and conclusions, and indicate the nature of the relations between them. Both recognize that some standard of validation must be established for the sources of evidence used. By and large all researchers, whatever their methodological and philosophical predispositions, share similar goals: to explain and understand, to engage with evidence and use it well, to distinguish between those claims about the world that are fanciful and that are robust.

Our intention is not to privilege any one way of doing research over any other. Our view is that the method you use in conducting research will always depend on the answers to the following questions:

1. What research question are you trying to answer?
2. What evidence or data do you need to answer the question?
3. How are you going to analyse the data; and what are the practical steps needed to obtain and record them?

Our view is that any research will be clearer, more accessible, more persuasive, and more likely to achieve its aims, if the researcher articulates a central question/puzzle/problem, provides a rationale for it, reviews the relevant literature, advances a hypothesis or argument, constructs a theoretical framework, defines concepts, variables, and relationships, and designs a 'test' of the hypothesis or argument. The distinctions drawn among and between qualitative and quantitative methods (discussed below), empirical and normative research, and positivism and interpretivism are important for purposes of reflection on how to go about finding credible answers to important questions. But, these distinctions are ultimately sterile. Research is either systematic, self-aware, clear, and transparent, or it isn't. Irrespective of what type of research you pursue and what methods you use, your research will be judged according to some generally accepted standard of research practice.

There is one last distinction that we wish to address: the distinction between quantitative and qualitative political research.

Quantitative vs qualitative research

To reap the rewards of methodological diversity, while ensuring that research is more problem-driven and relevant to important political questions, requires that we develop a notion of some shared standard, one that can be applied to a variety of different questions and diverse research traditions. The search for a unified set of standards, or a common definition of what constitutes good research, has tended to become bogged down in a debate about whether and how it is possible to bridge the divide between quantitative and qualitative methods and approaches. Quantitative research tends to be based on the statistical analysis of carefully coded information for many cases or observations (in whatever way those observations are defined). Qualitative research tends to be based on the discursive analysis of more loosely coded information for just a few cases. Some even go as far as to say that quantitative and qualitative traditions are so ontologically distinct as to be incommensurable. This position is based on a belief in a hard-and-fast connection between quantitative methods and the tenets of positivism, on one hand, and qualitative methods and interpretivism, on the other. We think that this represents a false dichotomy. Different methodological positions are not tied to any epistemological or ontological position. Nor are they tied to any particular type of research question or research design.

Others suggest that some methods are inherently better than others. This position has frequently been attributed to the book *Designing Social Inquiry* (1994), by Gary King, Robert Keohane, and Sidney Verba. *Designing Social Inquiry* began an important debate about methodology, and the book continues to occupy a central place in debates about methods. Its aim, according to its authors, is to bridge the quantitative/qualitative divide (King et al. 1994: 4). Its primary focus is causal inference in both qualitative and quantitative research and, more generally, scientific methods and elements of scientific research. The authors argue that 'All good research can be understood—indeed is best understood—to derive from the same underlying logic of inference. Both quantitative and qualitative research can be systematic and scientific', provided each submits to 'the rules of scientific inference—rules that are sometimes more clearly stated in the style of quantitative research' (1994: 4–5, 6).

The authors argue that quantitative and qualitative research are substantively the same and only differ in the types of techniques the employ; that 'the differences between the quantitative and qualitative traditions are only stylistic and are methodologically and substantively unimportant' (1994: 4). Both are seeking scientific insights into social phenomena, and both require rigorous scientific method to ensure such results. But critics of *Designing Social Inquiry* argue that, in offering an abstract formal model of scientific methods and elements of scientific research that will be applicable to all sorts of research, the authors develop a 'quantitative template for qualitative research'—one that presupposes the superiority of the former over the latter (Brady and Collier 2004: 3), and that imposes positivist concepts like hypothesis testing on qualitative researchers.

While we think some of these objections have been overstated, we do not agree that some methods are better than others. However, there are certainly better ways to carry out a method. It is therefore less important *which* method is used, than *how* the method is used. Our concern with all the methods we discuss is with their specific procedures, techniques, or strategies for collecting and analysing data or information necessary to demonstrate an argument. The link between theory and evidence is central to sound research, to how we actually go about collecting and analysing the information or evidence that we need to support (or just as importantly undermine) an argument. And while it is true that there is no such thing as a correct method, there is such a thing as convincing evidence and analysis, and this is far more important. Evidence can be gathered and interpreted and analysed in a variety of different ways. There are good ways and bad ways of doing research using each of the methods we discuss. No method is perfect. All have their strengths and weaknesses, and it is important to be aware of what they are.

The research process

There are a large number of texts available that address themselves to research methods, to specific aspects of the research process, and to debates relating to social science methodology: books on theories and methods, on research design, and on political analysis.

This book is also concerned with research design, analysis, and theory (though it does not devote chapters to specific theoretical approaches, such as rational choice or feminism). However, it is primarily designed as an introduction to the *research process*. The aim of this book is to introduce (1) key issues in the philosophy of social science that bear on the choices researchers must make in pursuing research; (2) a step-by-step delineation of the process of asking and answering a research question—formulating a question, reviewing the relevant literature, advancing a hypothesis or argument, constructing a theoretical framework; defining concepts, variables, and relationships; and designing a 'test' of the hypothesis or argument; and (3) the array of methods used in political research and how scholars utilize these methods to answer questions about political phenomena.

Before elaborating on these aims, we wish to raise a point about the array of methods we introduce in Part III of the book. As we noted earlier in this chapter, we are methodological pluralists. We are enthusiastic about the diversity of the field and about new methods of inquiry that are developing. But we do not cover every method and approach in this book. We doubt that it is possible to adequately survey, in a single volume, the vast array of methods and approaches available to political researchers; and we do not attempt to do so. Instead, we provide an in-depth discussion of a range of widely used methods that we think can provide a base on which to build greater expertise and explore more specialized techniques; and we signal, where appropriate, how these can be further developed in more specific ways. Our Guide to Further Reading in each chapter directs readers both to specialist texts on the subject matter of the chapter and to more specialized adaptations of the approach discussed. We expect that students, with the help of the further reading for each chapter, will be able to take these approaches in a variety of further directions.

This book is concerned with the process and practice of political research: the principles and procedures that guide scholars as they conduct research, the beliefs and assumptions they hold, the kinds of questions they ask, and the variety of decisions that they must make. Its aim is to answer two questions:

1. How does one formulate research questions?
2. Once these questions are formulated, how does one design and carry out research in order to answer them?

To address these questions we focus on three broad components of the research process: (1) key issues in the philosophy of social science (the problems of what we can know and how we can know it); (2) the 'nuts and bolts' or the 'how to' of research: *how to* find and formulate a research question; *how to* develop, through an engagement with the relevant literatures, an argument or answer that responds to your question; and (3) the specific methodological procedures and techniques utilized in carrying out a given research project. Below, we provide an overview of each of these components.

Part I: Philosophy of Social Science: Knowledge and Knowing in Social Science Research

Methodology refers to the conduct of inquiry. Among other things, this involves reflection upon the system of values, beliefs, principles and rules that guide analysis within a given discipline. Questions of ontology and epistemology—questions about the complexities and ambiguities of knowing and gaining knowledge of the social world—are a core part of this reflection. These questions are the focus of key debates within the philosophy of social science and, in our field, of on-going debates about scientific practice, forms of knowledge, age the world of politics.

Why, you might ask, should these philosophical issues and controversies concern political researchers? To start with, it is important to understand that all social scientific theorising adopts a position with respect to the issues that these controversies involve. If you are unaware of them, you will not fully understand the implicit assumptions and implications, either of what others are arguing, or of what you yourself are arguing. We have said that research methods build on and develop your own natural abilities to think and solve problems. In the same way, an understanding of philosophical positions concerning knowledge helps to make explicit and to develop the philosophical assumptions about, and approach to, knowledge that you already employ in your everyday life.

Furthermore, if we see the purpose of scholarly research as the generation of valid and reliable knowledge, and view truth as a central characteristic of valid knowledge, then we need to adopt and defend assumptions about the nature of truth and procedures for discovering the truth. In this way, philosophical presuppositions about 'reality' are intrinsically linked to the substantive issues that are central to inquiry in our field. Researchers cannot contribute to knowledge about something unless they adopt and defend a view of what is knowable about the social world and what sorts of things different methods enable us to know.

Philosophy of social science debates have implications for all areas of research; and, whether or not researchers follow ongoing debates in the philosophy of social science, they tend, either implicitly or explicitly, to reflect one or another of the different answers and positions that these debates have generated. All of us have stored in our minds a 'worldview' which provides the basis for the opinions we form about what goes on around us. This is constituted, most likely in large part, by 'an accumulation of the ideas and prejudices of others' (Kahane and Cavender 2006: 19). If the unexamined life is not worth living, as Socrates is said to have claimed, then it perhaps follows that unexamined beliefs are probably not worth holding. Learning how to systematically investigate ideas we hold about the world enables us to analytically engage with political affairs, rather than to remain passive consumers of the output of politicians, political analysts, and the news media. Reality is constantly being defined for us. The ability to identify the underlying structure of assumptions or the implicit theory which shapes a given account of reality, whether presented by scholars, politicians, or journalists, allows us to become more active analysts of contemporary politics.

In sum: understanding the terms of the major debates in the philosophy of social science, and sensitivity to their implications, is an important part of producing good research. What you presume is knowable about the social world will bear on the strategic choices you will need to make all through the process of research.

Each of the chapters in Section I of the book is devoted to a key controversy in the philosophy of social science:

1. What is knowledge? How do we know? (Chapter 2)
2. Can the pursuit of knowledge be 'objective'? (Chapter 3)
3. What is the nature of the social world? (Chapter 4)

The first controversy involves questions about what sort of knowledge we can gain about the social world. Is it the same sort of knowledge that scientists are able to obtain about the natural world? Or are the forms of knowledge concerning the social world and the natural world necessarily different? In **Chapter 2** we address three different approaches to answering these questions and their implications for conducting political research.

The first approach is 'positivism'. 'Positivism' is usually defined by the following three tenets: (1) scientific methods (i.e. the testing of hypotheses derived from pre-existing theories) may be applied to the study of social life; (2) knowledge is only generated through observation (empiricism); and (3) facts and values are distinct, thus making objective inquiry possible (Snape and Spencer 2006). A second approach, 'interpretivism' maintains that the social world is fundamentally different from the world of natural phenomena, and that it does not exist independently of our interpretation of it. The task of social science, then, is fundamentally different from that of natural science, because the objects of the social sciences' are different from those found in the natural world. The third approach, scientific realism maintains that knowledge is not limited to what can be observed but also includes theoretical entities (unobservable elements of social life).

Positivism maintains that it is possible to define a distinction between facts and values, and for us to acquire value-neutral, objective knowledge about social phenomena. Critics argue that knowledge produced by social-scientific research is not value-neutral, but is shaped by a variety of factors, including existing scientific theory, politics, and power relations, cultural beliefs and meanings, and the researcher's own motivations and values. Can knowledge produced through the study of the social world be 'objective'? We consider this question in **Chapter 3**.

Finally, we take up the issue of social ontology (**Chapter 4**): What is the 'social'? What is the social world made of? What is the basic unit of analysis in the study of the social world? Two contrasting views about the nature of the social world have dominated discussion of this question: 'individualism' and 'holism'. Methodological individualism argues that individuals are the basic units of society and that social life must be explained in terms of the actions of individuals. Methodological holism treats 'social wholes' as the basic unit of analysis, understood as distinct from, and not directly explicable in terms of, its parts.

In political research, discussion of this issue is carried on within a debate about the relationship between agents (the actors) and the structures which shape, give meaning to, or make possible their actions. How can we understand the relationship between individual agents and the social structures within which they act? Are societies reducible to the individuals who make them up? Or is society more than the sum of its individual members? What level of description—the individual or the collective—is necessary for explanation of social phenomena? The issues raised in each of these debates have implications for how you pursue research and develop explanations of political phenomena.

Part II: How to Do Research: An Overview

A second component of the research process involves the practicalities of doing research: the basic nuts and bolts of the research enterprise. By this we mean the steps involved in developing a plan for pursuing research on a topic. This involves developing a researchable question, locating applicable theory and literature, formulating testable hypotheses, and clarifying concepts and developing empirical indicators. The chapters in Part II of the book introduce basic elements of research: a research question, what requirements it must meet, and where to find and how to formulate one (**Chapter 5**); how to construct an argument, hypothesis, or theory that answers it (**Chapter 6**); and how to design research to test, investigate, or demonstrate it (**Chapter 7**).

Most political research originates from some general question or problem that arises, either from the events, issues, or processes we observe in the world around us, or from the theories and frameworks that our field has developed in order to understand them. But the research *process* only begins with the conversion of this general question or problem into a well-formulated, clearly focused, research question. *Step 1* of the research process involves finding and formulating a researchable question, and locating applicable theory and literature (**Chapter 5**). We discuss why research should be guided by well-formulated research questions, the role of the 'literature review' in providing both the inspiration and rationale for them, and the different types of questions scholars ask. We discuss the basic requirements of a research question and how to go about meeting them. We argue that a research question is one that (1) has significance for a topic or issue relating to the subject matter of our field, (2) is researchable (it can be answered through conducting research), and (3) has not yet been answered definitively.

Irrespective of the particular way researchers choose to structure their research, a carefully formulated research question will ensure that their research has a clear purpose with clear goals. A research question makes the research task specific; so that, rather than trying to gather all the information you can find on a topic, you direct your attention to just the information that addresses the question and helps you to develop an argument in answer to it. When you have a well-formulated research question, you can make decisions about what information should be included or excluded, what data you will need to collect, what to observe, or what to ask your interviewees.

To formulate a research question you need to be clear about what you want to know. We identify different types of questions and what each type commits you to doing; and also the logical fallacies that sometimes find their way into the statement of a question and lead to false conclusions. The third requirement of a research question requires that you show that others who have addressed it have failed in some way to provide a definitive answer to it. The literature review performs this function. It identifies what (range of) answers are found in the existing literature relating to the question and it develops an argument about what needs to be done in order to provide a better answer to the question than those that currently exist.

Once you have formulated a research question, you will be ready to move on to *Step 2* of the research process: how to answer it. We discuss the basic components of an answer to a research question, what requirements it must meet, and where to find and how to formulate one (**Chapter 6**). To get you started we offer a broad template. This is meant to serve as a starting point—a set of considerations to be revised to fit with the question and aims that animate a particular project. The template shows a research process that is structured in an idealized linear fashion. But we emphasize that the process as it actually unfolds is often not linear at all. The real process is often circuitous. Most researchers move back and forth between theory and evidence—between theorizing something that is the focus of their research, and mucking about in the 'dust of detail' (learning more about the specific facts of the case or question or issue, or the observations of other scholars that we treat as facts). As Philip Shively observes, 'one of the better-kept secrets' in our field, is that good researchers usually do not '"frame hypotheses" in any formal sense before they start to work, though they may have some operational hunches about what they expect to find. . . . They play with data, immerse themselves in what other people have written, argue with colleagues, and think' (Shively 1989: 25). In sum, we describe the research process as consisting of a set of components or series of steps but, in practice, the process of research does not unfold in the sort of linear fashion that this suggests. We rethink our views as a result of learning from the research process itself in ways that can feedback to our previous choices and lead us to revise them. So, what the template we present really shows is, not the *process* of research, but its ultimate *presentation*.

We organize our discussion of the various considerations and tasks involved in developing an answer to a research question around three basic requirements. The *first* requirement is that the answer be appropriate to the type of question that is being asked. Different types of questions demand different types of answers. For instance, *descriptive* questions will require that you describe the characteristics of something, or model how it works or behaves. *Explanatory* questions will require that you explain what factors or conditions are causally connected to a known outcome. *Normative* questions may require that you adjudicate among different understandings of how something should be, or what should or ought to be done, by considering the arguments of others, and submitting well-reasoned arguments for one's own.

The *second* requirement of an answer to a research question is that it makes a contribution to knowledge. Social science research is expected to address a question whose answer will contribute to collective knowledge in a particular field of study; so in developing an answer to a research question one must ask oneself: Why should we care about this answer or argument? In other words, your answer must matter. It is not enough to say that the question has not been asked before. After all, one very good reason why a question has not been asked is because no one cares about the answer. So you must always make a case for why the question is relevant and important.

The third requirement is that an answer must be clearly and fully specified with regard to the factors or variables you think must be taken into consideration in order to answer your question, and how you think these factors or variables are related to each other. For all types of research, we think it is useful to formulate a 'working hypothesis'—an operational hunch about what you expect to find. Initially, what argument motivates the research? What findings might be expected? By articulating in advance the contours and logic of the investigation, a hypothesis helps to guide research. Developing a hypothesis encourages you to be very precise about how your answer relates to those that others have offered to your question, and how your answer relates to what evidence you would expect to see in the real world. The term 'hypothesis' is often treated as applicable to only quantitative research and to a specific prediction about the nature and direction of the relationship between two variables. But we use the term 'hypothesis' to mean 'a hunch, assumption, suspicion, assertion, or idea about a phenomenon, relationship, or situation', with which research begins and which becomes the basis of inquiry (Kumar 2005: 74). The key thing is that the hypothesis should be empirically or logically verifiable (or not). That is, it should be falsifiable with evidence. A hypothesis which is not falsifiable is really just a tautology, and so is not going to tell us anything interesting about the political world.

If we are interested in the question we ask and the hypothesis we test, then we should also be interested in the answer we get; and that means that an answer which discredits our hypothesis is just as valid as one that confirms it. There is sometimes a tendency to think that research is only worthwhile if it produces results that support our hypothesis, but null findings can be interesting too. For example, the finding that the level of ethnic diversity within a country *does not* influence the level of democracy within a country has important implications for our understanding of what impedes democracy (and what does not).

Hypotheses can either be tested with evidence (**confirmatory research**), or operate as a guide to a process of discovery (**exploratory research**). Exploratory research begins with a question and perhaps a basic proposition, probes its plausibility against various types of data, and eventually generates a more concrete hypothesis, which can be more widely and rigorously tested.

Once you have a hunch or argument about the answer to your research question, you then need to develop a strategy for providing a convincing 'test' or demonstration of it. This is *Step 3* of the research process: how to demonstrate the validity of your answer (**Chapter 7**). The plan you develop to do this is what we call a **research design**. It sets out a plan for research, including what observations to make and how to make them. It is informed by and fulfills a logical structure of inquiry; and it specifies the sort of test or evidence that will convincingly confirm or disconfirm a hypothesis; the observations you need in order to demonstrate the relationships stated by your hypothesis, and how you will go about making them; the data relevant to demonstrating these relationships, and how and where you will collect them. The type of research design you use and the kind of information you collect, the sources of data and the data-collection procedures you choose, should be based on what will provide a convincing test, demonstration, or investigation of your argument or hypothesis.

Part III: How to Do Research in Practice

The third part of the book is devoted to examining the principles of different methods in political research, and how to use them in practice. These methods enable us to put a research design into practice and to carry out the research and analysis needed to answer a research question. Methodological principles are concerned with *how we obtain knowledge* about the political world; with the specific procedures or techniques that we use to tell us something about the world when we carry out research. Research methods are in a sense the tools of analysis. And, as with any tool, it is important to know how to use it in order to complete a task.

In Part III of the book we focus on different strategies for collecting and analysing evidence in order to test or develop specific hypotheses. In particular, we focus on the ways in which data is collected and the ways in which it can then be analysed. These are two distinct and crucial aspects of the research process. Failure to devote sufficient care and attention to either will lead to research results which are untrustworthy and unreliable, meaning that we may reject hypotheses that are actually true or accept hypotheses that are actually false. Obviously, we want to avoid the possibility of either of these outcomes occurring as far as possible. If we reject or accept a hypothesis, we want it to be because we have collected convincing data and analysed the data properly.

Research methods all involve two important components: **data collection** and **data analysis**. And it pays to think of these separately. We can therefore think about different methods of data collection, such as collecting information through the use of experiments (**Chapter** 8), comparative research (**Chapter** 9), surveys (**Chapter** 10), interviews or focus groups (**Chapter** 11), participant observation (**Chapter** 12), or collecting archival data or documentary records such as speeches, policy documents, or media reports (**Chapter** 13). The type of evidence that we use is important. But more important is how we collect and code the evidence in preparation for analysis. This relates to the issues of validity and reliability. We want the data we have collected to be good and solid and reliable and robust. It is what separates us from those who rely on rumour and hearsay and anecdotes. Data collection needs to be systematic, not haphazard. We must have guiding principles to ensure that the data we collect is of good quality.

Having obtained this data or information, we can then think about how to go about analysing it. It is common to distinguish between **quantitative** and **qualitative** approaches to analysing data. Quantitative analysis tends to rely on statistical techniques, which we discuss in detail in **Chapters 14, 15,** and **16**. But there is a wide variety of more qualitative analysis techniques that we can consider. It is worth remembering that this distinction between qualitative and quantitative analysis primarily refers to different methods of analysis rather than different methods of data collection. And although there is some overlap between how we collect evidence and how we analyse it, there is also a lot of diversity, and similar types of data can be analysed in different ways. In fact data from all the types of data collection methods that we discuss can be analysed using either quantitative or qualitative techniques. When we talk about 'quantitative data', we are only talking about evidence that has been coded in preparation for quantitative analysis. This involves coding and categorizing the data with numerical values. The actual form of the evidence can be almost anything. It is therefore important to be familiar with both qualitative and quantitative approaches, since failure to understand or engage with one approach is likely to cut you off from a lot of relevant research that is carried out on your topic of interest.

Much is often made about the relative strengths and weaknesses of different methods, in particular between quantitative and qualitative approaches. It is frequently asserted that quantitative research may be good at making generalizations, but is a blunt instrument for investigating hard-to-define concepts, such as power, globalization, and democracy or difficult-to-observe phenomena, like money laundering, criminal or anti-social behaviour, corruption, and terrorism. By contrast, one of the key strengths of qualitative research is often thought to be its ability to investigate these hard-to-define concepts and hard-to-reach populations. However, whereas qualitative research might be able to go into a lot of detail, there is sometimes a nagging suspicion that its findings might not have wider relevance to contexts outside the immediate vicinity of where the research was conducted. While there might be an element of truth in this, these strengths and weaknesses should not be overstated or viewed as inherent in the different methodological approaches.

These strengths and weaknesses are often presented in terms of a trade-off between description and detail (validity of measurement) and explanation and generalization (validity of inference). We reject this idea. The ability to make generalizations is not just the preserve of quantitative approaches, but about something more fundamental to the research process. It is about being able to rule out and control for theoretically plausible alternatives. All methods of analysis should take this issue seriously, otherwise we may end up with spurious findings. The only way to address this is by considering theoretically important variables, and the only way we can do this is by considering enough cases to make it manageable. For example, the concern that the findings from a *small N* (where *N* refers to *number*, as in number of cases or countries, etc.) study may not be applied more generally are to do with concern over omitted variable bias, which can cause spurious relationships. This we discuss in detail in **Chapter 9**.

To be able to estimate the effect of many variables you need lots of cases to see if your argument still holds up when you consider different factors across different contexts. Quantitative methods provide an efficient way of doing this. But qualitative methods can do it as well. And indeed they often do it, as we discuss throughout the book. But it is generally a slower and less systematic process which takes a great deal of time. Studies are repeated, findings are applied to new contexts, and, as this is done, theories or hypotheses are indirectly tested on a wide range of cases. But there is nothing to stop it being done quicker and more systematically. It would just involve more money. The difference is not one of method but of time and costs. There is no methodological reason to stop you repeating qualitative studies; you can do twenty in-depth interviews (see **Chapter 11**); but why stop at twenty? If time and resources are no obstacle, then it is possible to do 2000 interviews. And why not collect multiple ethnographies? Recent research is attempting to do just this, through collaborative comparative ethnographies that try and develop a firmer basis for wider inferences (see Gillespie, Gow, and Hoskins 2007, Gillespie and O'Loughlin 2009).

By contrast, it is often said that qualitative methods can provide more valid measures of political phenomena. They are better able to measure and study difficult-to-define political phenomena, whereas quantitative methods are too blunt and reduce complicated concepts down to numbers which can never capture the full meaning of what is being investigated. But this is not the case either. There may be an issue to do with the extent to which extant survey data can be used to answer new questions, but the answer to this is to design new surveys or collect new data and devote additional resources to the problem. The difference is one not of method, but of resources. It is possible to measure anything in a reliable and valid way with quantitative methods of data collection, but to do so if the object of investigation is difficult to observe or measure can be very costly. Studies using qualitative methods are often relatively cheap.

Our position is that, irrespective of whether a quantitative or qualitative approach is employed, the questions, decisions, concerns, and procedures, with which researchers have to deal in designing research, are similar. The main considerations are always to do with sampling and measurement. Whether we are doing quantitative research or qualitative research, we want the answers we arrive at to be meaningful and say something about the world. We don't want them to just reflect the way in which we have chosen to measure political phenomena or selected particular cases to analyse.

In discussing these different forms of data collection and data analysis, we draw on some of the most prominent approaches in political research. We do not discuss every method used in political research, but a selection of prominently used ones that can serve to introduce themes and research protocols generalizable to other methods.

We start this section with an introduction to the principles of experimental research in **Chapter 8**. The experimental approach is widely considered to be the most 'scientific' research design. Through the use of **control groups** and **experimental groups** the researcher is able to control what stimuli—or interventions—different subjects are exposed to, and then examine what impact this exposure has on the political outcome variable of interest. Controlled experiments of this type are very useful for testing causal hypotheses. Broadly speaking, there are three main experimental designs. There are **laboratory** experiments (where subjects are taken to a common location), **field** experiments (which take place in real-world settings), and **natural** experiments (which in a sense occur naturally, in so far as the researcher is not active in the data-gathering process). Despite the scientific potential of experimental research, the approach is not widely used in the study of politics. However, this is beginning to change. Experiments are now one of the fastest growing fields of political inquiry. We discuss some of the obstacles that have been traditionally associated with doing experiments in political research, and discuss the potential for developing and expanding its application.

In **Chapter 9** we focus on comparative research. Comparative research represents one of the largest fields of political inquiry, and to a certain extent is used by all investigators who engage in empirical research. The comparative method (or approach or design, as it is sometimes termed) actually involves a number of different methods and can be used in conjunction with any method of data collection. The logic of comparison is based on how many countries (or cases) are compared, and how the cases for analysis are selected. Both aspects of case selection are very important, as the cases you look at can affect the answers you get to any particular research question (as Barbara Geddes, 1990, has pointed out). Broadly speaking, there are three main approaches. There are **large-N** studies (involving the analysis of many cases), **small-N** studies (involving the analysis of a small number of cases, typically 2, 3, 4, but with no real upper limit), and **single-N** studies (otherwise known as **case studies**). Virtually all political research falls into one of these three sub-types. One of the key strengths of comparative research, particularly when it involves the analysis of several or more countries, is that it provides a bridge between looking at domestic factors (which take place within countries) and international factors (which take place between countries). Comparison helps us to broaden our intellectual horizons, and we can use comparison to see if what we think is a self-evident truth in one context also works in the same way in a different context.

The following chapters explore various methods of data collection and analysis. Among the most widely used forms of data collection in political research are **surveys**, which we discuss in detail in **Chapter 10**. One of the great strengths of survey research is that it helps us to make general claims about what different sections of society or different sub-groups of the population actually think and do. It thus gives voice to people who might not otherwise be heard. But a major weakness is that surveys can, and frequently do, misrepresent what people think and do and thus create misleading information. The extent to which surveys misrepresent the 'real' or 'true' attitudes and behaviour of the people they seek to study can be thought of as error. The purpose of a good survey is to try and minimize this error. There are two important sources of error that we consider. The first is to do with **measurement error**, and refers to the ways in which surveys use questions to try and measure different social and political phenomena, such as political attitudes, opinions, and behaviour. The second is to do with **sampling error**, and refers to the ways in which respondents are chosen or selected to complete the survey and the implications this has for the representativeness of the sample. These principles of sound survey design, to do with sampling and measurement, are relevant for all form of data collection.

In **Chapter 11** we focus on data collection using **interviews** and **focus groups** and explore issues concerning how these data can be analysed. Interviews are in a sense the qualitative cousin of surveys. Many of the principles are much the same for the two methods of data collection, but whereas surveys are typically concerned with generating large samples so that they can make valid inferences about a given population, interviews are more frequently used to ascertain more specialized knowledge, either about what so-called experts or elites think, or to explore the meanings that people attach to different concepts. It can be a very useful method to complement survey research, and indeed virtually all survey research draws upon semi-structured interview techniques at the design stage to pilot new questions. One of the great strengths of interviews and focus groups is that they can help a researcher understand people's perceptions, feelings, opinions, experiences, understandings, values, beliefs, attitudes, emotions, behaviour, formal and informal roles, and relationships. Interviewing individuals, either face-to-face or over the telephone, or through mailed questionnaires, helps researchers to learn about how people feel. The focus group is a good technique for exploring *why* people hold certain beliefs or feel the way they do. Exchanges among participants can lead to far more probing and reflection than is possible in individual interviews or questionnaires, and may provide more robust and revealing responses to the issues which are the subject of the focus group.

In **Chapter 12** we consider participant observation, the most intensive form of data collection of all. The distinctive feature of participant observation, and one of the great strengths of the approach, is that data collection is carried out in real time. This means that the researcher has a direct, first-hand opportunity to observe what people actually do, what they actually say to each other, and how they actually interact with different institutions or political processes, rather than just relying on what people say that they do. Participant observation (and ethnography more generally) therefore has a number of characteristics that overlap with other methods we consider (such as surveys, focus groups, and interviews) and a number of characteristics that are distinctive, particularly with respect to the role of observation. Whereas surveys are based on the ancient art of asking questions to find out what people think, say, and do, participant observation is based on something rather different. It recognizes that what people say they do, and what they actually do, can be and frequently are quite different. Accordingly, to get a 'true' sense of what people think and say and do, it is not enough to merely ask people questions and record their answers; it is also necessary to observe what people do in practice.

In **Chapter 13** we consider a different type of data collection. Whereas surveys, interviews, and participant observation are all to do with collecting information about what people think or say or do, either by asking them questions or by observing what they do, or some combination of the two, textual analysis is based on the analysis of archival data or documentary records such as speeches, policy documents, or media reports, to do with what people or institutions or organizations have actually done (or produced). These documents provide a rich source of information about the ways in which politics is practised. We discuss some of the different ways in which these sources of evidence are analysed, focusing on historical analysis, discourse analysis, and content analysis. Unlike asking people questions (e.g. through surveys or in interviews), using texts to collect data has the advantage of being non-intrusive. Researchers do not face the problem of influencing their data source through the questions they ask. And they can study past policy positions as they were recorded at the time. Once recorded, texts do not change.

Quantitative analysis is now one of the most widely used techniques of analysis in political research. Whether you love it or hate it, it is hard to avoid. And although many students are apprehensive about quantitative analysis, it is an important skill to acquire, which will not only stand you in good stead for conducting research (both in terms of what you can read and what you can do), but will also provide you with a transferable skill. In **Chapters 14 , 15, and 16** we provide a step-by-step guide to quantitative analysis, which will equip you with the skills to be able to interpret what others have done, and carry out quantitative analysis for yourselves.

Although it is easy to overstate the differences between these different methods, it is also important to bear in mind their similarities. All methods of data collection and analysis can (and frequently do) investigate similar political phenomena. There is no sense in which the investigation of certain topics or issues determines your method of inquiry. For example, if you are interested in what people think about politics; you can examine this through the use of surveys, interviews, and focus groups, and ask questions about what people think and say they have done. You can also explore this through ethnography and participant observation and record what they actually do and say. Rather than thinking about how to choose between different forms of data collection and analysis, the more pertinent issue is often to think about how to combine different methods.

There is no rule about which method should be used for which research design. From Table 1.1 we can see that there is considerable overlap between different research designs, methods of data collection, and methods of data analysis. For example, longitudinal studies may use qualitative historical analysis or quantitative statistical analysis. There is also considerable overlap between different methods of analysis and different methods of data collection. Although it is common to associate quantitative analysis with survey research, there is nothing to prevent this type of analysis being carried out on data collected using other methods. Indeed, a great deal of quantitative analysis has been done on interview data based on expert or elite interviews (such as Polity IV, Freedom House, or Transparency International data), and on documentary records and public records and media reports (see Chapter 12). Even focus groups can be analysed quantitatively if there are enough of them. This approach is frequently adopted in deliberative polling studies (see Luskin, Fishkin and Jowell 2002), which can be regarded as a type of experimental focus group. Indeed it is only really participant observation that does not appear to lend itself to quantitative analysis, though that is not to say that participant observation doesn't incorporate quantitative analysis or that it cannot be combined with quantitative analysis.

This all goes to show that some of the oppositions between qualitative and quantitative approaches have been somewhat overstated. They should not be seen as competing approaches to political research but as complementary approaches. They can both be used for similar research designs. And they can both be used to analyse similar types of data. It is not the case that there are some types of data that you can only analyse qualitatively or some types of data that you can only answer quantitatively. On the whole, there is a considerable amount of overlap. So if you are interested in conducting a longitudinal study to investigate

Table 1.1 Research design, data collection, and data analysis in political research

	Research Design				Method of Analysis	
	Experimental	Comparative	Cross-sectional	Longitudinal	Quantitative	Qualitative
Method of data collection						
Surveys	✓	✓	✓	✓	✓	✓
Interviews	✓	✓	✓	✓	✓	✓
Focus groups	✓	✓	✓	✓	✓	✓
Participant Observation	✓	✓	✓	✓	✗	✓
Texts	✓	✓	✓	✓	✓	✓
Method of data analysis						
Quantitative	✓	✓	✓	✓	—	—
Qualitative	✓	✓	✓	✓	—	—

changing patterns of the tone of political coverage in newspapers, why not employ both qualitative and quantitative research? If different methods of data collection can be employed for similar research designs, and different methods of data analysis can be employed for similar forms of data, then the question is not why you should choose one method of analysis or collection over another, but why you should not choose all over one.

Unfortunately, the answer is usually pragmatic rather than intellectual, and has more to do with constraints of time, money, and expertise. For example, participant observation can be very time-consuming and surveys can be very expensive. Moreover, once researchers have acquired one methodological skill-set, they are often reluctant to learn another. Although these constraints are not irrelevant, they should be openly acknowledged and not be obscured by pseudo-methodological,-epistemological, or even -ontological arguments. We hope this book will contribute to lowering at least one of these obstacles, and that it will enable you to be comfortable using a wide variety of different methodological approaches and skills.

Research methods are in a sense the tools of analysis. It is common to think about different methods being a bit like different tools. Which tool you want to use may then depend upon the job that you want to do. And whereas one tool might be appropriate for a particular type of task, it might be inappropriate for another. So a saw is good for cutting things, but less helpful if you want to fix something together. Although there is some truth in this metaphor, we think the idea of choosing different methods according to the job you want to do leads to a very narrow view of what constitutes research. We prefer to look at the bigger picture. No one wants to go around just using a saw to cut things in half all the time. Rather, a craftsman, a skilled carpenter, may want to build a table and to do that he will need to cut things and fix things and sand things and varnish things. He will need to use a wide variety of different tools to complete his task. Becoming a skilled researcher is a bit like learning a craft. And it involves learning many skills and being able to combine them together to do a thorough job.

Of course, for the lazy or time-pressed there is always flat-pack furniture. If we buy a flat-pack table from Ikea, we can assemble it all using a single tool—just an Allen key or a screwdriver is needed. But the quality of the table is not going to be in the same league as one hand-built by a master craftsmen, and it may well collapse under a slight amount of pressure. If we don't want our research findings to collapse in a similar way, we should aim to set our sights a little higher than trying to investigate complicated political phenomena through the prism of a single methodological perspective.

 ## Conclusions

One of the great strengths of political research is its diversity. The study of politics encompasses a wide variety of different ontological, epistemological, and methodological positions. And while it might be disconcerting or confusing that there are no concrete shared principles that governs the study of politics, this variety is a great source of vitality within the discipline. Different perspectives act to continually challenge what we think we know. Constant questioning means that we can never take things for granted. We always need to be conscious of whether or not we can defend ourselves from criticism, since our findings will be scrutinized on many different fronts.

One of the defining characteristics of politics as a field of study is the wide variety of approaches it incorporates. This can be both a strength and a weakness for the discipline. It is a strength when this diversity is embraced, and when researchers adopt and integrate the different approaches and engage with research from across the methodological spectrum. It is a weakness when this diversity fragments the field, and when researchers from different methodological traditions retreat into their own enclaves and do not engage with what other people are doing in the discipline. Our view is that, to appreciate the diversity and pluralism within political research, it is useful to be familiar and conversant with the whole array of methods and approaches available to us. Our hope is that this book will help you in this task.

 ## References

Baber, W. and Bartlett, R. (2005), *Deliberative Environmental Politics: Democracy and Ecological Rationality* (Cambridge, MA: MIT Press).

Brady, H. and D. Collier (eds) (2004), *Rethinking Social Inquiry: Diverse Tools, Shared Standards* (Lanham, MD: Rowman & Littlefield).

Buckler, S. (2010), 'Normative Theory', in D. Marsh and G. Stoker (eds), *Theory and Methods in Political Science*, 3rd edition (Basingstoke: Palgrave Macmillan), 156–80.

Elstub, Stephen (2010), 'The Third Generation of Deliberative Democracy', *Political Studies Review* 8(3): 291–307.

Finnemore, Martha and Kathryn Sikkink (2001), 'Taking Stock: The Constructivist Research Program in International Relations and Comparative Politics', *Annual Review of Political Science* 4: 391–416.

Gerring, John and Joshua Yesnowitz (2006), 'A Normative Turn in Political Science?', *Polity* 38(1): 101–33.

Gillespie, M. and B. O'Loughlin (2009), 'News Media, Threats and Insecurities: An Ethnographic Approach', *Cambridge Review of International Affairs* 22(4): 667–86.

——J. Gow, and A. Hoskins (2007), 'Shifting Securities: News Cultures Before and Beyond the Iraq Crisis 2003: Full Research Report', ESRC End of Award Report, RES-223-25-0063. Swindon: ESRC.

Kahane, H. and N. Cavender (2006), *Logic and Contemporary Rhetoric: The Use of Reason in Everyday Life*, 10th edition (Belmont, CA: Thomson Wadsworth).

King, G., R. Keohane, and S. Verba (1994), *Designing Social Inquiry: Scientific Inference in Qualitative Research* (Princeton, NJ: Princeton University Press).

Kumar, R. (2005), *Research Methodology: A Step-by-Step Guide for Beginners*, 2nd revised edition (London: Sage Publications Ltd).

Laitin, D. (2005), Contribution to 'Symposium I: Ian Shapiro's The Flight from Reality in the Human Sciences (Princeton University Press, 2005)', in *Qualitative Methods: Newsletter of the American Political Science Association Organized Section on Qualitative Methods* 3(2) (Fall): 13–15.

Luskin, R., J. Fishkin, and R. Lowell (2002), 'Considered Opinions: Deliberative Polling in Britain' *British Journal of Political Science* 32: 455–87.

O'Flynn, I. (2006), *Deliberative Democracy and Divided Societies* (Edinburgh: Edinburgh University Press).

Parkinson, J. (2006), *Deliberating in the Real World: Problems of Legitimacy in Deliberative Democracy* (Oxford: Oxford University Press).

Pollins, B. M. (2007), 'Beyond Logical Positivism: Reframing King, Keohane, and Verba', in R. N. Lebow and Mark Lichbach (eds), *Theory and Evidence in Comparative Politics and International Relations* (New York: Palgrave Macmillan), 87–106.

Shapiro, I. (2005a), *The Flight from Reality in the Human Sciences* (Princeton, NJ: Princeton University Press).

——(2005b), 'A Response to Mackie, Hochschild, and Laitin', in *Qualitative Methods: Newsletter of the American Political Science Association Organized Section on Qualitative Methods* 3(2) (Fall): 16–19.

Shively, W. P. (1989), *The Craft of Political Research*. 2nd edition (Englewood Cliffs, NJ: Prentice-Hall, Inc.).

Smith, R. (2004), 'Reconnecting Political Theory to Empirical Inquiry, or, A Return to the Cave?', in E. D. Mansfield and R. Sisson (eds), *The Evolution of Political Knowledge: Theory and Inquiry in American Politics* (Columbus, OH: The Ohio State University Press), 60–88.

Snape, Dawn and Liz Spencer (2006). 'The Foundations of Qualitative Research', in J. Ritchie and J. Lewis (eds.), *Qualitative Research Practice: A Guide for Social Science Students and Researchers* (Thousand Oaks, CA: Sage Publications).

Thompson, D. (2008), 'Deliberative Democratic Theory and Empirical Political Science', *Annual Review of Political Science*, 11(1): 497–520.

Part 1

Philosophy of Social Science: Knowledge and Knowing in Social Science Research

2

Forms of Knowledge: Laws, Explanation, and Interpretation in the Study of the Social World

 Chapter Summary

This chapter considers fundamental assumptions that researchers make about how we can know and develop knowledge about the social world, including assumptions about the nature of human behaviour and the methods appropriate to investigating and explaining that behaviour. The core concern is whether and how we can pursue a systematic and rigorous study of social phenomena in the way that scientists pursue study of the natural world. Without considering this issue, it is difficult to design or structure an approach to research into political phenomena, and to make any claim with respect to the findings that result from that research.

This chapter focuses on three different answers to the question of how to approach the study of social phenomena: those offered by positivism, scientific realism, and interpretivism. In exploring the differences among them and their implications for conducting political research, our discussion will engage with a number of questions, including the following:

- What form(s) of knowledge should be the goal of political research?
- Should the social sciences strive to emulate natural science methods, or is understanding social phenomena something essentially different from explanation in the natural sciences?
- Can we study politics scientifically? What does it means to be 'scientific?
- What distinguishes science from non-science?

Introduction

Every researcher must confront fundamental questions about the nature of knowledge and how we acquire it. These questions are the focus of key debates in political research, and the subject of an ongoing inquiry into scientific practice, forms of knowledge, and the world of politics. What sort of knowledge can we gain about the social world? Is it the same sort of knowledge that scientists are, able to obtain about the natural world? Or are the forms of knowledge concerning the social world and the natural world necessarily different? If they *are* different, is it still possible to produce knowledge that is reliable and objective? What counts as legitimate knowledge of the social world? These questions bear directly on research practice and, consequently, are of primary concern to those who seek to understand political processes and structures. The answer or answers *you* accept will determine the sort of research you pursue, the claims you make on the basis of that research, and your assessment of the findings of the research produced by others in our field.

We will consider three different approaches to these questions: positivism, scientific realism, and interpretivism. Each approach differs from the others with respect to its ontological, epistemological, and methodological premises. These differences are summarized in Box 2.3 in the concluding section of this chapter.

The terms 'ontology', 'epistemology', and 'methodology' relate to fundamental issues concerning research practice and knowledge. **Ontology** is concerned with '*what is*': with assumptions about the nature of the social world and the basic elements that make up this world. Questions of ontology relevant to political research include whether the social world is fundamentally different from the natural world; whether it is an objective reality that exists independently of us or is in important respects subjectively created. **Epistemology** is concerned with *what is knowable*, with what we *can* know about social phenomena, and, consequently, what type or form of knowledge we should pursue and treat as legitimate knowledge about the social world. It is only when we have considered these ontological and epistemological questions that we can move to a consideration of methodological questions. **Methodology** is concerned with *how we obtain knowledge*, with the means and methods that can provide us with legitimate knowledge of the political world. Box 2.1 shows how these key issues concerning knowledge are related.

We begin this chapter with a discussion of the development of positivist thought and practice, including classical and logical positivism, Karl Popper's critique of these, and the role of general laws and causation in social-scientific explanation. We then focus on two non-positivist positions: scientific realism and interpretivism. The three positions differ from one another in many ways and, in particular, with respect to their view of how the assumptions, logic, and methods of science can be used by scholars to study human behaviour. However, though each position has developed, in part, through a critique of the others, each of them produces useful forms of knowledge. Taken together, they have enabled us to broaden the range and type of questions that political research can effectively address.

BOX 2.1 Ontology   Epistemology   Methodology

Ontology	Epistemology	Methodology
What exists? What is the nature of the social world?	What sort of knowledge of it is possible? How can we know about it?	What strategies can we use to gain that knowledge?

Positivism

As a prelude to our discussion of positivism, it would be helpful to get a sense of its role in political research by briefly considering behaviouralism and the 'behavioural revolution' in the field of politics.

Behaviouralism is the term used for the application of positivism and empiricism to political research.[1] What has been called the 'behavioural revolution' was concerned to promote the systematic search for sound and reliable knowledge about politics based on a positivist approach to knowledge. For behaviouralists, political research involves studying and explaining the observable behaviour of individuals or aggregates of individuals (parties, classes, interest groups, governments, social movements).

Behaviouralist research focuses on the question of what political actors do and why they do it. Until the mid-1970s, behaviouralist researchers emphasized an inductivist approach to research which, as we shall see, is associated with classical positivism. An inductive approach to social inquiry is one in which 'knowledge is arrived at through the gathering of facts that provide the basis for laws' (Bryman 2004: 11). Although behaviouralist research can employ both quantitative and qualitative data, during the 1950s and 1960s behaviouralist researchers tended to focus on questions that could be answered by gathering and studying data conducive to exact measurement, as for instance voting data or data from public-opinion polls and social surveys. This tendency generated the criticism that, by focusing on phenomena that lent themselves more easily to measurement, the field had become preoccupied with technique rather than substance, and was failing to address significant problems.

These concerns triggered a 'post-behavioural revolution'. Despite its name, this 'revolution' was not concerned to displace behaviouralism, but to 'propel political science in new directions' (Easton 1969: 1051). Some of these new directions moved the field towards a further realization of positivist and behaviouralist goals, such as the trend towards 'positive political theory' or rational choice theory. Positive political theory assumes that rational self-interest, 'as opposed to attitudes, which are the subject of study in much behavioral research', provides the motivational foundation for behaviour; and that individual self-interested rational action combines to produce collective political outcomes (Amadae and Bueno de Mesquita 1999: 270). But while the post-behaviouralist revolution moved behavioural research forward, it also set in motion trends that moved the field in non-positivist directions, and encouraged the emergence of an array of theoretical approaches that represented a self-conscious rejection of behavioural and positivist assumptions. Normative theory, which we will consider in Chapters 3 and 6, witnessed a re-birth, and often self-consciously as a response to the influence of behaviouralist research. In addition, there emerged a set of approaches based on non-positivist assumptions and associated with 'interpretivism', including constructivism, feminism, post-modernism, and critical theory.

The behavioural revolution set in motion an important process of discussion and debate within political research about the methods and goals of the field. It began a discussion on the desirability and possibility of attaining reliable, empirical, causal knowledge about political life. It promoted more methodologically self-conscious research; and, though much behavioural research originally focused on what might be characterized as a narrow range of questions, it also succeeded in broadening the research domain, as behavioural researchers, seeking insights from the theories, research methods, and findings of other disciplines, opened the way to greater interdisciplinarity in the field. Behaviouralism established an emphasis on research based on empirical observation, testing involving systematic evidence, and falsifiable and causal explanation. By emphasizing the importance of research that is capable of replication by others, behaviouralism makes researchers more precise about what they want to know, what explanation they are advancing, and how they intend to demonstrate it.

We will gain a better understanding of this revolution, and of both its positivist and non-positivist legacy, as we explore the basic tenets and contours of positivist thought.

Positivism began as a movement to establish a sound basis for social-scientific inquiry. This is a fundamentally important issue in political research. Political researchers want to be able to offer credible answers to important questions, and they are concerned to ensure that the research practices and methods they employ enable them to do this. Positivism offers a particular approach to resolving these issues. It maintains that it is possible to arrive at factual, reliable, and objective answers to questions about the social world by employing the methods used in the natural sciences. Depending on your point of view, this position may strike you as highly controversial or as plain common sense. A large number of researchers in our field react to positivist thought in one or the other of these two ways. Consequently, it is likely that positivism will continue to occupy a central place in our field, both in providing a foundation for research and in stimulating the articulation of alternative methodological positions.

The term 'positivism' was invented by the French philosopher Auguste Comte (1798–1857) to describe what he saw as the last of three phases in the development of society and its search for truth. It was Comte's view that society had passed through a theological stage and then a metaphysical stage; and that now it had entered into a final 'positive' stage in which the search for truth is characterized by the systematic collection of observed facts. The term 'sociology', which refers to the scientific study of the social world, was also his invention. Both terms expressed the same belief: that the social world could be explained using similar methods to those used to explain natural phenomena.

This view of social science methodology, in common with the other approaches to be discussed in this chapter, commits us to a number of ontological and epistemological claims. The nature and implications of these claims and their relationship to a positivist methodology will become clear as we identify and discuss the basic tenets of positivism.

We begin discussion of these tenets by first considering the classical positivist tradition, and then focusing on the development of positivist thought through the movement of 'logical positivism' and Karl Popper's critique of logical positivist tenets. In discussing these developments, our purpose is not to provide an intellectual history of positivism: the ideas of classical positivism were not superseded by those advanced by logical positivists; nor were those associated with logical positivism supplanted or displaced by the ideas of Karl Popper. In other words, the development of positivism over time did not always or usually lead to the wholesale rejection of previous ideas, but rather to an expansion of the array of positions associated with it.

Classical positivism

The *first* tenet of positivism—one implied by our previous discussion—is **naturalism**. Naturalism is the idea that there are no fundamental differences between the natural and the social sciences. Note that this idea entails an ontological presupposition about the social world: if there is no difference between the social and natural *sciences*, it must be because there is no fundamental difference between the social and natural *worlds*. Both claims provide positivism with a basis for building a larger edifice of thought concerning the nature and goals of social-scientific inquiry. As we shall see, positivism maintains that, since the social sciences are no different from the natural sciences, they should have the same structure and logical characteristics as the natural sciences. We'll return to this notion in a moment when we discuss the third tenet of positivism. But first let's consider a *second* tenet of positivism: **empiricism**.

Empiricism is a philosophical theory of knowledge which claims that what we know of the world is limited to what can be observed. Knowledge is only that which originates in sensory experience: there is no *a priori* knowledge, no knowledge of reality that is acquired prior to sense experience. So, an empiricist epistemology commits positivism to the view that social reality can only be known through what is observed and that knowledge of the social world is therefore limited to phenomena that can be observed by the senses. Positivists maintain that social science should be empirical, based on evidence that is visible in the world. Its goal should be to gain knowledge of social reality through concepts which apply to or derive from what is observable and measurable.

Additional tenets of positivism provide further elaboration of its position concerning the basis of knowledge and the form it takes. Consider a *third* tenet of positivism: that the goal of social science is to explain and predict social phenomena by means of **laws**. The German logician Carl Gustav Hempel (1905–1997) argued that if the discovery of laws is necessary in the physical or natural sciences, then laws must be necessary also in social science. If the social world is like the natural world, then, like the natural world, it also must be regular, systematic, and law-governed. There are regularities in, and ultimately laws of, social and political processes; and we can explain social events and phenomena by means of law-like generalizations that have the same status as natural scientific laws.

The possibility of discovering laws in the social sciences is one of the key issues on which positivism and its critics divide. As we shall see, there is considerable debate concerning whether social laws exist. Some non-positivist approaches insist that there is a difference "'in kind" between the subject matter of natural and of social science, which precludes the use of laws in the explanation of human behavior and makes it impossible to establish social laws' (McIntyre 1994: 131). We will be considering this view later in the chapter.

We have said that positivism holds that the social world is regular, systematic, and law-governed, like the natural world; that social phenomena can be explained and predicted by means of laws that have the same status as natural scientific laws; and that the purpose of social science, therefore, is to discover these laws. But how do we go about discovering laws of social life? Classical positivist thought maintains that laws can be discovered through systematic investigation of observable events and happenings, and by means of inductive reasoning. **Induction** is a means of reasoning that begins with specific observations and measures. It moves to an identification of patterns and regularities and to the formulation of some tentative hypotheses that can be explored; and it ends by developing some general conclusions or theories. An inductive approach to social inquiry is, as we noted earlier, one in which 'knowledge is arrived at through the gathering of facts that provide the basis for laws' (Bryman 2004: 11). We will have more to say about induction and other means of reasoning (i.e. 'deduction' and 'abduction') further on in our discussion of the development of positivist thought.

We are still discussing the third tenet of positivism: the view that explanation of social phenomena should proceed by the discovery of laws. But, for positivism, there is another key element in social science explanation: explanation must not only proceed with reference to law-like generalizations, it must also establish a cause–effect relationship between events in the world. Positivism sees the social world as comprising phenomena that are causally related to each other; consequently, to explain a social outcome we are required to show the factors or conditions that combined to bring it about or caused it to be more likely to occur in the circumstances.

Virtually all social research is concerned to discover causes. But there are different conceptions of causation. The positivist conception of causation is an empiricist conception which was introduced by the Scottish philosopher, economist, and historian, David Hume (1711–1776). Most of us probably carry in our minds an idea of causation as a relation between two events, the cause and the effect, which expresses some type of 'necessary connection' between them. But Hume pointed out that we cannot directly perceive causal relationships. He points out that 'when we look about us towards external objects, and consider the operation of causes, we cannot in any instance discover a power, necessary connexion, or quality which binds the effect to the cause and renders one an infallible consequence of the other' (1966: 51). Instead, we observe only the 'constant conjunction' of events; we observe only that one thing follows the other. Our experience of observing this 'constant conjunction' between events conveys to our minds a necessary relation between these events. So the causal conclusions we reach are based, not on 'knowledge of causal mechanisms and the generative properties of things', but only 'on the observation of how a certain event is followed again and again by a certain other event' (Ekström 1992: 108).

According to this conception, then, causation is constituted by facts about empirical regularities among observable variables. There is no underlying power or necessity deriving from the laws of nature. All we can do is observe that one thing follows another with regularity; and, because of this observation, we develop a psychological expectation that Y will occur whenever X does. But we cannot know that X is the *cause* of Y by observing that X is constantly followed by Y. Consequently, in establishing the basis of causal explanations, positivists are concerned with observing empirical regularities rather than in discovering causal mechanisms. This is a subjective conception of causation: causation as a perceived regular association among variables. An objective conception of causality, one involving causal necessity or causal mechanisms is, according to positivism, metaphysical. This objective conception of causation features prominently in the critique of classical positivism articulated by logical positivism, a subject to which we will turn next. But before moving on, we need to briefly note a *fourth* tenet of positivism: that it is possible to make a *distinction between facts and values*.

Positivism maintains that we can gain knowledge of the social world through application of the scientific methods used in the natural sciences. According to this fourth tenet of positivism, the pursuit of knowledge through these methods can be value-free or objective, because statements of fact (confirmed by the senses) can be distinguished from normative statements. Science is concerned with the discovery of facts, whereas values relate to ethics or policy studies. The argument that it is possible to distinguish between facts and values, and to treat 'facts' as independent of the observer and of his or her values, represents a key difference between positivists and adherents of alternative approaches. However, we will leave discussion of this issue for the time being, since we

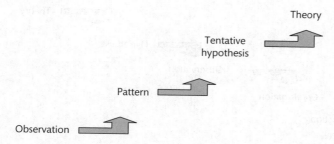

Figure 2.1 Induction
Source: Trochim 2006.

will be exploring it in some detail in Chapter 3. Instead, we turn to a consideration of the further development of positivist thought as a result of logical positivism and Karl Popper's critique of it.

Empiricism and logic as the basis of truth claims

The ideas of classical positivism were developed by a movement that adopted the name 'logical positivism', as well as by the highly influential critique of Karl Popper.

Logical positivism began in the early twentieth century as a movement within philosophy. Inspired by developments in twentieth-century logic and mathematics, its goal was to introduce logical reasoning and mathematics as sources of knowledge in addition to empiricism. It advanced the idea that social inquiry should combine induction (based on empiricism) and deduction (in the form of logic) as methods of reasoning.

We have previously discussed induction as a means of discovering laws. Induction, you will recall, is a process of reasoning from particular facts to a general conclusion. As Figure 2.1 shows, in induction we begin with particular observations or cases and then develop generalizations about them. **Deduction** works the other way around. As Figure 2.2 shows, deduction moves from broader generalizations and theories to specific observations. We start, not with an observation, but either with a theory that has already been confirmed or with a logical argument, and then we draw out the meaning or implications this has for explaining some particular case or phenomena.

To digress from our discussion of logical positivism for a moment, it should be noted that, in practice, researchers do not use solely one method or the other. Scientific inquiry typically involves a process of continuous interaction between theory and observation, in which the researcher moves from observation to theory (induction) and from theory back to observa-

BOX 2.2 Induction, Deduction, Retroduction	
Induction	observation ⊗ theory
Deduction	theory ⊗ observation
Retroduction	observation « theory

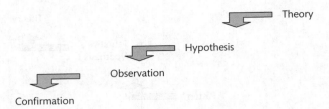

Figure 2.2 Deduction
Source: Trochim 2006.

tion (deduction). Box 2.2 illustrates how this process contrasts with and combines induction and deduction. The compiling of evidence (induction) leads the researcher to theory (deduction); and once a hypothesis is formed, the researcher brings it 'backward' for readjustment or redefinition. The term 'retroduction' describes this interaction of induction and deduction in an evolving, dynamic process of discovery and hypothesis formation.

We have said that logical positivism introduced the idea that social inquiry should combine both induction and deduction. It also established 'verification' (of statements or propositions) as the goal of social science research. Verification was held to be the main criterion for establishing truth claims and a means of defining a clear line of division between science and metaphysics.

Both of these tenets of logical positivism became the target of a critique by Karl Popper (1902–94), a philosopher of science who also wrote extensively on social and political philosophy. Popper's critique had a decisive impact on social-scientific thought. In fact, its influence was so great that logical positivism's most important contribution to social science, it might be argued, is the role it played in having served as the focus of this critique. This does not diminish its contribution: in the quest to establish a sound basis for scientific inquiry, logical positivism raised important questions about the concepts and practices of science which continue to have relevance for social-scientific inquiry today. Moreover, while Popper was a critic of logical positivism, there are also many affinities between his views and those held by logical positivists.

Logical positivists had argued that both inductive and deductive methods of reasoning should be used to acquire knowledge of social phenomena. But Popper argued that induction must be rejected entirely. Moreover, the argument he advanced for rejecting induction also provided grounds for rejecting **verifiability** as a basis for establishing truth claims.

Popper elaborates these arguments in his book, *Logik der Forschung*, published in 1934, and later published in English under the title *The Logic of Scientific Discovery* (1959). The book addresses two issues. The first is what David Hume calls 'the problem of induction'. The problem is whether experience can provide the basis for gaining general theoretical knowledge. Since experience is particular, while knowledge is general or even universal, how do we achieve universal knowledge on the basis of particular experience? How can we reach general statements of scientific law on the basis of experiences that are necessarily limited and particular? Popper argues that no matter how many experiences we have of observing something, this does not permit the deduction of a general statement of scientific knowledge.

The reasoning that leads him to this conclusion begins with David Hume's argument about the limits of inductive reasoning. Hume argued that since we cannot observe the universe at all times and in all places, but are only able to observe particulars, we are not justified in deducing general laws based on inductive evidence. Popper's now famous story of the black swan illustrates what happens when we attempt to formulate laws based on observation. The story is that, once upon a time, Europeans thought that all swans were white because, having found nothing but white swans for thousands of years, Europeans concluded on the basis of their experience that all swans were white. But one day Europeans went to New Zealand (as Popper had), and there they found black swans. What this story tells us is that no matter how many observations confirm a theory, it only takes one counter-observation to falsify it: only one black swan is needed to repudiate the theory that all swans are white. And since it only takes a single unforeseen or seemingly improbable event to invalidate a generalization based on empirical observation, then empirical observation alone cannot generate 'laws'. Popper therefore concludes that, rather than endeavouring to discover laws through induction, what scientists should be doing is testing theory deductively.

Popper's critique of induction leads him to reject another tenet of logical positivism: the notion that scientists should seek to verify hypotheses. Popper argues that, since a single exception to the rule destroys inductively generated theory, then conclusive verification of a hypothesis is not possible. So Popper proposes that we reverse the logical positivist assumption about verifiability: he argues that rather than continually attempting to *prove* a theory, scientists should attempt to *disprove* it. Since we cannot *verify* a **hypothesis**, our aim should be to *falsify* it. We should formulate propositions in such a way as to enable them to be refuted. By doing this, it will be possible for us to show a theory to be wrong; and we can then introduce a new theory which better explains the phenomena. This, Popper argues, is how we achieve progress in science.

The notion of **falsifiability** is the basis of Popper's argument concerning the second issue he addresses in *The Logic of Scientific Discovery*: the problem of demarcation. This refers to the problem of determining how to differentiate science from non-science. It is a key problem in the philosophy of science and the subject of ongoing debate. For Popper, it is falsifiability —and not verifiability, as logical positivists argued—that defines the boundary between science and pseudo-science or metaphysics. Anything non-falsifiable is outside science.

Consider religions and ideologies in this regard. Religions and ideologies are logically consistent statements which provide a guide for understanding the world. But they cannot be proved false: potentially disconfirming or anomalous facts do not prove them false, but are incorporated within them. A scientific theory, however, must state what evidence would disconfirm it or prove it to be false. If you cannot think of anything that might disconfirm a theory, then it is not a theory at all but a set of self-verifying statements—an ideology.

To sum up: in rejecting induction, Popper was rejecting the idea that observation provides the basis for the formulation of scientific theories. Theories cannot be derived from observation (induction), because at any time a single observation can disconfirm the theory. Popper concludes that social inquiry must proceed deductively, through a process in which observations are not the basis of theories, but are derived from and used to 'test', or falsify, them. According to Popper's notion of falsifiability, we endeavour to falsify hypotheses. We reject those which are falsified and we continue to test those that are not until they become so thoroughly tested that we can consider them to be 'confirmed', though it remains possible that some day someone may falsify or significantly modify them.

Two objections have been made to this formulation. The first objection is to the distinction which Popper seems to make between facts and theories. Popper seems to assume that the observations or facts that we pursue as a means of testing theories can be established independently of the theory that they are meant to test. We consider the debate concerning this issue in some detail in Chapter 3. A second objection is that Popper's notion of falsifiabilty is at odds with how scientists actually go about developing and testing theories. Do researchers seek to disprove or falsify their own theories? Do they discard their theories when they are confronted with disconfirming evidence? We will consider Thomas Kuhn's and Imre Lakatos' answers to these questions, and the further evolution of Popper's falsificationist position that developed as a response to them, in Chapter 3.

Here, however, we have still to consider a further question: how do we use deductive reasoning to discover laws of social life as a basis for explanation? Previously we have discussed the classical positivist approach to explanation: inductive reasoning based on systematic investigation of observable events and happenings. As we have seen, logical positivists maintain that both induction, based on empiricism, and deduction in the form of logic could be used to discover laws. Popper argues that we can establish laws of social life as a basis for explanation only through deduction. But, what is the process through which deduction operates as a means of explaining social phenomena? For the answer to this question, we turn, again, to Carl Gustav Hempel.

Hempel maintains that explanation in the social and natural sciences is the same, not only because both involve the search for and discovery of law-like generalizations, but because the social and natural worlds are subject to laws *in the same way* (see Hempel 1994). The logic and function of laws, what Hempel calls 'general laws', are the same. In both the natural and social sciences, individual events can be subsumed within hypotheses about general laws of nature: what this means is that to explain some fact is to cite some law or laws and other conditions from which the fact can be deduced.

Hempel formalizes this definition of explanation in his **deductive-nomological model**.

A deductive-nomological explanation is deductive because the phenomenon to be explained (*explanandum*) is logically deducible from that which does the explaining (the *explanans*); and it is nomological because the *explanans* includes at least one law ('nomos' is the Greek word for law). According to this model, then, something is explained when it is shown to be a member of a more general class of things, when it is deduced from a general law or set of laws. A full explanation of an event requires that we give an account of how a phenomenon follows deductively from a well-confirmed general law. For instance, 'To explain fully why an actor votes (a "fact") we must do more than just isolate the particular cause of this particular event (for example, the intensity of the voter's concern about unemployment). We must subsume this act of participation under a "law" that explains why, under certain conditions, the voter had to vote: "persons with intense preferences for candidates or issues", everything else being equal, will become "active in politics"' (Milbrath 1965: 53; quoted in Schwartz 1984: 1123). Given the general law, the particular case in question was to be expected.

But, how do we confirm a regularity or generalization that what we take to be a 'law' is, in fact a law? A regularity might be true, accurate, or supported by evidence; but it might be only 'accidentally true': true only as a result of circumstance or coincidence. Explaining how to distinguish law-like generalizations from those that are 'accidental' is one of the central problems in the philosophy of science. However, in general, we can say that a law expresses a necessary connection between properties, while an accidental generalization does not. If a necessary connection exists between its properties, then we should be able to test a law by its ability to predict events. If we predict something on the basis of a law and find that the prediction was true, then the law can be said to be confirmed.

This is what Carl Hempel proposes that we do in his **hypothetico-deductive model** of confirmation. We confirm that the generalization is a law (rather than an accidental generalization) by treating it as a hypothesis and then we test the hypothesis by deducing from the hypothesis a sufficient number of explicit predictions of further phenomena that should be observable as a consequence of the hypothesis. Observations that run contrary to those predicted are taken as a conclusive falsification of the hypothesis; observations which are in agreement with those predicted are taken as corroborating the hypothesis. It is then supposedly possible to compare the explanatory value of competing hypotheses by looking to see how well they are sustained by their predictions.

An example of what is regarded as a law or, at least, a law-like generalization in our field is Duverger's Law. The sociologist, Maurice Duverger, proposed that the plurality rule for selecting the winner of elections favours the two-party system. Duverger offers two theoretical explanations for why a plurality rule election system tends to favour a two-party system. The first is the 'mechanical effect' of under-representing losing parties; and the second is a 'psychological factor': voters don't want to waste their votes on losers (Riker 1982: 761). William Riker explains: 'when the definition of winning forces candidates to maximize votes in order to win (as in plurality systems), they have strong motives to create a two-party system; but when the definition of winning does not require them to maximize votes (as in runoff and proportional systems), then this motive for two parties is absent' (Riker 1982: 755).[2]

To sum up: the deductive-nomological model holds that an observed phenomenon is explained if it can be deduced from a law-like generalization. The hypothetico-deductive model confirms that a generalization is a law by treating the generalization as a hypothesis, and testing it by its deductive consequences. To explain some fact is to cite a law or laws plus other relevant conditions from which the *explanandum* may be deduced (the deductive-nomological model of explanation). To confirm a hypothesis is to deduce some observed phenomenon from the hypothesis plus other relevant known conditions (the hypothetico-deductive model of confirmation).

We have traced the development of positivist thought through a consideration of the basic tenets of classical and logical positivism and the arguments advanced by Karl Popper. We turn now to approaches that emerged as a challenge to positivist thought and research.

Challenges to positivist approaches within the social sciences

There are a number of approaches to social inquiry that challenge the positivist position and that articulate a fundamentally different basis for inquiry. Here, we focus on two alternative positions—those represented by scientific realism and interpretivism.

Scientific realism

Scientific realism is concerned to elaborate a non-positivist version of science, one that its adherents claim is *more* scientific than positivism. Their message, as Ruth Lane puts it (Lane 1996: 373), is that 'we don't have to be positivists to be scientific!'

Scientific realism appears to be similar to positivism in some ways because it accepts a number of assumptions of positivism that other non-positivist approaches reject. For instance, scientific realism assumes, like positivism, that the social and natural worlds are essentially similar, and that the social and natural sciences are therefore fundamentally similar, as well. These assumptions are based on another shared assumption: **realism**. Realism holds that the world exists independently of our knowledge of it, that reality has an independent existence (it exists independently of human beings and their perceptions), and that it impacts directly upon the human mind without any reflection on the part of the human knower. We can therefore gain objective knowledge of the world because our knowledge of it is directly determined by an objective reality within the world.

So, positivism and scientific realism share some key assumptions. However, there is a key difference between the two approaches—and it is an important one! Let's recap for a moment before stating this difference. Both approaches maintain that the subject matter of scientific research and scientific theory exists independently of our knowledge of it, that we can therefore gain objective knowledge of it, and can treat 'facts' as independent of the observer and of his or her values. Now, where the two approaches differ is that, while positivists maintain that reality consists of only that which we can directly observe, for scientific realists, reality consists of observable elements as well as observable ones.

You will recall that positivists assume that statements not based on observable data are metaphysical. Scientific realists break decisively with this assumption. They assume that there are knowable, mind-independent facts, objects, or properties that cannot be directly observed but which are, nonetheless, *real*. They argue that unobservable elements of social life, such as structural relations between social phenomena, are crucial to an understanding and explanation of what goes on in the world. They point out that the central role of unobservable elements in shaping outcomes is one of the features that makes the social world similar to the natural world; that this ontological conception of the social world is not metaphysical, but more scientific, and more closely aligned with the tenets of the natural sciences, than the positivist conception.

Consequently, for scientific realists, the goal of scientific research is to describe and explain both observable and unobservable aspects of the world. But how do we know these unobservable elements exist? According to scientific realism, we know they exist because we can observe their *consequences*: unobservable elements of social life can be treated as 'real' if they produce observable effects. To posit the existence of unobservable entities to explain observable outcomes is consistent with well-established scientific practice. We treat gravity and subatomic particles as real because, even though we cannot see them, we can see their effects. Similarly, there are many elements in social and political life that are not directly observable—social structures, capitalism, society—but they have observable effects; and because their effects are observable, researchers in our field treat them as real.

Given these assumptions, it follows that, for scientific realists, scientific knowledge does not take the form solely of empirical regularities, and scientific research cannot be solely concerned with the goal of formulating law-like generalizations based on observations. To state this differently, if scientific realists reject the notion that only entities of which we have direct sensory experience are 'real', then they cannot depend on an epistemology that places emphasis on direct observation for pursuing knowledge of the social world.

It follows that scientific realists also cannot accept the empiricist (Humean) conception of causality that positivists employ. Recall that positivists treat causation as constituted by facts about empirical regularities among observable variables, and seek to establish causal relationships by observing these regularities rather than by discovering causal mechanisms. They treat the notion that causal mechanisms produce outcomes in social life as metaphysical, since we are unable to have knowledge of causal mechanisms through direct observation only. But scientific realists assume that unobservable elements are part of reality and are knowable, and so they treat causal mechanisms and causal powers as 'real', as a legitimate object of scientific investigation, and as fundamental to explanations of social outcomes. For scientific realists, explaining social outcomes entails providing an account of the causal mechanism that brought about a given outcome; and with developing empirically justified theories and hypotheses about causal mechanisms.

A causal mechanism can be defined as 'a series of events governed by lawlike regularities that lead from the *explanans* to the *explanandum*' (Little 1991: 15); or 'the pathway or process by which an effect is produced or a purpose is accomplished' (Gerring 2007: 178). Charles Tilly identifies three sorts of mechanism. Environmental mechanisms are 'externally generated influences on conditions affecting social life'; cognitive mechanisms 'operate through alterations of individual and collective perception'; and relational mechanisms 'alter connections among people, groups, and interpersonal networks' (2001: 24). Michael Ross defines an environmental mechanism—the nature of a government's resource base—to explain the apparent link between oil exports and authoritarian rule. He calls this mechanism a 'rentier effect': 'when governments derive sufficient revenues from the sale of oil, they are likely to tax their populations less heavily or not at all, and the public in turn will be less likely to demand accountability from—and representation in—their government' (2001: 332). Explanations of a variety of political outcomes might link them to the effect of increases or decreases in the government's resource base (see e.g. Chapter 6). Cognitive mechanisms have been identified to explain ethnic conflict as, for instance, changing conceptions of racial, ethnic, gender, religious, or class differences (e.g. Hoffmann 2006). Relational mechanisms, such as governmental absorption and destruction of previously autonomous patron–client networks, or bureaucratic containment of previously autonomous military forces, have been held to effect 'the likelihood of civil war, the level of domestic violence, and even the prospect that a given state will engage in international war' (Tilly 2001: 38). Robert Gilpin (1981) has argued that there is a tendency for a disjuncture to arise between the costs and benefits of hegemony, and that, when it does, the hegemonic state begins to decline. Gilpin identifies a number of mechanisms that cause this disjuncture. One is the 'law of the increasing costs of war': military techniques tend to rise in cost, and the increasing cost of war produces a fiscal crisis within the hegemonic state. Another is the 'law of expanding state expenditures': private and public consumption grows faster than the GNP as a society becomes more affluent (the rich indulge increasingly in lavish consumption; the poor begin to clamour for welfare).

Those who emphasize the importance of mechanisms in causation have different views about the nature or types of social mechanisms that operate to produce social outcomes. These are linked to different assumptions about what we should treat as the basic unit of analysis in social inquiry. So, for instance, those who treat individuals as the basic unit of social analysis favour agent-based models, or individual-level mechanisms to explain outcomes. This is characteristic of rational choice approaches, which assume that the instrumental rationality of individuals is the causal mechanism that produces social outcomes. Structural models, on the other hand, attempt to demonstrate that there are structural or institutional mechanisms that cause social outcomes. In Chapter 4 we will be exploring the differences between the individualist and collectivist (or holist) ontologies on which these different models are based. We will also discuss how what Peter Hedström and Richard Swedberg (1998) call 'social mechanisms' produce outcomes through macro–micro interactions and linkages.

We have been discussing the assumptions of scientific realism with regard to basic questions concerning the nature of the social world, forms of knowledge, and the goals of social science. We have said that, for scientific realists, the goal of scientific research is to describe and explain both observable and unobservable aspects of the world. It still remains to say how scientific realists establish that claims regarding unobservable social phenomena are true.

Scientific realists argue that knowledge of unobservable elements of social life can be obtained through the development of theoretical constructs. But how can we know whether our theories about unobservable elements of social life are true? The answer is that we can accept as true the theory or hypothesis which, from among those that have been advanced to explain a phenomenon, offers the best explanation. The 'best' explanation or hypothesis is the one that, based on various 'rules of method', explains a fact better than other available hypotheses. For instance, it may be 'best' because it has been tested and not refuted, while the others have not; because it accounts for more, or better meets the standard of explanation we accept for other phenomena. 'If a theory is certified by such rules of method, a scientist is rationally justified in accepting the theory' (Sankey 2008: 28). Scientific realism maintains that we can accept that a theory is true if there is rational justification for accepting it to be true; and it is rational to accept as true the best available explanation of any fact.

This position is summed up in the phrase 'Inference to the Best Explanation'. Scientific realists maintain that inference from some data to the 'best explanation' justifies our acceptance of a hypothesis as true. By **inference** we mean the reasoning involved in the process of drawing conclusions based on facts or logical premises; and, according to scientific realists, the kind of inference that justifies our accepting a hypothesis as true emerges from a type of reasoning called '**abduction**'. Contemporary philosophers use 'inference to the best explanation' and 'abduction' interchangeably.

Abductive reasoning is prior to and distinct from induction and deduction. Abduction starts with a hunch that a set of seemingly unrelated facts are connected in some way. The hunch or hypothesis can then be affirmed by induction or deduction. Abduction may be used to explain singular events rather than, as in inductive reasoning, to form generalizations on the basis of a large number of token instances; and, unlike induction, it can employ both observables and unobservables to explain events. Abductive reasoning requires that we choose from among competing explanations the best available explanation: the one that best explains a particular event or phenomenon given all the available evidence. The abduction is provisional: new evidence may later undermine it. But it is reasonable for us to believe it if it is the best explanation we have. We may later find out that the explanation is wrong and then it will no longer be reasonable for us to believe it; but it remains the case that it was not wrong or unreasonable for us to have believed it prior to our finding out that it was wrong. When a detective infers that a murder was committed by a suspect, he does so because this hypothesis provides the best explanation for the murder; and it is the 'best' explanation because it fits better with the forensic evidence, and/or provides a better account of motive and opportunity. Later information may reveal this explanation to be false; but this does not make it unreasonable for the detective to have made the original inference.

We now have introduced some of the key terms of reference in a continuing debate about the scientific status of unobservable elements of social life. Because political researchers continually refer to unobservables such as 'society' and 'structures of power' to explain political events and processes, we will be returning to this debate in later chapters. But, before moving on from discussion of scientific realism to a consideration of other non-positivist approaches, it is worth noting a related position that has emerged within the field of politics: **critical realism**.

We have said that scientific realism, like positivism, assumes that there exists a reality separate from our description of it. *Critical* realism represents a move away from this position. As we have seen, scientific realism is committed to identifying the unobservable structures that work to generate observable outcomes. This, as Roy Bhaskar points out, is *critical* in that it opens up the possibility or our being able to change our world (1998: 2). But critical realism also rejects the view, accepted by scientific realists and associated with what adherents of critical realism call 'naïve realism', that the external world is as it is perceived. Instead, it holds that perception is a function of the human mind, and that we can therefore only acquire knowledge of the external world by critically reflecting on perception. While some political researchers see the terms 'scientific realism' and 'critical realism' as synonymous (see e.g. Brown 2007: 409), this would seem to be a position that moves us further in the direction of the interpretivist approaches that we will be discussing next. Some examples of how a critical realist position informs political research are in Chapter 13, where we discuss critical discourse analysis, a type of textual analysis inspired by, and to a large degree consistent with, a critical realist philosophy of science.

We have been discussing scientific realism, an approach to social inquiry that provides an alternative to positivism. As we have seen, its main difference with positivism is that it does not place emphasis on direct observation in pursuing knowledge of the world; rather, it assumes that reality consists of both observable and unobservable elements. We have also seen that there are some respects in which scientific realism and positivism are more similar than dissimilar. For instance, both agree that the world exists independently of our knowledge of it. This assumption has important implications for what we treat as legitimate knowledge and how we conduct research. We turn now to a set of approaches that break decisively with this assumption, and promote ontological and epistemological positions that stand in diametric opposition to those of positivism.

Interpretivism

Interpretivism maintains that the social world is fundamentally different from the world of natural phenomena, and so we cannot understand it by employing the methods used to explain the natural world. It argues that it is impossible for us to gain knowledge of the social world by searching for *objective* regularities of behaviour that can be summed up in social-scientific laws analogous to the laws of physics, because the social world does not exist independently of our interpretation of it. The social world is what we experience it to be: it is *subjectively* created. The task of social science, then, is fundamentally different from that of natural science, because the objects of the social sciences are different from those found in the natural world. Social phenomena are socially or discursively constructed; so we cannot explain and predict social phenomena by means of laws. The primary goal of social science must be to achieve an understanding of human behaviour through an interpretation of the meanings, beliefs, and ideas that give people reasons for acting.

Let's consider the implications of this view for how we conduct political research.

Recall our earlier discussion about behaviouralism. Behaviouralist research is positivist and empiricist. Its concern is with the question of what political actors do and why they do it. It seeks to discover the causes of behavioural outcomes by understanding the motivations of political actors. It uses public-opinion polls and social surveys to learn about the beliefs, attitudes, and values that motivate behaviour; or rational choice theory to explain how individual self-interested rational action motivates behaviour. However if, as interpretivists contend, people act on the basis of the meanings they attach to their own and to others' actions, then understanding human behaviour requires an understanding of these meanings. Consequently, social science must be concerned, not with discovering causes of social outcomes, but with piecing together an interpretation of the meanings of a social outcome or production.

Intepretivists seek to understand human behaviour through interpretation and interpretive theory. These are forms of social science 'that emphasize understanding the meaning that social behaviour has for actors' (Gibbons 2006: 563). These forms include a multiplicity of approaches, most notably hermeneutics, cultural anthropology, *verstehen* social theory, critical theory, and post-structuralism. In what follows, we will focus on hermeneutics as a means of highlighting the differences between interpretivist and positivist approaches. We will then consider how approaches based on interpretivist and positivist assumptions analyse a specific area of political inquiry.

'Hermeneutics' originally referred to a method used to interpret theological and legal texts. In fact, 'the literal English translation of the German word "hermeneutics" is interpretation' (Gibbons 2006: 563). Today, 'hermeneutics' refers to theories and methods that are used in the interpretation of texts of all kinds. These texts include not just written documents, but any object or practice that can be *treated as a text* and which can, therefore, be the subject of interpretation. But can human beings and their actions be treated as a text and the subject of hermeneutical interpretation? Interpretivists argue that they can. Hermeneutics can be used to study behavioural outcomes because, if behaviour is a product of the meanings and intentions employed by social actors, then the social scientist endeavouring to understand that behaviour is involved in an interpretive exercise not unlike that engaged in by the translator of a text.

The philosopher Charles Taylor elaborates this argument in an influential essay entitled 'Interpretation and the Sciences of Man' (1994). Taylor explains that any field of study can be the object of hermeneutics if it meets two requirements. First, it must contain an object or a field of objects that is a text, or a 'text-analogue'. Second, this text must be 'confused, incomplete, cloudy' or 'seemingly contradictory'; that is, it must be in some way 'unclear'. When these criteria are met, hermeneutical interpretation can be used 'to bring to light an underlying coherence or sense' with respect to the objects defined by the field of study and, in this way, enable us to understand them (Taylor 1994: 181). Does the study of politics meet these criteria? Yes. We can treat the behaviour we are concerned to understand—the actions of a government, or the behaviour of members of a group towards one another—as 'texts'; and, since the motives and goals of this behaviour are often unclear or at odds with the pronouncements of the political actors involved, we can use interpretative methods in order to make sense of this behaviour.

Interpretivists argue that it is necessary not only to employ a hermeneutical approach, but also to reject empiricist scientific methods for studying human behaviour. Empiricist methods treat social reality as consisting only of what Charles Taylor calls 'brute data'. By 'brute data', Taylor means 'data whose validity cannot be questioned by offering another interpretation or reading, data whose credibility cannot be founded or undermined by further reasoning' (Taylor 1994: 184). These data capture political behaviour involving actions that have an identifiable physical end state. When actors raise their hands at a meeting at the appropriate time we can give this action a 'brute data' description and say that the actors are 'voting for the motion'. However, the action may have meanings for the actors that are not captured by the 'brute data description' of it. It may be the case that when an actor votes for a motion, she is also expressing loyalty to her party or defending the value of free speech (Taylor 1994: 190). But a 'behavioural' (or positive, or empiricist) political science deals only with brute data and their logical consequences, and avoids addressing the meaning of political behaviour.

As Taylor points out, brute data captures more than behaviour that has an identifiable end state: it also captures the subjective reality of individuals' beliefs, attitudes, and values 'as attested by their responses to certain forms of words, or in some cases, their overt non-verbal behaviour' (1994: 198–9). But while these data capture subjective meanings, there are *non*-subjective (intersubjective and common) meanings constitutive of social reality that they cannot capture such as, for instance, inter-subjective meanings and common meanings. Inter-subjective meanings are meanings that do not exist only in the minds of agents but are rooted in and constitutive of social relations and practices such as paying taxes and voting. Common meanings involve recognition or consciousness of shared beliefs, aspirations, goals, values, and a common reference point for public life of a society. Common meanings are the basis of community, in that they are expressed by collective aspirations, actions, and feelings (1994: 197). Taylor argues that we need to study these non-subjective (inter subjective and common) meanings in order to comprehend political issues such as social cohesion, stability, disorder, and legitimacy. Moreover, they are crucial for 'a science of comparative politics': without them, we 'interpret all other societies in the categories of our own' (1994: 200), rendering invisible important differences among societies and making comparison impossible.

To stay with this point for a moment longer, analyses based on positivist epistemological assumptions, like those offered by rational choice theory, depend on an abstract description of human agency, one that pays little attention to differences across social, cultural, and historical settings. Rational choice theory seeks to explain social phenomena as the outcome of purposive rationality, and of material and structural factors exercising causal influence on individuals. Its concern is to show how a given outcome is the result of purposive choices by individuals within a given set of material and structural circumstances. As Daniel Little puts it: 'Agents like these in structures like those, produce outcomes like these' (Little 2009). But interpretive approaches see individuals as unique, and human activities, actions, and social formations as unique historical expressions of human meaning and intention. Consequently, they are concerned, not with abstract descriptions of human agents, but with detailed interpretive work on specific cultures.

These differences between positivist and interpretive approaches can be illustrated by reference to a key area of research in our field: political participation. Positivist studies typically equate political participation with voting. However, interpretivists would argue that a particular voter may 'not understand voting as participation at all, in contrast, say, to party activism. (It is neither practically nor logically impossible that an actor could say, "No, I do not participate in politics, but I do vote")' (Schwartz 1984: 1118). But positivists tend to treat participatory acts as 'brute facts', as having an 'objective' ontological status: as existing 'in some sense "in the world" separate from the theoretical stance of the observer or of the participant' (Schwartz 1984: 1119).

Joel Schwartz points out that there is no objective point of view from which to describe and understand participation, that participation 'is a "subjective" phenomenon much like "justice" and "virtue"' (Schwartz 1984: 1119). Consequently, 'any successful attempt to describe and explain participatory acts must begin, not by imposing the observer's theoretical framework onto the data, but rather with a sensitivity to the frameworks of the participants themselves' (Schwartz 1984: 1120). While positivist studies typically equate political participation with voter turnout, participation involves a variety of political acts. By imposing their own concept of 'participation', researchers are prevented 'from seeing the plural forms that participation in fact takes in the world. Whether acts (of an American voter or demonstrator, a French revolutionary, a Muslim revolutionary, a Solidarity member, and so on) count as acts of participation depends on those actors' subjective understanding of what they are doing' (Schwartz 1984: 1117).

In sum, interpretivism maintains that all social action is framed by a meaningful social world. To understand, explain, or predict patterns of human behaviour, we must first understand the meanings concrete agents attribute to their environment (social and natural); the values and goals they possess; the choices they perceive; and the way they interpret other individuals' social action. Social science is, therefore, fundamentally different from natural science, and it is the importance of meaning that distinguishes social science from natural science. Humans act because of what things mean, so an understanding of human behaviour requires that we develop an understanding of meanings and intentions employed by social actors.

Many researchers have pointed to the tendency to cast positivism and interpretivism approaches as 'two grand traditions in social science epistemology' and to exaggerate the differences between them (Pollins 2007: 93). Positivism and interpretivism have different ontological and epistemological commitments, but they don't necessarily represent opposing or competing traditions. Researchers working in both traditions generally follow the same methodological conventions, and so can understand what those working within the other tradition are doing. Researchers depend upon different assumptions, and may be interested in and test different questions. But while they may 'be tackling different kinds of questions', 'practical investigation of these questions often leads them to similar methodological tasks' (Finnemore and Sikkink 2001: 395). Ted Hopf argues that there is, in fact, 'a certain methodological unity' between the two traditions. The methodological conventions they share include the following:

a. clear differentiation of premises from conclusions;
b. acknowledgement that sampling strategies matter;
c. recognition that some standards of validation must be established for the sources of evidence used;
d. differentiation of causes from correlations;
e. recognition that the spectre of spuriousness haunts all correlations;
f. acceptance of deductive logic;
g. belief in the need for the contestability of findings (2007: 56).

These shared methodological conventions may, in fact, be seen as reflecting a common research practice founded in the hypothetico-deductive method. As Brian Pollins puts it: some researchers 'assess whether the information they have gathered fits with the interpretation they have posited', and others 'consider the fit of competing interpretations with the facts they have gathered', but 'in either case they are practicing the hypothetico-deductive method' (Pollins 2007: 100). In fact, according to Dagfinn Føllesdal, the hermeneutic method that we discussed in our consideration of interpretivism, above, 'is actually the hypothetico-deductive method' applied to materials that are 'meaningful', i.e. material that expresses an actor's beliefs and values' (1994: 233). Interpretation-hypotheses can be judged by deducing consequences from them and confronting them with data, such as, for instance, a given text and related works bearing on it.

So interpretivists and positivists do not necessarily use different approaches to gathering relevant evidence. However, they do differ in their conception of what constitutes explanation (recall our discussion, above, about political participation). They also differ in their understanding of evidence.

The differences between positivist and interpretivist conceptions of both explanation and evidence might be described by defining a distinction between 'external' and 'internal' explanation and evidence. External explanations are associated with positivist research: they tend to work via correlations or deductions on the basis of *ascribed* reasons, and so need not concern themselves with actors' understandings of the world. Interpretive explanations, on the other hand, are 'internal' in the sense of their being concerned with the world of meanings inhabited by the actor (Hampsher-Monk and Hindmoor 2009: 48). The distinction can be applied to different types of evidence, as well: 'external evidence' consists of empirical evidence about the behaviour, and the effects of the behaviour, of particular actors; while 'internal' or interpretive evidence consists of evidence about the beliefs of actors whose actions comprise the phenomena to be explained.

To highlight these distinctions, let's compare the analysis offered by a specific positivist approach (rational choice theory) and a specific interpretivist approach (constructivism) with respect to a particular area of political inquiry: the eruption of ethnic conflict within the former Yugoslavia.

The analysis of ethnic conflict: a positivist (rational choice) and interpretivist (constructivist) approach

A number of rational choice and constructivist explanations have been offered for why ethnic conflicts erupted in Yugoslavia in the 1990s. Both types of explanation have been concerned to offer an alternative to the cultural, 'ancient hatreds' explanation for the war between the Serbs and Croats. As many people have noted, the vast majority of Serbs and Croats lived together peacefully until the spring of 1991, when Croatia declared its independence. There is no evidence to suggest the existence of deep and widespread hatred in relations among Serbs and Croats during the sixty-year history of Yugoslavia. Moreover, even if evidence could be found for the persistence of 'ancient hatreds', they still cannot explain a key 'puzzle': why relations among communities that had been living together peacefully became polarized *so quickly*, before finally dissolving into savage violence.

Rational choice theory is the study of strategic political interactions, of how people (agents or players) determine strategies in different situations. It explains outcomes as the result of rational choices made by individuals within a given set of material and structural circumstances. It shows that, given a particular set of circumstances, the strategic interactions of agents will produce predictable, law-like outcomes. Much of the analysis of strategic political interactions focuses on how individual actors make decisions in game-like situations. A 'game' is any situation in which a fixed set of agents or players, with a fixed set of strategies available to them, compete against one another, and receive a payoff as a result of the strategies they and their fellow actors choose. The assumption is that all players know all possible outcomes and have preferences regarding these possible outcomes based on the amount of value or utility they derive from each of them. All players behave rationally; and they make rational decisions about what strategy to pursue based on a calculation of the costs and benefits of different strategies for achieving their preferred outcome.

In a series of articles (1994, 1995, 1998), James Fearon used rational-choice assumptions as a basis for exploring the causes and conditions of ethnic conflict and war.

In order to explain the 'puzzle' of the rapid polarization of Serbs and Croats in Croatia in 1991, James Fearon develops a game-theoretic model: a model of how groups of people interact when confronted with a situation of uncertainty, based on assumptions of game theory. Fearon points out that, just months before the eruption of war between Serbs and Croats in Croatia, journalists had reported that 'most people seemed to have had no use for or interest in the exclusivist arguments pushed by the minority of extremists' (1998: 114). 'With the exception of a relatively small number of extremists . . . Serbs and Croats in the mixed population areas recognised that war would be costly and viewed it as unnecessary.' But in spring 1991, 'Serbs and Croats who had resisted the extremists appeals finally opted for division and war' (Fearon 1998: 115).

Fearon argued that, following the collapse of the Soviet Union, ethnic conflict erupted in Yugoslavia as a result of a 'commitment problem'. The problem arises when 'two political communities find themselves without a third party that can guarantee agreements between them' (1995: 2). If, in a new state, ethnic minorities don't believe that the state can guarantee that the ethnic majorities will not infringe on their rights, they will prefer to fight for succession while the state is still weak. This, he argues, helps to explain the rapid polarization of ethnic groups in Croatia following the declaration of Croatian independence in June 1991.

Explanation consistent with the hypothetico-deductive model here consists of (1) a set of initial determining conditions (circumstances pertaining at particular times and places); and (2) a general law or laws which connect these conditions to the type of events to be explained ('hypotheses' which are capable of being confirmed or disconfirmed by suitable empirical findings). First, Fearon specifies the set of initial conditions. The commitment problem, Fearon tells us, arises whenever three conditions hold: (1) the groups interact in anarchy, without a third party able to guarantee and enforce agreements between them; (2) one of the groups anticipates that its ability to secede or otherwise withdraw from joint arrangements will decline in the near future; and (3) for this group, fighting in the present is preferable to the worst political outcome it could face if it chooses continued interaction (1995: 10). Second, on the basis of a game-theoretic model he develops of the commitment problem, Fearon generates hypotheses about what makes ethnic war more or less likely. The key mechanisms include (1) the expected change in size in the relative military power between groups that would result from formation of a new state; (2) the relative size of the ethnic minority; (3) whether majority and minority groups' costs for fighting are low; and (4) whether institutions can be created that give minority groups political power that is at least proportional to their numbers.

Fearon then applies the model to the war in Croatia in 1991–2. When Croatia declared its independence from Yugoslavia, minority Serbs living in Croatia faced the prospect of being in a state with no credible guarantees on their political status, or economic and even physical security. 'If the commitment problem model does capture something of what was going on in Croatia, then we might expect to find evidence of Croatian leaders trying to work out guarantees with Serb leaders' (1998: 119). This, he finds, occurs on numerous occasions. Croatian President Tudjman met with the leader of the Serbs in Croatia, Jovan Raskovic, 'to discuss the issue of commitment to guarantees on the Serbs' status and "cultural autonomy"' (1998: 119). But despite Tudjman's efforts to construct a credible set of guarantees for the Serb minority, his efforts to solve the commitment problem were ultimately unsuccessful. With the 'prospect of entering the new state of Croatia with no credible guarantees on their political status, or economic or even physical security', the prospect of a war then appeared better to the Serbs than the prospect of fighting later, by which time the Croatian state would have grown stronger (Fearon 1998: 116).

The evidence, then, consists in showing that there is a 'fit' between the deductions of the theory and the observed behavioural outcomes; that the outcome is consistent with the theoretical predictions. Fearon also endeavours to demonstrate that his explanation offers a better 'fit' with the facts than other explanations do. Finally, he argues that the basic commitment problem that he describes 'appears either to lurk or to have caused interethnic violence' in other cases, as well: in Azerbaijan, Georgia, Moldova, Ukraine, Estonia, Zimbabwe, South Africa, and Northern Ireland (1995: 21).

Let's consider how an interpretivist approach, **constructivism**, explains the rapid ethnic polarization that occurred in the former Yugoslavia in the 1990s.

Constructivism is an approach that has had an important influence on political inquiry. Consistent with interpretivist assumptions, constructivism maintains that reality does not exist as something independent of us and is not, therefore, merely discovered by us: it is socially, and actively, *constructed*. Constructivists assume that social phenomena are social constructs in the sense that their shape and form is imbued with social values, norms, and assumptions, rather than being the product of purely individual thought or meaning. We live in 'a world of our making', as Nicolas Onuf (1989) has put it. Actors are not totally free to choose their circumstances, but make choices in the process of interacting with others and, as a result, bring historically, culturally, and politically distinct 'realities' into being. In this respect, the world of politics is a social construction rather than something that exists independently of human meaning and action. States and other social institutions take specific historical, cultural, and political forms that are a product of human interaction in the social world.

In contrast with positivist approaches which emphasize a single objective reality, the idea of social construction suggests difference across context. It is not only the material environment, but also the cultural and institutional environment that provides incentives and disincentives for behaviour. Society is more than just the site of strategic interaction to pursue pre-defined interests in a rational, utility-maximizing manner. It is a constitutive realm, an environment that forms and influences the identities and interests of actors and makes them who they are. Moreover, social interaction also influences the identity of actors. The properties of actors are not intrinsic to them: they are socially contingent, they depend on social interaction: bargaining/negotiating, arguing, communicating in general. Both the identities and interests of actors are constituted (formed, influenced) through interaction and by the institutionalized norms, values, and ideas of society. Since the interests and identities of actors are not given—but result from social interaction—they cannot be abstracted from the social conditions which produce them; and they are subject to change as a result of political processes.

Consistent with these assumptions, constructivism, like rational-choice approaches, rejects explanations of nationalist and ethnic phenomena as the outcome of essential cultural identities. But, unlike rational-choice approaches, it sees nationalist and ethnic conflict as a phenomenon that has assumed a variety of forms across space and time; and it emphasizes the role of identities that are multiple and fluid and politically malleable: influenced by surrounding structures and 'constructed' for political purposes.

Murat Somer (2002, 2001) addresses the same 'puzzle' as Fearon: the rapid ethnic polarization that occurred in Yugoslavia in the 1990s. Somer emphasizes the significance of public discourses in forming individuals' ethnic identities, and in suppressing and reviving dominant perceptions of ethnic identities. He argues that ethnic conflict is a result of processes of ethnic identity construction in the public arena that construct a divisive image of identities. Public ethnic activities and expressions are immediately observed and they immediately affect the decisions of others.

Ethnic polarization changes the dominant images of ethnic categories in society through cascades of individual reactions. A cascading process changes behaviour and attitudes and, once begun, is very difficult to stop. In Yugoslavia, ethnic polarization in public discourses was engineered by ethnic entrepreneurs who constructed and promoted a divisive image of ethnic identities as mutually exclusive and incompatible with belonging to the same nation. This triggered a 'cascade process', which resulted in the creation of a critical mass of opinion around a new image of ethnic identities. People who secretly held this divisive view, as well as people who now felt compelled to support it, jumped on the bandwagon. Hence, the divisive image became the norm, and it became 'inappropriate, even blasphemous, to defend interethnic mixing and brotherhood' (Somer 2001: 128).

Somer draws a distinction between public and private ethnic polarization and highlights the way people publicly 'falsify' their private beliefs. During the communist era, state policies had 'aimed at eradicating the public expression of the divisive image of ethnic relations in the country; but they had insufficiently encouraged its elimination in private'. Consequently, the public discourse in Yugoslavia had exerted pressure for 'downward falsification' to discourage people from openly expressing their ethnic prejudices. This 'downward preference falsification concealed, to most observers, the private importance of the divisive image'; consequently, 'even analysts who had a fair idea about the private significance of the divisive image were surprised by the severity of polarization' in the 1990s (2001: 136). During the 1990s, 'the dominant public discourse emphasizing unity and brotherhood' turned into one that emphasized 'radical ethnonationalism' (2001: 136). But this 'public polarization far exceeded private polarization' (2001: 143). Consequently, there was widespread 'upward ethnic preference falsification', the exaggeration of public support for the divisive image, as the new nationalist regime exerted pressure for people—including liberal and moderately tolerant individuals—to think and act in an ethnically intolerant manner.

Somer uses survey research which indicates decreases in self-identification with the overarching Yugoslav identity between 1981 and 1991. The respondents were anonymous, so these surveys were able to capture changes in people's private preferences. During the 1980s there was a striking upsurge in 'the public expression of the divisive image' (Somer 2001: 143). But, 'in 1989, when public polarization had reached an advanced state, anonymous surveys continued to reveal that interethnic tolerance levels were high by global standards'. So, 'while the public discourse was becoming increasingly more divisive and less tolerant of interethnic differences, private attitudes remained quite tolerant of interethnic differences'. In fact, 'the highest levels of tolerance were found in Bosnia, the site of the most violent crimes' (Somer 2001:144). 'Desertion and call-up evasion were very common during the civil war when public support for the divisive image was at its peak' (Somer 2001: 144).

Let's sum up by comparing the two approaches to understanding ethnic polarization in Yugoslavia. Both highlight the significance of social and political institutions in forming individuals' ethnic identities. But Fearon, like other rational-choice theorists, tends to stress the structural and constraining features of institutions. Somer, on the other hand, emphasizes their social and cognitive aspects. Both are constructivist in the sense that they see changes in an actor's identity constructions as likely to occur in moments of crisis and dilemma. But Fearon, consistent with rational choice approaches, emphasizes the role of strategic calculation in identity construction, while Somer emphasizes cognitive features, such as norms of behaviour and inter-subjective understandings (though these don't necessarily operate to the exclusion of the calculative element stressed in the rational choice explanations offered by Fearon and others).

Let's consider how the two analyses illustrate the distinction between 'internal' and 'external' explanation and evidence that we previously discussed. The analyses that Fearon and Somer offer are consistent with the assumptions, respectively, of rational choice and constructivist approaches regarding actors' interests: rational-choice theories assume that agents act on the basis of fixed interests and preferences; constructivists assume that interests can only develop from the image an actor holds of himself and of others, that identities are the source of interests (and, therefore, the basis of action) (e.g. Wendt 1994; Ringmar 1996).

Fearon models external 'behaviour', and then seeks evidence by way of deductive fit with that model. Empirical evidence consists of statements and activities of Croatian leaders that indicate a concern for providing the Serb minority with a commitment to guarantee their status and cultural autonomy. But there is no direct evidence of the existence of a commitment problem among the Serb population, of strategic behaviour on the part of individuals or groups, or of the relationship between belief and action. Direct evidence concerning whether the individual or group choices which led to ethnic polarization were made for the reasons stated in his model might be impractical or impossible to obtain. Instead, the 'test' of the model involves (1) deducing the factors that, in the given circumstances, might be expected to lead groups to resort to violence; and (2) observing the outcomes. Where we observe that circumstances favour the behaviours that the model tells us are most likely to occur, we can infer that there is a line of cause and effect that relates those circumstances and the outcome. Somer identifies a mechanism, the 'cascade' process, which links popular beliefs, public political discourse, and relations across groups. He then combines survey data with detailed examination of the historical events to provide evidence of the changing nature of public and private views and suggest the relationship between them.

Both analyses have implications for politics and policy: which of the explanations for ethnic conflict we choose to favour has implications for how people relate to each other and how governments act. The choice of which set of assumptions will provide the best starting point for your own research on a specific political issue or problem is one which you will need to carefully consider.

Conclusions

This chapter has begun our consideration of some fundamental ontological, epistemological, and methodological problems posed by social inquiry. These problems mostly branch out from one central question: are the methods of the social sciences essentially the same as, or essentially different from, those of the natural sciences? We have reviewed the basic tenets of three different answers to this question: positivism, scientific realism, and interpretivism. How these answers differ is presented in Box 2.3.

All of these define a position with respect to how we study and conduct research in the social sciences. As Box 2.3 shows, all are based on fundamentally different assumptions about how we can know and develop knowledge about the social world; and all of them remain important perspectives for contemporary social research. The question of whether and how we can pursue a systematic and rigorous study of social phenomena in the way that scientists pursue study of the natural world and, more generally, philosophical presuppositions about 'reality' implicit in social science research, bears on how we design or structure an approach to research into political phenomena, and the claims we can make with respect to the findings that result from that research.

At the heart of the debate among these perspectives is the question of what sort of knowledge we can gain about social phenomena. This question is also central to the controversy that we take up in Chapter 3, which is the debate about whether the knowledge produced through the study of the social world is or can be 'objective'; and in Chapter 4, where we consider the question of what is the 'social'.

Reality— is constantly being defined for us—by political scientists, by historians, by politicians in their speeches, by media analysts in their news reports. The ability to identify the underlying structure of assumptions or the implicit theory which shapes a given account of reality, whether presented by scholars, politicians, or journalists, allows us to become more active analysts of contemporary politics, rather than depending on the analysis of others.

BOX 2.3 Positivism, Scientific Realism, and Interpretivism Compared

	Positivism	Scientific realism	Interpretivism
Ontology: What is the nature of the social world?	No different from the natural world: an objective reality that exists independently of our knowledge of it (a 'naturalist' ontology).	No different from the natural world: an objective reality that exists independently of our knowledge of it (a 'naturalist' ontology).	Fundamentally different from the natural world. Reality is not mind-independent: it is subjectively created.
Epistemology: What sort of knowledge of the social world is possible?	Scientific knowledge of the social world is limited to what can be observed. We can explain and predict social phenomena by discovering empirical regularities, formulating law-like generalizations, and establishing causal relationships.	Scientific knowledge is not limited to what can be observed but also includes theoretical entities (unobservable elements of social life). We can explain and predict social phenomena based on theories about these entities and certify the truth of these theories by employing various rules of method.	Scientific knowledge can be gained through interpreting the meanings which give people reasons for acting. We can, in this way, understand human behaviour; but we cannot explain or predict it on the basis of law-like generalizations and establishing the existence of causal relationships.
Causality: what do we mean by 'causes'?	A reflection of the way we think about the world; established by discovering observable regularities.	A reflection of reality; established by discovering unobservable underlying generative mechanisms.	We cannot seek causes, but only uncover meanings that provide the reasons for action.
Methodology: How can we gain knowledge of the social world?	Through direct observation.	Through direct observation and logic applied to both observable and unobservable structures.	Interpretive theory and textual strategies. The social world is like a text and has to be interpreted to discover hidden meanings and subtexts.

 Questions

- What is involved in providing an explanation of social phenomena? How is explanation distinct from and related to interpretation?

- What place does the concept of 'law' have in social-scientific explanation?

- What does 'causality' mean? How, according to different conceptions of causality, do we establish that something causes something else?

- How is describing, interpreting, and explaining human action different from describing, interpreting, and explaining non-human events?

- Should the primary goal of social science be to provide law-like explanations, capable of supporting predictions? Or are law-like explanations impossible, or unnecessary, within social science?

Guide to Further Reading

March, D. and P. Furlong (2002), 'A Skin not a Sweater: Ontology and Epistemology in Political Science', in D. Marsh and G. Stoker (eds), *Theory and Methods in Political Science,* 2nd edition (Basingstoke: Palgrave), 17–41.
The authors discuss positivism, interpretivism, constructivism, and also realism, as different approaches to ontology and epistemology in political science, and illustrate their differences with case studies.

Martin, M. and L. C. McIntyre (eds) (1994), *Readings in the Philosophy of Social Science* (New York: MIT Press).
This volume brings together a collection of important texts on the disputed role of general laws in social-scientific explanation (Part II), and on interpretation and meaning (Part III).

Gibbons, M. T. (2006), Hermeneutics, Political Inquiry, and Practical Reason: An Evolving Challenge to Political Science'. *American Political Science Review* 100: 4 (November), 563–71.

Lane, R. (1996), 'Positivism, Scientific Realism and Political Science'. *Journal of Theoretical Politics* 8 (3): 361–82.
This article explores the implications of scientific realist principles for political science, political research, and political theory, providing examples of a scientific realist approach in studies utilizing a variety of theoretical approaches, including rational choice, new institutionalism, and comparative politics.

Little, D. (1991), *Varieties of Social Explanation: An Introduction to the Philosophy of Social Science* (Boulder, Colorado: Westview Press), chapter 2 ('Causal Analysis'), pp. 13–38.

Russo, F. (2009), *Causality and Causal Modelling in the Social Sciences* (New York: Springer).
This book offers an overview of debates, and it provides a valuable analysis of reasoning about causation by looking at the causal arguments advanced in specific social science studies.

Sankey, H. (2008), *Scientific Realism and the Rationality of Science* (Aldershot: Ashgate), chapter 1.
This chapter provides a clear exposition of the doctrines of scientific realism, which distinguishes between core and optional doctrines; and the principal arguments that have been advanced for scientific realism.

 ## References

Amadae, S. M. and B. Bueno de Mesquita (1999), 'The Rochester School: The Origins of Positive Political Theory', *Annual Review of Political Science* 2: 269–95.

Benoit, K. (2007), 'Electoral Laws as Political Consequences: Explaining the Origins and Change of Electoral Institutions'. *Annual Review of Political Science* 10 (June): 363–90.

Bhaskar, Roy (1998), *The Possibility of Naturalism: A Philosophical Critique of the Contemporary Human Sciences,* 3rd edition (Hemel Hempstead: Harvester Wheatsheaf).

Brown, Chris (2007), 'Situating Critical Realism', *Millennium: Journal of International Studies* 35(2) (March): 409–16.

Bryman, A. (2004), *Social Research Methods* (Oxford: Oxford University Press).

Colomer, J. P. (2005), 'It's Parties that Choose Electoral Systems (or, Duverger's Laws Upside Down)', *Political Studies* 53: 1–21.

Easton, D. (1969), 'The New Revolution in Political Science', *American Political Science Review* 63(4) (December): 1051–61.

Ekström, M. (1992), 'Causal Explanation of Social Action: The Contribution of Max Weber and of Critical Realism to a Generative View of Causal Explanation in Social Science', *Acta Sociologica: Journal of the Scandinavian Sociological Association* 35: 107–22.

Fearon, D. James (1994), 'Ethnic War as a Commitment Problem', paper presented at the annual meeting of the American Political Science Association, New York, http://www.stanford.edu/~jfearon/papers/ethcprob.pdf.

——(1995), 'Rationalist Explanations for War', *International Organization* 49(3): 379–414.

——(1998). 'Commitment Problems and the Spread of Ethnic Conflict', in David Lake and Donald Rothchild (eds), *The International Spread of Ethnic Conflict* (Princeton, NJ: Princeton University Press), 107–26.

Finnemore, M. and K. Sikkink (2001), 'Taking Stock: The Constructivist Research Program in International Relations and Comparative Politics', *Annual Review of Political Science* 4: 391–416.

Føllesdal, D. (1994), 'Hermeneutics and the Hypothetico-Deductive Method', in Michael Martin and Lee C. McIntyre (eds), *Readings in the Philosophy of Social Science* (Cambridge, MA: MIT Press).

Gerring, J. (2007), 'Review Article: The Mechanismic Worldview: Thinking Inside the Box'. *British Journal of Political Science* 38: 161–79.

Gibbons, M. T. (2006), 'Hermeneutics, Political Inquiry, and Practical Reason: An Evolving Challenge to Political Science', *American Political Science Review* 100: 4 (November), 563–71.

Gilpin, R. (1981), *War and Change in World Politics* (Cambridge: Cambridge University Press).

Grix, J. (2002), *The Foundations of Research* (Basingstoke: Palgrave/Macmillan).

Hampsher-Monk, I. and A. Hindmoor (2009), 'Rational Choice and Interpretive Evidence: Caught between a Rock and a Hard Place?' *Political Studies* 58(1): 47–65.

Hedström, P. and R. Swedborg, eds (1998), *Social Mechanisms: An Analysis Approach to Social Theory.* (Cambridge : Cambridge University Press).

Hempel, C. G. (1994), 'The Function of General Laws in History', in Michael Martin and Lee C. McIntyre (eds), *Readings in the Philosophy of Social Science* (Cambridge, MA: MIT Press), 43–54.

Hoffmann, M. J. (2006), 'Social (De)Construction: The Failure of a Multinational State', in Jennifer Anne Sterling-Folker (ed.), *Making Sense of International Relations Theory* (Boulder, CO: Lynne Reiner), 123–38.

Hopf, T. (2007), 'The Limits of Interpreting Evidence', in R. N. Lelbow and M. I. Lichbach (eds), *Theory and Evidence in Comparative Politics and International Relations* (Basingstoke: Palgrave/Macmillan), 55–84.

Hume, D. (1966), *Enquiries Concerning the Human Understanding* (Oxford: Clarendon Press).

Lane, R. (1996), 'Positivism, Scientific Realism and Political Science', *Journal of Theoretical Politics* 8(3): 361–82.

Little, D. (1991), *Varieties of Social Explanation: An Introduction to the Philosophy of Social Science* (Boulder, CO: Westview Press).

——(2009), 'McIntyre and Taylor on the Human Sciences'. 16 July. http://understandingsociety.blogspot.com/2009/07/macintyre-and-taylor-on-human-sciences.html.

May, T (2003), *Social Research: Issues, Methods And Process*, 3rd edition (Buckingham: Open University Press).

McIntyre, L. C. (1994), 'Complexity and Social Scientific Laws', in Michael Martin and Lee C. McIntyre (eds), *Readings in the Philosophy of Social Science* (Cambridge, MA: MIT Press), 131–44.

Onuf, N. (1989), *World of Our Making: Rules and Rule in Social Theory and International Relations* (Columbia, SC: University of South Carolina Press).

Pollins, B. (2007), 'Beyond Logical Positivism: Reframing King, Keohane, and Verba', in R. N. Lelbow and M. I. Lichbach (eds), *Theory and Evidence in Comparative Politics and International Relations* (Basingstoke: Palgrave/Macmillan), 87–106.

Popper, Karl, (1959), *The Logic of Scientific Discovery* (London: Hutchinson of London).

Riker, W. H. (1982), 'The Two-Party System and Duverger's Law: An Essay on the History of Political Science', *American Political Science Review* 76 (December): 753–66.

Ringmar, E. (1996), *Identity, Interest and Action* (Cambridge: Cambridge University Press).

Ross, M. (2001), 'Does Oil Hinder Democracy?' *World Politics* 53: 325–61.

Sankey, N. (2008), *Scientific Realism and the Rationality of Science* (Aldershot : Ashgate).

Schwartz, J. D. (1984), 'Participation and Multisubjective Understanding: An Interpretivist Approach to the Study of Political Participation', *Journal of Politics* 46: 1117–41.

Somer, M. (2001), 'Cascades of Ethnic Polarization: Lessons from Yugoslavia', *The ANNALS of the American Academy of Political and Social Science* 573(1): 127–51.

——(2002), 'Insincere Public Discourse, Trust, and Implications for Democratic Transition: The Yugoslav Meltdown Revisited', *Journal for Institutional Innovation, Development and Transition* 6 (December): 92–112.

Taylor, C. (1994), 'Interpretation and the Sciences of Man', in Michael Martin and Lee C. McIntyre (eds), *Readings in the Philosophy of Social Science* (Cambridge, MA: MIT Press), 181–212.

Tilly, C. (2001), 'Mechanisms in Political Processes', *Annual Review of Political Science* 4: 21–41.

Trochim, W. M. (2006), *The Research Methods Knowledge Base*, 2nd edition. Available at: http://www.socialresearch methods.net/kb/.

Wendt, A. (1994), 'Collective Identity Formation and the International State', *American Political Science Review* 88(2) (June): 384–96.

 ## Endnotes

1. Note the difference between the terms 'behaviourism' and 'behaviouralism': 'behaviourism' is a school of psychology which studies observable behaviour, rather than 'unobservable' behaviour such as mental processes and intentions, and emphasizes experimentation and causal analysis. 'Behaviouralism' is the term adopted by political scientists. The key tenet of behaviouralism is that only observable behaviour may be studied.

2. In recent years some researchers have modified Duverger's Law by suggesting that 'it is the number of parties that can explain the choice of electoral systems, rather than the other way round' (Colomer 2005: 1; see also Benoit 2007).

Objectivity and Values

 Chapter Summary

This chapter explores a key debate in the philosophy of social science: whether it is possible to separate facts and values in social science research. The debate raises fundamental questions about how values influence social-scientific inquiry, the role and responsibilities of the researcher in social-scientific inquiry, and the ways in which areas of study are shaped by the norms and values of research communities and environments. Consequently, the answers researchers give to these questions have important implications for how they approach research and understand its findings. Among the questions this chapter explores are the following:

● Can social science be 'value-free'?

● Are the findings of the natural sciences less biased than those of the social sciences?

● To what extent, and in what ways, do 'values' present problems for the analysis of the social world?

● To what extent, and with what effect, do a researcher's own values intrude into research?

● To what extent do the values associated with a set of shared social practices intrude into the search for knowledge?

Introduction

The aim of this chapter is to explore the question of whether social science can be 'value-free'. Political researchers want to be able to offer credible answers to important questions. They are concerned, therefore, to employ research practices and methods that enable them to do this. The question of whether and to what extent values influence scientific research bears directly on this concern. Scholars in all areas of research are concerned with this question; and, whether or not they follow ongoing debates on this issue in the philosophy of social science, their views tend, either implicitly or explicitly, to reflect the different answers and positions that these debates have generated.

The answers philosophers of science give to the question of how values influence scientific research differ according to how they answer a larger and more fundamental question: whether it is even possible to distinguish between facts and values in scientific inquiry. These are difficult and unsettling questions. They not only complicate our efforts to produce research findings that are unbiased and, therefore, reliable; they also raise doubts about whether it is possible to produce unbiased research at all.

In Chapter 2 we noted that the distinction between facts and values is a central tenet of positivism. Positivism maintains that facts are fundamentally different and distinguishable from values, and that they exist independently of the observer and the observer's values. Science is 'value-free'—it is concerned with facts, not values; and any intrusion of values in the research process contaminates the objective character of science.

Recall that this methodological position is the basis of another tenet of positivism: 'naturalism'. Naturalism claims that the social world is no different from the world of natural phenomena, and social scientists should therefore approach the study of social phenomena in the same way, according to the same scientific principles, that scientists use to study natural phenomena. To be scientific, social inquiry must seek comprehensive and systematic explanations of events, and it must be objective or value-free. The distinction between facts and values is what differentiates science from non-science, and what defines the boundary between the 'scientific' study of society and ideology. Consequently, arguments that suggest it is not possible to distinguish between facts and values would seem to undermine the possibility of understanding the social world through scientific study—the possibility, that is, of social science.

The aim of this chapter is to explore the question of whether social inquiry can be 'value-free'. How we answer this question depends on whether we think it is possible to distinguish and keep separate the realms of facts and values. In the following introduction to the fact/value debate, we, of necessity, present a somewhat stylized version of it. We first consider how this issue has been addressed in the study of politics. We then consider various ways that 'values' intrude into social-scientific inquiry: how the observer's values and other biases influence research, how the act of observation itself intrudes on the object of study, and the extent to which observation is 'theory-laden', i.e. shaped by shared social practices and inseparable from the interpretations to which those practices give rise.

Normative and empirical theory in political research

The influence on political research of positivism and its fact-value distinction is reflected in the institutionalization of a division between empirical and normative research and theory. This division is predicated on the assumption that it is possible to separate questions about what is (empirical questions) from questions about what should or ought to be (normative questions). According to positivism, it is this ability to separate empirical and normative questions that makes it possible for social science to be objective and value-free.

Empirical theory is concerned with questions that can be answered with empirical data (data gathered through observations of the world around us). Normative theory is theory that concerns itself with questions of what ought to be the case. It is often associated with 'moral' issues in politics; with questions concerning human rights, distributive justice, and intervention, and with questions of what is morally just: what is a just government, international order, distribution of resources, way of treating the environment for future generations? When, if ever, is war just, and what is just conduct in war? Positivists insist that propositions concerning such questions cannot be addressed by empirical theory and subjected to formal empirical tests; and that hypotheses about what *is* are constitutive of the domain of non-normative, value-free empirical theory. Research practice tends to reflect this view: normative questions tend to be addressed by political theorists in ways that do not involve 'rigorous, methodologically informed empirical study'; while empirical questions tend to be addressed by researchers concerned with the discovery of 'facts'; but not with undertaking 'rigorous, philosophically informed normative study' (Gerring and Yesnowitz 2006: 103). Scholars will assume, for instance, that federalism and civil society are good for democracy, or strong parties are good for governance, but will make no attempt to provide empirical proof of the assumption. Authors of empirical studies will suggest implicitly that their particular object of study 'has a broader significance', that the subject 'affects society', but fail to make explicit how, or to what extent, it does so (Gerring and Yesnowitz 2006: 107).

In recent years, critics of positivist social science have challenged this disciplinary divide. They argue that the notion of 'normative theory' assumes, wrongly, that we can distinguish between questions about *what is* and those concerned with *what ought to be*; and that all theory is normative theory. They argue that, though not all theory is expressly concerned with reflection on normative issues, no theory can 'avoid normative assumptions in the selection of what data is important, in interpreting that data, and in articulating why such research is significant' (Cochran 1999: 1). Robert Cox neatly sums up this overall position: 'all theory is for some one and for some purpose'. All theories reflect values (Cox 1981: 128). The claim that all theory is normative in this sense, is also a claim about the impossibility of separating facts and values. We begin our exploration of this issue in the next section.

Values, the researcher, and the research process

[O]ne can do a good job predicting what a study will find by knowing the preferences of the scholars who undertook it.

(Jervis 2002: 188)

The statement, quoted above, expresses a perhaps commonly held view. It is generally assumed that a researcher's values have at least some influence, not only on the conclusions reached, but on every aspect of research, including the selection of research questions, data gathering, observations, and conducting experiments. But does this preclude the possibility of separating facts and values, and of pursuing objective scientific study of the social world? Some scholars argue that it is impossible for social inquiry to be objective and value-free; others argue that objectivity in the social sciences, while perhaps difficult to maintain, is possible.

The sociologist Max Weber (1864–1920) developed a somewhat complicated and highly influential position on this question. Weber argued that (1) there *is* a distinction between facts and values: questions of value are independent of or separable from questions of fact; but that it nevertheless remains the case that (2) value-neutrality is *not* possible in the social sciences; however, despite this, (3) we must strive for a value-neutral social science. Let's consider each of these points a bit further.

Weber argued that facts can be distinguished from values because knowing the facts of something is not the same thing as knowing its value; and knowing the value of something does not lead us to a factual description. We can therefore distinguish between questions of fact and questions involving values. Social scientists should deal only in questions of fact and remain ethically neutral on questions of values. He emphasized, however, that values are unavoidable in the practice of social science. Values enter into the selection of problems, the determination of conclusions, the identification of facts, and the assessment of evidence. 'There is no absolutely "objective" scientific analysis. . . . of "social phenomena" independent of special and "one-sided" viewpoints' (1994: 535).

Researchers focus on 'only those segments of reality which have become significant to us because of their value-relevance'. Only a small portion 'of concrete reality is interesting and *significant* to us, because only it is related to the *cultural values* with which we approach reality' (1994: 539). Only those things that we perceive to be meaningful will become objects of investigation for us. Undertaking research on something presupposes that it is connected in some way to our values. A researcher's own 'point of view' also influences the conceptual scheme that he or she constructs in order to pursue inquiry. So researchers inevitably bring their own presuppositions into the research field. They cannot remain neutral; there is no 'view from nowhere'. Weber argues, however, that though many elements of research are subjective and value-relevant, it is nonetheless possible to conduct research in a value-neutral manner if researchers adhere to the norms and practice of good social science, and if they 'make relentlessly clear', both to their audience and themselves, 'which of their statements are statements of logically deduced or empirically observed facts and which are statements of practical evaluations' (Weber 1948: 2). As long as researchers adhere to scientific standards, then social science can make reference to values without making value judgements. It can provide a factual and objective assessment of actors and their practices, an objectively true account of how the world functions, without attempting to tell us what goals we ought to pursue, what direction policy ought to take, or what values ought to be promoted.

Weber's views have remained influential and continue to inform discussions of the role of values in scientific inquiry. Many contemporary scholars follow Weber in arguing that social inquiry can be objective, despite the intrusion of a researcher's own values in the research process; that, while 'important practical obstacles' are frequently encountered in social science research, that doesn't mean that it is *intrinsically impossible* to secure unbiased conclusions in the social sciences (Nagel 1994: 583). The philosopher, Ernest Nagel, argues that while the selection of problems may be value-orientated, 'It is not clear . . . why the fact that an investigator selects the material he studies in light of problems which interest him and which seem to him to bear on matters he regards as important', presents any greater challenge to the logic of social inquiry than for that of any other branch of inquiry (1994: 572). Nagel cites as an example a researcher who believes that 'a free economic market embodies a cardinal human value' and who wishes to inquire into which activities are important to its operation. Why, Nagel asks, should we assume that his interest in a free market economy will bias his evaluation of the evidence on which he bases his conclusions about what is needed for its operation? The fact that the interests of the researcher determine what he selects for investigation 'by itself, represents no obstacle to the successful pursuit of objectively controlled inquiry in any branch of study' (1994: 572).

Nagel acknowledges that researchers concerned with social phenomena are often committed to social values and that these enter into the assessment of evidence and the content of conclusions. But he argues that 'steps can be taken to identify a value bias when it occurs, and to minimize if not to eliminate completely its perturbing effects' (1994: 573). One way to do this is for social scientists to 'abandon the pretence that they are free from all bias' and 'state their value assumptions as explicitly and fully as they can' (1994: 572). He acknowledges that 'unconscious bias and tacit value orientations are rarely overcome by devout resolutions to eliminate bias'; but there are ways, he argues, to recognize and correct for prejudices. For instance, researchers can 'sift warranted beliefs' and 'retain only those proposed conclusions . . . that survive critical examination by an indefinitely large community of students, whatever their value preferences or doctrinal commitments' (1994: 574). While he recognizes that this mechanism may not work as effectively as in the natural sciences, he insists nonetheless that we are not warranted on these grounds to conclude that reliable knowledge of human affairs is unattainable (1994: 574).

Though much consideration focuses on the bias that a researcher may pass on to a subject, it may as likely be the case that bias arises in the interaction between researcher and subject. This likelihood can arise in all research, but it has received a good deal of attention in relation to ethnographic research. In ethnographic research, the researcher, while becoming more immersed in the community of study, may find it difficult to remain objective. In some cases, researchers come to identify so much with the subjects that they lose the capacity for objective criticism (this is often referred to as 'going native'). This source of bias in ethnographic research is discussed in Chapter 12.

While consciousness of biases and concerted effort to limit their impact may overcome some of the difficulties involved in separating facts and values, some biases that influence research findings may be more difficult for researchers to identify and control.

One bias of this sort is the influence which a researcher's *expectations* exercise on the results of an inquiry. Researchers call this type of bias the 'Rosenthal Effect', after psychologist Robert Rosenthal. Rosenthal conducted a series of studies that were designed to determine whether the expectations of researchers can bias their results. In one study, two groups of subjects were shown photographs of people and asked to rate the photographs according to whether the people in them had recently experienced success or failure. The experimenters who administered the test were told what result their group, on average, was expected to produce. Each time this experiment was replicated the results for each group conformed to the expectations that had been communicated to the experimenters. A second study tested the effect of experimenters' expectations on the performance of animals; a third experiment tested the effect of a teacher's expectations on student performance. The results of all the studies showed the same thing: that the expectations of the experimenters influenced the behaviour of their subjects. Further study led to the conclusion that experimenter bias influences *human* subjects through 'subtle and complex auditory and visual cues'; and it influences *animal* subjects through the way they handle and observe them (Martin 1994: 585–7). So, a researcher's expectation about the results of an experiment affects the outcome of the experiment. But this type of bias, Michael Martin argues, does not preclude the possibility of value-free inquiry. Experimental techniques that minimize contact between experimenter and subjects, and statistical methods that can correct for bias, mean that the Rosenthal Effect need not foreclose the possibility of objective social science research (Martin 1994: 593).

In sum, these and other scholars conclude, like Weber, that even though values *do* influence research, it is nevertheless still possible for social science to be objective and value-free. There are important practical difficulties in securing value-free and unbiased findings in the social sciences, but these are not insurmountable.

However, while it may be possible to limit or eliminate a researcher's own values or biases, a more difficult issue to address is the tendency for the act of observation *itself* to contaminate the subject of study and produces biased and unreliable conclusions. There are a number of related arguments about how this operates.

One argument is that human behaviour changes while we study it, because those we are studying alter their behaviour when they know they are being observed. This phenomenon is known as the 'Heisenberg Effect'. The 'Heisenberg Effect' derives from Werner Heisenberg's Principle of Indeterminacy in particle physics. Heisenberg's principle asserts 'that the very process of trying to observe tiny particles inside the atom alters the situation being studied' (Morgan 1994: 30). Some political scientists have pointed out that the behaviour of government officials and bureaucrats changes when they know they are under observation. This, in fact, 'is one of the justifications for having a free press': the scrutiny of the press is supposed to deter politicians 'from taking actions that would be to their benefit but costly to the public interest' (Morgan 1994: 30).

The philosopher Charles Frankel found many instances of the 'Heisenberg Effect' in the course of working as a United States Assistant Secretary of State in charge of education and culture from 1965 to 1967. Frankel discovered that 'when he sent out letters merely to get information about what US officials were doing with regard to particular programmes, he got back replies indicating that the officials to whom he had written had changed what they were doing after receiving his letter' (Morgan 1994: 37). He reported that merely in an effort to inform himself, he had 'apparently produced changes in policy', i.e. in the phenomena which he was studying (Frankel 1969: 83; quoted in Morgan 1994: 37).

The problem, then, is that human behaviour changes while, and because, we are trying to study it. However, there is a variety of techniques for dealing with this difficulty. For instance, some researchers in our field get around the problem by using 'content analysis' (see Chapter 13). By systematically analysing an official's statements for clues to his perceptions and attitudes, researchers can get material on decision-making without interviewing the decision-makers.

But the problem of altering behaviour as a result of studying it has another facet: behaviour may change as a consequence, not only of the process, but of the results, of studying it. The problem here is how we can know if the theories we use to explain outcomes are true if they themselves have the effect of altering the practices that produce those outcomes. An example of this is the effect deterrence theory had on weapons deployments, contingency planning, arms-control proposals, and relations among allies. If theory alters practice, it becomes, in effect, a self-fulfilling prophecy. How then can we claim to be able to separate and distinguish between the realms of fact and value? Generally speaking, the physical sciences do not face this problem: planets do not move differently because of the process or the results of studying them. But in the social sciences, theory can be a self-fulfilling prophecy.

If, using the authority of science, you convince policy-makers that, for instance, war is inevitable given the anarchical nature of the international system, than it *is* inevitable and it becomes impossible to test the proposition scientifically (Morgan 1994: 31–2).

There are two other arguments concerning how the act or process of observation compromises our ability to separate facts and values. Perhaps the best way to make clear their substance and implications is by briefly revisiting Karl Popper's 'falsificationist thesis' (1959), which we discussed in Chapter 2. Popper argued that falsification, not verification, should be the aim of science; that social inquiry must proceed deductively, through a process in which observations are derived from and used to 'test' theories; but that the aim of our tests must be to 'falsify', rather than verify, them. We reject those which are falsified but continue to test those that are not until they become so thoroughly tested that we can consider them to be 'confirmed', though it remains possible that someday someone may falsify or significantly modify them.

One objection that has been made to this argument is that Popper's argument about falsification seems to assume that observations or facts we use to test theories can be established independently of the theory that they are meant to test. But Thomas Kuhn (1962) and others have argued that observation is 'theory-laden': that our observation of 'facts' cannot be separated from the theoretical notions which give intelligibility to what we observe. Observation is the interpretation of a phenomenon in the light of some *theory* and other background knowledge. In fact, we might say that a phenomenon is an already interpreted regularity (or event). For instance, as Kuhn explains (1962: 114), when we look at the picture shown in Figure 3.1 we do not merely observe curved lines on a page: we see either a rabbit or a duck.

Figure 3.1 Duck or rabbit?
Source: Jastrow, J. (1899).

Can we perceive what these lines produce irrespective of an act of interpretation? While the same data lend themselves to different interpretations, the perceptual experience and theoretical interpretation are simultaneous: the 'facts' do not present themselves to us independently of our theoretical beliefs. What we observe this object to be is dependent on how we describe it. That is, if we are told that 'this is a picture of a duck', we will likely see a duck; if we are told that it is a rabbit, we will probably see a rabbit. The reality is not independent of a description of that reality.

A second objection to Popper's notion of falsifiability highlights another problem with the fact-value distinction. Popper assumes that the scientific enterprise involves the rigorous, systematic application of reason, so that when theories are falsified by experience they are thrown out, irrespective of how many important people have invested themselves and staked their careers in promoting them. But some people question whether this assumption is warranted. Is this actually the way scientists go about developing and testing theories? Is it actually the case that researchers seek to disprove or falsify their own theories? *Do* they discard their theories when they are confronted with disconfirming evidence?

The philosopher of science, Thomas Kuhn, argued that Popper presents an idealization of true science; that, rather than unrelenting criticism and testing, science has tended towards paradigmatic conformity and conservatism. In *The Structure of Scientific Revolutions* (1962), Kuhn argues that science is a social institution. It consists of a community within which there is a common view—what Kuhn calls a 'paradigm': a conceptual scheme, about which some community of scholars agree, and which defines the objects of investigation and the ways in which they are to be investigated. The implications of this argument for the fact-value distinction and, thus, for the objectivity of scientific knowledge, has made Kuhn's book a focus of controversy for nearly half a century.

In the next section we consider Thomas Kuhn's influential arguments concerning paradigms and how they change through scientific 'revolutions'. After reflecting on their implications for the possibility of value-free social inquiry, we then explore the implications of Imre Lakatos' rival notion of 'scientific research programmes'.

Values and social practice

So far, the discussion has focused on how a researcher's values intrude on the research process. But to adequately address the question of how values influence social research we need also to consider the influence of values associated with a more general set of shared social practices.

Social-scientific research is often portrayed as being unaffected by the context and environment in which it is conducted. However, researchers live within a given society, and they work within a system of academic incentives and disincentives that reward some activities and discourage others. It would seem unreasonable to suppose that this system, including the gate-keeping functions of the academy, the creation and enforcement of disciplinary norms, 'rewarding good behaviour and punishing—or at least ignoring—bad behaviour' (Gerring 2001: 5), public and private funding, publication outlets, universities, government, and the mass public, *does not* affect researchers and their work. The question is whether such influences invalidate the possibility of a neutral social science. In the next section, we discuss two influential perspectives on this question.

Thomas Kuhn and scientific revolutions

Thomas Kuhn (1922–96) is widely considered to have been 'one of the most influential philosophers of science of the twentieth century, perhaps the most influential' (Bird 2009). His book, *The Structure of Scientific Revolutions* is 'one of the most cited academic books of all time' (*Stanford Encyclopedia of Philosophy*). By highlighting the value-laden social practices within which scientific inquiry takes place, the book presents a compelling challenge to the notion that it is possible to separate facts and values in scientific science research.

In *The Structure of Scientific Revolutions* (1962), Kuhn looks at the history of science and concludes that the growth of knowledge is not a *logical* process but a *social* one. Science does not simply progress by stages based upon neutral observations, and through cumulative, gradual knowledge acquisition. Science is an essentially *social* institution. Scientists are socialized, not to pursue unrelenting criticism and testing, but to accept the reigning values, beliefs, concepts, and rules of their profession. Consequently, there is no 'theory-independent' view of the world; the world appears to us in the context of theories we already hold: it is 'theory-laden'.

Kuhn argued that science tends to be dominated by 'paradigms'—conceptual schemes about which some community of scholars agree, and which define the objects of investigation and the ways in which they are to be investigated. Once a paradigm is established, it directs scientific investigation through the operation of what Kuhn calls 'normal science'. The aim of 'normal science' is not 'to call forth new sorts of phenomena', but 'to force nature into the preformed and relatively inflexible box that the paradigm supplies'; indeed 'those that will not fit the box are often not seen at all' (1962: 24).

Though Kuhn's book was concerned with the natural sciences, it caused a great crisis of objectivity in both the natural and the social sciences. Kuhn's arguments threw open to question the status of science as a rational and progressive development towards 'truth', challenging the distinction between natural and social science, and between social science and ideology.

As we have previously discussed, positivists maintain that if the study of politics is to be scientific, it must adopt the same scientific principles that the natural sciences use to study natural phenomena. But Kuhn challenges the notion that the natural sciences are objective or value-free; that scientists apply the neutral instrument of 'scientific method' to independently existing reality, that the growth of scientific knowledge is piecemeal and cumulative; and that theories are discarded as 'falsified' if they fail (Ball 1976: 158). Based on his reading of the history of science, Kuhn argues that the validity of truth-claims is grounded in the consensus of some scholarly community; that what science means by 'truth' is the consensus of those it defines as competent and full members of its community. Academic journals, hiring, and curricula are orientated towards certain explanatory frameworks and conceptual schemas, and research using other frameworks and schemas is undervalued and marginalized within the profession.

These arguments challenge the distinction in science between fact and value and, consequently, our faith in the authority of 'science'. Science is essentially social. It consists of a community within which there is a common view. This common view is what Kuhn calls a 'paradigm'.

Paradigms and paradigm change

In *The Structure of Scientific Revolutions*, Kuhn describes the developmental pattern of science in terms of paradigm shifts. For Kuhn, the history of science is the history of transition from one paradigm to another via 'revolution'. What Kuhn calls a 'paradigm' is a conceptual scheme, about which some community of scholars agree, and which defines the objects of investigation and the ways in which they are to be investigated. A paradigm shift occurs when an anomaly or anomalies arise which violate the assumptions of the reigning paradigm.

Kuhn elaborates a model of the development of science that focuses on the consolidation of paradigms, and processes which shift the commitment of a community of scholars from one paradigm to another. The model starts by elaborating the features of what Kuhn calls *pre-paradigmatic scientific investigation*. This is a pre-scientific phase in the development of a scientific field in which investigation is random and diverse. The absence of a paradigm or some candidate for one means that 'all of the facts that could possibly pertain to the development of a given science are likely to seem equally relevant'. As a result, 'fact-gathering is a far more nearly random activity than the one that subsequent scientific development makes familiar' (Kuhn 1962: 15).

During the period of pre-paradigmatic investigation, a variety of schools of thought compete for our attention. But in the next step in the model, one of the pre-paradigmatic schools triumphs, leading to the *establishment of a paradigm*. It is then that scientific investigation becomes highly directed and focused. Paradigms generate 'particular coherent traditions of scientific research', reflected in textbooks, departments, degrees, appointments, promotions, journals, conferences, and honours and awards (1962: 10). The establishment of a paradigm inaugurates a period of what Kuhn calls '*normal science*', of science that operates within the limits of a paradigm and concerns itself with testing and working on 'puzzles' via bits of research that are implied by the paradigm. It consists primarily of developing the paradigm 'by extending the knowledge of those facts that the paradigm displays as particularly revealing, by increasing the extent of the match between those facts and the paradigm's predictions, and by further articulation of the paradigm itself' (1962: 24). This involves both empirical and theoretical work. The empirical work consists of fact gathering, improving the accuracy and scope of factual determinations, matching facts with theory, coming up with quantitative measures, and applying the paradigm to new areas and different settings. Normal theoretical work involves using the theories generated by the paradigm to predict, and developing new or more precise applications of them. But whether empirical or theoretical, the work of normal science does not raise questions about the paradigm itself. It treats the paradigm as a given; it does not pursue critical exploration of its core assumptions. It engages, instead, in 'a strenuous and devoted attempt to force nature into the conceptual boxes supplied by' the paradigm (1962: 5). Normal science proceeds on the assumption 'that the scientific community knows what the world is like', and scientists aggressively defend that assumption.

It is possible, however, for research within the framework of the paradigm, or real world events and processes, to bring to light anomalies for the paradigm. An *anomaly* is something which deviates from the general rule; something which is inconsistent with the basic assumptions. But anomalies are not grounds for rejecting a paradigm; they generally do not even cause a critical review of it. However, if the anomalies grow, or if an anomaly is very fundamental—if it threatens to undermine the very foundation of the paradigm—this may lead to a *crisis*. An anomaly may also evoke a crisis if it has some immediate practical import. In that case, the field starts to revolve around the problem and a search for its solution, and the field may consequently begin to look different. However, scientists resist change. They will set the problem aside, or devise modifications in order to shoehorn the anomalous fact into the existing paradigm. And even when the crisis begins to blur the paradigm—to loosen the rules of normal research in the field—theorists will not declare the crisis-ridden paradigm invalid unless there is some alternative paradigm available to take its place.

Once a candidate for a new paradigm emerged, there is a battle over its acceptance. Finally, there is a *transition* from a paradigm in crisis to a new one from which a new tradition of normal science emerges. This constitutes a revolution in the field. As in a political revolution, in a 'scientific revolution'

1. a malfunction leads to crisis;

2. there is a loosening of rules as basic institutions are rejected;

3. competing camps form: there are those who seek to defend the old order, and those who seek to institute something new;

4. the competing camps seek support by resorting to techniques of mass persuasion;

5. scientists transfer their loyalties from the old to the new paradigm, and this inaugurates a new era of normalcy or 'normal science'.

Figure 3.2 depicts these steps and how they are related.

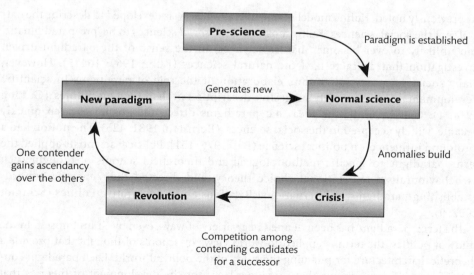

Figure 3.2 Thomas Kuhn, *The Structure of Scientific Revolutions*

The implications of this model are significant for the way we understand scientific claims. The notion of 'normal science', as elaborated by Kuhn, suggests that the rationality of science is limited; that just as adherents of an ideology or religion will discard an anomaly or disconfirming fact or incorporate it within the ideology, scientists will 'often suppress fundamental novelties because they are necessarily subversive' of their 'basic commitments' (1962: 5). Similarly, the shift from one paradigm in favour of another is not the result of a rational decision but something rather more like a conversion experience. Paradigms shift when scientists change their minds about fundamental matters.

This represents a clear challenge to the positivist ideal of scientific progress. Positivists see the choice between two competing theories as resolved by a 'crucial experiment' whose results supports one theory and refutes the other. But, for Kuhn, the shift from one paradigm to another neither results from nor produces cumulative knowledge because different paradigms produce *incommensurable* knowledge. Paradigms are incommensurable because they disagree about what the data actually are; so paradigm choice can never be settled by logic and experiment alone. It involves, at least in part, an act of faith.

In sum, a paradigm consists of a set of theories that share, not only common assumptions, but incommensurable content with respect to some other paradigm. This is because paradigms do not contain theory-neutral facts that can serve as a basis of comparison. All observation is theory-laden: 'When Aristotle and Galilei looked at swinging stones, the first saw constrained fall, the second a pendulum' (Kuhn 1962: 121). They relied on such different ontological assumptions that they were incommensurable; so no neutral measure could be found to assess one against the other. The arbiter, Kuhn argues, is peer consensus. And the new 'paradigm', or way of looking at the world, may not contain any of the ideas of the old one.

Kuhnian paradigms and political studies: the case of development theory

As previously noted, Kuhn's model of scientific progress was developed to describe the natural, not the social, sciences. Kuhn considered the *social* sciences to be 'pre-paradigmatic' and unlikely to ever become 'mature sciences', in the sense of the paradigm-driven investigation that characterized the natural sciences (Kuhn 1962: 164–5). However, many social scientists saw Kuhn's elaboration of the role of paradigms in scientific development, 'as an extremely suggestive description of their own disciplines' (Gutting 1984: 1). Consequently, the idea that paradigms direct and shape research quickly became 'widely accepted in the social sciences' (Bernstein 1981: 425). The notion had a 'profound influence' on political science (Ball 1976: 151). Political scientists applied the term 'paradigm' to specific methodological and theoretical schools of thought such as behaviouralism and rational choice theory, and directed their energies towards establishing paradigms in International Relations and Comparative Politics (Schmidt 2002: 9).

The term 'paradigm' has been defined in a variety of ways, even by Kuhn himself. In the study of politics, the term is applied to world views or schools of thought that provide a theoretical architecture for pursuing the study of the political world. Each paradigm consists of a set of assumptions that provide a basis for the development of theories that explain particular events or categories of events, and that enable us to decide, from among the universe of political phenomena, which are important to study. Different behaviours and prescriptions for action flow from different sets of assumptions. If you assume people are capable of altruism, mutual aid, and collaboration, you might be in favour of pursuing cooperation and collective action to resolve problems and advance global welfare. If you assume that humans are driven, first and foremost, by an instinct for power, your choices might be more fatalistic and survivalist. If you assume that people are basically a product of the material conditions and social relations which dominate their life, then, if you wish to change the world, you may seek to change the material environment which shapes human thought and action. This general usage of the term 'paradigm' in the study of politics is summarized in Box 3.1.

Let's consider an example of how the notion of 'paradigm' has been applied to a specific area of inquiry within politics: the study of development.

Paradigms and the study of development

Since World War II, the field of development studies has been dominated by two theoretical perspectives: 'modernization theory' and 'dependency theory'. These perspectives have been frequently referred to as 'paradigms' (Bodenheimer 1971; Foster-Carter 1976; Valenzuela and Valenzuela 1979; Pavlich 1988; Geddes 2003). Barbara Geddes argues that, while neither perspective has operated as a 'Kuhnian hegemonic paradigm', they have 'most of the other features Kuhn attributes to paradigms' (2003: 6–7). Each is comprised of 'collections of theories, hypotheses, applications, and favoured methodologies' (2003: 21). In each, a set of theories structures research, including identifying what questions need to be addressed and what constitutes evidence. Modernization theory is based on Liberal and neo-Liberal assumptions, while dependency theory is based on Marxist and neo-Marxist assumptions. Each consequently describes and explains 'third world' underdevelopment in strikingly different ways.

A paradigm for the study of development emerged in the United States during the immediate post-World War II decades, and it reflected the social context of that place and

---

BOX 3.1 Paradigms in Political Research

Paradigms

- arise within a specific social context
- consist of a set of assumptions about the nature of an area of study
- help to explain events and processes, and provide a guide to action or policy
- lose their usefulness when events or circumstances arise which violate the assumptions of the paradigm, and are supplanted by other paradigms, containing different assumptions

time. US foreign policy following World War II was concerned to ensure that the 'developing world' would not be drawn into the Soviet communist bloc; and it was this concern that animated the US government to enlist social scientists to study and devise ways of promoting capitalist economic development and political stability (Gendzier 1985; Diamond 1992; Simpson 1999). By the early 1950s, the study of 'development' was established as a key scholastic project and, through generous funding and institutional inducements, it continued to attract a steady and ever-expanding flow of research and writing from across the social sciences. Within a couple of decades, the study of development had markedly converged around a common set of analytic conventions and general themes. These conventions and themes eventually became the basis for what is referred to as 'modernization theory'.

Modernization assumed that underdevelopment was a stage in development through which all nations must pass, and that progress would eventually come about through the spread of modern capitalism to backward, traditional areas. But, consistent with strands of neo-Liberal thought current in post-World War II America, it maintained that development was not something that could be achieved through more-or-less natural processes of economic growth, but only through the intervention of more advanced countries. Problems of development, it maintained, result from weaknesses in the various factors of production—land, labour, and capital—within the developing countries; and the way these weaknesses could be overcome is through trade, foreign investment, and aid from advanced capitalist countries. Ultimately, and through contact with the developed market economies, the diffusion of capital and technology would produce economic development in the backward countries.

By the end of the 1960s, a key anomaly had emerged for the modernization paradigm: 'modernization' did not appear to be occurring. The paradigm had generated the expectation that the development of industrial capitalism in 'third world' countries would enable them to achieve the conditions of life that exist in the advanced industrial countries of 'the West'. However, it soon became clear that converging levels of industrialization had not produced a concomitant convergence of incomes; and that the divide in income and wealth between the 'developed' and 'developing' worlds was, in fact, widening. For whole societies and large populations within them, industrial 'development' appeared to be producing conditions of life that were worse and not better.

In the late 1960s, a theoretical perspective emerged that offered an explanation for this anomaly. The overall conception it advanced was of capitalist development as a worldwide process that, as the result of the appropriation of surplus by advanced countries from those in the 'developing' world, delivers unequal benefits and produces structurally different developmental outcomes. This perspective formed the basis of what came to be known as 'dependency theory'.

Dependency theory not only challenged many of the core assumptions of modernization theory, it turned modernization theory on its head. While modernization theorists focused on the benefits of free trade, foreign investment, and foreign aid, dependency theorists argued that international market relations occur in a framework of uneven relations between developed and underdeveloped countries and work to reinforce and reproduce these relations. Dependency theorists argued that the international economy is under the monopolistic control of the developed economies. Free, unregulated international trade and capital movements tend to favour the already well-endowed and work to accentuate, not diminish, international inequalities. A more equitable distribution of benefits, they argued, could not occur within the international capitalist system; and, in consequence, 'third world' countries will be unable to move beyond limited industrialization.

But modernisation theorists and other critics soon pointed to a key anomaly for dependency theory: the demonstrated capacity of some 'third world' countries to industrialize and achieve rapid economic growth. The response of dependency theorists was to insist that, though the manufacturing sector in many 'third world' countries has grown dramatically, these sectors are controlled by multinational corporations with headquarters in the advanced countries; and, whatever benefits they may bring in the form of managerial and technological know-how, they take more than they give and make it impossible for these countries to achieve the conditions of life that exist in the advanced countries. While critics acknowledge that many problems of development persist in countries that have achieved substantial industrial growth, they argue that the explanation that dependency theorists offer for them is unconvincing, that it fails to sufficiently account for different developmental outcomes, vastly exaggerates the power of the international system to shape outcomes in developing countries, and systematically ignores the role of internal factors in producing and reproducing these problems.

The debate remained at a stalemate. Adherents of both perspectives failed to undertake the sort of vigorous criticism, empirical testing, or theoretical investigation that might open the way to radical revision, synthesis, or consensus. Instead, modernization theorists and dependency theorists continued to reassert their commitment to the core assumptions of their respective paradigms: one set of theorists continually urged the necessity for greater market freedom; another set continued to focus on the enduring legacy of colonialism and the continued relevance of imperialism. With development theory at an impasse, many theorists simply undertook to reduce expectations of development, so that, by the second half of the 1990s, 'the normal usage of the term "development" had mutated to mean a modest increase in "industrialisation"... an improved capacity to produce textiles, sports shoes, furniture, or even a solid GDP based on the export of resources, agricultural products, or low-tech industries' (Mason 1997: 409).

The field of development studies appears to many observers to have been driven, less by the findings of rigorous scientific investigation, than by incommensurable and irreconcilable ideological commitments. Barbara Geddes has argued that inquiry into development has been characterized by the succession of one untested theory after another, bringing us no closer to truth but, instead, embroiling us 'in fruitless, often ideologically weighted debates' (2003: 223). The problem with the two perspectives, she argues, is not so much their incapacity to resolve anomalies, as the paradigmatic conformity that led researchers to ignore disconfirming evidence. In each paradigm, 'evidence was available that should have called them into question at the time of their creation'. Yet, it took 'decades to notice the plethora of inconvenient facts' (2003: 7–8), because researchers failed 'to make use of all available information' in the formulation of theories, and consumers were willing 'to accept theories without strong supporting evidence' (2003: 17). Analysts used evidence selectively 'to develop, support, or test theories': the modernization paradigm 'used evidence from only a few North Atlantic countries'; while earlier versions of dependency theory 'ignored readily evidence of rapid growth' in developing countries' (2003: 17–18).

Dependency theory was revised in response to evidence of industrial growth in developing countries. However, 'cross-national studies that challenged the implications of the revised dependency paradigm were ignored' (2003: 15). She notes that scholars find persuasive and are drawn to a theory because of its intuitive, emotional, and ideological appeal. They prefer one theory over another less for its explanatory abilities than because of its consistency with their own interests, beliefs, values, and personal morality; and when a theory fits with their personal experience or ideological commitments, they are less inclined to dig deep for disconfirming evidence. What researchers see is essentially related to their theories and beliefs. Available information that is inconsistent with a researcher's preconceptions is disregarded. In this way, paradigms become, in effect, a means of excluding other interpretations and their policy implications.

These reflections are consistent with Kuhn's notion of science as 'social', as are Geddes' account of the shift from one developmental model to another. Barbara Geddes observes that 'Each paradigm lost its power to structure research when evidence of gross inconsistency between expectations arising from theories within the paradigm and real-world events became impossible to ignore' (2003: 7–8). When this occurred, modernization theory was overthrown by dependency theory in the same way that political regimes are toppled: by 'well-organized, coherent, mobilized opposition'. The subsequent demise of dependency theory was due to its own 'internal contradictions and inability to deal with the inconvenient facts thrown up by the world'; and, like the collapse of a regime, the fall of the dependency paradigm was followed by a period of 'chaos and contention' (2003: 7).

While Kuhn's arguments continue to provoke reflection on the nature of the social-scientific enterprise, a second, contrasting conception of the nature of science and how it advances has also proved highly influential. But, before turning to a consideration of this second perspective, it is worth noting a position that takes seriously Kuhn's notion of 'normal science' and calls for a 'post-normal science'.

The notion of 'post-normal science' was advanced by Silvio Funtowicz and Jerome Ravetz (1992, 1993) to describe an approach that is complementary to, but different from, conventional or 'normal' science. They argue that, while 'normal science' is appropriate in situations with low levels of uncertainty and risk, it is not suitable in situations when either decision stakes or system uncertainties are high. With low levels of uncertainty and risk, the standard techniques and procedures of scientific inquiry, and the peer review process for ensuring the quality and validity of results, remain appropriate. But Funtowicz and Ravetz argue that 'traditional problem-solving strategies of science . . . need to be enriched to solve the problems that our science-based industrial civilization has created'. They call for a 'democratization' of science that entails, not only incorporating multiple viewpoints into the process of inquiry, but extending the peer community. Their notion of post-normal science is summed up in this excerpt, below.

The problem situations that involve post-normal science are ones where, typically, facts are uncertain, values in dispute, stakes high, and decisions urgent. Because applied science and professional consultancy are inadequate, something extra must be added onto their practice which bridges the gap between scientific experts and a concerned public. This is post-normal science, comprising a dialogue among all the stakeholders in a problem, regardless of their formal qualifications or affiliations. For the quality assessment of the scientific materials in such circumstances cannot be left to the experts themselves; in the face of such uncertainties, they too are amateurs. Hence there must be an *extended peer community*, and they will use *extended facts*, which include even anecdotal evidence and statistics gathered by a community. Thus the extension of the traditional elements of scientific practice, facts, and participants creates the element of a new sort of practice. This is the essential novelty in post-normal science. In this way we envisage a democratization of science, not in the sense of turning over the research labs to untrained persons, but rather bringing this relevant part of science into the public debate along with all the other issues affecting our society. (Funtowicz and Ravetz 1992: 254–5; emphasis in original)

While this perspective shows how Kuhn's arguments continue to inform thinking about the nature of the social-scientific enterprise, it leaves unanswered questions about the research methods, and processes of validation, that are appropriate for post-normal science. Let's turn, now, to a contrasting conception of the nature of science.

Imre Lakatos and scientific research programmes

In his essay, 'Falsification and the Methodology of Scientific Research Programs' (1970), the philosopher of science, Imre Lakatos (1922–74), emphatically rejects Kuhn's model of scientific progress. Kuhn's model, he argues, is relativistic and reduces science to 'mob-psychology' (1970: 178). Lakatos' aim, therefore, is to elaborate a model of scientific change that highlights how scientific change involves, at every step, a process that is both critical and rational. He replaces Kuhn's 'paradigm' with the notion of a '*scientific research programme*', and describes how the incremental, cumulative, and progressive articulation of scientific research programmes lead to the growth of scientific knowledge. He rejects the notion that there is anything like 'normal science' where everyone agrees on the basic assumptions defining a subject of investigation and the way in which it is to be investigated. He argues that there are always alternative, competing theories in existence. What Kuhn calls 'normal science', he argues, is nothing but a research programme that has achieved monopoly; but research programmes rarely achieve complete monopoly and, when they do, they do so only for relatively short periods (1970: 155).

A 'scientific research programme' consists of two main elements: the 'hard core' and the 'protective belt'. The relation of these two elements is defined by two methodological rules: the 'positive heuristic' and the 'negative heuristic'. Box 3.2 provides a definition of these terms, as well as a number of other terms relating to them.

The *hard core* of a research programme consists of very general hypotheses. It is a 'hard' core because of its *protective belt* of auxiliary assumptions. The *negative heuristic* of a research programme is a convention or methodological rule that stipulates that scientists should not question the hard core of the programme, that they should not modify or abandon it, and should avoid paths of research that bear directly on it. The *positive heuristic* tells scientists to pursue research related to the hypotheses that make up the protective belt; and provides general guidelines for changing or augmenting them in the face of an anomaly. The protective belt can be modified or changed without abandoning the

BOX 3.2 Imre Lakatos and the Methodology of Scientific Research Programmes: Basic Terms

Scientific research programme	The development of a theory, which remains constant (the 'hard core'), in combination with its protective belt of auxiliary hypotheses, which changes over time
Hard core	Basic axioms and hypotheses that remain constant and are accepted (for a time) without question
Protective belt	Specific falsifiable theories or 'auxiliary hypotheses' based on the hard core; these, but not the hard core, can be falsified
Auxiliary hypotheses	Additional specific hypotheses generated by a theory
Heuristic	A rule or recommendation for developing an idea or theory
Negative heuristic	The stipulation that the hard core of the program not be abandoned or modified
Positive heuristic	Instructions as to how to adjust the theories and auxiliary hypotheses in the protective belt in the face of an anomaly
Anomaly	A departure from what is expected or predicted in a specific set of circumstances
Progressive research programme	When adjustments to the protective belt predict hitherto unexpected facts, the research programme is *theoretically progressive*; it is *empirically progressive* if some of these predictions are corroborated
Degenerating research programme	When adjustments to the protective belt are made that fail to explain and corroborate new facts

programme itself, so when we get a falsifying observation, we should attribute it to problems with auxiliary hypotheses that constitute the programme's protective belt. We are free, in fact, encouraged, to question, modify, and change these hypotheses in order to protect the hard core.

A research programme changes, then, by modifying auxiliary assumptions and hypotheses in the programme's protective belt. These are tested, adjusted and re-adjusted, and even completely replaced. As Figure 3.3 shows, this process may produce a problem-shift. Lakatos was deeply hostile to Kuhn's argument that paradigm shifts depend ultimately on the consensus of the scientific community. He saw this as tantamount to a claim that scientific change is non-rational, essentially a process of arriving at 'truth by consensus' (Lakatos 1970: 92). Consequently, his concern was to show that there are objective reasons for why scientists favour one theory, or research programme, over another; that the process by which we choose from among competing research programmes is a rational process (and not a political battle, as is suggested in Kuhn's account).

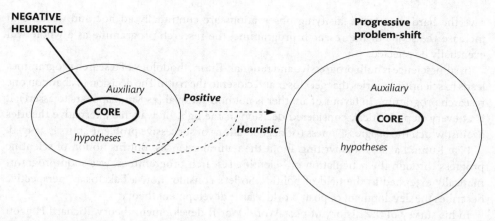

Figure 3.3 Imre Lakatos' methodology of scientific research programmes

A progressive problem shift leads to the discovery of novel facts. If a research programme increases in content through progressive problem-shifts, it is progressive; if it fails to do this, it is degenerating. Here is how Lakatos describes these processes:

> Let us take a series of theories, T1, T2, T3, . . . where each subsequent theory results from adding auxiliary clauses to . . . the previous theory in order to accommodate some anomaly, each theory having at least as much content as the unrefuted content of its predecessor. Let us say that such a series of theories is *theoretically progressive (or 'constitutes a theoretically progressive problemshift')* if each new theory has some excess empirical content over its predecessor . . . Let us say that a theoretically progressive series of theories is also *empirically progressive (or 'constitutes an empirically progressive problemshift')* if some of this excess empirical content is also corroborated . . . Finally, let us call a problem shift *progressive* if it is both theoretically and empirically progressive, and *degenerating* if it is not. (Lakatos 1970: 118; emphasis in original)

In general, we can assess the relative merits of competing research programmes by comparing the degrees to which they are progressive or degenerating—the degree to which the problem-shifts through which each is developing are progressive or degenerative. Again, and as Figure 3.4 shows, we do this by determining whether the problem-shift leads to the acceptance of a theory which has produced a higher ratio of novel facts to anomalies.

Research programme A is preferable to competing research programme B if either A is more *progressive* than B or is *degenerating* less than B. Although not everyone will come to reject a research programme at the same time, if the changes made to the protective belt to

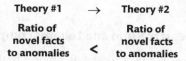

Figure 3.4 Imre Lakatos' methodology of scientific research programmes: comparing theories

save the hard core from falsifying observations are continually ad hoc and do little to increase the scope of the research programme, the research programme as a whole will eventually be rejected.

In sum, science is both progressive and rational. The methodology of research programmes leads to scientific theories that get closer and closer to the truth. The decision to abandon one research programme in favour of another is not non-rational (as Kuhn appears to assert); it is at every step a critical, considered decision in the light of available alternative theories against which the progressiveness (or degeneration) of successive problem-shifts is gauged.

Like Kuhn, Lakatos was writing about the natural sciences. But his notion of scientific progress through the articulation of 'scientific research programmes' was soon programmatically extended to the field of politics. So let's consider how a Lakatosian perspective describes the development of post-World War II development theory.

In his survey of the history of post-World War II development theory, Richard Higgott argues that the two dominant approaches to development—modernization theory and what he refers to as 'Marxist' theory ('broadly defined')—are best understood as Lakatosian 'research programmes'. The 'study of underdevelopment', Higgott explains, 'has been marked by a polarization into [these] two broad based schools of thought' (1983: 14), But neither of them are 'tightly-paradigmatic' in the sense popularized by Kuhn (Higgot 1983: 43). Neither achieved 'an ascendancy which would allow for a process of normal and revolutionary science' (1983: 6). Moreover, there was no 'paradigm shift' from one to the other.

Recall that, in Barbara Geddes' account, *modernization theory* had been 'toppled' and replaced by dependency theory; that, subsequently, *dependency theory* had collapsed due to its own 'internal contradictions and inability to deal with the inconvenient facts'; and that this collapse was followed by a period of 'chaos and contention' (Geddes 2003: 7). But Higgott insists that the crisis within modernization theory led, not to a paradigm shift, but to internal restructuring. Consequently, with the rise of dependency theory, there was no 'wholesale migration of scholars' from one to the other (1983: 9), no 'transference of allegiance, or conversion', such as occurs in a Kuhnian paradigm shift (1983: 42). Nor, in Higgott's account, did dependency theory collapse and inaugurate a period of 'chaos and contention'. According to Higgott, dependency theory arose in the 1960s as a 'crude radical alternative' to modernization theory (1983: 5), but it exhibited 'highly pluralistic tendencies' (1983: 46), and ultimately served as a springboard to a richer, more sophisticated Marxist analysis (1983: 52).

Consequently, neither perspective 'was killed off (or falsified)'. Rather than one succeeding the other, the two traditions co-existed and, not only endured, but prospered. At times they seemed 'at risk', especially in the 1960s and early 1970s when testing 'appeared to be degenerative or "content decreasing"'. But both proved to be 'extremely durable' because 'the essence of these research programmes' was 'basically sound'; and the modifications introduced within each perspective were progressive adjustments to their theoretical hard cores (1983: 8).

The role of values in research: Kuhn and Lakatos compared

It was Lakatos' intention to elaborate a contrasting model to the one Kuhn had developed. However, in their respective accounts of how science actually operates, the two models appear more similar than dissimilar. Both assume that scientists work within a framework of theoretical assumptions; and that scientists maintain a framework's central set of propositions by convention. To this extent, it seems right to argue, as Kuhn does, that the Kuhnian notion of 'paradigm' and the Lakatosian conception of 'research programme' describe the same phenomenon. Kuhn argues that:

> in discussing research conducted within a tradition . . . I have repeatedly insisted that it depends, in part, on the acceptance of elements which are not themselves subject to attack from within the tradition and which can be changed only by a transition to another tradition, another paradigm. Lakatos, I think, is making the same point when he speaks of the 'hard core of research programs,' the part which must be accepted in order to do research at all and which can be attacked only after embracing another research program. (Kuhn 1970: 137)

But, while both agree that scientists maintain a tradition's core assumptions, they offer different explanations for why scientists do this. Kuhn argues that the defence of a research tradition's core assumptions is often due to a tendency on the part of scientific communities to encourage paradigmatic conformity; Lakatos insists that it is the outcome of rational methodological decisions. Both invoke the history of science to support their claims. Based on the historical evidence they present, it could be argued that Kuhn's evidence suggests that the commitment of a scientific community to a research tradition does not always have an entirely objective basis. On the other hand, Lakatos does not really attempt to show that, historically, it is actually the case that scientists direct criticism away from the hard core of a research programme because they make a methodological decision to do so. It would seem, then, that while Kuhn's argument is concerned with what, historically, scientific practice has been, Lakatos is making a normative argument about what scientific progress *should* entail.

Kuhn points to what he sees as a second way in which the two models appear to be similar: the description of what Lakatos calls the 'degenerating stage' in the evolution of a research programme. Lakatos characterizes this as a stage in which the programme ceases to lead to new discoveries, and ad hoc hypotheses accrue to it that do little to increase its scope. Kuhn writes that 'I cannot myself tell the difference between what he has to say about this important stage and what I have said about the role of crisis in scientific development' (1970: 139).

But Lakatos insists that it is their differing accounts of what ensues from degeneration or crisis that distinguishes his model from Kuhn's. For Kuhn, the shift from one scientific 'paradigm' to another reflects political and cultural factors; for Lakatos, theory development through 'research programmes' is a rational process. Scientists make a rational determination of when to give up on a particular theory. When it stops incorporating new facts it can be considered to be degenerating and, thus, abandoned for a theory that offers an increase of empirical content.

Lakatos was hostile to what he saw as the subjectivist aspects and implications of Kuhn's model and, in particular, the prominent role that Kuhn ascribes to subjectivity in the choice among competing theories and in the shift from one paradigm to another. However, Lakatos does not entirely escape his own critique: subjectivity appears to play a prominent role in his own model, as well.

According to Lakatos, a theory is to be judged on the basis of whether it is able to put forward 'novel facts', some degree of excess empirical content over its predecessor. But progress cannot always be judged in these terms, because not all empirical facts are of equal significance. Novel facts can be either trivial or important, and which they are depends on the values and normative concerns of the individuals making the assessment. It is up to the individual scientist to judge whether a programme that is not generating progressive problem-shifts is merely experiencing a temporary lull or has begun to degenerate; and this, Lakatos says can, in any event, only be known retrospectively. Thus a scientist's 'theory choice' is as much a 'subjective' judgement as the decision to change paradigms is in Kuhn's account.

In comparing these supposedly contrasting views of the nature of the scientific enterprise, what becomes apparent is that, irrespective of whether research employs a positivist or interpretivist approach, or addresses empirical or normative questions, the researcher's subjective valuations are likely to enter into the research process. No approach or type of research ensures a value-free process of inquiry; none can free researchers from the need to be explicit and self-critical concerning their own underlying assumptions and values.

 ## Conclusions

Where does this consideration of the debate about the fact/value distinction leave us?

We began our discussion in this chapter by considering how this distinction has been institutionalized in political research in the division between empirical and normative research and theory. As John Gerring and Joshua Yesnowitz argue, the separation between normative theory and empirical analysis generates problems for both sides of the divide. As a result of the division between empirical and normative research, both lack relevance to important problems (2006: 104). Empirical study of social phenomena 'is meaningless if it has no normative import; and it is misleading if its normative content is present, but ambiguous', if we don't know how it matters. Normative arguments that propose or justify one value system over another will lack relevance if they make no attempt to relate to the facts of actual practice or public life. In sum, good social science 'is both empirically grounded and relevant to human concerns' (2006: 133). Normative theorizing 'must deal in facts' and empirical work 'must deal in values' (2006: 108). While we must be sensitive to the difference between normative and empirical questions and statements, we must also recognize that they are not independent of each other, and that there are costs in keeping them separate.

The chapter then explored various ways that 'values' intrude into social-scientific inquiry. It began by considering whether, how, and with what effect, a researcher's own values intrude into research. It then focused on how the act of observation itself intrudes on the object of study. Finally, it took up the question of whether and how research is shaped by shared social practices and is inseparable from them.

To explore this last issue, we considered two different views concerning the role of social factors and practices in scientific inquiry. Thomas Kuhn claims that scientific investigation often reflects relations of power, professional ambition, and wider political and cultural factors; that scientists often accept a theory based, not on observable evidence, but on political and cultural factors. Imre Lakatos emphatically rejects this view of established scientific practice. He argues that scientific inquiry is rational and leads to progressive theory development.

These differing views are really the product of different concerns. Kuhn is concerned with the question of how science advances *in practice*; Lakatos is chiefly concerned with a normative question: how *should* science advance? Kuhn attempts to produce a factual account of science. Critics are right to be concerned with its normative implications. But rather then shooting the messenger, we would be better off treating the message as a cautionary tale about how subjectivity and paradigmatic conformity can intrude into research. Lakatos' elaboration of a 'methodology of scientific research programmes' is less a model of how science is actually done, than a proposal for how it *should* be done. It contributes to our thinking about what procedures would allow for a more consistently objective assessment of research findings and pursuit of theory development.

Ernest Nagel has argued that 'steps can be taken to identify a value bias when it occurs, and to minimize if not to eliminate completely its perturbing effects' (1994: 573). To do this we need to proceed with an awareness of the various ways that values intrude into the research process. With this awareness, we can then be in a position to pursue the ideal that Lakatos elaborates: a process of inquiry that, at every step, is both critical and rational.

 ## Questions

- Is political research value-free?

- To what extent, and in what ways, do 'values' present problems for political analysis?

- According to Kuhn, what is scientific progress? Under what circumstances does scientific progress occur? How is Kuhn's view of scientific progress different from the conventional wisdom about how scientific knowledge develops?

- What is a paradigm? Is the concept of a paradigm relevant for the social sciences? Why or why not?

- How is Kuhn's conception of a 'scientific revolution' similar to a political revolution?

- What is Lakatos' notion of a research programme? What aspects of Kuhn's model does it correspond to and differ from?

- Is the notion of 'normal science' applicable to the study of politics?

 ## Guide to Further Reading

Ball, T. (1976), 'From Paradigms to Research Programs: Toward a Post-Kuhnian Political Science', *American Journal of Political Science* **20(1) (February): 151–77.**

Critical Review; Special Issue: Rational Choice Theory and Politics 9(1–2) (1995).
This issue contains a wide-ranging symposium on the criticisms launched against rational choice theory by Donald P. Green and Ian Shapiro, in *Pathologies of Rational Choice Theory: A Critique of Applications in Political Science* (New Haven: Yale University Press, 1994). At least six of the contributions, both pro and con, based themselves in part on their interpretations of Lakatos' theory of research programmes.

Fleck, L. (1979), *Genesis and Development of a Fact* **(Chicago: University of Chicago Press).**
A fascinating study of the genesis of a theory in medical science that attempts to identify the process by which an idea achieves the status of a fact. Fleck shows that, among other things, a fact must be plausible, and that its plausibility is rooted in a given era. A fact must also be 'suitable for publication', i.e. stylistically relevant within a given culture.

Gerring, J. and J. Yesnowitz (2006), 'A Normative Turn in Political Science?' *Polity* **38(1) (January): 10–33.**
The authors provide arguments concerning how and why a more normatively orientated study of politics can contribute to theoretical development, empirical inquiry, and disciplinary unity.

Lakatos, I. and A. Musgrave (eds) (1970), *Criticism and the Growth of Knowledge* **(Cambridge: Cambridge University Press).**
This volume arose out of a symposium on Kuhn's work held in London in 1965. The book begins with Kuhn's statement of his position, followed by seven essays offering criticism and analysis, and finally by Kuhn's reply.

Martin, M. and L. C. McIntyre (eds) (1994), *Readings in the Philosophy of Social Science* **(Cambridge, MA: MIT Press).**
This volume brings together a collection of important texts on objectivity and values (Part VII).

Riley, G. (ed.) (1974), *Values, Objectivity, and the Social Sciences* (Reading, MA: Addison Wesley Longman Publishing Co).
A collection of articles on research objectivity, values, and partisanship by prominent social scientists.

Science, Technology & Human Values 36:3 (May 2011). **Special issue on 'Post-Normal Science'.**

Taylor, C. (1994), Neutrality in Political Science', in Michael Martin and Lee C. McIntyre (eds), *Readings in the Philosophy of Social Science* (Cambridge, MA: MIT Press), 547–70.
In this influential article, the philosopher Charles Taylor argues that value-neutrality in the social sciences, and the possibility of separating facts and values, is a myth: it is a myth that researchers consider the facts of something and, on the basis of the facts, move to a judgement or valuation of them.

Vasquez, John A. et al. (1997), Forum on 'The Realist Paradigm and Degenerative vs Progressive Research Programs', *American Political Science Review* 91 (December): 899–934.

 # References

Ball, T. (1976), 'From Paradigms to Research Programs: Toward a Post-Kuhnian Political Science', *American Journal of Political Science* 20(1) (February): 151–77.

Bernstein, H. R. (1981), 'Marxist Historiography and the Methodology of Research Programs', *History and Theory* 20(4) (December): 424–49.

Bird, Alexander, 'Thomas Kuhn', in Edward N. Zalta (ed.), *The Stanford Encyclopedia of Philosophy (Fall 2009 Edition)*, http://plato.stanford.edu/archives/fall2009/entries/thomas-kuhn/.

Bodenheimer, S. (1971), *The Ideology of Developmentalism: The American-Paradigm-Surrogate for Latin American Studies* (Beverly Hills, CA: Sage).

Cochran, M. (1999), *Normative Theory in International Relations* (Cambridge: Cambridge University Press).

Cox, R. (1981), 'Social Forces, States and World Orders: Beyond International Relations Theory', *Millennium: Journal of International Studies* 10(2): 126–55.

Diamond, S. (1992), *Compromised Campus* (New York: Oxford University Press).

Foster-Carter, A. (1976), 'From Rostow to Gunder Frank: Conflicting Paradigms in the Analysis of Underdevelopment', *World Development* 4(3) (March): 167–80.

Frankel, C. (1969), *High on Foggy Bottom: An Outsider's Inside View of the Government* (New York: Harper & Row).

Funtowicz, S. O. and J. R. Ravetz (1992), 'Three Types of Risk Assessment and the Emergence of Post Normal Science , in S. Krimsky and D. Golding (eds), *Social Theories of Risk* (Westport, CT: Praeger), 251–74.

——(1993), 'Science for the Post-Normal', *Futures* 25(7): 739–55

Geddes, B. (2003), *Paradigms and Sand Castles Theory Building and Research Design in Comparative Politics* (Ann Arbor: University of Michigan Press).

Gendzier, I. (1985), *Managing Social Change: Social Scientists and the Third World* (Boulder, CO: Westview).

Gerring, J. (2001), *Social Science Methodology: A Criterial Framework* (Cambridge: Cambridge University Press).

——and J. Yesnowitz (2006), 'A Normative Turn in Political Science?' *Polity* 8:(1) (January): 101–133.

Gutting, G. (1984), 'Paradigms and Hermeneutics: A Dialogue on Kuhn, Rorty, and the Social Sciences', *American Philosophical Quarterly* 21 (1) (January): 1–15.

Higgott, R. (1983), *Political Development Theory: The Contemporary Debate* (Beckenham, Kent: Croom Helm).

Jastrow, J.(1899). 'The Mind's Eye', *Popular Science Monthly* 54: 299–312. From wikipedia, http://en.wikipedia.org/wiki/file: Duck-Rabbit_illusion.jpg.

Jervis, R. (2002), 'Politics, Political Science, and Specialization, PS', *Political Science and Politics*, 35(2) (June): 187–9.

Kuhn, T. (1962), *The Structure of Scientific Revolutions* (Chicago: University of Chicago Press).

——(1970), 'Notes on Lakatos', *Proceedings of the Biennial Meeting of the Philosophy of Science Association* (1970): 137–46.

Lakatos, I. (1970), 'Falsification and the Methodology of Scientific Research Programs', in I. Lakatos and A. Musgrave (eds), *Criticism and the Growth of Knowledge* (Cambridge: Cambridge University Press), 91–196.

Martin, M. (1994), 'The Philosophical Importance of the Rosenthal Effect', in Michael Martin and Lee C. McIntyre (eds), *Readings in the Philosophy of Social Science* (Cambridge, MA: MIT Press), 585–96.

Mason, M. (1997), *Development and Disorder: A History of the Third World since 1945* (Hanover and London: University Press of New England).

Morgan, P. M. (1994), *Theories and Approaches to International Politics: What Are We to Think?* 4th edition (New Brunswick, NJ: Transaction Publishers).

Nagel, E. (1994), 'The Value-Oriented Bias of Social Inquiry', in Michael Martin and Lee C. McIntyre (eds), *Readings in the Philosophy of Social Science* (Cambridge, MA: MIT Press), 571–84.

Pavlich, G. (1988), 'Re-Evaluating Modernisation and Dependency in Lesotho', *The Journal of Modern African Studies* 26(4) (December): 591–605.

Popper, Karl (1959), *The Logic of Scientific Discovery* (London: Hutchinson of London).

Schmidt, B. (2002), 'On the History and Historiography of International Relations', in W. Carlnaes, T. Risse, and B. Simmons (eds), *Handbook of International Relations* (London: Sage), 3–22.

Simpson, C. (ed.) (1999), *Universities and Empire* (New York: New Press).

Valenzuela, A. and S. Valenzuela (1979), 'Modernization and Dependence: Alternative Perspectives in the Study of Latin American Development', in J. Villamil (ed.), *Transnational Capitalism and National Development* (Sussex: Harvester Press), 31–65.

Weber, M. (1948), *The Methodology of the Social Sciences* (New York: The Free Press).

——(1994), 'Objectivity in Social Science and Social Policy', in Michael Martin and Lee C. McIntyre (eds), *Readings in the Philosophy of Social Science* (Cambridge, MA: MIT Press), 535–46.

Methodological Individualism and Holism

 Chapter Summary

This chapter considers the perennial debate in the philosophy of social science concerning '**individualism**' and '**holism**'. These represent contrasting views about the nature of the social world and how we can gain knowledge of it. The chapter explores the various positions—ontological, epistemological, and methodological—which the terms 'holism' and 'individualism' are used to represent, and their implications for how we pursue research and develop explanations of political phenomena. The questions which we consider include the following:

- What is 'society'? Is it something distinct from and more than the individuals that comprise it?
- What is the proper unit of sociological analysis?
- Should explanation in social research give primacy to individuals or to social collectives?
- Do social explanations need to 'reduce' to arguments about the actions of individuals?
- How do structures and agents relate to produce outcomes in politics and international relations?

Introduction

This chapter addresses the third in a series of key debates concerning how we know about and study the social world. Previously we considered the debate about whether knowledge of social phenomena can be gained through a process similar to that which is used to gain knowledge about the natural world: whether we can explain social phenomena in the way that scientists explain natural phenomena, or whether it is possible only to interpret what people do and why (Chapter 2). We then focused on debates about how values influence social-scientific inquiry, whether it is possible to define a distinction between facts and values, and whether pursuit of knowledge of the social world can be value-free and objective (Chapter 3).

This chapter explores debates concerning 'individualism' and 'holism' in social inquiry and their implications for how we conduct political research. Individualism and holism represent different positions with respect to questions of ontology, epistemology, and methodology. The debates we consider thus involve three interrelated issues. First is the issue of social ontology. What are the basic elements that make up the social world? What sorts of things constitute 'social facts'? What are the sorts of things we are investigating when we do research on, for example, nations, political parties, or classes? Can we treat these social 'wholes' or collectives as more than their individual constituents, as actors in their own right? The second issue concerns epistemology. In pursuing knowledge of the social world, what should we treat as the basic unit of sociological analysis?[1] What constitutes legitimate knowledge of social phenomena? These ontological and epistemological issues are related both to each other and to a third issue: the nature of social explanation. Is **methodological individualism** or **methodological holism** more appropriate to explanation in social research? Should social explanation give primacy to individuals or to social collectives?

We will begin our consideration of these questions in this chapter by discussing the ontological and epistemological positions that the terms 'individualism' and 'holism' are used to define. The chapter then discusses methodological individualism and holism, debates concerning these positions in social science research, the normative concerns (i.e. the politics of individualism and collectivism) that have intruded on these debates, and difficulties in keeping normative issues separate from analytic ones. Finally, the chapter considers how methodological individualism and holism are reflected in the debate concerning the nature of, and relationship between, social structures and human agents ('the structure-agency problem') in the field of politics.

Individualism and holism

Before considering the debate about individualism and holism as *methodological* positions, we need to distinguish it from two different but related, areas of debate: the debate about *ontology*—about what *is*, or what is real; and debates about *epistemology*—about what constitutes knowledge of the social world. Recall how we defined these terms in Chapter 2: 'ontology' is the study of what exists and the nature of what exists; 'epistemology' is concerned with what is knowable. The ontological question that we focus on in this chapter concerns the nature of, and the basic elements that make up, the social world. The epistemological question that we consider concerns what sort of knowledge of the social world is possible.

As ontological positions, individualism and holism represent two different answers to a fundamental question regarding the nature of society: are societies reducible to the individuals who make them up? Or is society something more than, and distinct from, the sum of its individual members? According to *ontological individualism*, all that exists in the world are individual persons.[2] We cannot say, for instance, that the world consists of entities such as universities *as well as* teachers, students, and administrators: it contains *only* individual persons. The social entity, 'university', is nothing more or less than the individuals who are involved in university activities. Though we talk about institutions such as the state, the church, or the university, these entities are really just individual people organized in a particular way. We talk about social groups, but these are simply collections of individuals co-existing. The individual elements draw on resources around them, but they are nonetheless independent entities that have self-contained properties. Thus, in studying social institutions or groups, analysts must study individuals.

Ontological holism claims that social wholes are more than, and distinct from, the sum of their individual constituents. The whole affects and is affected by the qualities of its constituents. These constituents are not, as individualism maintains, independent entities that have self-contained properties: they are internally related in the sense that each is imbued with, and constituted by, the qualities of others. So we cannot consider the whole as simply consisting of independent individuals sequentially summed together, one after the other. Much —perhaps all—human interaction consists of actions, and generates outcomes, that cannot be comprehended and explained as a sum of individual actions.

Ontological individualism and holism entail corresponding *epistemological* positions: claims concerning how we know about and what constitutes knowledge of the social world. An *individualist epistemology* claims that, since only individuals exist, all that it is possible for us to know is what individuals do. Social science is, therefore, the study of individual behaviour, of how individuals act, and of individual attributes, beliefs, perceptions, and attitudes. A *holist epistemology* maintains that, because individuals are part of a social whole, part of a system of relations that constitute them, an individual action is not fully intelligible until the whole of which it is a part is taken into account. As we shall discuss, further along in this chapter, one might adopt an ontological position without necessarily accepting the corresponding epistemological position. For instance, one might concede that the social world consists of social entities, such as institutions or classes (ontological holism), but still maintain that explanations must be reducible to statements about individuals (epistemological individualism).

Methodological individualism and holism

Thus far we have discussed the claims of ontological individualism and holism (different views of what really exists), and of epistemological individualism and holism (different views about what constitutes knowledge of the social world). We turn now to a consideration of *methodological* individualism and holism.

Methodological individualism

Debates about methodology in the social sciences have to do with the principles and procedures of inquiry that can provide us with legitimate knowledge of the social world.

Methodological individualism claims that, since all that it is possible for us to know are the actions of individuals, then explanations of social phenomena such as classes, power, or nations must ultimately be explicable in terms of facts about individuals. Unless we can account for an outcome in terms of individuals and their desires and beliefs, we do not have an explanation of that outcome.

The case for methodological individualism is generally based on two key claims. The first is what has been called 'the doctrine of reducibility'. According to this doctrine, statements referring to holistic sociological entities can be reduced to statements referring only to individuals and their actions or dispositions. To illustrate how this reduction can be made, consider this statement: 'the party voted unanimously to accept the proposed platform'. It is possible to replace this sentence with one that does not use the holistic term 'party'. We can assume that the party consists of *n* members; and we can then state that '*n1* decided to endorse the proposed platform, *n2* decided to endorse the proposed platform, *n3* decided to endorse the proposed platform . . .' , etc. The individualist would argue, therefore, that by saying that the party unanimously took some action, we are simply saying that each individual member of which it is composed took that action.

A second claim used to establish the case for methodological individualism is that any explanation of a given social phenomenon is only *final* and *satisfactory* once it is provided in language which refers solely to individuals and their actions. Much of the discussion of this claim has focused on what J. W. N. Watkins called 'rock-bottom' explanations and 'half-way' ones: those that do, and those that do not, specify what Talcott Parsons called 'the action frame of reference' (Parsons 1937). Watkins maintains that we will only have a 'rock-bottom' explanation for a given social phenomenon once we have an explanation solely in terms of individuals and their dispositions (1957: 106).

Watkins identifies two areas, however, in which methodological individualism does not work. The first involves probability situations 'where accidental and unpredictable regularities in human behaviour have a fairly regular and predictable result'. These statistical regularities in social life—such as the generally stable rate of automobile accidents annually—'are inexplicable in individualistic terms' (Watkins 1994: 443). The existence of these statistical regularities, Watkins makes emphatically clear, does not 'support the historicist idea that defenceless individuals like you and me are at the chance mercy of the inhuman and uncontrollable tendencies of our society' (Watkins 1994: 443). We can control these regularities 'insofar as we can alter the conditions on which they depend. For example, we could obviously abolish road accidents if we were prepared to prohibit motor traffic' (Watkins 1994: 444). A second area in which methodological individualism does not work 'is where some kind of physical connection between people's nervous systems short-circuits their intelligent control and causes automatic . . . bodily responses'. For instance, individuality may 'get submerged beneath a collective physical rapport' at revivalist meetings or among panicking crowds (Watkins 1994: 444).

So, with these exceptions, Watkins maintains that 'we shall not have arrived at rock-bottom explanations of . . . large-scale [social] phenomena until we have deduced an account of them from statements about the dispositions, beliefs, resources, and interrelations of individuals' (Watkins 1957: 105–6).

However, there have been challenges to both claims used to establish the case for methodological individualism. Critics argue that the 'doctrine of reducibility'—that social terms 'reduce' to individual ones—runs into the problem of 'multiple realizability' (Little 1991: 190–95; Kincaid 1996: 145–55; Sawyer 2002; Zahle 2003). In the example of the political party, it appears that there is an equivalence between social and individual terms, and that the term 'party' can be reduced to individual terms. But critics argue that there are cases where social terms refer to events or entities 'that can be realized by a multitude of different configurations of individuals'. Social terms such as 'revolution', 'primary group', 'power elite', 'peer group', and 'bureaucracy' can be realized by any number of different individual configurations. Even specific institutions (the UK bureaucracy, the US power elite) can experience significant changes in the configuration of individuals realizing them (Kincaid 1994: 500). The problem of 'multiple realizability' provides the basis for the methodologist *holist* argument that where a single macro-level generalization is instantiated by several micro-level mechanisms, the macro-level relationship will be invariant under a broader range of circumstances than any particular micro-mechanism and will consequently offer a better explanation. Arguments that seek to establish the case for a holist methodological position also challenge the second claim used to establish the case for methodological individualism—that an explanation of social phenomena is only *final* and *satisfactory* if it refers solely to individuals and their actions. We will explore this challenge to methodological individualism further when we turn, in the next section, to a consideration of methodological holism.

Finally, in what Geoffrey Hodgson calls a 'devastating' critique of methodological individualism (2007: 220), critics have argued that methodological individualism, in one of its two versions, has never been achieved in practice, whereas its second version is tantamount to abandoning the position altogether.

According to this argument, there are two different versions of methodological individualism. The strong (or narrow) methodological individualist position holds that explanations of social phenomena must be reducible to statements about individuals only. A weaker (or broader) version of this position maintains that explanations may also include *interactions* among individuals, or *social* relations (Udehn 2001: 346–9). Both positions recognize that an understanding of individuals must involve consideration of cultural and institutional factors. The strong version holds that social phenomena must, nonetheless, be explicable in terms of facts about individuals. Hodgson argues that this type of explanation is 'unattainable in practice' (2007: 220). It has a problem of infinite regress: the emergence of the institutions and cultures that influence individuals must themselves be explained; and these would at least in part be explained by other individuals. As long as we are addressing social phenomena, we never reach an end point where there are isolated individuals and nothing more. We are involved in an apparently infinite regress, similar to the puzzle 'which came first, the chicken or the egg?' (Hodgson 2007: 219).

As for the weak version of methodological individualism, that explanation may also include interactions among individuals, Hodgson points out that admitting 'interactive relations between individuals' in explanations 'opens the door to 'emergent properties'—to the possibility that novel properties may emerge, i.e. 'properties that are not possessed by the entities taken in isolation' (Hodgson 2007: 220). The notion of emergence allows for a conceptualization of society as not completely external to individuals; as having an objective character, but one that is located within the practices of individuals. Certain aspects of society are not reducible to the individual, even though these aspects of society are still rooted in individual practice. This blurs the line separating methodological individualism and holism so that 'the two doctrines no longer appear as clear-cut opposites'. Instead, we get 'a mix, or synthesis, of individualistic and holistic elements' (Udehn 2002: 502).

Methodological holism

Methodological holism assumes that social institutions, collectives, and organizations are prior to, and fundamentally independent of, individuals and can therefore be taken as 'primitives' in social science explanation: they can serve as the primary independent variables determining individual and collective behaviour and outcomes.

The case for this methodological position rests on a number of arguments. The first argument derives from Émile Durkheim's argument that there are 'social facts' that 'govern' individuals. These 'social facts' are not merely an aggregation of facts about individuals. They are distinct from facts about individual life; and they function independently of an individual's use of them. They consist of 'ways of acting, thinking, and feeling external to the individual', and they are endowed with a power of coercion that exercises a check or constraint on individual action (1994: 434). The power of external coercion which a social fact exercises or is capable of exercising over individuals may be recognized 'either by the existence of some specific sanction or by the resistance offered against every individual effort that tends to violate it' (1994: 434). Social facts include social organizations ('legal and moral regulations, religious faith, financial systems, etc.') and social currents: 'great movements of enthusiasm, indignation, and pity in a crowd [that] do not originate in any one of the particular individual consciousnesses'; that 'come to each one of us from without and carry us away in spite of ourselves' (1994: 434). An example of the coercive force of social facts can be seen, for instance, in education, and in its 'continuous effort to impose on the child ways of seeing, feeling, and acting, which he could not have arrived at spontaneously' (1994: 435).

A second argument used to establish the case for methodological holism concerns the existence of 'emergent properties'. These are properties that emerge when entities interact and which are 'novel' in the sense that they are properties not possessed by the entities taken in isolation (Hodgson 2007: 220). To illustrate how interaction among individuals produces properties that are 'emergent', consider the following description of two boys carrying a log.

> The boys are fitting their actions to each other and to the object and are involved in a give-and-take requiring considerable sensitiveness. The two do not apply force in succession, or in opposite directions; they bring a common force to bear simultaneously. If one moves somewhat faster or swerves slightly, the other adapts his movement correspondingly. There is an immediate, direct communication between them through the object. The amount of movement, timing, pace, and direction are regulated and continuously checked by the corresponding action of the partner. Here is a unity of action that embraces the participants and the common object. The performance is a new product, strictly unlike the sum of their separate exertions....Neither boy would act in just the same way in the absence of the other; what each contributes is a function of his relation to the other in the task. (Asch 1952: 173–4)

In this example, the interaction of individuals produces 'novel' properties—properties that are not possessed by the individuals taken in isolation. Analogously, society in certain of its aspects is not reducible to the individuals that comprise it, even though these aspects of society may be rooted in individual practice. In modern social theory, structures are typically defined 'as sets of interactive relations between individuals'; and these relations might produce properties that are separate and distinguishable from the individuals themselves.

Another argument for the holist methodological position relates to the claim advanced by methodological individualists that any explanation of a given social phenomenon is only *final* and *satisfactory* once it is provided in language which refers solely to individuals and their actions. Recall that J. W. N. Watkins recognized that there are two areas in which methodological individualism does not work: statistical regularities in social life which are inexplicable in individualistic terms, and crowd or situational dynamics that cause automatic or instinctive bodily responses (Watkins 1994: 444). But holists argue there are other areas of research in which the 'rock-bottom' explanations demanded of methodological individualism either don't work or aren't necessary. One of these involves explanations of deep underlying causes of intentional states that operate at a sub-intentional level. For instance, it might be the case that a behaviour is generated by a compulsion or bias that has not penetrated into consciousness and that consequently functions at a sub-intentional level. In this case, an explanation in terms of intentional states will not be 'rock bottom': explanation will need to be sought, instead, at a deeper, more fundamental, level, perhaps at the level of some evolved behavioural/physiological function.[3]

There are other types of social-scientific inquiry in which 'rock-bottom' explanations are not necessary. For instance, there are explanations provided by statistical analyses in which knowledge of intentional states does not necessarily contribute anything essential to their 'adequacy'. As an example, consider current research on civil wars. One of the strongest findings in the existing civil war literature is that poorer countries are more likely to experience civil war (e.g. Fearon and Laitin 2003; Collier and Hoeffler 2004). Studies conclude, however, that income inequality between individuals does not increase the likelihood of civil conflict (e.g. Collier et al. 2003) but, rather systematic social and economic inequalities that coincide with ethnic cleavages or regions within a country (e.g. Stewart 2002; Østby 2008). Total population size is also known to affect the probability of the onset of civil war. Population pressures have been shown to play a role in internal conflict as, for instance, in the existence of 'youth bulges', large cohorts of youths that may serve as recruiting grounds for rebel movements if society is unsuccessful in integrating them (Urdal 2004, 2006). These findings lack micro-foundations: they are not linked to data on the intentional states of those who participate in internal conflicts. But such data are not necessary to making these findings on these macro-level variables a useful and important discovery. These findings don't tell us anything about the individual decisions that lead to the initiation of civil war, but they have succeeded in identifying particular macro-level factors, such as territory and population, and ruling out others, as having utility in explaining the causes of internal conflicts.

Causal-structural studies are another type of social-scientific inquiry that provides explanations that are not 'rock-bottom' but are, nonetheless, 'satisfying'. These depend on the relations between various elements of social structure without identifying individual-level processes that give rise to them. Theda Skocpol's, *States and Social Revolutions* (1979) is a well-known example. Skocpol argues that social revolution is brought about by factors such as military defeat that change the relationship of state organizations to domestic political and social groups. *Ancien régimes* cannot respond to external events ('international military threats arising in the modern era') and as a result states experience 'revolutionary crises'. When this occurs, 'revolts from below' accomplish 'changes in class relations that otherwise would not have occurred' (1979: 23). Skocpol identifies a small class of relevant cases, specifies the social variables to be empirically evaluated (state structure, land tenure systems, forms of military organization), and then determines whether there are credible causal sequences among these variables in the several cases. Though it may be possible to provide explanations such as these with micro-foundations (Skocpol does not), this sort of structural explanation, Daniel Little (1992) argues is, nonetheless, adequate.

Other arguments focus on the advantages of the interpretivist techniques favoured by a holist methodological position; and, in particular, their ability to draw attention to potentially important contextual factors often overlooked or obscured by positivist research instruments. Positivist instruments based on principles of methodological individualism tend to study separate, self-contained, and homogeneous variables that can be combined arithmetically to explain outcomes. In Chapter 2 we said that a variable is a characteristic that can assume different values or characteristics. But if we treat a variable as separate, independent, and self-contained, we isolate it 'from any qualitative, or internal, relationship with others that could modulate its quality' (Ratner 2007: 4). Variables, then, will vary only quantitatively, and remain qualitatively the same. Consequently, the order in which we measure them is irrelevant. So, for instance, in questionnaires, each item 'is a separate (discrete) element that supposedly taps a discrete attribute; and each response is treated as a separate element that is accorded equal weight, and can be summed, with the others.

However, holism views the constituent elements of a whole, not as independent entities that have self-contained properties, but as internally related. If the whole is not simply the sum of independent individuals, an individualistic form of methodology that explains social phenomena as a sum of individual actions can obscure just what a researcher might want to learn. This can be illustrated by contrasting the approach described above, with a hermeneutical, holistic analysis. Instead of treating each response as separate and independent, this type of analysis examines patterns of interrelated responses which indicate the quality and significance of each.

Consider the example of a study designed to determine the level of 'interest in politics' among a population. George Bishop and his colleagues found that people were more likely to think they were 'very interested' in politics following the 1980 presidential campaign in the United States when they were asked the question immediately after, rather than just before, a set of questions about who they thought would win the election, how close they thought the race would be, and whether they personally cared which party won the election (Bishop et al. 1982). In a similar experiment, they also discovered that people were less likely to think they followed 'what's going on in government and public affairs' when asked about it right after, instead of just before, a difficult group of questions concerning what they knew about the record of their member of Congress. They concluded that questions such as these 'may not measure what they are intended to measure: an individual's general interest in politics'; instead, they may be measuring, among other things, 'whatever response has been made most plausible and accessible in memory by the wording of the question and by the context in which it is asked' (Bishop et al. 1984: 160–1). By 'context' they mean not just the immediate questionnaire, but also the electoral environment in which a question is asked. For instance, if

> people are asked how interested they are in politics in the midst of an exciting presidential campaign, we would expect them to say they are more interested than if we asked the same question during a dull, local election campaign. Similarly, we would expect people to think they were more interested in following a political campaign if they are asked the question shortly after the election than if they are asked about it several weeks later. We would also expect people who have voted in the election to think they were more interested in the campaign than people were who did not vote. (Bishop *et al* 1984: 161)

As this example makes apparent, context is often crucial, both in shaping the responses to individual items and to evaluating them; and, in this regard, a holist, interpretivist approach may offer important advantages over an individualist approach.

However, holistic approaches are prone to analytic weaknesses, as well. Where structure has been placed at the forefront of sociological explanation, it has tended to imply a causal determinism in which the efficacy of human agency is lost. Structures invariably seem to exist separately from, but nevertheless to determine, motivated social action. This leads to what is perhaps the most characteristic problem of holistic analyses: their tendency to treat macro-social entities as if they had a concrete, material existence; as analytically independent of their constituent elements; inert, unchanging, and unmediated by human agency. The 'reification' of social entities is apparent, for instance, in many discussions of globalization. Some analysts trace the emergence of globalization to the interests and activities of specific groups and governments. But the predominant tendency is to locate the origins and driving force of globalization in macro-sociological entities like markets and capital. Globalization, in this view, is the outcome of the 'logic' of markets or of international capital, or of institutional and technological innovation and change, or of the evolutionary development of capitalism and capitalist production. Globalization appears, from this perspective, as a more-or-less natural outcome of a natural spatio-temporal spread of more-or-less natural economic and technological developments, 'Markets', 'technology', 'capital', and 'capitalism' are treated as primary and autonomous agents in the process of globalization. Human agents (individuals, or collections of individuals organized in groups, governments, and states) appear as mere bystanders; and can act only within the limits set by markets and the 'logic' of capital. Note how this conceptualization is reflected in the following statements.

The historian, Eric Hobsbawm, asserts that, as a result of 'the transnational economy', the territorial nation state 'can no longer control more than a diminishing part of its affairs' (1994: 424). Susan Strange enlarges on this view: 'impersonal forces of world markets . . . are now more powerful than states to whom ultimate political authority over society is supposed to belong. Where states were once the masters of markets, now it is the markets which . . . are the masters over the governments of states' (1996: 4). The former Secretary General of the United Nations, Boutros Boutros-Ghali, makes the same point: 'individual states have less and less capacity to influence things, while the power of global players—in the realm of finance, for instance—grow and grow without being controlled by anyone' (in Martin and Schumann 1997: 185). And, finally, this from former British Prime Minister Tony Blair, in a radio interview: 'we are going to live in a market of global finance and there will be investors that decide to move their money in and out of countries . . . . I'm afraid I'm someone who says look, this is a situation you live and work with and try and prepare yourselves for, but cannot really change' (*Today Programme*, BBC R4, 30.9.98; quoted in Held 1998: 26).

The politics of individualism and collectivism

Philosophical discussions about individualism and holism go back to the nineteenth century. But, in the twentieth century, arguments about individualism and holism as methodological positions in social analysis generated political controversy when they appeared to conflate these positions with normative arguments concerning the values of individualism and collectivism in political life. The conflation of debates about individualism and holism as methodological doctrines, and normative arguments concerning the nature of 'the good society' (arguments upholding the virtues of competitive individualism, on the one hand, and of community and social and economic equality on the other), has complicated discussion on these issues ever since.

The controversy arose when Karl Popper, in a series of essays entitled 'The Poverty of Historicism' (1944a, 1944b, 1945) and in *The Open Society and its Enemies* (1945), appeared to associate holism with the values of collectivism in political life. This conflation of analytic and normative issues seemed to be the basis of his endorsement of methodological individualism: he appeared to endorse methodological individualism as a counter to holism, which, he believed, promoted the adoption of collectivist ideologies in political life and, as he argued, consequently advanced the cause of totalitarianism. The controversy that was generated by this conflation of methodological and normative arguments has confused debates about methodological individualism and holism in the social sciences. Popper seemed to invoke 'methodological individualism' as a means of countering the notion that the social world consists of collective entities such as classes. But one might adopt *methodological* individualism without accepting *ontological* individualism; that is, one might concede that the social world consists of social entities, such as institutions or classes, but still maintain that explanations must be reducible to statements about individuals. The correspondence of ontological and epistemological positions is illustrated with reference to individualism in Table 4.1.

The rise of interest in rational choice theory reignited the controversy. Rational choice attempts to explain all social phenomena in terms of the rational calculations made by self-interested individuals. It maintains that social interactions are based on the individualistic competition of self-interested, rational individuals; and that rational individuals do not cooperate to achieve common goals unless coerced. This challenged a common premise in

Table 4.1 The individualistic research tradition

	Definition of social concepts	Explanation of social phenomena	Reduction of social laws
Ontology	Social phenomena are made up of individuals, their physical and psychic states, actions, interaction, social situation, and physical environment.	Social phenomena are caused by individuals, their physical and psychic states, actions, interaction, social situation, and physical environment.	Social laws are laws about individuals, their physical and psychic states, actions, interaction, social situation, and physical environment.
Epistemology	Social concepts can in principle be *defined* in terms of individuals, their physical and psychic states, actions, interaction, social situation, and physical environment.	Social phenomena can in principle be *explained* in terms of individuals, their physical and psychic states, actions, interaction, social situation, and physical environment.	Social laws can in principle be reduced to laws about individuals, their physical and psychic states, actions, interaction, social situation, and physical environment.
Methodology	Social concepts should be defined in terms of individuals, their physical and psychic states, actions, interaction, social situation, and physical environment.	Social phenomena should be explained in terms of individuals, their physical and psychic states, actions, interaction, social situation, and physical environment.	Social laws should be reduced to laws about individuals, their physical and psychic states, actions, interaction, social situation, and physical environment.

Source: Udehn 2002: 499.

the tradition of pluralist political thought: that groups of individuals who share a common interest will have an incentive to promote that interest; that 'groups arise on the basis of common interests, that they are maintained through member support of group policies, and that group policies are an expression of underlying common interests' (Moe 1980: 2).

The problem of collective action had already been revealed to social scientists before the rise of rational choice theory. Mancur Olson had shown, in *The Logic of Collective Action* (1965), that the existence of common interests among individuals does not necessarily produce an incentive to pursue concerted political action. The reason, he argued, was that, rather than working to promote a common interest, individuals are just as likely to let others do the work and to 'free-ride': after all, once a common interest (or 'collective good') is achieved, everyone gains from its provision irrespective of whether or not they worked for it. So social scientists were already aware of collective action problems. However, rational choice theory provided simple, powerful models that showed why, as a result of this problem, rationally calculating individuals will act against collective interests.

The rise of interest in rational choice theory gave renewed impetus to one of its core principles: methodological individualism. Adding to this impetus was the emergence of the movement known as 'analytical Marxism' and, in particular, Jon Elster's rational choice version of it. Elster argued that much of Marxian class analysis overlooks the potential for collective action problems; that Marxist theorists ignore the incentives that individuals face and that motivate individual action, and so fail to consider the possibility that the working class faces a collective action problem when it comes to engaging in revolutionary activity. What Marxist theory needed, he argued, was a micro-analysis of the incentives that motivate individual workers to contribute to achieving a collective good. Rational choice theoretical tools such as game theory could enable analysts to do this. Using methodological individualism to interpret Marxist theory, and tools provided by rational choice theory, Elster sought to show how Marxist theory could be reconstructed so as to provide explanations of 'exploitation, struggle, revolution' and other macro-social phenomena (1982: 453), with 'microfoundations: with an account of the intentional states that motivate individual action'.[4]

The attempt by Elster and other 'analytical Marxists' to ground Marxist analysis on principles of methodological individualism generated considerable controversy. But it also inspired a constructive debate on whether and how to provide explanations of macro-social phenomena with micro-foundations, a debate that succeeded, as previous debates had not, in keeping the issue separate from the strong (or narrow) methodological individualist position (that we previously discussed) and other efforts at reducing macro phenomena to micro-foundations.

Coleman's bathtub

In an influential discussion of how to provide explanations of macro-social phenomena with micro-foundations, James Coleman introduced a useful visualization of macro–micro relations. In a diagram which is often referred to as 'Coleman's Bathtub' or 'boat' (because of its trapezoidal shape), Coleman depicts (1) causal relations going down from macro phenomena (e.g. institutions) to the *conditions* of individual actions, which (2) then give rise to individual *actions*, that (3) in turn aggregate up to macro outcomes (Coleman 1990: 8). Coleman developed his account of these linkages through a discussion of Max Weber's famous explanation, in *The Protestant Ethic and the Spirit of Capitalism* (1905), of how Protestant religious doctrines contributed to the rise of capitalist economic organization.

Coleman argued, in effect, that Weber's argument lacked 'micro-foundations'. Social change comes about through changes in individuals and their interactions, so explanations of social change that refer to macro-level factors only are incomplete. More specifically, macro phenomena have to be explained by *the interaction of micro-and macro-levels*. Coleman's 'bathtub' figure, together with a depiction of Weber's argument, is shown in Figure 4.1. Weber explained Macro Factor *Y* (e.g. capitalism) in terms of Macro Factor *X* (Protestant religious doctrine). Coleman argued that this explanation is incomplete. But a full explanation, Coleman argued, must explain how Protestant religious doctrine affected the values of individuals (a transition from the macro-to the micro-level) and how the actions and interactions of individuals in turn contributed to the rise of capitalism (a transition from the micro-to the macro-level). In sum, a full explanation requires an explanation of the macro-to-micro and the micro-to-macro transitions: how Macro Factor *X* creates constraints on actors (arrow 1); how actors choose actions under the constraints (arrow 2); and how the actions accumulate to the macro level (arrow 3).

In Chapter 2 we discussed causal mechanisms and, in particular, the notion that there are 'social mechanisms' that produce social outcomes. Drawing on Coleman's scheme, Peter Hedström and Richard Swedberg describe a 'social mechanism' as a process of beginning with a macro phenomenon with micro implications, followed by (1)a causal process on the micro-level that leads to a new micro-level; followed finally by (2)a macro-social change that reflects the micro-social situation (Hedström and Swedberg 1998). This seems a useful way to think about how, through macro–micro and micro–macro interactions, these mechanisms operate to produce outcomes.

What methods are there for generating and assessing evidence on causal mechanisms?

An increasingly popular method for exploring causal mechanisms, primarily in case studies, is process tracing. Alexander George and Timothy McKeown (1985) define process tracing as a method to identify the causal chain and causal mechanisms that connect hypothesized causes and outcomes. In process tracing the researcher 'explores the chain of events or the decision-making process by which initial case conditions are translated into case outcomes. The cause–effect link that connects independent variable and outcome is unwrapped and divided into smaller steps; then the investigator looks for observable evidence of each step'

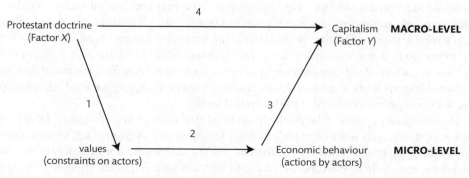

Figure 4.1 Macro–micro linkages (Coleman's 'Bathtub', and *Weber's Protestant Ethic and the Spirit of Capitalism*)

(Van Evera 1997: 64). Using case studies and within-case analysis, the researcher searches for evidence of the causal process a theory hypothesizes or implies in a case, through examining data from histories, archival documents, interview transcripts, or other sources. These might help reconstruct the sequence or structure of events, or reveal the motives or perceptions of government officials or decision-makers. In this way, process tracing can help to uncover the micro-foundations of individual behaviour.

Fallacies

While there is, as of yet, no definite solution to the methodological problem of linking individual and collective action, there is at least a recognition that, in the absence of a solution, analysts must be alert to falling victim to one or another of two common fallacies or errors of reasoning. The first of these is what is called the '**ecological fallacy**': the error of inferring individual characteristics from group characteristics based on aggregate data. For instance, and as Elster argued, when we ignore the potential for collective action problems in groups, we move too easily from an identification of a group interest to the ascription of an individual interest. When inferences about the nature of specific individual behaviour are based solely upon population-level or 'ecological' (i.e. group) data, this can lead to very wrong conclusions.

The classic example of an ecological inference problem is provided by W. S. Robinson. In a widely cited article, Robinson (1950) noted that, on the basis of census data, several geographic districts in the United States in 1930 showed a positive correlation between the literacy rate and the proportion of immigrants: the greater the proportion of immigrants in the unit, the higher its average literacy rate. However, when individuals instead of aggregates were considered, the correlation turned negative: immigrants were on average less literate. The positive correlation at the aggregate level was because immigrants tended to settle in areas where the population was already more literate. Moreover, when Robinson was writing, districts with large percentages of African Americans (then located mainly in the South) generally elected segregationist candidates; but, as Robinson demonstrated, this relationship was not reproduced at the individual level: blacks did *not* vote for segregationist candidates. This did not mean that the aggregate level relationship was 'spurious'. Districts with large numbers of African Americans really *did* elect segregationists.

The ecological fallacy appears to be an inherent problem in political studies. The observation that most armed conflicts take place in poor countries with low education standards leads, wrongly, to the conclusion that poor and uneducated young men are more likely to join a rebel group; the fact that wealthier *states* in America are more liberal should not lead us to conclude that *liberal voters* are richer than conservative voters; that a decrease in income is correlated with an increase in crime at the county level does not mean that low personal income leads to an increase in criminal behaviour. Aggregate-level relationships are *not* necessarily reproduced at the individual level!

However, the opposite fallacy—the 'individualistic' or 'reversed ecological' fallacy—is just as common. This is the error of deducing conclusions about groups (e.g. organizations, societies) using findings from the individual level of analysis. So, for instance, in the case of Robinson's study of electoral outcomes in districts with large percentages of African Americans, the fact that African Americans were not segregationist did not mean that the district-level linkage between racial composition and segregationist policies was spurious. In contemporary France, 'the vote for the xenophobic National Front tends to be highest in districts with high percentages of Muslim immigrants'. The *ecological* fallacy is to assume that the immigrants are supporting the National Front. They are not (Inglehart and Welzel 2003: 63). The *individualistic* fallacy is to assume that, because Muslim immigrants do not support the National Front, the vote for the National Front will not be high in districts with high percentages of Muslim immigrants. It is. If we focus too much on the characteristics of individuals, we may wrongly attribute these characteristics to a group or population. It may be the case that at an individual level, high income or other markers of material success are associated with a lower rate of suicide. But this does not mean that populations or societies which are rich have a lower rate of suicide or better mental health. In fact, it may be that the opposite is true.

Both fallacies, Todd Landman, argues, 'originate from the same source: the ontological predisposition of the researcher' (Landman 2008a: 43). An individualist ontology predisposes a researcher to collect data on individuals to provide insight into collective behaviour; while a holist ontology may focus the attention of a researcher on macro-social phenomena in order to better understand the circumstances that shape individual behaviour.

While explanations that *combine* macro- and micro-foundations would likely be better able to avoid fallacies associated with individualist and holist methodological positions, they would also provide more comprehensive explanations of political outcomes. We will consider this issue in the next section.

Agents and structures in the study of politics

There are two broad tendencies in explanations of political outcomes as they relate to agents and structures: intentionalism (agential explanations) and structuralism (structural explanations). **Intentionalism** refers to approaches that give primacy to the intentions and actions of individual agents in explaining events. Approaches which pursue this type of 'agential' explanation include rational choice and public choice theories. The term '**structuralism**' refers to approaches that privilege the role of structures in explanations of social phenomena. These approaches assume that there are structures that individuals cannot see and of which they may not have any awareness, but that nonetheless shape or influence their actions; that constrain, and also provide opportunities for, individual action.

Questions relating to the relative importance of structural and agential factors, and to the role of both in explaining political events, are at the heart of debates about many political outcomes, with explanations for many political phenomena tending to stress *either* agents *or* structural factors.

For instance, explanations for the variation in human rights abuse across countries have tended to be either agential or structural. Agential explanations focus on 'the intentionality of individual and state choices, the strategic interaction of state and non-state actors, and the human rights implications of the multiple outcomes of these interactions'. Structural explanations focus on the impact on human rights of macro patterns and holistic structures: 'broad socio-economic change, institutional differentiation and transition, and particular structural constraints at domestic and international levels of analysis' (Landman 2008b: 4).

Studies of revolutions have also tended to offer either one type of explanation or the other. Theda Skocpol, in *States and Social Revolutions* (1979), argued for a structural and 'non-voluntarist' study of revolutions. Samuel Popkin, in *The Rational Peasant* (published the same year, 1979), argued for a study of peasant revolutionary action based upon the axioms of rational choice. Skocpol's analysis focuses exclusively upon social structures, and Popkin focuses exclusively upon individual action. Skocpol views individual revolutionary action to be a function of social-structural dynamics. Similarly, Popkin views social change (revolution) as a function of intentional maximizing behaviour on the part of individuals. Theoretical inconsistencies emerge in both studies because of the emphasis on one set of factors to the exclusion of the other. Skocpol argues that a structurally generated collapse of effective peasant sanctioning enables peasants to gain sufficient tactical freedom to launch concerted attacks against the landed elite. But Skocpol's analysis doesn't account for individual choices to revolt; it doesn't acknowledge impediments to collective action. On the other hand, Popkin's emphasis on the ability of revolutionary organizations, and the political entrepreneurs who lead them, to provide and create incentives that induce participation, leaves out of the analysis the role of the social-structural environment within which these activities take place. As Jeffrey Berejikian (1992) points out, an understanding of how agents and structures *interact* would enable us to develop more comprehensive explanations of social change.

The agent–structure problem

In recent years, debate over methodological individualism and holism in the field of politics has tended to focus on the question of how to define the relationship between structures and agents. This question is at the core of what is known as the structure–agency problem. Which are most important in explaining political outcomes: agential factors or structural factors? Which of these have explanatory primacy? Can they be combined to produce better explanations of social phenomena?

The subjects of politics are human beings who exercise agency (personal autonomy) within a structure (the material conditions which define the range of actions available to actors). A central problem in social and political theory, however, is to explain the outcomes that we observe in terms of both the individual agent and the social structure within which it acts. As Stuart McAnulla points out, 'We have an intuitive understanding of the importance of both structural and intentional factors in social reality' (2002: 274). The problem is to find a way in which to define (1) how human agents act in politics; (2) the social structure or system within which they act; and (3) the relationship between the two. It is really the third of these that represents the heart of 'the structure–agent problem'. How do we do justice to both sides of this relationship?

In a highly influential article, 'The Agent Structure Problem in International Relations Theory' (1987), Alexander Wendt criticized the two solutions that had been offered to this problem by International Relations theorists. Wendt points out that Neo-Realist theory and World Systems theory had answered the ontological question of which came into existence first—agents or structures?—by making agents prior or primitive, thus adopting an individualist ontology; or making structures prior or primitive, which is a holistic ontology. Both variants are reductionist solutions. By defining structure in terms of the distribution of capabilities among the pre-existing units, Neo-Realism reduces the notion of 'structure' to attributes of pre-existing, individual units that are not theorized.

In World Systems theory, structure is treated as analytically independent of its constituent elements. It is conceived of as something more than, independent of, and existing in the absence of, interacting individual elements. Agents have no impact on it. So the structure is inert, unchanging: reified. There is no theory of the structure, of how it emerges, of what produces it. Wendt argued that we need to conceive of social structures as ontologically dependent upon, but not reducible to, their units; and develop mediating concepts that can link structure and agency in concrete situations. For Wendt, the solution lies in some version of 'structurationism', a position that has provided the basis for a number of influential theoretical perspectives regarding the structure–agency relationship. We consider two of these, below.

The dialectical relationship between structures and agents

In contrast to analyses which either give agents or structures primary ontological status, dialectical approaches attempt to give weight to both structure and agency without falling into the traps of structuralism and intentionalism.

In his theory of structuration, Anthony Giddens attempts to develop a dialectical synthesis of the two. His structuration theory reconceptualizes the dualism of structure and agency as a 'duality of structure' (1984). Structuration theory states that structures are themselves dual in that they are 'both the medium and the outcome' of social action (1981: 27). He thus recasts the two independent sets of phenomena, structure and agency, as concepts which are dependent upon each other and recursively related.

According to structuration theory, structure shapes people's practices, but these practices constitute and reproduce social systems. Agents and structures co-exist and co-determine each other. This dialectical synthesis of the two makes structures and individuals ontologically equivalent and irreducible (not reducible to the other). They are mutually constitutive, but ontologically distinct, entities. Each is the effect of the other; they are co-determined.

However, critics argue that the conception of structure and agency as co-determined, or mutually constitutive, ends up conflating them. This makes it difficult to examine their independent properties and the relationship or dialectic between them. The notion that structure and agency are mutually constitutive—that they are, in fact, the same thing, or two sides of the same coin—makes it very difficult to examine the interrelationship or dialectic between the two.

A second dialectic approach, Margaret Archer's 'morphogenetic approach', was elaborated as an alternative to this conflation of structure and agency. Archer argues that while rejecting the 'upward conflation' of methodological individualism and the 'downward conflation' of holism, structurationism offers yet another conflation of structure and agency: a 'central conflation'. We must not conflate the two at all, Archer argues. Unless we maintain the analytic distinction between structure and agency and treat them as irreducible to one another, we cannot examine how they relate to one another over time.

Archer points out that structures and agents are irreducible because they are fundamentally distinct. The distinction between them rests on the fact that social structures, unlike agents, don't possess self-awareness. In whatever way we conceptualize the 'social'—as an objective and emergent stratum of reality, or as a negotiated and objectified social construct—the social remains fundamentally different from its component members in this lack of self-consciousness. We must not only keep structures and agents analytically distinct; we must also make it our task to discover what difference 'the self-awareness of its members make to the nature of the social' (Archer 2007: 40).

Archer proposes that we should understand society as the *interaction over time* of objective structure, on the one hand, and individual, subjective agency, on the other. Though she makes structure analytically prior to agents—because the temporal pre-existence of structure is a condition for individual action (1995: 15)—she argues that there is never a moment at which *both* structure and agency are not jointly in play. Structural conditioning (which is temporally prior, and relatively autonomous, yet possessing causal powers) shapes social interaction; and social interaction, in turn, generates structural elaboration. This scheme of *Structural Conditioning → Social Interaction → Structural Elaboration* is stretched out over time.

The difference between the 'morphogenetic approach' proposed by Archer, and structurational models, such as that elaborated by Anthony Giddens, is represented schematically in Figure 4.2, below. Though both concerned with the time–space dimension of the structure-agent relationship, the morphogenetic approach does not conflate structure and agency.

Figure 4.3 illustrates the ontological dualism and temporal interaction described in Archer's morphogenetic approach. 'T' represents time. 'T1', then, refers to an initial point in time in which structures condition social interaction. The period of time between 'T2' and 'T3' is one in which processes of social interaction impact structures; so that at 'T4' we find that, as a result of prior social interaction, the initial structures have been elaborated in some way. Though Archer's morphogenic approach has been criticized for making the temporal pre-existence of structure a condition for individual action, many theorists see this 'morphogenetic' approach as representing another step forward on the road to resolving the structure–agency problem.

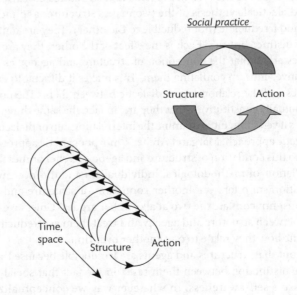

Figure 4.2 Structurational models
Source: Rose 1999.

Structural conditioning
T1

Social interaction
T2   T3

Structural elaboration
T4

Figure 4.3 The morphogenetic approach

Source: Archer 1995: 157.

 ## Conclusions

Researchers in our field are confronted with two 'truisms' about the social world. 'First, individuals are often agents whose intentional, self-conscious, actions both reproduce and transform social reality. Second, society consists largely of interconnecting social relationships (structures) that condition the interaction between agents, as well as the outcomes of agent action' (Berejikian 1992: 647). However, the methodological problems stemming from the simultaneity of individual and collective action have yet to be solved. There is growing consensus that there exist macro phenomena—systems of norms, social and political structures, institutions and organizations—but that we must be able to provide 'micro-foundations' for entities and causes at the macro-level.

All social-scientific theorizing adopts, either implicitly or explicitly, a position with respect to the relationship between agents (the actors) and the structures which shape, give meaning to, or make possible their actions. We have considered influential accounts of how we might understand and conceptualize this relationship; but debates about methodological individualism and holism, the relationship between 'macro-' and 'micro-' factors, between society and the individual, and between structures and agents remain unresolved. What, then, is to be done? Stuart McAnulla suggests that 'the debate should not focus upon an effort to find the Holy Grail of a solution. Rather, structure–agency issues should be acknowledged as an *unavoidable problem*.' It is 'an issue on which we cannot avoid adopting a position . . . we are bound to appeal to some understanding of structure–agency whenever we offer explanation of political events' (McAnulla 2002: 273; emphasis in original). We cannot seek a solution 'in the way one might look for an answer to a riddle'. What we can do is to continue to look for useful conceptualizations of how structure and agency relate (McAnulla 2002: 274). This seems a commonsensical way in which to approach these issues in research.

 ## Questions

- In what sense is a society more than the sum of its individual members?
- Can an explanation of a social phenomenon which only makes use of holistic social terms ever be fully satisfactory?
- *Are* there social concepts which cannot be defined by reference to individuals only?
- What difference does the self-awareness of its members make to the nature of the social?

 ## Guide to Further Reading

Birnbaum, P., J. Leca, and J. Gaffney (eds) (1990), *Individualism: Theories and Methods,* **trans. John Gaffney (Oxford: Oxford University Press).**
A collection of essays by eminent social scientists from several countries on the question of individualism from historical, methodological, hermeneutical, political, and sociological points of view.

Hedstrom, P. and R. Swedberg (eds) (1998), *Social Mechanisms: An Analytical Approach to Social Theory* (Cambridge: Cambridge University Press).
Papers from a symposium held in Stockholm in 1996, by a number of prominent social scientists, including Thomas Schelling, Jon Elster, and Timur Kuran.

Hodgson, G. (2007), 'Meanings of Methodological Individualism', *Journal of Economic Methodology* 14(2) (June): 211–26.
A discussion of ambiguities, contradictions, and vagueness in how the term 'methodological individualism' is used.

Little, D. (1990), *Varieties of Social Explanation: An Introduction to the Philosophy of Social Science* (Boulder, CO: Westview Press), chapter 9 ('Methodological Individualism'), 183–201.

Martin, M. and L. C. McIntyre (eds) (1994), *Readings in the Philosophy of Social Science* (New York: MIT Press).
This volume brings together a collection of important texts on reductionism, individualism, and holism (Part VI).

Udehn, L. (2001), *Methodological Individualism: Background, History, and Meaning* (New York: Routledge).
This book addresses comprehensively and analytically the large literature on methodological individualism.

Wendt, A. (1987), 'The Agent–Structure Problem in International Relations Theory', *International Organization* 41(3) (summer): 335–70.
The two most influential structural explanations for international outcomes, Neo-Realism and World Systems theory are the focus of Alexander Wendt's influential, widely-cited decision. He shows that each of these theories represents a different approach to solving the agent–structure problem.

 # References

Archer, M. S. (1995), *Realist Social Theory: The Morphogenetic Approach* (Cambridge: Cambridge University Press).

——— (2007), 'The Trajectory of the Morphogenetic Approach: An Account in the First-Person', *Sociologia, Problemas e Práticas* 54: 35–47.

Asch, S. (1952), *Social Psychology* (Englewood Cliffs, NJ: Prentice-Hall).

Berejikian, J. (1992), 'Revolutionary Collective Action and the Agent-Structure Problem', *American Political Science Review*, 86(3) (September): 647–57.

Bishop, George F., Robert W. Oldendick, and Alfred J. Tuchfarber (1982), 'Political Information Processing: Question Order and Context Effect', *Political Behavior* 4(2) (June): 177–200.

——— (1984), 'Interest in Political Campaigns: The Influence of Question Order and Electoral Context', *Political Behavior* 6(2) (June): 159–69.

Coleman, J. (1990), *Foundations of Social Theory* (Cambridge, MA: Harvard University Press).

Collier, P. and A. Hoeffler (2004), 'Greed and Grievance in Civil War', *Oxford Economic Papers* 56(4): 563–95.

———L. Elliott, H. Hegre, A. Hoeffler, M. Reynal-Querol, and N. Sambanis (2003), *Breaking the Conflict Trap: Civil War and Development Policy* (Oxford: Oxford University Press and Washington, DC: World Bank), available at http://econ.worldbank.org/prr/CivilWarPRR.

Durkheim, E. (1994), 'Social Facts', in Michael Martin and Lee C. McIntyre (eds), *Readings in the Philosophy of Social Science* (Cambridge, MA: MIT Press), 433–40.

Elster, J. (1982), 'Marxism, Functionalism and Game Theory', *Theory & Society* (July): 453–82.

——— (2007), *Explaining Social Behavior: More Nuts and Bolts for the Social Sciences* (Cambridge: Cambridge University Press).

Fearon, J. D. and D. Laitin (2003), 'Ethnicity, Insurgency, and Civil War', *American Political Science Review* 97(1): 75–90.

George, A. L. and T. J. McKeown (1985), 'Case Studies and Theories of Organizational Decision Making', *Advances in Information Processing in Organizations* 2: 21–58.

Giddens, A. (1981), *A Contemporary Critique of Historical Materialism* (Berkeley, CA: University of California Press).

——(1984), *The Constitution of Society: Outline of the Theory of Structuration* (Berkeley, CA: University of California Press).

Hedström, P. and R. Swedberg (1998), 'Social Mechanisms: An Introductory Essay', in P. Hedstrom and R. Swedberg (eds), *Social Mechanisms: An Analytical Approach to Social Theory* (Cambridge: Cambridge University Press), 1–31.

Hobsbawm, E. (1994), *The Age of Extremes* (London: Michael Joseph).

Hodgson, G. (2007), 'Meanings of Methodological Individualism', *Journal of Economic Methodology* 14(2) (June): 211–26.

Inglehart, R. and Christian Welzel (2003), 'Political Culture and Democracy: Analyzing Cross-Level Linkages', *Comparative Politics* 36(1) (October): 61–79.

Kincaid, H. (1994), 'Reduction, Explanation, and Individualism', in Michael Martin and Lee C. McIntyre (eds), *Readings in the Philosophy of Social Science* (Cambridge, MA: MIT Press), 497–514.

——(1996), *Philosophical Foundations of the Social Sciences* (Cambridge: Cambridge University Press).

Landman, T. (2008a), *Issues and Methods in Comparative Politics*, 3rd edition (London: Routledge).

——(2008b), 'Empirical Political Science and Human Rights', *Essex Human Rights Review* 5(1) (July): 1–7.

Little, D. (1991), *Varieties of Social Explanation: An Introduction to the Philosophy of Social Science* (Boulder, CO: Westview Press).

——(1992), 'Jon Elster', in W. Samuels (ed.), *New Horizons in Economic Thought: Appraisals of Leading Economists* (Aldershot: Edward Elgar).

Martin, H.-P., and H. Schumann (1997), *The Global Trap* (London: Zed).

Masters, R. (2001), 'Biology and Politics: Linking Nature and Nurture', *Annual Review of Political Science* 4: 345–69.

McAnulla, S. (2002), 'Structure and Agency', in D. Marsh and G. Stoker (eds), *Theory and Methods in Political Science*, second edition (Basingstoke: Palgrave), 271–91.

Moe, T. (1980), *The Organization of Interests* (Chicago: University of Chicago Press).

Olson, M. (1965), *The Logic of Collective Action: Public Goods and the Theory of Groups* (Cambridge, MA: Harvard University Press).

Østby, G (2008), 'Polarization, Horizontal Inequalities and Violent Civil Conflict', *Journal of Peace Research* 45(2): 143–62.

Parsons, T. (1937), *The Structure of Social Action* (New York: Free Press).

Popper, K. (1944a), 'The Poverty of Historicism I', *Economica* 11: 86–103.

——(1944b), 'The Poverty of Historicism II', *Economica*, 11: 119–37.

——(1945), *The Open Society and its Enemies*, vol. I: *Plato*, vol. 2: *Hegel and Marx* (London: Routledge & Kegan Paul).

——(1945), 'The Poverty of Historicism III', *Economica*, 11: 69–89.

Popkin, S (1979), *The Rational Peasant: The Political Economy of Rural Society in Vietnam* (Berkeley, CA: University of California Press).

Ratner, C.(2007), 'Contextualism versus Positivism in Cross-Cultural Psychology', in G. Zheng, K. Leung, and J. Adair (eds), *Perspectives and Progress in Contemporary Cross-Cultural Psychology* (Beijing: China Light Industry Press).

Robinson, W.S. (1950), 'Ecological Correlations and the Behavior of Individuals', *American Sociological Review* 15: 351–7.

Rose, J. (1999), 'Towards a Structurational Theory of IS, Theory Development and Case Study Illustrations', in J. Pries-Heje et al. (eds), *Proceedings of the 7th European Conference on Information Systems* (Copenhagen: Copenhagen Business School).

Sawyer, R. K. (2002), 'Nonreductive Individualism Part I—Supervenience and Wild Disjunction', *Philosophy of the Social Sciences* 32: 537–59.

Sidanius, J. and R. Kurzban (2003), 'Evolutionary Approaches to Political Psychology', in D. Sears, L. Huddy, and R. Jervis (eds), *Oxford Handbook of Political Psychology* (New York: Oxford University Press).

Skocpol, T. (1979), *States and Social Revolutions: A Comparative Analysis of France, Russia, and China* (New York: Cambridge University Press).

Somit, A. and S. Peterson (eds) (2003) *Human Nature and Public Policy: An Evolutionary Approach* (New York: Palgrave/Macmillan).

Stewart, F. (2002), 'Horizontal Inequalities: A Neglected Dimension of Development', Queen Elizabeth House Working Paper Series 81, University of Oxford, available at http://www. qeh.ox.ac.uk/pdf/qehwp/qehwps81.pdf.

Strange, S. (1996), *The Retreat of the State: The Diffusion of Power in the World Economy* (New York: Cambridge University Press).

Urdal, H. (2004), 'The Devil in the Demographics: The Effect of Youth Bulges on Domestic Armed Conflict, 1950–2000', Social Development Paper (Washington, DC: The World Bank).

—— (2006), 'A Clash of Generations? Youth Bulges and Political Violence', *International Studies Quarterly* 50: 607–29.

Udehn, L. (2001), *Methodological Individualism: Background, History, and Meaning* (New York: Routledge).

—— (2002), 'The Changing Face of Methodological Individualism', *Annual Review of Sociology* 28: 479–507.

Van Evera, Stephen (1997), *Guide to Methods for Students of Political Science* (Ithaca, NY: Cornell University Press).

Watkins, J. W. N. (1957), 'Historical Explanation in the Social Sciences', *British Journal for the Philosophy of Science* 8(2) (August): 104–17

—— (1994), 'Historical Explanation in the Social Sciences', in Michael Martin and Lee C. McIntyre (eds), *Readings in the Philosophy of Social Science* (Cambridge, MA: MIT Press), 441–50.

Weber, Max (1905), *The Protestant Ethic and the Spirit of Capitalism*, trans. Talcott Parsons (London and Boston, MA: Unwin Hyman, 1930).

Wendt, A. (1987), 'The Agent Structure Problem in International Relations Theory', *International Organization* 41:3 (summer): 335–70.

Zahle, J. (2003), 'The Individualism–Holism Debate on Intertheoretic Reduction and the Argument from Multiple Realization', *Philosophy of the Social Sciences* 33: 77–99.

 ## Endnotes

1. See the discussion in Chapter 1 concerning units and levels of analysis. In the study of politics, a 'unit of analysis' is the entity that a researcher analyses, the 'what' or 'whom' that is studied, in order to explain a political event or process. This is not the same as the specific *unit of observation* on which data are collected. Units of analysis commonly employed in political studies include individuals, social groups, legislatures, texts, bureaucracies, and states. To distinguish units of analysis from 'levels of analysis', recall that this latter term refers to a conceptual scheme which divides up the world into different aggregations of social phenomena or 'levels' of social organization. An entity that serves as the unit of analysis for a study might also be defined in terms of one or another level of analysis. For instance, international organizations become a unit of analysis when they are selected as the focus of a specific study, and they are also associated with the international level of analysis. What makes an entity a unit for analysis is its selection by a researcher for analysis.

2. *Epistemological* individualism claims, not that only individuals exist, but that knowledge of social phenomena can only consist of knowledge of separate individual elements.

3. There are several perspectives on how human biological evolution influences political behaviour. See, for instance, Masters 2001, Sidanius and Kurzban 2003, and Somit and Peterson 2003.

4. Elster has, to some extent, changed his mind about the utility of rational choice theory: 'I now believe that rational-choice theory has less explanatory power than I used to think. Do real people act on the calculations that make up many pages of mathematical appendixes in leading journals? I do not think so' (2007: 5).

Part 2

How to Do Research: An Overview

5

Asking Questions: How to Find and Formulate Research Questions

 Chapter Summary

In this chapter we move from issues in the philosophy of social science to a consideration of the research process. This chapter focuses on *step one* of this process: the formulation of a well-crafted research question. A research question not only initiates the research process, it is crucial to every other step along the way. The chapter discusses why your research should begin with a research question, how a research question structures the research process; the difference between a topic or general question, on the one hand, and a focused research question, on the other; where to find and how to formulate research questions, the various types of questions scholars ask, and the role of the 'literature review' as a source and rationale for research questions. In discussing these issues, the chapter asks and answers a number of questions, including the following:

● What is a research question?

● Why begin political inquiry with research questions?

● What kinds of questions stimulate good research?

● How can you develop a research question from the existing literature relating to your area of interest?

● What is the role of the 'literature review' in a research project?

● What form does a good research question take?

Introduction

> Questions are the engines of intellect, the cerebral machines which convert energy to motion, and curiosity to controlled inquiry.
>
> (Fischer 1970: 3)

Most political research originates from some general question or problem that arises, either from the events, issues, or processes we observe in the world around us, or from the theories and frameworks that our field has developed in order to understand them. But the research *process* only begins with the conversion of this general question or problem into a well-formulated, clearly focused, research question. As we shall explain, there is an important difference between a *general* question, topic, or idea that you may wish to investigate, and a *research* question. It is the formulation of a research question that enables you to channel your interest, intellectual energy, and curiosity into the pursuit of structured, systematic inquiry. The step you take which moves you from identifying a topic to defining a research

Identify an area of research interest

Specify a research question

Figure 5.1 Step 1

question, illustrated in Figure 5.1, can be challenging, frustrating, and time-consuming. But once it's accomplished, you are on your way!

This chapter focuses on formulating a research question. It will discuss the requirements for a research question, where research questions come from, surveying the literature to gain an overview of the topic that you are interested in, the role of a 'literature review' in providing both the inspiration and rationale for research questions, the different types of questions scholars ask, and how to formulate a research question so that it addresses an issue of significance in both the real world and the scholarly community devoted to the study of politics.

There are three misconceptions about research questions we should clear up at the outset.

The first has to do with the role and function of a research question. When we say that good research *begins* with a well-formulated research question, this might be interpreted as meaning that a research question is important as a means of *initiating* the research process. But a research question plays a continuous role throughout the research process. It establishes the basis for every decision a researcher makes in every phase of a project. So, getting the research question fully in focus not only gets you off to a good start: it informs every other part of the research process.

A second misconception concerns the task of formulating a research question. This may sound like a relatively straightforward task—one that is easily and quickly accomplished; and maybe you are wondering why we need to devote an entire chapter to discussing how to go about it. However, formulating a good research question is not as easy as it might first appear. It often demands considerable time and thought and, for many researchers, may be the most difficult part of a research project. But however much time it might take to accomplish, once you have formulated a good research question, the rest of the research process becomes far easier and clearer, and moves along much faster.

A third misconception about research questions has to do with their relevance to different types of research. Some people may think that the formulation of a specific research question is relevant only to quantitative research; that qualitative research is more open-ended and doesn't require the framing of a research question. But, irrespective of whether you are pursuing qualitative or quantitative research, there are good reasons why your research should be based on and shaped by a research question. Below, we list six reasons why the formulation of a research question should be step one of the research process.

1. It forces you to get clear about what you want to know.
2. By requiring that it addresses an issue of significance in the real world, it ensures that your answer, if systematically developed, will make it possible for your research to contribute to knowledge about important issues.

3. By requiring that it addresses an issue of significance to the field of politics, it ensures that your answer in some way contributes to, rather than merely reproduces, existing knowledge.

4. It organizes, and is the basis for, everything else that follows.

5. It focuses and narrows your search for information.

6. It enables you to decide what to include and exclude from your research.

Consider the steps involved in conducting research outlined in Box 5.1: what it shows is that every component of the process flows from and is directly connected to a research question. We will be discussing each of these components over the course of this and the following two chapters.

There are two things that you should note about the outline of research components presented in Box 5.1, as well as the discussion throughout this chapter.

First, this outline is meant to provide a *general template* for formulating a research question and structuring research. The design of *your* research will ultimately be shaped by your topic and the aims of your project, and by the guidelines that your thesis/dissertation supervisor or course tutor requires that you follow. 'The Answer' part of this outline suggests a focus on hypothesis generation and theory testing, an approach not equally relevant to all types of research. It might be argued, too, that this is an approach not accepted in the different forms of knowledge (positivism/interpretivism) discussed in Chapter 2. But as Chapter 2 pointed out, though positivist and interpretivist researchers tend to be guided by different assumptions, they also tend to share a common set of research practices founded in the hypothetico-deductive method. Some researchers 'assess whether the information they have gathered fits with the interpretation they have posited', and others 'consider the fit of competing interpretations with the facts they have gathered', but 'in either case they are practicing the hypethetico-deductive method' (Pollins 2007: 100). Consequently, they generally follow the same methodological conventions. But, again, Box 5.1 serves as a starting point and set of considerations to be revised or elaborated consistent with the question and aims that animate your own project.

Second, what Box 5.1 shows is a research process that is structured in an idealized linear fashion. The real process is different. For instance, though researchers may start with 'some operational hunches about what they expect to find', they generally do not '"frame hypotheses" in any formal sense before they start to work' (Shively 1989: 25). Good researchers generally are engaged in learning and creative re-thinking all along the way. As Chapter 6 will discuss, our aim in presenting the outline shown in Box 5.1 is to offer some clear and obvious procedures to get you started. As you gain experience, you will develop your own process of work and way of fulfilling the requirements of good research.

Irrespective of the particular way you choose to structure your research, a carefully formulated research question will ensure that your research has a clear purpose. If you are not clear what question or questions your research is designed to address, you will produce research that is unfocused and, ultimately, uninteresting to others. More specifically, a research question ensures that your research will be focused on and clearly linked to the realization of a specific aim that contributes to our knowledge of some significant problem or issue. A research question also provides, as a general question or topic does not, a logic of inquiry to guide

---

BOX 5.1 Outline of Research Components

1. The question

   A. What do you want to know? What is *the central question/problem/issue/puzzle?*

   B. Why do you think it is worth doing/knowing? What is *the rationale for pursuing research on this question?*

2. The literature

   A. Who else has asked and answered your question? What (range of) answers to this question are found in *the existing literature relating to it?*

   B. What are the *positive elements* in the current literature? What in the literature can you highlight, underline, expand, extend, improve, build upon, continue?

   C. What needs to be done? Delineate the crucial aspects of the problem requiring investigation. *What need to be done in order to provide a better answer to the question than currently exists?*

3. Your answer

   A. *Theoretical Framework.* What are *the theoretical elements and guiding assumptions of the study?*

      1. What factors or variables of the problem must be investigated in order to answer your central question?

      2. What is/are *your hypothesis/es* (how are these factors linked)?

         a. What is the source of your hypothesis/es? What in theory would lead us to expect the relation(s) you assert?

         b. How would you demonstrate the relationships stated by the hypothesis/es?

      3. What is *the spatial/temporal domain of the study?* What is the rationale for defining this domain for the study?

   B. *Data and sources*

      1. What are *the data relevant to demonstrating the relationships you hypothesize?*

      2. What *sources* are there *for these data?*

---

decisions about the design and methods of the research. Moreover, a properly formulated research question ensures that you are building on existing knowledge. A research question makes the research task specific; so that, rather than trying to gather all the information you can find on a topic, you direct your attention to just the information that addresses the question and helps you to develop an argument in answer to it. When you have a well-formulated research question, you can make decisions about what information should be included or excluded, what data you will need to collect, what to observe, or what to ask your interviewees.

Research questions: What are they? Where do they come from?

What is a research question? A research question is one that (1) has significance for a topic or issue relating to the subject matter of our field; (2) is researchable (it can be answered through conducting research); and (3) has not yet been answered definitively. To say that a question 'has not yet been definitively answered' means that the question has not been addressed; or that the answers that have been offered have not succeeded in resolving debates about the question; or that there is still more that can be done to improve the answers that have so far been offered by, for instance, providing a more systematic, thorough answer; or by considering the question in light of different cases or perspectives that might provide further illumination. We will expand on this further along in the chapter.

All three of these requirements reflect a basic attribute and requirement of social science research: that it addresses a topic or issue relating to the subject matter of a field of study in a way that contributes to our knowledge of that topic. The first requirement compels you to relate a specific topic that interests you to a broader issue or area of inquiry within the field of politics (#1B in Box 5.1). The requirement that a question be researchable means that it must be formulated in a way that makes it possible for you to provide an answer to it through conducting research (#3 in Box 5.1). To be researchable it will have to be sufficiently focused to permit an answer that can in some way be tested or demonstrated, and free of errors of reasoning that might generate false answers or conclusions. Research is expected to contribute empirically, conceptually, or theoretically to our knowledge of something. Consequently, the third requirement—that a question must be one to which we 'don't know the answer'—requires that you explicitly locate your research within the framework of an existing social scientific literature (#2 in Box 5.1). Doing this ensures that you will proceed with an awareness of the 'state of the art' in terms of existing knowledge on the topic or issue that interests you and, so, minimize the chance of duplicating what has already been done.

We will discuss each of these requirements a bit further on, when we consider how to formulate a good research question. First, let's consider how to go about finding a research question.

Finding research questions

Research *topics* in our field originate from our observation of real-world problems and events such as conflicts, elections, or revolutions. But an important source for finding research *questions* is the literature in the field of politics, as well as social science literatures relevant to the subject matter of our field. Please note that, while a *topic* is usually a statement, a *research question* is a question: it is a sentence with a *question mark* at the end of it.

Before we discuss how to use the literature to find a research question, there are two caveats worth noting.

First, though the literature in our field is an important source for research questions, you should not approach the literature with too accepting a frame of mind. As Barbara Geddes points out, in our field

> [t]he literature on some subjects contains only a few arguments generally accepted as true; many controversies in which the hypotheses on both sides lack both clarity and strong empirical support; and large amounts of opinion and conjecture, unsupported by systematic evidence but nevertheless often referred to as theory (2003: 29).

Students are frequently advised to 'look for holes in the literature' in order to find research questions. But, if we accept Geddes' characterization of some of the literature in our field, it appears that this may not always be a good strategy. In fact, Geddes sees the literature as important to the formulation of a research question, *not* because it suggests gaps that need to be filled, but because it stimulates 'indignation, annoyance, and irritation' (Geddes 2003: 29–30). It should be noted, too, that our understanding of the political world usually increases, not through finding and filling gaps in existing knowledge—as Patrick Dunleavy points out, there are often good reasons why gaps remain unfilled (2003: 274)—but by well-crafted research that produces incremental extensions and revisions of it.

In any case, it is worth emphasizing that you should approach the literature on any subject analytically. To be 'analytical' is to ask questions: to subject something to questions in order to discover its meaning or essential features. So our advice is to approach the literature with a questioning frame of mind: one that combines respect for the efforts and achievements of the scholars who produced it, with a healthy degree of scepticism.

Our second caveat about using the literature as a source for research questions is that you should avoid getting drawn into questions that are politically insignificant. Here we are referring to those questions that, as they become the focus of dispute among academic researchers, lose connection with the real-world problems that they originally were meant to address. Research is expected to contribute to our knowledge of a real-world problem or issue, either through empirical research which will improve the theories and methods relevant to understanding that problem and its solution, or through directly addressing conceptual or theoretical shortcomings in existing theories and methods. Since we do not yet have fully effective tools for investigating the many important problems that researchers want to address, much research in our field is concerned with making more effective the tools we use to understand a given problem. But, as Gary King, Robert Keohane, and Sidney Verba argue, research should be driven, not by methods, but by questions and problems. Research which focuses 'too much on making a contribution to a scholarly literature without some attention to topics that have real-world importance', runs the risk of 'descending to politically insignificant questions'. But they also emphasize that 'attention to the current political agenda without regard to issues of the amenability of a subject to systematic study within the framework of a body of social science knowledge leads to careless work that adds little to our deeper understanding' (1994: 17). The best research, as King and his co-authors observe, manages to do both these things: 'to be directly relevant to solving real-world problems and to furthering the goals of a specific scientific literature' (1994: 18). Box 5.2 sums up this view.

BOX 5.2 What Do We Mean When We Say That a Research Project Should Be 'Significant'?

FIRST: *a research project should pose a question that is 'important' in the real world.* The topic should be consequential for political, social, or economic life, for understanding something that significantly affects people's lives, or for understanding and predicting events that might be harmful or beneficial.

SECOND: *a research project should make a specific contribution to an identifiable scholarly literature by increasing our collective ability to construct verified scientific explanations of some aspect of the world* (King, Keohane, and Verba 1994: 15).

With these caveats duly noted, it should be emphasized that reading the literature on a specific topic of interest to you is an important means of gaining knowledge both of existing research and current debates, and of suggesting questions about the topic.

Any issue relating to the political world is likely to be the subject of debate. Experts are likely to produce a variety of conflicting views about how to define it; where, when, and why it originated; how it developed or evolved, what its impact is, what its likely future trajectory will be, and what decision-makers or specialists can or should do with respect to it. If you plan to pursue research on an issue, you will need to sort through the various opinions and judgements about it and come to your own conclusions. You will then be able to figure out how to make visible some dimension of the issue that brings added strength to one or another of the positions represented in that debate, produce a synthesis of their elements, or show how the debate itself is based on erroneous assumptions or logic. But first you will need to get a feel for the debates—for the different positions, and the current 'state of play'.

A good way to go about doing this is to survey the literature on the topic that interests you. We are not referring here to a literature *review*, which is something you write *after you have formulated your research question* (we will be discussing this later in this chapter). A *survey* of literature on your topic helps you to focus your interest and your search for a question on a narrower, more specific, aspect of the topic.

Let's say, for example, that you are interested in problems of democracy, and that you want to learn more about it and make it the focus of a research project. This is a topic of great importance and interest to researchers throughout the social sciences, and the literature relating to it is immense. So, how can you convert your general interest in this large subject into a well-formulated, clearly focused research question; one that will engage your interest, channel your energies, and enable you to contribute to current discussions and debates about some aspect of the subject?

One way is to *survey* the literature about democracy in order to find out what questions other researchers are asking about the topic and what key debates and issues their research addresses. Look at the list of questions in Box 5.3. These represent only a small sample of the questions that researchers ask about democracy. But each question alerts you to a different avenue of research and directs your attention to a more specific literature and set of research questions. You can then select those you think you might be interested in pursuing and compile a bibliography of previous research and writing on them. This, then, is the aim of the survey: to compile a starting bibliography on a narrower aspect of the general topic that interests you. With this done, you read the titles on your bibliography (and the abstract or summaries of the entries, as well); and this will either inspire ideas about how to extend, refine, or critique this literature, or direct your attention to other literatures and avenues of research.

Here is a simple strategy you can use to get this process going.

1. Go to the library and use the online catalogue to get the title of *one* book on your topic. When you go to the library shelf where the book is kept you will discover that it is located in a neighbourhood populated by many other books on the same topic. You can then do a 'neighbourhood search' (peruse the titles of the books on the surrounding shelves) to get a sense of the variety of facets of and entry points into your topic. Pick a book whose title seems to promise either an introduction to an interesting facet of your topic or a good general survey

BOX 5.3 Twenty Questions about Democracy

Democracy

1. What are the problems of democratization in newly decolonized countries?

2. What are the implications for democracy of globalization?

3. Do democratic states have more in common with each other than with undemocratic states?

4. Are there different models of democracy in different cultural contexts?

5. What are the different institutional manifestations of democracy?

6. Is democracy always liberal?

7. Can democracy be imposed upon countries from outside or must it draw upon the established practices of countries *even if* these practices are not obviously democratic?

8. To what extent and on what conditions might democracy be imposed (hence undemocratically) by a foreign power?

9. Are interest groups a threat to democracy?

10. Is the concentration of media ownership a threat to democracy?

12. How does electoral system design affect ethnic conflict regulation in ethnically divided societies?

13. How essential are political parties to representative democracy?

14. What is the relationship between nationalism and democracy?

15. What is a developmental state? Is democracy relevant to its conceptualization?

16. Can ethnic/religious/linguistic politics and democracy be positively related with each other?

17. Is democracy the best political system for promoting human rights in the developing countries?

18. Can democracy promote interstate conflict resolution?

19. Does democracy require an explicit understanding and justification of certain core values?

20. What are the institutional implications of deliberative democracy?

of the topic, and turn to its bibliography or list of references. The reference section of one well-chosen source will contain pages filled with titles that indicate questions and issues people are writing about. These will stimulate ideas of how you might narrow your focus.

In addition, or alternatively, you will want to search the JSTOR database: http://www.jstor.org/cgi-bin/jstor/gensearch. JSTOR reproduces the full image of articles in over 117 scholarly journals. Enter keywords in the full-text search. Make sure that the 'Political Science Journals' box is checked; and, if your topic involves specific geographical areas (e.g. the Middle East, Latin America) or issues and factors central to other disciplines (e.g. Economics, Anthropology, Psychology), you may want to select other journal categories, as well. Peruse the resulting list of articles for three or four that seem particularly relevant and read their abstracts, introductions, and conclusions. You will also want to search the Web of Science (http://webofknowledge.com/). This source includes five databases covering virtually all fields of knowledge. Two of the most useful are the *Social Sciences Citation Index* (*SSCI*) and the *Arts & Humanities Citation Index (A&HCI)*. When you find a scholarly article relevant to your particular research interest, you can also locate all subsequent journal articles that cite it. Also check Google Scholar (http://scholar.google.com/). *Always be sure to retain full bibliographic references (author, date, title, journal, volume, pages) for the articles of interest you find.*

2. A particularly useful source to get you started is a survey or 'state of knowledge'-type article. These often provide a breakdown of the literature on a topic according to its various entry points, debates, and perspectives; and a review of the evolution of thinking on the topic up to and including the most recent and influential works. See if you can spot an article on your topic whose title conforms to something along the lines of the following: 'The Study of Gender and Politics: The State of the Art', or 'Parliamentary versus Presidential Systems: A Survey of the Literature'. Relevant course syllabi or reading lists, which may be accessible online, can also provide this sort of introduction to the literature on a topic.

3. Pursue the line of investigation that seems most interesting to you by getting one of the relevant books or articles you find in a bibliography (or on a course reading list), and then turn to the back of *that* book or article to get additional titles (and also to get 'search terms' that you can put into a search engine).

Bibliographic or Reference Management Software packages allow you to save and store the bibliographic details of the references you find (articles, books, conference papers, websites, etc.). With these packages you have not only stored the bibliographic details of the references you think you may want to use, you also have a personal database of references that you can search and sort; and you can connect between your package and Word to create a customized bibliography in your preferred referencing style at the end of your document. If you change your mind about what referencing style you want or need to use, you can quickly and easily reformat the references. Some of the more popular packages are Endnote, Endnote Web, RefWorks, Reference Manager, Zotero, and Mendeley.

4. Once you have a bibliography of promising books and articles on a particular line of investigation, read the literature you have compiled and think, critically and creatively, about its insights and how to extend them, or its weaknesses and flaws and how to overcome and correct them.

Box 5.4 provides a snapshot of how a survey of the literature on a topic reveals numerous different dimensions or facets of a specific topic.

Institutional libraries offer abundant support to assist you, including online and paper-based guidance on searching databases and finding research literature, web searching, how to reference (including citing electronic resources) and managing references, and new developments in search tools and websites.

Define your topic in terms of 'keywords' that you can use to search various information sources. Think about alternative meanings and contexts for your keywords. Also think of ways of combining words to ensure that only the meaning you want is retrieved. And consider alternative spellings of the words you use. For instance, American and British English use different spellings for many words. So you may want to use a truncation that will capture both spellings (such as behavio*, which will retrieve behavior, behaviour, behavioural, and behavioural).

Look at ways to link your keywords. Do you want records which contain all of your keywords or are some alternatives? Do you want to relate two words so that they are near each other? Can you focus your search by excluding words which might appear with other words

BOX 5.4 Surveying the Literature to Narrow Your Search for a Research Question

Step 1

1. Identify a research area: *conflict.*

2. Identify a case, particular space of time, or geographic area in which you might want to investigate it: **Mexico.**

3. In Google Scholar type '**Conflict Mexico'.** Scan the titles of the listed articles. This identifies questions that scholars are asking about these conflicts, and suggests questions that they either fail to address or address insufficiently, including the following:

   a. What are the motivations behind the conflicts?

   b. What are the main economic determinants?

   c. What are their relationships with political and social issues?

   d. What type of conflicts persists in the country?

   e. What are the root causes of the conflicts?

   f. What are some of the politico-economic losses and gains?

   g. What have been the impacts on human development and poverty?

   h. How does the analysis of the conflicts relate to past and current theoretical discourse and debate?

   i. Which and where are the inflexion points of the conflicts?

   j. Have the causes and relationships changed over time? What dimensions have influenced them?

   k. What is the intensity of the conflicts?

   l. How does (do) the conflict(s) in Chiapas compare to other cases in Mexico? Are there any linkages?

   m. What issues have been addressed? Which ones remain unresolved?

   n. What politico-economic tools are needed to mitigate and overcome the conflicts?

   o. What are the lessons learnt for conflict prevention and conflict resolution?

5. Select an aspect or dimension of the research area and compile a bibliography on it: **the relation of environmental factors to persistent internal conflicts in south-eastern Mexico (the states of Chiapas, Guerrero, and Oaxaca).**

Step 2

6. Begin to assemble a bibliography on this research area by scanning one article, below:

   Environmental Scarcity and Violent Conflict: The Case of Chiapas, Mexico (Philip N., Howard, Thomas Homer Dixon), Occasional Paper, Project on Environment, Population and Security, Washington, D.C.: American Association for the Advancement of Science and the University of Toronto, January 1996.

Pick out the particularly interesting titles cited in this article and from among the 32 titles that *Google Scholar* shows as having cited this one, including this particularly useful looking one:

   Nils Petter Gleditsch, Armed Conflict and the Environment: A Critique of the Literature, *Journal of Peace Research,* Vol. 35, No. 3, Special Issue on Environmental Conflict (May, 1998), pp. 381–400;

7. Collect, and then read, the literature you have compiled on that specific aspect or dimension of the research area, and think of ways to extend or refine it.

you are searching for but in a different context? How you do this and what options are available are not the same with every database, so you will need to use the on-screen links and help system to familiarize yourself with how each of them works.

Set limitations on your search as, for instance, by publication date (how far back you want to search), range (the types of publication or documentation you wish to include), geographical or time scope, or country of publication. Be sure to keep a complete and accurate record of your searches. A detailed record of everything useful you find will enable you to provide an accurate bibliography at the end of your project.

As part of a strategy to narrow your search for a question, you might do an online search of fellowship and grant programmes that provide support for research in our field. There are various agencies and funding bodies that offer awards and grants to support research on topics related to the subject matter of our field. And often they issue calls for applications or proposals. These calls for proposals typically focus on a broad topic and include a breakdown of that topic into a set of narrower issues or questions relating to it. Box 5.5 shows a sample of a call for proposals in the field of politics. Government agencies also publish requests for proposals. These are likely to describe some problem that the agency would like researchers to address, and the approach they would like you to take in investigating it. We would not encourage you to actually respond to these calls while working towards a degree. But they might serve to spark your interest in a question and start you on the path that leads you to a research question.

We have discussed where and how to find a question. This is the best way we can think of to get you started. However, as you develop experience and confidence as a researcher, you will doubtless be able to find questions through other, and perhaps more creative, ways.

In any case, once you have a question, it is likely that there will still be some distance to travel before you have formulated it so that it satisfies the three criteria which define a research question (one that has significance for a topic or issue relating to the subject matter of our field, that is researchable, and that has not yet been answered satisfactorily). We take up the issue of how to formulate a research question, below.

How to formulate a research(able) question

Let's begin our consideration of how to formulate a research question by recalling the three requirements of a research question. For the moment, we will focus on the first two requirements; we will be discussing the third requirement a bit further along.

At the beginning of the research process, the requirement that a question be both (1) *significant* (for real-world problems or for academic debates or theories); and (2) *researchable* (answerable through research) can sometimes be a source of frustration. This is because a researcher often will start with an interest *either* in a general subject matter or broad question, *or* in a quite specific case or problem. Those who begin with an interest in a general subject matter sometimes have difficulty coming up with a more specific case or domain in which to investigate it; that is, they have difficulty coming up with a narrower, researchable question. Conversely, those who begin with a narrower issue or problem sometimes have difficulty relating it to a broader, more general area of interest. So we often have in hand a

---

BOX 5.5 Calls for Proposals as a Source for Research Questions

Global uncertainties: security for all in a changing world programme, under the auspices of Research Councils UK

ESRC/AHRC Fellowships on Ideas and Beliefs

The ESRC and AHRC invite full applications from researchers from across the social sciences, arts, and humanities for a number of high-profile research fellowships, as part of the RCUK Global Uncertainties: Security for All in a Changing World programme.

The cross-Council programme focuses on the nature and interactions of five global issues: conflict, crime, environmental degradation, poverty and terrorism, and their implications for various concepts and contexts of security and insecurity. Within this framework, this fellowship call focuses specifically on how ideas and beliefs of individuals, communities, and nation states relate to these five global phenomena. Fellowship applications under this call must address one or more of the following key research areas:

a. How do individuals and communities develop their ideas and beliefs about security and insecurity?

b. Why do some ideas and beliefs lead to conflict, violence, or criminal activity? What lessons can we learn from a) above that provide the basis for countering those ideas and beliefs that reinforce conflict, violence, and crime?

c. How do issues around the cycle of knowledge production and use interact with the creation, management, and resolution of insecurities?

d. How are risks and threats communicated, constructed, represented, and received by key actors and communities, using different media and cultural forms for different audiences, including the use of language, images, and symbolism?

e. Is there an acceptable balance between national security needs and the protection of civil liberties and human rights? If so, can one be secured? And how do we balance local needs against global responsibilities within a security context?

f. How should institutions with responsibility for different aspects of a broad security agenda, including security forces themselves, evolve to meet new risks and threats?

Proposals addressing the interaction between these questions/areas and applications which challenge existing policy or practice assumptions and/or consider alternative framing or approaches to addressing these priority research areas will be welcomed. The full specification document can be found below.

Source: http://people.bath.ac.uk/esscjs/Research_Office/GU_Fellowships_Spec.pdf

---

significant question that we don't know how to make researchable, or a researchable question whose significance for the field of politics we have not yet been able to determine or define.

To aid the process of developing a statement of the question that meets both these requirements, we introduce a tool, the 'research vase'. By providing a visualization of the research process, the 'research vase' may help you to locate where your question falls in the typical conundrum we have described, and to identify what you need to do in order to make it satisfy both requirements of a research question.

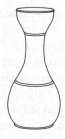
-- Top of vase: the broad question or topic
   relating to the subject matter of our field

-- Middle of the vase: the 'researchable' question
   that will enable you to investigate the question

-- Bottom of the vase: how the conclusions of your research
   help to illuminate the broad question at the top of the vase

Figure 5.2 The research vase

The research vase

Most research projects share the same general structure. We can think of this structure as following the shape of the vase that is pictured in Figure 5.2.

The vase in this picture has a broad top and base, and a narrow middle. Figure 5.2 shows how different aspects of the research process can be seen as corresponding to different parts of the vase. The top of the vase represents a large question that engages a broad theoretical perspective or area of inquiry relating to the subject matter of our field. Its narrower middle represents a narrower, more specific question which can be addressed through conducting research: a question which is, in other words, 'researchable'. After passing through this narrow middle, the vase broadens out again. This part of the vase represents the final stage of research: the stage in which the researcher reflects on the conclusions of the research for both researchers and practitioners (completed at the point of the process represented by the 'middle of the vase') and what these conclusions tell us about the broader question or larger area of inquiry which is represented by the top of the research vase.

The vase, then, enables us to visualize the first two requirements for a research question and how they are related to each other. The *top of the vase* represents the broader question or terrain within which you locate your research, and for which it is significant. It should be pointed out that when you 'fill in' this part of the research vase you not only satisfy the first requirement of a research question, you also establish part of the *rationale* for your question.

Look again at the components of the research process shown in Box 5.1. 'The question' includes two elements: a statement of the question which your research will address; and the rationale for pursuing research on it. We establish a rationale or justification for pursuing research on a particular question by showing that it meets the three requirements for a research question. The rationale for a question includes a statement of *the context* for its consideration. Does it engage a current real-world problem or issue? Does it arise from an issue that is the focus of debate in our field? It also provides a *justification of its importance for study*. Why do you think what the question asks is worth knowing? Why does it matter intellectually, theoretically, or empirically? So, the rationale for pursuing research on a question rests, in part, on a statement of its broader significance and how its answer will contribute to collective knowledge about politics and international relations. But a complete statement of the rationale also will include an explanation of why and in what respect the question has not yet been definitively answered.

The middle of the vase represents the narrower question that a researcher formulates in order to be able to address the topic or question which is at the top of the vase and which, as stated or in respect to what it asks, is too broad to answer. This narrower question enables the researcher to engage in direct measurement or observation of something. It indicates the specific observations of reality in a particular temporal and/or spatial setting, or the specific theoretical idea or conceptual system, which will be the focus of research. Finally, the *bottom of the vase* represents the stage in the process of research where the conclusions of the research are used to reflect back on the broad question or topic at the top of the vase.

We previously noted that it is often the case that, at the beginning of the research process, a researcher will have in mind *either* a question that is too broad to be researchable (the top of the vase), *or* a question that is very specific and needs to be related to a broader issue or problem of significance in our field (the middle of the vase). Those with an interest in a general subject matter will need to find an empirical case or domain—a specific aspect of the problem and/or a setting (a specific country or group)—which will enable them to investigate the subject matter and to derive conclusions relevant to the broader question; those who start with an interest in a particular case will need to identify it as a case, instance, or aspect of a more general issue of interest to scholars pursuing research in the field of politics.

Consider this question: 'Is the US winning its "War on Terror"?' This is a good question: it is significant, the subject of much debate, and one to which we do not yet have a definitive answer. But it is also a question that *in this form* is not possible to answer through research, because it is too broad to be studied directly. If you were interested in pursuing research on this question, you would need to express it in a form that is *researchable*. This would require you to find an aspect of the 'War on Terror'—one weapon, or policy—that can be the focus of research, and a setting in which to study it. For instance, you might focus on one initiative being pursued in the 'War on Terror': the securitization of Muslim charities. 'Securitization' means the representation of something (in this case, the representation of Muslim charities by governments) as a potential security problem. In the case of Muslim charities, they have been securitized because their finances may support groups classified by governments as connected to illegitimate violence. With this as a focus, you might ask: 'What has been the impact of the securitization of Muslim charities in Egypt since 9/11?' You might hypothesize that 'the securitization of Muslim charities in Egypt since 9/11 has *increased* tensions within the country'. Now you have developed an empirically testable hypothesis which can contribute to answering the broader question with which you began.

Alternatively, you might have begun the research process with an interest in a narrower question about the impact of new restrictions on Muslim charities in Egypt. Here, you begin with a specific research interest (the middle of the vase), and will need to 'fill in' the 'top of the vase' by considering what more general phenomenon or issue the research question addresses; how your question might be linked to a broader area of concern or inquiry in our field; what your findings might eventually tell us about more general issues. This, then, might lead you to position your research on Muslim charities in Egypt as part of a broader question concerning whether or not the US is winning its 'War on Terror'.

To continue, for a moment, with the issue of relating a specific question to a broader terrain: you can often identify the broader empirical or theoretical terrain or context relevant to your question by translating individual names into 'kind' names. For instance, an interest in the ASEAN security framework can provide insight into the more general phenomenon of 'regional integration'; a specific question about the north–south conflict within Sudan can engage an aspect of the literature on 'civil wars'. A researcher who wants to learn more about the tribal Pashtuns of south-eastern Afghanistan and north-western Pakistan might relate this research to a bigger question about the survival and continuing relevance of tribes as a form of political organization and authority.

But let's look more closely at what is entailed in the process of 'narrowing down' a broader question. Consider the following question: 'Does globalization undermine the basis of the nation state?' The question concerns the relationship between 'globalization' (concept 1) and 'the basis of a nation state' (concept 2). To make this question researchable, each concept will need to be defined specifically enough to allow us to observe or measure whether or to what extent one of them (globalization) is adversely affecting (undermining) the other (the nation state). We can do this by choosing one facet of globalization and one feature of the basis of the nation state that will enable us to explore more concretely the relationship between globalization and the basis of the nation state. We might choose, for instance, to focus on economic integration, which is a key facet of globalization; and on state autonomy, which is a key basis of the nation state. This will enable us to ask a narrower question: 'What impact does economic integration have on state autonomy?' Through further reading, we might discover that researchers measure the integration of a country into the world economy by using an index that combines measures of a country's various transnational links and its involvement in international organizations. Further reading will also enable us to better understand the core functions of the nation state; and we might decide that a state's ability to manage public finances is a critical indicator of the autonomy of a state, inasmuch as a state cannot enjoy autonomy if it must depend on external sources to fund its ongoing operations. We continue to explore existing research and find that researchers have measured the degree of a state's autonomy and whether it is increasing or decreasing by using data on the ratio of domestic to foreign sources of revenue in a state's budget at a given time, and changes in this ratio over time. Our question, then, might be: 'Do high levels of integration into the world economy (as measured by our index) decrease a state's ability to manage its public finances?' So here we have it: a research question which will enable us to investigate a narrower, more specific terrain relating to the broader question about globalization and the bases of the nation state.

There are two other issues involved in making a question researchable. The first has to do with whether you are asking the *kind of question* you want to ask. The second issue has to do with the inclusion of *errors of reasoning* in the statement of a question. We discuss both of these issues, below.

Types of questions: getting clear about what you want to know

Once you think you have a question, and before proceeding any further with the research process, it is worth giving some thought to what your question is asking and what you will need to do in order to answer it. Is your question, as stated, asking for something different from what it is that you really want to know and do?

In order to get clear about what you are asking and want to know, it is useful to consider various types of questions that researchers ask. Not all types of research question will be appropriate to the requirements of your dissertation or other type of project as defined by your department. For instance, some departments may require that a dissertation be based on an explanatory question. However, though the requirements of your department may limit your choice among different types of research questions, understanding something about all types of questions will help you to formulate your question and to be clear about what you will need to do in order to answer it. Consider the types of questions listed in Box 5.6. Each type of question is asking for a particular type of information. For instance, a descriptive question is one that asks for information about the characteristics or behaviour of something. This is perhaps stating the obvious. But by making this explicit you will be able to consider whether the question you have formulated is asking about the thing that you really are interested in knowing. Also, by making explicit what kind of question you are asking and what that question is asking for, you can begin to think about what you will be required to do in order to answer it. Let's consider each of the types of questions shown in Box 5.6.

Descriptive questions

Descriptive questions are concerned with the characteristics of what has happened, what is going on, or what exists; and with the characteristics of how something behaves. Descriptive questions often ask 'Who, What, Where, and When'. These can be research questions if they are significant and researchable, and if it can be shown either that people disagree about their

---

BOX 5.6 Types of Questions, What You Want To Know, and What You Will Do

Type of question:	What you want to know:	What you will do:
Descriptive	The characteristics of something or of how it works or behaves	Describe the characteristics of something; model how it works or behaves
Explanatory	The causes of something that has occurred or is happening	Explain what factors or conditions are causally connected to a known outcome
Predictive	The future outcome of current conditions or trends	Predict what outcome will occur as a result of a set of known factors or conditions
Prescriptive	The things that can be done to bring about some outcome	Prescribe what should be done to prevent something from happening or to bring something about
Normative	What is best, just, right, or preferable and what, therefore, ought to be done (or not done) to bring it about (or prevent it)	Adjudicate among different understandings of how something should be, or what should or ought to be done, by considering the arguments of others, and submitting rational reasons for one's own

answer or are, in some way, wrong about the answer on which most of them agree. For example, *who* killed Pakistan's Prime Minister, Benazir Bhutto? *What* national security doctrine guided US foreign policy under George W. Bush? *When* did the 'take-off' to industrial development occur in England? *Where* did nationalism, or the nation-state model, first emerge? But descriptive questions come in a variety of forms. The question 'Have the foreign policies of EU member states become Europeanized?' asks whether we can *describe* the foreign policies of EU member states as having become 'Europeanized'. 'Has class diminished in importance as a basis for voting?' is a question which asks whether, in describing the bases of voting preference, class is less important than it previously was. The question, 'What has been the impact of structural adjustment programmes on third world countries?' is asking for a description of the impact of these programmes. When we ask 'What proportion of people hold various opinions?' we are asking a descriptive question for which public opinion polls provide an answer. Some descriptive questions can be answered rather easily, as they have a clear factual answer that is readily accessible and uncontested. Others, however, are not easily resolved, may be the subject of much contestation, and can provide much scope for theoretical and empirical investigation.

Explanatory questions

Explanatory questions generally ask about *what is causing or has caused* an outcome, or *why* something exists or has happened: 'What accounts for the resurgence of "Hindu nationalism" in India in recent years?' 'Why are British citizens generally less favourably disposed towards the EU than their counterparts in other member countries?' 'Why was there a reversal of democratization in Georgia?' These questions are answered through identifying the outcome to be explained (dependent variable) and the factor or factors thought to be connected with it (independent variables); and then showing what the nature of the connection or relation between them is.

Explanatory and descriptive questions are both concerned with connections or relations between two or more variables. But while a descriptive question might ask what relationship exists between gender and voting preference, or of educational achievement and political participation, an explanatory question will be concerned with why that relationship exists. So, for instance, a descriptive question might ask what proportion of males and females say they would vote for a Democratic or a Republican candidate in the next US presidential election, while an explanatory question might ask why more women say they will vote for a Democratic candidate in the next US presidential election.

But there is not always a firm distinction between questions which ask for descriptions and those which ask for explanations. A question that asks about the causes of 'ethnic conflicts' is already suggesting something about their causes ('ethnicity'); and an elucidation of these causes will, in turn, confirm our description of them as 'ethnic' conflicts. The answer to the question of whether people with a college education are more apt to vote than those with only a grade school education, offers both a description of those who vote, and a possible explanation for voting (White and Clark 1983: 23).

It appears to many people that explanatory and descriptive questions are more valued by, respectively, positivist and interpretivist researchers. This is because positivists tend to stress the pursuit of law-like explanations as the goal of social science research, while interpretivists tend to emphasize the role of interpretation (see Chapter 2). But both are concerned with description as well as with explanation. Where they differ is in their conception of what constitutes explanation. The difference, as Iain Hampsher-Monk and Andrew Hindmoor point out, is that positivist explanations are 'external' in the sense that they tend to work via correlations or deductions on the basis of *ascribed* reasons, and so need not concern themselves with actors' understandings of the world; while interpretive explanations are 'internal' in that they are concerned with the world of meanings inhabited by the actor (Hampsher-Monk and Hindmoor 2009: 48).

Predictive questions

Predictive questions are concerned with the likely effect or outcome of something or the trajectory of existing trends. In our field, researchers tend to be concerned with questions about the outcome of government policies: 'What will be the effect of an intervention to bring about regime change in Zimbabwe?' 'What will be the impact of the "Arab Spring" on possiblities for democracy in the Middle East?' 'What will be the consequence of nationalizing insolvent firms?' Researchers are also concerned about the outcome of trends: 'What impact will increasing urbanization have on Egypt's unemployment rate?' 'Will coalition casualties in Afghanistan increase over the next year?' 'Will China and Japan develop more cooperative relations in the next twenty years?' 'Will ethnic conflict increase in European cities in the next twenty years?'

Predictive studies use explanations to speculate about what will likely occur or be the case in the future. So, for instance, if we analyse evidence and find that event A causes or explains event B (an *explanation*), we then can *predict* that if A continues to increase, we will likely have a greater amount of B in the future (White and Clark 1983: 23). Predictive questions require you to develop an argument that if certain conditions or circumstances prevail, a certain outcome is likely to occur or come into being.

Prescriptive questions

These are questions that ask about what we should do, or about what is right or wrong, or good or bad. A prescriptive question asks: 'How can we bring about X (or prevent Y and Z)?' Researchers in our field are concerned with prescribing what governments should undertake to do in order to bring about or to prevent something. What should the UN do to bring about an end to the war in Darfur? What steps should the international community take to reduce human trafficking? What can the British government do to stabilize its housing sector? While prescriptive and normative questions are often closely connected, they are not necessarily the same. Prescriptive questions are more concerned with ascertaining facts needed to solve political problems. The question, 'Is democracy the best form of government?', is a normative question; but questions about what governments can do to expand political participation, or to ensure sound electoral processes, or to facilitate peaceful transfers of power, are prescriptive questions.

Normative questions

While prescriptive questions are concerned with identifying the best means to given ends, normative questions are concerned with determining what the ends themselves should or ought to be. A normative question asks: 'What is best, just, right or preferable and what, therefore, ought to be done (or not done) to bring it about (or prevent it)?' When, if ever, is war and political violence justified? What makes a government or state legitimate? Are there transcendent or universal human rights? Should human rights limit the way states can treat their citizens? On what basis should trade-offs between liberty and security be decided? What constitutes political equality and does it require economic equality? To what extent should liberal democracies tolerate illiberal cultures?

Box 5.7 shows different forms that descriptive, explanatory, predictive, prescriptive, and normative questions take.

BOX 5.7 Types of Questions

Your question	What you will do
What is terrorism?	**Describe** the characteristics of terrorism.
How are terrorists and their actions similar to or different from traditional political or military actors and actions?	**Describe** the characteristics of terrorism and those of other forms of violence, and compare them.
What are the consequences of terrorism?	**Describe** what the consequences of terrorism have been.
How might we expect various audiences and people to react to terrorism?	**Describe** how different types of individuals/groups react to terrorism.
What type of individual becomes a terrorist?	**Describe** the types of individuals who become terrorists.
Why do people or groups engage in terrorism?	**Explain** why people engage in terrorism.
What factors act as a stimulus or facilitator to terrorism?	**Explain** the factors that stimulate or facilitate terrorism.
How do the media affect our view of terrorism?	**Explain** how media content affects views of terrorism.
Where are future terrorist attacks likely to occur?	**Predict** that terrorist attacks will occur as a result of a particular set of factors or conditions.
Will terrorist attacks increase over the next decade?	**Predict** the future trajectory of terrorist attacks as a result of a particular set of factors or conditions.
How can the ideas or actions of terrorists be influenced?	**Prescribe** what can be done to influence the ideas or actions of terrorists.
What is the most effective way that governments can respond to terrorism?	**Prescribe** policies that will enable governments to respond most effectively to terrorism.
How can governments control terrorism while maintaining democratic freedoms?	**Prescribe** policies that will enable governments both to control terrorism and preserve democratic freedoms.
When, if ever, are war and political violence justified?	**Make explicit the moral implications** of different points of view concerning when, if ever, war and political violence are justified; and present reasons why your own point of view is to be preferred.

Unanswerable questions: fallacies in framing research questions

We have established that a question must be sufficiently narrow or specific to permit empirical investigation, and that it should be formulated as a type of question that asks what you are really interested in answering.

However, a question that satisfies these conditions may still not be researchable if it contains errors of logic, or 'fallacies' that would generate false answers or conclusions. The most common errors of this sort are when a question is framed so that it

1. 'begs' another question;
2. presents a false dichotomy;
3. asks about a fictional event;
4. is metaphysical;
5. is a tautology.

An example of each of these fallacies should suffice to make clear the sort of error it entails and question that results.

Consider this question: 'Why was American slavery the most awful that was ever known'? As the historian David Hackett Fischer points out, this is an explanatory question (a 'why' question) that begs a second (descriptive) question: the question of whether American slavery was 'the most awful that was ever known' (Fischer 1970: 8). This second question 'goes begging' in the sense that it is not explicitly asked and answered, but is simply assumed. In other words, the question is formulated in a way that really poses two questions; but it is explicitly asking—and intending to answer—only one of them.

A question that is constructed so as to present a false dichotomy is one that forces us to choose between two answers that are neither mutually exclusive nor collectively exhaustive. Fischer describes what happens when questions such as these appear on an undergraduate essay examination: confronted with a question of this sort, the 'disgusted undergraduate' is forced to make a choice between 'unappetizing alternatives, or perhaps to combine them in some ingenious paradoxical contrivance of his own invention' (Fischer 1970: 10). Some of Fischer's examples will likely remind you of countless others: 'Napoleon: Enlightened Statesman or Proto-Fascist?'; 'Jacksonian Democracy: Myth or Reality?'; 'Plato: Totalitarian or Democrat?'

Then there is the fallacy of 'fictional questions'. Consider this example: 'Would US President Franklin Delano Roosevelt have decided to drop atomic bombs on Japan had he still been in office in August 1945?' The problem with this question is that there are no secure grounds on which to base an answer to it. We might be able to contrast the views of Roosevelt with those of his Vice President, Harry Truman, who succeeded him and whose decision it was to use these weapons. But how can we know that, if he had still been president, Roosevelt would not have done precisely what Harry Truman did? Empirical research cannot answer this question.

We encounter the same problems with the fallacy of metaphysical questions: these are questions that attempt to 'resolve a non-empirical question by empirical means' (Fischer 1970:12). Consider this question: 'Was World War I inevitable?' How can you answer a question about inevitability through empirical research? Using words like 'inevitable', 'unavoidable', and 'inescapable' commits you to an argument that goes beyond what your research can establish.

Finally, there is the problem of tautological questions. These come in a variety of forms. The most common consists of the statement that 'things that are X are in fact X'; or 'X is X'. Consider this question: 'Was George W. Bush unsuccessful because he was moving against the tide of history?' We would not know whether he was 'moving against the tide of history' except for the fact that he was unsuccessful. So this question asks if he was unsuccessful because he was unsuccessful. Here's another example: 'Did the assertion of separate national movements cause the centrifugal tendencies (i.e. the dispersal of political power away from the central government) that led to the dissolution of Yugoslavia?' This asks if centrifugal tendencies were the cause of centrifugal tendencies. If you ask, 'Do mainstream Americans believe that racism is unacceptable?', and further discussion reveals that 'finding racism unacceptable' is what you mean by 'mainstream', then what you are asking is whether mainstream Americans are mainstream.

'Researchability': a final consideration

To be researchable, your question must be within your ability to answer it. You need to consider the main practical issues involved in answering your question, including the availability and accessibility of data, and additional resources and training you might need. Will you be able to *access* people, statistics, or documents from which to collect the data you need to address the question fully? Can this data be accessed within the limited *time* and *resources* you have available to you? How long would you need to complete the research necessary to answer the question? What ethical constraints might be at issue? The answers to these questions (which we will consider further in Chapter 6) may lead you to redefine your research questions.

So far, we have considered (1) the need to formulate a question so that it relates to an issue or area of inquiry that is significant for the field of politics; and (2) the various considerations that ensure that a question is researchable. These considerations relate to two of the three requirements for a research question. In the next section, we address the third requirement of a research question: that the question does not yet have a definitive answer. The next section explains how the 'Literature Review' enables you to establish this.

The literature review

The commonly used term, 'literature review', sounds like something mundane and mechanical: an obligatory chore contrived to ensure that you have done some reading on your topic. This is unfortunate; and it is also misleading. A review of the existing literature is not only a crucial part of the research process, it is where you demonstrate your ability to engage *analytically* with politics, where we hear *your* voice and find out how you think and reason.

A literature review has a dual function. First, it explains why, and to what extent, a definitive answer to your question does not yet exist; so it provides the means by which you demonstrate that your question meets the third requirement for a research question. Second, and in the process of performing the first function, it prepares the ground for the elaboration of your own argument. Box 5.8 shows how asking and answering a few key questions about the literature advances each of these functions.

BOX 5.8 The Dual Function of a Literature Review

1. **Establish that a question has not yet been definitively answered, or that no one else has done what you are proposing to do, by asking:**

   A. Who else has asked and answered your question? What (range of) answers have been given to this question in the existing literature?

   B. What is missing, irrelevant, defective, unwarranted, or ambiguous in the existing literature on your topic?

2. **Set the stage for your own argument, by asking:**

   C. What are the positive elements in the current literature? What in the literature can you highlight, underline, expand, extend, improve, build upon, continue?

   D. What needs to be done? What requires further investigation or rethinking? What would provide a better understanding of the matter?

The literature review demonstrates that the subject has not been adequately dealt with in the existing literature; and it explains how you intend to address this state of affairs, either by doing something that has not already been done and that promises to yield further insight into the question; or by doing what *has* already been done—but better. This may require you to show that, though the question might already be the subject of mountains of articles and books, the answers that have been offered to it are in some way incomplete or flawed. What you will need to do is to identify other researchers who have asked and answered your question, and then say what in their answers is wrong, incomplete, or weak. In addition to identifying the weaknesses, you will also highlight the valuable elements in their answers. It is on the basis of both these positive and less positive elements that you build your case for what you yourself propose to do to contribute to the literature.

This is the second function of a literature review: to set the stage for a statement of how your research is going to address the weaknesses of existing studies, and/or underline, expand, extend, improve, or build upon their strengths. Students sometimes think there is no literature related to their topic. There may not be books and articles that address *exactly* the same topic, but there will always be related research that will provide a conceptual and theoretical context for your research. Ask yourself: 'What is my question a case of? Is there a broader literature on this type of phenomena?'

You should develop your literature review over three stages. There is always a first stage in which you read, follow leads to other promising books and articles, and then read some more. You will be reading *analytically*—that is, asking a lot of questions about what you are reading, and also trying to get a sense of different debates, theories, perspectives, and arguments. Eventually you will need to bring some kind of organization to the literature, by summarizing how the literature breaks down into different theoretical perspectives, entry points, or arguments. This is the second stage of developing a literature review. Finally, and as a result of the previous two stages, your own argument will begin to come into focus. You should now have answers to the questions listed under 'Literature' in Box 5.1 (Outline of Research Components). At this point you are ready to write the literature review: a discussion of the best research and writing on your question organized in a way that sets the stage, and helps to make the case, for your own argument.

Let's look more closely at each of the three stages in the development of a literature review.

Stage 1: Reading the literature

Recall our previous discussion about approaching the literature *analytically*. As you evaluate the major arguments or explanations in the existing literature on your question, ask yourself questions about their weaknesses. You should query the questions, answers, methods, and conclusions of each contribution to the literature you read. Scrutinize their ideas, definitions, concepts, information, or logic. Ask yourself what is missing, irrelevant, defective, unwarranted, or ambiguous. There are numerous questions you can ask about each aspect of the material you read. Consider, for instance, the questions, below.

1. What is *the* author's *central question* or subject of inquiry? How does the way the question is asked make it different from that which others have asked? How does it illuminate, or obscure, crucial dimensions of the phenomenon investigated? What is the author's *purpose* (to describe, explain, predict, prescribe)?

2. What is *the author's answer or argument*? What factor or factors is the author's analysis highlighting? Does the author define these factors clearly? (What is meant by 'technology', 'rapid change', 'instability'?)

2a. How does the author's argument or explanation differ from others? (Note that the title of the book or article is usually designed to communicate what differentiates this particular treatment of the subject matter from other books and articles; and the chapter titles and section headings provide clues to how the overall argument is developed.)

2b. If the purpose of the inquiry is to explain something, what are the author's major hypotheses? Are they developed *deductively* from a more basic theory? Are they developed *inductively*? What is the strength, nature, and generality of the relationship between the independent and dependent variables?

2c. What assumptions underlie the account of events that the author presents? Are the assumptions sound? Does the argument assume things that need to be demonstrated?

2d. Does the basic argument make sense? Is the chain of reasoning sound? If the author moves from one claim to another that supposedly follows from the first, does the author demonstrate a clear relationship between the two claims? Are there any leaps of logic, inconsistencies, circular arguments, or contradictions within and among the parts of the argument or the subsidiary arguments?

3. What *methods* are used to demonstrate the argument? Are there any shortcomings or flaws with respect to the methods used? Is the time frame too short, or artificial; or the spatial domain too limited or artificial, to generate sound conclusions? Are key definitions ambiguous, or too narrow or broad?

4. What *evidence* is presented in support of the claims that are made? Is the evidence well selected, or is it arbitrary? Does the author use many different kinds of examples, or ones that are chosen simply because they support a particular contention or case? Does the author address examples of what might be considered a 'hard case' for the argument—counter- examples that might undermine the central claims? Can you think of an anomaly—a case that

doesn't fit with or isn't explained by the theory? Has the author ignored, suppressed, overlooked, or slighted relevant evidence, alternative data sources or other interpretations of the data?

5. Do the *conclusions* fully draw the implications of the overall argument, all parts of the argument, and subsidiary arguments?

Stage 2: Summarizing the literature

You have read widely, but selectively in your topic area, asked questions of everything in the material you have read, and taken careful notes all along the way. It is time, now, to bring some organization to this literature: to summarize it in a way that identifies the major themes, issues, arguments, positions, or perspectives that constitute it and that highlights their major points of contact and division.

You will not be summarizing all the literature relating to your topic (or related more broadly to the focus of the research); but only the literature that directly addresses the specific question you are asking. So, for instance, if you were pursuing research on the question we discussed previously concerning globalization and the bases of the nation state, you would not review all the literature on international finance (a vast field of enquiry), but rather the literature that addresses sources of state revenue and the control by national states over capital flows.

It might be appropriate, depending on your question, to summarize the intellectual progression of the field, including major debates; alternatively, your question might require you to focus on sources that address the relevant subject matter within a certain time period. But, however you organize your summary, it should include the main conclusions of the most important and influential arguments and ideas in the existing literature relating to your question. What are the principal positions that experts take with respect to causes, consequences, or solutions? Do existing studies tend to divide between two or three different approaches or perspectives? Are there different schools of thought? If so, who are the major disputants, and what points of difference lie between them? What are the aspects of the topic about which experts appear to agree? What are the principal insights that have emerged from the literature?

These questions enable you to organize and summarize the literature. They will also raise additional questions: What puzzles, problems has the literature left unsolved? Is there an aspect of the field that is missing? Do the arguments and theories in the literature tend to focus on examples or cases drawn from one part of the world? Have they been/can they be applied to other parts of the world? These are the sorts of questions that will move you towards the third and final stage of the development of a literature review.

Stage 3: What still needs to be done? Setting the stage for your own argument

You have read, and you have thought creatively and critically about the arguments in the literature and the findings of previous research relevant to your topic (first stage). You have been able to bring some organization to the literature by breaking it down into the major points of contact and division among the various perspectives and arguments that it contains (stage two). In the process of doing this, you have identified strong and weak elements in the literature; and this has led naturally to a consideration of what might be done to build on those strengths and overcome those weaknesses. Consequently, in the process of analysing the positive and less positive elements in others' arguments, your own argument has begun to come into focus. You are now ready to move to the final stage in the development of a literature review: writing a discussion of the existing literature that presents *a recapitulation of your own process of evaluation and critique* of it and *the process by which your own argument began to take shape*. In sum: your 'literature review' discusses the best literature on your question in a way that shows how a reasoned analysis of its strengths and weaknesses leads naturally to a consideration of what you propose to do as a contribution to resolving the question. It leads, naturally, in other words, to the introduction of your own argument.

Here are some basic considerations and ground rules to guide the writing of your literature review.

1. A literature review should itself develop an 'argument'—a particular perspective on the literature. It should begin with a statement of that argument and use evidence to back it up. The argument of your literature review is just like any other argument: your interpretation of the material you discuss must be backed up with evidence to show that what you are saying is valid. The literature review should contain an introduction, the body of the review containing the discussion of specific sources, and a conclusion.

2. Your discussion should be organized around ideas, themes, theories, or issues that enable you to advance the argument of your literature review, and *not* the sources themselves (you are *not* writing an annotated bibliography—a list of sources with a discussion of each one of them, one at a time).

3. The number of sources you discuss depends on how many you need in order to persuasively demonstrate the argument of your literature review. You must satisfy a critical reader—as for instance one of the authors whose work you are challenging—that your argument is based on considerable thought and study and that you know what you are talking about. Comprehensive knowledge of the literature on a topic is essential to research on that topic; and the depth and breadth of knowledge that your literature review exhibits is what will give you credibility as a researcher.

4. Address the best arguments. Include those with which you agree and those with which you disagree. Don't leave out good arguments in order to make a case that there are no good arguments along the lines of what you yourself may want to develop. Don't downplay or misrepresent the sophistication and implications of the arguments advanced by a strong opponent; and don't go after a weak opponent (a 'strawman'). It may be the case that the only opponents *are* weak. Be sure, however, you haven't overlooked a stronger one.

5. The types of sources that should be included (books, journal articles, websites[1]) will depend on your topic. You are concerned with the state of the best current literature and previous research on this question. Focus on the articles and books that are most influential and widely cited. Concentrate your efforts on relevant articles published in the most credible research journals dealing with the general area of inquiry related to your question. Ideally,

these should be research journals that use a blind-review system. In a blind review, authors submit potential articles to a journal editor who solicits several reviewers who agree to give a critical review of the paper. The paper is sent to these reviewers with no identification of the author so that there will be no personal bias (either for or against the author). Based on the reviewers' recommendations, the editor can accept the article, reject it, or recommend that the author revise and resubmit it. Articles in journals with blind-review processes can be expected to have a fairly high level of credibility.

6. Select only the most important points in each source that relate directly to the argument of your literature review.

7. A good literature review is one in which the material is thoroughly 'processed': organized according to an overall argument and around key issues or themes, and rendered in the writer's own voice. While the literature review presents others' ideas, your voice and your own perspective should predominate. Use quotes sparingly and maintain your own voice by starting and ending the discussion of different issues, themes, or individual sources with your own ideas and words, using the sources to support what you are saying. Find models: read the literature reviews in books and articles written about your area of interest to get a sense of what style and organization is effective.

 ## Conclusions

This chapter has been devoted to the first step in the research process: finding and formulating a research question. We have discussed the following:

- three requirements of a research question. We have said that for a question to be a *research question* you will need to:
  (1) articulate a rationale for pursuing research on the question in terms of its significance for a broad issue or area of interest within our field;
  (2) formulate the question so that it is researchable—so that it can be answered through research; and
  (3) show that the question has not been definitively answered;

- how to go about meeting these requirements. We introduced a visual tool—the 'research vase'—which can help you to conceptualize the first two requirements of a research question. To meet the third requirement of a research question you must show how others who have asked this question failed in some way to provide a definitive answer to it. The literature review performs this function. It identifies who else has asked and answered your question, and what (range of) answers are found in the existing literature relating to it. It highlights the positive elements in the current literature, and makes an argument about what need to be done in order to provide a better answer to the question than currently exists;

- different types of questions and what each type commits you to doing;

- the logical fallacies that sometimes find their way into the statement of a question and that lead to false conclusions.

Once you have formulated a research question, you have completed step one of the research process. You will then be ready to move on to step two: developing an answer to your question. This is the focus of the next chapter (Chapter 6).

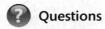

Questions

- What makes a question 'researchable'?
- How do you formulate a question so as to maximize its generality?
- How might errors of logic in the formulation of a question generate false answers or conclusions?
- What is the difference between a survey or summary of the literature and a 'literature review'?
- How are the requirements of a research question related to the rationale or justification for pursuing research on a question?

Guide to Further Reading

Browne, M. N. and S. M. Keeley (1994), *Asking the Right Questions: A Guide to Critical Thinking*, **4th edition (New York: Prentice Hall).**
The authors provide a wide range of questions that can be used to interrogate the existing literature on a topic.

Buttolph Johnson, Janet, H. T. Reynolds, and Jason D. Mycoff (2008), *Political Science Research Methods* **(Washington, DC: CQ Press), chapter 3.**
This chapter discusses the steps involved in specifying a research question and developing a hypothesis.

Geddes, Barbara (2003), 'Big Questions, Little Answers, How the Questions You Choose Affect the Answers You Get', in *Paradigms and Sand Castles* **(Ann Arbor, MI: Michigan University Press), chapter 2.**
This chapter makes the case for caution in using the literature in our field as a source of research questions, and argues that 'looking for gaps' in the literature may not be a good strategy for finding research questions.

Hedrick, Terry E., Leonard Bickman and Debra J. Rog (1993), 'Defining the Focus of the Research', in *Applied Research Design: A Practical Guide* **(London: Sage Publications), chapter 2.**
This chapter provides practical advice about getting clear about the problem or issue that interests you and identifying the research questions that can address it.

Hoover, Kenneth and Todd Donovan (2004), *The Elements of Social Scientific Thinking*, **8th edition (Belmont, CA: Thomson-Wadsworth), chapter 3.**
The authors present strategies for narrowing the focus of a research question, and discuss hypotheses, operationalizing concepts, and how to relate research questions to broader areas of concern.

Kahane, Howard and Nancy Cavender (2005), *Logic and Contemporary Rhetoric: The Use of Reason in Everyday Life*, **10th edition (New York: Wadsworth Publishing), chapters 1 and 2.**
These chapters discuss in detail common errors of reasoning or fallacies that prevent clear thinking and the formulation of good research questions.

King, G., R. Keohane, and S. Verba (1994), *Designing Social Inquiry* **(Princeton, NJ: Princeton University Press), chapter 1.**
The authors discuss the value of formulating a research question so that it both addresses a real-world issue and contributes to a scholarly literature in a given field. They suggest a variety of ways that the literature can be used as a source of developing a research question.

References

Dunleavy, P. (2003), *Authoring a PhD: How to Plan, Draft, Write and Finish a Doctoral Thesis or Dissertation* (Basingstoke: Palgrave Macmillan).

Fischer, D. H. (1970), *Historian's Fallacies: Towards a Logic of Historical Thought* (New York: Harper).

Geddes, B. (2003), *Paradigms and Sand Castles* (Ann Arbor, MI: Michigan University Press).

Hampsher-Monk, I. and A. Hindmoor (2009), 'Rational Choice and Interpretive Evidence: Caught between a Rock and a Hard Place?' *Political Studies* 58(1): 47–65.

King, G., R. Keohane, and S. Verba (1994), *Designing Social Inquiry* (Princeton, NJ: Princeton: University Press).

Pollins, B. M. (2007), 'Beyond Logical Positivism: Reframing King, Keohane, and Verba', in R. N. Lebow and Mark Lichbach (eds), *Theory and Evidence in Comparative Politics and International Relations* (New York: Palgrave/ Macmillan), 87–106.

Shively, W. P. (1989), *The Craft of Political Research*, 2nd edition (Englewood Cliffs, NJ: Prentice-Hall, Inc.).

White, L. G. and R. P. Clark (1983), *Political Analysis: Technique and Practice* (Monterey, CA: Brooks/ Cole Publishing Co.).

 ## Endnote

1. The internet is a fast and easy way to access information. It is a source of good information, but it is also a source of half-truths and complete falsehoods. Consequently, you will have to figure out what is a legitimate source and what is not. In general, authoritative sources are ones that are known to verify their facts and information to a reasonable extent before publication. Reputable academic journals, for example, normally only publish articles that have been at least twice blind-reviewed by experts in the field who agree that the information is essentially correct and that the material is usefully contributing to a body of knowledge. Major news sources, which are liable under libel legislation and have an interest in being trusted by their readership, also attempt to meet a high standard of journalism.

    There are, however, millions of publications and websites which are geared towards presenting opinions and rumours rather than research and certifiable facts. These include blogs, 'quasi' news, and gossip sites. Essentially, the key comes down to verifiable information. Can the source verify the facts given—or can the author prove their case? In the case of blogs and opinion-based websites or user content-generated sites, probably not. Examples of academic or authoritative sources online include articles from major sources (BBC, CNN, AFP), government websites, and reputable NGOs (e.g. International Committee of the Red Cross, Amnesty International, National Union of Journalists). *Information sources such as Wikipedia, About.com, or Infoplease.com are not* academic sources. Wikipedia and other sites like it do not provide sufficient monitoring of what information goes up, and frequently the information is wrong and misleading.

6

Answering Research Questions: Requirements, Components, and Construction

 Chapter Summary

The previous chapter was devoted to a discussion of how to find and formulate a research question. This chapter, along with Chapter 7, focuses on how to develop an answer to it. We begin our discussion, in this chapter, by addressing the following issues:

- What are the requirements and components of an answer to a research question?
- What is a 'theory' and what is its role in social science research?
- What is a 'theoretical framework'?
- What is a hypothesis?
- What are the components of a hypothesis?
- What types of hypotheses are there and how do they guide different kinds of research?
- Why do you need, and how do you formulate, conceptual and operational definitions of your key terms?
- How do you go about answering normative questions?

Introduction

We have discussed *Step 1* of the research process: the formulation of a well-crafted research question (Chapter 5). We turn, now, to *Step 2*: how to develop a hypothesis or argument that answers it. We discuss the basic components of a hypothesis or argument that answers a research question, what requirements it must meet, and where to find and how to formulate one.

What does answering a research question involve? The various considerations and tasks involved can best be understood in relation to three basic requirements. The first requirement is that the answer be appropriate to the type of question that is being asked. *Different types of questions demand different types of answers* (see discussion in Chapter 5 and, also, Box 5.7). The second requirement of an answer to a research question is that it makes a contribution to knowledge. Social science research is expected to address a question whose answer will contribute to collective knowledge in a particular field of study; so, as you develop an answer to your research question, you must ask yourself: Why should we care about this answer or argument? How does it contribute to the development of knowledge about politics? In other words, your answer must matter.

You contribute to the development of knowledge in our field by relating your question and answer to existing theory. The reason for this is that in order to achieve progress in a field of study, research must be cumulative; and theory facilitates cumulative research. It links one study with another, and helps to ensure that the work of researchers enters into dialogue with and builds on the work of others. As we discussed in Chapter 5, researchers develop both a question about a topic, and an answer to it, through a critical analysis of existing theory and research relevant to that topic. All research questions and answers are informed by a set of expectations derived from previous research and theories. Recall that the function of your 'literature review' is to articulate the contribution you intend to make by indicating what gap or need in the existing literature on the topic your answer or argument will fill. What contribution will the research you intend to pursue make to our knowledge of something? How, specifically, does it contribute empirically, conceptually, or theoretically to our knowledge of that topic? *Different types of research provide different contributions to knowledge.*

In order to contribute to knowledge in a field of study, an answer to a research question must meet a third requirement: it must be clearly and fully *specified*. It must be specific with regard to (1) the factors or elements you think must be taken into consideration in order to answer your question; and (2) how you think these factors or elements are related to each other. Together, these factors and their relations constitute a '*hypothesis*': a reasoned, clearly specified hunch or expectation with which you begin your research and which helps to guide and focus your research. An answer or argument in response to a research question consists of a hypothesis and an investigation of it. Developing a hypothesis encourages you to be very precise about how your answer relates to those that others have offered to your question.

The term 'hypothesis' is often treated as applicable only to quantitative research and to a specific prediction about the nature and direction of the relationship between two 'variables' (we will be discussing this term presently). We use the term 'hypothesis' in a far more expansive way. What we mean by 'hypothesis' is 'a hunch, assumption, suspicion, assertion, or idea about a phenomenon, relationship, or situation', with which research begins and which becomes the basis of inquiry (Kumar 2005: 74). Hypotheses can either be tested with evidence (confirmatory research), or operate as a guide to a process of discovery (exploratory research). Confirmatory research begins with a hypothesis and uses observations to test it. We begin with a statement, on the basis of a theory, of what we would expect to find, and then see whether what we expect is fulfilled. Exploratory research begins with a question and perhaps a basic proposition, probes its plausibility against various types of data, and eventually generates a hypothesis as a conclusion rather than as a preliminary to conducting the research itself (Schmitter 2008). In this type of research, we might develop an answer through (1) a preliminary hunch; (2) an investigation; and then (3) a more concrete hypothesis. Whether you are addressing a descriptive, explanatory, predictive, prescriptive, or normative question, thinking in terms of formulating a hypothesis can help you to clarify your argument and the kinds of evidence that will provide a meaningful demonstration of your answer.

We see a hypothesis as a basic infrastructural element whose function, in all research, is to help to make explicit the argument that is being developed. For all types of research, we think it is useful to formulate a 'working hypothesis'—an operational hunch about what you expect to find. Initially, what argument motivates the research? What findings might be expected? By articulating in advance the contours and logic of the investigation, a hypothesis helps to guide research. As we shall see, *different types of research are guided by different types of hypotheses.*

We pointed out in Chapter 2 that, irrespective of whether researchers see themselves as positivists or interpretivists, practical investigation of research questions often leads them to undertake similar methodological tasks and research practices. As a number of scholars have argued, these common practices are founded in the hypothetico-deductive method. Researchers either 'assess whether the information they have gathered fits with the interpretation they have posited', or they 'consider the fit of competing interpretations with the facts they have gathered'; but, in either case, as Brian Pollins points out, 'they are practicing the hypothetico-deductive method' (2007: 100).

We want to draw a distinction between the *process* of research and its *presentation*. The *process* of research is often circuitous. Most researchers engage in a dialogue between ideas and evidence (Ragin 2000), moving back and forth between theory and evidence —between theorizing something that is the focus of their research, and mucking about in the 'dust of detail' (learning more about the specific facts of the case or question or issue, or the observations of other scholars that we treat as facts). As W. Philips Shively observes, 'one of the better-kept secrets' in our field, is that good researchers usually do not '"frame hypotheses" in any formal sense before they start to work, though they may have some operational hunches about what they expect to find. . . . They play with data, immerse themselves in what other people have written, argue with colleagues, and think' (Shively 1989: 25). As this chapter explains, the research process can be conceptualized as a series of steps. However, in practice, the process of research does not unfold in the sort of linear fashion that these suggest. We re-think our views as a result of learning from the research process itself in ways that can feedback to our previous choices and lead us to revise them.

However, we agree with Shively that starting with 'clear and obvious procedures' that are 'more methodical and easier to apply for the beginning researcher' is a good way to learn how to do research (Shively 1989: 25–6). As students gain more experience, they will doubtless become more creative and develop their own process of work.

Political inquiry encompasses a variety of types and processes and possible starting points. But whatever the *process*, we suggest that the *presentation* of research makes clear the logic behind your reasoning and the assumptions upon which you are relying. All types of research should be arranged carefully, systematically, clearly, and logically. What we read should be a coherent narrative whose story line moves through research question, relevant literature, hypotheses, procedures and methods, findings, conclusions, implications.

The sections that follow will elaborate on all these points, using the three requirements of an answer to a research question we've just discussed. We discuss the components of, and answer to, a research question; approaches to developing hypotheses and the elements that constitute them (variables, and the relationships that can be established among them). We also consider the ways you must specify your argument or answer: the need to use terms that mean what you want them to mean, and that can be understood by others in precisely the way you want them to be understood; the necessity of providing a conceptualization (or *conceptual definition*) of your basic terms or variables, as well as an even more specific

---

BOX 6.1 Outline of Research Components, Revisited

1. **The question**[1]
   A. What do you want to know? What is *the central question/problem/issue/puzzle?*
   B. Why do you think it is worth doing/knowing? What is *the rationale for pursuing research on this question?*

2. **The literature**[1]
   A. Who else has asked and answered your question? What (range of) answers to this question are found in *the existing literature relating to it?*
   B. What are the *positive elements* in the current literature? What in the literature can you highlight, underline, expand, extend, improve, build upon, continue?
   C. What needs to be done? Delineate the crucial aspects of the problem requiring investigation. *What need to be done in order to provide a better answer to the question than currently exists?*

3. **Your answer**[2]
   A. *Theoretical framework.* What are *the theoretical elements and guiding assumptions of the study?*
      1. What factors or variables of the problem must be investigated in order to answer your central question?
      2. What is/are *your hypothesis/es* (how are these factors linked)?
         a. What is the source of your hypothesis/es? What in theory would lead us to expect the relation(s) you assert?
         b. How would you demonstrate the relationships stated by the hypothesis/es?
      3. What is *the spatial/temporal domain of the study?* What is the rationale for defining this domain for the study?
   B. *Data and sources*
      1. What are *the data relevant to demonstrating the relationships you hypothesize?*
      2. What *sources* are there *for these data?*

   [1] Discussed in Chapter 5.
   [2] Discussed in the present chapter and in Chapter 7.

---

definition which identifies empirical referents for them (an *operational definition*). Chapter 7 will continue our discussion of how to answer a research question by focusing on research design and on data and sources. Box 6.1, which reproduces the outline of research components we presented in Chapter 5, indicates the elements that we have already covered, and those that we will be covering in both this and the next chapter.

Answers to research questions: general requirements

An answer to a research question (1) provides the type of answer appropriate to the question you are asking; (2) contributes to the development of knowledge in the field of politics by relating itself to existing theory and research on a topic; and (3) clearly and fully specifies its key elements and how they are related to each other.

What type of answer does your question require?

A research question, as Chapter 5 emphasized, not only initiates the research process, but is crucial to every step along the way. The kind of question you ask determines the type of answer you provide, the research you pursue (confirmatory, exploratory), and the means by which you pursue it. *You must provide the type of answer that your question requires.* If you were asked in an exam to '*Describe what* the key differences are in Chinese and Iranian policies used to address population growth issues', a response designed to *explain why* Iran and China have pursued different population growth policies would be inappropriate. The point, of course, is that the type of answer must be appropriate to the type of question. That means that, since, as we maintain, an answer to a research question entails an investigation of a hypothesis, different types of questions will require different kinds of hypotheses. So, let's review the different types of questions researchers in our field ask and then consider what sort of hypothesis might be formulated to order to answer them.

In Chapter 5 we identified five different types of question that researchers in our field ask: descriptive, explanatory, predictive, prescriptive, and normative questions. (We pointed out in Chapter 5 that not all departments will permit you to use all these types of question as the basis of a research or dissertation project; some departments may require that your dissertation be based on an explanatory question; other departments may allow other types, or all types, of questions.)

There is a tendency to treat hypotheses and hypothesis-testing research as applicable only to explanatory and predictive questions *Explanatory questions* are concerned with what is causing or has caused an outcome, or why something exists or has happened. An *explanatory hypothesis* advances a guess as to the cause of, or reason for, something by identifying what factors or conditions are connected to a known outcome. They state, for instance, that X is caused, or made possible, by Y. *Predictive questions* are concerned with what will occur or be the likely outcome of something. A *predictive hypothesis* generalizes from an understanding of current or past events to predict the future outcome of current conditions or trends. Using evidence on current events, accumulated knowledge of general patterns, and relevant theories and theoretical research, it starts with conditions that are thought to be causal, and predicts the resulting phenomena. A predictive hypothesis claims that factor X will cause event or state Y, that outcome Y will occur as a result of a set of known factors or conditions X, or that in conditions ABC, event or state Y will tend to occur.

While explanatory and predictive questions are types of questions most usually associated with hypothesis-driven research, we maintain that all research questions and answers are informed by a set of expectations (hypotheses) derived from previous research and theories and that, for all types of research—including descriptive, prescriptive, and normative research—it is useful to formulate a 'working hypothesis' or operational hunch about what you expect to find.

Let's consider the sort of hypothesis that might be formulated in response to a descriptive question. *Descriptive questions* are concerned with the characteristics of what has happened, is going on, or exists; or of how something behaves. The function of a hypothesis in descriptive research is to select, based on an assessment of what we think will prove most relevant, just those factors from the world of facts and figures, people and events, that we think are most useful for directing and focusing our research. We cannot simply describe everything relating to a phenomenon. We must always select and organize, out of the universe of possibilities, those aspects we think will prove important to explore and highlight. We can start with a theoretical construct or theoretically informed notion, hunch, or expectation that will serve as a *descriptive hypothesis*; perhaps an ideal type—a set of characteristics that we expect to find in some relationship to each other in a given case. A descriptive hypothesis might state, for instance, that X has A, B, C characteristics and/or behaves in D, E, F ways.

Description often involves an effort to set up definitions and classifications, or to make sense of alternative conceptualizations of a topic. The basis of this type of descriptive analysis might be a hypothesis that something can be *meaningfully described*, or usefully defined, seen, or interpreted, *as something else*; that a given concept is useful for describing or understanding something; that we shall understand this thing better if we see it in this way, or if we interpret it as being divided into these three types. We might call this sort of descriptive hypothesis an *interpretive* hypothesis. When we state, for instance, that all X belong to class Y; or that X can be interpreted as Y, we are hypothesizing that we can make good sense of X if we classify it, or interpret it as representing or 'meaning', Y. Does 'democracy' or 'political participation' in China *mean the same thing* as these terms do in the United States or Peru? Can we interpret (meaningfully describe) older democracies today as facing a 'crisis of political participation'? The 'test' of this sort of hypothesis is showing the usefulness of describing or interpreting X *as* Y.

Hypotheses can also be formulated as a basis for addressing prescriptive and normative questions. *Prescriptive questions* ask *what we should do* to bring about, or prevent, some outcome; what course of action we should follow to achieve a particular objective or goal. A prescriptive question might ask, for instance, 'How can the "brain drain" be reversed in South Africa?' A *prescriptive hypothesis* states that to achieve desired end X, we should do Y. To investigate this kind of hypothesis, the researcher will inventory available options, weigh the pros and cons of each for achieving the desired outcome, and, based on this analysis, advance an argument for a policy, using existing theoretical and empirical research to verify the argument's factual and theoretical assumptions. *Normative questions* deal with questions of what is right and wrong, desirable or undesirable, just or unjust in society. A *normative hypothesis* is an argument or suggestive proposition about *what ought to be* that is advanced for further discussion, analysis, and investigation. A normative hypothesis might state that the best type of X is Y; that the basis for deciding or justifying X ought to be Y, the legitimacy of X ought to be based on Y, or that X is just when conditions A, B, C are present. Investigation of these hypotheses would entail elaborating an argument about why this should be the case and establishing the plausibility and coherence of the argument. The 'test' of a normative hypothesis is the rigour of logic and internal consistency of the argument.

In sum, it is useful to formulate a 'working hypothesis' for all types of research, but the hypotheses that are formulated must be appropriate to the type of question being asked. Box 6.2 shows the different kinds of hypotheses that different types of questions will require.

Some examples of different types of research questions and the hypotheses that might be offered in answer to them are shown in Box 6.3. Note that a hypothesis is stated affirmatively, i.e. not as a question.

Answers that contribute to the development of theory

We have said that an answer to a research question should contribute to the development of knowledge in the field of Politics by relating itself to existing theory and research on a topic. What is a 'theory' and why do we need it (what does it do for us)?

BOX 6.2 Types of Questions and Forms of Hypotheses

Type of Question	▶ Form of Hypothesis
Descriptive	X has A, B, C characteristics and/or behaves in D, E, F ways.
Explanatory	X exists as a result of A, B, and C.
Predictive	If circumstances X and Y prevail, Z is likely to occur or come into being.
Prescriptive	In order to bring about X, do (or don't do) A, B, C.
Normative	X is preferable to Y and Z, therefore A, B, C ought to be done (or not done) to bring about X (or prevent Y and Z).

BOX 6.3 Research Questions and Hypotheses

Type of Question	▶ Research Question	▶ Hypothesis
Descriptive	What is the effect of negative advertising on political participation?	As the number of hours of negative ads watched increases, the probability that an individual will vote decreases.
Explanatory	What are the root causes of the Chiapas conflicts?	Conflict resulted from the deterioration of conditions for the indigenous population due to the drop in coffee prices in 1989, the reform of article 27 of the Constitution of 1992 to facilitate the commercialization of land, and the North American Free Trade Agreement which came into effect in 1994.
Predictive	Will China and Japan develop more cooperative, or more conflictual, relations over the course of the next twenty years?	Economic and security interdependence will increase over the next two decades, leading to an easing of historical tensions and greater cooperation between the two countries.
Prescriptive	What steps should the international community take to reduce human trafficking?	Within complicit or non-cooperative countries, tax treaties should be used to create internal pressure on the governments and on their wealthiest citizens who have the political power to force change.
Normative	Are there transcendent or universal human rights?	All rights and values are defined and limited by cultural perceptions. There is no universal culture, therefore there are no universal human rights.

The world is complex. A theory is an attempt to make sense of the world by indicating that some factors are more important than others and specifying relations among them. A theory is always a skeletal version of reality: it encompasses only a portion of the real world, deals with only a few variables, and makes simplifying assumptions to keep variables and cases manageable. A good theory is parsimonious: it attempts to explain as much as possible with as little as possible (parsimony). It is also generalizable: it can be applied to a variety of contexts or settings.

The nature and function of theory in social research can be brought more clearly into focus by contrasting theory-driven research with an ideal-typical 'non-theoretical' research enterprise. Consider, for example, a study of the causes of World War I. The 'non-theoretical' researcher, unconcerned with either parsimony or generalizability, might choose to focus on any and all factors historians have recorded as present at the time of the outbreak of World War I. Here, for example, are a dozen of the possibly hundreds of factors relevant to explaining the outbreak of the war (note how some of these factors are themselves 'theoretical', i.e. the product of prior theorizing): (1) the international balance of power and the change in the configuration of the international system (a rigidified balance-of-power system, which heightened competition and tension, led to an arms race and a fear of losing allies); (2) British hegemonic decline and Anglo-German rivalry; (3) German nationalism and other attributes of the German state, which gave it a propensity for aggression; (4) Austria's struggle to survive and its effort to eradicate the threat of Serbian nationalism within its empire, and in the Balkans generally; (5) Russian geopolitical imperatives (its quest to gain control of the Dardanelles for access to the Mediterranean and thus to the world's commerce); (6) British fear of German control over the channel ports; (7) France's ambition to reacquire Alsace-Lorraine; (8) Germany's internal class relations, which caused the state to pursue foreign economic policies that soured relations with Britain and Russia; (9) the balance of power of ethnic groups within Austria-Hungary; (10) the impact of the rapid and total mobilization of the Russian army, due to the absence of a plan for partial mobilization; (11) the role and interests of military elements in the German government and their influence on foreign policy; (12) the personality of Kaiser Wilhelm of Germany (the propensity he had for war at that time, or the qualities of mind and personality which allowed him to be manipulated by others into declaring war).

A history of World War I will focus on all of these, plus many, many others from among the universe of factors possibly relevant to understanding why the war occurred. But a theory of the war focuses on just those few factors whose relations to each other can be shown to have been decisive in producing the particular outcome (war). Theory not only minimizes the number of factors to be treated as analytically relevant to an outcome, but, since it requires that we show how the factors are related to one another, it ensures that the selection of factors is non-random. Let's say that, after devoting some thought and study to the causes of World War I, you found your interest increasingly drawn to factors (4) and (12), above—Russian geopolitical ambitions and Kaiser Wilhelm's personality. Could you show that these factors not only helped to produce the war, but were also related to each other in some systematic and logical way? Later in this chapter we will look at a well-known theory of the causes of World War I, discuss the variables on which the theorist chose to focus, the reason he chose them, and his argument about how they were related to each other and to the outbreak of war.

We have endeavoured to define 'theory' by contrasting it with what might be described as 'non-theory'. We can further define the term by relating it to two others that tend to be used interchangeably with it: 'proposition' and 'hypothesis'. Together, the three terms can be seen as representing different stages in the development of an idea. The first stage would be a **proposition**: a hunch or guess that two or more variables are related. When put forward for investigation—stated in a way that enables us to determine whether it is right or wrong—a proposition becomes a hypothesis. So an idea may start as a proposition, a statement that identifies key factors that are thought to be related in some way; it might then be developed so that the factors and their relations to each other are more precisely defined. This more specific statement is what we call a 'hypothesis'. Though a hypothesis is stated in a way that enables us to evaluate, analyse, or investigate, it is still a provisional and untested idea. Once it has withstood repeated tests and has been found to have considerable explanatory power, it becomes a theory.

We can distinguish different types of theory according to scope and level of generalizability ('grand' versus middle-range theory), analytic process (inductive versus deductive theory), and the nature of the questions it addresses (empirical versus normative).

The sociologist, Robert Merton, defined a distinction between what he called '**grand theory**' and '**theories of the middle-range**' (Merton 1968). Grand theory is what he characterized as 'all-inclusive systematic efforts to develop a unified theory that will explain all the observed uniformities of social behavior, social organization, and social change' (1968: 39). Merton argued that grand and abstract theories of society provided no basis for an empirical social science. He called on theorists to apply themselves to the development of what he called 'theories of the middle range': theories that attempted to understand and explain a limited aspect of social life, a more restricted domain or set of social phenomena. These explanations could then be verified through empirical research and then perhaps systematized into theoretical systems of broader scope and content.

Theories also differ according to the analytic process that links theory and research, in particular whether theory guides research (deduction) or whether theory is an outcome of research (induction). We discussed these different processes in Chapter 2. Deduction moves from broader generalizations and theories to specific observations. We start either with a theory that has already been confirmed or with a logical argument, and then we draw out the meaning or implications this has for explaining some particular case or phenomena. So, in deductive theory, a hypothesis is deduced from current theory, which is then subjected to empirical scrutiny. Induction, you will recall, is a process of reasoning from particular facts to a general conclusion. We begin with particular observations or cases and then develop generalizations about them. Inductive theory is, therefore, the outcome of research.

Another analytic process that links theory and research is what has been called '**grounded theory**' (Glaser and Strauss 1967; Corbin and Strauss 1990). Grounded theory is an inductive research strategy. The researcher starts by collecting data. Concepts and categories are not applied to the data, but emerge from them. Hypotheses are not tested or formulated on the basis of data, but are developed through the interaction of theory and data. Theory is therefore produced through, and *grounded* in, data. What is most emphasized in grounded theory is that it is explicitly an emergent process: the aim is to discover the theory implicit in the data, to allow theory to emerge from the data as opposed to forcing it into preconceived frameworks.

Finally, we can distinguish different types of theory according to the nature of the questions they address (empirical versus normative). We have previously discussed (and raised some objections to) the distinction between empirical theory and normative theory (Chapters 1 and 3). Empirical theory is concerned with questions that can be answered with empirical data (data gathered through observations of the world around us). **Normative theory** is concerned with questions about what is right and wrong, desirable or undesirable, just or unjust in society. We will have more to say about answering normative questions later on in this chapter.

So, having reviewed different types of theory, we can now sum up how the terms 'proposition', 'hypothesis', and 'theory' differ from, and are related to, one another. A statement positing that two or more variables are related is a proposition: a provisional idea that merits evaluation. In order for us to evaluate its worth, its constituent terms need to be defined very specifically. Once you have done this, you have a hypothesis: a tentative answer or argument you wish to develop (investigate, demonstrate) in response to your research question. A theory identifies a small number of variables that must be taken into consideration in addressing the question, and how they are related both to each other and to the outcome that is being addressed.

Where do hypotheses come from?

Your answer (a hypothesis and investigation of it) must be situated in relation to existing theory and previous research relevant to your question. A researcher develops a hypothesis through a critical analysis of the strengths and weaknesses of both. This provides a way to identify what requires further investigation or re-thinking: what would provide a better understanding of the matter, or make visible some dimension that brings added strength to one or another of the positions in a debate; what would produce a fruitful synthesis of different perspectives, or reveal erroneous assumptions or logic in current understandings. As we discussed in Chapter 5, the analysis you undertake of existing theory and previous research relevant to your topic is presented in what is conventionally referred to as the 'literature review'.

Any issue relating to the political world is likely to be the subject of conflicting views about how to define it; where, when, and why it originated; how it developed or evolved, what its impact is, what its likely future trajectory will be, and what decision-makers or specialists can or should do with respect to it. In the process of sorting through the various opinions and judgements about these issues, you gain an understanding of the different positions, and the current 'state of play' regarding a given topic. Who else has asked and answered your question? What puzzles or problems have they left unsolved? Are there important issues or dimensions of a phenomenon that they have not addressed? Are there claims for which there is little systematic evidence; or relevant evidence or alternative data sources that have been insufficiently considered? Are there logical inconsistencies or errors in how variables or a relationship between two variables are specified, so as to cast doubt on the merit of the conclusions? Are concepts defined wrongly, ambiguously, too narrowly or too broadly, or in a way that obscures crucial dimensions of the phenomenon investigated? Do arguments and theories tend to focus on examples or cases drawn from only one part of the world? Do they fail to address or control for confounding factors or alternative explanation? Is the time frame too short, or artificial; or the spatial domain too limited or artificial? What is missing, irrelevant, defective, unwarranted, or ambiguous? What should be further highlighted, underlined, expanded, extended, improved, built upon, or continued (e.g. through application to other cases)?

Gradually your own point of view emerges. You start to identify good reasons for why you think one position is better, more persuasive, more accurate or comprehensive than another. You might start to develop a list of reasons for why you think one thing is true and another thing false. Eventually you develop clear, focused, and logically sound reasons for thinking what you think. This process is retold in your literature review. Your literature review sets the stage for your own argument or answer by identifying, and developing an argument about, weaknesses in the literature relevant to your question that need to be addressed or strengths that have been insufficiently exploited.

Illustration: how an analysis of existing studies provides the basis for a hypothesis

The process of reading and analysing literatures related to your research question can provide the basis for a hypothesis that escapes the weaknesses of existing studies and builds upon their strengths. Let's illustrate how a researcher's 'literature review' leads to the development of a hypothesis about an important area of inquiry in PIR.

In *States, Scarcity, and Civil Strife in the Developing World* (2006), Colin Kahl develops an argument about the relationship between environmental pressures and civil conflict through a critical review of relevant studies of the issue.

Kahl begins by observing that 'civil strife in the developing world represents perhaps the greatest international security challenge of the early twenty-first century'; and that 'a growing number of scholars and practitioners' are focusing on the role in these conflicts of rapid population growth, environmental degradation, and competition over natural resources (2006: 1–2). In order to engage with the literature on resource-related conflicts, Kahl must first sort through and organize the various arguments and judgements that it contains. It is this inventory and organization of existing knowledge on a topic that enables a researcher to begin the process of developing and making a case for his or her own point of view. Kahl concludes that the existing literature on resource-related conflicts can be divided into two broad perspectives: those linking conflict to scarcity and grievance, and those arguing that conflict is driven by abundance and greed. He then selects for sustained analysis those hypotheses from within each perspective that appear to be most robust and influential: two hypotheses linking conflict to resource scarcity (the 'deprivation hypothesis' and the 'state failure hypothesis'), and two that link conflict to resource abundance (the 'honey pot hypothesis' and the 'resource curse hypothesis'). After analysing the strengths and weaknesses of each of these, he is then ready to state his own hypothesis.

Here is a brief summation of Kahl's key points of agreement and disagreement with these hypotheses and how his own hypothesis addresses their weaknesses and builds on their strengths.

The 'deprivation hypothesis' maintains that population growth, environmental degradation, and poor distribution of natural resources create deprivation among the poorest elements of society and, in this way, increase the chances of civil strife. Population and environmental pressures contribute to falling wages, unemployment, and landlessness. This increases poverty and inequality, leads to frustration and grievances, and increases the risks of collective violence.

Kahl points to two key weaknesses with this hypothesis. First, it ignores collective action problems. We discussed the problem of collective action in Chapter 4. The 'problem' to which this refers is that the existence of common interests among individuals does not necessarily produce an incentive to pursue concerted political action; because, rather than working to promote a common interest, individuals are just as likely to let others do the work and to 'free-ride'. Kahl points out that the 'deprivation hypothesis' doesn't take this problem into account; it doesn't provide an explanation of when and why individuals are willing and able to make the sacrifices (in land, wages, and time) necessary to participate in organized violence under conditions of resource scarcity. The second weakness Kahl finds with this hypothesis is that it assigns no role to the state. The state, by virtue of its control over resources within a territorial domain over which it exercises its authority, must, Kahl reasons, play an important role in resource-related conflict.

The 'state failure hypothesis' escapes this weakness by placing the state at the centre of the story it tells about how, when, and why resource scarcity generates conflict. It argues that population and environmental pressures confront the state with increased demands for costly investments. This undermines state capacity and legitimacy and opens up 'political space' for violence. Kahl argues that this hypothesis doesn't go far enough in elucidating the role of the state in resource-related conflicts because it assumes that environmental and demographic pressures lead to conflict only in countries with weak state governance. But state strength can also provide an avenue for resource-related conflict, Kahl argues, because a strong state can enable state elites to politically exploit demographic and environmental pressures to engineer violence against social groups.

The 'deprivation hypothesis' and the 'state failure hypothesis' both focus on resource scarcity. Other hypotheses focus on situations in which resource abundance leads to conflict. The general argument advanced by this perspective is that resource abundance leads to conflict by encouraging rebel groups to form and fight over valuable natural resources. This is what the 'honey pot hypothesis' argues. The problem with this hypothesis, Kahl argues, is that the 'greed-based logic' on which it depends is chiefly applicable to non-renewable mineral resources rather than to renewable ones. Non-renewable resources—oil, diamonds, copper—are those most likely 'to be implicated in violent conflicts' in situations in which there are abundant resources, because these 'tend to be much more valuable per unit of volume, geographically concentrated, and easily tradable than most renewable resources'. The 'vast majority of examples of honey pot–driven conflicts', Kahl argues, 'revolve around oil, precious metals, diamonds, and other valuable minerals' (2006: 18).

The same weakness attaches to what is perhaps the best-known resource hypothesis about resource abundance and conflict: the 'resource curse hypothesis'. According to this hypothesis, state control of abundant supplies of valuable resources contributes to corrupt, authoritarian governments that become prime targets for rebellion. Like the 'honey pot hypothesis', resource curse accounts apply 'much more to countries dependent on the export of non-renewable resources than renewable resources' (2006: 19). Moreover, these accounts, Kahl argues, take insufficient account of the ways in which social and political factors affect the relationship between resource endowments and violence (2006: 21).

To sum up these points: Kahl shows that the most important hypotheses concerning resource-related conflict are weak in one or more of three ways. First, they don't provide an understanding of the role of the state in resource-related conflicts. Either they assign no role to the state or, if they do, they fail either to take into account the possibility both of state weakness (failure) and state strength (exploitation), or to provide a sufficient understanding of the variables that affect state capacity. The second weakness with these hypotheses is that they pay insufficient attention to collective action problems. Third, they are applicable to countries with non-renewable mineral resources rather than those with chiefly renewable resources.

Kahl then draws these different lines of critique together to produce a hypothesis of his own. The state, he argues, plays a crucial role in resource-related conflicts in developing countries: resource pressures can lead to conflict because they either push a state towards failure or provide the state with opportunities for exploitation. Scarce resources can lead to state weakness (failure), which, in turn, leads to conflict; resource abundance can contribute to state strength and exploitation, which, in turn, generates rebellion and conflict. Whether environmental pressures push a state towards failure or exploitation depends on social and political factors which affect the relationship between resource endowments and the state. Kahl conceptualizes these factors in terms of 'groupness'—the ease with which countries divide into ethno-cultural, religious, or class factions, which helps to overcome collective action problems; and 'institutional inclusivity or exclusivity', which relates to the influence wielded by groups or organizations over the state. Kahl hypothesizes that the potential for conflict will increase where there's a high degree of groupness, and where exclusive institutions short-circuit cooperation and leave state elites free to instigate violence. Conversely, the potential for conflict decreases where there is a low degree of groupness and where institutional inclusivity facilitates societal cooperation in the face of a weakened state.

Figure 6.1 shows the main hypotheses in the existing literature, and the hypothesis that Kahl produces as a result of his analysis of their strengths and weaknesses. It is useful to reconstruct your hypothesis, in the same way as the hypotheses in Figure 6.1, using an arrow diagram to identify key theoretical variables and the direction of the hypothesized relationship between them.

You will recall from Chapter 5 that we discussed the need to provide a rationale for your research question. You need to provide a rationale for your hypothesis, as well. You must identify the source of your hypothesis—what in theory or practice gives rise to it. Is it developed deductively from a more basic theory? Is it based on assumptions of a general 'approach' (rational choice, institutional, Marxist, etc.), or a blend of aspects of two or more approaches? Or is your hypothesis developed inductively from a body of empirical evidence? Are you hypothesizing that the lessons drawn from another domain of experience can be usefully employed to address the domain relating to your research question?

All hypotheses are based on a set of expectations derived from existing theory and previous research. Whether the question you are addressing is descriptive, explanatory, predictive, prescriptive, or normative, there will be something in theory or previous research that provides the basis for a hypothesis about the way the world works or should work, about future developments or policy proposals. The key components of some theory or explanatory approach or body of research are what lead you to expect the relation(s) your hypothesis states. These components comprise what we refer to as a 'theoretical framework'. This framework is like a story or a set of assumptions that connects the dots represented by your key factors or elements. We said previously that theory ensures that contributions to knowledge are cumulative. But theory also furthers the research enterprise by providing patterns for the interpretation of data; by supplying 'frameworks within which concepts and variables

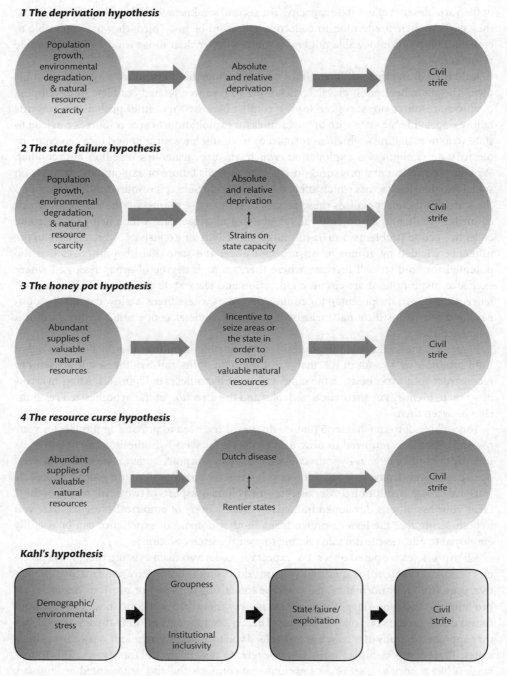

1 The deprivation hypothesis

Population growth, environmental degradation, & natural resource scarcity → Absolute and relative deprivation → Civil strife

2 The state failure hypothesis

Population growth, environmental degradation, & natural resource scarcity → Absolute and relative deprivation ↕ Strains on state capacity → Civil strife

3 The honey pot hypothesis

Abundant supplies of valuable natural resources → Incentive to seize areas or the state in order to control valuable natural resources → Civil strife

4 The resource curse hypothesis

Abundant supplies of valuable natural resources → Dutch disease ↕ Rentier states → Civil strife

Kahl's hypothesis

Demographic/ environmental stress → Groupness / Institutional inclusivity → State faiure/ exploitation → Civil strife

Figure 6.1 Hypotheses about how demographic and environmental pressures generate conflict

acquire substantive significance', and by allowing us 'to interpret the *larger meaning* of our findings for ourselves and others' (Hoover and Donovan 2004: 37).

Hypotheses can be investigated in two ways. A hypothesis can be tested with evidence (confirmatory research), or it can operate as a guide to a process of discovery (exploratory research). Both contribute to the development of theory. Hypothesis testing uses logical or empirical evidence to evaluate existing theories; hypothesis-generating research produces findings that can be used in the development of theory.

Hypothesis testing begins by stating, on the basis of a theory, what we would expect to find, and then sees whether that expectation is fulfilled. Hypothesis-testing or confirmatory research is deductive in that it is driven by a particular hypothesis: the researcher has a specific, focused statement in mind and his/her objective is to prove or disprove that hypothesis. Hypothesis-generating research begins with a question and perhaps a basic proposition, examines a set of cases, and comes up with a more specific set of propositions. Hypothesis-generating or exploratory research is inductive, in that the researcher observes a phenomenon in order to generate questions or hypotheses for subsequent research. Both kinds of research are 'part of the overall scientific method' (Gerring 2001: 23). Both types of research must ultimately specify the relationship between variables. Both require one to make an argument. Both are part of a single, evolving, dynamic process of discovery and hypothesis formation. As we pointed out in Chapter 2, scientific inquiry typically involves a process of continuous interaction between theory and observation, in which the researcher moves from observation to theory (induction) and from theory back to observation (deduction). Figure 6.2 illustrates this process.

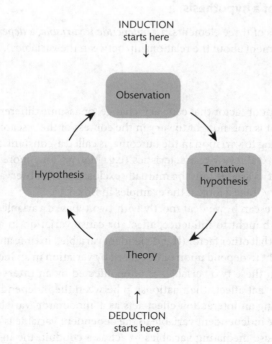

Figure 6.2 Induction and deduction

At the beginning of this section we stated that in order to contribute to knowledge in a field of study, an answer to a research question must meet three requirements. The first requirement is that the answer be appropriate to the type of question that is being asked. The second requirement of an answer to a research question is that it makes a contribution to knowledge in our field by relating your question and answer to existing research and theory. We have not yet discussed the third requirement of an answer to a research question: that it must be clearly and fully *specified*. We address this requirement in the next section.

Specifying your argument or answer: the nuts and bolts

Hypotheses can be assessed on the basis of a variety of criteria: empirical data, added value (increased understanding), plausibility in comparison with other available hypotheses, usefulness, internal logic, elegance, parsimony. But in order to assess a hypothesis you must clearly and fully *specify* its component factors and relations. You must not only specify its essential elements—the variables and their relationship to one another; you must also make sure you are using terms that mean what you want them to mean, and are defining them so that they can be understood by others in precisely the way you want them to be understood. This requires that you, first, develop a conceptualization, or conceptual definition, of the terms or variables you use. Second, you must develop an even more specific, operational, definition that identifies empirical referents for them.

The components of a hypothesis

A hypothesis consists of three elements: an *independent variable*, a *dependent variable*, and *a proposition* (a statement about the relationship between the variables).

Variables

A variable is a concept or factor that can vary, change, or assume different values or characteristics. A factor that is not thought to vary in the context of the research and, hence is not capable of contributing to variation in the outcome, is called a 'constant'. A variable assumes at least two different values or characteristics (e.g. high vs low, more vs less, present vs absent). The values of a variable must be mutually exclusive: each observation must fit in one and only one category. Take a look at the examples in Box 6.4.

In social science research, we deal mostly with two types of variables. An **independent variable** is a factor thought to influence, affect, or cause variation in another variable. It always comes before that other factor (the 'dependent variable') in time and space. A **dependent variable** is thought to depend upon or be caused by variation in an independent variable. The relation between these two variables is often affected by an **intervening variable**. An intervening variable that affects the relationship between the independent and dependent variables by producing an interaction effect acts as a 'moderator' variable. One that transmits the effects of the independent variable to the dependent variable is called a 'mediating' variable. Without these mediating variables to act as a conduit, the independent variable would not affect the dependent variable. Recall our discussion, in Chapter 2, on causal

BOX 6.4 Variables and Values

Variables	Values
Resources	Abundant/scarce
Interdependence	Vulnerability/sensitivity
Domestic support for war	Strong, neutral, weak
Form of government	Democracy, dictatorship
Socio-economic and political changes	Rapid/slow
Organization size	Large/small
Democracy	Stable/unstable
Economic development	Low/moderate/high
Gender	Male/female

BOX 6.5 Variables

Variable: a factor or characteristic that can assume different values or characteristics

A **dependent variable** is the variable in which you are primarily interested, and which you assume is dependent upon a second variable. Our dependent variable is some political outcome (events or process) we are endeavouring to explain.

An **independent variable** is the variable thought to, directly or indirectly, cause or influence the dependent variable. Within this particular relationship it is independent because it does not depend on the other variable/variables. Our independent variable(s) are factor(s) that bring about the outcome we wish to explain—the factor or set of factors are determinative of this political outcome. The value of the dependent variable is influenced (or depends) on the value of the independent variable/variables.

An **intervening variable** influences the relation between two others and thus produces an interaction effect (*'moderator' variable*) or transmits the effects of the IV to the DV (a *'mediating' variable*).

mechanisms and the notion that there are 'social mechanisms' that produce social outcomes. In Chapter 4, we addressed this issue again in the context of a discussion concerning how to provide explanations of macro-social phenomena with micro-foundations. Remember James Coleman's contention that macro phenomena have to be explained by the interaction of micro and macro-levels ('Coleman's bathtub')? One of the functions that mediating variables might fulfil is to show how micro and macro phenomena are linked to each other. Box 6.5 summarizes the role of independent, dependent, and intervening variables.

We can illustrate variables, their values, and how they provide the nuts and bolts of an argument with reference to the argument developed by Colin Kahl that we just discussed. The question Kahl is addressing is: What effects do environmental pressures have on conflict within developing countries. His dependent variable (what he wants to explain) is the likelihood of conflict. This variable can assume two values: *increased* likelihood or *decreased* likelihood. His independent variable (what he thinks effects this outcome) is demographic and environmental stress. These pressures can vary between two values: *high* and *low*. He identifies an important intervening variable that enables the independent variable to affect the dependent variable. This is the state: a mediating variable that links the effects of environmental pressures to the likelihood of conflict. This variable has two values: it can be *strong and exploitive*, or *weak and failing*. Which of these two values it assumes depends on other intervening variables having to do with the social and political institutions of a given country: 'groupness' (values: *high/low)* and institutional inclusivity (*high/low*). He argues that these variables affect whether environmental pressures push a state towards failure or exploitation.

Relationships

All types of research questions are concerned with connections or relations between two or more variables. A descriptive question might ask *what* relationship exists between gender and voting preference, or between educational achievement and political participation; an explanatory question would ask *why* that relationship exists. A predictive question would ask how that relationship might be expected to change in the future; a prescriptive question might be concerned with what steps might be taken to strengthen a relationship. While we don't think of normative political theory as requiring a dependent and independent variable, normative questions nonetheless are concerned with connections and relations, and with whether they are just or desirable.

There are two types of relationships in political research: two ways that variables can be connected or related to each other. In practice, these two types tend to converge.

The first relationship is one of **association**. In this relationship, a variable, e.g. 'unemployment', is in some way associated with, related to, or linked with another variable, e.g. 'inflation'. This term is roughly synonymous with **correlation** (two things vary together in a linear fashion) and with **co-variance** (the alleged cause varies with the supposed effect). All these terms refer to a relation between variables such that changes in one variable *occur together* with changes in the other. A relationship of association can be positive or negative. Two variables are *positively related* when they change in the same direction: when the occurrence of high values on one variable are associated with the occurrence of high values on the other, and low values on one are associated with low values on the other. For instance, a positive correlation between inflation and unemployment means that when inflation is high, unemployment also tends to be high; and when inflation is low, unemployment also tends to be low. When two variables are *negatively related*, the values of the variables change in opposite directions, so that when one variable (inflation) decreases, the other (employment) increases.

The second type of relationship between two variables is **causality**. With this type of relationship, changes in one variable *bring about* changes in another. To establish that a causal relationship exists between two variables you must show that four conditions have been met. The first condition is that the hypothesized cause or independent variable (IV) is temporally prior to the effect, i.e. the dependent variable (DV). In other words, the IV must precede the

DV in time. The second condition is that the two variables are correlated or co-vary. Of course, correlation does not establish that two variables are causally related. That is why we need the third condition: that a causal mechanism or process links the two variables. We discussed causal mechanisms in Chapter 2, and the desirability, more generally, of showing the 'micro-foundations' that connect variables—the intentions and choices of individuals, or of social and political units that have acquired the capacity to act collectively. You have to be able to tell a plausible story that you think probably connects the independent variable(s) with the outcome that you are trying to explain, often including an 'intervening variable' that gets us from the hypothesized cause (IV) to the effect (DV). The fourth condition is that the correlation between the IV and the DV is not spurious. This requires that you rule out the possibility of a variable that is causally prior to both the IV and the DV, so that the correlation that appears to exist between the two variables does so only because a third (antecedent) variable is affecting both.

A well-known and puzzling finding about US Congressional electoral campaigns can illustrate how a third variable can render a seeming correlation spurious. In a study of the effects of campaign spending in congressional elections, Gary Jacobson (1978) found that increased spending by incumbents correlates with increased odds of failure. So, it might be assumed from this finding that *spending more* by incumbents somehow *causes* electoral failure. However, Jacobson found that there was a third variable that was antecedent to both spending and electoral failure: the nature of the electoral battle, i.e. whether it was expected to be tough or easy. Incumbents who expect a tough fight spend more than incumbents who expect to win easily. If spending more is evidence of a tough fight, there is nothing puzzling at all about finding that increased spending appears to be correlated with electoral failure. The notion that somehow spending more by incumbents *causes* electoral failure is spurious: another variable, the toughness of the fight, explains both high spending and electoral failure.

In sum, when we assert that variation in independent variable X *causes* variation in dependent variable Y, we are making four assertions: (1) the change in X precedes the change in Y; (2) X and Y are correlated; (3) a causal mechanism or process can be identified that links the variables; and (4) the correlation between X and Y is not spurious or a coincidence.

We said that in practice the two types of relationship we've discussed—association and causality—tend to converge. To explain why they do, we need to explain that there are two different notions of causality that social scientists employ: deterministic causation and probabilistic causation. A *deterministic* causal relation states that 'if (x) then *always/invariably* (y)'. However, we generally tend to see human behaviour as, not determined, but constrained; consequently PIR research usually employs a *probabilistic* notion of causality rather than a deterministic one. A probabilistic causal relation states that 'if (x) then *maybe/sometimes/probably* (y)'. 'Probabilistic' means that when the values that an IV takes on increase, this *usually results* in the values of the DV increasing (or decreasing). This notion of cause focuses the efforts of researchers on finding factors that make an effect more likely: for example, the finding that the more educated a person is, the *more likely* he is to vote. The more robust we make our correlations—the more we seek to meet the conditions of causality discussed, above—the more the relation of correlation between two variables converges with one of probabilistic causation. Though a robust correlation cannot establish *why* X and Y co-vary, knowing that X is usually associated with Y can make a significant contribution to our understanding of political outcomes.

Conceptualization and operationalization

In order for research to be cumulative, the answers we offer to a research question must be clearly and fully *specified*. This means, among other things, that the terms we use must mean what we want them to mean and be formulated so that others will understand them in precisely the way we want them to be understood. We must provide both a conceptualization or *conceptual definition* of them, as well as a definition that identifies empirical referents to them: an *operational definition*. Specifying our terms in this way makes it possible for our ideas to be assessed and for our research to enter into dialogue with and build on the work of others.

Concepts and concept formation: what are you talking about?

A concept is a term applied to a collection or class of things that are to be regarded alike, because they either share a common characteristic or feature (e.g., gender, type of government) or are instances of some general type of behaviour (war, participation). A concept provides a label for instances or characteristics that are commonly found together. When we attach a label or general term (concept) to observations or events we can link separate observations or events together and form generalizations. We observe people voting and we refer to this as 'participation'. We observe that a legislator consistently takes certain positions on political issues and we call him a 'conservative'.

Translating knowledge into the more general categories represented by concepts enables knowledge to cumulate. We use concepts as a shorthand to refer to much of the substantive content and issue base of political studies: elites, bureaucracy, legislatures, judiciaries, policy, ethnicity, pluralism, alienation, human rights, government, federalism, public opinion, elections, power, development, democracy, culture, legitimacy, charisma, hegemony, institutionalization, exploitation, authority, interests, class, corporatism, civil society, racism, terrorism, egalitarianism, dependency, consensus, welfare state, social justice.

But, many concepts used in our field are anything but clear. There is often a lack of consensus about what concepts are important, what they mean, and how they should be defined and measured. What one scholar means by 'ideology' may be something quite different from what another person means. There is also a lack of consensus about what concept should be employed to describe a given phenomenon or outcome. Researchers frequently use different concepts to understand the same situation. What one researcher calls a 'terrorist organization', another might call a 'social movement'; an event that one researcher calls a 'revolution' another might call a 'coup'. Social science is characterized by a continuous conflict not only over how we define concepts, but which ones we should use to comprehend a given reality. Consequently, we need to spell out with as much precision as possible what a concept that we use (e.g. 'ideology') means in the context of our research. The point is not just to define the terms we use, but to consider very carefully *what* terms we should use and *how* we should define them.

Concept formation

The term 'concept' refers to a mental image (conception) that summarizes a collection of seemingly related observations and experiences. *Conceptualization*, or 'concept formation', is the process of selecting the term by which some collection of things should be known. As John Gerring points out, it concerns 'the most basic questions of social science: *What are we talking about?*' (2001: 35). Much thought has been devoted to the question of what distinguishes a *good* concept from one that is less good or less useful. John Gerring identifies eight essential criteria for a good concept: familiarity, resonance, parsimony, coherence, differentiation, depth, theoretical utility, and field utility. Box 6.6 shows how Gerring defines each of these criteria.

A good concept must mediate among these criteria, usually through a series of trade-offs. For instance, you decide that a good place to start the process of conceptualization is with a term that meets the criterion of *familiarity* (established usage). You find, however, that the term has little *theoretical utility* (usefulness for theory). Your next step will be to find a term that does a better job of mediating between these two criteria. Perhaps you come up with a new term for something that offers *resonance* (a 'ring'). You may discover, however, that this comes at too high a cost with respect to *familiarity, theoretical utility*, or other criteria. *Parsimony* (explaining the most with the least) must be balanced with *depth* (the number of features shared by the observations or instances we want to regard as alike). *Coherence* (the internal consistency of the instances and attributes) often needs to be considered in relation to *differentiation* (of the observations and instances from similar concepts).

We can illustrate the problems and trade-offs that researchers face in concept formation by considering how researchers have struggled to arrive at a satisfactory definition of a key term of political analysis: power. Below, we provide a brief summary of the debate about how to conceptualize power. This is not intended as a full discussion of the debate, but only as an illustrative example of the problems researchers in our field confront when attempting to define key concepts.

BOX 6.6 Criteria for Conceptual Goodness

1. Familiarity	How familiar is the concept (to a lay or academic audience)?
2. Resonance	Does the chosen term ring (resonate)?
3. Parsimony	How short is the term and its list of defining attributes?
4. Coherence	How internally consistent (logically related) are the instances and attributes?
5. Differentiation	How differentiated are the instances and the attributes (from other most-similar concepts)? How bounded, how operationalizable, is the concept?
6. Depth	How many accompanying properties are shared by the instances under definition?
7. Theoretical utility	How useful is the concept within a wider field of inferences?
8. Field utility	How useful is the concept within a field of related instances and attributes?

Source: From Gerring 1999: 367.

Conceptualizing 'power': the search for theoretical utility

Researchers in our field generally agree that 'power' is a key concept in political inquiry, and that it is central to any understanding of politics. But what we mean when we use the term 'power' is anything but clear. Is 'power' a capability, an attribute, or a relation? A capacity to do something or control somebody, or an action? A property of actors or of relations? Is it necessarily conflictual, intentional, or effective, or all three? Who possesses and exercises it: individuals, groups, social institutions and organizations?

Difficulties of this sort arise, in part, because of the problem of differentiating 'power' from similar or related phenomena, such as coercion, authority, influence, domination, force, inducement, persuasion, manipulation. But attempts to achieve a high degree of *differentiation* in the conceptualization of power often entail a loss of *depth*. The term 'power' must not only be differentiated from other, similar concepts; it must also capture the many different ways that people can exercise power over each other (some of which cannot always be observed), and the very diverse sources of power: material resources like money, property, wealth, natural resources, information, military capabilities, good jobs; but also intangible factors like charisma, status, prestige, reputation, respect, honour, character.

Let's consider these difficulties in relation to two ways in which researchers have attempted to define 'power': in terms of relations between actors (power as control over actors, agendas, and preferences); and the outcome of those relations (power as control over events and outcomes).

A conceptualization of power as *control over actors* defines 'power' as the ability of one actor to impose its will on others. This fits our intuitive notion of power (*familiarity*); and it captures several dimensions of power (*depth*) by including control of actions, agendas, and preferences. In this conceptualization of 'power', to use Robert Dahl's oft-quoted formulation, power is the ability of A to get B to do something he would not otherwise do (Dahl 1957). One way this can be achieved is through controlling *agendas*—structuring or determining what issues are discussed, preventing 'the public airing of policy conflicts' (Bachrach and Baratz 1970: 8); keeping potential issues out of politics, 'whether through the operation of social forces and institutional practises or through individuals' decisions' (Lukes 1974: 24). The importance of controlling agendas is illustrated by the struggle of countries in the South to gain some control over the agenda relating to North–South issues; the agenda-setting power of media, NGOs, or global social movements, like the anti–globalization movement. 'Control over actors' can also be achieved through controlling *preferences*—through influencing what other actors desire. The ability to get what you want, not through the 'hard power' of military and economic strength, but through attraction, is what Joseph Nye has called 'soft power' (1990, 2002, 2004). Controlling preferences means the ability to generate consensus, through the manipulation of public opinion or propaganda (disinformation), through censorship (withholding information), or political correctness (thought control).

Controlling actors through control over actions, agendas, or preferences encompasses much of what we mean when we use the term 'power'. However, this conceptualization makes it difficult to distinguish between interactions in which one actor exercises power over another and those involving exchange relations. How do we know whether the outcome of an interaction between two actors (e.g. a negotiation) occurred as a result of the exercise of power by one actor over another, or because both sides had something to gain from the outcome? If the UK agrees to the demand by the US to impose taxes on offshore activities, does this show that the US exercised power over the UK with respect to this issue, or that some sort of exchange occurred in which both benefited? Can we interpret the outcome, more generally, as demonstrating something about current power relations in the international system, or something about the nature and content of exchange relations? A 'control over actors' definition of power often makes it difficult to distinguish one from the other.

But there is another problem with this conception of 'power'. It is tautological: you are defining power in terms of the outcome. Let's say that we think that some action by Actor B can be explained as a result of the power that Actor A was able to exercise over Actor B. We explain that B did what A wanted it to do because A had the power. But we can only know that A had this power because B *did do* what A wanted it to do. We only know that A has power over B by the result. 'Power' as a concept is only interesting if it can be used to explain events or outcomes; and a conceptualization of 'power' that is tautological is not *theoretically useful*.

Consider the second conception of power: *control over events and outcomes*. By focusing not on relations between actors, but on the outcome of those relations, this conception allows us to account for interactions between actors in which both actors benefit (exchange), though they may gain disproportionately. In a conception of power as control over the outcomes, we can not only account for shared power or exchange, but also for situations in which relatively weak countries exercise power through sharing control over mutually consequential outcomes. For example, during the Cold War, the small, relatively powerless Middle East states exercised power through their shared control over stability in the region. They could threaten to act in destabilizing ways: to escalate the Arab–Israeli conflict and cause a widescale confrontation in the region, or to lose militarily. But though this conception of power offers important advantages over the 'control over actors' conception, it doesn't escape the problem of tautology. Like the 'control over actors' conception, it defines power by the outcome; so there is no objective way of determining who has the power until we see how things turn out.

A more general criticism of both conceptions is that, in general, most of what happens in politics is not attributable to the direct exercise of power by actors, over each other or over outcomes. Power is usually exercised in a far less direct way. This is what the notion of *structural power* highlights: aspects of power which operate through indirect institutional, unintended, or impersonally created effects. Structural power operates through a network of (historically constituted) relationships that benefit some and disadvantage others (Guzzini 1993). Susan Strange (1994) identified four key structures through which power is exercised: the *security structure*, which provides protection to human beings; the *production structure*, the primary means of creating value and wealth in a society; the *finance structure*, which determines who has access to money, how, and on what terms; and the *knowledge structure*, which 'determines what knowledge is discovered, how it is stored, and who communicates it by what means to whom and on what terms' (1994: 121). When women of childbearing age in poor countries work at factory jobs that expose them to potentially dangerous chemicals, it is a result of the exercise of power, not by employers, but of production and financial structures that give poor women in these countries few other ways to survive. The US is able to indirectly influence other states' behaviour by controlling the monetary structures within which they must operate.

We have touched on only a few of the challenging and vastly complicated issues and considerations involved in the attempt to conceptualize 'power'. Hopefully, the example sufficed to alert you to the sort of ambiguity that attaches to terms that are commonly used in our field and the consequent need to provide a carefully considered conceptual definition of those that you use.

Conceptualizing 'democracy': mediating between coherence and differentiation

We achieve broader knowledge by generalizing; and we generalize by applying our conceptualizations to a wider range of observations or experiences. However, using existing concepts to cover instances that lie 'outside their normal range of use' (Gerring 1999: 360), either in application to new cases, or as a result of changes over time *within* cases—captured by Giovanni Sartori's (1970, 1984) notions of *conceptual travelling* (the application of concepts to new cases)—can create problems of *conceptual stretching* (Collier and Mahon 1993: 845)—the distortion that occurs when a concept does not fit the new case. We can illustrate the problem of 'conceptual stretching' and efforts to prevent it, by considering attempts to deal conceptually with the changing nature of political democracy over the past decades.

The great diversity of new post-authoritarian political regimes established in Latin America, Africa, Asia, and the former communist world in recent decades share important attributes of democracy. But they also differ in significant ways both from each other and from the democracies in advanced industrial countries.

The term 'democracy' has been applied to those political systems that meet a 'procedural minimum' definition of 'democracy': fully contested elections, full suffrage, the absence of massive fraud, and effective guarantees of civil liberties, including freedom of speech, assembly, and association (Collier and Levitsky 1997: 434). Those political systems that have this procedural minimum, plus some further differentiating attribute, provided the basis for defining the 'classical' subtypes of democracy as, for instance, 'parliamentary democracy', 'multiparty democracy', and 'federal democracy'. In order to capture the diverse forms of democracy that have emerged in recent decades, researchers have defined new sub-types: 'authoritarian democracy', 'neopatrimonial democracy', 'military-dominated democracy', 'limited', 'oligarchical', 'controlled', 'restrictive', 'electoral', 'illiberal', 'guarded', 'protected', and 'tutelary' democracy. The goal was to generalize our understanding of democracy to a wider set of cases. But because these 'subtypes' are cases that do not meet the definition of the root term, that do not represent *full* instances of the term, 'democracy', it could be argued that they really refer 'to a *different* set of cases' than those that we call democracies (Collier and Levitsky 1997: 430, 438).

Rather than referring to forms of democracy which are incomplete, i.e. which are missing attributes included in the procedural minimum definition, as different *types* of democracy, some analysts consider it more useful to refer to political systems as exhibiting different *degrees* of democracy (Collier and Levitsky 1997: 440).

This approach owes much to Robert Dahl's influential study, *Polyarchy* (1971). In this study, Dahl uses the term 'democracy' to refer to a political *ideal*. The term 'polyarchy' refers to *actual* political systems. Polyarchies are systems of representative government that 'to a relatively high degree' are characterized by (1) equal chances of all members of the community determining the agenda for, as well as the outcome of processes of political decision-making; and (2) the effective accountability of the elected officials during the time between elections (1971: 84). The notion that actual political systems can be characterized in terms of degrees or gradations of democracy has been widely accepted. Some analysts argue that 'democracy is *always* a matter of degree' (Bollen and Jackman 1989: 612; emphasis added; see also Bollen 1980, 1993; and Bollen and Paxton 2000; Dahl 1971, 1989; Coppedge and Reinicke 1990).

But others argue that this approach to conceptualizing democracy is fundamentally flawed. 'Political systems are *systems*', Giovanni Sartori argues. They are 'bounded wholes characterized by constitutive mechanisms and principles that are either present (albeit imperfectly) or absent (albeit imperfectly)' (1987: 184; emphasis added). Regimes 'cannot be half-democratic' (Alvarez et al. 1996: 21). The distinction between democracy and non-democracy should be treated, therefore, as exhaustive and mutually exclusive categories. The question of whether to conceptualize 'democracy' as a dichotomous variable (democracy versus non-democracy) or in terms of degrees continues to be much debated.

As the discussion of 'power' and 'democracy' shows, we must not just define our terms, but think carefully about the implications of how we use them and the trade-offs that must be made among a variety of considerations that enter into the formulation of good as a concept.

Operational definitions: how will you know it when you see it?

Even when there is a consensus about the importance of a particular concept and how it should be defined, researchers often will *dis*agree about whether, where, or to what degree it is occurring. For instance, since the 1970s, International Relations scholars have become increasingly preoccupied with the growing interdependence among states. Researchers generally agree on what the term 'interdependence' means; but they do not always agree about how significant it is, whether it is increasing or decreasing, regional or universal, new or old. Even though we may agree on the meaning of a term, unless we provide an 'operational' definition of it—define it in a way that will enable us to determine its presence or absence, strength, and extent—we may not know it when we see it. So, in addition to providing a conceptual definition of a factor or variable, we need an operational definition, as well. **Operationalization** means defining a variable, so that we know it when we see it.

Suppose you ask: 'Is Pakistan a failed state?' You adopt a definition of 'failed state' used by other researchers: 'a failed state' is a state experiencing high state vulnerability or risk of violence. You now have a conceptual definition of 'failed state'. But how do you know 'state vulnerability' when you see it? You cannot leave it to your subjective sense of what constitutes vulnerability on the part of a state. You need to decide what will enable you to judge the degree of vulnerability of a state. You might decide that 'state vulnerability' can be operationally defined as a state in which there exists (1) humanitarian emergencies as a result of massive movement of refugees or internally displaced persons; (2) sharp and/or severe economic decline; (3) a progressive deterioration of public services; (4) the intervention of other states or external political actors. You can then go and get evidence and data on each of these indicators of 'state vulnerability' in order to reach your conclusions about whether or not Pakistan is a failed state.

We will not be content to know your conclusions: we need to know how you reached them. You must make explicit what set of actions (operations) will lead another to achieve the same result when repeated. Other researchers should be able to follow your procedures and come up with the same findings. An operational definition provides travel instructions: sets of actions (operations) which will reveal to other researchers how you arrived at your findings. It specifies what empirical *indicators* or data will enable us to determine the presence or absence of a variable, or measure its extent. To operationalize the term 'speeding', we put a number on it: 70 mph. This becomes a proxy for 'speeding'. It also suggests the data that will enable us to determine when 'speeding' has occurred: a speedometer reading. Let's say you hypothesize that the higher someone's social class, the more likely they are to be conservative. You might choose to use different income levels to operationalize 'social class': less than $40,000 is 'lower' class, $40,000 to $79,999 is 'middle class', and $80,000 and over is 'upper class'; and to operationalize 'conservatives' on the basis of a series of questions about political issues. Perhaps you are interested in whether there is a difference in the 'personal adjustment' in the military of men and women. How do you know 'personal adjustment' when you see it? You decide that those who, in answer to the question 'How have you adjusted to being in the army?', responded that in general they were in good spirits, that they liked being in the army, and that they were satisfied with their army jobs and status, can be classified as well adjusted, personally.

Illustration: Lenin's explanation of World War I

Let's review the components of a hypothesis by considering how they combine to produce a well-known theory of the causes of World War I.

During World War I, a book by Vladimir Ilyich Lenin (1870–1924) was published, entitled *Imperialism, the Highest Stage of Capitalism* (1916). The book was inspired by a concern to understand the causes of the war that had engulfed Europe and was escalating into a global conflagration. In the process of developing an explanation of the war, Lenin also developed an argument about capitalism, imperialism, and revolution.

Lenin explains World War I as a consequence of intense imperialist rivalry among the major European powers. The source of his hypothesis was Marx's notion that the contradictions of capitalism would lead inevitably to revolutionary crisis and open the way to a transition to socialism. Marx had pointed to a number of contradictions of capitalist development:

1. Technological change under the direction of capitalism creates unemployment (a 'reserve army of labor'). This holds wages in check and depresses the consuming power of the working class.

2. Unemployment is an integral and essential element of the system: without it, capitalists would lose control over the labour market.

3. As capital accumulates, the rate of profit falls. This causes capitalists to interrupt the accumulation process, which produces economic crises and depressions.

4. The power of the working class to consume doesn't keep pace with the growth of production potential. As a result, production potential remains underutilized, and in place of actual economic expansion, stagnation and contraction eventually sets in.

Figure 6.3 shows how Lenin derived a hypothesis from Marx's theoretical work. Lenin observed that capitalist nations had avoided the crisis that Marx had predicted through overseas imperialism. He argued that:

1. finance capital responds to the falling rate of profit by combining into larger economic units—cartels, monopolies—in order to gain market power;

2. finance capitalists invest capital abroad in less developed regions to get a higher rate of return;

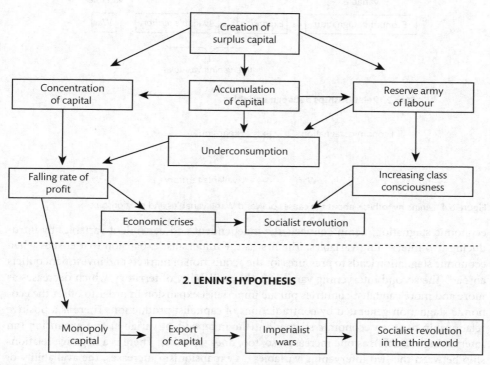

1. SOURCE OF HYPOTHESIS:
Marx's theoretical elaboration of the contradictions
of capitalism

Figure 6.3 The Source of Lenin's hypothesis about the causes of World War I
Source: Inspired by Gurley 1975: 54. Our thanks to David Lake, who used a variation of it in an undergraduate seminar at UCLA.

3. the flag follows finance capital: because government is needed to protect investment, to set up exclusive spheres of investment. As capital accumulates and profit rates fall, capitalist economies in competition with one another embark on an effort to divide up the world in order to secure external markets, investment outlets, and sources of food and raw materials;

4. once the entire world is split up, a re-division of territory can only come about through war. In the process of war, socialist revolutions occur abroad.

The imperialist solution to the problem of overproduction/under-consumption was to secure external markets and investment outlets abroad. This prevented socialist revolution at home (and, at the same time, made socialist revolution much more likely to occur in the underdeveloped regions due to the hyper-exploitation of workers there). Lenin's hypothesis was that World War I was the outcome of efforts by the imperialist powers to territorially re-divide the world among themselves. The temporal domain to which he intended this hypothesis to apply was 'the era of monopoly capitalism'.

We can identify the specific component of the hypothesis, as follows. The dependent variable is war in the era of monopoly capitalism; the hypothesized independent variable is

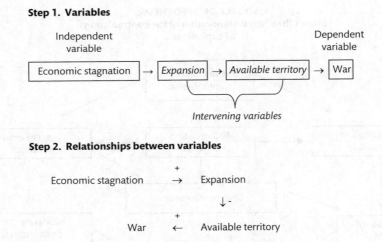

Figure 6.4 Lenin's hypothesis about the causes of World War I: variables and relationships

economic stagnation. Lenin connects the independent and dependent variables by introducing two intervening variables. The first is the imperialist expansion that ensues when economic stagnation leads to pressures for the acquisition of markets and investment outlets abroad. The second intervening variable is the availability of territory, which decreases as more and more capitalist countries pursue imperialist expansion in order to offset the economic stagnation generated by contradictions of capitalist production. There is a positive relationship between economic stagnation (the independent variable) and expansion (an intervening variable): as one increases, so, too, does the other. There is a negative relationship between the two intervening variables: as expansionism increases, the availability of territory decreases. There is also a negative relationship between the availability of territory and the potential for war: a decrease in the availability of territory increases the likelihood of war. Figure 6.4 provides a diagram of these variables and how they are related.

After formulating this hypothesis, Lenin investigated it by looking for evidence that would support it or prove it wrong. He presented data and evidence for each of his key variables, and relevant conclusions from leading scholars and economists, both Marxist and non-Marxist, including data on economic stagnation in the major belligerent countries, policies of imperialist expansion on the part of those states, and the decrease in the amount of available desirable territory into which these states might expand.

Answering normative questions

It is sometimes noted that normative political theorists tend not to be as explicit about their methods as are researchers concerned with empirical questions—that they are often 'silent on questions of method and approach' (Leopold and Stears 2008: 1). David Leopold and Marc Stears maintain that, in fact, 'the vast majority of students beginning advanced research in political theory in the United States and Britain' embark on their studies 'without any significant training in, and reflection on, the research methods that they will have to employ if they are to produce high quality work of their own' (2008: 2).

We have said that the research process we outline in this chapter is relevant to all types of research. Here we want to elaborate this point in relation to research that addresses normative questions. In our view, answers to normative and empirical questions can and should be developed in broadly similar ways.

Empirical and normative research

In previous chapters (Chapters 1 and 3), we discussed the distinction that has been institutionalized in political research between empirical and normative research. Empirical research is thought to concern questions about the 'real world', questions that can be answered with empirical data (data gathered through observations of the world around us); while normative research is seen as concerned with questions concerning what is best, just, right, or preferable in society, which are best answered through forms of argumentative discourse. But, as we have suggested in previous chapters, the distinction defined between empirical and normative research is overdrawn. Among other things, this has likely helped to obscure the extent to which generally similar methods are used to address both.

The empirical/normative distinction is predicated on the assumption that it is possible to wholly separate questions about what *is* (empirical questions) from questions about what *should* or *ought to be* (normative questions). However, as we pointed out in Chapter 3, many people engaged in political research have challenged this assumption, and this includes many normative political theorists, as well. In fact, there is an ongoing debate among political theorists concerning the relationship between normative political theory and empirical inquiry. The debate concerns what many perceive to be the gulf between 'ideal' foundational philosophical reflections on, for instance, rights, liberty, equality, or justice, and the real-world conditions and institutions in which problems relating to these issues arise and must be resolved. One position maintains that the point of normative political 'theory' is to arrive at a coherent *ideal*. The articulation of an ideal aids our practical understanding because it allows us to measure the distance between it (the ideal) and the real world. The other position argues that, since the ideal is constrained by what is possible, we need to integrate theory with a consideration of its implications and likely outcomes for the political world in which real citizens live. According to this view, the task of the political theorist is to investigate both political principles and the underlying 'facts' of political and social life that underpin them (Miller 2008). The aim of normative political theory is the clarification of underlying basic principles or arguments. But normative arguments that propose or justify one value system over another will lack relevance if they make no reference to related empirical and practical issues.

We can better understand the two positions by considering them in relation to theories of social justice. Theorists on one side of the debate argue that the fundamental principles of justice are logically independent of issues of feasibility and questions about human nature (e.g. Mason 2004, Cohen 2008); that only by removing itself from the world of empirical observation and the particularities of time and of place can normative political theory perform its proper task of identifying the actual meaning of 'justice', and of outlining the ways in which our world could be made to fit its demands (Stears 2005: 326). An example of what might be called 'ideal' theorizing is John Rawls' *Theory of Justice* (1971). In this highly influential work, John Rawls presents what he identifies as an 'ideal' theory of justice. This theory is 'ideal' in that it makes two idealizing assumptions: that (1) all comply with the principles of justice; and that (2) social conditions are such as to enable citizens and societies to abide by principles of political cooperation. Rawls says that, by abstracting from the world as it actually is (e.g. ignoring the possibility of law-breaking, or conditions that overwhelm the capacity of actors for moral reasoning), ideal theory allows us to find ideal principles of justice and to develop an understanding of how to reform our non-ideal world in line with these principles.

Theorists on the other side of the debate about normative theory and empirical inquiry argue that research on social justice has become detached from the real world; that theorists who focus on the question of what an ideally just society would look like neglect the empirical realities of real societies and the implications of their theorizing for pressing practical issues of social justice confronted by societies here and now. They argue that constructing a theory that can help resolve problems of social justice requires consideration of the non-ideal conditions and social institutions faced by actual political actors (e.g. Dunn 1990; Carens 2000; Farrelly 2007; Sen 2009).

In our view, analytically rigorous theoretical endeavour need not be comprised, but rather might be enhanced considerably, by giving due consideration to the diverse complexities that arise in real, non-ideal societies. Depending on the question, political theorists might combine the use of philosophical methods of logic, categorization, or conceptual analysis with any of the methods of data collection that researchers use to address empirical questions.

Empirical and normative questions, answers, and methods

Reflecting the views concerning ideal theory and empirical inquiry discussed above, is the tendency to think of normative questions as generally falling into one or the other of *two* basic *types*. The first are *questions in which principles, ideals, and concepts are the primary focus*. What *principles* ought to be adopted and enforced such that compliance with them will achieve social justice? What would an *ideally* just society look like? How is the *concept* of justice best understood? Theorists tend to address these sorts of questions by employing philosophical methods of logic, categorization, or conceptual analysis: by analysing the logical structure of a principle, systematizing the reasons that can validly be advanced for and against particular choices, or developing a conceptual framework. Theorists might engage in a form of argumentative discourse that, by drawing logical inferences and showing how the ideas presented were logically developed, convinces others that the conclusion reached is reasonable and plausible. Theorists might use any number of different methods of categorization to define the features that something has or doesn't have, by, for instance, comparing the similarity of an instance to a prototype. Theorists might break down or analyse concepts into their constituent parts using conceptual analysis: 'an attempt to provide an illuminating set of necessary and sufficient conditions for the (correct) application of a concept' (Audi 1983: 90), and a test of such sets using hypothetical examples and thought experiments.

The second type of questions normative political theorists ask are *questions that involve evaluating and criticizing substantive political, social, and economic practices and institutions*. Which institutions and practices are appropriate to implement the principles of distributive justice? Does equality of opportunity require inequality of liberty? These are at least in part answerable only by empirical inquiry and data from history and the social sciences. Consequently, theorists who address these sorts of questions often combine techniques from analytical philosophy (i.e., tools of logic, for analysing forms of language, and increasing argumentative clarity) with those from empirical social science.

Theorists might use any or all methods of gathering facts that empirical researchers use. A theorist addressing a question concerning existing beliefs might employ methods such as interviews, surveys, or the analysis of language or meaning in discourse and texts in order to chart expressed opinions and bring implicit assumptions to light. The research might engage with and incorporate the findings of sociologists, economists, and experts in social policy. It might seek to identify statistical correlations, and figure out causal mechanisms, as well. The question might concern how a value—justice, efficiency, national solidarity, welfare, security, democracy—ought to be understood. An argument might be developed concerning the implications of a particular conception of, or moral premise relating to, this value. It might be developed with reference to some particular policy or institutional area, and by appeal to logic and empirical evidence in varying. A researcher might reflect on the relevance and applicability of a theory to the clarification and solution of a normative issue or problem in a particular domain. For example, the research might involve analysing the usefulness of a particular theory of justice, or comparing the utility of several theories, for the study of problems relating to globalization, migration, nationalism, multiculturalism, education, ageing, changing gender roles, or global inequality.

In general, researchers addressing normative and empirical questions will develop answers to them in broadly similar ways. As in any research, the normative political theorists finds and formulates an interesting question, reads what others have written on that question, engages with this literature and, through that engagement, formulates an argument of his or her own.

We have previously argued that, irrespective of what kind of question a researcher addresses (descriptive, explanatory, predictive, prescriptive, or normative), thinking in terms of formulating a hypothesis in answer to it can help to clarify the argument and the kinds of evidence that will provide a meaningful demonstration of it. A *normative hypothesis* advances, for further discussion, analysis and investigation, an argument or suggestive proposition about what ought to be. Recall that a hypothesis consists of three elements: an independent variable, a dependent variable, and a proposition (a statement about the relationship between the variables). While we don't think of normative political theory as requiring a dependent and independent variable, normative questions nonetheless are concerned with connections and relations, with demonstrating relations between premises and conclusions, and indicating the nature of the relations between them. A normative hypothesis might state that the best type of X is Y; that the basis for deciding or justifying X ought to be Y, the legitimacy of X ought to be based on Y, or that X is just when conditions A, B, C are present. Investigation of these hypotheses would entail elaborating an argument about why this should be the case and establishing the plausibility and coherence of the argument, with the help, if relevant, of empirical or historical evidence.

We began this discussion by observing that normative political researchers are often silent about the methods they use. It is not a question of *whether* political theorists employ methods: they *do*. A variety of methods is used to address normative questions. What is at issue is their tendency not to reflect on the methods they use. Irrespective of what type of research is pursued, research should be systematic, self-aware, clear, and transparent. This enables others to evaluate the argument with respect to the kind and nature of its premises, the strength of the inferential links between premises and conclusions, and its possible criticisms or refutations.

Conclusions

We have organized our discussion of the various considerations and tasks involved in developing an answer to a research question around three basic requirements. The first requirement is that the answer be appropriate to the type of question that is being asked. The second requirement of an answer to a research question is that it makes a contribution to knowledge. The third is that your answer must be clearly and fully specified with regard to the factors or elements you think must be taken into consideration in order to answer your question, and how you think these factors or elements are related to each other.

We maintain that for all types of research, answers or arguments in response to research questions benefit from being formulated as a hypothesis and an investigation of it. We determine which ideas are most useful for understanding social life by turning our ideas into hypotheses and assessing them. A hypothesis articulates the contours and logic of the investigation. In all research, a hypothesis helps to make explicit the argument that is being developed and to guide research. Hypotheses can either be investigated by testing them with evidence (confirmatory research), or through their operation as a guide to a process of discovery (exploratory research).

Next up: How do you know if your hunch is right? What kind(s) of evidence would give you confidence that your proposition is probably correct or, alternatively, lead you to conclude that the proposition is probably wrong?

Questions

- What is the difference between a concept and a variable? How are the two related?
- What is a theory?
- What is the role of theory in political and social scientific inquiry? How does theory contribute to a furthering of our understanding of the political and social world?
- In what ways are the study of concepts important for political and social scientific inquiry?
- What is the function of operationalizing concepts?

Guide to Further Reading

Bell, Daniel and Avner De-Shalit (eds) (2003), *Forms of Justice: Critical Perspectives on David Miller's Political Philosophy* **(Lanham, MD: Rowman and Littlefield).**
Political philosophers have traditionally argued that there is a single, principled answer to the question of what justice is. But David Miller (*Principles of Social Justice*, Cambridge, MA: Harvard University Press, 1999) has theorized that justice can take many different forms. Taking this position as a starting point, this collection of articles consider whether justice takes one form or many by drawing real-world implications from theories of justice and examining in-depth social justice, national justice, and global justice.

Collier, David and Henry Brady (eds) (2004), *Rethinking Social Inquiry: Diverse Tools, Shared Standards* (Lanham, MD: Rowman and Littlefield).

Gerring, John (2001), *Social Science Methodology: A Criterial Framework,* Cambridge: Cambridge University Press. 'Concepts: General Criteria' and 'Strategies of Definition', pp. 35–86.

Goertz, Gary (2005), *Social Science Concepts: A User's Guide* (Princeton, NJ: Princeton University Press).

Leopold, David and Marc Stears (eds) (2008) *Political Theory: Methods and Approaches* (Oxford: Oxford University Press).

Sartori, Giovanni (ed.) (1984), *Social Science Concepts: A Systematic Analysis* (New York: Sage). Sartori's theoretical chapter, entitled 'Guidelines for Concept Analysis', explains how words acquire multiple meanings and provides a succinct discussion of the problems involved in defining concepts and finding suitable terms for them. It contains chapters examining key terms, e.g. consensus, development, ethnicity, integration, political culture, power, and revolution. In each of these chapters, the starting point is a word that has acquired a multiplicity of meanings.

Schmitter, P. (2008), 'The Design of Social and Political Research', in D. Della Porta and M. Keating, *Approaches and Methodologies in the Social Sciences: A Pluralist Perspective* (Cambridge: Cambridge University Press), 263–95.

Schramme, T. (2008), 'On the Relationship between Political Philosophy and Empirical Sciences', *Analyse und Kritik* 30: 613–26. Schramme argues that the findings of the empirical sciences might play a role in justifying normative claims in political philosophy. He describes how political theory has become a discipline divorced from empirical sciences, and outlines some functions that empirical studies might have in political philosophy.

 # References

Alvarez, M., J. A. Cheibub, F. Limongi, and P. Przeworski (1996), 'Classifying Political Regimes', *Studies in Comparative International Development* 31: 3–36.

Audi, R. (1983), 'The Applications of Conceptual Analysis', *Metaphilosophy* 14(2) (April): 87–106.

Bachrach, P. and M. S. Baratz (1962), 'Two Faces of Power', *American Political Science Review* 56(4) (December): 947–52.

Bollen, K. A. (1980), 'Issues in the Comparative Measurement of Political Democracy', *American Sociological Review* 45 (June): 370–90.

——(1993), 'Liberal Democracy: Validity and Method Factors in Cross-National Measures', *American Journal of Political Science* 37: 1207–30.

Bollen, K. A. and R. W. Jackman (1989), 'Democracy, Stability, and Dichotomies', *American Sociological Review* 54: 612–21.

Bollen, K. A. and P. Paxton (2000), 'Subjective Measures of Liberal Democracy', *Comparative Political Studies* 33(1) (February): 58–86.

Carens, J. (2000), *Culture, Citizenship, and Community* (Oxford: Oxford University Press).

Cohen, G. A. (2008), *Rescuing Justice and Equality* (Cambridge, MA: Harvard University Press).

Collier, D. and S. Levitsky (1997), 'Democracy with Adjectives: Conceptual Innovation in Comparative Research', *World Politics* 49(3) (April): 430–51.

——and J. E. Mahon (1993), 'Conceptual "Stretching" Revisited: Alternative Views of Categories in Comparative Analysis', *American Political Science Review* 87(4) (December): 845–55.

Coppedge, M., and W. H. Reinicke (1990), 'Measuring Polyarchy'. *Studies in Comparative International Development* 25: 51–72.

Corbin, J. and Strauss, A. (1990), 'Grounded Theory Research: Procedures, Canons and Evaluative Criteria', *Qualitative Sociology* 13: 3–21.

Dahl, R. A. (1957), 'The Concept of Power', *Behavioral Science* 2: 201–15.

——(1971), *Polyarchy: Participation and Opposition* (New Haven, CT: Yale University Press).

——(1989), *Democracy and its Critics* (New Haven, CT: Yale University Press).

Dunn, J. (1990) 'Reconceiving the Content and Character of Modern Political Community', in J. Dunn (ed.), *Interpreting Political Responsibility* (Oxford: Polity), 193–215.

Farrelly, C. (2005), 'Making Deliberative Democracy a More Practical Political Ideal', *European Journal of Political Theory* 4(2): 200–8.

——(2007), 'Justice in Ideal Theory: A Refutation', *Political Studies* 55 (December), 844–64.

Gerring, J. (1999), 'What Makes a Concept Good? A Criterial Framework for Understanding Concept Formation in the Social Sciences', *Polity* 31(3) (spring): 357–93.

——(2001), *Social Science Methodology: A Criterial Framework* (Cambridge: Cambridge University Press).

Glaser, B. G. and A. L. Strauss (1967), *The Discovery of Grounded Theory* (Chicago: Aldine).

Gurley, John G. (1975), *Challengers to Capitalism: Marx, Lenin, and Mao* (Stanford, CA: Stanford Alumni Association).

Guzzini, S. (1993), 'Structural Power: The Limits of Neorealist Power Analysis', *International Organization* 47(3): 443–78.

Hoover, K. and T. Donovan (2004), *The Elements of Social Scientific Thinking*, 8th edition (Belmont, CA: Wadsworth/Thompson).

Jacobson, G. (1978), 'The Effects of Campaign Spending in Congressional Elections', *American Political Science Review* 72 (June): 469–91.

Kahl, Colin H. (2006), *States, Scarcity, and Civil Strife in the Developing World* (Princeton, NJ: Princeton University Press).

Kumar, R. (2005), *Research Methodology. A Step-by-Step Guide for Beginners*, 2nd revised edition (London: Sage Publications Ltd.).

Lenin, V. I. (1916), *Imperialism, the Highest Stage of Capitalism: An Outline* (New York: International Publishers, 1939).

Leopold, D. and M. Stears (2008), 'Introduction', in D. Leopold and M. Stears (eds), *Political Theory: Methods and Approaches* (Oxford: Oxford University Press), 1–10.

Lukes, S. (1974), *Power: A Radical View* (New York: Palgrave Macmillan).

Mason, A. (2004), 'Just Constraints', *British Journal of Political Science* 34(2): 251–68.

Merton, R. K. (1968). *Social Theory and Social Structure* (Glencoe, IL: Free Press).

Miller, D. (2008), 'Political Philosophy for Earthlings', in D. Leopold and M. Stears (edssew), *Political Theory: Methods and Approaches* (Oxford: Oxford University Press), 29–48.

Nye, J. S. (1990), *Bound to Lead: The Changing Nature of American Power* (New York: Basic Books).

——(2002), *The Paradox of American Power: Why the World's Only Superpower Can't Go It Alone* (New York: Oxford University Press).

——(2004), *Soft Power: The Means to Success in World Politics* (New York: Public Affairs).

Pollins, B. (2007), 'Beyond Logical Positivism: Reframing King, Keohane, and Verba', in R. N. Lelbow and M. I. Lichbach (eds), *Theory and Evidence in Comparative Politics and International Relations* (Basingstoke: Palgrave/Macmillan), 87–106.

Ragin, C. (2000), *Fuzzy-Set Social Science* (Chicago: University of Chicago Press).

Rawls, J. (1971), *A Theory of Justice* (Cambridge, MA: The Belknap Press of Harvard University Press).

Sartori, G. (1970), 'Concept Misformation in Comparative Politics', *American Political Science Review* 64: 1033–53.

——(1984), 'Guidelines for Concept Analysis', in Giovanni Sartori (ed.), *Social Science Concepts: A Systematic Analysis* (Beverly Hills, CA: Sage), 15–85.

——(1987), *The Theory of Democracy Revisited* (Chatham, NJ: Chatham House).

Schmitter, P. (2008), 'The Design of Social and Political Research', in D. Della Porta and M. Keating, *Approaches and Methodologies in the Social Sciences: A Pluralist Perspective* (Cambridge: Cambridge University Press), 263–95.

Sen, Amartya (2009), *The Idea of Justice* (Cambridge, MA: Harvard University Press).

Shively, W. P. (1989), *The Craft of Political Research*, 2nd edition (Englewood Cliffs, NJ: Prentice-Hall, Inc.).

Stears, Marc (2005), 'The Vocation of Political Theory: Principles, Empirical Inquiry and the Politics of Opportunity', *European Journal of Political Theory* 4(4): 325–50.

Strange, S. (1994), *States and Markets*, 2nd edition (London: Pinter).

Research Design

 Chapter Summary

Previous chapters have focused on how to find and formulate a research question (Chapter 5) and how to develop a hunch about the answer to one (Chapter 6). In this chapter, we focus on designing research to investigate your hunch. Our discussion focuses on the following issues:

- basic principles of research design;
- types of research design;
- selecting cases and units of observation and analysis;
- types of evidence researchers use to answer the questions they ask;
- methods of collecting data;
- sources of data.

Introduction

You have a well-crafted research question. It is one that you have shown (1) has significance for a topic or issue relating to the subject matter of our field; (2) is researchable (it can be answered through conducting research); and (3) has not yet been answered definitively. You also have a hunch about the factors you think must be taken into consideration in order to answer your question, and how you think these factors are related to each other. Together, these factors and their relations constitute what we call a '*hypothesis*': a reasoned, clearly specified hunch or expectation about the answer to your question that will guide and focus your research. In Chapter 6 we said that your response to a research question will consist of a hypothesis and an investigation of it; and we discussed the basic components of a hypothesis, and how to formulate one. We turn now to a discussion of how to investigate it.

So you have a hunch or argument about the answer to your research question. How do you know whether your hunch is right? And how will you convince others that it is right? Your strategy for providing a convincing 'test' or demonstration of your hypothesis is what we call a 'research design'. A research design specifies the sort of evidence you need to investigate your hypothesis, and describes how the evidence will be collected and analysed.

In this chapter we first discuss the basic principles of research design. We then provide an overview of (1) types of research design; and (2) methods of data collection. Research designs and data collection methods are often confused with each other, and indeed there is a certain amount of overlap between them. The overall strategy you will employ to demonstrate or investigate your argument, is your *research design*. The sort of data that will enable you to implement this strategy, and where and how they will be obtained, is your *method of data collection.* A research design answers the question 'What sort of evidence will test my hypothesis?' The answer might be 'data on the perceptions, attitudes, and opinions of politicians'. A data-collection method answers the question 'How and where can I get this information?' It might specify, for instance, that we will use surveys or interviews, ethnographic research, or content analysis, or all four together. It will specify whether the data will be collected using qualitative or quantitative methods; and whether we will collect them ourselves or use data collected by others.

In some fields, the term 'research design' is also used to refer to the overall plan for addressing a research problem or question. In this usage, the 'research design' includes the definition of the research question, the hypotheses to be examined, including the number and type of variables to be studied and the relationship between them; and the schedule and budget for carrying out the research. While a research design and a data-collection method are closely related in the sense that a particular method of data collection must fit with the strategy defined by a research design, they represent two separate steps or components in the research process.

Often students will come to us and say something along the lines of the following: 'I am going to be in Egypt over the semester break and, as I want to write my thesis on Egyptian foreign policy, was wondering whether you think it would be a good idea to try and conduct some interviews while I am there?' In most cases our response will be, 'I don't know: it depends on the research question you intend to address and what hypothesis you decide to investigate.'[1]

The point is, you cannot collect data or gather information until you know precisely what sort of evidence you need. What you will need to be looking for is evidence that would confirm or disconfirm the argument you plan to advance or investigate; but you won't know what sort of evidence that *is*, unless you know what argument or hypothesis you are putting forward for investigation. To call upon the familiar 'toolbox' metaphor, it is as if you said 'There is something in the basement that we want to repair. Should we use a hammer or a wrench?' How can we know which tool to suggest if we don't know the nature of the problem and how you think you might go about solving it?[2] *First,* you formulate a research question and a hunch about what might provide an answer to it; *then* you can decide what information you will need to collect in order to confirm or disconfirm your hypothesis. Only then will you know whether it would be useful to conduct interviews, and if so, whom you should interview and what you should ask.

Basic principles of research design

Before you begin your research, you will need to think carefully and creatively about what sort of research will enable you to answer your question or test your hypothesis *in a convincing way.* Your research design is the culmination of this thinking. It specifies what will enable you to draw logical, valid, and reliable conclusions about your hypothesis. A good research design has the following attributes:

1. it specifies the type of research and techniques of data collection appropriate to the objectives of the project;

2. it makes explicit the logic which enables you to draw inferences—logical conclusions based on the information you collect or observations you make;

3. it identifies the type of evidence that not only confirms your hypothesis or argument, but provides a convincing 'test' of it;

4. it decreases threats to the internal and external validity of your findings;

5. it ensures that your findings are reliable.

Different types of research design and methods of data collection are not more or less rigorous than others; they are only more or less appropriate for the task at hand. A saw is not better or worse than a wrench; it is only more or less useful in relation to a specific task. A research design is good if it allows researchers to draw valid inferences. It should provide a structure of inquiry that enables us to draw *logical* conclusions on the basis of known facts or premises; and it should make explicit of the logic linking of the facts we know (that we collect or observe) to those we don't (those that are the subjects of our research questions and hypotheses). The process of using the facts we know to draw logical conclusions about facts we do not know is what we call inference (King, Keohane, and Verba 1994: 46). This is the basic logic that underlies most thinking. However, in conducting research, the process must be made explicit and follow certain rules.

Your research must be presented in a way that is clear, orderly, and systematic enough so that someone else will be able to retrace your steps and arrive at the same results and conclusions. Knowledge is the product of research that is open at every step to checking and double-checking by others. Consequently, you must be both transparent and explicit. You must describe what you did (or plan to do) in clear, simple language.

The components of a research project should be designed to provide a convincing test of your hypothesis. As David de Vaus puts it, rather than seeking *evidence that is consistent* with our argument or hypothesis, we should seek *evidence that provides a compelling test* of it (de Vaus 2001: 11). You can usually find empirical support for almost any hypothesis. So rather than marshalling evidence to fit an argument or hypothesis, you should seek evidence that can 'test' it against rival perspectives, arguments, or hypotheses (see the discussion of 'literature reviews' in Chapter 5) and show why your explanation or interpretation is to be preferred. Silence your sceptics by raising the objections or questions that they might raise. Assume their point of view and argue, on their behalf, against yourself. Think carefully about what sort of evidence will enable you to make comparisons and judgements between alternative possible explanations, and to provide the analytic leverage you need to demonstrate that your hypothesis is in some way better, more credible, useful, accurate, or illuminating than its rivals.

The better the research design, the more it decreases threats to validity. A study is valid if its measures actually measure what they claim to, and if there are no logical errors in drawing conclusions from the data. Researchers distinguish among a variety of different types of validity. We will discuss two types: internal validity and external validity.

Internal validity often refers to the extent to which we can be confident that the independent (causal) variable produced the observed effect. The more the structure of a study eliminates alternative interpretations, the better we are able to draw unambiguous conclusions from our results, and 'the stronger the internal validity of the study' (de Vaus 2001: 28). What is at issue is whether there are factors, other than your independent variables, that might be affecting the outcome. Is the independent variable responsible for variation in the dependent variable? What other possible causes might there be for the relationship between the variables? Could something else have been responsible for the variation in the dependent variable? Could there be confounding factors? These are the biggest threat to validity: if you do not design your research in a way that enables you to rule out other factors or alternative explanations, the internal validity of your study will be threatened. **External validity** refers to 'the extent to which results from a study can be generalized beyond the particular study' (de Vaus 2001: 28). Can you generalize your findings? Are your conclusions likely to apply more widely? Are they applicable to other similar situations or cases?

Research should be designed to ensure that your findings are reliable. **Reliability** refers to the 'repeatability' or 'consistency' of your findings. A research design is reliable if other researchers can perform exactly the same procedures and come up with the same results (your findings are repeatable). A reliable measure is reliable if it gives us the same result over and over again (assuming that what we are measuring isn't changing).

Now that we know what a research design does for us, let's consider different types of research designs used in political research.

Types of research design

The types of research design that are commonly used in our field include experimental designs, cross-sectional and longitudinal designs, and comparative designs. Below, we discuss experimental designs, which we discuss further in Chapter 8. Following that is a brief overview of what is conventionally called 'quasi-experimental' or 'non-experimental' designs. These are used in most social science research. They lack the characteristics of a true experiment, but endeavour to employ other means of controlling the environment and isolating the effects of particular factors or variables. We outline the basic principles of cross-sectional and longitudinal designs. We then provide a brief introduction to comparative designs, which we take up in greater detail in Chapter 9.

Experimental designs

Experimental designs are often thought to most closely resemble the true scientific method (see Chapter 2), and as such they are widely regarded as being the most effective design for testing whether or not two variables are causally related. They manage to do this thanks to the rigorous use of experimental control. This helps to overcome one of the main problems that researchers face when they want to investigate causal relationships: there are a vast number of potentially important variables that may influence any given political phenomena, and in the absence of rigorous controlled experiments (not dissimilar to those used in medical research), it is very difficult to know which are responsible for causing the phenomena under investigation. One of the great strengths of experimental research is that the researcher can control the environment and manipulate particular variables of causal interest with great precision. Indeed, the defining characteristic of experimental research is intervention by the researcher in the data-gathering process (Morton and Williams

2008). We call the data gathered by intervention (or treatment, as it is sometimes known) experimental data.

Broadly speaking there are three main ways of carrying out experimental research: in a laboratory, in the field, and by utilizing natural occurrences. In laboratory experiments, the subjects are recruited to a common location where the experiment takes place. The laboratory experiment is designed to ensure that the researcher has as much control over the environment to which subjects are exposed as possible. In this way the experimental group and the control group can be exposed to exactly the same environment except for the experimental intervention. Accordingly, any difference that is recorded on the post-test measurement of the dependent variable can be confidently attributed to the presence (or absence) of the intervention. However, because of concerns about the artificial environment of laboratory experiments, some political scientists favour the more natural setting of field experiments. In field experiments, the intervention by the researcher takes place in real-world environments, and subjects may not even know that they are participating in an experiment. This obviously raises some ethical issues, to do with informed consent and deceit (which we discuss in detail later in this chapter). But as Gerber and Green (2003: 94) observe, field experiments have two main strengths. First, random assignment ensures unbiased inference about cause and effect, and second, the natural settings ensure that the results will tell us something useful about the real world.

The third main type of experimental design is often referred to as a natural experiment. The natural experiment relies on naturally occurring events as interventions rather than interventions controlled by the researcher. Even though in this case the researcher is not doing the intervening, the approach taken with the data is as if the researcher has.

There is often thought to be a trade-off between these different types of designs. In particular, it is often argued that laboratory experiments tend to have relatively high levels of internal validity but low levels of external validity, whereas field experiments tend to have higher levels of external validity but lower levels of internal validity. That is, with lab experiments, the controlled setting in which the experiment takes place enables the researcher to have a high degree of confidence in the effect of the causal variable on the outcome of interest (high internal validity). However, at the same time, because of the artificial environment of the laboratory setting, it is less certain whether the findings from the experiment may be applied or generalized to real-world settings (low external validity). By contrast, since field experiments take place in the real world and reproduce as closely as possible the conditions under which different political phenomena occur, they tend to have higher levels of external validity, meaning the findings can be generalized with more confidence.

Given these different strengths and weaknesses, rather than prioritizing one approach over the other, or regarding one approach as inherently superior to the other, it makes more sense to think about how the two approaches can be combined. For a study to really stand up, it should be possible to try and examine it in both settings. As Elinor Ostrom (2007: 26–7) says, 'To test theory adequately, we need to use methods that together combine external and internal validity. One gains external validity in doing field research, but internal validity in the laboratory'.

Although experimental research has certain obvious strengths, particularly when it comes to testing causal hypotheses, it is still not used particularly widely in political research. However, there is the potential for it to be used much more widely than it is. In Chapter 8 we discuss some of the main reasons why it is not used more widely, with reference to some of the restrictions that ethical issues and practical considerations play in determining what sort of questions can be answered. But we also go on to discuss the potential avenues for future research.

However, even if experimental research is not used widely, it has still been incredibly influential in terms of shaping how we can study politics. Most of our research designs are, in effect, an effort to approximate the logic of experimental design as closely as possible and in the positivist hierarchy, Large N quantitative analysis is often seen as the next best thing to doing experimental research.

Quasi-experimental or non-experimental designs

'*Quasi-experimental*', or *non-experimental, designs* are employed in most social science research. In these designs, one characteristic of a true experiment will be missing, usually either randomization or the use of a separate control group. But, more generally, we can say that quasi-or non-experimental designs differ from experimental designs in the *degree of control* a researcher has over the subjects of research (that which is being studied) and the conditions in which the subjects exist. When researchers have complete control over an experiment, they allow one and only one variable to change. They then can trace the effects of that change to the dependent variable and measure how it responds. The greater the *degree of control* we have over our subjects and their environments, the better able we are to assess change in the dependent variable (DV) as a result of change in the independent variable (IV); and the greater the internal validity of our research.

Research in the social sciences rarely permits complete control over subjects and their environments. Instead, through the use of quasi-or non-experimental designs, we employ methods of observation and data collection which, as far as possible, hold all conditions constant but one. Types of quasi-experimental designs include **cross-sectional** and **longitudinal studies**, and comparative studies. We often use these designs to increase our ability to attribute changes in our DV to changes in our IV and, thus, to increase the internal validity of our research.

Cross-sectional and longitudinal designs

Cross-sectional designs involve analysing a sample, or cross-section, of a population at a single point in time. Longitudinal designs explore changes or trends over time. In a longitudinal study, research is repeated with the same sample or set of cases over two or more intervals. To illustrate how these two designs might differ in how they address the same question, consider the hypothesis that as countries get richer income distribution becomes more unequal. A researcher might employ either a cross-sectional research design or a longitudinal design to investigate this hypothesis. Using a cross-sectional design, a researcher might select sample of countries with different levels of economic growth (low, medium, high) and analyse the association between level of growth and change in inequality. With a longitudinal design, a researcher might select a country or countries that have moved from lower to higher levels of development to see whether income distribution *over time* was consistent with the trend suggested by the hypothesis.

A key feature of a cross-sectional design is that it is concerned with explaining variation between places or between people at a single point in time, rather than explaining variation within places over time. An example of a cross-sectional study is one conducted by Timmons Roberts, Bradley Parks, and Alexis Vasquez to investigate 'Who Ratifies Environmental Treaties and Why?' (2004). In this study, Timmons Roberts and his co-authors try to explain variation between different states' behaviour with respect to international environmental issues. To explore this question they conduct a cross-sectional study on the determinants of whether or not states have ratified international environmental treaties, using data from 177 countries. They find that most of the variance in the ratification of environmental treaties is accounted for by three variables: 'disadvantaged insertion into the world economy' (defined in terms of countries with a narrow export base), voice and accountability through domestic institutions (the degree to which citizens choose those who govern them and the independent role that the media plays in keeping government accountable), and civil society pressure (number of nongovernmental organizations, NGOs, in the country). In particular, 'the number of NGOs in a nation appears virtually synonymous with its likelihood to participate in environmental treaties' (2004: 39). While the dependent variable for this study is a measure of how many environmental treaties were ratified between 1946 and 1999, the independent variables (a country's position in the world economy, voice and accountability, number of NGOs per country) are drawn from a single point in time (mostly from 2000).

When data are collected at *a single point in time,* as in a cross-sectional study, analysts must be careful about drawing any conclusions about *changes over time*. In order to overcome this problem, repeated cross-sectional studies can be used to introduce a longitudinal element into the research design. An example of a repeated cross-sectional study is William Mishler and Richard Rose's (2007) investigation into how citizens, socialized by authoritarian regimes in quintessentially authoritarian cultures, can learn the attitudes and behaviours necessary to become loyal and effective citizens of new democratic regimes. William Mishler and Richard Rose address this question by constructing a repeated cross-sectional study to test two competing hypotheses drawn from two theories that dominate the study of processes of political learning and relearning.

Cultural theories hypothesize that basic political attitudes inculcated through early life socialization are deeply ingrained and change only slowly over extended periods. *Institutional theories* emphasize adult political experiences or political 'relearning' based on individuals' rational assessments of contemporary institutions and circumstances. Attitudes and behaviours are malleable and adaptable. 'Thus, later life experiences are expected to play a greater role in shaping adult opinions' (Mishler and Rose 2007: 823). The two theories yield different predictions: cultural theories 'predict substantial generational differences in political attitudes . . . that change little over an individual's lifetime'; institutional theories 'predict substantial changes among individuals across either generations or the life cycle' (Mishler and Rose 2007: 824). The authors test these competing perspectives using data from a series of national probability surveys conducted in Russia between 1992 and 2005. Each survey is an independent cross-section of the population and not part of a panel design (one in which a particular set of respondents are questioned repeatedly). Although the content of the surveys changes over time to reflect changing conditions in Russia, they include a core of questions asked consistently over time to facilitate comparisons. Their evidence suggested that 'individual assessments of contemporary political and economic experiences', and that 'Russians' lifelong socialisation into an authoritarian culture by an authoritarian regime is not in itself an insurmountable obstacle to the development of democracy in Russia' (Mishler and Rose 2007: 832).

While repeated cross-sectional studies can be used to measure trends or 'aggregate' change over time, they don't measure 'individual' development or change. This type of design might therefore be less satisfactory for investigating, for example, the relationship between individuals' civic orientations and political participation. As Jan Leighly points out, studies that rely on cross-sectional survey data on individuals' characteristics, such as civic orientations, as predictors of participation, assume that positive civic orientations are causally prior to acts of participation. But the direction of causality can run in the opposite direction: participation can lead to changes in individuals' political attitudes, and particularly in their sense of political efficacy and sophistication (1995: 186). Studies of political participation therefore need to look at individuals' acts of participation, and track how their participation decisions change, over time (1995: 198). This is what longitudinal designs allow us to do. They study processes of individual development and change over time, and the effects of earlier events or characteristics on later outcomes.

There are two main types of longitudinal design. In a 'cohort' study, the researcher selects a group of people within a delineated population, i.e. having a similar characteristic or experience (e.g. an age or ethnic group), and charts the individuals' development processes from a particular time point. In a panel study, the researcher chooses a sample, often a randomly selected national one, and collects information on it at two or more points over time. While panel studies gather information on the same people at each time point, the number of participants tends not to be constant over time, because of attrition. This can introduce bias into the results. Longitudinal data are particularly useful in answering questions about the dynamics of change. For example, under what conditions do voters change political party affiliation? What are the respective roles of mass media and friends in changing political attitudes? It is also useful in predicting long-term or cumulative effects that are normally hard to analyse in a cross-sectional study.

Comparative designs

Comparative research designs are perhaps the most widely used research design in political research. In a sense everything is comparative. We can have comparative experimental designs, comparative cross-sectional designs, and comparative longitudinal designs. We can even think of the single country case study as a type of comparative design, since it usually involves a comparison of some type or another, whether it is between regions within the country or between periods over time. Within the comparative framework it is common to distinguish between three main types of research design. There are large-N studies (where N refers to the number of countries—or cases—that are compared), small-N studies (involving the analysis of a small number of countries, typically 2, 3, 4 . . . but with no real upper limit) and single-N studies (otherwise known as case studies). These designs are distinguished primarily in terms of how many countries (or cases) are compared, but also in terms of how the countries for analysis are selected. Both aspects of case selection are very important. These are discussed in detail in Chapter 9.

There is often thought to be a trade-off between the in-depth, intensive knowledge derived from the study of a small number of cases, on the one hand, and the extensive, cross-case knowledge based on the study of a large number of cases, on the other—although this is often overstated. Small-N studies or single-country case studies are often used to uncover causal paths and mechanisms and assess specific mechanisms identified in theories. This is frequently referred to as **process tracing**. Research using a large number of cases may observe a strong statistical relation between two variables, and may use a theory to describe these statistical results. But if the researcher is unable to observe directly the key mechanisms of the theory, it will be difficult to know if the mechanisms producing the statistical relation are the same as those described in the theory. Selecting a small number of cases for in-depth investigation can enable a researcher to test for the existence of these mechanisms. The study of a small number of cases can also enable a researcher to investigate a case that is theoretically anomalous. Detailed study of a case that deviates from theoretical expectations may generate findings that lead us to substantially revise or altogether discard existing theories. Explaining anomalies can also be a source of new theories. In-depth investigation of a small number of cases can also help in generating hypotheses and theories in developing fields of inquiry.

Because case study designs can incorporate a broader history and wider context than can other designs, case study research is generally strong in dealing with two threats to internal validity: the threats which 'history' and 'maturation' present to the validity of a study. 'History' refers to historical or contextual factors, and 'maturation' to natural changes that affect the relationship between the independent variables and the outcome. Case study research is generally weaker in external validity (i.e. generalizability) because it includes only a small number of cases of some more general phenomenon (Gerring 2007: 43). Greater generality can be achieved by using a larger set of cases (as, for instance, in comparative case study designs). However, extending the analysis to broader contexts might lead to conceptual stretching and, thus, threaten the conceptual validity of the study (Collier and Mahony 1996: 69; see Chapter 6 for a discussion of 'conceptual stretching').

Research costs will also be a factor in the number of cases you select to study. If each case requires a limited amount of easily collected information, you might include many, or even all, relevant cases. If you need a great deal of information, or the information you need is harder to collect, you will examine fewer cases—perhaps only one or two. Cross-national studies of war that rely on quantitative measures that are easily computed from available statistical sources (e.g. United Nations annuals or computerized data banks) might include every country in the world. But, a study of the impact of privatization policies on social inequalities among multi-ethnic populations might require more detailed information that can be gathered only through close analysis and would lead the researcher to focus on only a few cases.

You must provide a rationale for why the specific case or set of cases you selected, from among all those in the larger population, were chosen. Researchers may select cases because they are *critical* (to testing a theory), *revelatory* (reveal relationships which cannot be studied by other means) or *unusual* (throws light on extreme cases) (Yin 1984).

But whatever the purpose they are chosen to serve, it is important that they are selected with care, and that the selection is based on the type of case that will provide the most convincing test or investigation of your hypothesis. Ultimately, the choice of how many and which cases you study and how you will study them will be determined by your research question and the hypothesis that you intend to investigate, though it is becoming more common to integrate these different research designs together, so as not to leave out either the general or the specific.

Types of research, types of design

Empirical questions (descriptive, explanatory, or predictive questions) are concerned with how something works, why things happened the way they did or what might be the outcome of current trends or conditions. An answer to a *descriptive question* might involve describing the characteristics of something; or modelling how it works or behaves. Common designs for these questions are case studies that provide an in-depth understanding of a process, event, or situation. *Explanatory questions* need a design that enables the researcher to determine whether one or more variables causes or affects one or more outcome variables, and to rule out other feasible explanations. *Predictive questions* require research designs that enable researchers to forecast future developments, based on an analysis of current events and relevant theories. We can analyse evidence and find that event A causes or explains event B (an *explanation*), and then predict that if A continues to increase, we will likely have a greater amount of B in the future (White and Clark 1983: 23). Predictive questions require you to show that if certain conditions or circumstances prevail, a certain outcome is likely to occur or come into being.

Prescriptive questions are concerned with finding information to solve political problems. To investigate a hypothesis about what would be best to do in response to a problem, the researcher will inventory available options, weigh the pros and cons of each for achieving the desired outcome, and, based on this analysis, advance an argument for a policy, using existing theoretical and empirical research (e.g. case studies). The researcher clearly defines the question to be answered or problem to be resolved; establishes relevant evaluation criteria so as to be able to compare, measure, and select among alternatives (e.g. cost, net benefit, effectiveness, efficiency, equity, administrative ease, legality, political acceptability); identifies alternative policies; and evaluates the costs and benefits of each, and the degree to which criteria are met in each of them.

Normative questions are usually settled through reflection on which view, when fully developed, offers the most coherent and convincing argument (Rawls 1993: 53). The 'test' of a normative hypothesis consists of two interrelated components: (1) the logical consistency of the ideas—the conclusion and all points leading up to it must follow from the original premises; and (2) consideration of the arguments of other theorists who have written about these issues, both those that provide support for your own, and those that raise criticisms and concerns that you will need to address if you are going to make a convincing case for your point of view. The appropriate research design, therefore, involves tracking down, as far as possible, persuasive arguments that certain conclusions follow logically from certain basic principles—principles over which, we can reasonably hope, far-reaching agreement can be reached. The method is to render such arguments—in respect to both basic and derivative principles—as clear, open, and logical as possible.[3]

In normative political analysis, the chief concern is with advancing an argument that is clear, logically sound, and rationally convincing. The researcher finds an interesting question, reads what others have written on the subject, engages with these works, and forms a carefully reasoned argument in reaction to them, with help, if relevant, of empirical or historical evidence. Depending on the research question, the research might be analytic, critical, genealogical, deconstructive, or interpretive; and draw on methods employed in analytical or applied philosophy, or the history of political thought. The aim might be to provide conceptual frameworks for deliberation, to analyse the logical structure of a principle, or to record and systematize the reasons that can validly be advanced for and against particular choices. In these cases, the researcher might employ the philosophical method of conceptual analysis, logic, and classification. The aim might be to draw out implications of a moral premise within some limited problem area, appealing to logic and empirical evidence in varying degrees in the process. Some researchers might be concerned with the interpretation of existing beliefs. Their aim is to ascertain what people actually think by charting expressed opinions and bringing implicit assumptions to light. The analysis might be concerned to uncover and examine a value—justice, efficiency, national solidarity, welfare, security, democracy—that informs political policies and institutions and offer an interpretation of how that value ought to be understood. In these cases, the research might employ interpretive methods concerned with working out exactly what a text is saying and why it's saying it in the way it does.

Data-gathering strategies: how the data are collected

Part of your research design involves determining what data and which data sources you will use to answer your research question. You should describe the data required to investigate your hypotheses and explain how and where you will obtain it. What sources are there for these data? Are they generally available to political researchers? Do the data exist at all? Are there problems of availability, reliability, standardization? Can they be successfully overcome?

Data collection involves setting the boundaries for the study, and collecting information through observations, interviews, documents, visual materials, and published statistical and other data. You must set the boundaries for the study in advance of data gathering, including (a) the time frame, or *temporal domain;* (b) the place, or *spatial domain*; (c) the *actors* or units that are the relevant focus of the examination; and (d) the *variables* or factors you think are important for arriving at an answer to your research question and that are, in fact, components of your hypothesis (answer). You are then ready to collect information. This information can be gathered from a variety of different sources.

There are many different ways to collect data: through ethnographic research, surveys and questionnaires, interviews, observations, or the analysis of existing documents and texts. Data can be gathered using more, or less, structured methods: for instance, using open-ended and flexible questions, or questions to be answered by respondents selecting from among a fixed set of choices. The main instrument for gathering data might be the researcher herself (it may be that data are not 'collected' at all, but rather are co-produced by the observer and what is being observed), or instruments such as standardized surveys that are administered in a fashion that minimizes researcher bias. The method might entail gathering data through direct contact with the subject, as in the use of focus groups or ethnographic methods; or without direct contact, as in the case of mailed surveys. You can collect the data yourself through any of these means; use data collected by others, including statistical sources, oral histories, memoirs, newspapers, government documents, public opinion surveys, and interviews; or use a combination of both. *Any data collection method can be used for any type of research design.* No single source has a complete advantage over the others; and various combinations of methods might be complementary and used in tandem. Your hypothesis determines in large part the kind of data required and suggests methods for collecting it. However, practical limitations (e.g. time, money, skill, ethical concerns) will also enter into your calculations and choices.

Let's briefly consider some main data-collection methods, what each entails and what sort of data or evidence each provides.

Questionnaires and surveys

Sometimes we need to know the personal experiences, perceptions, opinions, and attitudes of influential individuals in order to answer a research question. To get this information we can use questionnaires and surveys that ask people questions about particular topics that can reveal inside views of the political process. These can be mailed, handed out, or conducted in interview format (see Chapters 10 and 11).

Survey research is a method of gathering data from respondents thought to be representative of some population, using an instrument composed of closed or open-ended items (questions). It involves selecting the people to be approached (sampling), translating the broad objectives of the study into questions that will obtain the necessary information (questionnaire design), collecting data through questionnaires or interviews (fieldwork), and coding and inputting the responses (data processing). This is a major form of data collection in the social sciences, and is frequently used in political research.

Surveys combine a method of obtaining information from people by asking questions and modern random sampling procedures that allow a relatively small number of people to represent a much larger population (Schuman and Presser 1996: 1). They are a valuable resource for examining a wide range of topics, and can provide an accurate and reliable insight into what ordinary people think about politics and how they do politics. They rely on samples, which are selected from a particular group of people or other units (such as households, businesses, schools, etc.) that the researcher wishes to study. If we were to interview everybody in a population (e.g. all voters, all asylum seekers), it would be incredibly time-consuming and expensive. Surveying a representative sample of the population allows the researcher to make generalizations about the attributes of a given population without having to actually interview everyone in that population. If the sample is chosen in a haphazard or subjective way, then there is little hope of making accurate generalizations about the wider population we are interested in.

Interviewing and focus groups

We have said that one of the ways researchers try to find out about the social world is to ask people questions, and that this can be done by asking people to fill in questionnaires (surveys). It can also be done through interviews conducted via telephone, internet, through formal face-to-face interviews, or more informally, in the context of focus groups (see Chapter 11).

Interviews can be structured and unstructured. In the structured interview, interviewees are asked a set of identical questions in exactly the same way, and are usually asked to select their answers from a limited range of options. More structured techniques might include surveys and questionnaires. Structured interviews are better for making comparisons and less structured interviews may be more appropriate for early exploratory phases of research. Unstructured interviews are more like ordinary conversations: there is no set interview structure and interviewees answer in their own words. These allow for longer questions and more in-depth probing, and are most frequently used in ethnographic research. The interviewer initiates the conversation, presents each topic by means of specific questions, and decides when the conversation on a topic has satisfied the research objectives. Researchers sometimes use a combination of interview methods, using structured questions to obtain factual information (such as age or income), and unstructured questions to probe deeper into people's experiences.

Focus groups

Focus groups involve a form of unstructured interviewing that generates different data from other forms of interviewing. A focus group is a group of people selected because they are believed to be related to some phenomenon of interest. The researcher meets with the group and facilitates an organized discussion related to something the participants have experience of, or beliefs about.

Discussion can bring out insights and understandings in ways which simple questionnaire items may not be able to tap, such as emotional and unconscious motivations not amenable to the structured questions of conventional survey research. The interaction among focus group participants may reveal more than they would in the more formal interview setting. Using focus groups, researchers can learn how things are discussed in a particular culture, test hypotheses about beliefs, mix people who wouldn't normally mix, test questions for future interviews, or test policy ideas to see how citizens react to them.

Ethnographic research

Ethnographic research provides data on social phenomena by placing researchers 'in the midst of whatever it is they study so they can examine various phenomena as perceived by participants' (Berg 2004: 148). The objective of ethnographic research is to describe the lives of people other than ourselves with accuracy and detailed observation honed by first-hand experience. It involves participating, overtly or covertly, in people's daily lives in a way that can 'throw light on the issues that are the focus of research' (Hammersley and Atkinson 1995: 1). The idea is that a researcher must enter the environment of those under study to observe and understand their behaviour (see Chapter 12).

In political research, ethnographic studies have been conducted with the purpose of developing a better understanding of different institutions (e.g. the military, the BBC, the World Bank), or cultures (migrants in the US, fundamentalist religious groups in the EU), events (a war, a summit), or roles (campaign worker, news editor).

Participant observation involves the actual participation of the researcher in the events or environment being studied. This technique provides an 'insider' account of the activities and daily lives of the people being studied. By taking part in this way, researchers are able to construct an account of the way in which the group perceives their world. The personal insights of the researcher can be cross-validated through repeated, in-depth interviews with a broad cross-section of informants; and through conventional archival research, consultation with experts, use of surveys, and other techniques. The use of multiple researchers is an additional way to ensure reliability.

Discourse/content analysis

Content analysis generates data by analysing documents, reports, statistics, manuscripts, and other written, oral, or visual materials. These materials permit researchers to access subjects that may be difficult or impossible to obtain through direct, personal contact (such as, for instance, interviews with decision-makers) or to increase the sample size above what would be possible through either interviews or direct observation (see Chapter 13).

Content analysis involves coding the 'content' of written documents, audio transcripts, radio programmes, television programmes, public speeches, or internet pages. It allows us to explore the beliefs, attitudes, and preferences of actors (even after they are dead).

Content analysis provides evidence about subjectivity: What were they (the actors) thinking? What were their intentions? Questions about subjective phenomena arise in virtually all types of social research. Narrative data (e.g. autobiographies, literature, journals, diaries, first-hand accounts, newspapers) often provide important keys to both process (and thus mechanisms) and subjectivity. These records provide different sorts of evidence. Verbal accounts from politicians, eyewitnesses, journalists, and contemporary historians constitute an important source of information for political research. These come increasingly with visual data via photographs, films, and videos. Participants in the political processes we study (e.g. civil servants, members of advisory councils, and representatives of pressure groups involved in decision-making processes), generate party programmes, parliamentary proceedings, resolutions, speeches, treaties, press conferences and press reports, television and radio interviews, and correspondence. Through content analysis, we can systematically analyse these materials for clues to decision-makers' perceptions and attitudes. The method is often used in conjunction with other methods in order to establish a firmer causal link. For example, a researcher might explore whether a rise in racist statements in radio and television cable shows precedes the rise of racist attitudes in public opinion polls (using a survey).

Using data from existing archives allows you to widen the scope of your work far beyond what you could collect for yourself, and makes possible comparisons and the study of trends over time; and they can be used for purposes quite different from those for which they were originally collected. For instance, the ESRC Data Archive holds almost 4000 data sets, including those from many large and important government-produced surveys and censuses, as well as academic research and historical materials. The Appendix contains a listing of data sources for political research, including databanks, consortia, data archives from state and independent government agencies, policy-making organizations, international organizations, academic institutions, scholars, think tanks, and private organizations.

It is also a good idea to use multiple sources of data and methods of data collection whenever possible. Doing this enables you to approach a research problem from different angles, something that is called 'triangulation'. Triangulation of evidence increases the reliability of the data and the process of gathering it. In the context of data collection, triangulation serves to corroborate the data gathered from other sources: the use of different data sources can enable researchers to cross-check findings. Triangulation yields more complete data and results in more credible findings; and it also enables researchers to find agreement between different perspectives. It might involve the use of different research methods to study a single research problem: a comparison of the results of these different methods can enable a researcher to identify whether differences are due to biases in one or another of these methods. It might also involve the use of different researchers to study the same research problem with the same people and with the same methods: if the same results are discovered, the findings and interpretations have stronger validity because of this corroboration. Triangulation might also involve using different theoretical perspectives to look at the same data: examining the same data from different theoretical perspectives can enable the researcher to identify bias.

Ethical research

To conclude this chapter, we want to discuss the ethical principles to which all political research should conform.

Ethical issues have become increasingly important in guiding research since the late 1990s or so. Before then, ethics was not something that researchers (not just ethnographers, but pretty much all political researchers) would have had to think very much about, as there was little in the way of ethical scrutiny of research. But this has now changed. Ethical scrutiny is now something that nearly all research is required to go through, even for graduate and undergraduate research projects. Most universities have ethics committees that issue guidelines about ethical practice, and these guidelines or codes are often based on the codes of professional organizations such as the British Sociological Association or the American Sociological Association.

Although one of the main goals of research is to accumulate knowledge or develop an understanding of a particular phenomenon, it is also recognized that achieving these goals should not come at the cost of all else. And in particular, the social cost (or potential cost) of those involved in the research (the informants) needs to be taken into account in order to ensure that they are not unduly exploited or harmed. Ethical scrutiny is therefore designed to protect research participants. It is also designed to try and protect the university institutions themselves, so that researchers are deterred from engaging in ethically dubious research activities that could come back to haunt the institution in the form of legal action or unwanted publicity.

Broadly speaking, ethical issues can be summarized under six main headings: voluntary participation, informed consent, privacy, harm, exploitation, and consequences for future research. In practice, there is considerable overlap between these different principles.

Voluntary participation

The researcher should always stress that participation in a study is completely voluntary, and that a person who declines to participate will not incur any penalty. Not only should people know that they are not required to participate in a study; they should also know that they can withdraw from a study at any point without penalty (de Vaus 2001: 83).

Informed consent

This is closely related to voluntary participation. The principle of informed consent requires that the researcher tell participants about the purpose and likely benefits of the study, the process through which participants were selected, procedures that will be followed, and any risks for the subject.

The issue of informed consent is one of the most hotly debated ethical principles. The bulk of discussion focuses on what is called disguised or **covert participation**. This type of observation happens against the informants' knowledge, and they are thus not provided with an opportunity to express whether they would like to take part in the research or not. Most ethical codes of conduct now regard this type of research as unjustified. It is often seen as a type of infiltration or spying (Bulmer 1982), and is even thought to contravene the human rights of autonomy and dignity of participants (Hammersley and Atkinson 2005). For this reason, covert studies are rarely carried out anymore. The defence that the ends can sometime justify the means tends not to carry much weight.

The principle of informed consent not only requires that the researcher should make their identity known, but that they should also make the purpose of their research known, and provide informants with the opportunity to withdraw from the research process at any stage. The Social Research Association (SRA) *Ethical Guidelines* (2003: 27) goes as far as to say:

> Inquiries involving human subjects should be based as far as practicable on the -freely given informed consent of subjects...They should be aware of their entitlement to refuse at any stage for whatever reason and to withdraw data supplied. Information that would be likely to affect a subject's willingness to participate should not be deliberately withheld.

The issue of deception is one that requires careful thought. It might be reasonably argued that any deception in the conduct of research involving human subjects is inconsistent with informed consent and is unethical. But it also may be necessary for participants to remain uninformed about the hypotheses under investigation, so as to ensure that the results of the study will not be biased as a result of this knowledge (McDermott 2002: 41). This is an issue, in particular, for experimental research. If deception is involved, researchers should explain to participants 'what the deception was and why it was deemed necessary for the unbiased collection of the data. In particular, subjects should be reassured that all their data will be confidential and that the experimenter will obtain subjects' written permission before any of their information is shared publicly' (McDermott 2002: 41).

Privacy

A third area of ethical concern relates to the right to privacy of the informants. This is partly related to issues of informed consent, and provides an opportunity for the informant to decide what information they are prepared to make public. But it also refers to the identity of the informant, and their right to anonymity. This is important in all areas of research, but is particularly important when there is a risk that information that is provided to the researcher might be used against the informant at a later date. Protecting the privacy and confidentiality of what informants tell you can therefore be a very serious issue. At one level, in ethnographic research, it is easy to use pseudonyms for the informants so that they cannot be identified by name. But this may not always be enough to ensure privacy. Informants may be identifiable by information you have revealed about them. Some ethnographers therefore prefer to make the field site anonymous.

Harm

Another area of ethical concern relates to the harm of participants. Research that is likely to harm participants is generally regarded as unacceptable. But harm can occur in a variety of ways. Although political research doesn't tend to endanger informants directly, the research process can nonetheless have consequences for informants which may cause them harm or distress. Sometimes this can come about from the act of research. For example, research on racism might reinforce racist practices (see discussion by Troyna and Carrington 1989) or research on football hooligans might incite informants to violence as a way of impressing the researcher. But harm can also come from the publication of research, and the making public of details of people's lives or opinions that may cause them distress or even put them in danger from the authorities. The identity of informants should be kept confidential; but more than that, it should not be possible to identify them.

All of these issues are discussed in more detail in the Social Research Council's online publication, *Ethical Guidelines*, posted at http://www.the-sra.org.uk/guidelines.htm#ethic.

 ## Conclusions

Perhaps more than any other academic discipline political research incorporates a wide variety of different methods and approaches. This has both its advantages and disadvantages. It strengthens the discipline as a whole when this diversity is embraced, and when researchers adopt and integrate the different approaches and engage with research from across the methodological spectrum. It weakens the discipline when this diversity becomes segregated, and when researchers from different methodological traditions retreat into their own enclaves and do not engage with what other people are doing in the discipline. In the following chapters we present chapter-length treatments of some of the most widely used and influential methods and approaches in the study of politics. Each method has its own strength and weakness, but rather than getting bogged down in petty discussions about which method is best, or which method is best for which type of topic or question, the challenge that faces serious researchers is to think about how these methods can be incorporated with each other, and the strengths of one approach used to balance the weaknesses of another.

 ## Questions

- What is meant by 'research design'?
- What are the various types of research designs used in political research?
- Why should researchers be concerned with research design? Can politics be studied rigorously without attention to issues of research design?
- What are the major components of research designs?
- What are the general criteria for evaluating research designs?

Guide to Further Reading

Creswell, John W. (2003), *Research Design: Qualitative, Quantitative, and Mixed Methods Approaches* (Thousand Oaks, CA: Sage Publications).
An introduction to different types of research design, and how to combine qualitative and quantitative research strategies.

Davies, R. B. (1994) 'From Cross-Sectional to Longitudinal Analysis', in A. Dale and R. B. Davies (eds), *Analyzing Social and Political Change: A Casebook of Methods* (Thousand Oaks, CA: Sage Publications).
Davies argues that more data are required to characterize empirically the dynamic process that lies behind the cross-sectional snapshot; and these data can be supplied through longitudinal analysis.

de Vaus, David (2001), *Research Design in Social Research* (Thousand Oaks, CA: Sage Publications).
Presents key types of social science research design, including case studies, cross-sectional, experimental, and longitudinal; with a discussion, for each, of tools required, possible issues, and data analysis.

Druckman, J. N., D. P. Green, J. H. Kuklinski, and A. Lupia. (2006), 'The growth and Development of Experimental Research in Political Science', *American Political Science Review* 100(4): 627–35.
This article documents how thinking about experimentation has evolved over the century, and demonstrates the growing influence of laboratory, survey, and field experiments.

Flyvbjerg, B. (2006), 'Five Misunderstandings about Case-Study Research', *Qualitative Inquiry* 12(2) (April): 219–45.
This article discusses five misunderstandings of case study research: (a) theoretical knowledge is more valuable than practical knowledge; (b) one cannot generalize from a single case; therefore, the single-case study cannot contribute to scientific development; (c) the case study is most useful for generating hypotheses, whereas other methods are more suitable for hypotheses testing and theory building; (d) the case study contains a bias toward verification; and (e) it is often difficult to summarize specific case studies.

George, A. L. and A. Bennett (2005), *Case Studies and Theory Development in the Social Sciences* (Cambridge, MA: MIT Press).

Gerring, J. (2004), 'What is a Case Study and What is it Good For?' *American Political Science Review* 98 (May): 341–54.
This article clarifies the meaning, and explains the utility, of the case study method. It argues for the complementarity of single-unit and cross-unit research designs.

—— (2001), *Social Science Methodology: A Criterial Framework* (Cambridge: Cambridge University Press); 'Research Design: General Criteria' (chapter 8), 'Methods' (chapter 9), 'Strategies of Research Design' (chapter 10).

McDermott, R. (2002), 'Experimental Methods in Political Science', *Annual Review of Political Science* 5: 31–61.
This article discusses issues of central concern to experimentalists, including impact versus control, mundane versus experimental realism, internal versus external validity, deception, and laboratory versus field experiments; and summarizes the advantages and disadvantages of experimentation.

Munck, Gerardo (1998), 'Canons of Research Design in Qualitative Analysis', *Studies in Comparative International Development* 33(3) (September): 18–45.
Advances the idea of multi-method approach to political research.

Ragin, C. (2000), *Fuzzy-Set Social Science* (Chicago: University of Chicago Press).
The difference between research designs aimed at testing theory and those aimed at building, developing, and refining theory.

 # References

Berg, B. L. (2004), *Qualitative Research Methods for the Social Sciences* (Boston, MA: Allyn and Bacon).

Bulmer, M. (1982), 'The Merits and Demerits of Covert Participant Observation', in M. Bulmer (ed.), *Social Research Ethics* (Basingstoke: Macmillan), 217–51.

Collier, D. and J. Mahoney (1996), 'Research Note. Insights and Pitfalls: Selection Bias in Qualitative Research', *World Politics* 49(1): 56–91.

de Vaus, D. (2001), *Research Design in Social Science* (London: Sage).

Gerber, A. and D. Green (2000), 'The Effects of Canvassing, Telephone Calls, and Direct Mail on Voter Turnout: A Field Experiment', *American Political Science Review* 94(3) (September): 653–63.

Gerring, J. (2007), *Case Study Research: Principles And Practices* (Cambridge: Cambridge University Press).

Hammersley, M. and P. Atkinson (1995), *Ethnography: Principles in Practice*, 2nd edition (London: Routledge).

King, G., R. Keohane, and S. Verba (1994), *Designing Social Inquiry: Scientific Inference in Qualitative Research* (Princeton, NJ: Princeton University Press).

Leighly, Jan (1995), 'Attitudes, Opportunities and Incentives: A Review Essay on Political Participation', *Political Research Quarterly* 48 (March): 181–209.

McDermott, R. (2002), 'Experimental Methods in Political Science', *Annual Review of Political Science* 5 (June): 31–61.

Mishler, W. and R. Rose (2007), 'Generations, Age and Time: The Dynamics of Political Learning during Russia's Transformation', *American Journal of Political Science* 51(4) (October): 822–34.

Morton, R. B. and K. Williams (1999), 'Information Asymmetries and Simultaneous versus Sequential Voting', *American Political Science Review* 93: 51–67.

Ostrom, E. (2007), 'Why Do We Need Laboratory Experiments in Political Science?' Paper presented at the 2007 American Political Science Association annual meeting, Chicago, IL, 30 August–2 September.

Rawls, J. (1993), *Political Liberalism* (New York: Columbia University Press).

Roberts, T. J., B. C. Parks and A. A. Vasquez (2004), 'Who Ratifies Environmental Treaties and Why? Institutionalism, Structuralism and Participation by 192 Nations in 22 Treaties', *Global Environmental Politics* 4: 22–64.

Schuman, H. and S. Presser (1996), *Questions and Answers in Attitude Surveys* (Beverly Hills, CA: Sage).

Shively, W. P. (1989), *The Craft of Political Research*, 2nd edition (Englewood Cliffs, NJ: Prentice-Hall, Inc.).

Social Research Association (2003), *Ethical Guidelines*, Social Research Association, available at http://www.the-sra.org.uk/documents/pdfs/ethics03.pdf.

Troyna, B. and B. Carrington (1989), 'Whose Side are We On?', in R. G. Burgess (ed.), *The Ethics of Educational Research* (Lewes: Falmer Press), 205–23.

White, L. and R. P. Clark (1983), *Political Analysis: Technique And Practice* (Monterey, CA: Brooks/Cole Pub. Co.).

Yin, R. (1984), *Case Study Research: Design and Methods*, 2nd edition (Thousand Oaks, CA: Sage Publications).

Endnotes

1. Of course, it wouldn't hurt for the student in the example, above, to take advantage of an opportunity to interview government officials in Egypt, as it might provide useful insights and perhaps generate an idea for a research question. But we would, nonetheless, use the query as an opportunity to make the point that research questions and hypotheses, not methods, should drive research.

2. We made the point, in Chapter 5, that research should be driven, not by methods, but by questions and problems. But, to continue with the toolbox metaphor, there are researchers who will start the research process by selecting their preferred tool from the research methods toolbox, and then go looking for something to use it on.

3. It cannot be scientifically demonstrated that certain normative standpoints are more correct (in the sense of closer to the truth) than others. Normative questions typically require research that combines given political facts with moral arguments. In contrast to empirical types of research, the researcher is not 'required to produce the full factual basis for his/her argument'. It is often the case that the researcher will 'need to assume facts which cannot possibly be tested against reality' (Shively 1989: 9).

Part 3

How to Do Research in Practice

Experimental Research

 Chapter Summary

This chapter examines the principles of experimental research design and discusses the issues and problems associated with different aspects of the approach. In doing so we pay special attention to the issue of internal and external validity, the common obstacles associated with experimental research, and what can be done to try and avoid or minimize them. The chapter examines:

- basic principles of experimental research;
- field experiments;
- laboratory experiments;
- natural experiments;
- internal and external validity;
- problems;
- ethical issues.

Introduction

The use of experimental designs to study political phenomena has grown considerably in recent decades. Although there is a long history of experimental political research, with some early pioneering studies dating back to the 1920s and 1930s (see in particular Harold Gosnell, 1927), in recent years there has been a marked increase in the use of the approach. Indeed, experimental research is now perhaps the fastest growing area of political research. Researchers in politics have used experimental designs to study political mobilization (Gerber and Green 2000; John and Brannan 2008), voting (Lodge et al. 1989), negative campaigning (Wattenberg and Brians 1999), coalition bargaining (Fréchette et al. 2005), electoral systems (Morton and Williams 1999); clientelism (Wantchekon 2003), culture (Henrich et al. 2004), identity (e.g. Habyarimana et al. 2007), foreign policy decision-making (Geva and Mintz 1997), international negotiations (Druckman 1994), justice (Frohlich and Oppenheimer 1992), and deliberation (Simon and Sulkin 2001).

The appeal of the approach is easy to appreciate. Experimental designs are often thought to most closely resemble the true scientific method (see Chapter 2), and as such they are widely regarded as being the most effective design for testing whether or not two variables are causally related. They manage to do this thanks to the rigorous use of experimental control. This helps researchers to isolate the impact of a specific variable and to overcome one of the main problems that researchers face when they want to investigate causal relationships. Since there is a vast number of potentially important variables that may influence any given political phenomenon, in the absence of rigorous controlled experiments (not dissimilar to those used in medical research), it is very difficult to know which variable is responsible for causing the phenomena under investigation. One of the great strengths of experimental research is that the researcher can control the environment and manipulate particular variables of causal interest with great precision. One of the defining characteristics of experimental research is intervention by the researcher in the data-gathering process. Morton and Williams (2008) describe this as 'playing God'. We call the data gathered by intervention (or **treatment**, as it is sometimes known) experimental data.

In this chapter we discuss some of the main issues in experimental research and some of the main ways in which the approach has been used in the study of politics. In the first part of this chapter we provide a brief overview of the basic principles of experimental design, and how experiments can be used to test causal hypotheses. We then go on to discuss some of the main ways in which experimental research works in practice. Experiments can be carried out in a number of different locations. Experiments can be carried out in a laboratory, in the field, and by utilizing natural occurrences. In laboratory experiments, the subjects (the participants in the study) are recruited to a common location where the intervention takes place. In field experiments, the intervention by the researcher takes place in real-world environments, and subjects may not even know that they are participating in an experiment. This obviously raises some ethical issues (which we discuss in detail in Chapter 7). By contrast, natural experiments rely on naturally occurring events as interventions rather than interventions controlled by the researcher.

With the rise of internet-based experiments, the distinction between some of these approaches is becoming more blurred (see Morton and Williams 2009). In addition, surveys are frequently used to carry out question-wording experiments, where some respondents are asked a question in a certain way and other respondents are asked the question using slightly different words. These types of experiments can be used to examine how respondents react to different types of information, and information framed in different ways. We discuss these types of experiments in Chapter 10.

We then discuss some of the main issues to do with the reliability and validity of experimental research. This has to do with whether or not we are confident that a causal relationship really exists between two variables (sometimes known as internal validity) and whether or not we are confident that our findings can be generalized to subjects outside the confines of the experiment (sometimes known as external validity). We will also discuss some of the practical and ethical problems associated with doing different types of experimental research.

Basic principles of experimental design

Experimental research relies on the use of control groups (in which no intervention takes place) and experimental groups (in which interventions do take place) and the **random assignment** of subjects (participants) to control and experimental groups.

The control group provides a point of reference to which the effect of the intervention can be compared. The random assignment of subjects to control and experimental groups ensures (as far as possible) that the two groups are similar to each other (see Chapter 10 on sampling). These groups are then treated in the same way in every respect apart from the intervention that is carried out on the experimental group. Any differences that are then observed between the groups on the outcome variable of interest (the dependent variable) can then be attributed to the intervention that took place.

The classic version of the experimental design comprises five steps (see de Vaus 2001: 48):

1. two groups: one group that is exposed to the intervention (the experimental group) and one group that is not exposed to the intervention (the control group);

2. random allocation of subjects to the groups before the pre-test;

3. one pre-intervention (pre-test) measure on the outcome variable;

4. one intervention (test/treatment);

5. one post-intervention (post-test) measure on the outcome variable.

Table 8.1 provides a conceptual overview of this method. The columns refer to the groups to which subjects are randomly assigned. Once subjects have been assigned to a control group and an experimental group, both groups are pre-tested on the outcome variable of interest, the dependent variable (Y). This provides a baseline measure which later results can then be compared to. In the next step, a treatment (or an intervention) is administered to the experimental group but not the control group. The treatment refers to the key independent variable (X) of interest. This is related to the causal hypothesis which we wish to test. To see whether the hypothesis is confirmed or not we need to carry out a post-test on both groups on the dependent variable. If our hypothesis is supported, then we should observe that the test statistic for our dependent variable Y has changed for the experimental group (which received the treatment) but has not changed for the control group. The test for the effect of the intervention is therefore carried out by comparing changes in the experimental group before and after the intervention to changes (if any) in the control group.

This classic design is often simplified in practice by dropping the pre-test stage. Valid inferences about the causal significance of the treatment variable can still be drawn so long as the groups are large enough. The key thing is that subjects are randomly allocated to the experimental and control groups. In effect this means that any differences between experimental and control groups are random and will not account for group differences in outcomes (see de Vaus 2001: 60). With this sort of design, rather than looking at the *amount of change* between the groups, the analysis is based on the post-test *differences* between the groups. Because subjects have been randomly allocated to their groups, the post-test differences should be the same as the difference in change scores of the experimental and control groups in the classic set-up.

Table 8.1 Experimental design

	Control group	Experimental group
Pre-test	Measure on outcome variable (Y)	Measure on outcome variable (Y)
Intervention	No treatment	Treatment
Post-test	Measure on outcome variable (Y)	Measure on outcome variable (Y)

There is also a number of issues to do with **case selection** in experimental research. The first issue is to do with how subjects (or participants) are selected for the study. The second issue is to do with how subjects are assigned—or allocated—to control or experimental groups within the study. Generally speaking, researchers who carry out experiments are more concerned with assignment than selection, particularly in laboratory experiments.

It is the random assignment of subjects to groups, rather than the random selection of subjects in the first place, that is most important for testing causal hypotheses. For this reason, many laboratory experiments do not rely upon representative or random samples of subjects. It can be very difficult, time-consuming, and expensive to select a random sample of participants from across the country and then transfer them to the location of the laboratory. It is often far more convenient to recruit people to the study who live near the lab. Indeed, since laboratory experiments frequently take place on university campuses where academics are based, the most convenient and accessible sample is often an all-student sample. This is precisely what a lot of experimental research relies upon. As long as the students are randomly assigned to treatment and control groups, the fact that they are not representative of the wider population does not undermine the internal validity of the study (see Druckman and Kam 2011 for an extended discussion on this topic). However, it might compromise the external validity of the study and the extent to which the findings can be generalized, at least in so far as the findings can be generalized to non-students.

We will illustrate how these designs are carried out in practice with reference to some specific examples. In particular, we focus on laboratory, field, and natural experiments. The main purpose of this chapter is to provide a brief overview of the three main types of experimental design. Politics researchers have conducted a great deal of both laboratory research (e.g. on the impact of campaign commercials) and field experiments (e.g. on the effects of canvassing, telephone calls, and direct mail on voter turnout: Gerber and Green 2000; John and Brannan 2008). And, where possible, they have also exploited 'natural experiments' (e.g. on the effects of gender quotas on female political representation). In the following sections, we discuss each of these experimental design types in turn.

Laboratory experiments

In laboratory experiments, the subjects are recruited to a common location where the experiment takes place. The laboratory experiment is designed to ensure that the researcher has as much control over the environment to which subjects are exposed as possible. In this way, the experimental group and the control group can be exposed to exactly the same environment except for the experimental intervention. Accordingly, any difference that is recorded on the post-test measurement of the dependent variable can be confidently attributed to the presence (or absence) of the intervention.

The controlled environment of a laboratory is particularly well suited to examining a wide range of political phenomena that might otherwise be difficult to investigate. In particular, Morton and Williams (2008: 346) suggest that they have three main strengths as a setting for experimental research. Laboratory experiments allow the researcher to have a great deal of control over what the subject is exposed to. In a natural setting, people might be exposed to many different types of stimuli each day, so it is difficult to investigate what impact if any each specific stimulus has on their attitudes or behaviour. In a laboratory, different stimuli can be manipulated one at a time, holding everything else constant. This allows causal hypotheses to be tested with far more precision. Second, laboratory experiments also allow the researcher to have a great deal of control over what variables are manipulated, and even to manipulate variables that might be difficult to vary in the real world. Third, laboratory experiments allow the researcher to create environments that simply don't exist in the real world. For example, they can explore how decision-making is influenced by entirely new voting systems.

However, laboratory experiments are not without their problems. An example can help to illustrate both the potential strengths and weaknesses of this approach. An area of political research that has received a great deal of attention is to do with the study of media effects on public opinion. In many ways, this type of research lends itself well to the experimental setting of the laboratory, since the causal significance of media 'effects' on political attitudes is notoriously difficult to unravel. Most people are exposed to multiple, competing media messages each day, so it is very difficult to establish what messages matter and how. One particular aspect of media effects that has received a great deal of attention is the impact of negative campaigning by political parties and, in particular, whether or not 'attack ads' have a demobilizing effects on voters during an electoral campaign.

One influential attempt to answer these questions was carried by Stephen Ansolabehere and his colleagues. Through a set of innovative controlled experiments in laboratory conditions, Ansolabehere and colleagues (1997) examine the extent to which subjects who view negative campaign adverts are less likely to say they will vote than subjects who view more positive campaign adverts. In the study, subjects were randomly assigned to different groups. Subjects in each group then watched identical public information broadcasts. Each broadcast had an advertisement break which consisted of three adverts, and one of these adverts varied across the groups. In one experimental group, subjects were exposed to an advert which was political in content and negative in tone; in another experimental group, subjects were exposed to an advert which was political in content and positive in tone. Subjects in the control group were not exposed to a political advert, and just watched a product advert. The results of their study are reproduced in Table 8.2. Controlling for a variety of other factors that influence whether or not someone votes, Ansolabehere and colleagues find that people who are exposed to political adverts with positive political messages are about 6 percentage points more likely to vote than people who are exposed to negative political adverts. They thus conclude that 'attack' adds have a demobilizing effect.

Given the random allocation of subjects to groups, any observed differences between the experimental and control group can therefore be confidently attributed to experimental intervention. These types of experimental study therefore have a high level of internal validity.

Table 8.2 Exposure to negative campaigning and likelihood of voting

	Control group	Experimental group 1	Experimental group 2
Intervention	Product advertisement	Negative political advert	Positive political advert
Post-test (Y)	61% likely to vote	58% likely to vote	64% likely to vote

Source: Adapted from Ansolabehere and colleagues (1997).

This means that we can be confident that the change in the outcome variable really was brought about by the key independent variable (the intervention), rather than some other factor. That is, it really is the variation in the tone of the political adverts that is responsible for the variation in willingness to vote. However, laboratory experiments are often criticized for lacking external validity. Since they take place in an 'artificial' environment, their findings cannot be easily generalized to the 'real world'. We might be confident that exposure to attack ads has a demobilizing effect in the laboratory setting, but does this effect also hold in the real world? Could attack ads be responsible (at least partly) for a decline in turnout?

Experimental laboratory research allows us to test hypotheses under controlled conditions designed to maximize internal validity. However, exercising a high degree of control over subjects can often lead to a reduction in the external validity of the findings and, in particular, that variant of external validity that is called **ecological validity**. This means that, because they do not reflect a real-life situation, the findings of laboratory experiments may not be generalizable (or extended) to the 'real world'. When we take people out of their natural environment and study them in the laboratory, we are exerting some control over them. Consequently, we are possibly limiting how much we can generalize the findings to all people in natural settings. The laboratory study may therefore lack ecological validity because the controlled environment in which it is conducted is so unlike the real world that whatever results are obtained will be inapplicable to people in non-laboratory settings. The question, then, is to what extent a laboratory study is true to life. Could it be replicated anywhere, using natural settings and conditions? Another reason why a laboratory study may lack ecological validity is because of **reactivity**. Reactivity occurs when research study participants alter their behaviour as a result of being aware of participating in a study. Reactivity threatens ecological validity because, when it occurs, the results of the experiment might be *generalizable only to other people who are also being observed*.

To illustrate some of these points, we can return to Steven Ansolabehere's study of 'attack ads'. One concern with the external validity of the findings might be that, since the behavioural and attitudinal consequences of exposure to the different types of campaign ads were measured by a survey conducted shortly after exposure occurred, it is unclear what the long-term impact of this was and how it might translate into actual electoral outcomes. If, for example, intention to vote declines immediately after exposure to negative advertising by 3 percentage points in the lab, does that imply that the mud-slinging senate campaign under study lowers actual turnout in the electorate by 3 percentage points? As Green and Gerber (2003: 101) argue, intention to vote is not the same thing as actual turnout; nor is one-time laboratory exposure the same thing as multiple attempted exposures in the course of an actual campaign.

Field experiments

Although some scholars prefer laboratory experiments to field experiments because the lab offers the researcher tighter control over the treatment and how it is presented to subjects, others take the view that the generalizations from these types of study will be limited unless treatments are deployed, and outcomes assessed, unobtrusively in the field (Druckman et al. 2006). Because of concerns about the artificial environment of laboratory experiments, political scientists have carried out experiments in real-world environments. These field experiments attempt to reproduce as closely as possible the conditions under which different political phenomena occur, thus increasing the external validity or generalizability of the findings. As Green and Gerber (2003: 94) observe, field experiments have two main strengths. First, random assignment ensures unbiased inference about cause and effect, and second, the natural settings ensure that the results will tell us something useful about the real world. Field experimentation can therefore be an incredibly powerful tool for enabling researchers to draw unbiased and externally valid causal inferences about different social and political processes.

There is a long history in political research of field experimentation or what Green and Gerber (2003) term controlled interventions into the political world. They use the term 'controlled intervention' since many of the early studies did not assign subjects to treatment and control conditions on a purely random basis. However, in most other respects, they closely resemble field experiments. An early example of this kind of controlled intervention was carried out by Harold Gosnell (1927) on voter registration and turnout in Chicago prior to the 1924 and 1925 elections. Gosnell gathered the names, addresses, and background information of thousands of voting-age adults living in various Chicago neighbourhoods. He then divided these neighbourhoods into blocks, assigning (though not on a strictly random basis) certain blocks to the treatment condition of his experiment, which consisted of a letter urging adults to register to vote. Comparing the registration and voting rates in his treatment and control group, Gosnell found his letter campaign to have produced a noticeable increase in political participation across a variety of ethnic and demographic groups.

A more recent and scientific example of this kind of experiment was carried out by Peter John and Tessa Brannan (2008) in Manchester prior to the 2005 British election. John and Brannan randomly selected the names of 6,900 people from the electoral register of a constituency in Manchester. The subjects were then randomly allocated to three groups (one control and two treatment). The researchers then selected one treatment group to receive a telephone call (the telephone group); and the other treatment group to receive a visit (the canvassing group). For both groups, the main purpose of the contact was to persuade the citizen to vote, both by providing reasons why it is important and by attempting to respond to any concerns about the voting process. The researchers had no contact with the control group. Comparing participation across the groups, John and Brannan found that turnout was significantly higher among the treatment groups than it was among the control group, with both telephone and canvassing having much the same effect on boosting turnout.

These studies not only provide strong evidence about the causes of turnout in the real world, but they also provide strong evidence about what factors can increase turnout. Experimental field research can therefore be a very effective way of evaluating different policy initiatives and pilot programs, since they provide a direct test of whether the initiative (or intervention) brings about a direct change in the outcome of interest. For this reason, field experiments can often be used to great effect in collaboration with political parties, policymakers, or other agencies who are seriously interested in trying to understand the impact of some type of policy or intervention. For example, Wantchekon (2003) carried out a remarkable field experiment on clientelism in Benin during a national election, in which he was able to persuade political parties to randomize the types of appeal they made to voters in different villages (between programmatic appeals and patronage based clientelist appeals). He was able to do this because there was considerable interest among the leading parties in Benin in learning about the effectiveness of alternative campaign strategies.

Wantchekon selected a number of villages and the inhabitants were then exposed to purely clientelist platforms and campaign strategies by one party and purely programmatic public policy platforms and appeals by the other party. The type of appeal that each party put forward varied between the different selected villages. The public policy message emphasized general policy goals, such as national unity and peace, eradicating corruption, alleviating poverty, developing agriculture and industry, and protecting the rights of women and children. The clientelist message emphasized specific promises made to the village for things like government jobs or local public goods, such as establishing a new local university or providing financial support for local workers.

Comparing these two experimental groups to the control group, where the platform was not manipulated and voters were exposed to the usual mixed platforms of the parties, Wantchekon found that parties which adopted the clientelist appeals tended to be much more successful than the parties which adopted the programmatic appeals, particularly for incumbent candidates. He also found that some groups of people responded to these appeals in different ways, and that women had a stronger preference for public goods messages than men.

Another great strength of experimental research is to try and uncover the way in which variables are related to each other when the direction of causality is uncertain. For example, a great deal of academic research has tried to unpick the relationship between newspaper readership and political attitudes and support. Does the newspaper someone reads influence their political preferences? Or do people's political preferences influence which newspaper they read? These so-called chicken-and-egg problems can be very difficult to solve. Politicians certainly believe that newspapers can be very influential, as do the newspapers themselves. After the Conservative Party victory in the 1992 UK election, the *Sun* (a British tabloid) brazenly declared 'It's the Sun Wot Won it'. Yet hard empirical evidence to support this view is hard to come by.

One way around the chicken-and-egg problem is to carry out experimental research. Gerber, Karlan, and Bergan (2009) report on an experiment they conducted during the 2005 Virginia gubernatorial election, designed to see if biased information sources affected voter behaviour. Washington has two national newspapers, the *Washington Post* and the *Washington Times*. Whereas the *Washington Post* is generally viewed as a liberal newspaper, the *Washington Times* is widely considered to be a more conservative paper. Gerber and his colleagues selected a large sample of subjects about a month before the election, and then, after discounting any people who already read the *Post* or the *Times*, randomly assigned subjects to one of three groups. The first group received a free one-month subscription to the *Post*, the second group received a free one-month subscription to the *Times*, and the third group received neither. Subjects completed a survey at the beginning of the study (pre-test) and after the election (post-test). Gerber, Karlan, and Bergan found that subjects who had been assigned to the (liberal) *Washington Post* were 8 percentage points more likely to vote for the (liberal) Democratic candidate than those not assigned a free newspaper. The results therefore provide evidence that political biases in newspapers can affect voting behaviour and political attitudes.

However, field experiments are not without their problems either, and in tackling the problem of external validity often associated with laboratory experiments, it is often argued that they introduce a new problem to do with internal validity. As we discussed in the previous section, when researchers exert a lot of control over a study (such as when they carry it out in a laboratory), it creates a degree of artificiality. This reduces the external validity of the experiment and makes it harder to generalize the findings. However, when researchers attempt to deal with this problem and carry out their experiments in the field, they have less control over the study and so can be less sure about the causal significance of the intervention. This can reduce the internal validity of the experiment. To illustrate this problem, we can return to the series of studies conducted by the psychologist Robert Rosenthal and his colleagues that we discussed in Chapter 3. Rosenthal and his colleague, Lenore Jacobson, conducted a study designed to determine the impact of teachers' expectations on student performance. The research question that Rosenthal and Jacobson (1968) addressed was: 'Does a teacher's expectations affect students' performance?' Their hypothesis was that favourable expectations of teachers will lead to an increase in students' intellectual ability. The dependent variable was intellectual achievement (measured by IQ tests). The independent variable was teachers' expectations (those that resulted from the information communicated to them by the researchers). The researchers conducted a pre-test of their dependent variable: they had IQ tests administered to elementary school students (grades 1–6). They randomly selected 20% of the students who were assigned to serve as the experimental group; the remaining 80% of the students represented the control group. The teachers were told that the students in the experimental group were academic 'bloomers', and would show unusual academic development over the coming year. At the end of the school year, Rosenthal and Jacobsen retested all of the students. The IQs of students whom they had characterized as academic 'bloomers' (the experimental group) had statistically improved, and they had improved at a faster rate than those of the other children (the control group).

This study appears to meet the conditions of a valid experiment. In the ideal experimental design, we are able to hold constant all variables but one, and do so in a controlled unchanging environment. But Rosenthal and Jacobson did not have complete control over the subjects and their environment, because the experiment occurred in a 'natural' setting. Consequently, student performance may have been affected by variables other than the teachers' expectations. Teachers may have introduced concrete changes that enhanced the learning environment of those students who had been characterized as 'intellectual bloomers', by, for instance, giving them extra or more difficult work, or choosing them to undertake more enriching classroom or extracurricular activities. They may have communicated to parents that their children were more advanced, thus bringing about changes in home environments. There is thus sometimes thought to be a trade-off between ensuring high levels of internal validity and ensuring high levels of external validity.

In order to have confidence in the results of an experiment, it is important to have high levels of both internal validity and external validity. Given that internal validity can sometimes be a problem in field experiments and external validity can sometimes be a problem in laboratory experiments, some critics argue that, since both designs are flawed, there is not much point in using either method. But a more reasoned approach might be to try and incorporate both types of design together. For a study to really stand up, it should be possible to try and examine it in both settings. As Elinor Ostrom (2007: 26–7) says, 'To test theory adequately, we need to use methods that together combine external and internal validity. One gains external validity in doing field research, but internal validity in the laboratory'.

Natural experiments

The third main type of experimental design is often referred to as a natural experiment. The natural experiment relies on naturally occurring events as interventions rather than interventions controlled by the researcher. According to Morton and Williams (2009), when natural interventions occur on a particular variable of interest, we can sometimes treat the intervention as if an experimentalist manipulated the variable. Even though in this case the researcher is not doing the intervening, the approach taken with the data is as if the researcher has. Such experiments have been utilized by scholars in a wide variety of fields, including political participation (Lassen, 2005; Krasno and Green 2008), ballot design (Gordon and Huber 2007; Carman et al. 2008), political psychology (van der Brug 2001), ethnic politics (Abrajano et al. 2005), comparative politics (Posner 2004), and bureaucracy (Whitford 2002).

The attraction of a natural experiment is that it removes many of the problems associated with carrying out laboratory and field experiments. First, since a natural experiment is naturally occurring, there is not the problem of artificiality associated with the laboratory experiment. And second, since the intervention occurs independently of the actions of the researcher, there are not the ethical issues which can create obstacles to doing field experiments. However, for a naturally occurring event to approximate a 'proper experiment', it is essential that the principles of experimental research are not violated. In particular, the condition of exogeneity is crucial. For a natural experiment to be valid, there must be variation in a causal variable that is independent of all other competing factors that may affect the outcome of interest. In practice, this often difficult to achieve. Naturally occurring interventions are often not entirely random. For example, when a country changes its electoral system, we might think that this represents a good opportunity to examine the impact of institutional design on some aspect of political behaviour, such as turnout. We might even regard this as a natural experiment, since we have variation in our independent variable of interest (electoral system) while many other important factors appear to stay the same. But a problem arises if not all factors do stay the same. For example, if the decision to change the electoral system is driven in part by concerns about citizen apathy and low levels of political support, then the variation in our variable of interest will be correlated with other important factors that drive turnout.

It is therefore important to try and ensure as far as possible that the principle of random allocation is not violated. This can often be effectively achieved when government officials manipulate policies or when policies are based on near-random processes. Under these conditions, researchers may be able to exploit near experimental conditions to examine a wide variety of different issues. For example, Miller, Krosnick, and Lowe (1998) examined the effects of ballot order (the order in which candidates' names appear on the ballot) on votes for political candidates in the United States, by exploiting the fact that, in certain Ohio counties, candidates' names are rotated from one precinct to the next. Miller and colleagues found that candidates at the top of the ballot win an average vote share of 2.5 percentage points more, with the largest effects turning up in contests without an incumbent contestant and where candidates' names appeared without party affiliations.

In an 'unfortunate' natural experiment, Carman, Mitchell, and Johns (2008) examined the effects of ballot design and voting instructions on the number of spoiled votes (ballots which had not been correctly filled in) in Scotland, by exploiting the fact that two different ballot designs were used in the Scottish Parliamentary elections of 2007 (one which provided full instructions and one which provided abbreviated instructions). Carman and colleagues found that, even after taking into account other potentially important factors, such as social deprivation, the predicted number of spoiled votes was 65% greater for ballots with abbreviated instructions. Carman and colleagues call the experiment 'unfortunate' because the decision to abbreviate the ballot instructions was not an intentional one, and only came to light after the election, when academics and the media began to investigate why there were so many spoiled ballots.

But natural experiments can also arise out of specific policy interventions. In an unusual natural experiment from India, Rikhil Bhavnani (2009) examined the impact of electoral quotas on women's representation in the *Panchayat* (village council). In particular, Bhavnani examined whether electoral quotas for women alter women's chances of winning elections even after the quotas are withdrawn. He was able to answer this question by exploiting the fact that randomly chosen seats in local legislatures are set aside for women for one election at a time. Bhavnani found that the probability of a woman winning office in a seat which had previously been reserved for women (but was not anymore) was five times higher than if the constituency had not been previously reserved for women.

Issues in experimental research

Despite the obvious strengths of experimental research for testing causal hypotheses, and despite the many examples of interesting and valuable research that has been carried out using experimental methods, experimental designs are still much less common in the social sciences than in the natural sciences. Indeed, experimental research is often viewed with a great deal of suspicion, and is sometimes thought to work better in theory than in practice. This view is neatly summed up by Arendt Lijphart: 'The experimental method is the most nearly ideal method for scientific explanation, but unfortunately it can only rarely be used in political science because of practical and ethical impediments' (1971: 684–5).

The practical and ethical obstacles to experimental research have received a great deal of attention. One of the main practical objections is that, with respect to many key areas in politics, researchers simply cannot randomly assign subjects to groups and manipulate the independent variable in order to measure their impact on the dependent variable. It is one thing to randomize whether or not voters are exposed to campaign material, but it is another thing to randomize the foreign policies of governments. The really big political science variables, like culture, electoral system, level of economic development, ethnic heterogeneity, cannot be manipulated. As Green and Gerber (2003) note, it is difficult to imagine how one could randomly assign presidential and parliamentary regimes for the purpose of evaluating their relative strengths and weaknesses. Similarly, it is simply not possible to go around randomizing the determinants of war to see which given set of factors is most likely to cause two countries to start a conflict. For these reasons, it is commonly thought that political research can never fully embrace experimental methods, and that it will remain something of a niche method. This view is put forward by Smith (2002), who suggests that experimental research can only be conducted on a relatively small (and minor) fraction of the political questions that most interest people.

Although there is some truth to this criticism, it is perhaps wise not to overstate it. With a bit of imagination, the prospects for innovative field experiments are much greater than is commonly assumed. Experimental research has been carried out on big issues, such as crime and security (Keizer et al. 2008), clientelism (Wantchekon 2003), police discrimination (Heussenstamm, 1971), and the influence of the media (Gerber et al. 2007). Moreover, as Green and Gerber (2003) argue, there is a balance that political researchers need to strike between answering 'big questions' badly and 'small questions' well. As they put it: 'If we think of the expected value of research as being the product of the intrinsic value of a research question times the probability that knowledge will be advanced by the evidence flowing from that research, this trade-off comes into sharper focus.' Experimental research can therefore be an extremely effective method for helping to answer narrow tractable questions.

There are also ethical issues that must be considered when conducting experiments. Ethical issues are relevant to all types of social inquiry, and we address them in detail in Chapter 7, but they also have special significance for experimental research. As Gerry Stoker (2010) points out, ethical issues tend to be more pronounced in experimental research than in purely observational research. The act of intervening to change something raises more ethical issues than simply observing what is happening, particularly if that intervention causes harm or distress to participants or relies on some sort of deception. A seminal psychology laboratory experiment carried out by Stanley Milgram (1963) is probably the most famous example of this kind of deception. It tested the willingness of participants to harm another person 'while only following orders' by getting them to administer electric shocks to others who appeared to be suffering pain. The study raises a number of ethical issues. The first is to do with deception: participants were lied to. They did not really administer electric shocks. The second is that it may have caused participants distress: participants may have been upset to learn that they were capable of basically killing someone just because a person in a position of authority told them to do so. However, these ethical challenges are not insurmountable; and there are a number of strategies that can be employed to try and deal with them.

 ## Conclusions

Experimental research has a number of strengths. It allows researchers to investigate causal hypotheses with a great deal of confidence. There is no other research design that is quite so effective at establishing causal connections, and the principles that underpin experimental research inform much of what we do in political research. Even if experimentation is not used widely in political research (though this is beginning to change), most of our research designs are, in effect, an effort to approximate the logic of experimental design as closely as possible. In particular, the ideas of experimental control permeate much of what we do, even if it is dealt with in different ways. To compensate for our inability to completely control any one case, researchers in our field can study many cases through the use of statistical analysis (see Chapters 14 to 16). We can also try and control for important factors using comparative research (see Chapter 9).

But experimental research also has a great deal of practical and, specifically, policy relevance. Experimental research can be a very powerful tool for monitoring and assessing the implementation of different policy actions. There is certainly a great deal of potential for academics and policy-makers to work more closely together to develop experimental studies. And, as Stoker (2010) suggests, pursuing this strategy would really help to make political research more relevant to politics, political actors, and citizens. The benefit for academics is that they are able to collect data to test hypotheses that they would not otherwise be able to investigate. For example, Wantchekon would not have been able to carry out his study on clientelism in Benin without the support of the main political parties who participated in his experiment. The benefit for policy-makers is that they will get valid and reliable evidence on what difference, if any, their policy intervention makes. Policies can be very expensive to implement and can also be very ineffective at bringing about the desired change. They are thus ripe for experimental research. Indeed, just as new medicines and drugs are required to undergo rigorous trial before they are approved, there is a lot to be said for adopting the same standards for policy initiatives.

The prospects for experimental research therefore look bright. Experiments provide a rigorous and scientific way to test causal hypotheses. They also offer the potential to engage with policy-makers in order to assess the effectiveness of new policies. With a little imagination, experiments can be used to answer a wide variety of questions which tackle a range of theoretical and empirical puzzles.

Questions

- What are the strengths of experimental research?
- Why is the experimental approach not used very often in political research?
- What are the practical and ethical obstacles to experimental research? How can these obstacles be overcome?
- Experimental research can only be used to answer small questions which are of minor interest to most people. Do you agree?
- What kind of research questions may be particularly well suited to experimental designs?
- What are the relative strengths and weaknesses of laboratory and field experiments?

Guide to Further Reading

Druckman, J. N., D. P. Green, J. H. Kuklinski, and A. Lupia (eds) (2011), *Cambridge Handbook of Experimental Political Science* **(Cambridge: Cambridge University Press).**
This book contains a collection of 36 articles on experimental research in political science, covering topics such as internal and external validity, and using students as subjects, as well as detailed chapters on laboratory experiments, field experiments, survey experiments, and more. The collection also includes a number of chapters that use experiments in practice to answer questions of substantive and theoretical interest.

Morton, Rebecca B. and Kenneth C. Williams (2009), *From Nature to the Lab: The Methodology of Experimental Political Science and the Study of Causality* **(Cambridge: Cambridge University Press).**
This book provides a detailed discussion of the different ways in which experimental designs can be used in political research. It provides a comprehensive account of the different issues researchers must engage with, and is full of engaging examples to illustrate their points. Is essential reading for anyone interested in knowing more about experimental research.

Stoker, G. (2010), 'Exploring the Promise of Experimentation in Political Science; Micro-Foundational Insights and Policy Relevance', *Political Studies:* **58: 300–19.**
This article examines the ways in which experimental research can be used in mainstream political science and the potential the approach has to engage with policy-relevant research.

References

Abrajano, M., J. Nagler, and R. Alvarez (2005), 'Race Based vs. Issue Voting: A Natural Experiment', *Political Research Quarterly* 58(2): 203–18.

Ansolabehere, Stephen and Shanto Iyengar (1997), *Going Negative: How Political Advertisements Shrink and Polarize the Electorate* (New York: Free Press).

Baumrind, D. (1985), 'Research using Intentional Deception: Ethical Issues Revisited', *American Psychologist* 40: 165–74.

Bhavnani, R. (2009), 'Do Electoral Quotas Work After They Are Withdrawn? Evidence from a Natural Experiment in India', *American Political Science Review* 103(1): 23–35.

Carman, Christopher, James Mitchell, and Robert Johns (2008), 'The Unfortunate Natural Experiment in Ballot Design: The Scottish Parliamentary Elections of 2007', *Electoral Studies* 27(3): 442–59.

de Vaus, D. (2001), *Research Design in Social Science* (London: Sage).

Druckman, D. (1994), 'Determinants of Compromising Behavior in Negotiation: A Meta Analysis', *Journal of Conflict Resolution* 38: 507–56.

Druckman, J. and Cindy D. Kam (2011), 'Students as Experimental Participants: A Defense of the "Narrow Data Base"', in James N. Druckman, Donald P. Green, James H. Kuklinski, and Arthur Lupia (eds), *Cambridge Handbook of Experimental Political Science* (Cambridge: Cambridge University Press).

——, D. P. Green, J. H. Kuklinski, and A. Lupia (2006),' The Growth and Development of Experimental Research in Political Science', *American Political Science Review* 100(4) (November): 627–35.

Fréchette, G., J. Kagel, and M. Morelli (2005), 'Behavioral Identification in Coalitional Bargaining: An Experimental Analysis of Demand Bargaining and Alternating', *Econometrica* 73(6): 1893–937.

Frohlich, N. and J. A. Oppenheimer (1992), *Choosing Justice: An Experimental Approach to Ethical Theory* (Berkeley, CA: University of California Press).

Gerber, A. and D. Green (2000), 'The Effects of Canvassing, Telephone Calls, and Direct Mail on Voter Turnout: A Field Experiment', *American Political Science Review* 94(3) (September): 653–63.

——, Dean Karlan, and Daniel Bergan (2007), 'Does the Media Matter? A Field Experiment Measuring the Effect of Newspapers on Voting Behavior and Political Opinions', *American Economic Journal: Applied Economics* 1: 35–52.

Geva, N. and A. Mintz (1997), *Decision-Making on War and Peace: The Cognitive-Rational Debate* (Boulder, CO: Lynne Rienner Publishers).

Gordon, Sanford C. and Gregory A. Huber (2007), 'The Effect of Electoral Competitiveness on Incumbent Behavior', *Quarterly Journal of Political Science* 2 (2 May): 107–38.

Gosnell, Harold F. (1927), *Getting-out-the-vote: An Experiment in the Stimulation of Voting* (Chicago: University of Chicago Press).

Green, D. and A. Gerber (2003), 'The Underprovision of Experiments in Political Science', *Annals of the American Academy of Political and Social Science* 589: 94–112.

Habyarimana, J., M. Humphreys, D. Posner, and J. M. Weinstein (2007), 'Why Does Ethnic Diversity Undermine Public Goods Provision?' *American Political Science Review* 101: 709–25.

Henrich, J., R. Boyd, S. Bowles, C. Camerer, E. Fehr, and H. Gintis (eds) (2004), *Foundations of Human Society* (Oxford: Oxford University Press).

Heussenstamm, F. K. (1971), 'Bumper Stickers and the Cops', *Society* 8: 32–3.

John, P. and T. Brannan (2008), 'How Different are Telephoning and Canvassing? Results from a "Get Out the Vote" field experiment in the British 2005 General Election', *British Journal of Political Science* 38: 565–74.

Keizer, K., S. Lindenberg, and L. Steg (2008), 'The Spreading of Disorder', *Science* 322: 1681–5.

Krasno, Jonathan and Donald Green (2008), 'Do Televised Presidential Ads Increase Voter Turnout? Evidence from a Natural Experiment', *Journal of Politics* 70(1): 245–61.

Lassen, David (2005), 'The Effect of Information on Voter Turnout: Evidence from a Natural Experiment', *American Journal of Political Science* 49: 103–18.

Lijphart, A. (1971), 'Comparative Politics and the Comparative Method', *American Political Science Review* 65(3): 682–93.

Lodge, M., K. M. McGraw, and P. Stroh (1989), 'An Impression-Driven Model of Candidate Evaluation', *American Political Science Review* 83: 399–419.

Milgram, Stanley (1963), 'Behavioral Study of Obedience', *Journal of Abnormal and Social Psychology* 67(4): 371–8.

Miller, Joanne M., Jon A. Krosnick, and Laura Lowe (1998), 'The Impact of Candidate Name Order on Election Outcomes', *Public Opinion Quarterly* 62: 291–330.

Morton, R. B. and K. Williams (1999), 'Information Asymmetries and Simultaneous versus Sequential Voting', *American Political Science Review* 93: 51–67.

—— (2008), 'Experimentation in Political Science', in Janet Box-Steffensmeier, David Collier, and Henry Brady (eds) *The Oxford Handbook of Political Methodology* (Oxford: Oxford University Press).

—— (2009), *From Nature to the Lab: The Methodology of Experimental Political Science and the Study of Causality* (Cambridge: Cambridge University Press).

Ostrom, Elinor (2007), 'Why do we Need Laboratory Experiments in Political Science?', paper presented at the 2007 American Political Science Association annual meeting, Chicago, IL.

Posner, D. (2004), 'The Political Salience of Cultural Difference: Why Chewas and Tumbukas are Allies in Zambia and Adversaries in Malawi', *American Political Science Review* 98(4) (November): 529–45.

Rosenthal, R. and L. Jacobson (1968), *Pygmalion in the Classroom* (New York: Holt, Rinehart & Winston).

Simon, A. and T. Sulkin (2001), 'Habermas in the Lab: An Experimental Investigation of the Effects of Deliberation', *Political Psychology* 22: 809–26.

Smith, Rogers M. (2002), 'Should We Make Political Science More of a Science or More About Politics?' *PS: Political Science and Politics* 35(2) (June): 199–201.

Stoker, G. (2010), 'Exploring the Promise of Experimentation in Political Science: Micro-Foundational Insights and Policy Relevance', *Political Studies* 58: 300–19.

van der Brug, W. (2001), 'Perceptions, Opinions and Party Preferences in the Face of a Real-World Event: Chernobyl as a Natural Experiment in Political Psychology', *Journal of Theoretical Politics* 13(1): 53–80.

Wantchekon, L. (2003), 'Clientelism and Voting Behavior', *World Politics* 55: 399–422.

Wattenberg, Martin P. and Craig L. Brians (1999), 'Negative Campaign Advertising: Demobilizer or Mobilizer?' *American Political Science Review* 93: 891–900.

Whitford, A. (2002), 'Decentralization and Political Control of the Bureaucracy', *Journal of Theoretical Politics* 14: 167–93.

9 Comparative Research

Chapter Summary

This chapter examines the principles of comparative research design and discusses the issues and problems associated with different aspects of the approach. In doing so, we pay special attention to the issue of **case selection**, the common sources of error that are associated with comparative research, and what can be done to try and avoid or minimize them. We examine:

- case selection;
- case study;
- small-N comparison;
- large-N studies;
- selection bias;
- measurement.

Introduction

This chapter examines the principles and uses of comparative research. The comparative method is one of the most widely used methods in political research and is frequently used to study a wide range of political phenomena, from democratization to civil war to institutional design to public policy. The scope for comparative research is almost limitless. However, often the term 'comparative politics' is used rather vaguely to simply mean the study of 'foreign' countries outside the UK and USA (van Biezen and Caramani 2006). But the term 'comparative methods' really implies something more than this. As Arend Lijphart (1971) wrote, the term 'comparative politics' indicates the *how* of the analysis, but not the *what*. Comparative politics is first and foremost a methodological approach, rather than an area of substantive interest. What unites and defines comparative studies therefore has little to do with the sort of questions asked, but rather with the method used. Following Peter Mair (1996) and van Biezen and Caramani (2006), we understand the comparative method primarily in terms of the rules and standards and procedures for identifying and explaining differences and similarities between cases (often, but not always, defined in terms of countries), using concepts that are applicable in more than one case or country.

There are many different ways in which this can be done. Indeed, the comparative method actually involves a number of different methods. These methods can be distinguished primarily in terms of how many countries (or cases) are compared (denoted by the letter **N**), and how the cases for analysis are selected. Both aspects of case selection are very important. Broadly speaking, there are three main approaches. There are large-N studies (involving the analysis of many cases), small-N studies (involving the analysis of a small number of cases, typically 2, 3, 4, but with no real upper limit) and single-N studies (otherwise known as case studies). In this chapter we discuss these different comparative approaches, provide an overview of the methodological issues that they raise, and evaluate the strengths and weaknesses of each approach.

The principles of comparison

Comparison, either directly or indirectly, forms an essential part of almost all empirical analysis. In a sense it is impossible not to compare. We do it all the time, whether we are aware of it or not. Any discussion of cause and effect relies on comparing the presence of one factor against the absence of another. This has led some scholars to define the comparative method rather broadly. For example, Gabriel Almond (1966) equates the comparative method with the scientific method generally, and says 'it makes no sense to speak of a comparative politics in political science since if it is a science, it goes without saying that it is comparative in its approach'. According to this understanding, all empirical research is comparative. We might even regard the statistical analysis of survey data as a form of comparative analysis, where the **unit of analysis** is an individual. For example, we can compare young people with old people to see if there is an association between age and turnout (see Chapter 15). But the comparative method more usually refers to the study of social and political *aggregates* rather than individuals. In particular, comparative politics is frequently based on comparing differences (or similarities) between countries. But it can also be used to compare differences between units within countries, such as regions, organizations, political parties, pressure groups, or whatever.

Like all methods, comparative methods are only as useful as the purpose to which they are put. If the research project has clear theoretical goals, then comparative research can be a valuable tool for helping to answer questions about different political phenomena. But if there is little theoretical justification for the comparison, or the justification is not made clear, then comparative research is unlikely to be of much use developing or testing theory. It is very important then to think carefully about the purpose of the comparison, and to avoid falling into the trap of just comparing different countries for the sake of it, without any clear theoretical goals guiding the selection of countries to analyse.

Broadly speaking, comparative methods can be used in three main ways: (i) to apply existing theory to new cases; (ii) to develop new theory or hypotheses; and (iii) to test theory.

One of the key strengths of comparative research is that it helps to broaden our intellectual horizons. We can use comparison to see if what we think is a self-evident truth in one context also works in the same way in a different context. Comparison therefore has a number of advantages over the single country case study, and helps us to guard against the twin dangers of what Rose (1991) has labelled *false uniqueness* and *false universalism*. False uniqueness emphasizes the specificity of the case, entirely ignoring the general social forces at work, and does not move beyond 'thick description'. Problems to do with false uniqueness can sometimes be found in area studies, where researchers emphasize how unique—or exceptional—their chosen country of analysis is, and seal themselves off from wider engagement with what is being written about in other countries. By contrast, false universalism assumes that the theory tested in one country/context will be equally applicable to other countries. For example, what is found to matter in the United States, whether it is the importance of 'resources for political participation', 'the association between social diversity and trust', or 'the impact of lobby groups on government policy' is often assumed to refer to universal truths about the way politics works, rather than context-specific findings particular to one country. The only way we can ever establish uniqueness or universalism is through comparison.

An important function of comparison is therefore descriptive. Do the same things work in the same ways across different contexts? We can use comparison to apply theory developed in one context (or **case**) to another context. Rokkan (1966: 19) refers to this as a 'micro replication', which is designed 'to test out in other national and cultural settings a proposition already validated in one setting'. This type of approach is often described as theory-infirming or theory-confirming (Lijphart 1971). For example, one influential theory in studies on political behaviour which emerged in the United States is that rich people and well-educated people tend to be more politically active because they possess the 'civic skills' that reduce some of the obstacles to participation (Verba et al. 1995). This theory is not framed in a context-specific way that is peculiar only to the United States (where the research was carried out), and so might be thought to apply across different contexts and be applicable to other countries. One useful purpose of comparison is therefore to try and establish whether this is the case or not, and whether the general theory proposed really is a general theory or not (false universalism). Subsequent research carried out in different countries has found that there is in fact substantial variation in terms of how important these so-called 'civic skills' are for political participation. In Britain, for example, although they appear to be important, they are less important than in the US (Parry et al. 1992). And further afield, in India, they are not important at all, and if anything, it is those who are the most disadvantaged in society who tend to participate the most (Yadav 2000; Michelutti 2008).

Comparison can therefore serve a useful descriptive purpose, and be used to map the extent to which different theories apply (or can be replicated) across different contexts, and the extent to which different social and political phenomena will occur across different countries. But at the same time descriptive comparison only takes us so far. It is one thing to show that there is variation across contexts, or that some accounts of political participation work better in one country than in another; it is another thing to try and develop and test theories in order to explain these differences.

It is to this end that comparative methods are most frequently used. Comparison can be used to try and generate and test hypotheses about the factors that explain these variations. The advantages of comparative cross-national analysis are manifold. First, comparative methods can be used to merge different levels of analysis, and link international, national, and domestic factors in order to explain a particular political phenomenon. For example, by comparing individuals nested within countries, we are able to examine the impact of country-level factors (such as institutional arrangement) on individual behaviour. For example, comparative research on voter support for extreme right-wing parties shows that whether or not someone votes for the far right is influenced both by individual factors, such as a person's attitudes towards immigration and national factors, such as whether the person lives in a country that uses proportional representation or not. Without comparison, we would not be able to examine the importance of these 'aggregate level' factors, and so our explanation of a particular phenomenon would be partial and underdeveloped. Comparison thus allows the researcher to move beyond a purely individualistic explanation of political phenomena.

How we compare

The comparative method is primarily a method for case selection. Do we compare many or few cases? And if we compare few cases, then on what basis do we select them? In the following sections we discuss the three main forms of comparison (case study, small N, and large N). In particular, we focus on how we select cases for analysis, the different ways in which this can be done, and some of the problems and trade-offs that are involved with each approach. Whereas small-N studies are better suited to generating hypotheses than testing hypotheses, large-N studies are able to do both.

Case study

The great advantage of the case study is that by focusing on a single case, that case can be intensively examined. For this reason, case studies remain one of the main forms of research in Comparative Politics (Geddes 2003; George and Bennett 2005). On the face of it, it might appear to be a contradiction in terms to talk about a comparative case study, since it is not immediately obvious where the comparison comes from if there is only one case involved. But good case studies are nearly always situated in a comparative context. They address theory or issues that have wider intellectual relevance, use concepts that are applicable to other contexts, and may even seek to make inferences that apply to countries beyond the original case. For example, Arend Lijphart's (1977, 1999) studies of consociationalism in the Netherlands, Robert Putnam's (1993) study of social capital in Italy, and Paul Brass's (2003) study of ethnic violence in India, are all regarded as classic 'comparative studies', even though each is only based on the analysis of a single case. What sets them apart is that they have all managed to develop arguments and theories that are relevant to many other contexts, and not only say something meaningful and interesting about the case in question, but also say something meaningful about general political phenomena.

Good case studies therefore possess two important characteristics. The first is that they say something interesting and meaningful about the case that is being studied. For example, a case study of ethnic violence in India should help to shed light on the sources of conflict in India, and contribute to the academic literature that has been written on the subject with reference to the particular case. That is, the findings of the study should be *internally valid*. However, a good comparative case study should also aim to say something more general, and engage with wider academic debates that might be applicable to other contexts and other cases. For example, does the study only shed light on the sources of ethnic violence in India, or could the implications of the argument and analysis also be relevant for helping to explain the sources of ethnic conflict in other parts of the world, such as in Africa? This involves setting the case in comparative context, and proposing theories or explanations that are also *externally valid* (at least hypothetically).

Although there is a widespread assumption that case studies represent a type of qualitative research, this is not strictly true. Case studies can be based on a wide variety of different data-gathering strategies, such as interviews, surveys, ethnography, focus groups, historical documents, policy documents, and speeches, to name just a few. Indeed, many single-country case studies are based on the quantitative analysis of survey data, for example on voting behaviour in Britain, or public attitudes towards the environment in Germany, or on public attitudes towards immigrants and ethnic minorities in the Netherlands. In the following chapters, we will explore some of these methods of data collection in more detail, so the focus here is more concerned with issues of case selection.

It is the extent to which the case study engages with wider comparative themes that makes it comparative. It can do this in one of two main ways. First, it can apply theory developed in one context to another context in order to assess whether the original theory 'works', thus addressing issues to do with false uniqueness and universalism. Or, second, it can seek to develop a new theory, and generate hypotheses that can be applied to other cases. However, because the case study is only based on the analysis of a single case, a case study cannot really be used to directly test theory. For this reason, we should always treat the inferences made from a case study with a certain degree of caution. They may sound plausible, but until they have been tested on a large number of countries, we have no way of knowing.

These two main types of case study can be used in a variety of ways (Lijphart 1971; Gerring 2004, 2007a; Yin 2009). Broadly speaking, we can distinguish between case studies that (i) provide descriptive contextualization; (ii) apply existing theory to new contexts; (iii) examine exceptions to the rule; and (iv) generate new theory. Issues to do with case selection and what makes a good country to study depend upon the purpose of the case study. You must provide a rationale for why the specific case or set of cases you selected, from among all those in the larger population, were chosen. Researchers may select cases because they are *critical* (to testing a theory), or *revelatory* (reveal relationships which cannot be studied by other means) or *unusual* (throw light on extreme cases) (Yin 2009).

One function of the case study is contextual description. Purely descriptive case studies do not seek to advance or apply theory, but rather provide a thick description of a particular event or phenomenon in a particular country. These types of study are most closely associated with ethnography (see Chapter 12) and can be a valuable source of data for secondary analysis. Given that these types of study do not engage with theoretical literature, it does not make much difference how the cases are selected for analysis, since there is no attempt made to use the case to make any wider inferences. However, this approach is not used very often.

More commonly, case studies are used to *apply theory* from one context to see if it still holds in another context. Research in Politics and IR is full of examples of this type of research. In the field of electoral behaviour, many concepts have been exported from research on the United States to other countries. Perhaps one of the most important of these 'exports' is the concept of party identification or party attachment, which states that some voters develop an attachment to a political party which is so strong that it forms a part of their identity (like a religious, national, or ethnic identity) and in turn shapes the way in which they interpret political information and events. This concept was developed in the United States in the 1950s by Angus Campbell and his colleagues at the University of Michigan, and was then applied to the British context by Butler and Stokes in the 1960s (see Campbell et al.

1960; Butler and Stokes 1969). It has since been applied to many other countries in order to explain a wide variety of political behaviour.

Case studies are an incredibly powerful tool for examining whether concepts and theories travel, and whether (or not) they work in the same way in cases other than where they were originally developed. When choosing a case study to analyse for these purposes, Geddes (2003) suggests two main criteria for case selection. The first is that the case should be representative of the domains of the theories they are intended to test. That is, the case should provide a fair test of the theory. One must therefore identify the universe of cases to which the theory (or hypothesis) applies. The second criterion is that cases used for testing arguments should be different from the cases from which the arguments were induced. In this way, each case study provides a new test of the theory, and contributes to the gradual accumulation of knowledge in favour (or against) the theory.

Case studies can be used to examine specific **outliers** or **deviant cases**, and to examine countries (or cases) that do not fit existing theory and are known to deviate from established generalizations. This type of case study is still based on developing existing theory, and seeks to uncover the reasons why the theory does not apply to the case in question. Case studies of this type have often focused on countries that are thought to be 'exceptional' for one reason or another, such as why there is no socialist political party in the United States, even though experience of industrialization suggests there should be one, or why there is no democracy in rich countries like Saudi Arabia, when modernization theory suggests there should be. Rogowski (2004: 82) notes the central importance of a deviant case in which the outcome is unexpectedly wrong: 'A powerful, deductive, internally consistent theory can be seriously undermined . . . by even one wildly discordant observation.' George and Bennett (2005: 114–15) suggest that such deviant cases may also yield information about previously unidentified causal mechanisms that may also operate in other cases (see also Brady and Collier 2004).

Case studies of this type can therefore be theory-confirming or theory-infirming (Lijphart 1971). A theory-confirming case study is one which tends to support the original theory, and shows that it has wider applicability beyond its original context. It thus adds further empirical support to the original theory. By contrast, a theory-infirming case study is one that does not support the original theory, and shows that it is found wanting in some way. However, it is not possible to go as far as to say that a theory-infirming case study can be used to reject the original theory, since just because the theory is found not to apply to a single case, it does not mean that it does not (or will not) apply to other cases.

For this reason, the idea of what has been termed a **crucial case** (Eckstein 1975) is controversial. A case is crucial if it can be regarded as crucial for the confirmation or disconfirmation of a theory. Case selection is based on the likelihood or unlikelihood of the outcome of interest occurring (Bennet and Elman, 2006). According to Gerring (2007b: 232) 'a most-likely case is one that, on all dimensions except the dimension of theoretical interest, is predicted to achieve a certain outcome and yet does not. It is therefore disconfirmatory. A least-likely case is one that, on all dimensions except the dimension of theoretical interest, is predicted not to achieve a certain outcome and yet does so. It is confirmatory.' The 'least-likely' case study relies on what Levy (2002: 144) has labelled the Sinatra inference: if the theory can make it here, it can make it anywhere. However, despite providing a tough empirical test for the theory in question, it is debatable whether any one-off case can ever be regarded as critical to confirming or disconfirming a theory (see Gerring 2007b for a detailed discussion).

But perhaps the most important use of the case study is to *generate new theory* and hypotheses in areas where no theory exists. The generation of new hypotheses and theory often develops from the analysis of particular case studies. Such case studies can be of great theoretical value, as the examples mentioned earlier attest. They tend to work best when the case selected for analysis provides what Naroll (1966) calls a sort of 'crucial experiment' in which certain variables of interest happen to be present in a special way.

Recently, there has been a great deal of discussion about the merits of using case studies to investigate causal mechanisms underpinning the association between two variables (Brady and Collier (eds) 2004; George and Bennett 2005). This is often described as **process tracing**. It involves looking for evidence of the pressures, incentives, motivations, and decision-making calculus in any given instance of action (George and Bennett 2005), often through the use of elite interview (see Chapter 11). It thus refers to a method of data collection and analysis, and although it is frequently associated with the case study, it can also be used for small-N analysis. Indeed, quantitative analysis often tests for the presence of causal mechanisms as well.

Case studies are widely used in comparative politics. They have a number of key strengths. They allow for a detailed analysis of political phenomena, with rich textual description. Because of this they do not tend to operate at a high level of theoretical abstraction and there is a good match between theory and evidence. They thus generally have relatively high internal validity. However, despite these strengths, they also suffer from a number of fairly obvious limitations, particularly in terms of how far the findings from one case study may be generalized to other contexts. It is not always apparent what lessons, if any, may be learned from a case study until the same type of analysis is repeated elsewhere. Indeed, even when apparently similar hypotheses have been tested in different contexts, it can still be difficult to draw any firm conclusions about whether or not the results confirm (or infirm) the original theory unless the hypotheses have been tested in exactly the same way in each case. Differences in the results may be down to differences in method, model specification (which factors are considered) or measurement (how key concepts are operationalized). One obvious way to reduce some of these problems, then, is simply to increase the number of cases considered in the analysis. This type of comparative research is known as small-N comparison, where N refers to the number of cases that are examined.

Small-N comparison

A lot of comparative research is based on small-N samples. These typically involve the comparison of two or more cases, and although there is no real upper limit to the number of cases that may be examined, it normally does not exceed more than a dozen or so. Small-N comparative studies of this type are widely used in political research, and in some respects are the quintessential form of comparative analysis. Indeed, Lijphart (1971) defines the comparative approach in terms of small-N analysis (in contrast to the statistical approach of large-N studies). Classic small-N studies include Michael Lewis-Beck's (1986) four-nation study of economic voting in Britain, France, Germany, and Italy; Seymour Martin Lipset's (1959) study of the social requisites of democracy in Europe and South America;

Thelda Skocpol's (1979) study of revolution in Russia, France, and China; Barrington Moore's (1966) study of democracy and dictatorship, and Almond and Verba's (1963) study of civic culture in the UK, United States, Germany, Italy, and Mexico. In addition, there are numerous area studies that rely on small-N comparisons to examine a variety of topics, such as ethnic politics in Africa (Posner 2004), party systems in East Europe (Kitschelt et al. 1999), and democratic stability in Latin America (Mainwaring and Scully (eds) 1995), to name but a few.

Comparisons of this type, based on the systematic analysis of several countries, have many advantages. They allow for the detailed in-depth analysis of the case study, but at the same time provide greater scope for contextualization. As such, they leave out neither the particular nor the general. However, although these small-N studies can be extremely useful for generating new ideas and answering questions, they are also fraught with problems, and the careless selection of cases for analysis can lead to the production of very misleading results. When we only analyse a few cases, it makes a great deal of difference which cases we analyse. Indeed, if we wanted to, it would be very easy to fix the results to get almost any answer that we wanted by just handpicking three or four cases that appear to confirm our hypotheses and ignoring all the other cases which do not.

Therefore to make an argument convincing, a number of important considerations need to be taken into account, and the justification for case selection needs to be made clear. If cases are selected in a haphazard way or without care and attention, then there is the very real risk of introducing **selection bias**. This is something that the researcher needs to be acutely aware of. To a greater or lesser extent problems associated with selection bias affect all small-N comparisons, since we are only dealing with a limited number of cases. We therefore have to pay special attention to how we select cases in order to try and minimize the risk of it occurring.

Small-N comparisons are based on the strategic selection of cases, appropriate to test a theory. Which cases we select therefore depends upon the theory we are interested in testing. But at the same time, there are a number of general principles that guide case selection. We are rarely if ever interested in comparing two (or more) cases that are exactly the same in every respect or completely different in every respect. Besides the almost practical impossibility of finding two such countries, even if we could, there would be little analytical point to such an exercise, since the comparison would be redundant (we would basically just be looking at the same thing twice). Rather, we are generally interested in comparing cases that are similar in some respects and different in other respects. We try to take advantage of the similarities and differences we see in the real world to see if the pattern of observed variations is consistent (or not) with our theoretical expectations. In this way, we can test hypotheses that move beyond the purely domestic to examine how the characteristics of countries and the relationship between countries influence political phenomena.

There are two main approaches that have been used to select cases for small-N studies. These are the **Most Similar Systems Design** (MSSD) and **Most Different Systems Design** (MDSD) (Przeworski and Teune 1970). These are based, respectively, on Mills' Method of Difference and Method of Disagreement. Each approach makes slightly different use of the observed similarities and differences that we observe between countries, though the logic of each is quite similar. We discuss each of these in detail below.

Most Similar Systems Design

The Most Similar Systems Design is based on selecting countries that share many (theoretically) important characteristics, but differ in one crucial respect (related to the hypothesis of interest). This sort of approach is frequently used in area studies (Przeworski and Teune 1970: 33), where countries within a specific region, such as Africa (or Latin America, East Europe, or South Asia, etc.), are similar in many important respects, perhaps to do with their culture, history, level of economic development, and social structure. The shared characteristics act as a control in order to test whether the crucial difference between the countries is associated with the variation in the dependent variable.

Table 9.1 provides a conceptual overview of this method. The columns refer to the selected cases and the rows refer to the variables of interest. We can see that the selected cases are similar with respect to variables A, B, and C. These variables constitute the control, and cannot meaningfully explain the variation in the dependent variable, since they are the same for all cases. However, importantly, the selected cases do vary on variable X. This is the variable related to our key hypothesis, which we think helps to explain the variation in our dependent variable Y. If our hypothesis is supported, then we should observe that our dependent variable Y varies in accordance with the variation in X. Thus the presence (or absence) of the key explanatory factor is able to account for the variation in the outcome of interest.

Example 1: the political salience of ethnic cleavages

We can illustrate the logic of this selection method with an example. A classic study of this type was carried out by Daniel Posner (2004) on the political salience of ethnic cleavages. Posner wanted to explore the factors that are associated with the political salience of cultural difference, and in particular, the factors associated with whether different ethnic groups were political allies or rivals. His hypothesis is that the political salience of ethnic difference is related to the population size of the groups in question. When the ethnic groups are both large, they constitute a viable base for political support, and so politicians will mobilize the groups, and the cleavage that divides them will become politically salient. If, however, the groups are both small, then they will go unmobilized and the cleavage that separates them will remain politically irrelevant. The cultural differences between the groups will still exist, but there will be no political importance attached to them.

Table 9.1 Most Similar Systems Design (MSSD)

	Case 1	Case 2	Case n	
	A	A	A	Overall similarities
	B	B	B	
	C	C	C	
	X	Not X	Not X	Crucial differences
	Y	Not Y	Not Y	

Using a Most Similar Systems Design, Posner examined the political salience of ethnic differences between two tribes, the Chewas and Tumbukas, who constituted a large proportion of the electorate in Malawi, but only a small proportion of the electorate in Zambia (Table 9.2). In doing so, Posner was able to control for a wide variety of factors that previous research suggested was important. The key thing to remember is that the selection of cases is based, in theory, on the independent variables, not on the dependent variable. The control variables are the factors that the ethnic groups in each country share. Ideally, our control variables should include variables that are theoretically important, since failure to include an important factor may result in **omitted variable bias**. Omitted variable bias, as the name suggests, occurs when we fail to take into account important explanatory factors. The consequence of this is that factors that are not really causally important may appear important because they are associated with (or have even influenced) the unmeasured missing variable. This can cause **spurious association** (see Chapter 16). The extent to which we can have confidence that our results will stand up and be robust is therefore dependent in part upon how adequately we have managed to control for other potentially important factors.

Posner's study controls for four important factors, variables A to D, which are all thought to increase the salience of ethnic differences. Variable A refers to the racial differences between the two groups, variable B refers to the cultural differences between the two groups, variable C refers to the historical development of the political system, and variable D refers to the experience of colonialism. Since these factors are the same for each of the countries, they act as a control. If we control for theoretically important variables, and our variable of interest appears to matter, then we can have greater confidence in the results. Importantly, then, the variable that relates to the hypothesis we are interested in testing varies across our cases. In Posner's example, variable X refers to the size of the ethnic groups.

Following Posner, our expectation is that the variation in the size of the ethnic groups (our explanatory factor) will be associated with variation in the salience of ethnic cleavages (the thing we are trying to explain). That is, when the ethnic groups are both large, the cleavage that divides them will be politically salient and so they will be rivals, but when the groups are both small, the cleavage that separates them will remain politically irrelevant and so they will be allies. If we observe this pattern, then our hypothesis is supported. If we do not, then

Table 9.2 Most Similar Systems Design (MSSD): the political salience of ethnic differences

Zambia	Malawi	
A	A	
B	B	Overall
C	C	similarities
D	D	
E=0	E=1	Crucial
Low political salience	High political salience	differences

Notes: A = racial differences between groups
B = cultural differences between groups
C = historical development of political system
D = experience of colonialism
E = (0 = ethnic groups are small) (1 = ethnic groups are large)

our hypothesis is not supported. From Table 9.2 we can see that the hypothesis does indeed receive empirical support, and that the political salience of ethnic differences is higher in Malawi, where the ethnic groups are both large, than it is in Zambia, where the groups are both small.

Of course, when we are dealing with only a few cases, there are always going to be lots of potentially important differences between the cases, and it is impossible to completely control for everything that might be theoretically relevant. In this sense, as Przeworski and Teune (1970) suggest, it is easy to overdetermine the dependent variable. Lijphart (1971) describes this as the 'too many variables, too few countries' problem. Whichever cases we select there will always be a number of differences between them, which makes it very difficult to establish which are the crucial differences and which are not.

For example, suppose we were interested in explaining the sources of democratic stability. Our hypothesis might be that democratic stability is related to the institutionalization of political parties in society. That is, where political parties have deep roots and are embedded within society, democracy tends to be more stable. To test this hypothesis, we might compare India and Pakistan, since they share many important similarities. They shared the experience of colonial rule under the British, became independent at the same time, and were both poor with low literacy rates and a largely agricultural economy at the time of democratization. In many respects, then, they were similar on theoretically important independent variables. These shared characteristics are unable to explain any differences between the two countries, such as why democracy has persisted in India over the past 50 years, but struggled in Pakistan, with frequent episodes of authoritarian rule. Our key independent variable of party system institutionalization does, however, appear to vary in the expected way between the two countries. Whereas the Congress Party in India had a strong base right across the country, penetrating even the most remote rural villages, the Muslim League in Pakistan was much more weakly institutionalized.

However, there are also many potentially relevant differences between the countries, to do with leadership (Nehru versus Jinnah), social demography and religion, institutional capacity, international support, and so on. It is difficult to establish, using pair-wise comparison, which of these differences is the crucial causal difference, although some candidates will be more plausible than others. It is also difficult to establish what combination of these variables is important. If we were to add more cases to our analysis, we might be able to eliminate some of the spurious differences that we observe between the two countries, but in reality there are rarely enough cases to find the right combination of similarities and differences we need to exactly test our theory.

Most Different Systems Design

The logic of Most Different Systems Design is to select cases that are different in most respects and only similar on the key explanatory variable of interest. Thus, rather than comparing countries that are very similar to each other, we compare countries that are very different from each other, hence the name. With this approach, the observed differences on important variables act as a control in order to test whether the crucial similarity that the countries share is associated with the dependent variable.

Table 9.3 Most Different Systems Design (MDSD)

Case 1	Case 2	Case n	
A	Not A	Not A	Overall
B	Not B	Not B	differences
C	Not C	Not C	
X	X	X	Crucial
Y	Y	Y	similarity

Table 9.3 provides a conceptual overview of this method. Once again, the columns refer to the selected cases and the rows refer to the variables in the analysis. This time we can see that the cases are different with respect to variables A, B, and C. These variables constitute the control. Importantly, our cases are all similar with respect to the key independent variable of interest, X. If our hypothesis is supported, then we should observe that our dependent variable Y is also similar across our cases. Thus the presence of the key explanatory factor is associated with the presence of the outcome of interest.

Example 2: revolutions

We can illustrate this approach with the example of Theda Skocpol's (1979) famous study of revolutions, which was based in part upon a Most Different Systems Design, comparing the causes of social revolution in three very different countries, Russia (1917–21), France (1787–1800), and China (1911–49) (Table 9.4). (See Geddes (2003) for an extended discussion of this example.) Broadly speaking, Skocpol's main argument is that social revolutions occur when external military threats provoke a split in the ruling elite and peasant communities take advantage of this split and revolt. Accordingly, countries which experience state breakdown and peasant revolt will also tend to experience social revolutions, even if they differ in many other important respects.

In order to test this hypothesis, Skocpol selected three countries very different in social, economic, and political terms, but similar in terms of having autonomous peasant populations, and similar in that they all experienced periods of external military threats which produced splits in their ruling elite. The key thing to remember with classic MDSDs is that the

Table 9.4 Most Different Systems Design (MSSD): the causes of revolution

France	Russia	China	
A	Not A	Not A	Overall
B	Not B	Not B	differences
C	Not C	Not C	
X-Elite split	X-Elite split	X-Elite split	Crucial
Y-Revolution	Y-Revolution	Y-Revolution	similarity

Notes: A = political system
B = social and cultural context
C = economic conditions

selection of cases should be based on the independent variables, not on the dependent variable. In the case of Skocpol's study, it is debatable whether this decision rule was followed (we will return to this later). In this example, then, the control variables are the factors that are different for each country, such as their social, economic, and political backgrounds. The key independent variables of interest are the same for each country: they all had elite splits, peasant uprisings and state collapse, and crucially, the outcome variable is the same for each country as well: they all experienced social revolutions, thus confirming the initial hypothesis.

Issues in small-N research

The issue of case selection in small-N studies is extremely important because the cases we choose to analyse can influence the answers we get to a particular question, and this is particularly the case when we are only analysing a few cases. When this occurs, it is known as selection bias. If we do not think carefully about case selection, we can end up with answers that are not very robust, or are even somewhat misleading. That is, we will make faulty inferences. The best way to avoid this happening is to conduct a large-N study and select cases using random probability methods or to take a full census of cases. But this is not always a viable option. To a certain extent, then, selection bias, or at least the risk of selection bias, is always going to be a danger in small-N studies, particularly when the study is designed to try and shed light on a broader phenomenon, and make some sort of generalization, however tentatively put.

Discussion about the relative merits of different strategies for selecting cases in small-N research has been one of the most controversial and hotly debated issues in comparative research (see King et al. 1994; Ragin 2000, 2008; Geddes 2003; Collier et al. 2004; George and Bennett 2005 for different sides of the debate). One of the main strategies that has been proposed is to select cases according to their characteristics on the independent variables (see King et al. 1994; Geddes 2003). This strategy has been elevated to almost law-like status: never select on the dependent variable. Some have even gone as far as to say that selecting on the dependent variable is a type of 'inferential felony' (Achen and Snidal 1989). This position has been challenged by some scholars (see Collier and Mahoney 1996; Dion 1998), but before outlining the criticisms, which we will return to later, it is worth discussing the logic behind the initial decision rule.

The argument goes that if we select on the dependent variable and do not pay sufficient attention to the independent variables, we may unwittingly exclude important factors from our analysis, or fail to control for them adequately. This means that what looks like a strong causal relationship between two variables may in fact be spurious. For example, suppose we want to examine the representation of women in parliament. We might choose three countries which have a relatively high percentage of women in parliament, such as Sweden (45%), Norway (40%), and Finland (40%), and seek to identify what factors they have in common. Since all three cases have electoral systems based on proportional representation, we might conclude that this is an important factor, and infer that PR systems are conducive to promoting the representation of women in parliament. But this inference would be wrong. There are many other countries with PR systems that do not have a high percentage of women in parliament, such as Brazil (8%), Turkey (9%), and Uruguay (15%). The percentage of women in parliament in Scandinavia may therefore have little to do with the electoral system, and more to do with the strategy of political recruitment by political elites or the political culture of the general public, both of which may be exogenous to institutional design. However, because we have not taken these factors into account when selecting our cases, it is difficult to establish which, if any, are important. The problem with not selecting cases on the independent variable, then, is that it makes it very difficult to control for potentially important variables.

When research is theory-driven, or at least guided (see Chapters 5, 6, and 7), we should always have some hunch that guides our research, and accordingly we should design our research in order to provide an appropriate 'test' of this hunch. Therefore, if our hunch is that the type of electoral system is an important factor in determining the representation of women in parliament, we would want to select cases that allow us to explore this, which means selecting cases according to the independent variables. In small-N analysis, this can be done either by selecting cases that are very similar to each other but vary on the key independent variable (Most Similar Systems Design) or selecting cases that are very different to each other but are similar on the key independent variable (Most Different Systems Design). Both these approaches allow us to control for potentially important factors, and so reduce the risk of obtaining spurious relationships.

When carrying out MDSD, it is easy to fall into the trap of selecting cases on the dependent variable. Indeed, MDSD is often incorrectly characterized as being based on this strategy. For example, if we were interested in exploring the cause of revolutions, we might be tempted to select three countries which have experienced revolutions and see what they have in common. This is, in essence, what Skocpol did in her study of revolutions, which has been criticized by Geddes (2003). Although Skocpol's study has been incredibly influential, it is also widely regarded as being based on spurious inference, in so far as the main causes of revolution do not appear to be generalizable to other relevant cases (see Geddes 2003). Geddes argues that there are lots of cases that do not conform to Skocpol's theoretical expectations, where there have been instances of external threat which did not lead to a social revolution. Although in some ways this is part and parcel of small-N research, there are also some specific issues to do with case selection that may have contributed towards this problem in Skocpol's study. Geddes argues that, in essence, what Skocpol did was select her cases on the dependent variable. That is, she didn't select them because they had all experienced peasant uprisings and state collapse, but because they had all experienced a social revolution.

However, selection on the dependent variable can just as easily occur in Most Similar System Designs. For example, if would not be wise to select two cases that have populist leaders and two cases that do not and look to see how they are different, because if you do, you are just as likely to introduce the same kind of selection errors. In both cases, you risk leaving out or not properly considering important explanatory factors, which will bias the results. The best way of ensuring that this doesn't happen (or at least is less likely to happen) is to base the selection on the independent variables. If prior theory suggests, for example, that institutional weakness is an important source of populism, then it is a good idea to take this into account when you select your cases. Thus, whether you are carrying out MSSD or MDSD, in theory the values of the cases on the dependent variable should not be a criterion for selection, and all selection decisions should be based on the values of the cases on the independent variables only. Of course, in practice, we often cannot help but know what value the dependent variable takes for each of our cases, but the important thing is that this knowledge should not influence our selection decisions (and if it does, we risk introducing greater selection error).

With exploratory research, there is sometimes a justification for selecting on the dependent variable if the study is in a genuinely new field and prior research does not suggest any important explanatory factors. Under these rare circumstances, it is not possible to control for theoretically important independent variables because no such background literature exists. However, instances of new research areas that have absolutely no connection to previous research are exceptionally rare. And even where they do exist, the researcher generally still poses some guiding themes or foreshadowed problems (see Chapter 12) that they want to explore, and so these factors should also feed into the selection of cases.

In recent years, there has been a bit of a qualitative backlash against this principle of selection, perhaps partly in response to the overtly statistical language in which King et al. (1994) originally framed their decision rule (see Collier and Mahoney 1996; Ragin 2000, 2008; Collier et al. 2004: 85–102; George and Bennett 2005). In essence, what these qualitative methodologists argue is that when certain qualitative methodologies are employed, particularly process tracing, it is permissible to select on the dependent variable. According to George and Bennett (2005), process tracing is fundamentally different from methods that rely on 'co-variation', and the method's contribution to causal inference arises from its evidence on the process which connects the cause and the outcome. Accordingly, to scholars like Collier et al. (2004) and Bennett and Elman (2006), it is therefore not susceptible to selection bias, which means that the principles of case selection discussed above are largely irrelevant, and that cases may be selected on the basis of the dependent variable (see Bennett and Elman 2006 for further discussion on this point). This is fine up to a point, at least in terms of describing what happens within a given case (internal validity). But as soon as we are interested in comparison and making wider inferences (external validity), it is a good idea to take the issue of case selection seriously, or else we can easily end up with misleading results (see Chapter 10 on sampling principles).

A second criticism that is often made against the principle of never selecting on the dependent variable is that there is a distinction between necessary and sufficient causes. Accordingly, selecting on the dependent variable, and looking to see what the countries have in common, can reveal the necessary conditions (or causes) for an outcome of interest, even if these causes are not in themselves sufficient to produce or cause the outcome of interest (see Dion 1998; Braumoeller and Goertz (eds) 2000; and Goertz and Starr 2003). For example, with reference to Skocpol, Dion (1998) distinguishes between a claim based on a sufficient condition for something to happen, such as 'state crisis leads to social revolution', and a claim based on a necessary condition for something to happen, such as 'social revolutions arise only if there is a state crisis'. Whereas state crisis which does not lead to social revolution is evidence against the sufficient proposition, only a social revolution which did not experience state crisis is evidence against the necessary condition. Therefore, in order to test hypotheses based on necessary causes, it is permissible to select countries which all have the same outcome on the dependent variable and see what they have in common.

Although this is a valid point, it might be argued that it is often useful to know whether the condition is only necessary or whether it is necessary and sufficient, in which case selecting on the dependent variable is not of much help. It might also be argued that it is difficult to distinguish between a necessary condition and a spurious condition. For example, suppose we are interested in democracy, and want to investigate the claim that 'democracy only persists over the long term in mono-ethnic societies'. If we select on the dependent variable and only choose countries which have been democratic for more than 20 years, the chances are that they will be ethnically homogeneous, confirming our hypothesis. But this does not mean that ethnic homogeneity is a necessary cause for democratic persistence. It is in fact not a cause at all, and the apparent coincidence between democratic stability and ethnic homogeneity is spurious, driven by the association between ethnic diversity and economic development (see Chapter 16). The only way we can try and knock down spurious relationships is to take seriously the idea of controlling for theoretically important factors, and the most effective way in which we can do this is with reference to selecting cases on the basis of the independent variables.

This brings us to a second related point, which is often confused with the principle of not selecting on the dependent variable. Many people believe that it is a bad idea not to have any variation in the dependent variable. That is, it is desirable to have negative cases as well as positive cases, such as cases where there has not been ethnic conflict, as well as cases where there has been ethnic conflict. This suggests that a Most Similar System Design is preferable to a Most Different Systems Design, since the latter is often unfairly criticized as selecting countries with the same outcome variables. But the logic underlying this supposition is faulty. Selecting cases so that there is variation in the dependent variable is still selecting cases on the dependent variable. The problems of selection bias do not come from the fact that there is no variation in the dependent variable, but from the fact that important independent variables have not been properly controlled for.

The key then is to control for theoretically important independent variables in order to test a specific hypothesis. Whether the approach used is MDSD or MSSD, failing to control for theoretically important variables can introduce error into the analysis and risk producing unreliable results. The risk of this occurring is no greater when case selection is associated with similarities in the outcome variable than when it is associated with differences in the outcome variable. However, these problems can be compounded. The worst-case scenario is to select on the dependent variable and choose similar types of countries with a similar outcome variable, or conversely to select different types of countries with a different outcome variable. The former is perhaps more common in comparative research and is a particular problem in area studies, where the dependent variable is the same for all selected cases. For example, studies on the rise of the 'New Left' in Latin America may seek to identify the common factors underpinning the electoral success of leftist leaders like Hugo Chávez in Venezuela, Evo Morales in Bolivia, and Rafael Correa in Ecuador. Given that these countries share many similarities, and that many of these similarities may also be shared with other countries in the region which have not experienced the sudden rise of 'New Left' leaders, it would be easy to ascribe causal significance to similarities between the three countries that are not really that important at all.

When we are dealing with just a small number of cases, selection bias is always likely to be a problem. We cannot get rid of it completely, and the harsh reality is that we cannot aim to make robust generalizations when we have a sample of just two or three cases. For this reason small-N studies are generally better at generating theory than testing theory. It is difficult ever to say with confidence that a theory is good or bad when it is just tested against a small number of cases. It can apply or not, but until it has been applied to a large number of cases, it is difficult to draw any strong conclusions. The only way we can have confidence that our findings can be robustly generalized and are not based on spurious associations is to gradually extend the analysis and test the key hypotheses across more and more cases.

This can be done either by replicating small-N studies using different cases, or by carrying out large-N quantitative research that seeks to test more widely insights generated from small-N analysis.

Of course, under many circumstances, small-N research is the only option. Often the population of interest is not the whole world, but only a handful of countries. For example, if we are interested in the success (or failure) of market reforms in fragile democracies, then there is only a limited number of countries that would be eligible for inclusion (Weyland 2002). But this does not change the basic point. Until the theory has been tested on a large number of cases (whether they exist or not), then the wider implications of the findings must be treated with caution.

The comparative inferences we can draw from small-N studies are therefore much more tentative than the inferences we can draw from large-N studies. This is because the standard for finding supporting evidence in favour (or against) a hypothesis tends to be somewhat different. In quantitative analysis (as we discuss in Chapters 14 to 16), the presence (or absence) of causal relationships are defined probabilistically. That is, for a hypothesis to be supported (or rejected), we make a decision based on the balance of probability. However, in small-N studies, it becomes more difficult to talk about probabilistic causality. If we compare three cases and observe the expected relationship in two of them, do we reject or accept our working hypothesis? Generally, in small-N studies, causality is deterministic. That is, in order to find evidence to support a hypothesis, the expected pattern needs to be observed in all the cases. This obviously creates a problem in that it is quite easy to reject a hypothesis that is actually true, just because one of the cases deviates from the expected pattern.

Qualitative comparative analysis (intermediate N)

Recently, discussion of small-N comparison has moved in a number of different directions with the development of Qualitative Comparative Analysis (QCA). QCA draws on insights from the methodology of necessary and sufficient conditions, Boolean algebra, and fuzzy-set logic (e.g. Ragin 1987, 2000, 2008; Goertz and Starr (eds) 2003). QCA has grown in popularity over the past few years, and there are now a whole host of textbooks devoted to explaining the method (see Ragin 1987, 2000, 2008; Caramani 2009; Rihoux and Ragin (eds) 2009, http://www.compasss.org). Typically, qualitative researchers examine a few cases at a time in detail, and look at how the different parts of a case fit together, both contextually and historically. According to Ragin, by formalizing the logic of qualitative analysis, QCA makes it possible to bring the logic and empirical intensity of qualitative approaches to studies that embrace more than a handful of cases, which would normally be analysed using variable-orientated, quantitative methods. In some ways, then, QCA occupies an intermediary position between small-N analysis and large-N analysis, and is generally used for samples that range from about a dozen or so cases to several hundred.

Boolean methods of logical comparison represent each case as a combination of causal and outcome conditions. These combinations can be compared with each other and then logically simplified through a process of paired comparison. Computer algorithms can be used to provide techniques for simplifying this type of data. (Software is available on Charles Ragin's website at: http://www.u.arizona.edu/~cragin/fsQCA.) But when only a few cases are used, it is also possible to do it by hand. The data matrix is reformulated as a **truth table** (see Ragin 1987).

Broadly speaking, there are two main ways of doing QCA. The first is known as **crisp set** QCA, in which all the variables in the analysis are treated as simple dichotomies (that is, the hypothesized causal condition is either present or absent). The second is known as **fuzzy set** QCA, in which variables are allowed to take different values and are calibrated on an interval scale between 0.0 and 1.0 (see Ragin 2008: chapter 2). A conventional (or crisp) set is dichotomous: a case is either 'in' or 'out' of a set, for example, the set of democracies. Thus, a conventional set is comparable to a binary variable with two values, 1 ('in', i.e. democracy) and 0 ('out', i.e. non-democracy). A fuzzy set, by contrast, permits membership in the interval between 0 and 1, while retaining the two qualitative states of full membership and full non-membership. Thus, the fuzzy set of democracies could include countries which are 'fully in' the set (fuzzy membership = 1.0), some who are 'almost fully in' the set (membership = 0.90), some who are neither 'more in' nor 'more out' of the set (membership = 0.5, also known as the 'crossover point'), some who are 'barely more out than in' the set (membership = 0.45), and so on, down to those who are 'fully out' of the set (membership = 0). It is up to the researcher to specify procedures for assigning fuzzy membership scores to cases, and these procedures must be both open and explicit so that they can be evaluated by other scholars (see Ragin 2008). Despite these measurement differences, the general analytical principles of the two approaches are much the same. For the sake of simplicity, we will focus just on crisp sets to illustrate how the approach can work.

QCA is a powerful heuristic tool as it can be used for several purposes, such as summarizing data, producing typologies, and elaborating new theories or models, as well as for testing existing theories, models, and hypotheses (Rihoux 2006). In particular, QCA is well suited to unravelling causal complexity in order to detect the different conditions (or configurations) that can lead to the same outcome occurring (which is sometimes called equifinality or multiple causation). The way in which it does this is by utilizing what are known as truth

Table 9.5 Hypothetical truth table showing three causes of successful strikes

Condition			Outcome	Frequency
A	B	C	S	N
0	0	0	0	4
0	0	1	0	6
0	1	0	1	5
0	1	1	0	3
1	0	0	0	9
1	0	1	1	6
1	1	0	1	2
1	1	1	1	4

Notes: A = booming product market
B = threat of sympathy strikes
C = large strike fund
S = success of strike
N = number of cases

tables. Truth tables present all the logical possible combinations of conditions and the outcome associated with each combination. By examining all the possible different combinations of variables that are associated with an outcome occurring (or not), the main aim of the approach is to try and simplify these different combinations to as few distinct (necessary) combinations as possible. This is done using something called Boolean algebra (see Ragin 2008 for a step-by-step guide to how this works in practice).

We can illustrate how this approach works by drawing on a hypothetical example. Table 9.5 reproduces Ragin's (1987: 96) hypothetical truth table on the factors associated with the success of strike activity. In this example, the aim of the research is to explore how three main factors influence whether or not a strike is successful. The three causal conditions are A = booming product market; B = threat of sympathy strikes; and C = large strike fund. Data are collected on 39 strikes, and for each case the causal conditions are (hypothetically) coded 1 if they are thought to be present (and 0 otherwise). Similarly, the outcome variable is coded 1 if the strike was successful, and 0 if it was not. The first three columns of the truth table refer to the independent variables/causal conditions. The rows refer to all the logical combinations that these conditions can take. When there are three independent variables, there are eight possible combinations in which they can be arranged. In more complex analysis, the rows (representing combinations of causal conditions) may be quite numerous. The fourth column refers to the dependent variable, and shows the recorded outcome (whether or not the strike was successful) for each combination of conditions. The last column refers to the number of cases that were observed in each row (though these are not really used in the subsequent analysis).

From Table 9.5 we can see that the four different combinations of conditions all led to a successful strike (where S = 1). We can express these conditions in an equation as follows:

S = ABC + AbC + ABc + aBc,

where a capital letter indicates that the causal condition in question was present and a lower-case letter indicates that it was absent.

The first step in the Boolean analysis of these data is to try and combine as many compatible rows of the truth table as possible. In a sense, this involves eliminating all redundant terms. If two combinations differ in only one factor but produce the same result, then the factor they differ on can be thought of as irrelevant.

So for example, since ABC and AbC are both associated with the presence of outcome S = 1, we may suspect that B is superfluous. That is, when we have A and C together, it doesn't matter whether we have B or not in order for S to occur. We can therefore combine the first two terms in the equation to produce AC.

Similarly, when B is present and C is not present (Bc), it doesn't appear to make any difference whether or not A is present in order for S to occur. So we can combine the terms ABc and aBc to produce Bc.

We can therefore express the equation in slightly simplified terms as:

S= AC + Bc.

This final equation states simply that successful strikes occur when there is a booming market for the product produced by the workers *and* a large available strike fund (AC) or when there is the threat of sympathy strikes by workers in associated industries combined with a low strike fund (Bc). This finding suggests that strikes can be successful for different reasons.

It also suggests that whereas the impact of A and C is conditional on the presence of each other, the impact of B is conditional on the absence of C. That is, the threat of sympathy strikes is taken seriously only when the striking workers badly need the support of other workers.

In order to use the truth table presented above, it is necessary to determine an output value for each row that is either 1 or 0. With hypothetical data, this is not a problem, but the real world is not so neat and the use of truth tables is often complicated by the presence of contradictory outcomes. That is where cases which share the same causal conditions exhibit different outcomes on the variable of interest. It is therefore more difficult to illustrate how this method works with real data.

Nonetheless, this type of approach has been used, adapted, and developed for a variety of purposes and to explore a variety of different political phenomena. One common application of the approach is to examine the extent to which different pathways (or combinations of causal conditions) can lead to similar outcomes. Recent examples include Rihoux's (2006) analysis of the success of Green parties in Western Europe, Veugelers and Magnan's (2005) analysis of the success of Far Right parties in Western Europe, and Berg-Schlosser's (2007) analysis of the success of democracy in Africa. Berg-Schlosser (2007) uses QCA to identify the different pathways to democratic success in Africa. He identifies four main groups of countries, in which each group developed democracy under somewhat different conditions. For each group, 'loser acceptance' at the time of transition turned out to be a necessary condition for the long-term success of democracy, but by itself this factor was not sufficient for democracy to prevail, as the negative examples of Congo-Brazzaville, Gambia, and others where democracy was not sustained demonstrate.

Although QCA provides an interesting approach for examining causal complexity, it is also beset with many of the same problems that we discussed earlier with reference to case selection in small-N research. There are a number of issues we need to pay attention to when carrying out QCA. The first issue refers to how many cases we choose to examine in our analysis. In order to examine whether the impact of a particular factor is necessary or sufficient, and whether its impact is contingent on the presence or absence of other variables, it is desirable to have cases which capture the different possible combinations of causal conditions, so, wherever possible, outcomes are known for each row of the truth table. Of course, in reality, some combinations are simply not present in the real world. Nonetheless, when very small samples are used, there are going to be a lot of gaps in the truth table.

Second, there is also the issue of case selection. As with all comparative research, it is necessary to define the theoretical population of interest from which the cases are selected. Sometimes all the countries (or cases) in a given population can be examined, but at other times a sample will be needed. As soon as we are dealing with a sample, we need to think about case selection or else our results may end up being very misleading. However, even when we are analysing an entire population of cases, we should still think about how robust our findings are. When we use exploratory techniques such as QCA to mine the data for patterns, we have to be sensitive to the possibility that our findings are driven by quirks or anomalies in the data that might not be present if we were to try and reproduce our analysis with different (but similar) cases. For this reason, scholars who use QCA often go on to use other methods of inquiry to test their arguments more widely, and so will think about the ways in which QCA can be used to complement large-N research.

Quantitative analysis (large-N comparison)

Large-N comparative studies are widely used in political research. Studies of this type frequently employ quantitative analysis to answer questions on topics as diverse as the nature and direction of the relationship between economic development and democracy (Przeworski et al. 2000); the causes of ethnic conflict (Wilkinson 2004) and civil war (Gleditsch 2007); the impact of party competition on social welfare (Lipsmeyer 2002), the relationship between different electoral and political institutions and political stability, conflict, and breakdown, to name but a few.

The principles of inference and quantitative data analysis are discussed elsewhere in this book (see in particular Chapters 15 and 16) and so will not be dealt with here. Instead, we will briefly discuss issues to do with selecting cases and data collection. Large-N comparative research, based on the statistical analysis of many countries, has many advantages. It allows us to rigorously test different hypotheses and make inferences about how variables are connected. Many of the problems of selection bias associated with small-N analysis that we discussed earlier can therefore be mitigated by using this approach. Large-N comparisons also allow us to systematically examine the effect of many different variables and to knock down spurious associations. They also allow us to examine how different factors interact with each other to produce different consequences in different contexts.

This allows us to have greater confidence that our results are robust. This confidence comes in part from simply being able to analyse a large number of cases (which are broadly representative of the population we are studying) and in part from being able to examine the impact of many different variables simultaneously, so as to rule out plausible alternative explanations. To rule out plausible alternatives we need to analyse many cases, or else we may encounter the 'too many variables not enough cases problem' that we discussed earlier. However, despite these obvious strengths, analysing a lot of cases also brings its own problems. This is often presented in terms of a trade-off between internal and external validity. As Coppedge (1999: 464) puts it, although large-N quantitative analysis is the best method available for testing generalizations, especially generalizations about complex causal relationships, it is also often criticized for its 'thin' (reductionist or simplistic) concepts and theories.

Large-N comparative studies involve the tasks of case selection, data collection, and data analysis. The principle of case selection for large-N research is fairly clear-cut, and there is a generally agreed upon set of procedures of best practice. Ultimately, the goal of case selection is to achieve a representative sample of the **population** of interest which is of sufficient sample size to enable robust inferences to be made. The principles of sample design are discussed in detail in Chapter 10, and many of the same principles apply to case selection in comparative research. The main advantage of this approach is that it helps us to overcome many of the problems to do with selection bias that we discussed earlier in the chapter.

To test any theory or hypothesis one must first identify the domain of the argument or the universe of cases to which the hypothesis should apply. This is generally referred to as the population of interest. So, for example, if you are interested in exploring why some countries engage in war whereas others don't, the population of interest may be all the countries in the world, since every country either engages in war or doesn't. However, if you're interested in exploring why some countries engage in war in the face of provocation, whereas others don't, your population of interest may be all the countries in the world that have experienced provocation. (You would need to think very carefully about how you could define provocation and then how you could measure it.)

Having defined the population of interest, the next step is to select eligible cases for the study. If the population is very big, it may be necessary to draw a random sample (see Chapter 10). However, it is quite common in large-N comparative research to simply analyse all the cases in the population of interest, and there are even a number of studies which have created data sets for all the countries in the world. The problem with this though is that this is still rather a small sample. These studies generally have data on about 192 countries, and if we had a sample of just 192 people in a survey we would be a bit reluctant to draw any strong conclusions. The same applies to comparative research. The size of the sample in relation to the population doesn't make any difference to how reliable the findings from our sample are. When you have a small sample there is always the risk of drawing faulty inferences.

Comparatavists often try to get round this problem by looking at data over time in order to try and increase their sample size. So, for example, they may collect information on 192 countries at yearly intervals over say a 50-year period, which would give them a total sample of 9,600. But even quite modest increases in sample size can help to knock down many faulty inferences. Geddes (2003: 89–105) provides a particularly striking example of this, which both highlights the limitations of small-N research and the advantages of large-N research. Geddes recounts how analysts trying to explain why some developing countries have grown economically faster than others have tended to focus their analysis on a few successful new industrializing countries (NICs), such as Taiwan, South Korea, Singapore, Brazil, and Mexico. It was noted that these countries all had fairly repressed labour forces. Accordingly, some scholars asserted that repressive labour laws and weak unions constitute a comparative advantage in international economic competition. The problem with this sort of claim is that it makes sweeping generalizations from the basis of a very few cases. The hypothesis sounds as if it might be plausible. And as we discussed earlier, small-N research is very useful for developing theories. But to actually test this theory and see whether it really does stand up, we need to see whether it applies more generally. To do this Geddes collects data on economic growth and labour repression for 84 developing countries and examines whether the finding still holds.

The statistical techniques she used to do this are discussed in Chapters 15 and 16. However, the main point of interest is that she found that the theory did not stand up to wider generalization. Although it was true that Taiwan, South Korea, and the others did have repressive labour laws and high levels of economic growth, Geddes found that there were many other countries that also had repressive labour regulations, such as Iran and Argentina, but which had not experienced economic growth. Similarly, she also found that there were many countries which did not have repressive labour laws, such as Botswana, but had experienced high growth. In short, the initial assumption that labour repression influences economic growth was a faulty inference. It is easy to make these sorts of faulty inferences when we only examine a few cases. And the best way to overcome this problem is to examine many cases. If we are interested in testing theories rigorously, and seeing whether they hold up in the different contexts to which they are thought to apply, then we are inevitably drawn to large-N analysis.

Whereas almost any type of data can be used in small-N research, large-N research generally relies upon quantitative data. We call it quantitative data because all the information is assigned a numerical value. Sometimes how we assign this value is obvious, because the variable of interest is measured in numbers, such as votes or inflation, or GDP per capita, war casualties, or unemployment. At other times, how we assign a value is less obvious, and is the result of a coding decision based on a qualitative judgement to do with how democratic an 'expert' thinks a particular country is. There are many different sources of data that are used in large-N comparative research. Surveys are a valuable resource (discussed in Chapter 10), and there are now many cross-national surveys that have been carried out in almost identical fashion in many different countries around the world over a relatively long period of time. These surveys provide valuable information about how public perceptions of corruption, or support for democracy, or support for human rights vary between different regions. Some of the most widely used cross-national surveys of this type are the Comparative Study of Electoral Systems (CSES), the World Values Survey, Eurobarometer, Latinobarometer, and Afrobarometer.

But population surveys are not the only source of data that large-N studies can draw on. There are now many cross-national data sets that have been compiled from expert surveys (see Chapter 11), which measure perceptions about the level of corruption in a country (Transparency International) or the level of democracy in a country (which forms part of the Freedom House and Polity IV measures of democracy). Comparative research also draws on policy documents and speeches (see Chapter 13) to examine the ideology of governments and political parties (Budge et al. 2001; Benoit and Laver 2006) and leadership styles and populism (Hawkins 2009). These methods of data collection are discussed in detail elsewhere in the book, and so will not be considered here.

But whatever data is collected, it is important that it is both **valid** and **reliable**. Broadly speaking, validity refers to whether the data measures what it is supposed to measure. That is, how closely does the operational indicator match the concept of interest? For example, if you are interested in the level of corruption in a country, is a survey question on a businessman's perceptions of corruption a valid measure of this? The issue is not whether you have measured accurately or not whether the businessman thinks that the country in question is corrupt or not, but whether perceptions of corruption are a valid measure of actual corruption. Reliability refers to how well the operational indicator has been measured. That is, does the question really tap into what the businessman thinks about the country in question?

The principles of data collection in large-N research are that information about the world can be coded or summarized in ways that capture meaning. We start with concepts or constructs that we want to measure; we develop operational indicators for these constructs; and then we collect data to measure the operational indicators (see Chapter 6). Some constructs are fairly easy to measure. Suppose we are interested in conventional political participation. Our conceptual definition of political participation might be whether or not people vote in general elections. Our operational indicator—which is what we use to measure our conceptual definition, might therefore be official election returns from around the world which detail what proportion of the voting-age public actually cast a ballot. This is a pretty valid measure. The data clearly taps into our concept of participation. It is also likely to be a reasonably reliable measure, though practices of vote rigging may make it less reliable in some countries than others.

However, other constructs are more difficult to measure. Suppose you are interested in measuring a country's level of democracy. We must therefore provide a conceptual definition of what we mean by democracy. There is a vast literature on this, and scholars disagree about how democracy should be defined. Some authors favour a thin definition based on institutional arrangements, others favour a thicker or fuller definition based on civil and political rights. Suppose we go for a thin definition of democracy, in which we define democracy as a system of government in which governments are selected though competitive elections. Our operational definition may therefore be the competitiveness of elections, and our operational indicator of competitiveness might be the difference in vote share between the winning party or candidate and the second-placed party or candidate. So an election where the winner achieved 99% of the vote would be considered relatively uncompetitive, whereas an election where two parties each got approximately 50% of the vote would be considered highly competitive. Our measure might be reliable, but we might not say it is valid, since it doesn't capture the full definition of democracy.

One of the main challenges in comparative research, particularly large-N comparative research, is to do with establishing **equivalence of meaning**. That is, whether the theoretical concepts and empirical indicators of those concepts mean the same things and measure the same things in the different contexts to which they are applied. For example, the concept of populism may mean different things in different contexts. Thus, when we talk about populism in Latin America, we may be talking about something rather different to when we talk about populism in Europe. Different understandings of a concept can lead to different measures to tap into that concept (see Adcock and Collier 2001), which in turn can mean that even though we think we are talking about (and comparing) the same thing, we are actually talking about two very different things. Under these circumstances, the comparison is no longer particularly meaningful, because we are no longer comparing equivalent phenomena.

When we are only comparing a few countries, it is possible to explore these issues in some detail, and take steps to ensure that there is a close match between concepts and measures in each of the cases being analysed. However, when we compare many countries, we face a number of problems. One the one hand, our concepts may mean different things in different contexts, and so our measures are not valid. On the other hand, in order to establish equivalence our concepts and measures may become so broad, if not stretched (Sartori 1970), that their meaning becomes diluted. On the dangers of **concept-stretching**, see Chapter 6. It is only with careful analysis and detailed substantive knowledge that we can have confidence that our measures mean the same things in different countries.

 ## Conclusions

In this chapter we have examined a number of different ways of doing comparative research. Broadly speaking, we can distinguish between these approaches according to the number of cases that are compared, and how the cases are selected. Comparative research is therefore primarily defined as a method of case selection. Different approaches to case selection are associated with various different problems, and the approach that is preferred may therefore depend upon the purpose to which it is used.

In particular, there are two main problems. The first is to do with selection bias. The second is to do with equivalence of meaning. The main problem with small-N studies and single-country case studies is that there is the real risk of selection bias. The cases we select can influence the answers we get. This means that our findings might not be very reliable, and could just be an artefact of the cases we have selected. If we selected different cases, we would come up with very different conclusions. One way to get round this is simply to examine more cases. But this comes with its own problems. When there are many cases, it becomes more difficult to ensure that the variables under investigation are both conceptually and empirically comparable. To ensure comparability we can end up using very general concepts and measures, which become abstract and devoid of meaning, undermining the validity of the measures.

Although these problems affect all comparative research, they should not be overstated. With careful design, we can take steps to tackle them head on, and by combining approaches, we can attempt to integrate the strengths of one approach with the strengths of another. However, it is worth bearing in mind that these issues of case selection are only the first part of the research process, and having chosen a case (or cases) to study, you then need to think about how you are going to study it/them. These methods of data collection and data analysis are discussed in detail in the following chapters.

 ## Questions

- What are the problems with selecting on the dependent variable? Have these problems been overstated?
- If the cases you select affect the answers you get, does this mean that small-N comparison is inherently less reliable than large-N comparison?
- Under what conditions does it make more sense to adopt a Most Different Systems Design than a Most Similar Systems Design?
- If a topic is worth investigating, it is worth investigating comparatively? Discuss.
- What is concept-stretching? To what extent can it hinder comparative research?
- To what extent is a small-N comparative study a qualitative research design?
- What is the difference between methods for case selection, data collection, and data analysis? Does what we do at one stage influence what we do at the next?
- What are the strengths and weaknesses of small-N comparison and large-N comparison?
- How does QCA differ from small-N research?

 ## Guide to Further Reading

Brady, H. E. and D. Collier (eds) (2004), *Rethinking Social Inquiry: Diverse Tools, Shared Standards* (Lanham, MD: Rowman Littlefield).
Contains a selection of essays which describe the ways in which qualitative approaches can contribute to the study of political phenomena.

Geddes B. (2003), *Paradigms and Sand Castles: Theory Building and Research Design in Comparative Politics* (Ann Arbor, MI: University of Michigan Press).
Provides a detailed discussion on case selection and how the cases you choose for analysis can affect the answers you get.

George, A. L. and A. Bennett (2005), *Case Studies and Theory Development in the Social Sciences* **(Cambridge, MA: MIT Press).**

An important discussion of the place of case studies in social science methodology. Emphasizes the importance of within-case analysis, provides a detailed discussion of process tracing, and of the concept of typological theories.

King, Gary, Robert Keohane, and Sidney Verba (1994), *Designing Social Inquiry: Scientific Inference in Qualitative Research* **(Princeton, NJ: Princeton University Press).**

One of the classic methodology books. Provides a very influential perspective on small-N research, and how it can be carried out systematically and scientifically.

Landman, T. (2008), *Issues and Methods in Comparative Politics* **(London: Routledge).**

Provides an engaging treatment of issues in comparative research, with many examples drawn from the fields of democracy, human rights, and conflict. The book examines how case studies, small-N comparisons, and large-N comparisons have been used to answer a variety of different questions in comparative politics.

Ragin, C. C. (1987), *The Comparative Method: Moving Beyond Qualitative and Quantitative Strategies* **(Berkeley, CA: University of California Press).**

This book introduces the principles of Qualititative Comparative Analysis and Boolean Algebra using crisp sets. It provides an informative and engaging introduction to QCA and how it can be used to answer a variety of questions in comparative political research.

——(2008), *Redesigning Social Inquiry: Fuzzy Sets and Beyond* **(Chicago, IL: University of Chicago Press).**

This book develops Ragin's earlier work on QCA, and provides an in-depth treatment of how to calibrate fuzzy sets. It contains lots of helpful information on how to construct truth tables and how to analyse them.

 ## References

Achen, C. and D. Snidal (1989), 'Rational Deterrence Theory and Comparative Case Studies', *World Politics* 41(2): 143–69.

Adcock, Robert and David Collier (2001), 'Measurement Validity: A Shared Standard for Qualitative and Quantitative Research', *American Political Science Review* 95(3): 529–46.

Almond, G. (1966), 'Political Theory and Political Science', *American Political Science Review* 60: 877–8.

——and Sidney Verba (1963), *The Civic Culture: Political Attitudes and Democracy in Five Nations* (Princeton, NJ: Princeton University Press).

Benoit, Kenneth and Michael Laver (2006), *Party Policy in Modern Democracies* (London: Routledge).

Bennet, A. and C. Elman (2006), 'Qualitative Research: Recent Developments in Case Study Methods', *Annual Review of Political Science* 9: 455–76.

Brady, H. E. and D. Collier (eds) (2004), *Rethinking Social Inquiry: Diverse Tools, Shared Standards* (Lanham, MD: Rowman Littlefield).

Brass, P. (2003), *The Production of Hindu-Muslim Violence in Contemporary India* (Seattle, WA: University of Washington Press).

Braumoeller, Bear, and Gary Goertz (2000), 'The Methodology of Necessary Conditions', *American Journal of Political Science* 44 (October): 844–58.

Budge, Ian, Hans-Dieter Klingeman, Andrea Volkens, Judith Bara, and Eric Tanenbaum (2001), *Mapping Policy Preferences: Estimates for Parties, Electors and Governments 1945–1998* (Oxford: Oxford University Press).

Butler, D. and D. Stokes (1969) *Political Change in Britain* (London: Macmillan).

Campbell, Angus, Philip E. Converse, Warren Miller, and Donald Stokes (1960), *The American Voter* (New York: Wiley).

Caramani, D. (2008), *Introduction to the Comparative Method with Boolean Algebra*, Quantitative Applications in the Social Sciences (Beverly Hills, CA: Sage Publications).

Collier, D. and J. Mahoney (1996), 'Insights and Pitfalls: Selection Bias in Qualitative Research', *World Politics* 49(1): 56–91.

——, J. Mahoney and J. Seawright (2004), 'Claiming Too Much: Warnings about Selection Bias', in H. E. Brady and D. Collier (eds), *Rethinking Social Inquiry: Diverse Tools, Shared Standards* (Lanham, MD: Rowman Littlefield), 85–102.

Coppedge, Michael (1999), 'Thickening Thin Concepts and Theories: Combining Large N and Small in Comparative Politics', *Comparative Politics* 31(4): 465–76.

Dion, F. D. (1998), 'Evidence and Inference in the Comparative Case Study', *Comparative Politics* 30(2): 127–46.

Eckstein, H. (1975), 'Case Studies and Theory in Political Science', in F. I. Greenstein and N. W. Polsby (eds), *Handbook of Political Science: Political Science: Scope and Theory*, vol. 7 (Reading, MA: Addison-Wesley), 94–137.

Geddes, B. (2003), *Paradigms and Sand Castles: Theory Building and Research Design in Comparative Politics* (Ann Arbor, MI: University of Michigan Press).

George, Alexander L. and Andrew Bennett (2005), *Case Studies and Theory Development in the Social Sciences* (Cambridge, MA: MIT Press).

Gerring John (2004), 'What is a Case Study, and What is it Good For?' *American Political Science Review* 98(2): 341–54.

—— (2007a), *Case Study Research: Principles and Practices* (Cambridge: Cambridge University Press).

—— (2007b), 'Is there a (Viable) Crucial-Case Method?' *Comparative Political Studies* 40: 231–53.

Gleditsch, Kristian Skrede (2007),, 'Transnational Dimensions of Civil War', *Journal of Peace Research* 44(3): 293–309.

Goertz, G. and H. Starr (eds) (2003), *Necessary Conditions: Theory, Methodology and Applications* (New York: Rowman and Littlefield).

Hawkins, K. (2009), 'Is Chavez a Populist?: Measuring Populist Discourse in Comparative Perspective', *Comparative Political Studies* 42: 1040–67.

King, Gary, Robert Keohane, and Sidney Verba (1994), *Designing Social Inquiry: Scientific Inference in Qualitative Research* (Princeton, NJ: Princeton University Press).

Kitschelt, H., Z. Mansfeldova, R. Markowski, and G. Toka (1999), *Post-Communist Party Systems: Competition, Representation, and Inter-Party Cooperation* (Cambridge: Cambridge University Press).

Levy, J. S. (2002), 'Qualitative Methods in International Relations', in F. P. Harvey and M. Brecher (eds), *Evaluating Methodology in International Studies* (Ann Arbor, MI: University of Michigan Press), 432–54.

Lewis-Beck, Michael (1986), 'Comparative Economic Voting: Britain, France, Germany, Italy', *American Journal of Political Science* 30: 315–46.

Lijphart, A. (1971), 'Comparative Politics and the Comparative Method', *American Political Science Review* 65(3): 682–93.

—— (1977), *Democracy in Plural Societies: A Comparative Exploration* (New Haven, CT: Yale University Press).

—— (1999), *Patterns of Democracy* (New Haven, CT: Yale University Press).

Lipsmeyer, Christine S. (2002), 'Parties and Policy: Evaluating Economic and Partisan Influences on Welfare Policy Spending during the European Post-Communist Transition', *British Journal of Political Science* 32 (4): 641–61.

Lipset, Seymour Martin (1959), 'Some Social Requisites of Democracy: Economic Development and Political Legitimacy', *American Political Science Review* 53: 69–105.

Mainwaring, S. and T. Scully (eds) (1995), *Building Democratic Institutions: Party Systems in Latin America* (Stanford, CA: Stanford University Press).

Mair, P. (1996), 'Comparative Politics: An Overview', in R. E. Goodin and H.-D. Klingemann (eds), *A New Handbook of Political Science* (Oxford: Oxford University Press), 309–35.

Michelutti, L. (2008), *The Vernacularisation of Democracy* (London and Delhi: Routledge).

Moore B. (1966), *Social Origins of Dictatorship and Democracy: Lord and Peasant in the Making of the Modern World* (Boston, MA: Beacon).

Naroll, R. (1966), 'Scientific Comparative Politics and International Relations', in R. Barry Farrell (ed.), *Approaches to Comparative and International Politics* (Evanston, IL: Northwestern University Press).

Parry, Geraint, George Moyser, and Neil Day (1992), *Political Participation and Democracy in Britain* (Cambridge: Cambridge University Press).

Posner, D. (2004), 'The Political Salience of Cultural Difference: Why Chewas and Tumbukas are

Allies in Zambia and Adversaries in Malawi,' *American Political Science Review* 98(4) (November): 529–45.

Przeworski, A. and H. Teune (1970), *The Logic of Comparative Social Inquiry* (New York: Wiley).

——, Michael E. Alvarez, Jose Antonio Cheibub, and Fernando Limongi (2000), *Democracy and Development. Political Institutions and Well-Being in the World, 1950–1990* (Cambridge: Cambridge University Press).

Putnam, Robert (1993), *Making Democracy Work: Civic Traditions in Modern Italy* (Princeton, NJ: Princeton University Press).

Ragin, C. C. (1987), *The Comparative Method: Moving Beyond Qualitative and Quantitative Strategies* (Berkeley, CA: University of California Press).

—— (2000), *Fuzzy Set Social Science* (Chicago: University of Chicago Press).

—— (2008), *Redesigning Social Inquiry: Fuzzy Sets and Beyond* (Chicago: University of Chicago Press).

Rihoux, B. (2006), 'Governmental Participation and the Organizational Adaptation of Green Parties: On Access, Slack, Overload and Distress', *European Journal of Political Research* 45: S69–S98.

—— and C. Ragin (eds) (2009), *Configurational Comparative Methods: Qualitative Comparative Analysis (QCA) and Related Techniques* (Thousand Oaks, CA: Sage).

Rogowski, R. (2004), 'The Role of Theory and Anomaly in Social-Scientific Inference', in Henry Brady and David Collier (eds), *Rethinking Social Inquiry: Diverse Tools, Shared Standards* (Lanham, MD: Rowman & Littlefield Publishers, Inc.).

Rokkan, S. (1966), 'Comparative Cross-National Research: The Context of Current Efforts', in Richard L. Merritt and S. Rokkan (eds),

Comparing Nations: The Use of Quantitative Data in Cross-National Research (New Haven, CT: Yale University Press).

Rose, Richard (1991), 'Comparing Forms of Comparative Analysis', *Political Studies* 39: 446–62.

Sartori, G. (1970), 'Concept Misrepresentation in Comparative Politics', *American Political Science Review*, 64:1033–63.

Skocpol, T. (1979), *States and Social Revolutions: A Comparative Analysis of France, Russia, and China* (Cambridge: Cambridge University Press).

van Biezen, I. and D. Caramani (2006), '(Non) Comparative Politics in Britain', *Politics* 26(1): 29–37.

Verba, S., Kay Schlozman, and Henry Brady (1995), *Voice and Equality: Civic Voluntarism in American Politics* (Cambridge, MA: Harvard University Press).

Veugelers, J. and A. Magnan (2005), 'Conditions of Far-Right Strength in Contemporary Western Europe: An Application of Kitschelt's Theory', *European Journal of Political Research* 44: 837–60.

Weyland, K. (2002), *The Politics of Market Reform in Fragile Democracies: Argentina, Brazil*

Wilkinson, S. (2004), *Votes and Violence: Electoral Competition and Ethnic Riots in India* (Cambridge: Cambridge University Press).

Yadav, Y. (2000), 'Understanding the Second Democratic Upsurge: Trends of Bahujan Participation in Electoral Politics in the 1990s', in Francine R. Frankel, Zoya Hasan, Rajeeva Bhargava, and Balveer Arora (eds), *Transforming India: Social and Political Dynamics of Democracy* (Delhi: Oxford University Press).

Yin, Robert K. (2009), *Case Study Research: Design and Methods*, 4th edition (Thousand Oaks, CA: Sage).

Surveys

Chapter Summary

This chapter examines the principles of survey research and discusses the issues and problems associated with different stages of the design process. In doing so, it examines questionnaire design, sample design, and interview techniques and discusses the common sources of error that affect survey research and what can be done to try and avoid or minimize them. The chapter examines:

- questionnaire design;
- measurement error;
- sampling design;
- sampling error;
- interview mode.

Introduction

This chapter examines the principles of survey research, and discusses the issues and challenges involved in carrying out a good survey. Despite a number of weaknesses, surveys continue to flourish and are frequently used in political research to investigate a wide range of political phenomena. They combine two things: the ancient but extremely efficient method of obtaining information from people by asking questions; and the modern random sampling procedures that allow a relatively smal l number of people to represent a much larger population (Shuman and Presser 1996: 1). As such, they are a valuable resource for examining a wide range of topics, and when done well, provide an accurate and reliable insight into what ordinary people think about politics and how they participate in politics.

A successful survey involves many different steps. Before thinking about questionnaires or samples, however, it is first necessary to establish what the main aims of the research project are, and to clarify they key concepts, issues, and theory that you want to examine (see Chapters 5 and 6). The survey will only give you the answers to the questions that are asked, and it is therefore important to have a clear idea about what it is that you want to find out before the survey is carried out, since it will be too late afterwards if a new idea comes to you when you are doing the analysis. The decisions that are made at this stage will influence each of the subsequent steps that are taken.

The next step—which is the focus of this chapter—is to decide how the questionnaire is going to be designed and how the sample is going to be selected. Surveys are about asking questions, and the type of question you ask can affect the sort of answer you get in three main ways. What question do you ask? Who do you ask the question to? And how do you ask the question? The purpose of this chapter is to examine each of these in turn. The first part of the chapter deals with *what* you ask and examines issues relating to questionnaire design. The second part deals with *who* you ask and covers sampling design, and the third part deals with *how* you ask questions, and looks at different types of interview technique.

The elements of a good survey

Surveys have both a descriptive purpose and an analytical purpose. The descriptive purpose is to try and provide accurate information about what people think and do in a given population; that is, to try and understand what happens. This is a valuable end in itself, and whether the survey is designed to produce population estimates about income or inequality, trust in parliament, or satisfaction with democracy, or how many people think terrorism is a legitimate form of political protest, the answers to these sorts of questions can be extremely revealing. However, surveys can be used for much more than just this. The analytical purpose is to provide data that can be used for theory testing or hypothesis testing to try and understand why things happen. It is one thing to know that a certain percentage of the population has lost faith in democracy; it is quite another to know the reasons why. Surveys are a powerful tool for trying to answer these questions. The researcher develops theories or explanations about why things happen, and uses surveys to collect data to test those explanations against what is observed in the real world. If the expectations are correct, then this lends support to the theory. If the expectations are wrong, there are two main possibilities. Either the theory is wrong, in which case it is back to the drawing board to try and come up with something more plausible, or the measurement or testing of the theory is wrong, and is somehow flawed. In this case, there may be nothing wrong with the theory or explanation per se, but the way in which key concepts have been operationalized (see Chapter 6) is bad. Obviously, we want to try and minimize the possibility of the latter occurring, and this means we must be very careful how we collect the information that we need, and how we then analyse it.

The focus of this chapter is on how surveys can be used to collect information. Chapters 14 to 16 deal with issues of analysis, but before we reach that stage it is necessary to be confident that the data we wish to analyse are reasonably sound. One of the great strengths of survey research is that it helps us to make general claims about what different sections of society or different sub-groups of the population actually think and do. It thus gives voice to people that might not otherwise be heard. But a major weakness is that surveys can, and frequently do, misrepresent what people think and do and thus create misleading information.

The extent to which surveys misrepresent the 'real' or 'true' attitudes and behaviour of the people they seek to study can be thought of as error. The purpose of a good survey is to try and minimize this error. In practice, it is rarely possible to eliminate all error (indeed, it is virtually impossible), but with good research design and careful administration, it is possible to reduce error, and perhaps more importantly, to be aware of what error remains.

This chapter focuses on survey error. It describes the main types of error that are found in surveys, and where possible provides information about what to do in order to try and reduce them. There are two important sources of error that we consider. These are highlighted in Figure 10.1 (see also Groves et al. 2004). The first is to do with measurement error,

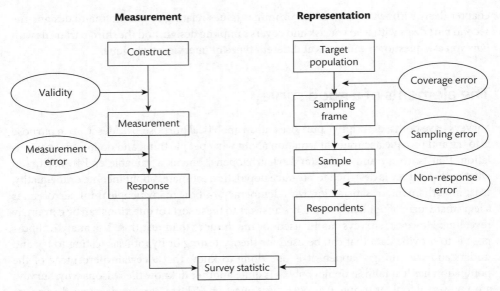

Figure 10.1 Sources of error in survey research

and refers to the ways in which surveys use questions to try and measure different social and political phenomena, such as political attitudes, opinions, and behaviour. The second is to do with sampling error, and refers to the ways in which respondents are chosen or selected to complete the survey and the implications this has for the representativeness of the sample.

What you ask: questionnaire design

Questionnaire design is a critical component of survey research. If questions are badly designed, then the results they produce will be flawed, no matter how large the sample size or how sophisticated the statistical analysis. Badly phrased questions or poorly measured concepts can render the research exercise useless before it has even begun and waste a lot of money in the process. It is therefore critical to make sure the **questionnaire** does what it's supposed to do as well as it can.

Validity: from concepts to survey questions

One of the most common uses of surveys is to measure the attitudes and behaviour of ordinary people. Many of these phenomena—or constructs—that we are interested in measuring are not directly observable. We therefore have to ask questions to try and measure the constructs we are interested in. Generally, it is thought that it is easier to measure behaviour, since this is more concrete. Past behaviour is in a sense a 'fact'; someone either voted or they didn't, they are either a member of a political party or they are not, and so on. By contrast, questions relating to attitudes and opinions are more abstract, and so more difficult to pin down and measure through the use of one or more questions. Although there is some truth in this, in reality there are difficulties associated with measuring both attitudes and behaviour. The harder a concept is to define, the harder it is to measure, so the first step is to clarify exactly what it is that we seek to examine (see the discussion of conceptualization and operationalization in Chapter 6). Concepts that are vague or multifaceted need to be pinned down and perhaps broken up into smaller parts.

Once we have a definition that we are happy with, the next step is to think about how it can be measured. This involves moving from the abstract to the specific. This is one of the hardest jobs in survey research, and it can easily go awry. What question (or questions) taps into the general idea that you are interested in exploring? These questions—or **indicators**—are the bread and butter of survey research. Whether we are measuring behaviour or attitudes, our primary concern is that the question we use is both valid and reliable. **Validity** means that the question measures what we think it does and reflects the concept that we are trying to address. It is an issue of how the question is used and the purpose it is used for. For example, if we are interested in a general concept, such as social status, we might use a question on educational level to try and measure this (de Vaus 2002: 53). The issue of validity is not whether we have measured education properly, but whether this is a suitable measure of our concept—social status. This is a frequent problem in social and political research. Often questions are used in ways for which they are not ideally suited. There may therefore not be anything wrong with the question per se, but the purpose that it is used for may not be appropriate. The validity of a measure therefore depends upon how we define the concept. This is always going to be open to debate, though is obviously more straightforward in some cases than others.

There are no easy ways to resolve this. But there are four basic ways in which we can try and assess validity (see Moser and Kalton 1971; de Vaus 2002 for an extended discussion). The first and most straightforward is **face validity**. Face validity simply means: on the face of it, does the question intuitively seem like a good measure of the concept? If the answer is no, then we definitely have a problem, but what is intuitively yes for one person may not be so for another. **Content validity** examines the extent to which the question covers the full range of the concept, covering each of its different aspects. **Criterion validity** examines how well the new measure of the concept relates to existing measures of the concept, or related concepts. **Construct validity** examines how well the measure conforms to our theoretical expectations, by examining the extent to which it is associated with other theoretically relevant factors. Ultimately, though, the matter of validity is one of judgement.

Reliability means the question is answered in the same way on different occasions. It is clear that an unreliable question lacks validity. But a reliable question need not be valid, because it could be measuring something other than what it was designed to measure, and reliability should not compensate for low validity.

Measurement error: developing indicators

A well-constructed question may or may not be valid. However, a badly worded question is never valid because it will not be a good measurement instrument. The next important issue to address then, as shown in Figure 10.1, is measurement error. By measurement error or error in observation, we mean the difference between what we record as the respondent's answer to a question and what is the respondent's real or true answer to that question.

On the whole, respondents will try to answer a question truthfully and to the best of their ability, but they may still not provide an accurate answer to the question they are asked for a number of reasons. It may be that they simply have not understood the question (which refers to problems of comprehension) or they cannot remember the answer (problems of recall). However, there are also more subtle reasons why they may not provide a 'true' answer. One reason is to do with the suggestibility of respondents. Some people may not be sure how to answer the question because they have never really thought about it before, and, rather than admit as much, they look for cues in the way in which the question is asked to give them clues how to answer. Another reason is that they may hold unfashionable or even unsavoury views, and thus be unwilling to reveal them. The following section discusses each of these potential sources of measurement error in turn.

Question wording comprehension

The literature on the wording of questions is vast (see Moser and Kalton 1971 and Tourangeau, Rips and Rasinski 2000 for good overviews). Respondents will interpret the question as best they can; but the more difficult a question is to understand, the more likely it is that respondents will interpret the question in different ways, introducing confusion about what exactly is being measured. We shall confine ourselves to some aspects of wording that are of general importance in survey research.

A common error is to ask a general question when a more specific question is needed. For example, if one is interested in the extent to which the general public trust their political representatives, it might be tempting to ask the following question: 'Do you trust politicians?' However, this question is unsatisfactory. It is not clear what trust means in this context. The respondent might trust politicians not to take bribes, but may not trust them to tell the whole truth when they are in a tight corner. The question fails to provide the respondent with the necessary frame of reference to give a meaningful answer. There may, of course, be a number of distinct frames of reference. One might be to tell the truth, one might be to put the interests of the country first, but whatever they are, they should be made explicit.

Ambiguity means that the question can be interpreted in different ways, and so in effect respondents may be answering different questions. A question can be ambiguous for a wide variety of reasons, and it may not always be obvious that it is ambiguous until you see how it is interpreted by different people. That is why it is so important to pre-test questions by carrying out exploratory research and piloting the survey (see Chapter 11 on interviews as a way of doing this). One particular type of ambiguity arises with **double-barrelled questions**. This is when the question incorporates two distinct questions within one. So, for example, consider the question: 'Do you agree or disagree with the following statement. "Tony Blair lied to parliament about Iraq and should be tried for war crimes".' You might think he lied but should not be tried for war crimes, and you might think he didn't lie but should be tried for war crimes, so how do you answer? Better to break the question up into two separate questions and ask about whether or not you thought he lied in parliament, and whether or not he should be tried for war crimes separately.

Related to the double-barrelled question is the question that relies on **faulty presupposition**. This means that the question assumes something that is not necessarily true. Moser and Kalton refer to these types of questions as **presuming questions**. For example, consider the following statement: 'Democracy is the best form of government because it makes leaders accountable.' This is difficult to decide because it rests on the premise that democracy is indeed the best form of government. In this context, it is hard to know what it means if a respondent disagrees with the statement. It could mean, 'I disagree; democracy is not the best form of government', or it could mean 'I disagree; accountability is not the main reason why democracy is the best form of government.' Likewise, the question 'Who did you vote for in the last General Election?' presupposes that the respondent voted. These types of question are best asked only after a **filter** question has revealed that the respondent did vote in the last election, and so, once again, are best asked separately.

The next three problems involve the meaning of words or phrases in the question. It is important that the question has the same meaning for different respondents. Vague concepts or vague quantifiers should therefore be made as concrete as possible. Vague questions encourage vague answers. If you ask someone whether they talk about politics regularly or occasionally, the meaning of their answer will be vague. As Moser and Kalton observe, this common choice of alternatives is strictly illogical since the word 'occasional' refers to frequency, whereas the word 'regular' does not. Many everyday terms are vague, and respondents may interpret them in different ways. This is a particular issue in comparative surveys, where the same term or word can have different connotations in different contexts. For example, the word 'nationalist' might have positive connotations in some countries, but negative connotations in other countries, particularly when 'nationalist' movements have been linked to acts of violence or repression. It is therefore important to investigate whether the question has the same (equivalent) meaning in the different countries where it is being asked. This is known as establishing equivalence of meaning.

Similarly, unfamiliar terms or jargon should be avoided. The aim in a question wording is to try and communicate with respondents as clearly as possible in a language they will understand. People who write surveys are often experts in the subject, and they may overestimate how familiar the respondents are likely to be with the terminology that they use. So, even if it is perfectly clear to the question designer what is meant by fiscal policy, democratic deficit, humanitarian intervention, or bilateral trade agreement, it might not be for the person answering the question. Moser and Kalton (1971) counsel question designers to put themselves in the position of their typical—or least educated—respondent. Many words which are common to university-trained survey experts are far from common in ordinary conversation. Even words like hypothetical, aggravate, deprecate, and hundreds more are in this category, and Gowers (1954) mentions many words which can often be replaced by simpler alternatives, such as 'help' instead of 'assist'; 'think' instead of 'consider'; 'begin' instead of 'initiate'; 'country' instead of 'state'; and 'enough' instead of 'sufficient'. For surveys of the general population (rather than elites, which is discussed in Chapter 11), Moser and Kalton (1971: 321) advise that the first principle in wording is that questions should use the simplest words that will convey the exact meaning, and that the phrasing should be as simple and informal as possible. The more questions sound like an ordinary (polite) conversation, the smoother the interview will be.

To ensure that respondents all understand the question and interpret it in the same way, it is therefore recommended to (1) define terms carefully; (2) avoid unfamiliar, ambiguous, or imprecise words; (3) avoid complicated wording/too many clauses; (4) avoid two or three questions in one. To help overcome comprehension problems, piloting the questionnaire is crucial. Observing how respondents answer questions can give a clear indication of how well they have understood them. Do they ask for the question to be repeated? Do they ask for clarification? Do they stare blankly at the interviewer?

Recall problems

However, even when respondents understand the question, measurement error can still arise in a variety of ways. Another potential source of error in survey responses is to do with memory failure—or **recall problems**. This is particularly relevant for questions about past behaviour or past actions that the respondent may have undertaken, such as whether they voted in the last election, and, if so, for which party (see Heath and Johns 2010). Sometimes respondents cannot remember the relevant events at all, and sometimes they partially remember or inaccurately remember. Wright (1993) suggests that one reason for this is that less politically engaged respondents are less likely to retain the information of who they voted for in their memory. Voters simply forget which party or candidate they voted for. Respondents struggling to remember how they voted are probably more likely to infer that they voted for the winner (Wright 1993; Atkeson 1999). This gives rise to the so-called **bandwagon** effect.

In addition, another type of memory-related problem is to do with what Belli et al. (1999) call source-monitoring error. This problem can affect questions about all sorts of behaviour, from turnout to protest to acts of aggression, particularly if the question is concerned with behaviour within a specific time frame, such as the past 12 months. Respondents can generally remember that they have done such an activity, but cannot recall accurately when it was, and so confuse real participation within the specified time frame with earlier experiences. This is also known as **telescoping**. As more time passes since the event, we make more errors in dating when it took place.

There are a number of strategies that can be used to try and deal with these problems. Perhaps the most sensible is not to put the respondent's memory under too much strain in the first place by asking them to recall events in the distant past, or to recount the number of times they have done something in a fairly lengthy time period. For this reason, questions tend to focus on events that have taken place in the past seven days for relatively common activities, such as reading the newspaper, or the past 12 months for less common activities, such as taking part in a protest.

Deliberate misreporting

However, even if respondents understand the question and can remember the answer, they may not always answer entirely truthfully. It is desirable that respondents answer the question. Non-response (or **item non-response** as it is known when it refers to a specific question) can introduce error. Refusals may happen for a variety of reasons, but are more common when the question deals with sensitive issues. Respondents may not want to declare how much money they earn, or which political party they support (particularly in polarized political contexts). For these reasons, sensitive questions tend to go at the end of questionnaires, although this needs to be balanced against issues relating to question order effects.

Respondents generally want to be helpful, but at the same time there is a tendency, which has been found in many studies, that they also want to present themselves in a good light. This is known as **social desirability bias**, in which respondents over-report socially 'desirable' behaviour and under-report 'undesirable' behaviour. At one extreme, respondents may be unwilling to admit that they hold racist views, or vote for extreme-right parties, and so instead will opt for another answer (perhaps saying they don't know). But even more moderate views and forms of behaviour are susceptible to the same biases. For example, surveys frequently find that respondents over-report the true extent to which they have voted. This in part may stem from a desire to appear a good citizen and to have fulfilled one's civic obligations (though the extent to which voting is considered a civic obligation obviously varies across contexts). One way to counteract this relatively mild social desirability bias is to load the question in a certain way that gives the respondent a ready-made excuse for not having done what they may think is expected of them. Loading a question means wording it in a way that invites a particular response, as discussed below with reference to leading questions. In this case, the question is loaded to try and invite the socially undesirable response. Sudman and Bradburn (1982) distinguish several strategies for doing this: ranging from the 'everybody-does-it' approach to the 'reasons for doing it approach'. Questions on voting generally borrow from these strategies, and ask something like this, which is taken from the British Election Study (BES):

> Talking with people about the general election on May 5th, we have found that a lot of people didn't manage to vote. How about you, did you manage to vote in the general election?

These strategies help to reduce the apparent sensitivity of the question. Similarly, embedding one sensitive question (for example, on vandalism) among other more sensitive questions (for example, on terrorism) may make the sensitive item of interest seem less threatening by comparison.

Question order effects

So far, the problems discussed have been relatively straightforward, but there is another set of measurement problems that is less easy to define. One of the major problems that affect survey research is to do with the order in which questions are asked—**question order effects**. Apart from sampling error, question order effects are probably the most commonly cited explanation for an unexpected or anomalous survey finding (Shuman and Presser 1996: 24). The context in which a question is asked or its position in relation to other questions can have a bearing on the answers that are given to it. The most obvious manifestation of this is when respondents try to appear consistent by answering one question to fit in with how they answered a previous question. To show the sort of effect that the order of questions can have, we draw on a survey experiment carried out by Schuman and Presser (1996: chapter 2), in which alternative versions of a questionnaire were asked to random halves of the sample. Respondents were asked two questions, about Communist journalists and American journalists. However, the order in which they were asked these questions varied across the two half-samples. Survey experiments of this type are frequently used in political research for a

Table 10.1 Order effects on Communist and American newspaper reporter items in 1980

Communist reporter first		American reporter first	
Yes to Communist Reporter	Yes to American reporter	Yes to Communist reporter	Yes to American reporter
54.7%	74.6%	63.7%	81.9%

Source: Adapted from Schuman and Presser (1996).

wide variety of purposes, and can be useful for trying to identify causal relationships (see Chapter 8).

> Do you think the United States should let Communist newspaper reporters from other countries come in here and send back to their papers the news as they see it?
>
> Do you think a Communist country like Russia should let American newspaper reporters come in and send back to America the news as they see it?

From Table 10.1, we can clearly see that respondents were much more likely to say that they would allow Communist reporters into the United States after they had answered the question on the American reporter first. When the question on the Communist reporter was asked first, only 54.7% of the respondents thought Communists should be let into the United States, but when the American question was asked first, this percentage increased to 63.7% (a statistically significant increase). Similarly, respondents were less likely to say they would allow American reporters in to Communist countries after they had answered the Communist question first, with the percentage dropping from 81.9% to 74.6% (also a statistically significant change). Schuman and Presser interpret this to suggest that respondents answer the question in terms of pro-American and anti-Communist sentiments, whichever question is asked first. But having answered the first question, they follow a norm of reciprocity, in which a substantial number feel compelled to provide an answer that is consistent with their previous response.

This type of problem can affect a wide range of questions, and it is not obvious how to deal with it. Generally, it is thought that it is preferable to ask the more important questions first, so they are not contaminated by responses to less important questions. For this reason, in most National Election Studies, questions on which party respondents voted for generally tend to come at the beginning of the questionnaire. However, the downside of this is that it risks contaminating subsequent questions that are aimed at measuring why people voted as they did. To try and reduce the possibility of this happening, it is perhaps a good strategy to leave gaps between questions where this type of contamination is thought to be most likely.

Question wording effects

Another group of problems arise from what can broadly be termed **question wording effects**. Respondents may be more (or less) likely to report certain types of behaviour or attitude, depending upon the way in which a question is phrased or the answer is recorded. A good example of this is the difference between **open-ended** and **closed questions**, and how response format can influence the answers that are given to the same question. A 'closed' question provides the respondent with a set of answers to the question and the respondent must select the response that reflects their view most closely. By contrast, an open-ended question does not provide the respondent with any answer-option to choose from, and the respondent must formulate their own response themselves, which the interviewer will then record verbatim.

There are pros and cons attached to each format. A major advantage of open-ended questions is that they give the respondent the opportunity to voice exactly what they think. They allow for a detailed and reasoned response, which can reveal the logic and rationale behind a respondent's answer. Answers are not prompted, and so reveal what the respondent actually thinks. However, there is also a number of disadvantages of using open-ended questions. They may provide a lot of information, but this information then needs to be coded in order to make sense of the answers. This can be very time-consuming. Many responses may be irrelevant or off-topic, and some groups of people may be more likely to respond than others, particularly those who are more educated or more interested in the topic.

For these reasons, closed questions are the standard procedure for most questions. Attitude questions almost always use a closed format, with the answer categories forming a scale. Closed questions provide the respondent with a predefined set of response alternatives. They are quick and easy for the respondent to answer and for the interviewer to code, and do not discriminate against the less talkative or eloquent respondents. They can also remind respondents of answers that they might not otherwise have retrieved from their memory (Schuman et al., 1986). However, this kind of prompting may be used by respondents to save themselves the mental effort of producing a valid answer themselves. Moreover, it is quite likely that the predetermined list of alternatives will exclude some issues that are genuinely salient to some people. This is a problem given survey respondents' general reluctance to insist on a response that is not explicitly offered (and thus legitimized) by the question.

These points are well illustrated by survey experiments comparing open and closed versions of questions on what respondents consider to be the most important political issue facing the country (Schuman and Presser 1996). Eight alternatives were offered in the closed format, though respondents did have the option of 'Other'. The distribution of responses in the two versions is shown in Table 10.2.

The first point to note is that, when unprompted, 36.5% of respondents named one of a wide variety of problems that were not included in the list of eight alternatives. In the closed version, hardly any respondents insisted on these 'other' issues; instead they chose from among the options explicitly offered. However, and this is the second key point, they did not choose between those eight issues in the same proportions as respondents to the open-ended version. Instead, they opted in disproportionately large numbers for 'crime and violence' and 'decreasing trust in government'. In contrast, the percentages for 'inflation' and 'unemployment' are barely different across the two versions. It seems that economic issues come to respondents' minds with or without prompting, but that crime is a problem of whose importance respondents need a reminder. (See also Heath and Johns 2010.)

It is not straightforward to assess which of these questions produces the truer picture of issue salience. It may be that respondents perceive crime to be a local issue, and so do not consider it when asked the open-ended version of the questionnaire. Thus the open question provides the narrower frame of reference. Which format is preferred is therefore difficult to resolve. The argument for closed questions is stronger in those cases where survey designers are confident that their list would cover most, if not all, of the more common responses. The best route to such confidence is to use open questions in a pilot survey, and then to base the closed list on the results from that pre-testing.

Table 10.2 Comparing open and closed questions measuring the most important issue facing the country

	Closed	Open
	Which of these is the **most important** problem facing the country at present?	What do you think is the **most important** problem facing the country at present?
Food and energy shortages	6.2	1.7
Crime and violence	36.1	16.1
Inflation	13.0	13.6
Unemployment	20.4	19.6
Decreased trust in government	10.2	3.1
Busing	1.1	1.1
Breakdowns of morals and religion	9.5	5.8
Racial problems	1.7	2.5
Other issues/problems	1.9	36.5
Total	100.0	100.0
N	422	449

Source: Adapted from Schuman and Presser (1996).

A further example of question wording effects relates to the tone of the wording. This is illustrated by other split ballot experiments that examine support for freedom of speech in the United States (Schuman and Presser 1996). The results from these experiments show that when respondents were asked if the government should *forbid* speeches against democracy, support for freedom of expression was much higher than when respondents were asked if the government should *allow* speeches against democracy.

The reason why logically equivalent questions can produce different responses according to the tone of wording that is used can occur for a variety of reasons. In general, those who are most susceptible to wording effects are probably those for whom the question does not have great resonance or importance. People who design questionnaires for political research tend to be very interested in the subject, and to have thought a great deal about the issues. However, these people also tend to be outliers, and, for many respondents, the subject matter may not be of any great personal importance. These respondents with weaker attitudes may therefore be responsive to a variety of external influences, ranging from a story on the previous night's news to a nuance in the question wording (Zaller 1992; Tourangeau et al., 2000).

Balanced questions

A similar way in which question wording can influence responses is to do with whether it is balanced or not. In general, questions should be neutral. In practice, this is difficult to achieve, and questions may vary considerably in terms of how neutral or balanced they are.

One example of an unbalanced question is what is often described as a **leading question**. A leading question indicates to respondents that certain responses are more useful or acceptable to those asking the question (Belson 1981). Generally, they are to be avoided, since they can prompt the respondent to answer the question in a certain way. One famous example of this type of question that is still widely used, is an item designed to measure whether respondents identify with a political party.

The original question developed for the National Election Studies in the United States is: 'Generally speaking, do you usually think of yourself as a Republican, a Democrat, an Independent, or what?' This question has been exported to many other contexts, including the British Election Study, which asks: 'Generally speaking, do you think of yourself as Labour, Conservative, Liberal Democrat, or what?'

The use of 'or what' at the end might be considered somewhat rude, even threatening, and could be taken to imply that not having such an identification is a bit odd. Respondents may therefore feel pressured to say that they do identify with one of the parties. Similarly, mentioning only the main parties may make respondents less likely to say that they think of themselves as partisans of other parties which are not mentioned. Certainly, alternative forms of asking this question in an open-ended format reveal much lower levels of identification (Heath and Johns 2010).

But questions can also be unbalanced in other ways. And a perfectly balanced question is difficult to achieve. **Acquiescence bias** refers to a tendency among respondents (or some types of respondent) to agree with attitude statements presented to them. There are several different interpretations for this. Implicit in many of these interpretations is that some groups of people, such as the poorly educated, are more likely to lack true attitudes on issues presented to them. Converse (1964) labelled these non-attitudes. Since they have no real answer to the question, they tend to just agree. Acquiescence bias is therefore likely to be more pronounced on issues or attitudes that are of low salience to the respondent, in which he or she lacks clearly defined views, or in cases where the question is not clearly understood. The most obvious remedy to this problem is to mix pro and anti statements, so that at least the extent of the problem can be identified. Related to acquiescence bias are something known as recency effects, which refer to the order in which responses are presented to the respondent in closed-format questions. Recency effects are said to occur when respondents select the last option they are offered. They are generally thought to be more likely to occur when the question is long or complicated, or when the respondent does not have a 'crystallized' opinion.

Response format

Another important aspect of questionnaire design relates to how to record the respondent's answer, or more specifically what types of response option to provide them with. There are many issues at stake here. The first concerns the number of response categories that are provided—and whether dichotomous (yes/no) or polytomous (e.g. levels of agreement) response categories are used. If polytomous response scales are to be used, then how many should be used and should a mid-point be included? There is little standard practice and there is considerable variation in terms of what is generally used, though, for most topics, five categories are probably sufficient.

Standard questions generally do not offer a 'Don't know' category, but will accept don't know as a valid response if it is spontaneously offered by the respondent. The rationale behind this approach is to try and probe an opinion. But in some cases this probing can invent data, as the respondent will be forced into providing an opinion that they do not really hold. Indeed, Converse (1964) suggests that much of the error that occurs in surveys comes from the random responses that are provided by people with no real opinion. To distinguish between 'real attitudes' and 'non-attitudes' it is therefore often a good idea to provide a question to gauge the respondent's level of interest or knowledge about the topic before (or after) asking about their opinion.

Who you ask: sample design

So far, we have discussed issues relating to questionnaire design, and how the questions you ask and the way in which they are asked can affect the answers you get. Equally important is the issue of sampling design. This is because surveys rely on samples, which are selected from the **populations** that we seek to study. In sampling terminology, the population of interest is a particular group of people or other units (such as households, businesses, schools, etc.) that the researcher wishes to study. Thus, for a study on voting behaviour in a given country, the population of interest may be all of the eligible voters. We rarely interview everybody in the population (when we do, it's called a census) because it is incredibly time-consuming and expensive, and so we must therefore choose who we select to interview. The purpose of the sample survey is to allow the researcher to make a generalization about the attributes of a given population without having to actually interview everyone in that population to find out what they think and do. In order to do this, the survey relies upon interviewing a sample of the population. How we do this has a big impact on the results we get. If the sample is chosen in a haphazard or subjective way, then there is little hope of making accurate generalizations about the wider population we are interested in. There are thus three main sources of error that can influence how representative the sample is of the population (see Figure 10.1). These relate to **coverage error** (what we choose our sample from), sampling error (how we choose our sample), and **non-response** (how many people from our sample complete the survey).

Defining the population: sampling frame

The **sample frame** is the set of the target population that has a chance to be selected in the survey sample. Once we have defined our population of interest, we must obtain a **sampling frame**, which contains a complete (or as complete as possible) list of all the population units. A frequently used sampling frame for national surveys is the Post Office Address file, which contains an almost complete list of addresses in the UK. It is important to remember that a random probability sample alone does not guarantee that a given sample will be representative if the sampling frame from which the sample is drawn does not cover the entire population. Under-coverage or coverage error can become a problem if certain segments of the population are left off the sampling frame. For example, the Electoral Register is one possible sampling frame for registered voters in the UK, but it will not tell us about people who are not registered to vote. It is therefore not such a good sampling frame for the population as a whole.

Choosing the sample: random probability sampling

A good sample is representative of the population from which it is drawn. This allows us to generalize our findings from the survey to the population. There are many different methods for drawing a sample. Since there is no way of knowing what our population looks like in every respect, it is difficult to assess how well we have matched our sample to the population. But there are some ways that will tend to produce better results than others. There are two main ways of drawing a sample: probability samples, which are drawn at random; and non-probability samples, which are selected more subjectively. To be representative in a sense appropriate for statistical inference, a sample must be a probability sample, where everyone in the population has a known, non-zero probability of being sampled. Generally, most academic surveys follow this approach. Non-probability samples are more frequently used in Market Research and 'Opinion Polls', and although they are not reliable in a statistical sense, they do often produce results that are reasonably accurate. However, when they do go wrong, they can do so spectacularly. (See Box 10.1.)

Probability samples assign each unit in the sampling frame a known non-zero chance of being selected. The important thing is that the probability of being selected is known for each unit; it does not have to be equal. For example, survey researchers frequently over-sample small but interesting groups in the population so they can be analysed in greater detail. There are four main types of sample design based on probability sampling. These are: (1) simple random sampling; (2) systematic sampling; (3) stratified sampling; and (4) cluster sampling.

Simple random sampling (SRS) is perhaps the most straightforward type of probability sampling. Every unit in the sampling frame has the *same* probability of being selected. The units are assigned numbers, and then random number tables are used to select the sample. This method, though, is not without drawbacks. The first is that it can be very expensive to carry out when investigators have to interview the respondents personally because they may need to travel long distances in order to attempt an interview. The other drawback is that

---

BOX 10.1 Sampling Design: How Not to Do It

A famous example of the dangers of non-probability sampling is the survey by the Literary Digest magazine to predict the results of the 1936 US presidential election. The magazine sent out about 10 million questionnaires on postcards to potential respondents, and based its conclusions on those that were returned. This introduced biases in at least two ways. First, the list of those who were sent the questionnaire was based on registers such as the subscribers to the magazine, and of people with telephones, cars, and various club memberships. In 1936, these were mainly wealthier people who were more likely to be Republican voters, and the typically poorer people not on the source lists had no chance of being included. Second, only about 25% of the questionnaires were actually returned, effectively rendering the sample into a volunteer sample. The magazine predicted that the Republican candidate Alf Landon would receive 57% of the vote, when in fact his Democratic opponent, F. D. Roosevelt, gained an overwhelming victory with 62% of the vote. The outcome of the election was predicted correctly by a much smaller probability sample collected by George Gallup.

interesting but small sub-groups of the population may not be selected in sufficient numbers to carry out meaningful analysis. It is therefore not used very often.

Systematic sampling is a slight variation on simple random sampling, and shares many of the same strengths and weaknesses. Researchers choose a random starting point on the sampling frame, and then select respondents at fixed intervals. So, for example, if there are 100,000 units listed on the sampling frame, and the aim of the survey is to interview 1,000 people, then the researcher will start at a random position, for example at number 876, and then interview every 100th person. By and large, this produces the same results as a simple **random sample**. The only difference that may emerge is if there is periodicity in the sampling frame, so that a certain type of person is listed at regular intervals within the sampling frame. For example, if the sampling frame is a database of married couples, and the data is arranged so that women are followed by their husbands, then every second person in the sampling frame will be a man. Accordingly, the 876th person on the list will be a man, as will every 100th person that follows this starting point. The sample that is drawn will therefore be entirely made up of men.

Probability sample designs can be made better by introducing special features to ensure that the sample adequately represents specific sub-groups of the population that may be of particular interest. Stratified sampling is an example of this. It involves setting different selection probabilities for different groups (or *strata*) in the population. It is frequently used to ensure that adequate numbers of people are selected from different regions of a country. For example, a survey of British adults based on simple random selection might by chance lead to a sample containing very few people from Wales or Scotland, and lots of people from England. To ensure that the sample represents the distribution of the population across these three regions, the sampling frame can be stratified (divided up) into separate lists for each country. Stratifying samples obviously requires that the sampling frame contains information regarding the stratifying variable (e.g. country). The sample can then de drawn from each list. The proportion of the sample drawn from each stratum can either be set to ensure that the sample is representative of Britain as whole, or can vary by strata so that it over-samples from those regions where fewer people live. This allows for the possibility of having a bigger sample size from Wales or Scotland than would otherwise be achieved, which in turn can facilitate the statistical analysis of people living in these regions. These unequal selection probabilities can then be corrected by **weighting the data** (see Box 10.2) to ensure that the overall sample is representative of Britain as a whole.

Although this method helps to ensure the representativeness of the sample, it does little to ease the costs of carrying out the survey that can make surveys based on simple random selection prohibitive. A technique to try and make this cost more manageable is cluster sampling. With cluster sampling, the units are not sampled individually but in groups (*clusters*). For example, a survey may sample households and then interview every adult within each selected household. Although this saves on transport costs, it increases sampling error, since people living in the same household might share certain characteristics, such as social class, which may not be representative of people living in other households. Multi-stage cluster sampling is an extension of this approach and is often used for large national surveys. This involves drawing several samples. At the first stage, the population is divided up into geographic regions, such as electoral constituencies, which form the clusters. These clusters are then selected using SRS. At the second stage, each of the selected clusters are then divided up into even smaller geographic units, such as electoral wards, which are again selected using SRS. At the third stage, addresses from within each electoral ward are selected, and then

BOX 10.2 Weighting the Data

People often talk about weighting the data, and about weighted and non-weighted data, though it is not always clear what this refers to. Broadly speaking, there are two main ways in which this can be done. The most straightforward form of weighting is to correct for unequal selection probabilities. So, for example, if we deliberately over-sample people living in Scotland, Wales, and Northern Ireland (so that we have a sufficiently large sample size to analyse people living in these countries separately), our combined sample will not be representative of the UK population as a whole. To correct this, we apply weights to the data, which adjusts our sample and statistically reduces the number of people living in Wales in our sample by the same degree to which we over-sampled them at the design stage. This brings the proportion of people living in Wales within our sample back into line with the proportion of people living in Wales within the UK. This is a relatively straightforward procedure, since the selection probability is known for every selected case.

The second way in which weights are often applied is to correct for unit non-response. This is more problematic, since it involves estimation. For example, suppose we find that response rates to our survey are higher among older people than younger people. Our achieved sample will therefore be skewed towards older people, and will not be representative of the population as a whole in terms of age. This can introduce bias if young people and old people differ in their political attitudes or behaviour. To compensate for this under-representation of young people, an adjustment is made to our sample which statistically increases the proportion of young people within our sample, so that it matches the proportion of young people in the population as a whole.

The problem with this strategy is that it assumes that non-response is random, and that young people who do not answer the survey are essentially the same as young people who do answer the survey. However, this assumption is not always valid. Young people who do not respond to the survey may be quite different in important respects. They may be less interested in politics, they may be less inclined to give up their time for nothing, or they may simply be occupied with work and going out. In these instances, applying non-response weights will do little to reduce any bias that has crept into the survey.

within each household a respondent is selected to interview. The advantage of this approach is that typically one investigator can carry out all the interviews within each cluster, since all the selected respondents will be within a relatively confined geographical area.

Non-probability sampling

Everything else being equal, for population surveys, probability samples are always preferred to non-probability samples. Non-probability samples are not only more likely to introduce error into the survey, but they are likely to do so in ways which are difficult to predict. This makes it much more difficult to have confidence in the results. The most common form of non-probability sampling is the quota sample.

Quota sampling requires investigators to interview a certain number (quota) of respondents, where quotas are set according to personal characteristics, such as age group, sex, and income group. These quotas are organized to try and get a spread of different types of people, which can then be weighted to ensure that the sample is representative of the population in these respects. Quota samples tend not to make explicit use of sampling frames and so are susceptible to coverage error. Quota sampling is non-random because interviewers can select any subjects they want that fit the selection criteria. This is usually done using some (unstated) form of purposive or convenience sampling, in which investigators approach those people who look most cooperative. Although quota sampling is quite common, and generally gives reasonable results, it is easy to introduce biases in the selection stage, and almost impossible to know whether the resulting sample is a representative one.

Other forms of non-probability sampling are even more unreliable. **Purposive sampling** involves investigators using their own 'expert' judgement to select respondents whom they consider to be typical or representative of the population of interest. It suffers from many of the same problems as quota samples, since it is very easy to introduce bias into the selection. Similarly, **snowball sampling** involves investigators finding respondents who meet some criteria of interest, such as being an animal rights activist or drug user, and then asking the respondent to suggest other similar types of people who they may know for the researcher to contact for interview. In this way, the researcher is able to build up a sample of respondents. However, the problem with this technique is that the cases that are selected are not independent of each other, and are often not independent of the initial starting point from which the snowball was generated. For example, using this sampling strategy, Becker (1963) attempted to interview drug users through his contacts in the music business. Unsurprisingly, the resulting sample was heavily biased towards musicians, who made up half of his sample. It was not therefore very representative of the population of interest. Snowball samples tend to be very unreliable, and are not a sound basis for making wider inferences. However, they are sometimes used in qualitative research, particularly when the population of interest is hard to reach, and does not have a reliable sampling frame (see Chapter 11).

However, perhaps the most unreliable of all sampling strategies is the **volunteer sample**. This is the sort of survey that is frequently carried out by morning television shows and internet sites, where viewers or readers are encouraged to express their opinions on various topical issues of interest. For example, consider what inferences you can draw from the following example of a Sky News viewers' poll:

Should Britain join the space race?

No—It's cosmic showboating	52%
Okay, but let's spend sensibly	30%
Yes—I'd be over the Moon!	18%

Putting aside issues to do with question wording, it tells us very little. We'd be unwise to infer that the British public is against joining the space race. We'd even be unwise to infer that Sky viewers are against joining the space race. All we learn from this type of exercise are the opinions of those readers or viewers who could be bothered to send in their response. For these reasons, volunteer samples (even the more serious ones) tell us essentially nothing about the average attitudes of the general population.

Sampling error

Even though probability samples tend to be more representative of the population than non-probability samples, they are still affected by different types of sampling error. Sampling error can occur for a variety of reasons. Two main factors that are important are to do with the response rate that the survey achieves and the sample size of the survey.

Ideally, everyone that is sampled will complete the survey. However, this rarely happens, and non-response can occur for a variety of reasons. Some people will refuse to participate, or will be unable to participate because they are too sick or because they are away on business. Non-response may therefore reduce sample size and introduce bias. Those people who do not answer the survey may be somewhat different in some key respects from those people who do answer surveys. If someone is not interested in politics, they might not want to spend an hour answering questions about the most recent election. Similarly, if someone is too sick to be interviewed, they might be too sick to do lots of other things as well, such as go out to vote.

An example of this relates to the measurement of turnout. It is not uncommon to find that the proportion of respondents who report voting in surveys far exceeds the official estimates of actual voter turnout. For example, in the 2005 BES, self-reported turnout was measured at 79%, well above the official turnout figure of 61%. This substantial discrepancy between survey estimates of self-reported turnout and official estimates of turnout is not just limited to Britain, and is common to most surveys carried out around the world (and has been a particular source of concern in, for example, the United States). A study by Swaddle and Heath (1989) examining the sources of this discrepancy found that a considerable portion of it was due to problems of response bias (where turnout among non-respondents is substantially less than turnout among survey respondents).

Non-response may introduce bias if those individuals who do not agree to be interviewed for the survey (or cannot be interviewed because they are away) are less likely to vote than those individuals who agree to be interviewed. Swaddle and Heath found that, according to the official turnout register, turnout among the survey respondents (83%) was substantially higher than among the non-respondents (75%). A substantial portion of the apparent over-report in turnout by surveys is thus attributable to issues of response and coverage. One obvious way in which survey measurement can be improved is therefore to ensure a high response rate. However, this is not easy to achieve, and in recent years response rates for face-to-face surveys have fallen to around 60%. Although researchers can try to correct for non-response bias by weighting the data, this is not a perfect remedy and does not get rid of the problem.

Survey organizations thus devote considerable time and energy trying to maximize response. Various strategies are employed, such as sending an advanced letter to the respondents, visiting the respondent in person, with repeat visits on different days at different times if the respondent is unavailable. One strategy that is becoming more common is the use of inducements, such as a cash incentive or gift. It is unclear how much difference these inducements actually make though. Research on different types of inducement show that entering the respondent into a prize draw has no impact on response, whereas an unconditional payment (whether they complete the survey or not) is most effective. However, this can obviously increase the costs of the project substantially.

How you ask: interview mode

The last stage of survey design that we consider is how the survey is administered. This is an important part of data collection. No matter how well a survey is designed, if it is poorly executed, then it will produce unreliable results. Over the past 25 years or so there has been a rapid expansion in the ways—or modes—that surveys can be carried out. The most common ways are face-to-face, by telephone, by post, and, more recently, by internet. The way in which the survey is carried out can influence both how people answer the questions, relating to issues of measurement error, and who answers the questions, relating to issues of sampling error (see Groves et al. 2004 for an extended discussion). We briefly describe the main differences between each of these modes of data collection, and then discuss some of the issues they raise.

Face-to-face interviews remain the gold standard in survey research, and most of the big academic and government surveys are carried out in this way. However, they are very expensive. Respondents are interviewed by trained investigators who administer the questionnaire personally, usually at the respondent's home. Investigators read out the questions to the respondent, show prompt cards with the responses (for closed questions) and record the verbal answers that the respondent provides. Traditionally, these interviews were carried out with pen and paper, but now they tend to be carried out using laptops (computer-assisted personal interviewing—CAPI), which can be used to play video clips and speeches. Face-to-face surveys can clearly establish who is answering the questions, and whether they are doing so freely and comfortably without intervention from other people. Telephone interviews are also administered personally by trained investigators, though obviously in a more remote way since they take place over the phone. They do not provide response cards and so lack visual cues. By contrast, both **postal surveys** and **internet surveys** are self-administered by the respondent, who must fill out written versions of the questionnaire by themselves. Internet surveys in particular are becoming more popular, and are frequently used in academic research. They have the advantage of being relatively cheap to administer, and there is now a whole host of websites on the internet which can be used to host the survey at relatively little cost, which can make it seem an attractive option for researchers with a limited budget.

Besides budget, there are a number of other important factors that need to be considered. The way in which a questionnaire is administered may influence the way in which respondents answer the questions in a number of different ways. First, face-to-face surveys (and to a lesser extent telephone surveys) can help to alleviate **comprehension problems**. The interviewer can make sure that the respondent has understood the question properly, and can repeat a question if necessary. Since personally administered interviews are carried out verbally, they also place less of a burden on the literacy skills of the respondent. By contrast, people with reading and writing difficulties may feel less confident and be less able to complete self-administered surveys.

However, there is another side to this. The presence of an investigator can in some cases inhibit the responses that are given. These are known as **interviewer effects**. To illustrate, Schuman and Converse (1971) carried out a study on whether the race of the interviewer influenced respondents' answers towards questions on race relations. They found consistent interviewer effects, whereby black respondents were much more likely to say that they trusted white people if they were interviewed by a white investigator than if they were interviewed by a black investigator. The more anonymous setting of internet and postal surveys may therefore help to alleviate these problems, and in the process may help to reduce social desirability bias which can affect certain sensitive questions. For these reasons, for sensitive topics, face-to-face surveys using CAPI often pass the laptop to the respondent and ask them to answer the questions on the screen by themselves. With respect to measurement issues then, the mode of interview that is preferred may vary, and depend in part upon the type of questions that are being asked in the survey, and whether they are complex on the one hand or sensitive on the other.

The way in which a questionnaire is administered can also influence the representativeness of the sample. In particular, problems to do with coverage error and non-response may vary by interview mode (see Groves et al. 2004). The best way to ensure that a sample is representative of the population is to draw a random sample, in which all members of the population have a known non-zero probability of being selected. To achieve this it is necessary to define the population and to select an appropriate sampling frame from which to draw the sample. However, the coverage of common target populations varies by different methods of data collection, and even where coverage is high, it is not always possible to find a reliable sampling frame. For face-to-face surveys and postal surveys, the most comprehensive national sampling frame from which to draw a sample is the Post Office Address file (or equivalent). This type of sampling frame tends to cover pretty much all the addresses in a country and so does not introduce much coverage error. However, obtaining a sampling frame with good national coverage is much more problematic for telephone interviews and internet interviews, and this can introduce greater coverage error.

For telephone surveys, even though the proportion of households with a telephone tends to be quite high in developed countries (typically over 90%), it is nonetheless difficult to obtain a comprehensive sampling frame. For example, the phone book (Yellow Pages or equivalent) is not very representative of the population because of the large number of people who are ex-directory (not listed). For example, in the UK about 25% of the population who have a telephone are not listed in the phone book. Even though the overall proportion of the population who have a telephone has increased in recent years, the proportion of the population who are not listed in the phone book has also increased. The phone book is therefore not a particularly good sampling frame, and researchers who do telephone surveys tend to use **random digit dialling** instead. This involves dialling numbers at random. Although this reduces coverage error, it involves making a lot of wasted calls to numbers that aren't in use, and does not distinguish between business and residential addresses. This can make it difficult to calculate response rates (see below).

For internet surveys, the past few years have seen a rapid increase in the proportion of British households with internet access, and according to the Office of National Statistics, about 70% of British households now have internet access. But this is still a long way away from full coverage, and any survey carried out through the internet will leave out a substantial proportion of the population. Moreover, the so-called 'digital divide' between those who are online and those who are not means that there are also likely to be important demographic differences between the two groups, which may introduce further bias (see Robinson, Neustadtl and Kestnbaum 2002). Moreover, for internet surveys, no good sampling frame has been developed for sampling the internet population (see Couper 2000, for a review). Survey companies therefore often rely upon drawing samples from a database of volunteers, which can then be weighted to make the sample representative of the population with respect to key demographic variables. This sampling strategy mixes elements of the volunteer sample and the quota sample, discussed previously.

However, despite these problems, recent research shows that in some cases there is very little observable difference between analyses using in-person data and internet data (see Sanders et al. 2007). David Sanders and colleagues carried out an experiment to compare the two modes of data collection following the 2005 British general election and found that, although there were some statistically significant, albeit small, differences in the distributions of key explanatory variables, the relative impact of these variables on turnout and party choice were virtually identical for the two types of data. They conclude that in-person and internet data tell very similar stories about what matters for turnout and party preference in Britain.

However, not all surveys are designed to study national populations, and in some cases it may be possible to acquire good sampling frames for internet surveys. For example, if the population of interest is students, then it may be possible to utilize University records to obtain a full list of students' email addresses. This sampling frame would have full coverage of the population of interest, and could be used to select a probability-based sample.

The way in which a questionnaire is administered can also influence the **response rate** to the survey. One of the main challenges for all types of survey research is how to obtain a high response rate, since non-response can introduce error if people who do not complete the survey differ in key respects from those who do. It is therefore important to try and achieve a high response rate, and also, to be aware of who does not respond to the survey and why. Traditionally, response rates for population surveys have tended to be higher for face-to-face surveys than for telephone surveys and mail and internet surveys (de Vaus 2002; Groves et al. 2004). However, there is also substantial variation across modes of interview depending upon how much effort is made to re-contact respondents, and according to Groves et al. (2004: 154), it is not clear whether there are any inherent differences between the modes that directly affect response rates.

Mode effects are more apparent when it comes to identifying the reasons for non-response, and for distinguishing between different types of non-response. For example, with face-to-face interviews, it is possible to distinguish between eligible units and ineligible units. An ineligible unit might be a business address or a derelict property where no one lives. In general, we are only concerned about the non-response of eligible units, so this information is important. However, in mail surveys it can be hard to distinguish between the two. If there is no response, it may be because the potential respondent did not complete the survey (eligible unit), or it may be because the survey was sent to a derelict property where no one lives (ineligible unit). Similarly, with telephone surveys, if the telephone rings but no one answers, it may be because the potential respondent is away or busy (eligible unit) or it may be because the telephone number is not in action (ineligible unit). Lastly, although emails sent to bad addresses are frequently bounced back, it is not always possible to tell whether it has reached its intended target.

In summary, although there are advantages and disadvantages in using each of the different interview modes, these are not fixed and vary according to the purpose of the survey and the target population. Moreover, modes of interview can be combined. For example, it is common practice to supplement face-to-face surveys with a mail back or internet follow-up, which can be a cheap and reliable way of gathering more data once the initial sample has been drawn.

Conclusions

As the examples in this chapter have shown, there are a wide range of difficulties that face researchers trying to undertake survey research. These difficulties come in many forms and can introduce error at various stages of the research process. But despite these difficulties, and perhaps because we are aware of them, surveys remain a valuable source of information. Some difficulties are easier to manage than others. By using random probability sampling, we can have confidence that our surveys are more representative of the population at large than surveys conducted by any of the other alternatives. And this representativeness can give us confidence that inferences we make from our sample are generalizable to the wider population. But ensuring representativeness is only part of the challenge.

Questionnaire design is not an exact science and the researcher is confronted with many measurement problems. Some of these problems can be at least partially remedied by careful question wording, but other problems persist and are harder to get rid of. Questionnaires are a very delicate instrument. Slight changes in how questions are worded or phrased can influence how people answer. This means that we should be very careful how we interpret the results from different survey questions. For example, if we are interested in the balance of public opinion for or against the decision to invade Iraq, we have to bear in mind that our survey estimate is influenced in part by how we have asked the question. A similar question framed in a slightly different way may produce a different estimate. If we want to know whether pubic opinion has changed, we therefore have to be careful to only compare survey questions that have been asked in exactly the same way. Even small changes in question wording could make the observed differences an artefact of measurement differences, rather than an indication of any real difference of opinion. For these reasons, when we analyse survey data, we tend to focus on whether responses to a particular question vary over time; or whether they vary by different sections of society.

 ## Questions

- What are the principles of good questionnaire design? Are these principles generally followed in survey research?
- If the way in which we ask questions affects the answers that we get, can surveys ever be trusted?
- What is measurement error? Can it be avoided? If not, what should we do?
- What is the difference between validity and reliability?
- How do we know if a survey question is valid?
- What is the difference between measurement error and bias? Which should we be more concerned about? Why?
- What are the strengths and weaknesses of different sampling techniques?
- Are non-probability samples really so bad? Why?
- What are the strengths of survey research? What are the weaknesses?
- What are the different types of error that affect survey research? What can be done to try and reduce them?
- As long as we are aware of the error we make, it doesn't matter if we make errors. Do you agree?

 ## Guide to Further Reading

de Vaus, David (2002), *Surveys in Social Research* (London: Routledge).
A detailed and accessible overview of survey design and administration. Contains many easy-to-read and helpful chapters on how to carry out a survey and how to analyse the results.

Groves, Robert, F. Fowler, M. Couper, J. Lepkowski, E. Stinger, and R. Tourangeau (2004), *Survey Methodology* (New Jersey: John Wiley and Sons).
A sophisticated examination of survey error and how to minimize it.

Moser, Sir Claus and G. Kalton (1971), *Survey Methods in Social Investigation* (London: Heinemann Educational Books).
A classic book on survey design. Provides a thorough examination of survey research, and offers advice on how to plan, design, and carry out a survey effectively.

Schuman, Howard and S. Presser (1996), *Questions and Answers in Attitude Surveys: Experiments on Question Form, Wording and Context* (London: Sage Publications).
A fascinating study reporting the findings from a number of survey experiments designed to investigate the impact of questionnaire design on the responses that are given.

 # References

Atkeson, L. (1999), '"Sure, I Voted for the Winner!" Overreport of the Primary Vote for the Party Nominee in the NES', *Political Behavior* 21(3): 197–215.

Becker, H. S. (1963), *Outsiders: Studies in the Sociology of Deviance* (New York: Free Press).

Belson, W. (1981), *The Design and Understanding of Survey Questions* (London: Gower).

Belli, Robert, Michael W. Traugott, Margaret Young, and Katherine A. McGonagle (1999), 'Reducing Vote Overreporting in Surveys', *Public Opinion Quarterly*, 63: 90–108.

Converse, Philip E. (1964), 'The Nature of Belief Systems in Mass Publics', in David Apter (ed.), *Ideology and Discontent* (New York: Free Press of Glencoe).

Couper, M. (2000), 'Web Surveys: A Review of Issues and Approaches', *Public Opinion Quarterly* 64: 464–94.

de Vaus, David (2002), *Surveys in Social Research* (London: Routledge).

Gowers, E. A. (1954), *The Complete Plain Words* (London: Penguin).

Groves, Robert, F. Fowler, M. Couper, J. Lepkowski, E. Stinger, and R. Tourangeau (2004), *Survey Methodology* (New Jersey: John Wiley and Sons).

Heath, O. and R. Johns (2010), 'Measuring Political Behaviour and Attitudes', in M. Bulmer (ed.), *Social Measurement through Social Surveys: An Applied Approach* (Aldershot: Ashgate).

Moser, Sir Claus and G. Kalton (1971), *Survey Methods in Social Investigation* (London: Heinemann Educational Books).

Robinson, J. P., A. Neustadtl, and M. Kestnbaum (2002), 'The Online "Diversity Divide": Public Opinion Differences among Internet Users and Nonusers', *IT & Society* 1: 284–302.

Sanders, D., H. Clarke, M. Stewart, and P. Whiteley (2007), 'Does Mode Matter for Modeling Political Choice? Evidence from the 2005 British Election Study', *Political Analysis* 15: 257–85.

Schuman, Howard and S. Presser (1996), *Questions and Answers in Attitude Surveys: Experiments on Question Form, Wording and Context* (London: Sage Publications).

——, Jacob Ludwig, and Jon Krosnick (1986), 'The Perceived Threat of Nuclear War, Open Questions, and Salience', *Public Opinion Quarterly* 50: 519–36.

Sudman, Seymour, and Norman M. Bradburn (1982), *Asking Questions* (San Francisco, CA: Jossey-Bass).

Swaddle, K. and Heath, A. (1989), 'Official and Reported Turnout in the British General Election of 1987', *British Journal of Political Science* 19(4): 537–51.

Tourangeau, Roger, Lance J. Rips, and Kenneth A. Rasinski (2000), *The Psychology of Survey Response* (Cambridge: Cambridge University Press).

Wright, Gerald C. (1993), 'Errors in Measuring Vote Choice in the National Election Studies, 1952–88', *American Journal of Political Science* 37: 291–316.

Zaller, J. (1992), *The Nature and Origins of Mass Opinion* (Cambridge: Cambridge University Press).

Interviewing and Focus Groups

 Chapter Summary

One of the ways in which researchers collect information about the social world is to ask people questions. This can be done by conducting structured and semi-structured interviews, face-to-face interviews, telephone or online interviews, or organizing focus group sessions. This chapter discusses different types and forms of interviewing, how interviews and focus groups (a form of interview) should be carried out; and coding and analysing interview data. The questions addressed in this chapter include the following:

- What are the different types and forms of interview?
- How can interview data be used to confirm or disconfirm a hypothesis or argument?
- How do you plan and conduct an interview?
- What do you need to consider when designing a questionnaire?
- What are the different types of question that might be included in an interview or questionnaire?
- How do the type and wording of questions, and the order in which you ask them, affect the responses you get?
- What interviewing skills will ensure a more successful outcome to an interview?

Introduction

Interviews are a prominent method of data collection in political research. *Interviews* as a method of collecting data in research can be distinguished from *surveys*, and also from interviews that are conducted for purposes other than research (such as job interviews or media interviews). There are similarities between interviews and surveys (discussed in Chapter 10). Both use questionnaires and interviewers. But these similarities relate mostly to structured interviews. This chapter focuses mostly on semi-structured interviews (including focus groups). In these types of interviews often the researcher wants to probe, which is rather like asking leading questions, to get the interviewee to open up and discuss something of relevance to the research question. This kind of technique is generally not used in survey research. The role of the interviewer is therefore somewhat different, and with the interview the interviewer is more active. More generally, we can say that the aims of interviewing and surveys can also be somewhat different (although they are frequently complementary). The aim of *surveys* is to produce standardized data which can be used to make generalizations about what a given population of people think about a particular issue. By contrast, *interviewing* is more concerned with obtaining detailed, often specialized information from a single individual or small number of individuals. The aim is not necessarily to make generalizations, but to gain valid knowledge and understanding about what the person in question thinks. Although both interviews and surveys take the issues of reliability and validity seriously, it may be argued that surveys tend to prioritize reliability (which allows them to make generalizations), whereas interviews prioritize validity (which allows them to gain a depth of knowledge).

In this chapter we will discuss types and forms of interviews, what considerations enter into designing a schedule of questions or a questionnaire, how to conduct an interview and organize a focus group, and how to analyse interview data.

I. Interviews

To decide whether interviews will enable you to investigate your hypothesis you must ask yourself, and answer, a number of questions. How will interviews enable you to investigate/demonstrate your hypothesis? What, specifically, do you need to find out, through interviewing, to enable you to investigate the relationships stated by your hypothesis? Is conducting interviews the best way to obtain this information? What kind of interview, and what sort of questions, will enable you to obtain this information? Of whom will you ask questions and what techniques will you use? Understanding the various types and forms of interview will enable you to answer these questions.

Types of interview

Different *types of interview* provide different ways of collecting interview data. Interview data can be collected by conducting individual face-to-face, telephone, or online interviews, or by organizing focus group sessions. These types of interview vary with respect to the degree of personal contact they entail between researchers and subjects. However, they all involve a situation in which a researcher asks respondents questions and then records and analyses their answers. For all types of interviewing, the primary purpose is to produce data that will help answer research questions.

Individual face-to-face interviewing

This type of interview is the best data-collection type for open-ended questions and in-depth exploration of opinions. The interviewer works directly with the respondent and has the opportunity to probe or ask follow-up questions. By being able to ask questions of subjects personally, the interviewer can probe unclear responses, resolve difficulties that lead to non-responses, and obtain useful information from body language and vocal cues. In sum, this type of interviewing can support longer and more detailed questions, is adaptable, and is a rich and dense source of data.

Telephone interviews

This type of interview enables a researcher to gather information rapidly. Most major public opinion polls that are reported are based on telephone interviews (see Chapter 10). Using telephone interviews gives researchers wide geographical access: people from all over the globe can be interviewed if they have access to a telephone or computer, as well as populations that are difficult to reach or interview by other means (e.g. people living in remote areas). Like face to-face interviews, they allow for some personal contact between the interviewer and the respondent, and they allow the interviewer to ask follow-up questions. Telephone interviewing supports longer questionnaires than mailed questionnaires, though not as well as face-to-face interviewing.

Online interviews

Online interviews are increasingly used as a data collection method by social scientists. These can be a useful technique for data collection on sensitive items, and they eliminate interviewer bias. But online interviews are a far less personal type of interview than other types; and they are not an appropriate tool for exploratory studies, which require intensive interaction with interviewees in order to gain better insight into an issue. They can be useful in small-scale studies on sensitive topics and in combination with other tools. This is a quick and easy way to reach geographically dispersed interviewees.

Focus groups

Focus groups generate different types of data from other types of interviewing. In this type of interview, a group of people is selected because they are related to some phenomenon of interest. The researcher meets with the group and facilitates an organized discussion related to something the participants have experience of, or beliefs about. The interaction among focus group participants may reveal more than they would in an individual interview, and bring out insights and understandings in ways which simple questionnaire items (used in face-to-face or telephone interviews or sent through the mail) may not be able to tap, such as emotional and unconscious motivations. Using focus groups, researchers can learn how things are discussed in a particular culture, test hypotheses about beliefs, mix people who wouldn't normally mix, test questions for future interviews, or test policy ideas to see how citizens react to them.

Let's compare the advantages and disadvantages of different types and forms of interviewing for specific purposes. Individual face-to-face interviews or focus groups provide more flexibility and can enable researchers to probe or ask follow-up questions. However, they always carry the possibility of interviewer bias, as well as respondent bias on sensitive items. They require skill to undertake well; they can also be very expensive, take a lot of time, and will usually be less feasible to do if the population you wish to interview is widely dispersed geographically. The data from both types are difficult to analyse—particularly in the case of focus groups, where the analysis may be concerned both with the content of what was said and the patterns of interaction. Telephone interviews enable the researcher to interview people who are not easy to access, but the interviewer does not see the interviewee, so body language and voice and intonation cannot be used as a source of extra information. Moreover, the interviewer has no control over the setting and ambience and cannot standardize the situation in which the interview takes place. And, telephone interviews have to be relatively short or energy levels will flag. Telephone interviews are not ideal if you want to ask lengthy questions, give the respondent detailed background for a question, or ask the respondent to select from a long list of possible options or answers. Online interviews have become increasingly popular. In cases where it is not possible to schedule a time to meet face-to-face or to speak on the phone, it might be the *only* way to conduct an interview. Online interviews present opportunities to interview individuals based anywhere in the world. And they provide more time for interviewer and interviewee to consider their questions and answers, allowing for increased flexibility and deeper reflection. Unlike more personal forms of interviewing (individual face-to-face, focus group, or telephone interviewing), they allow the interviewer to ask questions that may require the respondent to consult records in order to supply answers. However, they are a poor choice for complex questions, and the researcher cannot probe or collect additional data. As with telephone interviewing, the researcher has no control over whether and how a respondent is interacting with others while completing the questionnaire.

Forms of interview

You will not be able to select among these different *types* of interviewing—to fully weigh their advantages and disadvantages for different purpose—unless you are clear about how, within these types of interview, the *form* of interviewing can vary. What we want to clarify is: what are the different formats that interviews take, including the types of questions asked and the manner in which they are asked? Which of these forms or formats are supported by the different types of interviews that we just discussed?

There are three basic *forms of interview* that vary with respect to the degree to which the questions and responses are standardized across interview subjects. These are *structured*, *unstructured*, and *semi-structured* forms of interview. They differ with respect to the form of question employed (closed or open), how they are worded (shorter and simpler, or longer and more complex), and whether the same questions are asked the same way and in the same sequence across interview subjects (standardized or variable). **Structured interviews** consist of a standardized set of closed and shorter or simpler questions that are asked in a standardized manner and sequence. Of the types of interviewing we discussed previously, mailed questionnaires almost invariably use this form of interviewing. **Unstructured interviews** use open, and perhaps lengthier and more complex questions, which might vary in the way and order in which they are asked. Focus groups, which involve interviewing people together in flexible and exploratory group discussion formats are an example of a type of interview that uses this form of interview. Perhaps the most common type of interview used in political research is *semi-structured interviewing*: a form of interview that combines elements of both structured and unstructured interviews.

Structured interviews

Structured interviews often consist of **closed questions**. This means that both the questions asked and the coding of answers are standardized. This form of interview is primarily used in surveys, and is discussed in detail in Chapter 10. But whether thousands of respondents are interviewed in this way, or just a handful, the principles of questionnaire design are exactly the same. Interviewees—or respondents—are asked a set of identical questions in exactly the same way and in the same order; and they are usually asked to respond by selecting from a limited range of possible options or answers. Individual face-to-face and telephone interviews can use structured interviews, focus groups cannot use them, and mailed questionnaires generally must use them.

A key concern with the structured interview has to do with the limitations of asking standardized questions and presenting a standardized list of options from which respondents choose a response. Although this method may produce reliable results, in that everyone is presented with the same question and has the same opportunities to answer, it is often argued that it does not produce valid data. The problem is that the same word can mean different things to different people. Consider this example of a closed question:

How would you rate your course tutor?

Excellent	☐
Quite good	☐
Quite poor	☐
Useless	☐
Don't know	☐

The problem with this question is that people might mean very different things by 'excellent', but everyone who ticks that box in response to the question will be included in the percentage of people judging the course tutor to be 'excellent'. This raises questions about the validity of the data that these responses yield. As discussed in Chapter 10, there are four basic ways in which we can try and assess validity (see Moser and Kalton 1971; de Vaus 2002 for an extended discussion). The first and most straightforward is face validity. **Face validity** simply asks if, on the face of it, the question intuitively seems like a good measure of the concept. If the answer is no, then we definitely have a problem, but what is intuitively yes for one person may not be so for another. **Content validity** examines the extent to which the question covers the full range of the concept, covering each of its different aspects. **Criterion validity** examines how well the new measure of the concept relates to existing measures of the concept, or related concepts. **Construct validity** examines how well the measure conforms to our theoretical expectations, by examining the extent to which it is associated with other theoretically relevant factors. Ultimately, though, the matter of validity is one of judgement. The structural form of interview may lack validity in that it fails to fully capture the reality of people's lived experience. Because the structured interview allows researchers to be more detached from the people they are studying, it is difficult for them to explore what their subjects actually mean and how they actually behave in real situations.

Unstructured interviews

Unstructured interviews often use **open questions**, which allow for longer and perhaps more complex questions, as well as more in-depth probing and flexibility, than structured interviews. They are more like ordinary conversations: there is no set interview structure, and interviewees answer in their own words. The interviewer initiates the conversation, presents each topic by means of specific questions, and decides when the conversation on a topic has satisfied the research objectives. These elements of the interview process will likely vary with each individual interview, based on the responses of the interviewee.

Semi-structured interviews

Semi-structured interviews generally involve a small number of interviews in which the interviewer uses a combination of structured questions (to obtain factual information) and unstructured questions (to probe deeper into people's experiences). The interviewer prepares a schedule of questions, as well as supplementary questions to explore aspects of the response to each question asked. But the questions may be more general, and the interviewer may choose to vary the sequence in which they are asked, and to ask follow-up questions. Unstructured or semi-structured interviews can give greater insight into the meanings of a subject's experiences and hence provide more valid data. However, it is not as easy to compare responses of different groups or of the same group over time since each interviewee will have been asked slightly different questions to find out what they think. The data are not standardized and are thus hard to generalize from and, as the results cannot be quantified and re-tested, less reliable.

Box 11.1 shows how these types and forms commonly combine in political research.

Which type and form of interview to use?

When selecting the type of data collection technique and form of interview to use, there are a number of substantive and practical issues to consider.

Generally, structured interviews are better for making comparisons and less structured interviews may be more appropriate for early exploratory phases of research. Ultimately, it will be the nature of what you want to ask respondents that determines the type and form of interview you select. Are you going to need to get lots of detail in the responses (open questions); or can you anticipate the most frequent or important types of responses and develop reasonable closed-ended questions? Will the questions be complex and require multiple parts or sub-questions? Can you construct in advance a

---

BOX 11.1 Types and Forms of Interviews

	Forms of interview (types of questions, wording, and sequencing)		
	Structured (closed, shorter, standardized)	Semi-structured (combines structured/ unstructured forms)	Unstructured (open, longer/more complex, varied)
Types of interview (data collection techniques)			
Individual face-to-face	X	X	X
Focus-groups			X
Telephone	X	X	X
Online	X	X	X
Mailed questionnaire	X		

set of questions and the sequence in which they will be asked? Or will you need to proceed in a more exploratory manner, perhaps entailing lots of follow-up questions that you can't easily anticipate?

A key consideration is the likelihood of bias and of threats to the validity and reliability of your findings. A limitation with all types and forms of interviews is that researchers are dependent on what people tell them. Some people may have problems in recalling information accurately. But all people come to an interview with biases and prejudices; and people generally are prone to something known as the 'interview effect': the tendency for interviewees to give more 'socially acceptable' answers or answers they think the interviewer wants. The biases and prejudices of interviewers may also distort the interview process: they may not ask questions that make them uncomfortable, or fail to listen carefully to respondents on topics for which they have strong opinions. People may not tell the truth because they want to 'look good' in the eyes of the interviewer, or if they are asked something that either they don't know how to answer or that would be embarrassing for them to answer. Some types of interview are better able to reduce the effects of biases and prejudices. Anonymous questionnaires that contain no identifying information are more likely to produce honest responses than those identifying the respondent.

In selecting the type of data-collection technique, you will need to consider a number of practical considerations, such as cost, facilities, equipment, and time. Cost is often a major determining factor in selecting the type of interview to conduct. Costs can include travel expenses entailed in conducting personal interviews, or postal costs for an extensive mailing. Facilities are another consideration. You will require access to well-equipped phone-surveying facilities for telephone interviews, and a comfortable and accessible room to host focus groups. Equipment needs might include a transcription machine with a pedal-operated start–stop mechanism; or voice transcription software—such as *Dragon Naturally Speaking* speech recognition software from Nuance Communications—to record responses, and equipment or resources to pay for professional transcription.[1] Finally, will you have enough time to send out mail questionnaires and follow-up reminders, and to get responses back by mail? Will you have enough time to carry out all the personal interviews?

Each of the three forms of interview that we have discussed (structured, semi-structured, and unstructured) collect data in slightly different ways. An interviewer conducting face-to-face *structured* interviews will generally prepare an **interview schedule**: a list of questions to be asked of all interviewees. By contrast, an interviewer conducting unstructured or semi-structured interviews will generally prepare an interview guide: a set of questions that provide a list of talking points or areas to be covered. Below, we discuss each of these approaches to collecting data.

Designing a questionnaire or interview schedule for a structured interview

Designing a good questionnaire or interview schedule always involves decisions regarding the content, formulation, and sequencing of the questions.

► Content: choosing questions to ask

Take your hypothesis as a starting point. The research project should be designed to provide a convincing test of your hypothesis. Make sure that you are clear about exactly what you do need to find out and that the questions you ask supply you with the information you need. Formulate questions whose answers will contribute to confirming or disconfirming your hypothesis. Ensure that your questionnaire or interview schedule is designed to enable you to investigate your major analytic categories or variables and obtain the maximum quality of responses. Decide what questions will enable you to operationalize (measure or define) your variables. You might consider using questions employed by other researchers to tap the same information.

► Formulating questions

In discussing structured, unstructured, and semi-structured forms of interviewing, we referred to two types of questions: open-ended questions (allowing for completely open as well as partially categorized answers), and closed questions. Here we will look more closely at these types of questions. (See also our discussion in Chapter 10.)

Open-ended questions

Open-ended questions permit researchers to obtain in-depth information on issues with which they are not very familiar; opinions, attitudes, and suggestions of respondents; or sensitive issues. Open-ended questions ask: 'What did you think of the initiative? How did you feel about the decision? What do you like best about the proposed program?' The use of open-ended questions can be improved by preparing a list of further questions to keep at hand to 'probe' for answer(s) in a systematic way.

Closed questions

Answers to closed questions can be recorded in a number of different ways. However, it is important to ensure that the response alternatives provide a sufficient range of choices, and that they are mutually exclusive.

One of the most simple response formats is to invite respondents to select between two fixed alternatives. The respondent is offered two possible responses, only *one* of which may be selected (*dichotomous questions*): for instance, responses may take the form of Yes/No, True/False or Agree/Disagree. Although these questions are relatively simple, for many topics they are unlikely to cover the full range of responses that a respondent may want to give.

These types of questions can therefore easily be extended to cover a greater range of response alternatives. For example, a respondent may be offered a list of items and asked to select *one* of the responses:

Which party did you vote for in the general election?

Conservative ☐
Labour ☐

Liberal Democrat	☐
Scottish National Party	☐
Plaid Cymru	☐
Green Party	☐
Other party	☐

By contrast, respondents may also be provided with the option of selecting more than one response. For these questions the response is chosen from a list of items in which *any number* of items may be selected.

Which of these news sources have you consulted during the past month?

Television news programmes	☐
Radio news programmes	☐
Daily newspapers	☐
Internet news sites	☐
Weekly news magazines	☐
Monthly news magazines	☐
Other	☐

Another type of response format that is frequently used is one where the categories have an order, and answers involve rating, for instance, the level of agreement or disagreement with a statement from low to high. These are often referred to as numerical rating scales, and there are a number of ways in which they can be constructed. One of the most common types of rating scale is known as the Likert scale. This type of question generally provides a statement that reflects a particular attitude or opinion and asks respondents to indicate their level of *agreement* or *disagreement* with the statement. Usually respondents are given five different response alternatives:

The Government generally treats people like me fairly.

1. Strongly agree

2. Agree

3. Neither agree nor disagree

4. Disagree

5. Strongly disagree.

Rating scales can also be used to measure a respondent's level of *support* of level of *interest* in something.

How much interest do you generally have in what is going on in politics?

1. A great deal

2. Quite a lot

3. Some

4. Not very much

5. None at all.

Finally, we can also ask questions where the respondent is invited to rank different response options in order of *preference*:

> *Please rank the following items in order of what seem the most desirable to you, where 1 is the most desirable and 4 is the least desirable.*

Maintaining order in the nation	☐
Giving people more say in important decisions	☐
Fighting rising prices	☐
Protecting freedom of speech	☐

Questions asking respondents to rank items become increasingly difficult as the number of items increases, and this may make the answers less reliable. Generally, respondents should not be asked to order or rank a series of more than five items. For more details see Chapter 10.

Partially categorized questions

Pre-categorized questions combine elements both of open and closed questions. Respondents are asked an open question, but rather than recording their answer verbatim, the interviewer selects from a list of pre-coded responses and selects the answer category that s/he thinks comes closest to what the respondent said. Answers can be recorded quickly, and analysis is easier. But if one pre-categorizes too early, a lot of interesting and valuable information may just end up in the category 'Other'. Interviewers may try to force the information into the categories that are listed and, by merely ticking these, additional valuable information may be lost. Interviewers may stop after receiving the first answer, whereas more than one response could be applicable. If a question leads to an interesting discussion, it should be written down as completely as possible, in addition to being coded. Adequate space should be provided so that 'Other' responses can be recorded as close as possible to the respondents' own words. Otherwise categorization of these responses may be difficult afterwards.

Designing an interview guide for semi-structured or unstructured interviews

A semi-structured interview is a powerful research instrument which can help a researcher understand people's perceptions, feelings, opinions, experiences, understandings, values, beliefs, attitudes, emotions, behaviour, formal and informal roles, and relationships. In semi-structured interviews, the interviewer guides the interview, but permits various aspects of the topic to arise naturally and in any order. To do this, researchers will usually construct an 'interview guide': a basic checklist of areas to be covered in the interview in the form of questions. But, although the interviewer comes prepared with a list of areas to be covered, and may prompt and give direction to the interviewee, the interviewee is treated as an active subject, and not merely a reporter of facts or experiences.

Take a look at this draft of an interview guide on family life in border areas, below.

DRAFT INTERVIEW GUIDE

Introduction: purpose of research, tape recorder/confidentiality, conduct of interview.

BIOGRAPHY

1. *Tell me about your family background. What was it like when you were a child?*

   Prompt: Level/main source of household income
   Education of family members

2. *Are there holidays or special family events that your family celebrates?*

   Prompt: Could you tell me more about these?

3. *Tell me something about your extended family.*

   Probe: What sort of connections did your family maintain with this larger group of family members while you were growing up?

   Probe: How many family members live across the border?

FAMILY PRACTICES

4. *Does you family cross the border to see family members?*

5. *What is the pattern of your cross-border family visiting? How often do you cross the border to see family members?*

   Probe: Places you visit
   Usual length of visit

6. *Do you celebrate holidays and special occasions with members of your extended family who live across the border?*

7. *Do family members keep in touch with members across the border in other ways?*

CROSS-BORDER ACTIVITIES

8. *Do you cross the border to participate in family celebrations?*

   Prompt: Which ones?

9. *Do you cross the border for other purposes?*

   Prompt: Can you tell me briefly about these?

10. *Have there been any marriages in your family between individuals living on opposite sides of the border?*

    Prompt: Was the marriage considered a special marriage or was it treated like any other family marriage?

EXPERIENCE OF CROSS-BORDER VISITS

11. *What is it like travelling across the border? Does it take a long time to pass through the border control station?*

12. *What are your impressions of the places you have visited across the border?*

   Probe: What do you like/dislike about these places?

Another example of how an interview guide on social movements might be constructed is in Box 11.2, below.

   In conducting a semi-structured or unstructured interview, the aim of the interviewer is both to ask questions and to listen in a way that encourages the interviewee to talk. In particular, the interviewer tries to adopt a tone and manner that gives interviewees the freedom to open up, reflect, and express themselves. As interviewer, you must make sure not to lead the interview in a way that closes off discussion by the manner in which you ask questions and receive responses. Here are some general 'rules of thumb':

- Avoid questions phrased in a way that suggests or assumes a particular kind of answer. For instance, rather than asking what the respondent likes (or dislikes) about a candidate, an interviewer might ask, first, how the respondent feels about the candidate; and then follow up with a question about what the respondent most likes (or dislikes) about the candidate.

- Don't discourage long answers; instead, verbally and through body language encourage the interviewee.

- If you don't understand something, continue to listen rather than interrupt. You can ask for clarification during a break in conversation. Probe in ways that indicate your interest in what a person is saying and encourages the person to explain in more detail.

- Don't communicate, either verbally or through body language, your judgement about what the interviewee has told you. Make sure that your body language does not appear judgemental, or expose your negative judgement. Don't react to provocative statements but accept what the interviewee says.

- Use body language that signals interest (focus on interviewee, eye contact, nodding, smiling).

A semi- or unstructured interview will generally follow the same sequence.

- *Introduction.* The aim of the introduction is to explain the research, and the interview process, and to establish rapport with the interviewee. Explain the purpose of your research, what it is, and what you will do with the information you gather. Address confidentiality issues, and get permission to record the interview. Explain what the interview process will be like and how long it will take.

- *Warm up.* The aim is to help the respondent to relax. Emphasize that there are no wrong or right answers; and start with questions that are easy to answer and relatively impersonal.

- *Main body of the interview.* The main body of the interview consists of questions relating to the list of topics contained in the interview guide. These will consist of:

   - questions that introduce a topic (Would you please tell me about when your interest in the movement began? Have you ever…?);

BOX 11.2 Example of an Interview Guide on Social Movements

Overarching themes	Questions	Possible probes (follow-up questions)
Personal background	Please can you tell me a little about your own participation in the movement?	• How long have you been a member? • What led you to join? • Have you remained an active member continuously since the time you joined?
	Can you tell me what types of meetings you have attended?	• How many times have you attended? • Which ones do you find you have liked most? • Why was that?
About the movement	If you think about the movement, what do would you say that its major accomplishments have been?	• Raising awareness of key issues? • Encouraging wider participation in public life? • Raising funds for key activities and services?
	What do you think are the main strengths of the movement?	• Differences between the movement and other similar movements? • What has enabled the movement to develop these strengths?
	What do you think are the main challenges that the movement faces?	• What makes you think so? • Do you think others in the movement would agree?
Perceptions about the other members	In general, why do you think people become active members of the movement?	• What type of person becomes a member? • Have you ever talked with other members about this?
	Do you see members outside of meetings?	• Why not? • What sorts of things do you do or talk about with other members?
Perceptions about recent activities	Do you think the movement's recent campaign was successful in achieving its aims?	• Do you think anything should have been done differently? • How do you think the membership at large felt about the campaign?
	Do you think the movement should make any changes in how it promotes its interests?	• If you had a leadership position in the movement, would you have done anything differently?

- direct questions (Do you enjoy participating in these types of activities?); and

- probing questions. These include *follow-up questions* (Could you say more about…?), *specifying questions* (How did you react when you heard the news? What did you do after that?); and *interpreting questions* (Do you mean that your opinion of X changed?).

● *Cool-off*. When the main topics have been covered, the interviewer should begin to prepare for winding down the interview. In this 'cool-off' segment of the interview, the interviewer moves the discussion away from 'heavy' topics—those that have been most difficult to discuss or that have generated tension—and returns to more general questions. The aim is to end the interview on a lighter and brighter note.

● *Closure*. The interview will conclude with asking the respondent if they have anything they would like to add to what they have told you, and if there is anything they would like to ask you. You should not appear to be in a hurry to get away. Conclude the interview by offering the respondent sincere thanks for taking the time to talk with you.

Formulating questions

Whichever type of interview you conduct, or question you use, all questions should be formulated with the following considerations in mind.

1. *Avoid leading questions*. The wording of a question is extremely important. Researchers strive for objectivity in interviewing and, therefore, must be careful not to lead the respondent into giving the answer they would like to receive. A leading question is one that communicates the suggestion to respondents that certain responses are more useful or acceptable than others. A leading question is framed in such a way as to suggest that one answer is expected or preferred. Chapter 10 cited as an example of this type of question one developed for the National Election Studies in the United States: *Generally speaking, do you usually think of yourself as a Republican, a Democrat, an Independent, or what?* The phrase '*or what*' at the end of the question might give the impression that *not* having such an identification is somewhat odd, making it more likely that respondents will feel pressured to say that they *do* identify with one of the parties and less likely to say that they think of themselves as partisans of parties which are not mentioned.

2. *Avoid double-barrelled questions*. These are questions that ask for an answer on more than one dimension. For example, a researcher investigating the public response to a new legislative initiative asks, *Do you approve of the scope and cost-effectiveness of the measure?* If a respondent answers 'no', then the researcher will not know if the respondent disapproves of the scope or cost, or both. A question that asks for a response on more than one dimension will not provide the information you are seeking.

3. *Make questions non-confrontational or non–threatening*. In order to evoke the truth, questions must be non-threatening. When a respondent is concerned about the consequences of answering a question in a particular manner, there is a good possibility that the answer will not be truthful.

4. *Use simple, direct language.* You need to consider what your question might mean to different respondents. The questions must be clearly understood by the respondent. They must be specific and precise enough so that different respondents don't interpret them differently. Check that your language is jargon-free. Avoid ambiguity, imprecision, and assumption. Modifying adjectives can have highly variable meanings. Words like *usually, often, sometimes, occasionally, seldom,* and *rarely* may not mean the same thing to all people. Do not use uncommon words or unfamiliar abbreviations. Avoid ambiguous or technical terms, and long or very general questions. Make the wording of questions simple and to the point. Making them as brief as possible will reduce misunderstandings.

5. Finally, you should *pre-test questions.* Do a test-run to check whether the questions enable you to obtain the information you require and whether interviewers as well as respondents feel at ease with them. Pre-testing questions ensures that the research instrument functions the way it is meant to do. Pre-testing is usually considered only in structured interviewing; but it can be useful to (mentally) pre-test questions planned for an unstructured interview, as well. Consider each question and decide whether all respondents will be able to answer it. Ask the questions to yourself or to a friend and check whether the answers you get are the type of responses you want.

For more on pitfalls to avoid in the wording of questions, see Chapter 10.

▶ Question sequence

The sequence of questions must be logical. The interviewer should group together questions that are similar, rather than jumping from one unrelated topic to another. The interviewer should also use screening or 'filter' questions to determine whether the respondent has the requisite knowledge to answer a subsequent question. For instance, before asking someone who they voted for in the last election, you would first need to ask whether they voted. In this example, if the respondent answered 'no' to the screening question, the interviewer would skip the following question (about how the respondent voted), or the questionnaire would direct the respondent to the correct subsequent question.

The sequencing of questions should also allow, as much as possible, for a 'natural' conversation, even in more structured interviews. Within each group, transitions between questions should be smooth. Each question should follow comfortably from the previous question. You should start with questions directly related to the topic of the research—particularly questions most likely to secure the interest and attention of the respondent. Start with a question that is directly related to the subject of the study and that will raise the respondent's interest. More sensitive questions should be posed as late as possible in the interview.

Within every group of questions, general questions should come before more specific ones. The reason, as Alan Bryman points out, is that 'when a specific question comes before a general one, the aspect of the general question that is covered by the specific one is discounted in the minds of the respondents because they feel they have already covered it'. For example, if you first ask a question about a respondent's satisfaction with his salary, and afterwards ask about the respondent's satisfaction with his job (a more general question), the respondent may discount the salary issue, having already addressed it (Bryman 2004: 122). This is what is called **question order effect**. The context in which a question is asked or the position in which it appears in relation to other questions can have a bearing on the answers that are given to it. The most obvious manifestation of this is when respondents try to appear consistent by answering a question so that it fits in with how they answered a previous question. (We discuss this in more detail in Chapter 10.)

For example, George Bishop and his colleagues found that people were more likely to report that they were 'very interested' in the 1980 US presidential campaign when they were asked this question immediately after, rather than just before, a set of questions about who they thought would win the election, how close they thought the race would be, and whether they personally cared which party won the election (Bishop et al. 1984). In a similar experiment, they also discovered that people were less likely to think they followed 'what's going on in government and public affairs' when asked about it right after (instead of just before) a difficult group of questions concerning what they knew about the record of their member of Congress. They concluded that questions such as these 'may not measure what they are intended to measure: an individual's general interest in politics'; instead, 'they may be measuring, among other things, whatever response has been made most plausible and accessible in memory by the wording of the question and by the context in which it is asked' (Bishop et al. 1984: 160–1). By 'context' they mean not just the immediate question, but also the electoral environment in which a question is asked. For instance, if people are asked how interested they are in politics in the midst of an exciting presidential campaign, we would expect them to say they are more interested than if we asked the same question during a dull, local election campaign. Similarly, we would expect people to think they were more interested in following a political campaign if they are asked the question shortly after the election than if they are asked about it several weeks later. We would also expect people who have voted in the election to think they were more interested in the campaign than people were who did not vote (Bishop *et al.* 1984: 161).

As these examples make apparent, context is often crucial, both in shaping the responses to individual items and in evaluating them. This applies to all types of interview alike.

Conducting a face-to-face interview

Interviewing skills

Interviewing requires skill. A good interviewer (1) puts the interviewee at ease without becoming overly familiar; (2) tries to minimize the social distance between him/herself and the interviewee by dressing in a culturally acceptable and simple style; (3) is at ease and never in a hurry; (4) listens to answers, shows interest in what the interviewee says, and never shows any disapproval of the information received during the interview; (5) is sensitive to the respondents' mood, body language, time constraints, and different cultural norms; (6) probes and cross-checks in a thorough but sensitive manner; (7) makes sure the environment is free of noise and other people.

Recording the interview

If an interviewee hesitates or refuses to agree to audio recording, the only solution is to take notes. Usually, interviewees forget quickly that the recorder is on, but if they appear disturbed despite their consent that it be used, it should be stopped. However, even if you are using a tape-recorder (or, more likely, a dictaphone), you should take notes of important non-verbal events or observations. You should take notes in a discreet way without interrupting the flow of conversation.

Keeping control over the interview

The interviewer has to ensure that the interview begins well, and introduce the research to interviewees in a clear and comprehensive way. To ensure that the information provided by different respondents will be comparable, the interviewer must make sure that all topics are adequately covered. Responses that go on too long or off track should be politely stopped or steered back on track. The interviewer might say something in this case like: 'Thank you, this is interesting. Do you mind if I go back to the previous question? This (specify) is not yet fully clear to me.'

Probing

Open-ended questions tend to be very general (e.g. 'What do you think about . . .? Why do you feel that way?'). Consequently, respondents may answer in too general a way or use adjectives that are too general to convey a clear response. In addition to being unclear or incomplete, responses might be irrelevant to the question, offer no answer at all, or appear untruthful. Whenever a response is inadequate or unsatisfactory, the interviewer can use probing. Probing consists of asking questions to encourage further conversation, without influencing the answer. For instance, when a response is *unclear* or *incomplete,* the interviewer might gain clarity or additional information by asking for a more specific response, or an explanation of a term. For instance, the interviewer might ask: 'Could you elaborate a bit?' 'Could you mention more possibilities?' 'Why do you think so?', 'Why do you feel that way?', or 'Would you say some more about that?' Or, if the respondent has started to give an example but did not finish, the interviewer might probe with questions such as: 'When was that?', 'Why did you do that?', 'How often does that happen?' If the response is *irrelevant* to the question, the interviewer might say something like: 'That is not exactly what I meant to ask about' and repeat the question, slightly elaborated.

An answer might be *non-responsive*, either because the respondent did not understand the question or because the question touched on sensitive information that the respondent hesitated to divulge. In case of non-response, the interviewer should repeat or rephrase the question without suggesting a response. If it appears that the question was not understood, the interviewer might say: 'Perhaps, I wasn't really clear in the way I asked the question. What I meant to ask was . . .', followed by the question, phrased slightly more elaborately. If the respondent seems hesitant to answer, then the interviewer can stress again that the information will remain in confidence, and then repeat the question. If the respondent still objects to continuing, the interviewer can offer to skip the question. Sometimes an interviewer might suspect a response is *not truthful* because various parts of an answer contradict each other or because the respondent seems concerned to give the 'desirable' answer. The interviewer should communicate, not suspicion, but an interest in clarifying the situation, and say: 'I didn't ask the question clearly enough', or 'I didn't understand the answer'. S/he then might say: 'How should I interpret this'? Summarize the contradictory statements: 'You said X. You also said Y'; and then wait for the respondent to continue.

Ending the interview

At the end, the interviewer should not only summarize the interview, but also respond to questions that came up during the interview, give advice (if necessary or asked for), and give an opportunity for further questions of the respondent. Such 'after-interview' discussions and questions should *always* be recorded, like all spontaneous information, because discussions can shed light on complicated, not yet fully clear issues from many preceding interviews.

Conducting online interviews

Online interviews can be either synchronous or asynchronous. *Synchronous online interviews* resemble a traditional research interview in that they *take place in 'real time'*. The interviewer and interviewee are online simultaneously, in a virtual environment that allows real-time communication between two or more users. An example is an internet chat room, in which questions and answers are posted, read, and answered in 'real time'. *Asynchronous interviews take place in non-real time*, for example using email. Asynchronous online interviewing can also be conducted via bulletin boards, discussion groups, or web/internet forums.

Email interviews

An email interview can be an effective form of interviewing. Many people prefer email interviews because it is not necessary for a synchronous time to be scheduled. It might be the *only* way to conduct an interview (1) with a busy (or reclusive) public figure, with whom it is not possible to schedule a time to meet face to face or to speak on the phone; or (2) if the inconvenience and expense of travelling to an interview site would be prohibitive.

In email interviews, you should send an initial note to introduce yourself and to inform the individual of your affiliation, what information you are seeking, and how the information will be used. Indicate the length of time and the general time frame in which you foresee the interview process taking place. Ask the individual to specify a time for you to send questions that will be convenient and that will permit a timely response. Agree with the interviewee a follow-up exchange for clarifications or follow-up questions if the responses you receive are not clear or if you do not understand something that the interviewee writes. The researcher then sends out an email which contains the interview questions either in the body of the email or as a word attachment to the email. The participant responds to the interview questions, either in the body of the email or in a word document and returns the completed answers to the researcher. Often the interview will take place over a period of time and questions are sent in stages so that the interviewee is not overwhelmed with a long list of questions at the start of the process.

Email is the most familiar mode of online interaction, and is relatively simple in terms of technological requirements. Email interviews avoid all the practical difficulties of recording equipment and transcribing machines; and they eliminate travel and transcription costs. They present opportunities to interview individuals based anywhere in the world; and they tend to reduce interviewer bias. They also give interviewees time to think about questions and to give considered responses. The ability to redraft and edit questions and answers allows for increased flexibility and deeper reflection. It may be, too, that people tend to be more open with others in cyberspace than in real-world communication. The lack of visual clues can encourage candid interchanges and open up conversation in directions which otherwise might be avoided. Those individuals who are shy and reticent about speaking in face-to-face group interactions may find that the virtual environment encourages them to open up and engage in more candid exchanges.

There are, however, also disadvantages in conducting email interviews. The medium requires fairly simple questions, as there is less opportunity for the interviewer to probe or clarify. Greater motivation and interest will be required on the part of interviewees: they have to be willing to take the time and effort to sit in front of a computer screen and read text, think, type, and maintain a logical thread of answering. Respondents will not be able to express themselves at anything near the rate they communicate in speech, so less information can be exchanged within a given time frame. Moreover, while respondents may feel better able to discuss sensitive issues in an online environment than in a face-to-face interview, they might also be less open if they have concerns about privacy or sense a lack of control over the use of personal data. The lack of time restriction and the slowing down of the communication process may lead, not to greater openness, but to lack of engagement or to the production of 'socially desirable' answers, rather than the more spontaneous responses typical of synchronous interviews (both online and face to face). The delayed interaction and the inability to spontaneously direct the flow of conversation, or to prompt and probe participants, may lead to a paucity of data compared to synchronous interviews. Finally, though email and other types of online interviewing provide researchers with opportunities to interview individuals based anywhere in the world, not everyone has access to the internet. Young, wealthy, and educated people tend to use computers more than the elderly, poor, and uneducated.

Interviewing via video link and web camera

Asynchronous online interviewing can also be conducted via video link or web camera. Conferencing software is available for facilitating online synchronous interviews in a chatroom-type environment. The software packages can be downloaded by the participants. They provide a large 'chat' window in which the dialogue is displayed. Beneath this is a smaller window where users type their text, and press return; seconds later the contribution is displayed, prefixed with their name.

Using synchronous chat differs in a number of important ways from more traditional interviewing. Missing are the visual, non-verbal cues which the interviewer would normally rely on in order to build rapport and gain the trust of the interviewee. The interviewer must, therefore, give thought to ways of establishing rapport with interviewees. Virtual interviews also do not permit the natural flow of conversation in the way that telephone or face-to-face interviews do. Consequently, the number of questions should be limited. The number of open-ended questions should be limited, as well. More than a few questions in total will make the interview begin to feel laborious. If more information is needed, the interviewer can ask interviewees if they are willing to do a follow-up phone interview. If you will be asking confidential or personal questions, you must consider how to handle privacy issues.

Make sure you understand the equipment and process before the interview and, in particular, the type of microphone and what adjustments may need to be made in using it. Test your equipment and, if using a webcam, practice using it before the interview. Get a FAQ sheet on how to use the equipment and respond to possible glitches that might arise. Choose an area with a neutral background, and make sure the areas around you are clear and orderly. You will want to speak directly to the camera so that it appears you are speaking to the interviewee. Position your materials in close proximity to the camera so that when you glance at your notes, you will not appear to be looking away from the camera. Consider how to eliminate all potentially distracting noises, as the microphone on a webcam can magnify the slightest sound. If using Skype, you may experience some time lag when you're talking. Make sure you talk clearly so your voice will be easily picked up by the microphone.

Focus groups, which we discuss later on in this chapter, can also be conducted online. Online focus groups can be conducted using **listserv**, which is one of the key software applications for managing mailing lists. One advantage of this is that it eliminates the need to set up mutually convenient chat times. However, the interviewer does not communicate synchronously with participants. Respondents can post their replies at any time. This reduces the level of group interaction and the sense of immediacy. And the fact that the facilitator cannot always play an active role in moderating the discussion interview means that there is a greater likelihood of exchanges being unfocused or off-topic.

Elite interviews

Much political research is concerned with understanding political institutions and decision-making processes. Interviewing political elites is a key means of obtaining information about many aspects of these phenomena. Political elites are people 'who exercise disproportionately high influence on the outcome of events or policies in your research area' (Pierce 2008:119). We can identify three broad purposes for which interviewing elites can be useful.

The first purpose is to obtain new information. By virtue of the positions they hold, elites may have access to information that might not otherwise be available to a researcher. However, a second purpose of elite interviews is to 'confirm the accuracy of information that has previously been collected from other sources'. As Oisin Tansey explains,

When documents, memoirs, and secondary sources provide an initial overview of the events or issues under examination, interviews with key players can be used to corroborate the early findings. In this way, interviews contribute toward the research goal of triangulation, where collected data are cross-checked through multiple sources to increase the findings' robustness. (Tansey 2007: 766)

Finally, elite interviews can enable a researcher to make inferences about the beliefs or actions of a wider population of political elites. When analysts randomly select a sample of elites to interview from among a broader population, they can generalize from the findings of that sample to the wider group (see e.g. Aberbach and Rockman 2000).

One of the biggest challenges of conducting elite interviews is getting the individuals you select to agree to an interview. What you will need to do is to write to prospective interview subjects. This should be a brief letter 'on the most prestigious, non-inflammatory letterhead you have access to' (Aberbach and Rockman 2002: 674). The letter should state your purpose, but not in great detail. It should suggest, in a subtle way, why the interview would in some way benefit the prospective interviewee. Roger Pierce (2008: 120) lists a few reasons why elites might want to agree to an interview. These might include:

- 'you have persuaded them of the importance of your research and their potential contribution';
- they feel that their position obligates them to agree to interviews and that requests for interviews underlines their status;
- they want an opportunity either to 'set the record straight', or to reflect on the policies, politics, or institutions with which they are or have been associated.

Your initial letter should also inform the recipient of your intention to follow up with a phone call to see if a time might be arranged to meet. You must then follow up the letter with a phone call. Prepare for an exchange with the appointments secretary in which you will deliver a charming and persuasive account of your seriousness of purpose. Be persistent and 'insist firmly, but politely (and with a convincing explanation)' that no one but the targeted individual 'will do for the interview' (Aberbach and Rockman 2002: 674).

We haven't said anything about how to choose interview subjects. Roger Pierce suggests that you 'aim higher rather than low by approaching the "A-List elites" rather than lesser elites whom you may consider to be more approachable (Pierce 2008: 121). But, as George and Bennett point out, often lower-level officials may be better interview sources, given their day-to-day involvement with political processes (George and Bennett 2005: 103). As with all research decisions, you must let your research question and hypothesis determine your choice of interview subjects. We would like to point out, however, that you should not hesitate to pursue 'A-listers' that you feel would contribute to your research. A-listers are always happy to receive requests for their time and attention; they may, in fact, feel uneasy whenever such requests begin to thin out.

Let's move on. Once you have an interview scheduled, you must decide on a format. Elite interviews tend to be semi-structured and use open-ended, rather than closed-ended, questions. But there are a number of factors you should consider in deciding what type of question to use. One consideration is the degree of prior research on the subject of concern. The more that is known, the easier it is to use closed-ended questions. Conversely, the more uncharted the terrain, the more likely you will want to use exploratory, open-ended questions. A second consideration is 'response validity'. Open-ended questions increase the validity of the responses because they provide a greater opportunity for respondents to organize their answers within their own frameworks. The third major consideration is the receptivity of respondents. 'Elites especially—but other highly educated people as well—do not like being put in the strait-jacket of closed-ended questions. They prefer to articulate their views, explaining why they think what they think.' Reflecting on their experience in interviewing elites, Joel Auerbach and Bert Rockman noted that closed-ended questions 'often elicited questions in return about why we used the response categories we used or why we framed the questions the way we did' (Auerbach and Rockman 2002: 674).

Though elite interviews often rely on open-ended questions, a combination of open- and closed-ended questions might provide researchers with better opportunities to obtain the information they are seeking. For example, Sharon Rivera and her colleagues used a combination of open-ended and closed-ended questions to interview Russian elites. They started out with five open-ended questions, then followed with a couple of closed-ended questions, and then alternated between open- and closed-ended questions for the remainder of the interview. With this sequencing, they were able to realize a number of advantages. By starting with open-ended questions, they found it easier to elicit answers to closed-ended questions. As they describe it: 'We had demonstrated respect for the complexity of their views through the open-ended questions and thus had "earned" the right to ask questions posed exclusively from our frame of reference. Also, the closed-ended questions probably allowed respondents to recover a bit from the more demanding open-ended question format' (Rivera et al. 2002: 686).

In addition to, or as part of the process of, preparing questions for the interview, you must thoroughly research the subject. Make sure you know as much about him or her as possible. You should also check online for images so that you will be able to recognize your interviewee by sight. Arrive at the interview with your questionnaire, and/or interview schedule or guide, and an audio recorder. Whether or not you record the interview, you will want to take notes (to record non-verbal cues, as well as your own reflections); but you should not make the note-taking obvious, or let it deter you from maintaining eye contact. In conducting the interview, you will need to give space for the respondent to open up new areas, while making sure to cover the topics you feel you need to address. End the interview ten minutes early. The most revealing information is expressed by interviewees when the interview appears to have been formally ended. After the interview, type up your notes and transcribe your recording as soon as possible.

Expert interviews and surveys

Expert interviews and surveys might be thought of as a type of 'elite interview'. But the type of data researchers seek to collect through expert interviews and surveys will usually differ quite substantially from the data they might obtain through the use of elite interviews. Expert surveys are widely used in comparative research to measure a wide variety of different political phenomena, and can be analysed both qualitatively and quantitatively.

In an expert interview or survey, the researcher identifies individuals with specialized knowledge or expertise relating to a particular issue and asks them a common set of questions, either directly in face-to-face interviews, or through the administration of a postal survey. Rather than probing to discover what selected individuals think, and why they think what they think, the aim of expert interviews is to elicit specific information from individuals with specialized knowledge or expertise on a particular issue. Expert surveys perform the same function. Expert surveys enables researchers to summarize the consensus judgement of experts on a given issue and do so in a systematic way (Benoit and Laver 2006: 9).

Of course, the validity of expert-opinion data will depend on the quality of the experts. Expert judgements are valid and reliable in so far as the experts are well-informed about the subject in question. Some studies use a large pool of experts; others rely on a selected few. The use of multiple experts increases the validity of the data (Dorussen et al. 2005: 317). But in some instances knowledge may be limited to a handful of observers or participants, 'either because only a few persons are privy to the relevant information (e.g. government positions in behind-closed-doors negotiations) or because only a few persons have the relevant expertise' (Hooghe et al. 2009: 4).

Expert-opinion data has been used widely in studies of the European Union. An example is the Domestic Structures and European Integration (DOSEI) project. The purpose of the project was to determine the position of the EU members on the draft Constitution for the European Union. As part of the DOSEI project, 'country experts were asked to assess the national position on the draft Constitution. A total of 77 experts were interviewed, varying from one to six experts for any particular political actor' (Dorussen et al. 2005: 316). The project collected a wealth of information on all the relevant policy positions of all the main actors with respect to the draft European Constitution.

Expert surveys also have been used to identify the policy preferences of political parties. What these surveys seek to do is to obtain a consensus of specialists about particular policy positions in order to identify where parties stand on national issues. In a study that revealed the potential gains that could be produced from using expert surveys for this purpose, Francis Castles and Peter Mair (1984) used a postal survey to ask experts in 16 countries to locate parties in their 'own' countries on a ten-point scale between Left and Right. Kenneth Benoit and Michael Laver (2006) conducted a similar survey covering 47 countries. The 'experts' they surveyed were typically academic specialists in the political parties and electoral politics of their 'own' countries. Benoit and Laver defined four substantive policy dimensions as a basis for comparing policy scales among surveyed countries. For each policy dimension (economic policy, social policy, the decentralization of decision-making, and environmental policy), they used a scale running from 1 to 20, with the lower position indicating the typically 'left' position and the higher value the traditionally 'right' position.

Expert surveys are also used to collect a wide variety data in comparative research on topics such as democracy, corruption, human rights, and political repression, to name but a few (see Chapter 9). Often hard data on these issues is either unreliable or unavailable. For example, very few governments keep up-to-date records on how many political prisoners they torture. Nor is there much in the way of official data on how corrupt business practices are. To get round this problem researchers often rely on evaluations of different political phenomena by experts in the relevant field. So, who better to assess how corrupt business practices are in different countries than businessmen who frequently travel around the world? Transparency International has now been carrying out expert surveys on this issue for a number of years. It asks businessmen a series of questions about business practices and corruption in different countries. The data does not therefore strictly measure how corrupt a country is. Rather it measures perceptions of corruption. But the more businessmen agree on whether or not a country is corrupt, the higher we can regard the validity of the measure. We discuss this issue of the inter-coder reliability in more detail in Chapter 13, but the principles are much the same in expert interviews.

An example helps to illustrate this point. Expert surveys are frequently used to measure the level of democracy in a country. Two of the most widely used sources of data on this are Freedom House and Polity IV. Both draw on expert surveys (to differing degrees). Experts (defined as country specialists) are asked to evaluate the extent to which specific countries meet different criteria. For example, one question on the political environment asks 'To what extent are media outlets' news and information content determined by the government or a particular partisan interest? (0–10 points)'. Although there is a certain amount of subjectivity inherent in this approach (see Chapter 4) ideally, if all the experts are unbiased and well qualified to answer this question, then they should all agree and give the same rating. Under these circumstances inter-coder reliability is high, and we can think that perceptions are a valid measure of actual experience.

II. **Focus groups**

The focus group can be considered a form of group interview. However, it differs from a standard group interview in two ways. First, it involves a group of interviewees who are selected on the basis of their having had, or not had, some particular experience, or having a particular attribute. Second, rather than asking subjects to respond to the same question, as in a group interview, the focus group session is organized to address a theme or topic. Alan Bryman characterizes a focus group as combining a group interview with a focused interview (2004: 346).

Focus groups are a form of interviewing involving a group of six to ten people who meet in a conference-room-like setting, and are interviewed together in a flexible and exploratory group discussion format. Members of the focus group are selected because they share some attribute or are related to some phenomenon of interest. They might be chosen, for instance, because they are all between the ages of 35 and 50, or all have a child currently serving in the army and based overseas, or are all female police officers. The people selected to form a group can be unknown to each other, or already form some sort of pre-existing or natural group—people who know each other through clubs or social centres, who work together, or are classmates.

Rather than acting as an interviewer, the researcher performs the role of moderator or facilitator. The moderator initiates the session and moderates the ensuing discussion. The facilitator generally comes equipped with a relatively small number of questions and a willingness to relinquish a larger degree of control over the proceedings than would normally be the case in an individual interview, and to allow the discussion to develop and move in different directions with a certain degree of spontaneity. The emphasis is on interactions between participants rather than between the researcher and participants. The purpose is to explore people's ideas in a public setting so that the interviewer can observe how they react to each other's ideas and how their opinions are formed.

Why do focus group interviews rather than individual interviews? Interviewing individuals, either face to face or over the telephone, or through mailed questionnaires, helps researchers learn about how people feel. The focus group is a good technique for exploring social interactions, and how these shape attitudes and opinions. Exchanges among participants can lead to far more probing and reflection than is possible in individual interviews or questionnaires, and may provide more robust and revealing responses to the issues which are the subject of the focus group. The discussion can also bring into focus dimensions of an issue not previously considered by the interviewer. The unique contribution of a focus group among the array of interview methods is that it enables a researcher to study 'the ways in which individuals collectively make sense of a phenomenon and construct meanings around it' (Bryman 2004: 348).

In Chapter 2 we considered how understandings emerge as a result of interaction and discussion as individual participants contrast and fit their individual views with those of others. The understandings that emerges from interaction among individuals represent, not just the sum of their separate views, but something 'novel, not possessed by the individuals taken in isolation and that would not have emerged in the absence of their interaction'. Interactive relations between individuals can produce properties that are separate and distinguishable from the individuals themselves.

When a group of people with similar interests discuss an issue together, they are likely to produce richer insights and a wider range of information than individual responses obtained privately. One person's comment is likely to provoke a reaction from the other participants and generate more views. Since members of focus groups are selected for some shared attribute or experience, they are likely to feel more comfortable expressing their ideas and feelings; and, because they are not required to answer specific questions, respondents may be more spontaneous, and accurate, when expressing their views. However, a major determinant of focus group success and the quality of their results is the skill of the moderator. Also, focus groups are not representative of the general population; and the unstructured nature of the responses in focus group discussions makes coding, analysis, and interpretation difficult. Hence, the results of focus group discussions should be treated as exploratory, rather than conclusive.

Organizing and conducting a focus group session

Organizing and conducting a focus group session involves the following steps.

1. *Identify the major objective of the focus group session.* Just as is the case with questionnaires or interview guides, focus groups must be designed to produce data relevant to a hypothesis.

2. *Develop questions.* A session should last between 60 and 90 minutes. This is time enough to allow the moderator to ask at most five or six questions. Make sure these are formulated so as to elicit the information you want to be able to gather during the session.

3. *Membership*. Focus groups are usually conducted with six to ten members who have some similar attribute or experience. Select members who are likely to be participative and reflective, and who don't know each other.

4. *Plan the session*. Hold the session in a conference room, with participants sitting in a circle or around a seminar table so that everyone can see everyone else. Provide name tags for members, and refreshments. The *agenda* would normally look something like this: (1) welcome the participants; (2) review the agenda; (3) explain the goal of the meeting, and discuss the ground rules; (4) have group members introduce themselves; (5) questions and answers; (6) wrap up.

5. *Running the session*. The moderator will normally begin a session by introducing him/herself, the purpose of the research, the format of the session, and some ground rules, such as allowing everyone to speak and only one person to speak at a time. The moderator will also want to ask participants to fill out a form with some basic information about themselves: age, occupation, etc. In addition to an information sheet. participants should also be a given a consent form to sign before beginning the focus group.

All members should participate as much as possible. If one or two people are dominating the meeting, then call on others. Tell the individuals you want to hear from the others. Don't look at the individuals when you ask a question. Raise your hand as if to say stop when the individual tries to talk, and look at someone else. You might say something like 'Let's have someone else go first.' If the participant continues to dominate the session, you might suggest using a round-table approach, including going in one direction around the table, giving each person a minute to answer the question. If the domination persists, note it to the group and ask for ideas about how the participation can be increased.

Don't be abrupt with a dominating participant, as it may discourage participation from others. And if you feel your efforts to broaden the discussion have led to a withdrawal of participation by the dominating individual, try to re-establish rapport. If nothing else works, take a break and privately either discuss your concerns with the individual or ask the individual to leave. The discussion should remain focused, maintain momentum, generate useful information, and achieve closure on questions. After each question is answered, the moderator should reflect back a faithful summary of what was said.

6. *Record the session with either an audio or audio-video recorder*. The focus group session should be recorded, using microphones strong enough to pick up voices around the table or circle. It will be important to have a record, not just of what was said, but of how it was said and who said it. So there should be someone taking notes, as well.

III. Analysing interview data

Data analysis of interview data entails three main steps: data reduction, coding, and drawing conclusions. Indeed these steps of analysis are common to all types of data, though how we go about doing it in practice varies somewhat according to the type of data we have collected (for example, see the discussion of textual analysis in Chapter 13).

BOX 11.3 Different Processes of Data Analysis

Structured interviews	Unstructured interviews
Analysis is done using standardized statistics and procedures	Data is analysed by systematically organizing and interpreting information using categories, themes, and motifs that identify patterns and relationships
Results tend to summarize patterns of similarities, variability, size, direction, and/or significance of any differences between specific groups.	Results are in-depth explanations for patterns of behaviour

1. Data reduction

'Data reduction refers to the process of selecting, focusing, simplifying, abstracting, and transforming the data that appear in written up field notes or transcriptions' (Miles and Huberman 1994: 10). Data reduction can be achieved by noting redundancies in the data and discarding all but the most interesting and compelling statements concerning a particular issue or theme. Not only do the data need to be condensed for the sake of manageability, they also have to be transformed so they can be made intelligible in terms of the issues being addressed.

Data reduction is somewhat more straightforward for structured interviews than for semi-structured or unstructured interviews, since much less data are collected. Structured interviews generally ask questions that call for relatively short, simple, or quantifiable answers which the interviewer can easily record. The main goal in the analysis of structured interview data is to quantify the data and then subject it to statistical analysis so that hypotheses can be tested. The data from unstructured interviews is not as easy to code or quantify as data obtained from surveys. Great care needs to be taken in developing code frames to record the different types of answers, and attention also needs to be paid towards how interviewers' questions or probes vary across different respondents. Since there is often substantial variation in how questions are asked, the data cannot be tracked as easily over time, and the results of data analysis are not as easily compared, since in effect what is often being tracked or compared is answers to different questions. The more structured a question then, the easier it will be to analyse. Data for focus groups are difficult to analyse— particularly if the analysis is concerned with both the content of what was said and the patterns of interaction. Open questions permit free responses, which are recorded or written down as far as possible in the respondents' own words. This mass of data has to be organized and somehow meaningfully reduced or reconfigured. Box 11.3 gives a snapshot of how the analysis and results obtained from semi-structured and unstructured, and structured interview data differ.

The first step in data reduction is to transcribe the tapes or notes of the interviews. As part of this process, you should develop a 'profile' of each interviewee: a summary of the interviewee's background, experience, and opinions. Whenever possible, interviewee's opinions should appear in these profiles in their own words, to avoid the possibility that rewriting them may change their substance or emphasis.

Recording and transcribing interviews results in an unwieldy amount of verbal data. One of the central tasks of semi-structured and unstructured interview data analysis is to reduce the amount of data to a more manageable level by identifying and extracting the most important, meaningful, and interesting parts of the interview text. This should begin as a process of 'discovering what's in the material', rather than starting out with definite hypotheses in mind. When the transcripts have been completed, read them, first, as a whole to note your general impressions. Read carefully through each interview without taking notes. When you finish reading you might wish to write down a few general notes or impressions.

Next, review the interview transcripts, again, this time looking for very specific things—for similarities and differences and patterns and thematic connections in the data. Make marginal notes, highlighting key words and themes. For focus groups, make a note of major opinions and attitudes that are expressed by the groups. Underline or circle those items that you think will prove to be the most important or meaningful. This is the start of producing a list of terms that will be subsequently used for coding. Codes emerge from a process of refining the marginal notes you make on transcripts.

2. Coding

Coding means breaking down interview material and assigning them to different categories according to the variable to which they relate. In coding interview data you name and categorize phenomena through close examination of data. Closed questions are pre-coded. Open questions will require a coding frame—a list of categories and codes for each question used to analyse responses. Eventually, you will perhaps want to reduce the number of code words and categories of information; but as you begin this process you should not worry about placing too many initial restrictions on yourself.

Consider whether you are using two or more words or phrases to describe the same thing; or whether an item might be coded in more than one way. Some responses may refer to more than one issue or idea. These should be given more than one code word so that the response can be included in each relevant area. Consider, too, whether your codes might be replaced with concepts and categories in the literature relating to your research question and hypothesis. Look to see if certain codes tend to be associated with other codes, and whether you can perhaps code for these connections.

When you code the transcripts, you mark sections of the transcript in a way that indicates what the interviewee or focus group participant is talking about. For instance, every time a participant mentions a 'new report', the researcher marks the section to indicate this. Using code words will make this faster, e.g. NEWSREP (i.e. NEWS REPORT). So, in the end a transcript will have a list of code words running down the side of the page. This makes it easier to identify sections of interest later on, as all that will be needed when looking at the issue of XYZ is to look down the transcripts and take all the responses marked XYZ.

The information provided by open questions needs to be coded in order to make sense of the answers. This can be very time-consuming. Many responses may be uncodable; answers may be irrelevant or off-topic, and some groups of people may be more likely to respond than others, particularly those who are more educated or more interested in the topic. Each coherent interview segment should be given a code number to indicate the concept, category, theme, or argument it relates to. These segments can then be copied and separated from the transcripts (with either real or electronic scissors) and put back together thematically to serve as the raw material for an analysis of the general findings of the study and their implications for policy-or decision-making.

Throughout this process it is important to reflect on what significance these data have for your research question and hypothesis. The researcher must make choices about which aspects of the data should be emphasized, minimized, or set aside completely. At all stages of the research process, the researcher will be concerned to probe the generalisability, reliability (the consistency of findings/results), and validity (if the study in fact investigates what was intended).

Traditionally, coding involved gathering together those portions of a text belonging to a given label or name. Researchers used different coloured highlighters for each code and then cut and pasted together similarly coloured fragments using scissors and paste. Today, there is computer software that performs this task. Coding of data can be done using one of the computer-based analysis program packages, e.g. NUD*IST, NVivo, or Atlas.ti). However, whether computer software or highlighters are used, the process remains the same. It is the researcher who defines and names the categories of data. The result of both coding and analysis depends exclusively upon the researcher's interpretation of meanings hidden in the data.

Using the research question and hypothesis as a guide, every line, paragraph, or other section of text is coded for relevant themes. As themes are developed, the researcher assigns a working definition to each code. That way, in going through the transcripts, the definition is continually being challenged, and sometimes new codes must be developed because the properties do not fit the text. Also, codes that are rarely used are dismissed and some categories are broadened to accommodate the lost code. Important to note is that this type of analysis is not linear, but circular. Constant comparison (see Glaser and Strauss 1967) means that the researcher must continually compare the categories and codes of new transcripts with existing categories and codes in order to more fully develop the properties of the overarching categories for the individual codes. This process is ongoing until saturation is reached: that is, no new codes or categories emerge and coding more transcripts would only produce a repetition of themes.

Be aware that extracting and coding fragments will remove them from the context within which they appeared and disrupt or lose the narrative flow of what was said (Bryman 2004: 411).

3. Analysis

Once sequences of text are marked with codes (coding), sequences of text marked with each code are collected together (retrieving). The analysis should then connect up the codes to each other in order to bring into focus a web of meanings.

Drawing conclusions involves stepping back to consider what the analysed data mean and to assess their implications for the questions at hand. Verification, integrally linked to conclusion drawing, entails revisiting the data as many times as necessary to cross-check or

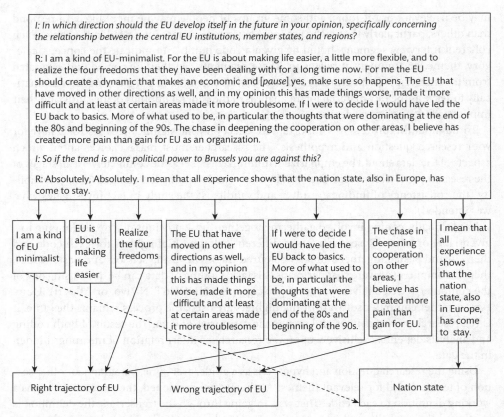

I: In which direction should the EU develop itself in the future in your opinion, specifically concerning the relationship between the central EU institutions, member states, and regions?

R: I am a kind of EU-minimalist. For the EU is about making life easier, a little more flexible, and to realize the four freedoms that they have been dealing with for a long time now. For me the EU should create a dynamic that makes an economic and [pause] yes, make sure so happens. The EU that have moved in other directions as well, and in my opinion this has made things worse, made it more difficult and at least at certain areas made it more troublesome. If I were to decide I would have led the EU back to basics. More of what used to be, in particular the thoughts that were dominating at the end of the 80s and beginning of the 90s. The chase in deepening the cooperation on other areas, I believe has created more pain than gain for EU as an organization.

I: So if the trend is more political power to Brussels you are against this?

R: Absolutely, Absolutely. I mean that all experience shows that the nation state, also in Europe, has come to stay.

| I am a kind of EU minimalist | EU is about making life easier | Realize the four freedoms | The EU that have moved in other directions as well, and in my opinion this has made things worse, made it more difficult and at least at certain areas made it more troublesome | If I were to decide I would have led the EU back to basics. More of what used to be, in particular the thoughts that were dominating at the end of the 80s and beginning of the 90s. | The chase in deepening cooperation on other areas, I believe has created more pain than gain for EU. | I mean that all experience shows that the nation state, also in Europe, has come to stay. |

Right trajectory of EU   Wrong trajectory of EU   Nation state

Figure 11.1 *An example of data reduction*
Source: Folkestad 2008: 6.

verify these emergent conclusions, to validate findings by cross-checking with other questions and information from other respondents. 'The meanings emerging from the data have to be tested for their plausibility, their sturdiness, their "confirmability"—that is, their validity' (Miles and Huberman 1994: 11). Validity means something different in this context than in quantitative evaluation, where it is a technical term that refers quite specifically to whether a given construct measures what it purports to measure. Here validity encompasses a much broader concern for whether the conclusions being drawn from the data are credible, defensible, warranted, and able to withstand alternative explanations.

Folkestad (2008) is interested in exploring Euroscepticism among various political parties in Nordic countries and Central Eastern Europe. He decided that conducting qualitative interviews with elites in political parties might provide him with insight into this phenomenon. To explore the content of Euroscepticism among the respondents that he interviews, he formulates conceptual categories concerning the trajectory of the EU, drawn from the categories that Kopecky and Mudde (2002) used to conceptualize support for and opposition to European integration.

Folkestad reduced the material from the interview into three categories: 'right and wrong trajectory of the EU, and a more ontological category, "Nation-state". Whereas the two first categories show the answer the respondent is giving to the question (right and wrong directions of the EU), the last category tells us something about what kind of political organization/polity he views as the most proper' (Folkestad 2008: 7). The data reduction process is shown in Figure 11.1.

 ## Conclusions

As with any method of data collection, the use of interviews or focus groups should be appropriate both to the research question and to the hypothesis you are investigating. You choose interviewing as a means of data collection because you are confident that the data that you collect through this means will provide a convincing test of your hypothesis, and will enable you to draw logical conclusions about your hypothesis. Questions should be designed so that the responses actually measure what they claim to.

As we discussed in Chapter 7, it is a good idea to use multiple sources of data and methods of data collection whenever possible. Doing this enables you to approach a research problem from different angles. This is called 'triangulation'. Triangulation of evidence increases the reliability of the data and the process of gathering it. In the context of data collection, triangulation serves to corroborate the data gathered from other sources: the use of different data sources can enable researchers to cross-check findings. Triangulation yields more complete data and results in more credible findings; and it also enables researchers to find agreement between different perspectives. It might involve the use of different research methods to study a single research problem: a comparison of the results of these different methods can enable a researcher to identify whether differences are due to biases in one or another of these methods. It might also involve the use of different researchers to study the same research problem with the same people and with the same methods: if the same results are discovered, the findings and interpretations have stronger validity because of this corroboration.

 ## Questions

- What are the advantages and disadvantages of semi-structured interviews compared to structured interviews and surveys?
- Some researchers are very critical of the widespread use of structured interviews. Why?
- Why might a researcher prefer to use a structured rather than an unstructured interview to gather data?
- What are the different *types of questions* that might be part of a questionnaire and what sorts of information do they enable you to obtain?
- In what ways does the order in which you ask questions affect the responses you get?
- What considerations would guide your choice of what type of interview to conduct?
- How can interview data be used to confirm or disconfirm a hypothesis or argument?

 ## Guide to Further Reading

Aberbach, J., J. Chesney, and B. Rockman (1975), 'Exploring Elite Political Attitudes: Some Methodological Lessons', *Political Methodology* 2 (1975): 1–27.
Uses data from interviews with American political elites to illustrate open-ended interviewing. Discussion on coding techniques for interview data analysis.

Denzin, N. K. and Y. S. Lincoln (eds) (1994), *Handbook of Qualitative Research* (Thousand Oaks, CA: Sage Publications).
This volume consists of 36 chapters on qualitative methods in social research. It covers historical and philosophical perspectives, as well as detailed research methods. Extensive coverage is given to data collection and data analysis, and to the 'art of interpretation' of findings obtained through qualitative research.

Gubrium, J. F. and J. A. Holstein (eds) (2002), *Handbook of Interview Research: Context and Method* (Thousand Oaks, CA: Sage Publications).
A comprehensive handbook covering virtually all forms of interviewing.

Hammer, D. and A. Wildavsky (1993), 'The Open-Ended, Semistructured Interview: An (Almost) Operational Guide', in A. Wildavsky (ed.), *Craftways: On the Organization of Scholarly Work* (New Brunswick, NJ: Transaction Publishers), 57–101.
Examines the procedures associated with semi-structured interviewing and provides useful discussion about the relationship between the researcher and the respondent.

Krueger, R. A. (1998), *Moderating Focus Groups* (Thousand Oaks, CA: Sage Publications).

Kvale, S. (1996), *InterViews: An Introduction to Qualitative Research Interviewing* (Thousand Oaks, CA: Sage Publications).
Covers all aspects of the interview process, including the theoretical and philosophical foundations of interviewing, and the influence those foundations have on the process, the content, and the analysis of qualitative interviews.

MacNaughton, P. and M. Jacobs (1997), 'Public Identification with Sustainable Development: Investigating Cultural Barriers to Participation', *Global Environmental Change* 7: 5–26.

McLellan, Eleanor, Kathleen M. MacQueen, and Judith L. Neidig (2003), 'Beyond the Qualitative Interview: Data Preparation and Transcription', *Field Methods* 15 (February): 63–84.
Outlines the consequences of inappropriate or inadequate preparation of transcripts from recordings and offers practical considerations that can help researchers systematically organize and analyse textual data.

Morgan, D. (1997), *Focus Groups as Qualitative Research*, 2nd edition (Newbury Park, CA: Sage Publications).
Compares participant observation and individual interviews; strengths and weaknesses; uses of focus groups.

O'Connor, H., C. Madge, R. Shaw, and J. Wellens (2008), 'Internet-based Interviewing', in N. Fielding, R. M. Lee, and G. Blank (eds), *The SAGE Handbook of Online Research Methods* (London: Routledge), 271–89.

Slapin, J. and S.-O. Proksch (2008), 'A Scaling Model for Estimating Time Series Policy Positions from Texts', *American Journal of Political Science* 52(8): 705–22.

Sudman, S., and N. Bradburn (1983), *Asking Questions: A Practical Guide to Questionnaires* (San Francisco, CA: Jossey-Bass).

'Symposium: Interview Methods in Political Science', *PS: Political Science and Politics* 35(4) (December 2002): 663–88. Beth L. Leech, 'Asking Questions: Techniques for Semistructured Interviews' (pp. 665–8); Kenneth Goldstein, 'Getting in the Door: Sampling and Completing Elite Interviews' (pp. 669–72); Joel Aberbach and Bert Rockman, 'Conducting and Coding Elite Interviews' (pp. 673–6); Laura Woliver, 'Ethical Dilemmas in Personal Interviewing' (pp. 677–8); Jeffrey M. Berry, 'Validity and Reliability Issues in Elite Interviewing' (pp. 679–82); Sharon Werning Rivera, 'Interviewing Political Elites: Lessons from Russia' (pp. 683–8).

Weiss, R. (1994), *Learning from Strangers: The Art and Method of Qualitative Interview Studies* (New York: Free Press, 1994).
Offers step-by-step introduction to method of qualitative interviewing: sample selection, development of an interview guide, the conduct of the interview, data analysis, and preparation of the data. Includes examples of successful and less successful interviews.

Software

Friese, S. (2004), *Software Overview*. Available online as a PDF at: http://www.quarc.de/software_overview_table.pdf.
A useful table comparing six software packages.

Matheson, J. L. (2007), 'The Voice Transcription Technique: Use of Voice Recognition Software to Transcribe Digital Interview Data in Qualitative Research', *The Qualitative Report* 12(4): 547-60. Retrieved from http://www.nova.edu/ssss/QR/QR12-4/matheson.pdf.

Rettie, R. (2005, Winter), 'Exploiting Freely Available Software for Social Research', *Social Research Update, 48*. Retrieved 4 September 2006, from http://sru.soc.surrey.ac.uk/SRU48.html.

References

Aberbach, J. D. and B. A. Rockman (2002), 'Conducting and Coding Elite Interviews',*PS: Political Science and Politics* 35(4) (December): 673-6.

Benoit, Kenneth and Michael Laver (2006), *Party Policy in Modern Democracies* (London: Routledge).

Bishop, George F., Robert W. Oldendick, and Alfred J. Tuchfarber (1984), 'Interest in Political Campaigns: The Influence of Question Order and Electoral Context', *Political Behavior*, 6(2): 159-69.

Bryman, A. (2004), *Social Research Methods*, 2nd edition (Oxford: Oxford University Press).

Castles, F. and P. Mair (1984), 'Left-Right Political Scales: Some Expert Judgements', *European Journal of Political Research* 12: 73-88.

de Vaus, David (2002), *Surveys in Social Research* (London: Routledge).

Dorussen, H., H. Lenz, and S. Blavoukos (2005), 'Assessing the Reliability and Validity of Expert Interviews', *European Union Politics* 6(3): 315-37.

Folkestad, Bjarte (2008), 'Analysing Interview Data: Possibilities and Challenges', Eurosphere Online Working Paper Series, Working Paper No.13 (December); at http://eurospheres.org/files/2010/08/Eurosphere_Working_Paper_13_Folkestad.pdf.

George, A. L. and A. Bennett (2005), *Case Studies and Theory Development in the Social Sciences* (Cambridge, MA: MIT Press).

Glaser, Barney G. and Anselm Strauss (1967), *The Discovery of Grounded Theory* (Chicago: Aldine).

Hooghe, L., R. Bakker, A. Brigevich, C. de Vries, E. Edwards, G. Marks, J. Rovny, and M. Steenbergen (2009), 'Reliability and Validity of the 2002 and 2006 Chapel Hill Expert Surveys on Party Positioning', http://web.me.com/rovny/Site/Academic_files/HoogheEtAl_EJPR_july2009.pdf.

Kopecky, P. and C. Mudde (2002), 'The Two Sides of Euroscepticism: Party Position on European Integration in East Central Europe', *European Union Politics* 3: 297-326.

Miles, M. B. and A. M. Huberman (1994), *Qualitative Data Analysis*, 2nd edition (Newbury Park, CA: Sage Publications).

Moser, C. A. and G. K. Kalton (1971), *Survey Methods in Social Investigation* (London: Heinemann).

Pierce, R. (2008), *Research Methods in Politics: A Practical Guide* (London: Sage Publications).

Rivera, S. W., P. M. Kozyreva, and E. G. Sarovskii (2002), 'Interviewing Political Elites: Lessons from Russia', *PS: Political Science and Politics* 35(4) (December): 683-8.

Tansey, O. (2007), 'Process Tracing and Elite Interviewing: A Case for Non-probability Sampling', *PS: Political Science and Politics* 40(4) (October): 765-72.

Endnote

1. There are various types of computer-assisted interviewing software. Computer-assisted telephone interviewing (CATI) is usually employed in conjunction with random-digit dialling (RDD) as a means of approximating random sampling. Computer-assisted personal interviewing (CAPI) allows the interviewer to enter responses directly into an uploadable database using a hand-held computer. Audio-CASI uses voice technology to prompt the respondent with items and receive responses by voice.

Ethnography and Participant Observation

 Chapter Summary

This chapter examines the principles of ethnography and participant observation: what they are, how (if) they became standardized as a research method, what form of evidence they constitute, and what place they occupy in the study of Politics. We look at the strengths of ethnographic fieldwork, and we try to identify what kind of material it produces and what aspects of social life it can reveal. We shall also discuss its weaknesses, especially issues of subjectivity, reliability, and generalizability. Topics discussed are:

- ethnography;
- participant observation;
- sampling;
- access;
- key informants;
- recording observations.

Introduction

Although participant observation was first developed by social anthropologists and sociologists, in recent years it has become a much more widely used research tool across the social sciences, and attention to political ethnographies in particular has grown (see Auyero 2006 and Schatz 2009). Political ethnographies have been carried out in a wide variety of contexts, from the study of political institutions and organizations, such as political parties and parliamentarians (Fenno 1978; Searing 1994), the judiciary (Latour 2010), local elites (Dahl 1961), international organizations (Weaver 2008), and NGOs, to the study of social movements (Blee and Currier 2006) and informal networks, such as terrorist groups, the mafia, drugs cartels, and betting syndicates (Parnell and Kane (eds) 2003). Political ethnography is also becoming more widely used in the study of International Relations (IR) (see Schatz 2009: 308). Gillespie led a team of ethnographers studying how British citizens, and British Muslims in particular, experienced securities and insecurities during the War on Terror (see Gillespie, Gow and Hoskins 2007; Gillespie and O'Loughlin 2009). Political ethnographies have also been carried out by Barnett (2006) on the US mission to the UN; by Pouliot (2007) on diplomacy and security; and Hopf (2002) on Russian foreign policy.

Political ethnographies have also been widely used in comparative research and have examined the political attitudes and behaviour of ordinary people living in different parts of the world, for example in India (Michelutti 2008), Senegal (Schaffer 1998), Uganda (Karlstrom 1996), and Chile (Paley 2001). Political ethnographies of this type have shed light on how marginalized social groups interact with modernization, globalization, and democracy, and how governmental policies and development programmes come to be reinterpreted, and accepted (or not) on the ground.

True, many of these issues can be, and frequently are, studied using other methods, but at the same time there is no substitute for getting out of the armchair, getting your hands dirty, and observing first hand what it is that you are writing about in its natural setting. Indeed, one of the key strengths of participant observation is that it provides the researcher with first-hand experience of the subject they are writing about. As Richard Fenno (1990: 56) wrote, 'as long as political scientists continue to study politicians, some of us certainly will want to collect data through repeated interaction with these politicians in their natural habitats'. This chapter examines the principles of the ethnographic method, its application to political research, and the issues that confront researchers who use this approach.

Ethnography is often described as an approach rather than a specific method. Indeed, ethnographers can and frequently do employ a variety of methods, from **participant observation**, to archival analysis, interviews, and surveys. The term 'ethnography' comes from Latin and literally means writing about people, where *ethnos* means people or folk and *graphia* means writing. The term therefore encompasses and recognizes two important components of the approach. The first is to do with the study of people, and how data are collected, and the second refers to how this data is then recorded and analysed (or written up). In this chapter we focus on both these components. First, we examine the method of participant observation, which is the method of data collection most closely associated with the ethnographic approach. Second, we examine how the observations and data from the fieldwork are recorded and reported.

The principles of ethnography and participant observation

Ethnography and participant observation can be defined in a number of ways, and these definitions frequently overlap with each other, and the two terms are frequently used interchangeably. According to Delamont (2004: 218) 'participant observation, ethnography and fieldwork are all used interchangeably...they can all mean spending long periods watching people, coupled with talking to them about what they are doing, thinking and saying, designed to see how they understand their world'. With reference specifically to ethnography, Brewer (2000: 6) writes that: 'ethnography is the study of people in naturally occurring settings or "field" by methods of data collection which capture their social meanings and ordinary activities, involving the researcher participating directly in the setting, if not also the activities, in order to collect data in a systematic manner'. Likewise Hammersley and Atkinson (2007: 3) describe the ethnographic approach in terms of the: 'ethnographer participating, overtly or covertly in people's daily lives for an extended period of time, watching what happens, listening to what is said, asking questions—in fact, collecting whatever data are available to throw light on the issues that are the focus of research'. Both these definitions of ethnography include reference to multiple forms of data collection. To some extent then ethnography refers to a multi-method approach. It encompasses a plurality of methods, all of which are used in conjunction with each other to generate a deep, first-hand understanding of what people do in their social environment.

The main method that is employed to do this is participant observation. In order to observe what people do in practice, participant observation involves 'research based on the close-up, on-the-ground observation of people and institutions in real time and space, in which the investigator embeds herself near (or within) the phenomenon so as to detect how and why agents on the scene act, think and feel the way they do' (Wacquant, 2003: 5). The distinctive feature of participant observation, and one of the great strengths of the approach, is that data collection is carried out in real time. This means that the ethnographer has a direct, first-hand opportunity to observe what people actually do, what they actually say to each other, and how they actually interact with different institutions or political processes, rather than just relying on what people say that they do, which is not always the same as what they actually do (as we discussed with reference to survey measurement error in Chapter 10).

Participant observation (and ethnography more generally) therefore has a number of characteristics that overlap with other methods we have considered in this book (such as surveys, focus groups, and interviews) and a number of characteristics that are distinctive, particularly with respect to the role of observation. Whereas surveys (see Chapter 10) are based on the ancient art of asking questions to find out what people think, say, and do, participant observation is based on something rather different. It recognizes that what people say they do, and what they actually do, can be, and frequently are, different. Accordingly, to get a 'true' sense of what people think and say and do, it is not enough to merely ask people questions and record their answers; it is also necessary to observe what people do in practice.

Participant observation, as the term implies, therefore involves the researcher living, and interacting, and participating in the daily life of the people (often referred to as **informants**) who she or he is studying. This can involve long periods of research, of many months, if not years, in the **field** (the research setting). This prolonged period of time spent in the field allows the researcher to embed themselves in the setting which they are studying and really get to know their informants, understand their behaviour, and get detailed information about what they think and say and do. As Ingold (2008) puts it, this involves the researcher getting out of the armchair, and actually interacting with the people whom he or she is writing about.

This research on the 'everyday practices' of human behaviour has a number of key strengths. It is particularly useful for studying sensitive topics, where people may not directly reveal their real thoughts or opinions to a stranger. One such sensitive topic is witchcraft, which, although an important part of social life in many parts of the world, is generally not something that people feel comfortable talking about to strangers. Adam Ashforth's (2005) book *Witchcraft, Violence, and Democracy in South Africa* draws on three years of fieldwork in Soweto (South West Township), an Apartheid-built black suburb of Johannesburg. In order to do his fieldwork, Ashforth learnt Zulu, Sotho, Xhosa, and the special brands of English Sowetans speak; he also learned to play the violin Zulu style, and was ready to defend his adopted brothers and sisters from recurrent threats of attack. Through first-hand observation, personal intervention, and long discussions with informants Ashforth was able to build up a detailed description of life under the shadow of extreme violence. This helped him to arrive at two revealing conclusions, first, that no one can make sense of local South African politics without understanding the enormous part played by fears about, accusations of, and reactions to witchcraft in Soweto's (and, by extension, South Africa's) everyday politics; second, that no one can hope to deal with South Africa's devastating AIDS epidemic or build local-level democracy without confronting witchcraft directly (see Tilley 2006 for an extended discussion of these findings).

Participant observation is also well suited to unpicking difficult-to-define or multifaceted political phenomena, where other research instruments such as surveys, interviews, or focus groups may provide too blunt an instrument to fully capture the diversity and meaning of a concept. For example, participant observation is able to shed light on and capture how Indians (Michelutti 2008), Senegalese (Schaffer 1998), Ugandans (Karlstrom 1996), or members of Chilean social movements (Paley 2001) understand what democracy means.

But perhaps the core strength of the method is to do with the act of observation. Participant observation allows the researcher to observe what people do on a day-by-day basis, and how their behaviour changes in response to different stimuli or different events. For example, using ethnographic, in-depth interviews, and document data on new and emerging social movement groups (SMGs) in Pittsburgh for 20 months before and after the 2004 US presidential election, Blee and Currier (2006) examine how SMG members think about elections and how groups decide to respond to national electoral campaigns. Participant observation also allows the researcher to observe first hand how and why unplanned or spontaneous events emerge—such as a riot or a fight, a strike that develops in a pitched battle, or a simple quarrel that escalates and gets out of hand. This kind of research is often described as **process tracing** (see Chapters 4 and 9). It involves looking for evidence of the pressures, incentives, motivations, and decision-making calculus in any given instance of action (George and Bennett 2005; Parsons 2010). Moreover, by observing people over a prolonged period of time, it is possible to build up a much more reliable impression of what they really think than would be possible after just a brief meeting or interview.

Theory and hypothesis testing

A key purpose of participant observation is simply to describe what people think, say, and do. By spending a long time in the field, repeatedly talking to informants over time and in different social settings, and observing what people do, the method is able to provide a **thick description** of the social and political lives of the informants. In doing so, it aims to provide a valid and reliable representation of how the subjects under study behave and think politically. In some sense, then, the method is concerned with understanding, with meaning, and with interpretation. This sort of data is valuable in its own right. Colonial 'ethnographies' of different communities in India provide a rich and detailed description of social life in the nineteenth century, which would otherwise have been lost. Ethnographies constitute a rich source of historical data, and in addition can give voice to people who otherwise would not be heard, and shine a light into corners of the political world that would otherwise go undetected.

But at the same time, this ethnographic description and focus on rich textual detail is often thought to create a trade-off in terms of how far findings can be generalized to other contexts and to shed light on theory more generally. Ethnography and participant observation have therefore often been derided as only capable of producing 'thick description'. According to Hammersley and Atkinson (2007), ethnographic research comprises a strong emphasis on exploring the nature of social phenomena, rather than setting out to test hypotheses about them. Since ethnography tends to focus on the specific rather than the general, it is therefore often regarded as an inappropriate method to use to test general hypotheses.

Whether or not ethnography can be used to test theory is a debate which has rumbled on for many years. Indeed, as far back as the 1960s, Edmund Leach complained about the tendency of ethnographers to focus on the specific rather than the general and lamented, 'most of my colleagues are giving up in the attempt to make comparative generalisations; instead they have begun to write impeccably detailed historical ethnographies of particular peoples' (Leach 1961: 1). To be sure, ethnography can be used in a purely descriptive, inductive way (and often is), but equally it can be, and sometimes is, also used more deductively.

As we discuss in Chapter 2, it is easy to overstate the differences between inductive and deductive approaches. But, in general, ethnographic research always begins with some problem or set of issues. At the very least, it starts from what Malinowski (1922) referred to as **foreshadowed problems**. Sometimes this is based on well-developed theory, sometimes it will be more exploratory, and sometimes it will lead to the formulation of specific hypotheses that are to be tested, or at least investigated.

Participant observation can be used for each of these purposes. That it is frequently not says more about the people who use the method than it does about the method itself. Thus, participant observation is concerned with producing descriptions and explanations of specific political phenomena, developing theories which may apply more generally, and applying theory to different social settings. It is a useful tool for generating theory in areas of research for which little is known, or where previous theory sheds little light. It is also a useful tool for applying theory, which is perhaps one of its most frequent uses. Ethnographers draw on insights from previous research and attempt to apply them to new contexts. Ethnographic studies frequently take well-developed ideas (or theories) about hierarchy or power or division of labour or social stratification, to name but a few, and see whether these ideas or theories apply in different contexts. If the theory is found to apply, and to provide a good framework for analysis, then the study in some sense corroborates or builds upon and develops the existing theory. But if the theory does not provide a convincing framework, then the study can be used to consider and reflect upon why it does not, and perhaps to propose some limitations to the original theory.

For example, Eliasoph's (1997) ethnography of different public and private spaces in a town on the US Pacific coast is a fantastic explanation of how political apathy is produced by contextual factors, and built up slowly through different phases and contexts of people's lives. She tests Noelle-Neuman's 'spiral of silence' theory, an explanation for why individuals feel unable to express their political views publicly, by spending years in this town getting to know groups and individuals, being a participant observer in social clubs, cake bakes, and town hall meetings, as well as talking to people in private.

The process of applying theory may over time, with repetition, lead (indirectly) to the testing of theories, in that some theories may be found not to apply so many times that they lose their relevance and can essentially be falsified, while other theories are found to apply to many different contexts and so are given more empirical support. But the key point is that the testing of theory comes from the gradual accumulation of knowledge, rather than from any particular one-off ethnography.

Participant observation methodology

The main research instrument for data collection in participant observation is the individual researcher who actually undertakes the exercise. There is thus an inherently personal component to the research process. Better researchers make for better data collectors, and better data analysers. As Bernard (2006: 344) observes, participant observation is a craft, and as with all crafts, becoming a skilled artisan at participant observation takes practice. It also takes talent and specific personal skills. Participant observation involves getting informants to open up, being allowed into their lives, and having the opportunity to observe and record personal and private events first hand. The extent to which the ethnographer is able to do this therefore depends in large part upon the ethnographer's personal characteristics, such as whether they are friendly and approachable, able to inspire trust and confidence, or whether informants think they are arrogant and standoffish.

Above all else, fieldwork involves the toil and dedication of the ethnographer, who has to spend thousands of hours in the field. Fieldwork relies on the tenacity and perseverance of the ethnographer, and the patience to sit through long, boring meetings in the hope that something interesting might come up. Ethnographers can spend months feeling as if nothing is happening and no progress is being made, only for things to suddenly take off. It can often feel like fieldwork is 99% perspiration for that 1% inspiration that unlocks the door to some specific issue of interest. Doing fieldwork is a long and arduous business, often in a very difficult environment, often among strange and unfamiliar people. It can be lonely and alienating, and is the most personally involved and challenging method of data collection that there is. Put simply, doing fieldwork is tough.

For many of these reasons, the idea of specific methodological training in participant observation was, for a long time, not taken terribly seriously. As Whiting recalls being told by a Yale University professor in the 1930s, method 'was a subject to be discussed casually at breakfast' (Whiting 1982: 156), not something worthy of a seminar. The skills for doing fieldwork were regarded as mysterious and unteachable (Bernard 2006: 343). Since so much depends upon the personal characteristics of the ethnographer, it is not really possible to know how someone is going to react to the pressures of doing fieldwork until they are out in the field, actually doing it. Ethnographers were therefore expected to basically just get on with it, and learn how to do participant observation on the job.

Although much of this still holds, it does perhaps represent something of a romanticization of what it means to do fieldwork. Participant observation is both a humanistic method and a scientific one (Bernard 2006: 342), and as such it entails a number of methodological principles that can affect the quality, reliability, and validity of the data that is collected. In recent years, there has been a growing recognition of this, and there are now many textbooks specifically on ethnographic methods (see Hammersley and Atkinson 2007 for a particularly in-depth example), and many undergraduate and graduate courses that address different methodological and ethical considerations connected to the process of collecting and analysing data.

Participant observation involves the researcher making a number of methodological decisions, and the decisions that are made can influence the quality of the data that is collected. These decisions face the ethnographer every day, and whereas it is not possible to discuss all of them in detail, it is nonetheless important to highlight some of the main issues that need to be confronted, and discuss their implications for the quality of data that is generated. Broadly speaking, participant observation involves three interrelated steps. The first step refers to **case selection** and gaining **access** to the field site. Participant observation relies (usually) on the detailed analysis of a single case study. The criteria and justification for the choice of case (and type of case) that is selected is very important, since the type of cases you choose to analyse can influence the answers you get to a particular research question (see Chapter 9). This problem is even more of an issue when only one case is being examined. The second step refers to issues related to carrying out research in the field and collecting data. The role the investigator adopts, the contacts they make, the informants they observe and speak to, and the ways in which this is done, all have a substantial bearing on the quality, reliability, and validity of the data that is generated. Finally, the third step refers to recording observations, and how the data that is collected is written up, coded, and used for analysis.

In some sense, these different issues are analogous to the sampling and measurement issues that we discussed with reference to survey research in Chapter 10, and to a greater or lesser extent the same issues underpin all empirical research, whether it is qualitative or quantitative. We have to be aware about how we select our cases, how we collect our data and code it. The decisions we make at each step can have a strong bearing on what our final results look like. Participant observation may prioritize internal validity over external validity, but it certainly does not ignore the latter. But even to be internally valid, it is necessary to pay special attention to how the data is collected and coded within the domain of study. It would be problematic, to say the least, if another ethnographer carried out research on exactly the same topic in the same location at the same time and came to very different conclusions.

Choosing a research site

In a sense, all ethnographies are a form of case study (though the reverse is not true). And, as with any case study, the selection of the case (or field site) poses a number of challenges, and there are many issues that need to be considered. Hammersley and Atkinson (2007: 28) suggest that case selection can proceed in one of two general ways. First, the issue, or research question, or foreshadowed problem comes first, and a case or setting is then selected in order to investigate the topic. Or second, in some special circumstances, the setting itself may come first. A spontaneous opportunity may arise to investigate an interesting situation or group of people, and the research questions spring from the nature of that setting. For example, Pieke (1995) recounts how five months into his fieldwork in Beijing, he witnessed the emergence of the 1989 Chinese People's Movement. He thought this presented an interesting opportunity, and so started to carry out research. The setting thus came first, and his research questions were thus largely driven by his choice of case, rather than the other way round. However, instances of this type of 'opportunistic research' (Riemer 1977) are relatively rare, and more usually the choice of research setting (at least initially) is guided by the research question and the issues or hypotheses that the ethnographer wants to investigate, though, of course, these may change somewhat during the course of fieldwork.

One of the key problems that ethnographers face is that they sometimes find that the field site they have selected is not an appropriate arena to investigate what they had initially hoped to explore. To a greater or lesser extent this problem is relatively frequent, and it is widely accepted that the collection of primary data often plays an important role in the development of the research question. What an ethnographer initially sets out to investigate may not therefore always be exactly the same as what they end up investigating. Although this isn't always a problem, and indeed it can sometimes lead to the elaboration of new and exciting research questions, if the initial question or issue was thought to be worth investigating in the first place, then it is worth seriously thinking about how this can be done.

In particular, there are two interrelated issues that need to be addressed. The first is to establish the type of site that the researcher plans to study, and second, once this is done, to decide which site in particular to select for investigation. That is, before selecting the site, it is first necessary to think about the population of potential sites that would be eligible (or appropriate) cases for selection. The more thought that is put into this at the planning stage, the less risk there is of ending up in a place that is ill-suited to examining the desired issues.

Types of research site

Early ethnographic studies using participant observation tended to be the preserve of anthropologists, who often worked in small, isolated, self-contained communities that had little to do with the outside world and state structures. However, ethnographers have increasingly turned their attention beyond village settings to investigate social and political phenomena in a wide variety of settings, from urban ethnographies to ethnographies of political parties, institutions, and social movements. Indeed, some of the most in-depth ethnographies rely on fieldwork in multiple settings. For example, Michelutti's (2008) study on how democratic ideas and practices were reinterpreted among the Yadavs, a historically marginalized community in India, was carried out in a neighbourhood where many Yadavs lived, in the temples and religious festivals that they attended, in the political parties to which they were affiliated, and in the cultural associations of which they were members. Although the main research setting was the urban area where they lived, the other settings stemmed from this, linking the local area to the wider region, the state, and even to the nation. In this sense, ethnography is often described as holistic, in that it examines how what people say and do plays out in different settings and domains over time. Linked to this, recent discussions of multi-sited approaches seek in a similar way to link the local to the regional and even the global (Marcus 1995; Comaroff and Comaroff 2003). Multi-sited approaches carry out fieldwork in different research sites. For example, research on the Punjabi diaspora might carry out research in the Punjab, on people living there, and then carry out research in a different site in Southall, in the UK, where large numbers of Punjabis live.

By contrast, other studies, particularly in political research, have tended to have a more specific focus and are often primarily based on fieldwork in organizations and institutions, such as political parties, the civil service, parliament, the EU, and NGOs, or loose networks, such as gangs, religious extremists, or freedom fighters. Members and participants may not all live in the same place, and so are primarily linked through the organizations. For these cases, the main field site is therefore the organization, such as the local political party headquarters, and other research sites may then stem from this (see, for example, Bale and Dann's

2002 study of New Zealand's Green Party). The definition of the primary research site and justification for why one type of site is appropriate rather than another is therefore a crucial first step, which needs to be related explicitly to the research question and objectives.

Selection of research site

Having defined the type of research site that is appropriate for the research project, the next step is to decide which specific site is to be selected for the study. Often practical considerations form a prominent basis for selection, and although these are important, they should not be entirely divorced from theoretical and methodological considerations. The factors that make access to a site easier might also make it peculiar in some important respects, which means that it might not be very representative or typical of the population of interest. For example, although there is a great deal of academic interest in the shanty towns, or *barrios*, that surround major cities in Latin America, these locations are often dangerous and violent places which make it risky for a researcher to just turn up. There is a tendency among researchers, therefore, to focus on the barrios which are relatively safe, and where there are active NGOs and religious organizations that can help with access arrangements and introductions. Although this paves the way for some incredibly valuable research, at the same time barrios which have these organized links with civil society are likely to be somewhat different from the ones where NGOs and religious organizations are not present. This is an important consideration when thinking about how far findings from the research may be generalized.

A useful starting point for guiding case selection should therefore be to try and define the population of eligible cases for selection. What are the theoretical criteria for selecting a particular case? And what other potential cases might fit these criteria? Is the case chosen because it is intended to be typical or because it is an outlier? For example, if the research project is on Hindu–Muslim relations in India, are you interested in examining a neighbourhood that is characterized by particularly high levels of conflict, or particularly low levels of conflict? Thinking about these questions will help to identify the population to which your findings might apply, and set the parameters for potential generalizations that may stem from the research.

Access to research site

Having selected a site to conduct fieldwork, one of the most difficult steps in carrying out participant observation is gaining access to the research site. It is all very well to have a clear idea about the type of place where you want to do research, and even to have selected a potential site. But if it is not possible to gain access to the field site, then it is back to the drawing board. Access issues can create problems in two main ways. First, if access is not possible, it may introduce response bias similar in nature to the selection bias discussed above. Places where you cannot gain access may be different in important respects from the places where you can (or can more easily) gain access.

Second, access issues can also affect the way in which you carry out research. How you enter the field can shape how you are perceived by informants, and so your point of entry may have long-term consequences for your research project. One obstacle ethnographers frequently face is to overcome the suspicion of the people they are studying. For many informants, the purpose of ethnography is hard to fathom. Why would anyone want to study us? It is sometimes much easier to assume that the investigator is a spy rather than a political scientist. With time and hard work, these suspicions can be overcome, but the extent to which this is possible and the amount of time it takes may be influenced by the level of distrust in the first place. And on this score, first impressions can count for a lot. In this section we discuss some of the strategies that can be employed to gain access to the research site, and the impact that these strategies may have on the way in which research is conducted.

The issues surrounding access vary in a number of ways according to the object of investigation. This is often discussed in terms of whether the research setting is **open** or **closed** or a public or non-public setting (Hammersley and Atkinson 2007). The distinction between the two types of setting is relevant for gaining access because a closed setting may require the permission of someone in order to gain access. Access to closed settings (non-public), such as formalized groups or institutions, political parties, law courts, the police, the European Union, UN, development organizations, NGOs, to name just a few, present a number of problems, since some sort of formal permission may be required in order to carry out research. Bryman (2004: 297) suggests a number of strategies for gaining access to closed (organizational) settings, such as using friends, contacts, or colleagues to try to get support from someone within the organization. In particular, it is highly likely that you will need permission to do research from a **gatekeeper**—senior management in the organization. Gatekeepers may be wary about letting researchers snoop about in the organization, particularly if they have concerns as to whether the organization will be presented in a good light or not. Similarly, government permissions, or permits, are often needed to carry out research in tribal areas or reservations, and these permits can be difficult to come by, particularly if the research is on a sensitive topic. It is often then a good idea to offer gatekeepers something in return, such as a report or summary of your main findings. In dealing with gatekeepers, Bryman also suggests that it is a good idea to provide a clear explanation of the aims and methods of the research, and the amount of time it will take (and take away from people doing their job or other duties). It is also important to negotiate. Full access may not be forthcoming, but with careful compromise it might be possible to have some sort of limited access that nonetheless enables the researcher to investigate their topic. As Schatz (2009: 307) writes, access is a 'sliding scale' on which the political ethnographer strives to 'achieve the *nearest possible vantage point* to study a given problem'.

Where permission is needed, it is obviously important to get the permission giver—or gatekeeper—on board. However, it is also important to bear in mind how the compromises you make (if any) and the relationship you develop with the gatekeeper will affect your research, and how it will shape how you are perceived by informants once you have gained access. The extent to which this is an issue may depend upon the type of setting, and the hierarchy within the organization, and how the gatekeeper is viewed by those with whom you will be doing research. For example, if you are working in a factory, and have been given permission to do research by an unpopular member of senior management, then there is the risk that by association you will be viewed by the workers in an unfavourable light, and perhaps seen as a spy.

Access to open settings (public sites) is in theory more straightforward, since there aren't the same bureaucratic obstacles that need to be negotiated. But in practice it is beset by many of the same issues that face gaining access to private settings, particularly when the object of study is defined as a hard-to-reach population. If the site is a neighbourhood, or village or other public space, then it is not necessary to obtain formal permission to be there, and so the researcher can arrive, check out the location, and simply start observing what is going on. To facilitate this process, researchers often choose field sites where they have some prior personal link or contact.

However, some types of open public sites can present substantial access problems, particularly if the group in question is hard to reach, or involved on the periphery of legal activity, or indeed completely immersed in it, such as mafia, terrorist groups, or freedom fighters. For these inaccessible groups, it is often necessary to develop contacts who can provide an introduction to the group in question. However, obtaining these contacts is far from straightforward. They rely on trust and so are often only made after many years of hard work.

The role of the ethnographer

One obvious way to reduce some of these access problems is to do away with the need for permission in the first place, and for the investigator to assume a **covert** role, in which they do not reveal the true purpose of their research, or even that they are a researcher at all. This strategy means that the researcher does not face the problems of having to persuade people to give their permission to be studied, and the researcher doesn't have to face awkward questions about why they want to do the research either. This distinction between **overt research** and covert observation also influences the way in which data is collected, and the role that the ethnographer adopts in the field. Broadly speaking, there are three main types of role the researcher can adopt: the participant, the participant observer, and the observer.

The participant is a fully functioning member of the social setting and his or her identity is not known to the informants. The participant is a covert observer. It is widely documented that the act of being studied can alter the behaviour of the subjects under investigation. This is known as **reactivity**. One way to reduce this reactivity is for the researcher to adopt a covert role so that the informants don't know they are being studied. The behaviour of informants will therefore be more natural, and this can often lead the researcher to gain much closer access. For example, Humphreys (1970) pretended to be gay in order to enter the world of those he was studying.

The participant observer is the most common approach used by the investigator in ethnographic research. It is much the same as the participant approach, in that the researcher participates directly in the informants' lives, but differs in that it is overt, and the informants are aware of the researcher's identity. By contrast, the observer (or observer-participant) is focused on observation rather than participation. The researcher acts mainly as an interviewer, or carries out unobtrusive observation.

Although there are some obvious attractions to the covert approach, particularly when the researcher is concerned that permission might not be given if asked for, or when the researcher is concerned that knowledge about their identity might alter the way in which informants relate to them, there is also a number of ethical issues related to carrying out covert research to do with deception and informed consent (see Chapter 7). It is therefore an approach that is not widely used anymore.

Doing participant observation

Once in the field, there is a number of issues that the researcher faces in terms of how they can do participant observation, and how this will influence the quality of data that is generated. In participant observation, the main instrument of data collection is the individual ethnographer. The reliability and validity of the data that is collected therefore depend in large part upon how they behave, who they talk to, what they observe, and where they go. In addition, there are also all sorts of personal issues—such as the gender, ethnicity, and age of the researcher—that may influence how they are perceived by their informants, and shape their role as a researcher within the community. This can introduce considerable subjectivity into the research process, which may bias the conclusions that are reached (see Chapter 3 for an extended discussion of this).

Having gained access to the field site, a requisite of participant observation is to build and develop a relationship with the people who are being studied. Part of this comes simply with time and contact. One of the most important factors that influences the quality and reliability of the data generated is therefore related to the amount of time spent in the field. All other things being equal, the ethnographer is likely to have much more reliable data if they have been doing fieldwork for 12 months than if they have only been doing fieldwork for 12 days. It is only by observing events and talking to people over a relatively long period of time that the ethnographer can build up a picture of how the community under study really thinks and behaves.

But the amount of fieldwork that is needed can also vary substantially according to the researcher's familiarity with the method of participant observation, the topic of study, and the location of fieldwork and the people. Since many of the skills of doing participant observation are learned on the job, the first major piece of fieldwork by an ethnographer might be as long as 18–24 months, but subsequent fieldwork might be much shorter. With practice, the ethnographer will be able to collect data more efficiently, they will have a better eye for what to look out for, and possess more finely tuned research skills. Moreover, if the ethnographer is going back to the same place as a previous fieldwork, then much of the background data is already in the bank. They already know the people and the language, and so can collect good data in just a matter of days or weeks.

In addition, in order to develop a relationship with informants, it is necessary for the ethnographer to learn the language of the people they are studying. This is a core skill in its own right, and the linguistic competence of ethnographers is a key part of being able to do research effectively. Although some ethnographers use interpreters, to pick up sensitive data it is advantageous to know the local language. 'Fluency in the local language doesn't just improve your rapport; it increases the probability that people will tell you sensitive things . . . and that even if people try to put one over on you, you'll know about it' (Bernard 2006: 361).

Choosing informants

One of the great strengths of participation is that it is thought to have high levels of '**internal validity**'. This means that the researcher can be confident that the findings from the research are valid with reference to the domain of study (field site), even if they are less confident that the findings can be generalized more widely to other potential sites. However, this point can easily be overstated, and should not be taken for granted. There are a number of issues that influence the internal validity of ethnographic research, and, without careful attention, it is easy to produce data that are neither internally nor externally valid.

As with surveys, doing participant observation involves sampling. Even just hanging around and chatting to people is a kind of convenience or **volunteer sample** (see Chapter 10). Ideally, the ethnographer would speak to everyone in the population of interest (field site), and observe everyone equally. However, in practice this is rarely possible. The ethnographer might speak to some people more than others and spend time with some people more than others. The sample of informants that the ethnographer primarily relies upon may therefore only be a relatively small subsection of the entire population. This is particularly the case for urban ethnographies, where hundreds if not thousands of people may live together in relative proximity, or for ethnographies of relatively large organizations that might contain many members. In these situations, the ethnographer needs to think very carefully about who they spend time with and why, as error and bias can easily be introduced into the sample, which will mean that it is not representative of the population of study, and so the internal validity of the findings will be compromised.

For example, suppose a researcher is conducting an ethnography of the House of Commons, and is doing participant observation among British MPs. Part of the research will involve watching what MPs do and say in public places, but part of the research will also be carried out in more private settings, where in-depth conversations and interviews with MPs can take place. Perhaps also the researcher will track different MPs, and get permission to observe who they have lunch with, who they talk to and meet, and so on to shed light on the links and contacts that MPs have with business and lobby groups and different social organizations. Basically, the ethnographer will try, as much as possible, to live the life of an MP in order to get a detailed first-hand impression of what they do. But undoubtedly the researcher will spend more time with some MPs than others. Perhaps they will only spend time with backbench MPs because senior ministers and shadow ministers may be less prepared to give full access to the researcher because they are concerned about leaks, confidentiality, secrecy, or are simply just too busy. So already there is some selection bias, and what started off as a study of MPs is now becoming a study of backbench MPs. But, even among these backbench MPs, some might be more helpful and accommodating and more prepared to give up their time. There is always a temptation to be drawn towards the cooperative informants and to spend time talking to the people whom you get on with best, who are most helpful and approachable, and who make the job of the ethnographer easier.

Some informants may therefore be more useful or helpful than others, and certain informants—or **key informants**—may become more central to the collection of data than others. These key informants can be a great asset. They may understand the purpose and aims of the research, and be able to direct the ethnographer to situations, or places or people, who may be useful for research. But they also carry risks. Overreliance on key informants can create a different set of problems, to do with the reliability and validity of the information that is generated. As Bryman (2004: 300) puts it, a reliance on key informants may mean that 'rather than seeing social reality through the eyes of members of the social setting, the researcher is seeing social reality through the eyes of the key informant'. It is therefore very important for the ethnographer to continuously bear in mind the representativeness of their informants, and to actively seek out different voices and speak to those who may be less forthcoming, as well as those who are helpful and amenable. The consequence of failing to do so (or not

doing so adequately) is to introduce error and bias, which can undermine the internal validity of the study.

Studying with informants

Because the nature of participant observation relies on so much social interaction, Ingold
characterizes it as study *with* a particular group of people, rather than just a study *of* people.
The social interaction is thus an important, but also potentially problematic, aspect of participant observation, as the researcher aims to become 'accepted' and 'trusted' by those that
they are working with. As Whyte (1993: 303) argues, 'if people accept you—you can just
hang around and you can learn the answers in the long run without even having to ask questions'. Building trust is thus a key part of the research process. It creates an environment
where informants can speak frankly about sensitive and private issues without embarrass-
ment, where they have the confidence to express their own views rather than the views they
think they should hold or are culturally expected to hold, all of which allows the ethnographer to collect rich, detailed, valid data. In addition, the more an ethnographer is accepted
by the community he or she is studying, the less likely informants are to respond to the presence of the ethnographer. Rather than sticking out like a sore thumb and constantly drawing
attention to themselves, the ethnographer can slip into the background, become part of the
mundane, and observe quietly what goes on around them. But if the ethnographer is not
really trusted—or viewed with suspicion—then there is a greater risk that the ethnographer,
just by their very presence, can influence what happens in the research site. Informants will
be guarded around the ethnographer, will change their behaviour when they think they are
being observed, and act in an 'artificial' way.

This is known as reactivity, which can be a major source of error in ethnographic research.
Reactivity occurs when the very presence of the researcher alters the way in which informants act. There are two main strategies for dealing with this (see Bernard 2006: 425). The first
is training. It is not possible to eliminate observer bias completely, but there is a wealth of
evidence to suggest that training and experience makes people better—more reliable and
more accurate—observers (Hartmann and Wood 1990). The second is to build trust. When
informants are comfortable in the presence of the ethnographer, they become more
unguarded and less likely to change their behaviour when the ethnographer is around. This
helps to reduce (though never entirely eliminates) the problem of reactivity. Becoming
accepted and gaining trust is thus an important part of doing fieldwork. In doing so, the
ethnographer will have greater opportunity to observe and talk about things that are perhaps on the borders of social acceptance or legality—and enter worlds of criminality, corruption, usury. Informants will also be more likely to reveal personal information and allow
the ethnographer to ask direct and personal questions, examine sensitive areas of research,
and be invited to private settings.

But this acceptance can also be a double-edged sword. Becoming accepted within one
part of the community of study can also isolate the researcher from other groups. For example, a researcher interested in studying Hindu–Muslim relations in India might find that as
they become accepted by Hindus, they become distrusted by Muslims. Their research therefore becomes skewed—or biased—towards one side of the story. Similarly, during Stacey
et al.'s (1975) research on local party politics, the research team hired offices in the same

building as the local Labour Party headquarters. This gave the researchers good access to Labour Party workers, and they soon built up good relations with them. But in the process of doing this, they realized that they were now being viewed with suspicion by Conservative Party workers, who thought that the researchers were too close to Labour, and somehow 'on their side'. These problems can compound the access problems discussed previously, if the group that the researcher is perceived to be closer to is also the group that they gained access through.

A related problem associated with building trust and acceptance is to do with the nature of the researcher's relationship with the people they are studying. Although the ethnographer needs to cultivate good relations in order to collect good data, they also need to be able to maintain some emotional distance from the people they are studying so they retain the capacity for critical analysis. As the researcher becomes more immersed in the community of study, they may find it harder to be **objective** (see Chapter 3). In extreme circumstances observers may even '**go native**' and identify so much with the subjects that they lose the capacity for objective criticism. They may even become an advocate for the group and campaign and lobby on their behalf.

It can be incredibly difficult to stay neutral and impartial when the act of data collection involves so much close social interaction in order to gain the trust of informants. This can make it difficult to present a 'warts and all' betrayal of real life, and the ethnographer may not want to present their informants in a bad light, particularly if they would like to go back to the field site to do research in the same place again. The practical difficulties of maintaining this balancing act can be hard to pull off, and there is no easy solution. While it is desirable to become accepted within the group, there can also be unintended consequences of doing this. Indeed, it can sometimes feel like an act of betrayal and raise ethical issues. The art of gaining acceptance is often described as a euphemism for 'impression management' or deception.

Identity of the researcher

The ability of the ethnographer to build a relationship with informants, and the type of relationship that they are able to build, depends not only on what the ethnographer does in the field, but also to a certain extent on who the ethnographer is. There is a large reflexive literature on how the identity of the ethnographer influences how informants perceive them. In particular, much of this discussion has focused on the sex of the ethnographer, but other social characteristics, such as age, ethnicity, nationality, and even marital status and whether or not the ethnographer has children, have all been identified as having an important impact on how the researcher is received by informants and the kinds of access to different social worlds that they are granted.

As far back as the 1930s anthropologists such as Margaret Mead had already started to highlight the impact that the gender of the ethnographer could have on the collection of data in terms of the consequences it had on (i) access to information; and (ii) on how others perceive the ethnographer. Some social characteristics have a fairly restrictive impact on what the ethnographer can or cannot study. Men, for example, would not be able to carry out participant observation with Muslim women in *purdah*, since they would be prohibited from being in the same room as them. Similarly, much of the discussion on gender has also examined the obstacles that gender stereotypes create for women researchers, who have often been restricted to the study of domestic realms involving other women, children, and elderly people (Hammersley and Atkinson 2007). The gender of the researcher can thus both help and restrict access to different areas of social life, depending upon the cultural norms of the informants. What you can and can't do as a man or woman (or where you can and can't go) is more fixed in some cultures than in others, and in many cultures there is a certain amount of elasticity in gender roles that creates lots of individual variation.

The gender of the researcher can also have a less obvious impact, and influence the way in which informants respond to questions.

In addition, the ethnicity and nationality of the researcher can also influence how informants react. Sometimes it can actually be an advantage if the ethnographer belongs to a different ethnic or national group than the informants. For example, Hannerz (1969) carried out research in a black ghetto in the United States, and commented that although he was often jokingly referred to as 'blue-eyed blond devil', the fact that he was Swedish rather than American helped to distance him from other whites, who were not favourably received by his informants. Similarly, an Indian Brahman studying Indian Dalits, or an upper-class English man studying Welsh coalminers might take much more 'baggage' into the field with them than would someone from a different country less closely tied to the people they were studying.

The extent to which the ethnographer shares social characteristics with the informants can therefore be both a help and hindrance to building a relationship, depending upon the context. It is not therefore that the ethnographer should allow these factors to determine what they do in the field, but rather that they should be aware of how they might influence both what they can do and how people respond to them.

Critics of ethnographic research often challenge it as a method which is inherently subjective (see Chapter 3). Accordingly, these subjective influences can affect what type of data is collected, how it is collected, and from whom it is collected, all of which means that the data collected and the findings that come from them may tell us more (or more than we would ideally like) about the researcher who carried out the project than about the people or place that were actually being studied. This creates a serious problem in terms of **replicability**, which is one of the hallmarks of robust research (see Chapter 2). If different researchers studying the same phenomenon in the same place come to different conclusions, how can the findings from either be trusted? In what sense, if any, can the findings from ethnographic research therefore be regarded as internally valid?

Political ethnographers have long struggled to answer these questions (Schatz (ed.) 2009; Wedeen 2010). For some the task becomes too daunting, and so they retreat ever further into self-reflexivity, producing 'descriptive analysis of the most limited, self-referential sort—explanation phobic' (Comaroff 2010: 526) and reducing 'ethnography to a solipsistic literary practice, one so obsessively reflexive as to be of no interest to anybody outside of itself' (Comaroff 2010: 525). For others, the only way to get around these problems is to incorporate ethnographic research within other methodologies, so for scholars like Laitin (2003, 2006) 'narrative' approaches (such as ethnography) are 'by themselves inadequate, but when combined with large-N statistical work and formal models . . . can help generate robust findings' (Wedeen 2010: 259). See also discussion in Pachirat (2009) and Hopf (2006). Both these views represent somewhat extreme positions. And whereas it is probably true that subjectivity is inherent in ethnography, as it is to a greater or lesser extent in all social research, particularly qualitative research, this should not be overstated. As we discuss in Chapter 3, no approach or type of research ensures a completely value-free process of inquiry, and none can therefore free researchers from the need to be explicit and self-critical concerning their own underlying assumptions and values and behaviour, and how this might influence the research process. But this self-criticism is only of any use if it helps to guide the research process.

Recording observations

Ethnography involves two distinct but related processes: collecting data through participant observation, and recording and writing up that data. The quality of data that is collected in an ethnography rests not only on how the fieldwork was conducted, but also on how the fieldwork was recorded. Some forms of data can be relatively easy to record. For example, an interview or speech can be digitally recorded and transcribed (see Chapter 11). But other types of data are more difficult to record, and the distinction between recording or preserving data and analysing that data becomes blurred. Indeed, in many ways it is almost unavoidable that researchers will interpret their data—and to a certain extent construct their data—because as they write up and record what they have seen or heard, the process of recording data is filtered through the ethnographer. It is not therefore a simple record or representation of objective information, but a construction of that information that is in part interpretation, part analysis, and part observation. In this section we examine how different types of data can be recorded in preparation for analysis.

Fieldnotes

Fieldnotes are the traditional way of recording observational and interview data in ethnography. Originally they were handwritten in field journals, but now there is a wide variety of computer software programs that can be used to record and organize fieldnotes. For a detailed discussion about the production of fieldnotes, see Emerson et al. (1995) and Sanjek (1990). The writing of fieldnotes is something that needs to be done with great care and attention. Poor quality note-taking can severely hamper the research process, and undermine the study. It is important that notes are comprehensive, but at the same time fieldnotes are always selective. It is not possible to record everything, and so the ethnographer must prioritize what is interesting or relevant to the research project. As Hammersley and Atkinson (2007) note, taking good fieldnotes is not just about writing down what you see and hear, but about knowing what to write down, how to write it down, and when to write it down.

The *when* is extremely important. As a general rule, the quality of notes diminishes with time, and the researcher should therefore aim to make notes as soon as possible after the observed action or conversation has taken place. Details can easily be forgotten or confused, and the longer the passage of time between the event and the record of the event, the greater the likelihood that this will happen. Ideally, then, notes should be made in real time, as events or conversations are taking place. But this is not always practical, and can be disruptive to the activity of carrying out participant observation. It is often necessary to wait until a time when the researcher is not directly involved in carrying out the research, and can spend time writing up the day's activities and expanding upon any brief notes that have been jotted down during the course of the day. Bernard (2006: 387) recommends spending two to three hours per day doing this.

In some sense, field journals and recordings provide the raw data that the researcher then uses for analysis, though the distinction between data and analysis is not always clear-cut. Bernard (2006) distinguishes between descriptive notes and analytical notes, though in practice there is likely to be considerable overlap between the two. In preparation for writing up and analysing field notes, there are now many software programs that can be used to index and code the data. It is important to draw on the full breadth of the fieldwork data when writing up the results, rather than selectively using only the data and evidence that is convenient to the argument, and modern software programs can help to ensure that this is done more systematically.

One of the main problems with ethnographic research is that it is very difficult for the reader to know whether this has been done, which makes it difficult to assess the reliability and validity of the research. In recent years there has been some discussion of whether ethnographic data should be deposited in archives and made available, similar to the standard practice with survey and interview data. This would help to remove the veil of secrecy that surrounds much of fieldwork and ethnographic data collection. The advantage of this is that it would create a firmer distinction between data and analysis. People would be able to see how data was collected, what data was collected (and what was not) and how it was then analysed. This would create a stockpile of evidence and information that could be reanalysed—perhaps with differing conclusions from the original author's. This could help make better use of data which are already collected. Doing this would no doubt improve the transparency of data collection, and reduce the probability of ethnographers 'making up' evidence to fit their argument.

For example, the 2004–7 Shifting Securities ethnography project, led by Marie Gillespie (mentioned earlier), which investigated ordinary people's understandings of security, was required by its funding body to deposit all ethnographic transcripts and reports on a secure website (http://www.mediatingsecurity.com). As a collaboration between 18 ethnographers, the project website became a resource for the project team itself to exchange information, preliminary papers, and of course the notes and reports of others. This allowed for the coordination of research questions and emerging hypotheses across the team. It also enabled the team leader to pay attention to issues of internal validity within the study, since patterns and outliers could be observed as findings came in across the 18 individual ethnographers' studies. Moreover, it allowed researchers working across the fields of political and social science to access this data, compare it with their own studies, and use that data to develop their own projects. It was important that the Shifting Securities website required secured access. For ethical reasons (see Chapter 7), this enabled the project leader to restrict the transcripts and reports to selected guest researchers and maintain ethical fidelity to the informants.

However, there is also considerable resistance and opposition to this developing trend. One objection is based purely on a matter of scale. Dingwall (1992: 169) wrote, 'it is no more possible to reproduce all the data than it is for a film-maker to show every inch of film. . .' . But even selective appendices present problems. There is the issue of confidentiality, and whether or not the identity of informants would be compromised or not. There is also the issue of how the data would be used, and whether it is (or could be) meaningful to people who did not write the notes and do the research themselves. Despite these objections, there is growing pressure among research councils and funding bodies to make at least some forms of ethnographic data more publicly available. But the monograph is still an important source of data in its own right.

Conclusions

Ethnographic methods and participant observation have tended to be overlooked as a research tool in politics and IR. However, this is beginning to change and in recent years there has been a renewed interest in political ethnography. Ethnography and participant observation are well suited to the investigation of political phenomena that other more formal techniques are ill-equipped to examine, such as hard-to-define topics or hard-to-access groups, like guerilla movements, revolutions, riots, racisim, and terrorism.

Participant observation is also well suited to uncovering what people actually do, particularly when, for whatever reason, what people say they do might be different from what they actually do. If you want to know how a riot broke out, you can ask people afterwards, speak to witnesses, and even speak to participants themselves. But this will provide a different, potentially less reliable source of data, than actually observing first hand what happens. Participant observation can produce two important sorts of data. The first is to do with what people say. This can either be in the form of answers to questions (like surveys and interviews and focus groups), or revealed statements that come to light in the course of other events. But perhaps the key advantage of participant observation over all other methods is the observational data that it reveals.

However, despite these undoubted strengths of participant observation, it is very difficult to assess the quality of data generated. The problem with participant observation is that it is very difficult to tell whether the data has been collected rigorously or not. We generally only know how long the researcher was in the field, the location of the field site (though sometimes this is anonymized), and the group of people among who the researcher worked. More methodological appendices would help to establish the reliability and validity of the research, and how far it could be generalized to other contexts. Some of these problems can be overcome. Carrying out comparative ethnography, or replicating existing ethnographies in other contexts, can help to establish the extent to which findings can be generalized. Combining ethnography with other methods of data collection can be used to derive testable hypotheses from the ethnographic data, which can then be examined more generally, using, for example, survey data.

Questions

- What are the particular strengths of ethnographic study? When might it be an appropriate method of analysis? When might it not be so helpful?
- To what extent does ethnography reflect the ethnographer's own worldview rather than that of the people it purports to represent?
- Is ethnography only concerned with description? How can it be used to develop explanations?
- Is ethnography always biased? If so, does it matter? If not, how can we avoid or minimize bias?
- Are the limits of ethnographic generalization overstated?
- Should ethnographers deposit their fieldnotes in data archives?
- What are the ethical obstacles to doing participant observation? Are these an unnecessary inconvenience?
- How might ethnography and survey data be meaningfully combined?

Guide to Further Reading

Bernard, H. (2006), *Research Methods in Anthropology: Qualitative and Quantitative Methods* (Lanham, MD: Altamira Press).
A very detailed and comprehensive account of the different aspects of ethnography, and the ways in which ethnographic research can be combined with other research strategies and methods. Although written primarily for anthropologists, it is full of engaging examples and is an extremely useful resource for all students interested in political ethnography.

Fenno, R. (1978), *Home Style: House Members in their Districts* (New York: Harper Collins).
This is one of the classic ethnographies in political research. Fenno conducted research with 18 members of Congress as they travelled around their constituencies, spending time with them, and observing what they did and who they spoke to on a day-to-day basis. The book offers fascinating insights into how congressmen interact with their constituents, and how this translates into their legislative effectiveness.

Hammersley, M. and P. Atkinson (2007), *Ethnography: Principles in Practice* (London: Routledge).
A very clear and comprehensive book on the different aspects of ethnographic research. It contains everything you need to know, with informative and detailed chapters on specific issues such as access, field relations, writing ethnography, and ethics. A must read.

Michelutti, L. (2008), *The Vernacularisation of Democracy: Politics, Caste and Religion in India* (London: Routledge).
This is a fascinating ethnography of everyday practices and beliefs about democracy among a historically marginalized caste group in Northern India. The book clearly illustrates what ethnography can contribute to the study of politics. Michelutti examines how culture and social practices inform politics and vice versa. In doing so, she examines how ideas about democracy get ingrained in domains of life, such as marriage, kinship, and religion, which in turn serves to 'vernacularize' democratic politics.

Schatz, E. (ed.) (2009), *Political Ethnography: What Immersion Contributes to the Study of Power* (Chicago and London: University of Chicago Press).
This book contains a collection of essays on how ethnographic approaches have been used to study a variety of issues in political research, with chapters on topics such as ethnic nationalism, civil war, public opinion, and authoritarianism.

 ## References

Auyero, J. (1999), 'From the Client's Point(s) of View: How do Poor People Perceive and Evaluate Political Clientelism?', *Theory and Society* 28: 297–334.

Ashforth, A. (2005), *Witchcraft, Violence, and Democracy in South Africa* (Chicago: University of Chicago Press).

Bale, T. and C. Dann (2002), 'Is the Grass Really Greener: The Rationale and Reality of Support Party Status: A Case Study', *Party Politics* 8(3): 349–65.

Barnett, M. (2006), *Eyewitness to a Genocide: The United Nations and Rwanda* (Ithaca, NY: Cornell University Press).

Bernard, H. (2006), *Research Methods in Anthropology: Qualitative and Quantitative Methods* (Lanham, MD: Altamira Press).

Blee, K. and A. Currier (2006), 'How Local Social Movement Groups Handle a Presidential Election', *Qualitative Sociology* 29: 261–80.

Brewer, J. (2000), *Ethnography* (Buckingham: Open University Press).

Bryman, A. (2004), *Social Research Methods* (Oxford: Oxford University Press).

Comaroff, J. L. (2010), 'The End of Anthropology, Again: Toward a New In/Discipline', *American Anthropologist* 112(4): 524–38.

Comaroff, J. and J. Comaroff (2003), 'Ethnography on an Awkward Scale: Postcolonial Anthropology and the Violence of Abstraction', *Ethnography* 4: 147–79.

Dahl, R. (1961), *Who Governs?: Democracy and Power in an American City* (New Haven, CT: Yale University Press).

Delamont, S. (2004), 'Ethnography and Participant Observation', in C. Seale, G. Gobo, J. Gubrium, and D. Silverman (eds), *Qualitative Research Practice* (London: Sage Publications).

Dingwall, R. (1992), 'Don't Mind Him—He's from Barcelona: Qualitative Methods in Health Studies', in J. Daly, I. MacDonald, and E. Willis (eds) *Researching Health Care: Designs, Dilemmas and Disciplines* (London: Routledge).

Eliasoph, Nina (1997), *Avoiding Politics: How Americans Produce Apathy in Everyday Life* (Cambridge: Cambridge University Press).

Emerson, R., R. Fretz, and L. Shaw (1995), *Writing Ethnographic Fieldnotes* (Chicago: University of Chicago Press).

Fenno, R. (1978), *Home Style: House Members in their Districts* (New York: Harper Collins).

—— (1990), *Watching Politicians: Essays on Participant Observation* (Berkeley, CA: Institute of Governmental Studies, University of California).

George, A. and A. Bennett (2005), *Case Studies and Theory Development in the Social Sciences* (Cambridge, MA: MIT Press).

Gillespie, M. and B. O'Loughlin, B. (2009), 'News Media, Threats and Insecurities: An Ethnographic Approach', *Cambridge Review of International Affairs* 22(4): 667–86.

——, J. Gow, and A. Hoskins (2007), 'Shifting Securities: News Cultures Before and Beyond the Iraq Crisis 2003: Full Research Report', ESRC End of Award Report, RES-223-25-0063 (Swindon: ESRC).

Hammersley, M. and P. Atkinson (2007), *Ethnography: Principles in Practice* (London: Routledge).

Hannerz, U. (1969), *Soulside: Inquries in Ghetto Culture and Community* (New York: Columbia University Press).

Hartmann, D. and D. Wood (1990), 'Observational Methods', in A. Bellack, M. Hersen, and A. Kazdin (eds), *International Handbook of Behaviour Modification Therapy* (New York: Plenum).

Hopf, T. (2002), *Social Construction of International Politics: Identities and Foreign Policies, Moscow 1955 and 1999* (Ithaca, NY: Cornell University Press).

—— (2006), 'Ethnography and Rational Choice in David Laitin: From Equality to Subordination to Absence', *Qualitative Methods* 4(1): 17–20.

Humphreys, L. (1970), *Tearoom Trade* (London: Duckworth).

Ingold, T. (2008), 'Anthropology is Not Ethnography', *Proceedings of the British Academy* 154: 69–92.

Karlstrom, M. (1996), 'Imagining Democracy: Political Culture and Democratization in Buganda', *Africa* 66: 485–505.

Laitin, D. D. (2003), 'The Perestroikan Challenge to Social Science', *Politics and Society* 31(1): 163–84.

—— (2006), 'Ethnography and/or Rational Choice: A Response from David Laitin', *Qualitative Methods* 4(1): 26–33.

Latour, Bruno (2010), *The Making of Law: An Ethnography of the Conseil d'Etat* (Cambridge: Polity).

Leach, E. (1961), *Rethinking Anthropology* (London: Athlone Press).

Malinowski, B. (1922), 'Introduction: The Subject, Method and Scope of this Inquiry', *Argonauts of the Western Pacific: An Account of Native Enterprise and Adventure in the Archipelagoes of Melanesian New Guinea* (London: Routledge), 2–25.

Marcus, G. (1995), 'Ethnography in/of the World System: The Emergence of Multi-Sited Ethnography', *Annual Review of Anthropology* 24: 95–117.

Michelutti, L. (2008), *The Vernacularisation of Democracy: Politics, Caste and Religion in India* (London: Routledge).

Pachirat, T. (2009), 'The Political in Political Ethnography: Dispatches from the Kill Floor', in E. Schatz (ed.), *Political Ethnography: What Immersion Contributes to the Study of Power* (Chicago and London: University of Chicago Press).

Paley, J. (2001), *Marketing Democracy: Power and Social Movements in Post-Dictatorship Chile* (Berkeley, CA: University of California Press).

Parnell, P. and K. Kane (eds) (2003), *Crime's Power: Anthropologists and the Ethnography of Crime* (New York and Basingstoke: Palgrave Macmillan).

Parsons, C. (2010), 'Constructivism and Interpretive Theory', in D. Marsh and G. Stoker (eds), *Theory and Methods in Political Science* (Basingstoke: Palgrave Macmillan).

Pieke, F. (1995), 'Witnessing the 1989 Chinese People's Movement', in C. Nordstrom and A.Robben (eds), *Fieldwork Under Fire: Contemporary Studies of Violence and Survival* (Berkeley and Los Angeles: University of California Press).

Pouliot, V. (2007), 'Pacification without Collective Identification: Russia and the Transatlantic Security Community in the Post-Cold War Era', *Journal of Peace Research* 44: 605–22.

Riemer, J. (1977), 'Varieties of Opportunistic Research', *Urban Life* 5: 467–77.

Sanjek, R. (1990), 'Ethnography', in A. Barnard and J. Spencer (eds), *Encyclopedia of Social and Cultural Anthropology* (London: Routledge).

Schaffer, F. (1998), *Democracy in Translation: Understanding Politics in an Unfamiliar Culture* (Ithaca, NY: Cornell University Press).

Searing, D. (1994), *Westminster's World: Understanding Political Roles* (Cambridge, MA: Harvard University Press).

Stacey, M., E. Batestone, C. Bell, and A. Murcott (1975), *Power, Persistence and Change: A Second Study of Banbury* (London: Routledge and Kegan Paul).

Tilley, C. (2006), 'Afterword: Political Ethnography as Art and Science', *Qualitative Sociology* 29: 409–12.

Wacquant, L. (2003), 'Ethnografeast: A Progress Report on the Practice and Promise of Ethnography', *Ethnography* 4: 5–14.

Weaver, C. (2008), *Hypocrisy Trap: The World Bank and the Poverty of Reform* (Princeton, NJ: Princeton University Press).

Wedeen, L. (2010), 'Reflections on Ethnographic Work in Political Science', *Annual Review of Political Science* 13: 255–72.

Whiting, J. (1982), 'Standards for Psychocultural Research', in E. Hoebel, R. Currier, and S. Kaiser (eds), *Crisis in Anthropology: View from Spring Hill* (New York: Garland).

Whyte, W. (1993), *Street Corner Society: The Social Structure of an Italian Slum* (Chicago and London: Chicago University Press), First published 1943.

13 Textual Analysis

Chapter Summary

Texts have always been a major source of information and evidence for political researchers. This chapter discusses two forms of textual analysis that have become increasingly prominent in Politics and International Relations research: discourse analysis and content analysis. It also offers a brief discussion of using documents, archival sources, and historical writing as data. Among the questions the chapter addresses, are the following:

- What is a discourse?
- What can an analysis of discourse reveal about the social world?
- What is content analysis?
- How do discourse analysis and content analysis differ?
- What are the differences between qualitative and quantitative content analysis?
- What procedures are involved in both quantitative and qualitative content analysis?
- What special considerations need to be made in using documents, archival sources, and historical writing as data?

Introduction

Government reports, political pamphlets, newspapers, and other texts have long provided important sources of information for students of politics. However, in recent decades, growing awareness of the importance of language and meaning for political analysis and of the power of the mass media has produced a dramatic upsurge of interest in textual analysis, not only in Politics and International Relations, but throughout the social sciences. In political research, two forms of textual analysis have become particularly prominent: discourse analysis and content analysis.

Discourse analysis is a qualitative type of analysis that explores the ways in which discourses give legitimacy and meaning to social practices and institutions. *Discourses* consist of ensembles of ideas, concepts, and categories through which meaning is produced and reproduced in a particular historical situation. The elements of a discourse can be brought to light through analysing the language, semiotics (latent meaning in text), and conventions found in a variety of written, oral, and visual 'texts'. But while textual analysis can reveal the elements of a discourse, the *meaning* that they produce or reproduce can only be understood in relation to some broader context. Consequently, discourse analysis is concerned with analysing, not just the text itself, but the relation of a text to its context (its source, message, channel, intended audience, connection to other texts and events), as well as the broader relations of power and authority which shape that context.

In contrast to discourse analysis, **content analysis** is concerned with the study of the text itself, rather than with the broad context within which it was produced. This analysis can be either quantitative or qualitative. The aim of *quantitative content analysis* is to draw inferences about the meaning and intention of a text through an analysis of the usage and frequency of words, phrases, and images, and the patterns they form within a text. *Qualitative content analysis* is a more interpretive form of analysis concerned with uncovering meanings, motives, and purposes in textual content.

Qualitative content analysis and discourse analysis have much in common. But a discourse analyst and a content analyst will tend to approach the exploration of an issue in somewhat different ways.

Consider, for example, issues of race and ethnicity, which the upsurge in identity politics (the politicization of ethnic, regional, gender, and sexual identities) has made a key focus of research in recent years. A discourse analyst exploring these issues might examine how ethnic and 'racial' inequality is 'expressed, enacted and reproduced by discourse as one of the practices of a racist society' (van Dijk 2004: 354). In his studies of racism, Teun van Dijk investigates a recurring set of 'underlying mental models and social representations' in 'influential public discourses' (those of elites and elite institutions), and attempts to understand the conditions, consequences, and functions of these discursive elements by exploring the contexts in which they are produced (van Dijk 2002, 2004). A content analyst would be more typically concerned with identifying ethnocentric and racist representations in the content of mass media, literature, and film. For example, in order to find out how the media represented Whites, Blacks, and Latinos as crime victims, Travis Dixon and Daniel Linz (2000) conducted a content analysis of a random sample of television news programmes aired in Los Angeles and Orange Counties. Their examination of the frequency of certain words, phrases, and images, revealed that *Whites* are more likely than African Americans and Latinos to be portrayed as *victims* of crime on television news; and that *Blacks and Latinos* are more likely than Whites to be portrayed as *lawbreakers* than as crime victims. With these data as a basis, the authors were then able to explore the theoretical implications of these findings.

What this example shows is that, despite similarities, discourse analysis and content analysis offer researchers a means of asking and answering different types of questions. In the next section, we discuss these two forms of textual analysis in greater detail, including the types of research questions they address, what they can reveal about the social world, and the procedures that each entails.

Discourse analysis

Discourse analysis is an interpretive and constructivist form of analysis that draws on diverse theoretical and methodological approaches from linguistics, anthropology, and sociology.

As an approach to understanding political phenomena, discourse analysis is **interpretive**. In common with interpretivist approaches (see Chapter 2), it assumes that people act on the basis of beliefs, values, or ideology that give meaning to their actions; and that to understand political behaviour, we must know about the meanings that people attach to what they're doing. Consequently, its aim is to reveal the meanings that the political world has for agents who participate in it and that give people reasons for acting.

But discourse analysis is also **constructivist**: it assumes not only that people act towards objects, including people, on the basis of the meanings which those objects have for them, but that these meanings are socially and discursively constructed. The aim of discourse analysis, therefore, is not only to reveal meanings through an examination of the language and discourse we employ in our interactions, but to uncover how discursive practices construct meanings through the production, dissemination, and consumption of various forms of texts, including formal written records, TV programmes, advertisements, and novels.

Speech act theory, post-structuralism, and critical discourse analysis

To further elaborate on this constructivist dimension of discourse analysis, it is useful to briefly consider some key ideas on which the constructivist understanding of discourse is based.

Speech act theory

The notion that meanings are discursively constructed is based on a fundamental assumption of discourse analysis: that language is a medium orientated towards action and function; that when we speak (or write), we do so, not only in order to say something, but also to *do* something. This idea—that language is used as much to do things as to make statements—lies at the heart of **speech act theory**, an approach to the explanation of language pioneered by the philosophers John L. Austin and John Searle in the 1960s. 'The issuing of an utterance', wrote John Austin, 'is the performing of an action' (1962: 6); or, as the Austrian philosopher, Ludwig Josef Johann Wittgenstein put it: 'Words are deeds' (1980: 46). All discourse-analytic approaches are based on this fundamental idea. Thus, discourse analysis is concerned with language, not as an abstract system, but as something that people use to do things. People use language to promise, threaten, insult, plead, and demand. More broadly, certain things become real through language: 'attitudes', points of view, particular 'subject positions' (ways in which objects or people take up or are placed in particular positions), entities, states-of-affair (what is going on), events, processes, activities, and relationships.

So people use *language* to create different kinds of social and cultural meaning, and to construct different accounts, or versions, of the social world. *Discourse* is 'a system of texts that brings objects into being' (Hardy 2001: 26). It constructs social reality by helping to construct what is knowable, sayable, and doable *within a particular historical context*. To highlight the distinction further, we can think of language as a set of rules of grammar and logic that can produce infinite possible sentences (language) or propositions (logic). However, a discourse is a system, or ensemble, of ideas, concepts, and categories, that is linked to, and functions within, a specific context. Consequently, we can say that discourse analysis is an exploration of 'language in context'. It is not interested simply in how something is represented by language, but in how it is actually constructed by the ways in which it is intelligible and legitimate to talk about it in a particular time and place.

Post-structuralism

The most important representative of post-structuralist thinking, Michel Foucault (1929–84), focused attention on the various ways discourses 'systematically form the objects of which they speak' (Foucault 1972: 49). This work suggested a variety of channels of inquiry to explore the construction of social reality through discourse, including:

1. how ways of talking about a topic are embedded in sets of power relations;
2. how these power relations are supported by institutions (asylums, governments, prisons, and schools) in particular historical contexts; and
3. how these institutional and historical configurations of discourse constructed new kinds of human subjects.

A particularly resonant avenue of inquiry that Foucault opened up was the exploration of how reiterated key words and statements that recur across texts of all kinds enable and delimit fields of knowledge and inquiry, and govern what can be said, thought, and done within those fields. In his *Archaeology of Knowledge*, Foucault analyses the history or genesis of the 'discursive practices' that lay claim to revealing knowledge, showing how the development of knowledge is intertwined with the mechanisms of (political) power. 'Discourse' can be understood in this context as a system of statements, expressing rules, roles, and boundaries that form a body of knowledge. For instance, we can speak of 'discourses of politics', 'discourses of democracy', or 'authoritarian politics'. In *Encountering Development* (1994), Arturo Escobar traces the emergence of a 'development discourse' ('developmentalism') after World War II, and shows how this discourse constructed a particular representation of the Third World that, over time, 'created a space in which only certain things could be said and even imagined' (1994: 39).

Poststructuralist theory questions whether there are essential human subjects, individual agents, and social realities independent of their dynamic historical construction in social and cultural discourses. For instance, Foucault asks whether the natural and social worlds are indeed knowable, accessible, and analysable without recourse to the constitutive forces of discourse. He did not think that there were definite underlying structures that could explain the human condition; and he thought that it was impossible to step outside of discourse and survey the situation objectively.

Building on this perspective, post-structuralist discourse theory assumes that the way people talk about the world does not reflect some objective truth about the world, but the success of particular ways of thinking and seeing. These ways of thinking and seeing become invisible because they are assumed to be truthful and right. In this way people's thought processes themselves can come to represent and reinforce particular regimes of power and coercion.

Critical discourse analysis

Post-structural thinking made important contributions to the field of discourse studies. However, it came under attack for its tendency to treat reality as little more than something constituted in and through discourse, and to ignore pre-existing social structures and power relationships. This line of critique was developed in what came to be known as 'critical discourse analysis'.

Critical discourse analysis (CDA) is 'critical' because it seeks to expose connections between language, power, and ideology (Fairclough 2001: 4). It is principally concerned with the role of discourse in enacting, reproducing, and resisting social power abuse, dominance, and inequality (Van Dijk 2001: 300, 352).

Hypotheses linking discourses to power can be investigated through an analysis of how powerful groups control public discourse, and of how discourse controls the minds and actions of less powerful groups, and the social consequences of such control (Van Dijk 2001: 355).

Discursive power—control over a discourse—is a crucial constituent of social power, and a major means of reproducing dominance and hegemony. Members (and particularly leaders) of more powerful social groups and institutions

> have more or less exclusive access to, and control over, one or more types of public discourse. Thus, professors control scholarly discourse, teachers educational discourse, journalists media discourse, lawyers legal discourse, and politicians policy and other public political discourse. Those who have more control over more—and more influential—discourse (and more discourse properties) are by that definition also more powerful. (Van Dijk 2001: 356)

Controlling people's minds is another crucial constituent of social power. Those groups who control the most influential discourses also have more chances to control the minds and actions of others, because people tend to accept beliefs, knowledge, and opinions 'through discourse from what they see as authoritative, trustworthy, or credible sources, such as scholars, experts, professionals, or reliable media . . . '. Moreover, 'in some situations participants are obliged to be recipients of discourse, e.g. in education and in many job situations' (Van Dijk 2001: 357).

CDA developed in association with a critique of post-structural and other discourse analytic approaches. But it has also been the target of critique. A key aspect of CDA that distinguishes it from other forms of discourse analysis is the degree to which the analyst depends on a prior theoretical perspective to analyse the data. For CDA, you start with a theory of dominance or power, then you explore materials in order to discover how discourse promotes or challenges one group's power over another (Fairclough 2001). As Ted Hopf points out, critical discourse analysis 'is in fact a political theory as much as a method of inquiry'. It assumes that language is a medium within which prevailing configurations of power are articulated and reproduced. Disrupting and challenging these power relations 'is one of the central features of what we call politics. This means that the meaning of any given text for DA often points to some underlying political problem or question' (Hopf 2004: 30). This dependence on prior theory brings it into conflict with those discourse analysts who want to stay closer to the materials in their data (see e.g. Wetherall 1998; Billig and Schegloff 1999).

Analysis

We have said that a *discourse* is 'a system of texts that brings objects into being' (Hardy 2001: 26) within a particular institutional and historical context. The goal of *discourse analysis* is to explore the relationship between discourse and reality in a particular context. Thus, the hypothesis to be investigated will typically be that that there is a co-variation or association between a discourse and a given context.

To investigate this hypothesis, the analyst will choose a discrete body of written work (e.g. a newspaper over a specific period of time, a set of speeches) and conduct an analysis of what reality its language, metaphors, and/or symbols help to construct. Texts are selected to enable the analyst to explore a hypothesized association between text features and context features, between some change in the context or circumstances and a systematic change in discourse features that are the focus of interest in a study (Lemke 1998). The analysis entails retroduction: reasoning backward from a particular discursive production to establish structure from its empirical manifestations. 'It asks what the conditions of possibility are of this or that particular discursive production' (Laffey and Weldes 2004: 28). (See Chapter 2.)

Establishing a co-variation or association between discourse and context is only a first step. A second step is to provide details of the process through which the power of a discourse has demonstrable effects.

Let's give some further consideration to each of these two steps.

1. The context

All approaches to discourse assume that, to understand the constructive effects of discourses, researchers must place them in their historical and social contexts. As we stated previously, discourse analysis is the study of language use in context. Discourses construe aspects of the world in inherently selective and reductive ways. The question to ask, therefore, is: 'Why this particular selection and reduction, and why here and now?' Thus, discourse analysis 'produces its greatest insights when rich contextual information can be factored into the analysis of each text or episode' (Lemke 1998: 1185). But how do we determine the relevant contextual factors of a text or discourse event? 'Context' is difficult to determine with any precision. It is difficult to know what aspects of context are potentially relevant to a textual analysis.

Let's first consider the different sorts of contexts that can be explored. We can distinguish between *local* and *broad* contexts (Titscher et al. 2000). The local context includes the immediate task and situation, the source, message, channel, and intended audience of the communication. The broad context consists of cultural norms and assumptions, knowledge, beliefs and values, the resources and strategies characteristic of a community's general cultural resources. Another way of characterizing different contexts are through the use of the terms *micro-discourse* (specific study of language) and *macro-discourse*. 'Language use, discourse, verbal interaction, and communication belong to the micro-level of the social order; power, dominance, and inequality between social groups are typically terms that belong to a macro-level of analysis' (van Dijk 2001: 354), the broad, societal currents that are affecting the text, being studied. Teun van Dijk explains that 'In everyday interaction and experience the macro and micro level (and intermediary "meso-levels") form one, unified whole. For instance, a racist speech in parliament is a discourse at the micro-level of social interaction in the specific situation of a debate, but at the same time may enact or be a constituent part of legislation or the reproduction at racism, at the macro-level' (van Dijk 2001: 354).

In his studies of discourse and racism, van Dijk focuses on *communicative, interactional*, and *societal* contexts. What he is interested in investigating is how 'influential public discourses' (those of elites and elite institutions) reflect 'similar underlying mental models and social representations', and 'similar ways of social interaction, communication, persuasion, and public opinion formation' (van Dijk 2002: 157). To understand the conditions, consequences, and functions of these discursive elements, he explores the communicative, interactional, and societal contexts in which they are produced. Figure 13.1 represents the way in which these contexts operate.

These contexts together include biased or stereotypical news, produced by journalists and other professionals, under the control of editors, in media organizations. In the wider society, the content of these texts is produced, and also reproduced, by members of many different professional and other social groups, and as part of daily routines and procedures: legislative debates conducted by politicians; textbooks, lessons, and scholarly publications produced by teachers and scholars. 'Racist societies and institutions produce racist discourses, and racist discourses reproduce the stereotypes, prejudices and ideologies that are used to defend and legitimize white dominance' (van Dijk 2004: 354).

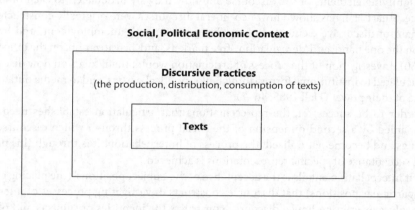

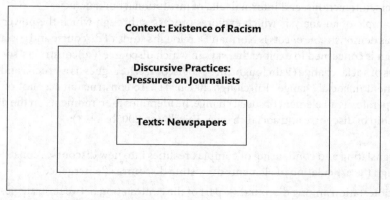

Figure 13.1 Text and context in discourse analysis

Source: Fairclough (1995: 59).

2. Analysing the process thorough which the power of a discourse has demonstrable effects

In addition to establishing an association between discourse and context, discourse analysis also seeks to show that discourse has demonstrable effects. In order to do this, discourse analysts have sought to delineate the process through which discourse becomes naturalized so as to become common sense—the mechanisms through which it 'fixes' meanings and becomes naturalized. These mechanisms can best be understood as a social process with two distinct dimensions: articulation and interpellation (Weldes 1996: 284).

The term 'articulation' refers to 'the process through which meaning is produced out of extant cultural raw materials or linguistic resources' (Weldes 1996: 284). 'Articulation' fixes meanings 'through a process of repeatedly establishing associations between different elements, so that these elements come to be seen as inherently or necessarily connected and the meanings they produce come to seem natural, to be an accurate description of reality' (Weldes 1996: 285).

In an investigation of the process of articulation, the researcher would, first, identify the main signifying elements of the discourse and how they are articulated to each other. For instance, Stuart Hall has shown how neo-liberal discourses were originally constructed out of a chain of discursive elements linking 'big government', 'unemployment', and 'welfare state', on the one hand; and 'deregulation', 'free markets', and 'privatization', on the other (Hall 1988: 50). Investigation of the process of articulation would, then, focus on how discourses are articulated to institutional forms (think tanks, political parties, and to media outlets) and partake of their power (Hall 1988: 46–7).

In order to be successful, the representations that articulation establishes need to be accompanied by a second dimension of the social process through which discourses 'fix' meanings and become naturalized: the process of 'interpellation'. It is through this process that the acceptance of specific representations is achieved.

What interpellation entails is the acceptance of the 'subject positions' (the placing of people in particular positions) that discourse constructs. Investigating processes of interpellation involves examining how a discourse constructs the identities of subjects and objects, and how these identities are then embodied in the spoken, written, and symbolic texts, the encounters, interactions, and informal talk, of institutional bureaucracies.

An example of an analysis which explores processes through which the power of a discourse has demonstrable effects is Norman Fairclough's study of discourse and social change. Fairclough is concerned to explore the ways in which discourse '(re)constructs' social life in processes of social change (Fairclough 2005a). Discourse, he argues, is a 'crucial and irreducible' element in social change (Fairclough 2005b: 41). To construct an account of how discourse operates as an element of social change, he identifies four 'moments' in the dialectical relationship of discourse and social change (Fairclough 2005b: 42–3):

1. the translating and condensing of complex realities into new discourses constructed through the articulation of elements of existing discourses ('emergence');

2. the contestation among discourses—part of the contestation between strategies and between groups of social agents—which may lead to particular discourses (and strategies) becoming hegemonic ('hegemony');

3. the dissemination of discourses and their recontextualization in new organizations, institutions, or fields, or at new scales ('recontextualization'); and

4. the 'enactment of discourses as new ways of (inter)acting, their inculcation as new ways of being, or identities, their materialization in features of the physical world' ('operationalization').

Fairclough applies this schema to an investigation of the 'discourse moment' in 'the emergence of a new regime of international security and the use of force, as evidenced recently in Kosovo, Afghanistan, and Iraq': the effort to develop and diffuse a new hegemonic discourse of international relations and international security. The focus of Fairclough's analysis is the contribution of one key 'player' in this process: the UK Prime Minister, Tony Blair. To explore Blair's contribution to elaborating a new doctrine of 'international community', he analyses '"doctrinal" speeches which elaborate policy' that Blair delivered in April 1999, April 2002, and January 2003 (Fairclough 2005b: 41).

While his analysis is not able to reveal all four 'moments' in the dialectic of discourse and social change, it does suggest what avenues of research this might entail. He finds that the texts he examines reveal, to some extent, the moment of *emergence* of a new discourse through articulating elements of existing ones; and that the second moment, *hegemony*, is revealed inasmuch as Blair is a major international statesman and opinion-former—though, as Fairclough notes, a wider range of material would need to be analysed over a longer period of time 'to get a sense of hegemonic struggles over international relations and international security'. The third moment, *recontextualization*, might be revealed in a further study charting the 'trajectories of the emergent hegemonic discourse in its structural and scalar dissemination'. This might entail 'investigating how the emergent hegemonic discourse of international relations and international security both "colonizes" and is appropriated' within government policy and media texts. He suggests, further, that the operationalization of a change in hegemonic discourse 'in new strategies, institutions, exchanges' might be revealed in case studies of processes of policy formation and implementation' by, for example, studying 'the process of decision making and implementation in the procurement of new military hardware' (Fairclough 2005b: 59).

Validity and reliability

Judgements of validity focus on the extent to which a plausible case has been made that patterns in the meaning of texts are constitutive of reality in some way. Does an interpretation adequately account for observations in relation to relevant contextual factors? Does it minimize potential researcher bias, and provide explanatory coherence within a larger theoretical frame?

In addition to plausibility, the validity of a discourse-analytic study can be judged in terms of its credibility—its ability to impart 'coherence' to a text, showing how it fits together in terms of content, functions, and effect; and its 'fruitfulness'—its ability to provide insights that may prove useful (Potter and Wetherell 1994). A discourse-analytic study should demonstrate a careful reading of the text; provide an interpretation that is clearly related to the textual evidence; and present an analysis which aims to be credible, plausible, coherent, and fruitful. Research should be open and transparent both about the textual evidence under review and about the basis of the claims made about it (Rapley 2008).

Content analysis

Content analysis involves the systematic analysis of textual information. In PIR, researchers tend to study election manifestos, news media, and political leaders' speeches. But there is a wide variety of texts that researchers might choose to analyse, including:

(1) *official documents*: government reports and administrative records, programme evaluations, descriptions of programme activities, legal reports, judicial decisions, company accounts; records from schools, hospitals, law courts; judicial decisions; and transcripts of speeches, conversations, discussions, and oral answers to questions;

(2) *cultural documents*: newspaper articles or editorials, magazines, TV programmes, films, videos, art works, photographs, advertising copy; reports from journals, magazines, and newspapers); and

(3) *personal documents*: letters, diaries, and emails.

Content analysis is an unobtrusive method of data collection. Gathering data through unobtrusive means has a number of advantages over obtrusive methods of data collection, such as surveys, unstructured and semi-structured interviews, focus group discussions, ethnography, and participant observation. The chief advantage is that they can reduce bias. For instance, in all types and forms of interviews, people can be expected to come to the interview with biases and prejudices. Moreover, all are generally prone to the 'interview effect': the tendency to give 'socially acceptable' answers or ones that they think the interviewer wants. People may not tell the truth because they want to 'look good' in the eyes of the interviewer; or because they are asked something either that they don't know how to answer or that would be embarrassing for them to answer. Of course, the researcher also comes to the interview with biases and prejudices, and these can distort the interview process, as well.

In addition to these problems, obtrusive methods are also prone to the 'Heisenberg Effect', which we discussed in Chapter 3. This is the tendency for people to change their behaviour when they know they are under observation. We described, as an illustration of this, the experience of Charles Frankel, who worked as a United States Assistant Secretary of State in the 1960s. When Frankel sent out letters merely to get information about what US officials were doing with regard to particular programmes, he got back replies indicating that 'the officials to whom he had written had changed what they were doing after receiving his letter' (Morgan 1994: 37). Merely in an effort to inform himself he had 'apparently produced changes in policy', i.e. in the phenomena which he was studying (Frankel 1969: 83; quoted in Morgan 1994: 37).

Researchers in our field can get around these problems by using unobtrusive methods of data collection. Using content analysis, researchers can get material on decision-making without interviewing the decision-makers. They can systematically analyse an official's statements for evidence concerning his or her perceptions and attitudes. They can analyse transcripts of a public hearing rather than depend on what government officials remember or choose to tell them about those hearings. In addition to reducing bias, analysing textual information can also enable researchers to gain access to subjects that may be difficult or impossible to research through direct, personal contact; and they can study larger populations and more documents than would be possible through either interviews or direct observation.

In sum, content analysis might be a way to reduce some types of bias and investigate a wider range of topics among a larger population of people. But whether content analysis is the appropriate analysis for your research project will depend on what evidence you need in order to investigate your hypothesis, and whether the evidence is at least partially embodied in texts.

Qualitative and quantitative content analysis

Content analysis can be either quantitative or qualitative. We tend to agree with Klaus Krippendorf, that '[u]ltimately, all reading of texts is qualitative, even when certain characteristics of a text are later converted into numbers' (2004: 16). However, quantitative and qualitative content analysis differ in the types of questions they address, as well as in the procedures they use both to analyse text and to record, process, and report data. Which method you employ will depend on your research question and the hypothesis you intend to investigate.

The development of *quantitative content analysis* was inspired 'by the need to develop a more objective and systematic method for analysing the rapidly increasing volume of communications produced by governments, companies, and other organizations' (Burnham et al. 2004: 236). It has been generally concerned with the **manifest content** of communications. This is the content that is easily observable—that resides on the surface of communication. An example would be to count the number of times a particular word, phrase, or image occurs in a communication. Quantitative analyses generally are concerned to tell us 'How often?' or 'How many?'

However, not all research questions can be answered by focusing on the manifest or surface content of texts. The meaning of the text, or the variables of interest to the researcher, may not reside on the surface of the content but 'between the lines'. *Qualitative content analysis* is more concerned with this **latent content**. Qualitative content analysis assumes that it is possible to expose the meanings, motives, and purposes embedded within the text, and to infer valid hidden or underlying meanings of interest to the researcher (Weber 1990: 72–6). It is generally more sensitive to the context in which texts are produced, and better able to tell us about meanings, norms, values, motives, and purposes. However, as we shall discuss later in this chapter, recent advances in computer-aided content analysis have also enabled quantitative analyses of content to uncover latent dimensions of texts.

Irrespective of whether you choose to conduct a quantitative or a qualitative content analysis, you will need to address the same considerations before embarking on a content analysis. You will need to decide what population of documents would provide evidence relevant to your hypothesis, what content you will examine and why, what kinds of data are required, whether they are available or they need to be collected, the kind of analysis that is required, and the resources needed. And, irrespective of whether your analysis is quantitative or qualitative, the procedures that you will need to follow to collect data are generally the same.

Steps

Quantitative and qualitative content analysis generally involves the same four steps. We can think of each of these steps as relating to a specific question that the researcher must ask and answer.

Step one

Question: What set of documents is germane to your research question, and what sample from this set will you analyse?

Answer: Select both the population of texts you will use and how much of this material is to be analysed.

The first step is to *select the material to be analysed*. This requires that you first *identify the population of texts* (documents or other communications) that will provide evidence appropriate to an investigation of your hypothesis. Once the population of relevant texts has been identified, you will need to be sure that all of the documents that you need from this population are available and accessible. If some cannot be located—if, for instance, there are missing years in a series of annual reports that you want to investigate—you may risk introducing bias into your analysis. Once you identify the population of relevant documents and ensure that they are available, you must decide whether to analyse the full set or a partial set of the material. If the document population is too large to be analysed in its entirety, you will need to *select a representative sample* of the material to investigate and analyse. Probability sampling may be the right choice if your intention is to generalize from the sample to the population. Non-probability sampling can be used if generalization is not necessary or if probability sampling procedures are not practical.

Depending on the aims of the analysis, you may choose textual data that belongs to a single semantic domain, e.g. political speeches, or that cuts across a number of semantic domains. Your data might consist of one particular text type (party manifestos, annual reports) or include texts belonging to different text types. The texts you select might contain only texts produced by a specific speaker or author, either of the same, or different, types; or they may be produced by different persons—as in the case of open responses to questions in surveys. The data can be obtained from an existing archive, or they may need to be collected. There exist a large number of electronic text archives containing text data from a large variety of sources, and online text databases with a wide variety of text material which can be directly accessed and downloaded. In addition, full texts of a variety of publications are available online.

Step two

Question: What will you examine these texts *for*?

Answer: Define categories.

Once you have selected both the population of texts you will use and how much of this material you will analyse, the second step is to *define the categories* or topics of interest that you will search for in the material you have selected to analyse. For a quantitative content analysis, this requires you to be clear about the variables you want information about: the subjects, things, or events that vary and that help to answer your research question. Then you must identify categories for each variable. For example, you might identify three categories related to the variable 'attitude towards the war': negative, neutral, and positive. Or you might often define five categories for the variable 'attitude towards the incumbent': greatly dislike, moderately dislike, indifferent to, moderately like, and greatly like.

Step three

Question: What segments of the text will contain what you are searching for?

Answer: Choose the recording unit.

The third step is to *choose the recording unit* (unit of content)—the portion or segment of text to which you will apply a category label. There are five recording units normally used in content-analytic studies.

1. A *single word or symbol*. This is generally the smallest unit that is used in content analysis research, and is an appropriate unit if you are studying the use of language. When words are the recording unit, researchers are usually interested in investigating the choice of certain words or counting the frequency with which they occur. *Word sense*—words that convey values (positive, negative, indifferent) or ideological positions—is a variation on words as recording units; and they can be counted just as if they were words.

2. A *sentence or paragraph*.

3. A *theme*. The boundary of a theme delineates a single idea, or 'a single assertion about some subject' (Holsti 1969: 116). This might be the recording unit in research on propaganda, values, attitudes, and beliefs.

4. A *character*. This might be the recording unit in studies of fiction, drama, movies, radio, and other forms of entertainment materials.

5. An *item or whole text*. This might be an entire article, film, book, or radio programme; a newspaper item, a magazine article, a web page or book, an episode of a TV programme, or a transcript of a radio interview.

Quantitative content analysts are generally more likely to divide texts into smaller segments: to count individual words, or examine phrases, word-strings, sentences, or paragraphs. Qualitative analysts tend to study documents in their entirety. In all cases, selection of recording units must be based upon the nature of the variables and the textual material to be coded. However, trade-offs among different options should also be considered. A recording unit that is objectively identifiable—one that has obvious physical (e.g. a whole text) or semantic boundaries (paragraphs, sentences, or words)—makes the coder's task relatively easy. However, while a recording unit that is objectively identifiable has its advantages, it may not properly encompass the categories being investigated. Sometimes a paragraph embraces too many ideas for there to be consistent assignment of the text segment to a single category. In fact, the larger the size of the recording unit, the more difficult and subjective is the work of coding, because as the size of the unit expands, so does the likelihood that the unit will encompass multiple variables.

Step four

Question: How will you identify, and signal the presence in your recoding units of, the categories you are looking for?

Answer: Creating (a) a coding protocol; and (b) a code for each variable, or a tag for each theme or topic, you are looking for; and (c) marking the text with the codes or tags.

Once these steps are completed, you are ready for the fourth step: **coding**. This involves (a) *creating a protocol* for identifying the target variables and categories; (b) *creating codes* that will signal their presence in the text; and (c) *coding* the texts using the protocol and codes.

(a) *Creating a protocol* involves developing a set of rules to ensure the reliability of the coding. The protocol will reflect a set of decisions that ensures that the researcher will code things consistently throughout the text, in the same way every time. For instance, the researcher has to decide whether to code only a predefined set of categories, or whether relevant categories not included in the set can be added as they are found in the text. Using a predetermined number and set of concepts allows the researcher to examine a text for very specific things. On the other hand, providing for flexibility allows new, important material to be incorporated into the coding process that could be significant for the findings of the analysis. Much quantitative analysis uses predetermined categories, though advances in computer technology (to be discussed later) have made it possible for quantitative analysis to uncover latent categories, rather than using predefined categories. Most qualitative content analysts prefer not to pre-set categories but to allow categories to emerge out of the data (Bryman 2004: 183).

Another decision is whether to code only for a given word, or also for words that imply that word. Can words be recorded as the same when they appear in different forms? For example, 'agree' might also appear as 'agreement'. The researcher needs to determine if two words are similar enough that they can be coded as being the same thing, i.e. 'agreeing words'. Researchers concerned to draw conclusions about the importance of a topic in the print or broadcast media might measure newspaper space (column inches) or radio or television air time.

These two decisions might best be understood as completing a sequence of steps in which you (1) ensure your analysis will be focused on the variable of interest to you (Step One, above); (2) determine the possible values each variable can take (Step Two, above); and (3) provide operational definitions of the variable's values that specify what phenomena you must observe to identify its existence (Step 3).

(b) Once you have created a protocol, you can then create a **code**, or short tag, for each variable's categories. Codes are simply abbreviations, or tags, for segments of text. Typically, a code will be an abbreviated version of a category. For example, a researcher coding three categories related to the variable 'attitude towards the war'—negative, neutral, and positive— might label these categories 'attwar*n*' (for negative), 'attwar*0*' (for neutral), and 'attwar*p*' (for positive).

(c) The final step is *coding*: marking recording units with the appropriate tags that you've designed to identify the categories being sought in the text. (Before you start, make sure each document from the set of working documents is recorded in a log and given a unique number. As the coding proceeds, record additional information, such as the name of the coder, the date it was coded, and unusual problems.)

Coding

Coding involves the identification of passages of text (or other meaningful phenomena, such as parts of images) and applying labels to them that indicate they are examples of some thematic idea. The coding process enables researchers quickly to retrieve and collect together all the text and other data that they have associated with some thematic idea so that they can be examined together, and different cases can be compared. We can distinguish between two broad approaches to coding: those using a priori codes, and those relying on grounded codes. A priori codes are based on a research hypothesis or a range of sources relating to it, such as previous research or theory, or topics from your interview schedule. Relying on a priori codes is what is often referred to as 'closed coding'. Grounded codes emerge from the data as the researcher reads it. The researcher puts aside presuppositions and previous knowledge of the subject area and concentrates, instead, on finding themes in the data. This is often referred to as 'open coding'. The most common way to go about developing grounded codes is through 'constant comparison'. What this means is that every time a researcher selects a passage of text and codes it, it is compared with all the passages that have already been coded that way. The researcher asks: 'What is this about?' and 'How does it differ from the preceding or following statements?' A list of the codes is drawn up, with a short definition attached to each one. Each time you find a passage that appears as though it might be coded with an existing code, you can check the coding frame or list to be sure that it fits with the definition. If there isn't an appropriate code, or the text doesn't fit with the definitions, then you can create a new one. Eventually, you may want to sort codes into groups. You may find several codes group together as types or kinds of something; that they refer to different ways that people react to, categorize, or cause something and so might be seen as dimensions of that thing (Strauss and Cobin 1990).

Of course you can move from one coding approach or strategy to another. For instance, some researchers suggest a three-stage coding process. In the first, 'open coding' phase, the researcher carefully reviews a small sample of the documents, making general notes about the broad themes that characterize each individual document, as well as the entire set of texts. In the second stage, all the documents are reviewed with these themes in mind. Patterns are labelled, and passages are 'tagged' as belonging to one or more categories. In the third stage, these labels and tags are checked and re-checked to ensure that they are applied properly (Neuman and Robson 2007: 337–42).

Manual and computer-assisted coding

Textual material can be coded manually, i.e. reading through the text and manually writing down concept occurrences; or it can be coded on the computer through the use of various computer programs.

In manual coding, the coder transcribes notes and interviews and copies transcripts and images; and then makes multiple copies of everything, as each item may represent an example of more than one theme or analytic idea. In open coding, perhaps using coloured highlighters, the coder marks the text by circling or underlining words, or running lines down the margins to indicate different meanings. In closed coding, the coder simply marks the boundaries of the recording unit and writes the code in the margin of the document, perhaps using different coloured pens for each variable. Next, the coder will cut up the transcripts and collect all the text fragments that are examples of similar themes or analytic ideas (open coding), or that are coded the same way (closed coding), into piles, envelopes, or folders. Each group of fragments can then be set out and re-read to discover more specific patterns or features of significance.

Coding can also be performed automatically with computer software that codes specific parts of text according to the particular categorization scheme you construct. A large number and variety of increasingly user-friendly computer software programs have been developed for this purpose.

Quantitative content analysis programs allow you to examine very large amounts of data, and a wide range of texts, quickly and efficiently. Among the widely used programs for quantitative content analysis are: General Inquirer, VBPro, Wordsmith, Textpack, TACT—Text, Analysis Computing Tools, and Textstat—a freeware program for the analysis of texts. There are also software programs that have been developed specifically for qualitative content analysis, including *Atlas/ti*, *NUD*IST*, and *HyperQual*. These allow the researcher to identify the recording unit in the text and assign the text to a coding category that has been defined either in advance or in the analysis process. They allow multiple coding of individual passages, and multiple coders to work on a single coding task while maintaining identification of the coder for calculation of reliability. A wide variety of reports can be generated from these packages, including counts of codes with illustrative quotations from the text.

Computer Assisted Qualitative Data Analysis Software (CAQDAS) allows researchers to use computer-based directories and files rather than physical files and folders, and to use word processors to annotate texts. CAQDAS packages, like QSR NVivo, help to organize and analyse data in documents, as well as in pictures, audio, and video.

Dictionary-based content analysis programs provide a 'basic handful' of text analysis functions, including word and category frequency counting and analysis, sorting, and simple statistical tests. 'Word frequency' refers to how often each word occurs in a document. Most operating systems (Windows, Mac OSX, Unix/Linux) have utilities to perform basic word counting and sorting. But software packages allow you to exclude 'stopwords', common words like 'in' and 'the' which add little meaning but get in the way of the analysis. They can produce a key words in context (**KWIC**) concordance—a list of the principal words in the document, in alphabetical order, and their immediate context. They also include lemmatization, which involves combining all words with the same stem, such as intend, intended, intends, intending, intent, intention, intentions, etc. For *category frequencies*, programs will group synonyms into categories and then show how many times each category occurs in the document. For example, the Linguistic Inquiry and Word Count (LIWC) dictionary maps onto the category 'death' the following words: ashes, burial*, buried, bury, casket*, cemet*, coffin*, cremat*, dead death*, decay*, decease*, deteriorat*, die, died, dies, drown*, dying fatal, funeral*, grave*, grief, griev*, kill*, mortal*, mourn*, murder*, suicid*, terminat* to LIWC category 59, death. The asterisks tell the program to treat all words matching a stem or stem word as belonging to the same category (Lowe 2007: 2). By collecting into a single category different words or phrases that represent a concept, category counts helps to make manifest the latent content in texts.

Another set of programs contains *annotation aids* (e.g. Win MAX-97 PRO; QSR NUD*IST; ATLAS.ti). These consist of an electronic version of the set of marginal notes and cross-references that researchers use when marking up transcripts by hand in order to analyse them and discover patterns.

An instructive example of the purposes for which researchers use the systematic analysis of political texts is the work of the Comparative Manifestos Project (CMG). The CMG is a large and influential quantitative content analysis project concerned with measuring the policy positions of political parties. The Comparative Manifesto Project produced quantitative content analyses of parties' election programs from 51 parliamentary democracies covering all democratic elections since 1945. This has become a widely used data set for party positions.

The Comparative Manifestos Project (previously known as the Manifesto Research Group) was formed in 1979.[1] The CMP undertook to measure the political preferences of parties across time and space through a comparative content analysis of political parties' election manifestos. Party manifestos are the programmes political parties issue for elections in some parliamentary democracies. They are authoritative party policy statements which set out both their strategic direction and the legislative proposals they intend to pursue should they win sufficient support to serve in government. The political researchers involved in the project were interested in addressing two questions: (1) what political issues divided post-war political parties; and (2) were they converging or diverging in ideological or policy terms? Anthony Downs' influential model of two-party competition leads to the expectation of party convergence to the policy position espoused by the median voter (Downs 1957: 112–19). MRG researchers were concerned to find out whether this actually occurred.

To estimate the policy position of a particular party on a particular matter at a particular election, the CMP used a trained human coder to manually code the party's election manifesto.[2] First, a classification scheme was developed consisting of 57 policy-coding categories. The unit of analysis that was used was a 'quasi-sentence'. A quasi-sentence is defined as 'an argument or phrase which is the verbal expression of one idea or meaning' (Klingemann et al., 2006: xxiii). Since long sentences may contain more than one argument, breaking up text into quasi-sentences enables researchers to isolate individual ideas so that they can be analysed. Coding consisted of allocating every quasi-sentence contained in a party's manifesto to one, and only one, of the 57 categories (one of which was 'uncoded'). A left–right position measure is calculated by grouping issue categories into 'right' and 'left' categories and subtracting one from the other.

Once text units were allocated to each category and counted, the CMP then defined the relative salience for the party of the policy area defined by each category as the percentage of all text units allocated to that category. The coding scheme derived from the documents themselves. Researchers found that relative emphases were the way in which British parties expressed themselves. Parties compete with each other by emphasizing different policy priorities, rather than by directly opposing each other on the same issues. So, for instance, political opposition was expressed by emphasizing peace, as opposed to military strength, freedom as opposed to planning. So the analysis was not concerned with counting *positive* or *negative* references made to different policy areas, but the *relative emphasis* parties placed on these categories.

The CMP data are generated by party manifestos coded once, and once only, by a single human coder. Though manual coding has advantages, the coding protocol had disadvantages. The manual analysis of party manifestos is an extremely time-consuming and costly process. Moreover, there is a potential for coding bias because human coders are inevitably aware of the authorship of the texts they are coding. These flaws in its manual coding encouraged CMP researchers to develop computer programs for the content analysis of party positions. A major step forward was the development of a fully automated text analysis program for measuring policy positions of texts called Wordscores (Laver et al. 2003). Wordscores uses references texts and references values in order to predict policy positions. The basic idea is that we can estimate policy positions by comparing two sets of texts: 'reference texts', documents for which we know the policy positions (e.g. by relying on expert surveys), and 'virgin texts', documents about which we do not know anything apart from the words they contain. A more recent innovation in quantitative content analysis of party positions, *Wordfish*, is a program that uses a statistical model of word counts, rather than anchoring documents. *Wordfish* estimates the policy positions of political actors based on the assumption that words are distributed according to a poisson distribution (the probability of a number of events occurring in a specified interval) (Proksch and Slapin 2009).

Computerized coding is easier, more flexible, less costly and labour intensive; and by removing the human factor from the coding process, it can significantly enhance the reliability of the content analysis. Thus, efforts to develop programs that resolve shortcomings in these methods are continuing; and because of the salience of the work generated by the CMP, the innovations of CMP researchers in this area have become one of the primary impetuses behind the move to computerized content analysis in political research, more generally.

Analysis

Analysis is the process of making sense and attaching meaning to the data we have gathered, and applying the resulting knowledge to our research question.

Once the coding is done, the researcher examines the data for patterns and insights relevant to the key research issues. The codes might be combined or sorted into families for more meaningful analysis. The data is analysed either to describe the target variable(s), or to identify themes or relationships between variables. The researcher then attempts to draw conclusions and generalizations by linking the data back to the research question. Irrespective of whether the data are quantitative or qualitative, the analysis will involve an attempt to inferentially link the textual data to the specific events, behaviour, or phenomena that are of interest to the researcher.

In a quantitative content analysis, analysis involves examining numerical data in relation to pre-operationalized variables, and drawing inferences based on the frequency, amount, salience, or intensity of a category (i.e. the intensity of a person's opinions or attitudes). The inferences drawn will be based on what resides on the surface of communication, i.e. what has been said, and on the observation of patterns that are explicitly present, but which may have been hard to see just by reading all the texts. The researcher may also be able to discover relationships among those patterns, and to identify much larger trends or ideas from the patterns; and, if the research involves charting changing language or other textual features over time, the researcher can draw inferences about political change. Qualitative data is non-numerical (words, images). Its analysis is conceptual, and involves identifying themes that emerge from the data. Quantitative content analysts report their data largely in numeric form, be it statistical, graphical, tabular, or figural. They may use frequency scores to generate 'word clouds' (or 'tag clouds'), which use the frequency of words in a given piece of text to generate a visual representation of the document. Qualitative content analysts rely on quotations and narrative as their primary modes of presentation. Some also draw concept maps, charts, diagrams, or other figures to visually represent the patterns in their data. The differences in how quantitative and qualitative researchers typically conduct a content analysis are summarized in Box 13.1, below.

BOX 13.1 Quantitative and Qualitative Content Analysis

	Quantitative	Qualitative
Objects of observation	Manifest content: word usage, sequences	Latent content: meanings, motives, purposes
Recording units (units of observation)	Segments of text	Whole texts
Procedures of observation	Counting, rating, logging	Themeing, tagging, memoing
Discovery of patterns	Calculated during analysis	Developed throughout process
Presentation of data	Graphs, tables, statistics, figures, word clouds	Quotations, concept maps, narrative
Data format	Numerical (frequency, amount, salience, intensity)	Non-numerical (words, images)
Data reduction	Variables (operationalized a priori)	Themes (emergent)
Substance of data	Meaning is inherent	Meaning is contingent
Data recording	Standardized instrument	Variable instrument
Data processing	Mathematical	Conceptual
Data reporting	Statistical, graphical	Verbal
Standards of evidence	Probability	Plausibility

Source: Adapted from Wesley (2011: table 6.2).

Validity and reliability

As with any method of data collection, researchers using content analysis must be concerned with the validity of their analysis and the reliability of their results.

In quantitative studies, validity refers to the extent to which we can draw unambiguous conclusions from our results, and whether our conclusions are likely to apply to other similar situations or cases. A study is valid if its measures actually measure what you claim they measure, and if your inferences follow from the data. Reliability refers to the 'repeatability' or 'consistency' of your findings. A study is reliable if anyone else following the same procedures would get the same results. The reliability of a content analysis study depends on three elements. The first is *coder stability*: does the same coder consistently re-code the same data in the same way over a period of time? Second, is *reproducibility*: do the coding schemes lead to the same text being coded in the same category by two or more coders?[3] Different people should code the same text in the same way. The third element is *objectivity*. **Intercoder reliability** reveals objectivity by showing the extent to which different coders, each coding the same content, come to the same coding decisions (Rourke et al. 2001: 13).

There are a number of common sources of unreliability:

1. a document is poorly written or vague;

2. word meanings, category definitions, or other rules in the coding instructions are ambiguous;

3. there is a lack of objectivity in the process of category definition and in the coding of sections of text;

4. the coder makes mistakes.

In qualitative analysis, the results of a study are valid and reliable to the degree that they are plausible to others: i.e. if the researcher explains how s/he came up with the analysis in a way that the reader can make sense of.

Both quantitative and qualitative content analysts should make both their data and raw materials available for verification (i.e. coding databases, memos, and the original documents). In quantitative content analysis, which uses a standardized coding instrument, this is most efficiently accomplished through the publication of the coding manual, including a comprehensive list of coding rules. Qualitative analysts must provide their readers with a detailed account of the coding 'protocol', including how conclusions were reached (Altheide 1996: 25–33). As Holliday suggests, all research 'needs to be accompanied by accounts of how it was really done... [Analysts must] reveal how they negotiated complex procedures to deal with the "messy" reality of the scenarios being studied' (2007: 7).

Using documents, archival sources, and historical writing as data

It is worth briefly considering documents, archival sources, and historical writing as sources of data. It is usual to distinguish between *primary* and *secondary* sources, with documents and archival material of various sorts falling within the former category, and historical writing belonging to the latter.

Primary sources refer to those materials which are written or collected by those who actually witnessed events which they describe. A primary source provides direct or first-hand evidence about an event, object, or person; and shows minimal or no mediation between the document/artefact and its creator. Examples of primary sources include letters, manuscripts, diaries, journals, newspaper and magazine articles (factual accounts), speeches, interviews, memoirs, documents and records produced by government agencies, recorded or transcribed speeches, interviews with participants or witnesses of an event, or with people who lived during a particular time; photographs, maps, postcards, posters, audio or video recordings, research data, and objects or artefacts such as works of art, buildings, tools, and weapons.

Participants in the political processes we are concerned to understand generate official records in the form of party programmes, parliamentary proceedings, resolutions, speeches, treaties, press conferences and press reports, television and radio interviews, and correspondence. These come from a variety of participants, including civil servants, members of advisory councils, and representatives of pressure groups involved in decision-making processes. Primary sources are also called archival data because they are kept in museums, archives, libraries, or private collections. There are many different types of archival sources. Some documents (e.g. government surveys and research projects) are produced with the aim of research in mind; others (e.g. diaries) are produced for personal use. The archive repositories (or record offices) maintained by national and local governments contain a wide range of official records, but also considerable quantities of 'private' material of potential value to researchers. Other types of archives containing material such as autobiographies, memoirs, or oral histories are found in university and other libraries or more specialized locations. Documents vary in their degree of accessibility, from closed (e.g. secret police files) or restricted (e.g. medical files and confidential corporate reports), to open-archival (e.g. census reports) and open-published (e.g. government budget statistics).

To assess the evidentiary value of a primary source, it is important to consider its intended audience, and the circumstances in which it was produced. Alexander George and Andrew Bennett counsel researchers to ask four questions when assessing primary documents: (1) who is speaking; (2) to whom are they speaking (even unsolicited documents for personal use are addressed to an audience); (3) for what purpose are they speaking; and (4) under what circumstances (2005: 99)?

A great deal of political research relies on secondary sources. *Secondary sources* are materials produced sometime after an event happened. They contain information that has been interpreted, commented, analysed, or processed in some way. Biographies, histories, encyclopedias, newspaper articles that interpret, or journal articles and books written by social scientists are all secondary sources. Ultimately, all source materials of whatever type must be assessed critically. But here we want to focus on the particular issues that arise for political research that relies on the work of historians for data and evidence.

Many political researchers draw on historical studies to find out what history can tell us about contemporary events, to develop typologies of political phenomena, or to account for different patterns of political and socio-economic development. Political researchers who draw on historical sources for evidence must consider two related issues.

The first issue concerns the extent to which we can treat the work of historians as reliable reports of past political or social realities. Political researchers need to recognize that the work of historians cannot be treated as unproblematic sources of 'facts', and that it is not possible to use an historical account as a 'theoretically neutral' background narrative. Historical accounts contain errors, biases, exclusions, and exaggerations. They reflect the historian's personal commitments and, more generally, their implicit theories of or perspectives on human behaviour. Recall our discussion in Chapter 3 about the argument, advanced by Thomas Kuhn and others, that observation is 'theory-laden'. According to this argument, our observation of 'facts' cannot be separated from the theoretical notions which give intelligibility to what we observe. What we call 'observation' is the interpretation of a phenomenon in the light of some *theory* and other background knowledge.

Consequently, as Ian Lustick points out, 'the work of historians... cannot legitimately be treated by others as, an unproblematic background narrative from which theoretically neutral data can be elicited for the framing of problems and the testing of theories' (Lustick 1996: 605). He points out that what we think we know about a period is not the 'result of an objective sifting and reporting of what primary sources and artifacts contain, but the result, first and foremost, of imaginative constructions of lives and events, which, woven into particular overarching narratives, seemed natural, convincing, or useful to these historians as vehicles for the claims they wished to advance' (Lustick 1997: 606).

This raises a second issue that political researchers must confront when they use historical studies as evidence. If there is no theoretically neutral historical record, if different authors offer vastly different interpretations about the same historical events, how are the background historical narratives which we use in historically grounded research to be chosen from among the available accounts? In the absence of a single 'historical record' on which we can rely, what set of rules can guide us in distinguishing 'accurate' from 'inaccurate' historical accounts?

The problem for political researchers is to choose from the available sources in a way that avoids 'selection bias'—i.e. a bias towards those accounts which fit with the argument being investigated and defended. The danger of selection bias arises whenever we must choose among conflicting, or partially conflicting, available historical accounts. The 'nub of the issue', as Ian Lustick points out, is that the search for available studies in order to form an evidentiary base for an argument 'may well entail, and can logically be supposed to entail, a heavy selection bias toward works by historians using implicit theories about how events unfold and how people behave very similar to the theory under consideration by the social scientist' (Lustick 1996: 607). It is natural that we will find most interesting those accounts that seem to best fit with the concepts and categories that our arguments employ. The chosen interpretation will likely coincide with or be supportive of the argument that is being 'tested'. We tend to adopt sources that suit the theory that we are testing, because we tend to find most convincing those accounts that fit with our theory (Lustick 1996: 614).

How do we choose from among these differing accounts of the past? Lustick suggests several strategies to address this issue. First, include an analysis of patterns across the range of historical accounts relating to your topic. Second, look for regularities that appear across otherwise different or contradictory accounts—accounts based on different approaches or on different archival sources, or which develop different perspectives or reach different conclusions. Third, note alternative versions, other sources that are available and that contradict those on which you rely, i.e. those that tell a different story. Justify your choices. You can limit the amount of additional space this might take by 'limiting use of this technique to elements of the background narrative that are either particularly controversial within existing historiography or that are particularly salient for the theoretical argument under review'.

We conclude with two points regarding the use of documents, archival sources, and historical writing as data.

The first point is that the choice of sources, as in every choice made in the research process, depends on what is required for developing a meaningful and persuasive investigation of your research question. The second point is the need for self-consciousness in the selection of source material. You must be critical and rigorous, both in terms of how you do your own research and how you evaluate the research of others. Researchers must be self-aware and critical about the choices they make, and make the considerations that enter into those choices clear and transparent to others.

 ## Conclusions

This chapter has outlined two main forms of textual analysis. Each of the two forms of textual analysis—discourse analysis and content analysis—provides insights into political phenomena: discourse analysis through examining how discursive practices construct the identities of subjects and objects and exercise power; qualitative content analysis through exploring the meanings, motives, and purposes of political action embedded within texts; and quantitative content analysis by drawing inferences about opinions or attitudes from an analysis of the usage and frequency of words, phrases, and images, and the patterns they form within a text. Despite their very real differences, similar standards apply to both forms of textual analysis. Both must be trustworthy in their treatment of documents. Both must be concerned with the validity and reliability of their procedures and conclusions.

Box 13.2 summarizes the differences and similarities among these forms and approaches to textual analysis.

Which of the two forms of textual analysis is 'better' than the others can only be determined in relation to a specific research project, and will depend on the research question, what sort of analysis will provide a useful response to it, and what data are needed and from whom. As we have previously emphasized, techniques of data collection are always employed in the service of a research question. As with any method of data collection, the use of discourse and content analysis should be appropriate to the research question and hypothesis you are investigating. The data collected by these means do not 'speak for themselves'. They are only interesting and significant to the extent that they provide a means of investigating a research question and hypothesis. You choose these means of data collection because you are confident that the data that they provide will enable you to investigate and draw logical conclusions about your hypothesis.

Unlike asking people questions (e.g. through surveys or in interviews), using texts to collect data has the advantage of being non-intrusive. Researchers do not face the problem of influencing their data source through the questions they ask, and they can study past policy positions as they were recorded at the time. Once recorded, texts do not change.

 ## Questions

- What do discourse and content analysis offer to political analysis?
- How do you know when you've identified a discourse? Where are its boundaries? Do discourses overlap? In what context or set of conditions does a discourse exist?
- How can you evaluate whether, when, and how political texts have effects on political life?

BOX 13.2 Discourse Analysis and Content Analysis Compared

	Discourse analysis	Content analysis	
		Qualitative	Quantitative
Ontology	Constructionist—assumes that reality is socially constructed	There is no inherent meaning in the text; meanings are constructed in a particular context; and the author, consumer, and researcher all play a role	Realist—assumes that an independent reality exists
Epistemology	Meaning is fluid and constructs reality in ways that can be posited through the use of interpretive methods		Meaning is fixed and reflects reality in ways that can be ascertained through the use of scientific methods
Data source	Textual meaning, usually in relation to other texts, as well as practices of production, dissemination, and consumption		Textual content in comparison to other texts, for example over time
Method	Qualitative (although can involve counting)	Qualitative (although can involve counting)	Quantitative
Categories	Exploration of how participants actively construct categories	Categories emerge from the data, though the research question, existing empirical research, and theory provide ideas for what to look for	Analytical categories taken for granted and data allocated to them
Inductive/ deductive	Inductive	Inductive	Deductive
Subjectivity/ objectivity	Subjective	Subjective	Objective
Role of context	Texts can be understood only in discursive context	Can only understand texts in discursive context	Does not necessarily link text to context
Reliability	Formal measures are not a factor, but coding is justified according to academic norms; different interpretations are not a problem and may be a source of data	The results are reliable to the degree that they are plausible to others: i.e. does the researcher explain how s/he came up with the analysis in a way that the reader can make sense of?	Formal measures of intercoder reliability are crucial for measurement purposes; differences in interpretation are problematic and risk nullifying any results

| Validity | Validity in the form of demonstrating a plausible case that patterns in the meaning of texts are constitutive of reality in some way | The results are valid to the degree that they show how patterns in the meaning of texts are constitutive of reality | Validity is in the form of accuracy and precision—demonstrating that patterns in the texts are accurately measured and reflect reality |
| Reflexivity | Necessarily high—author is part of the process whereby meaning is constructed | Considers the extent to which the author plays a role in making meaning; and different ways a meaning might be consumed | Not necessarily high—author simply reports on objective findings |

Source: Adapted from Hardy et al. (2004: 20-1).

- With what general type of research questions is content analysis concerned?
- What is the difference between manifest and latent content? What are the implications of this distinction for content analysis?
- If politics is about power, and language has power, is political analysis a matter of analysing language?
- In what ways might your analysis address the issue of selection bias when using historical writing as data?

 ## Guide to Further Reading

Discourse analysis

Clayman, S. and J. Heritage (2002), *The News Interview: Journalists and Public Figures on the Air* (Cambridge: Cambridge University Press).

Fairclough, N. (2002), *Analysing Discourse: Textual Analysis for Social Research* (London: Routledge).
An introduction to discourse analysis, drawing on a variety of texts, from political speeches and television news reports to management consultancy reports and texts concerning globalization, to illustrate key issues in discourse analysis.

Gee, J. P. (2005), *An Introduction to Discourse Analysis: Theory and Method*, 2nd edition (New York: Routledge).
This is an introduction to discourse analysis that presents both a theory of language-in-use and a method of research. Its aim is to demonstrate how language, both spoken and written, enacts social and cultural perspectives and identities.

Hopf, T. (2004), 'Discourse and Content Analysis: Some Fundamental Incompatibilities', *Qualitative Methods Newsletter* (Spring): 31-3.

Howarth, D. R. Norval, J, Aletta, and Y. Stavrakakis (eds) (2000), *Discourse Theory and Political Analysis: Identities, Hegemonies and Social Change* (Manchester: Manchester University Press).
Case study chapters show how discourse analysis can be applied.

Milliken, J. (1999), 'The Study of Discourse in International Relations: A Critique of Research and Methods', *European Journal of International Relations* 5(2) (June): 225-54.

Multi-Author Symposium (2004), 'Discourse and Content Analysis', *Qualitative Methods* (Spring): 15–38.

Raymond, G. (2000), 'The Voice of Authority: The Local Accomplishment of Authoritative Discourse in Live News Broadcasts', *Discourse Studies* 2: 354–79.

Ricento, T. (2003), 'The Discursive Construction of Americanism', *Discourse & Society* 14(5): 611–37.

Shenhav, S. R. (2006), 'Political Narratives and Political Reality', *International Political Science Review* 27(3): 245–62.

Symposium: Discourse Analysis and Content Analysis (2004), *Newsletter of the American Political Science Association Organized Section on Qualitative Methods* 2(1): 15–39.

Content analysis

Hopkins, D., and G. King (forthcoming), 'A Method of Automated Nonparametric Content Analysis for Social Science', *American Journal of Political Science*, available at http://gking.harvard.edu/files/abs/words-abs.shtml.

Johnston, A. I. (1995), *Cultural Realism: Strategic Culture and Grand Strategy in Chinese History* (Princeton, NJ: Princeton University Press).
A highly effective example of content analysis using ancient Chinese texts to assess beliefs and predicted behaviour.

Kohlbacher, Florian (2005), 'The Use of Qualitative Content Analysis in Case Study Research', *Forum: Qualitative Social Research* 7, available at http://www.qualitative-research.net/index.php/fqs/article/viewArticle/75/153.
A basic introduction is given to qualitative content analysis as an interpretation method for qualitative interviews and other data material. Useful for understanding how content analysis can contribute to qualitative case study research.

Krippendorff, K. (2004), *Content Analysis: An Introduction to its Methodology*, 2nd edition (Thousand Oaks, CA: Sage Publications).

—— and M. A. Bock (eds) (2008), *The Content Analysis Reader* (Thousand Oaks, CA: Sage Publications).
Fifty-one papers grouped around the following topics: the history and conception of content analysis, unitizing and sampling, inferences and analytic constructs, coders and coding, categories and data language, reliability and validity, computer-aided content analysis.

Lewis, R. B. (2004), 'NVivo 2.0 and Atlis.ti 5.0: A Comparative Review of Two Popular Qualitative Data-Analysis Programs', *Field Methods* 16(4): 439–69.

Mayring, Philipp (2000), 'Qualitative Content Analysis', *Forum: Qualitative Social Research* 1, available at http://www.qualitative-research.net/index.php/fqs/article/view/1089.
The author describes an approach of systematic, rule-guided qualitative text analysis, including the central procedures of qualitative content analysis, inductive development of categories, and deductive application of categories.

Monroe, B. L., M. P. Colaresi, and K. M. Quinn (2008), '"Fightin" Words: Lexical Feature Selection and Evaluation for Identifying the Content of Political Conflict', *Political Analysis* 16: 372–403.

—— and P. A. Schrodt (2008), 'Introduction to the Special Issue: The Statistical Analysis of Political Text', *Political Analysis* 16: 351–5.

Neuendorf, Kimberly A. (2002), *The Content Analysis Handbook* **(Thousand Oaks, CA: Sage Publications).**
Covers the history of content analysis, sampling message units, handling variables, reliability, and use of NEXIS for text acquisition. Also covers PRAM, software for reliability assessment with multiple coders.

Riffe, D., S. Lacey, and F.G. Fico (2006), *Analyzing Media Messages: Using Quantitative Content Analysis in Research* **(Mahwah, NJ: Lawrence Erlbaum).**
A comprehensive guide to conducting quantitative content analysis. Provides step-by-step instruction on designing a content analysis study; and detailed discussion of measurement, sampling, reliability, data analysis, and validity.

 # References

Altheide, D. L. (1996), 'Reflections: Ethnographic Content Analysis', *Qualitative Sociology* 10(1): 65–77.

Austin, J. L. (1962), *How to do Things with Words* (Oxford: Clarendon Press).

Benoit, K., M. Laver, and S. Mikhaylov (2009), 'Treating Words as Data with Error: Uncertainty in Text Statements of Policy Positions', *American Journal of Political Science* 53(2) (April): 495–513.

Billig, M. and E. Schegloff (1999), 'Critical Discourse Analysis and Conversation Analysis: An Exchange between Michael Billig and Emanuel A. Schegloff', *Discourse & Society* 10(4): 543–82.

Bryman, A. (2004). *Social Research Methods*, 2nd edition (Oxford: Oxford University Press).

Burnham, P., K. Gilland, W. Grant, Z. Layton-Henry (2004), *Research Methods in Politics* (Basingstoke: Palgrave Macmillan).

Dixon, T. and D. Linz (2000), 'Race and the Misrepresentation of Victimization on Local Television News', *Communication Research* 27(5) (October): 547–73.

Downs, A. (1957), *An Economic Theory of Democracy* (New York: Harper).

Escobar, A. (1994), *Encountering Development: The Making and Unmaking of the Third World* (Princeton, NJ: Princeton University Press).

Fairclough, N. (1995), *Media Discourse* (London: Edward Arnold).

—— (2001), *Language and Power* (London: Longmans).

—— (2005a), 'Critical Discourse Analysis, Organizational Discourse, and Organizational Change', *Organization Studies* 26: 915–39.

—— (2005b), 'Blair's Contribution to Elaborating a New Doctrine of "International Community"', *Journal of Language and Politics* 4(1): 41–63.

Foucault, M. (1972), *The Archaeology of Knowledge and the Discourse on Language* (New York: Pantheon).

Frankel, C. (1969), *High on Foggy Bottom: An Outsider's Inside View of the Government* (New York: Harper and Row).

George, A. and A. Bennett (2005), *Case Studies and Theory Development in the Social Sciences* (Cambridge, MA: Belfer Center for Science and International Affairs).

Hall, S. (1988), *The Hard Road to Renewal: Thatcherism and the Crisis of the Left* (London: Verso).

Hardy, C. (2001), 'Researching Organizational Discourse', *International Studies in Management and Organization* 31(3): 25–47.

Hardy, C., B. Harley, and N. Phillips (2004), 'Discourse Analysis and Content Analysis: Two Solitudes?' *Qualitative Methods: Newsletter of the American Political Science Association Organized Section on Qualitative Methods. Symposium: Discourse and Content Analysis* (Spring): 19–22.

Holliday, Adrian (2007), *Doing and Writing Qualitative Research*, 2nd edn (Thousand Oaks: Sage Publications).

Holsti, O. R. (1969), *Content Analysis for the Social Sciences and Humanities* (Reading, MA: Addison-Wesley).

Hopf, T. (2004), 'Discourse and Content Analysis: Some Fundamental Incompatibilities', *Qualitative Methods: Newsletter of the American Political Science Association Organized Section on Qualitative Methods. Symposium: Discourse and Content Analysis* (2004): 31–3.

Klingemann, H.-D., A.Volkens, J. Bara, I. Budge, and M. McDonald (2006), *Mapping Policy Preferences II: Estimates for Parties, Electors, and Governments in Eastern Europe, European Union and OECD 1990–2003* (Oxford: Oxford University Press).

Krippendorf, K. (2004), *Content Analysis: An Introduction to its Methodology*, 2nd edition (Thousand Oaks, CA: Sage Publications).

Laffey, M.and J. Weldes (2004), 'Methodological Reflections on Discourse Analysis', *Methods: Newsletter of the American Political Science Association Organized Section on Qualitative Methods* (Spring): 28–30.

Laver, M., K. Benoit, and J. Garry (2003), 'Estimating the Policy Positions of Political Actors Using Words as Data', *American Political Science Review* 97(2): 311–31.

Lemke, J. L. (1998), 'Analysing Verbal Data: Principles, Methods and Problems', in B. J. Fraser and K. Tobin (eds), *International Handbook of Science Education* (Dordrecht: Kluwer), 1175–89.

Lowe, W. (2007), *Software for Content Analysis— A Review*, 22 March, available at http://kb.ucla. edu/system/datas/5/original/content_analysis. pdf.

—— (2008), 'Understanding Wordscores', *Political Analysis* 16(4): 356–71.

Lustick, I. (1996), 'History, Historiography, and Political Science: Multiple Historical Records and the Problem of Selection Bias', *American Political Science Review* (September): 605–18.

Morgan, P. M. (1994), *Theories and Approaches to International Politics: What Are We to Think?* 4th edition (New Brunswick, NJ: Transaction Publishers).

Neuman, W. L. and K. Robson (2007), *Basics of Social Research: Qualitative and Quantitative Approaches* (Toronto: Pearson).

Potter, J. and M. Wetherell (1994), 'Analysing Discourse', in A. Bryman and R. Burgess (eds), *Analysing Qualitative Data* (London: Routledge), 47–66.

Proksch, S.-O., and J. B. Slapin (2009), 'Position Taking in European Parliament Speeches', *British Journal of Political Science* 40(3): 587–611.

Rapley, T. (2008), *Doing Conversation, Discourse, and Document Analysis* (London: Sage Publications).

Rourke, L., T. Anderson, D. R. Garrison, and W. Archer (2001), 'Methodological Issues in the Content Analysis of Computer Conference Transcripts', *International Journal of Artificial Intelligence in Education* 12: 8–22.

Searle, J. R. (1969), *Speech Acts: An Essay in the Philosophy of Language* (Cambridge: Cambridge University Press).

Strauss, A. and J. Corbin (1990), *Basics of Qualitative Research: Grounded Theory Procedures and Techniques* (Newbury Park, CA: Sage Publications).

Titscher, S., M. Meyer, R. Wodak, and E. Vetter (2000), *Methods of Text and Discourse Analysis* (London: Sage Publications).

van Dijk, T. A. (2001), 'Critical Discourse Analysis', in D. Tannen, D. Schiffrin, and H. Hamilton (eds), *Handbook of Discourse Analysis* (Oxford: Blackwell), 352–71.

—— (2002), 'Discourse and Racism', in D. Goldberg and J. Solomos (eds), *The Blackwell Companion to Racial and Ethnic Studies* (Oxford: Blackwell), 145–59.

—— (2004), 'Racist Discourse', in E. Cashmore (ed.), *Routledge Encyclopedia of Race and Ethnic Studies* (London: Routledge), 351–55.

Weber, R. P. (1990), *Basic Content Analysis*, 2nd edition (Newbury Park, CA: Sage Publications).

Weldes, J. (1996), 'Constructing National Interests', *European Journal of International Relations* 2(3): 275–318.

Wesley, Jared J. (2011), 'Observing the Political World: Quantitative and Qualitative Approaches', in Keith Archer and Loleen Youngman-Berdahl (eds), *Explorations: A Navigator's Guide to Research in Canadian Political Science*, 2nd edition (Toronto: Oxford University Press).

Wetherell, M. (1998), 'Positioning and Interpretive Repertoires: Conversation Analysis and Post-structuralism in Dialogue', *Discourse & Society* 9(3): 387–412.

Wittgenstein, L. (1980) *Culture and Value* (Oxford: Blackwell).

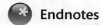

Endnotes

1. The MRG was formed by Ian Budge and David Robertson, both at that time in the Department of Government, University of Essex. It was constituted formally as a Research Group of the European Consortium for Political Research (ECPR), which obtained funding to support most of its work in the 1980s.

2. The full coding process is described in Benoit et al. (2009).

3. The simplest and most common method of reporting intercoder reliability is the *percent agreement* statistic. This statistic reflects the number of agreements per total number of coding decisions. 'Percent agreement after discussion' refers to reliability figures that were obtained through discussion between coders. Holsti's (1969) coefficient of reliability (CR) provides a formula for calculating percent agreement:

    CR = 2m/n1 + n2, where:

    m = the number of coding decisions upon which the two coders agree

    n1 = number of coding decisions made by rater 1

    n2 = number of coding decisions made by rater 2.

Quantitative Analysis: Description and Inference

 Chapter Summary

This chapter provides an introduction to quantitative analysis with a focus on description and inference. We discuss the different ways in which we can summarize data for a single variable from our sample and use it to make inferences about the wider population from which the sample was drawn. In particular, we focus on two of the key building blocks in quantitative research to do with measures of central tendency and measures of dispersion. The chapter contains:

- overview of analysis;
- univariate analysis;
- levels of measurement;
- methods of analysis;
- descriptive statistics;
- central tendency;
- dispersion;
- inferential statistics.

Introduction

Quantitative methods are one of the most widely used techniques in political research. They are used to answer a wide variety of questions, to do with democracy and democratization (Przeworski et al. 2000; Gleditsch and Ward 2006), civil war (Gleditsch 2007) and ethnic conflict (Wilkinson 2004), and to do with public opinion (Wlezien 1995; Bartle et al. 2011), elections, and voting behaviour (Clarke et al. 2004, 2009; Franklin 2004). Whatever topic you are interested in studying in political research, it is hard to avoid coming across literature that uses quantitative methods. It is therefore an important method to understand. Yet for many students this is an off-putting prospect. To the untrained eye, quantitative research can seem intimidating and difficult to understand—closer to the study of statistics than politics. Yet in reality things are not as difficult as they first appear. What can look complicated on the surface is actually relatively straightforward, even sensible, in practice, and familiarity with just a few basic concepts and techniques can take you a very long way in a short space of time. It is therefore well worth the effort of trying to learn how to use and understand quantitative methods, even if this involves some initial discomfort. It will not only help you understand the work of others, but, perhaps more rewardingly, it will also enable you to do your own original research yourself. And these data-analysis skills are hard transferable skills that are also highly valued in the work place, and can help you get a job after you graduate.

In our experience students are sometimes apprehensive about learning quantitative methods. Yet in our experience this apprehension is also soon overcome. Indeed, learning how to do quantitative research is often an incredibly rewarding experience. It is not only rewarding to overcome your initial anxieties, but in the process, new possibilities also open up, providing you with new skills which you can take with you in your own research and in your future career. Moreover, the actual statistical component of quantitative research is actually a relatively minor part of the research process. Good quantitative research is based upon good research design, interesting hypotheses, and a careful reading and understanding of the relevant literature. These research skills are common to all types of political research.

This chapter, and the chapters that follow, provide an introduction to the principles of quantitative research and a step-by-step guide on how to use and interpret a range of commonly used techniques. We start with the basics. The first part of the chapter looks at the building blocks of quantitative analysis. We focus on different ways in which data can be summarized, both graphically and with tables. We introduce two important measures: the **mean** and the **standard deviation**. In the second part of the chapter, we move on to inferential statistics, and discuss how we can make generalizations. In doing so, we introduce the concept of confidence intervals, often known as the margin of error.

Descriptive and inferential statistics

The research process involves the dual goals of description and explanation (see King et al. 1994: chapter 2). Each is essential. We cannot construct meaningful explanations without a sound knowledge of what it is that needs to be explained. For example, there is a great deal of research which describes the political landscape. By describing the world around us, collecting data and information, we build up a picture of what is usual, or strange, or salient in some way, and what it is that is interesting to explain. Many of the questions we are interested in are therefore descriptive ones, the answers to which tell us something meaningful about the world we live in. Have people become less politically engaged? Is the media becoming more powerful? Are politicians corrupt? Is inequality increasing? How much power do domestic governments have over economic policy? Is there global warming? What is globalization? Has it increased? To what extent do Iraqis support democracy? To what extent do Afghanis support the Taliban? These sorts of questions are all descriptive (see Chapter 5). Sometimes we are interested in describing the present, such as how much people know about politics, and sometimes we are interested in describing patterns over time, such as whether Iraqis' support for democracy has increased or decreased since the US–UK-led invasion. Related to these descriptive questions, we then develop explanations that we can seek to test. Why are some people more politically engaged than others? Why has Iraqi support for democracy changed since the invasion?

In the following chapters we will examine the statistical association between two variables (**bivariate analysis**) and three or more variables (**multivariate analysis**). This allows us to test hypotheses about causality, and answer questions about why things happen. But before getting into explaining why something happens, it is first a good idea to describe what happens in the first place.

Description in quantitative research comprises two parts. The first is to describe the data that we have collected. Whether it is from survey data (Chapter 10), expert interviews (Chapter 11), textual data (13), or comparative aggregate data (Chapter 9), we can use descriptive statistics as a way of summarizing our sample data for a particular **variable**. But we can also use this information to try and make generalizations about the wider **population** from which the **sample** was drawn; that is, to make inferences. With inferential statistics, we can go from just talking about how many people in our sample support the far-right British National Party (BNP), to making inferences about what we think the true level of support for the BNP is in the population as a whole. Our ability to make this jump from describing our sample to making generalizations about the population rests on how we have collected the data in the first place. This is why probability samples are so important, because they create a statistical link between sample data that we have and the population that we want to make an inference about.

Levels of measurement

Quantitative analysis requires that the information or evidence that we have collected is converted into numbers. Sometimes it is fairly obvious what these numbers refer to, such as when we are recording a respondent's age or a country's GDP per capita. However, at other times it is not so intuitive, such as when we are recording a respondent's religion or a country's electoral system. How we interpret the numbers we assign to different variables then depends upon what the numbers actually refer to, and whether they are in a sense 'real numbers' or arbitrary codes for distinct categories.

There are different methods of summarizing data and the method that we use depends upon the type of variable we are examining, and how this variable is measured. We can distinguish between these different types of variable according to what is known as their **level of measurement**. Broadly speaking, there are three levels of measurement: nominal (also called categorical), ordinal, and interval (also called continuous or scale). We describe each of these below.

Nominal comes from the Latin for name. A **nominal** variable is one where the numbers assigned to the variable are interesting only in so far as the labels—or names—that are attached to them are interesting. To interpret the variable, we must know what the values refer to and the names of the different categories. For example, consider the following questions from the British Election Study. We can see that each response to the question is assigned a number, but these numbers do not refer to anything other than the label that they represent.

> Talking to people about the general election **on June 7th**, we have found that a lot of people didn't manage to vote. How about you? Did you manage to vote in the general election?

1. Yes, voted.

2. No.

[IF YES] Which party did you vote for in the general election?
[DO NOT PROMPT]

1. Conservative

2. Labour

3. Liberal Democrat

4. Scottish National Party

5. Plaid Cymru

6. Green Party

7. Other Party.

The fact that people who didn't vote are coded 2 and people that did vote are coded 1 does not mean that non-voters are twice as apathetic as voters. Although each of these responses is assigned a numerical value, the number is of no interest itself, we are only interested in what the number refers to.

By contrast, in the case of **ordinal** variables, the numbers assigned to the different response categories do have some meaning. They have an order. Consider the example below:

Let's talk for a few minutes about politics in general. How much interest do you generally have in what is going on in politics?

1. None at all

2. Not very much

3. Some

4. Quite a lot

5. A great deal.

Once again, each response category is assigned a value, but this time we can interpret the values according to the order in which they are arranged. We can think of the numbers as referring to levels of political interest, so someone who replies that they have not very much interest in politics is coded 2, and from this we can see that they have less interest in politics than someone whose response is coded 4. But there is a limit to the extent that we can draw meaningful conclusions about how much more or less interested they are. We cannot say thatnsomeone who is coded 4 is twice as interested in politics as someone who is coded 2. Nor can we say that the difference in interest between 4 and 5, which is 1, is the same as the difference in interest between 1 and 2, which is also 1. In short, we can only make meaningful statements about the order of the responses, not the magnitude of the differences between them.

With **interval**—or scale—variables, the numbers do make sense. Indeed, there is no distinction between the value and the label. An example of this type of variable is age.

Now, a few questions about yourself and your background. What was your age last birthday?
Age in years __

If someone is 34 years old, they are coded as 34. The numbers have an order, so someone who is 40 is older than someone who is 30, and the numbers also have a magnitude that we can interpret, so someone who is 60 is twice as old as someone who is 30. The difference between 25 and 30 is 5 years, and this distance is the same as the difference between someone who is 45 and 50. For this reason, interval variables are often referred to as real numbers.

Summarizing the data

Next we turn to how the data from these different types of variables can be summarized. There are a number of ways in which we can do this. We can use tables, figures, and statistics. We can look at the **frequency distribution**—which describes the entire distribution of responses, and summarizes the number of cases for each given response code. We can also summarize various aspects of this distribution, relating to measures of **central tendency**—such as averages—and measures of **dispersion** or variation—such as the standard deviation. The appropriate method for summarizing data depends upon the level of measurement. We discuss each of these below.

Examining the distribution of variables also serves as a way of checking the data. One serious problem that affects quantitative analysis is **missing data**—or item non-response. For a variety of reasons, data for some cases in our data set may be unavailable. Respondents may not have answered some questions, or may have answered but given ineligible responses. Missing data of this kind can introduce error or bias into the analysis if those people who did not answer the question are different in some important respect from those who did answer. It is not straightforward what to do about missing data, but there are a number of strategies that are available (see Box 14.1). The other thing to keep an eye out for is **sparse categories**, which are much easier to deal with. This occurs when relatively few observations are found for a particular response category. This can create problems when analysing the data, and so the best thing to do if this problem arises is to combine responses into larger, more general categories.

Tables

Frequency tables are the normal tabular method for presenting distributions of a single variable. The table provides information on the distribution of responses across all response categories. They are therefore most appropriate when there are not too many different response categories (otherwise the tables become too big to easily interpret), and so are mainly used for nominal and ordinal variables. Tables should be clear and easy to understand. A good table presents the relevant information in a straightforward and transparent way. It should contain:

- a clear self-explanatory title;
- clear labels;
- an appropriate level of precision (round percentages to nearest whole number);
- sample size;
- a data source.

BOX 14.1 Missing Data

Missing data is a common problem in survey research (and other types of data collection). Running frequency tables allow you to identify the scope of the problem. Missing data can take different forms. Item non-response occurs when a respondent (for whatever reason) does not provide a valid answer to a question. It can reduce the sample size (especially in a multivariate analysis or when combining variables when several small amounts of missing data may accumulate) and risks introducing selection bias. Selection bias occurs when the sources of 'missingness' are not random, and are structured so that some types of people (or people holding some types of attitude or opinion) are less likely to provide a valid response than others. The structure of missing responses may vary from one variable to another, so there is no straightforward remedy that can be applied. The strategy for how to deal with this should depend in part on your theory about what has caused it. Below we discuss the common approaches to dealing with item non-response.

Listwise deletion is often the default choice, and simply involves deleting all missing values from the analysis. The danger with this approach is that you are throwing away information, reducing sample size, and more importantly, may be introducing bias if the missingness is not random. However, in cases where there are only a small number of missing values, this is probably the most practical solution. However, when there is a large number of missing values, it may be advisable to retain missing as a separate category.

More sophisticated techniques involve trying to predict what respondents would have answered to the question from information that is available elsewhere in the questionnaire. This is known as **imputation**. The simplest form of imputation is just to set the missing values to the midpoint or mean. This approach is quick and easy, but makes best sense if you believe the missing is random. In general, however, this is rarely the case, and setting missing to any constant value is regarded as unsophisticated and somewhat questionable. More advanced methods of imputation use regression methods (see Chapter 16) to impute values on the basis of other information provided by the respondent elsewhere in the questionnaire. Although this is statistically sounder, it can become quite technical, and is only useful in so far as good predictors are available.

All tables should be clearly labelled and easy to understand. They should have a self-explanatory title, and be properly referenced with the source of data. The response codes should be clearly labelled, and the sample size should be reported. If there is missing data, this needs to be reported too. If there is a large amount of missing data, it is important to be clear whether you are reporting percentages based on what is often called the total per cent (which includes missing values in the calculations) or the valid per cent (which does not include missing values).

For example, Table 14.1 summarizes the responses to the variable on vote choice that was asked in the 2005 British Election Study. It is a nominal variable. The first column contains a list of all the main response categories (the names of the main political parties in Britain). The second column (Frequency) contains information on the number of respondents from the survey who selected each response. At the bottom of this column in the last row, labelled 'Total', we can see that 4,161 people were interviewed for the survey. Of these people, 1,198 said they voted Labour, 867 said they voted Conservative, and 1,079 said they did not vote. We can use these numbers to calculate the percentage of the sample that provided each response. This is done in the next column, labelled 'Per cent'. The percentages are based on the total count. So, for example, 1,198 people out of 4,161 said they voted Labour, and this corresponds to 29% of our sample (1,198 divided by 4,161 multiplied by 100 = 29).

Table 14.1 Voting behaviour in the 2005 British General Election

	Frequency	Per cent	Valid per cent
Labour	1198	29	40
Conservative	867	21	29
Liberal Democrats	645	16	21
Scottish National Party (SNP)	137	3	5
Plaid Cymru	69	2	2
Green Party	20	0	1
United Kingdom Independence Party (UKIP)	45	1	1
British National Party (BNP)	6	0	0
Other	36	1	1
Did not vote	1079	26	
Don't know	13	0	
Refused	46	1	
Total	4161	100	100

Source: British Election Study 2005.

We should note, however, that some respondents did not provide an answer to the question. Some people did not vote, so if we are interested in the relative shares of the vote that each party received, we should exclude these people from the analysis. Also some people did not know, or could not remember, which party they voted for, and for whatever reason, some people refused to answer the question. These 'missing values' are a common problem in survey research, and can pose a bit of a headache in terms of how we treat them. Do we regard them as valid answers, or do we discount them from our analysis?

Missing data can introduce error, since we cannot be sure what those people actually did. We can hope that they are a random selection of the sample. But it is also possible that they are more likely to be certain types of voter. For example, those that refused to answer the question may be more likely to be Conservative voters (the so-called 'shy Tories') or BNP voters (who may be unwilling to reveal their true behaviour because of **social desirability bias**; see Chapter 10), and so excluding them will bias our results, since it means that we are undercounting some response categories. When the number of missing cases is small (as in this case), this error or bias will also be small, but when the number is relatively large, it can be a problem and we need to think carefully about what to do about it.

The most straightforward option (though not always the most appropriate) is simply to discount the missing values from the analysis. We can then re-calculate the percentages to refer to just the people who provided valid responses. This is done in the next column, labelled valid per cent. Here the base excludes all those who said that they did not vote and all those who did not know who they voted for or who refused to answer. We can see that the percentages in this column are somewhat different. Now our base is just 3,023. So, for example, 1,198 out of 3,023 respondents said they voted Labour, which corresponds to 40% (1,198/3,023*100 = 40).

We should also note that we have very few responses for some of the minor parties. For example, only 1% of our sample reported voting for the Green Party and UKIP, and less than

1% reported voting for the BNP. Sparse categories such as these can pose a number of problems for analysis, and it is generally advisable to combine them together where possible. In this instance, they could be incorporated within the 'Other party' category.

The next example we consider is from a question designed to measure whether respondents think of themselves as being ideologically left wing or right wing. The frequency distribution is presented in Table 14.2, and the exact survey question is reproduced under the table. The variable is ordinal. Again, we can summarize the data in terms of the frequency, the per cent, and the valid per cent, in the same way as before. However, we should note that there are quite a lot of people who selected the 'Don't know' option. People may not have understood the question, or may have been unable to place themselves. This in a sense is a valid answer. Not everyone thinks of themselves as being on the left or the right, and for analytical purposes we therefore need to think carefully about how we treat this data.

One option is simply to ignore the 'Don't knows' and exclude them from the analysis. For descriptive purposes, we might be interested in the percentage of those who are able to place themselves on the left–right scale. This is reported in the column labelled 'Valid per cent'. Here we have to be careful to be clear about what the data now refer to. They no longer refer to the ideological disposition of everyone (the British adult population), but only to those people who were able to place themselves. So, for example, of those who were able to place themselves on a left–right scale, 36% placed themselves in the centre, and just 1% placed themselves on the far left, and 2% placed themselves on the far right. With ordinal variables we can also look at the cumulative per cent. The cumulative per

Table 14.2 Left–right ideology self-placement, British adults in 2005

	Frequency	Per cent	Valid per cent	Cumulative per cent
0 Left	36	1	1	1
1	41	1	1	2
2	124	3	3	6
3	241	6	7	12
4	366	9	10	23
5	1295	31	36	59
6	532	13	15	74
7	454	11	13	87
8	295	7	8	95
9	78	2	2	97
10 Right	82	2	2	100
Don't know	613	15		
Refused	4	0		
Total	4161	100		

Note: Question: 'In politics, people sometimes talk about parties and politicians as being on the left or right. Using the 0 to 10 scale on this card, where the end marked 0 means left and the end marked 10 means right, where would you place yourself on this scale?'
Source: British Election Study 2005.

cent is a useful way of aggregating different responses. It adds up the percentages in order for each response category. From this, we can clearly see that 23% of respondents who were able to place themselves on a left–right scale placed themselves to the left of centre (giving answers 0 to 4).

With interval variables it is generally not feasible to report the data in tables, since there will be a lot of different response categories, and so the table will require a lot of rows. A table of age, for example, in which respondents' age varies from 18 to 100 would require 82 rows, which would go on for several pages. There would also be a lot of sparse categories. The purpose of tables is to present data in a clear and transparent way. Too many rows can distract from this. Moreover, it would not be very easy to interpret. One option then is to recode data into bands. So rather than displaying the distribution for all ages, we can band the ages into age groups (e.g. 18–30 years old, 31–40 years old, 41–50 years old, 51–64 years old, and 65 years and over). There are a number of different ways in which data like this can be grouped together. The data can be grouped into equal intervals, so that each band contains, say 20% of the sample; it can be grouped into equal intervals, so that each band spans, say, 15 years; or they can be grouped into distinctive categories of theoretical interest, so that bands refer to specific groups of interest, such as young adults, or retired people. It doesn't really matter which approach is used, but it is advisable to avoid having groups with either a very small or a very large sample size.

Graphs and figures

Sample distributions can also be displayed graphically. This is often a more accessible way of presenting data, and can be easier to analyse. The purpose of graphs and figures is to present the data as clearly and accurately as possible. People can often get very creative when it comes to displaying graphs, but it is wise not to get carried away, and to focus on just trying to present the information in the clearest terms possible. In most cases, a **bar chart** or **histogram** is the best option for summarizing the distribution of a single variable. **Line graphs** are also frequently used for summarizing data over time. However, the alternatives, such as pie charts, generally are not to be recommended. They may look pretty, but it can often be difficult to distinguish between the relative sizes of the different 'slices'. However, this is not such a problem with histograms and bar charts, which generally present the data more clearly.

The choice between bar charts and histograms depends upon the level of measurement of the variable. For nominal and ordinal variables bar charts are used, and for interval variables histograms are used. In practice, bar charts and histograms look quite similar to each other. The principal difference is that bar charts have a space between the bars to indicate that the response categories are distinct—or **discrete**—whereas with histograms the bars all touch each other to indicate that the response categories are **continuous**.

Figure 14.1 presents the data from Table 14.1 as a bar chart. Along the x-axis (the horizontal axis), the different response categories are labelled. The y-axis (the vertical axis) records the share of the vote in per cent. It is important to clearly label the axis so that the reader can interpret the information. Presenting the data in this way conveys all

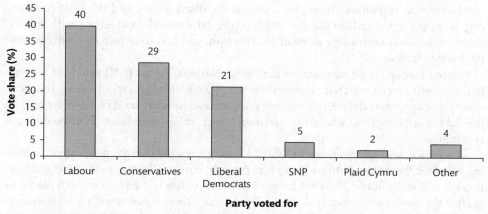

Figure 14.1 Bar chart of party vote in the 2005 British General Election
Source: British Election Study 2005.

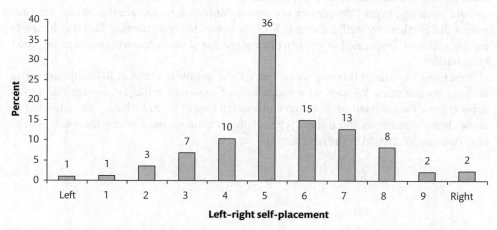

Figure 14.2 Bar chart of left–right self-placement
Source: British Election Study 2005.

the relevant information, and clearly shows which parties received the most votes and which the least.

Figure 14.2 depicts a bar chart for left–right self-placement. This variable is ordinal, and so there are spaces between the bars, although 0–10 scales are often treated as interval variables and so it could be presented as a histogram. Presenting the data in this way is in some respects an improvement on just presenting the data in tabular form, since we now get a clearer sense of the overall distribution of the variable. We can see that the most common responses are in the centre of the distribution, and the least common responses are in the **tails** of the distribution (the extreme values at either end). In fact, the variable looks quite like a **normal distribution**, which is something we will be coming back to later on.

Figure 14.3 depicts a histogram for the British National Party's (BNP) share of the vote in the constituencies which it contested for the 2005 British General Election. This is an example of **aggregate data**. Since share of the vote is an interval-level variable, we display the data in a histogram, where the bars touch each other to indicate that the data are continuous.

As we discussed with reference to Table 14.1, very few survey respondents reported having voted for the British National Party (the far-right party in Britain) in the 2005 election. Indeed, nationally only 0.7% voted for the BNP. Survey data is therefore not well placed to analyse the factors associated with the BNP vote, since there is not enough information to draw sensible conclusions. An alternative approach then is to examine the official election returns, and see how well the party did in each constituency which it contested. This is reported in Figure 14.3. The BNP stood in 119 constituencies, and in these constituencies its share of the vote ranged from a low of 0.8% to a high of 17%. We can see from Figure 14.3 that in 29 constituencies the BNP got around 4% of the vote, and in only seven constituencies did it manage to get 10% or more of the vote. Moreover, we can see that in one constituency it did particularly well, gaining 17% of the vote. This constituency, Barking, is clearly exceptional, and is separated from main body of the distribution. It can therefore be regarded as an **outlier**.

Presenting the data in this way we can get a sense of how the level of BNP support varies across constituencies. We can get a rough idea of how well it did on average (about 4% appears to be the most common value) and a rough idea of how much its vote varied, but to make clearer statements about these types of observation we need to employ special statistics. These are discussed in the next section.

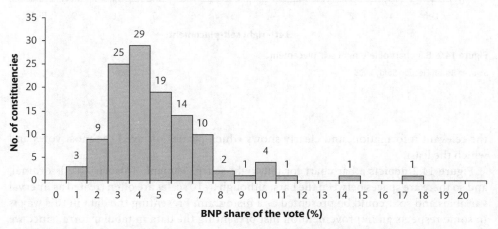

Figure 14.3 Histogram of BNP share of the vote in constituencies in the 2005 British General Election
Source: The British Parliamentary Constituency database, 1992–2005.

Summarizing the distribution using statistics

As well as summarizing the entire distribution, we can also choose to summarize some specific aspect of the distribution. This allows us to more easily make comparisons, either over time or between groups of people, countries, or places. In making these comparisons, it is useful to have information on the centre of the distribution, and how scattered or dispersed the data are around this point. These measures are known as measures of central tendency and measures of dispersion.

Measures of central tendency

There are three measures of central tendency: the mode, the median, and the mean. Each measure provides a summary of the 'central value' of the distribution in some sense, although how they do this varies somewhat. These measures are generally only appropriate for ordinal and interval-level data, since for nominal-level variables it does not really make much sense to talk about the central value because the values do not have any underlying order to them. However, for nominal variables, we are often interested in the mode, which refers to the most common value, or the largest group. So we might say that the modal religion in India is Hinduism, or the modal ethnic group in Kenya is Kikuyu, or the modal political party in the UK parliament is the Conservative Party.

To illustrate how these measures of central tendency are calculated, consider the following example. Suppose we were interested in the financial status of students, and decide to ask each of the students in a class how much money they receive from all sources per year. There are 11 students in the class, and each is asked to estimate their total annual income in pounds (to the nearest thousand). From this we obtain the following values. This is our distribution:

4, 6, 8, 8, 10, 10, 10, 12, 14, 16, 20

The **mode** is simply the most common value in the distribution. We can see that three students have an income of about £10,000. This is the most common value in the distribution and so is the mode. It is possible to have more than one mode in a distribution; in such cases, the distribution is bimodal or multimodal. The **median** refers to the middle value of the distribution. It is defined as the point which divides the observed values into two equal parts. All the values are arranged in ascending order (as above) and the median is simply the one in the middle. Since we have 11 students, in this case the median refers to the value of the sixth observation, which is also £10,000. If there is an even number of observations in the distribution (and so there is not one value that is directly in the middle), the median is calculated as the difference between the two middle values.

Whereas the mode and the median can be directly observed from the distribution, the mean needs to be calculated (though most computer programs will do this for you). The mean is the measure of central tendency that most of us think about when we hear the term 'average'. It is symbolized in two different ways, according to whether we are describing the population mean or the sample mean. For the time being, we just consider the sample mean. This is denoted as $\overline{X}$ (pronounced x-bar), where x is the variable of interest (in this case, student income). The mean is the measure of central tendency that is used most often in quantitative analysis, and is one of the building blocks for more advanced quantitative analysis techniques that we will encounter in the following chapters. It is calculated by adding up all the values of x that are observed in the distribution, and then dividing the total by the number of observations (students). It is expressed as follows:

$$\bar{X} = \frac{\sum x_i}{n}$$

where

$\bar{X}$ = the mean;
Σ = 'the sum of' (pronounced sigma);
x_i = the values of x to be summed;
n = the number of observations (sample size).

Using the above example, we can plug in all the values of x, add them up, and then divide by the number of observations (11). This gives us:

$$\bar{X} = \frac{4+6+8+8+10+10+10+12+14+16+20}{11}$$

$$\bar{X} = \frac{118}{11} = 10.72.$$

So, in the above example, the mean is £10,720. When the mode, the median, and the mean are all the same, we have a perfect normal distribution. However, it is not uncommon to find that sometimes the different measures produce very different values. Under these circumstances, it is natural to ask which measure is the best, and it is easy to suppose that it must be the mean, since this appears to be the most scientific. But this is not always the case.

The mean can be sensitive to extreme outliers, especially when we are dealing with relatively small samples. Suppose the day after we collected the above data, a new student entered the class who had a trust fund which gave him an annual income of £2 million. Including this person in our calculation dramatically changes the mean. Whereas the mode and the median are still £10,000, the mean is now a whopping £166,676. Clearly, the mean no longer appears to be very typical of what the average student has to live on. It is therefore always important to check for the presence of outliers (particularly when the sample size is relatively small), as these can dramatically distort the results and make what is highly unusual appear typical.

But at the same time, the problem with the median is that it is quite a blunt measurement instrument. If we are interested, for example, at looking at how public opinion has changed over time, we might prefer a more sensitive measurement instrument. For example, Eurobarometer routinely asks people to place themselves on a 0–10 left–right scale, where 0 is left and 10 is right (as discussed earlier). Figure 14.4 plots the median position since 1973. We can see that in the 1970s the median position fluctuated between 5 and 6, and since the late 1980s has remained constant at 5, suggesting that there has not been a great deal of change in public attitudes. By contrast, Figure 14.5 plots the mean position since 1973. From this measure we can see that since the late 1980s there has been a gradual shift to the left in public opinion.

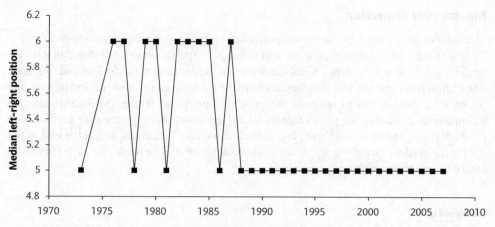

Figure 14.4 Left–right self-placement in the UK–median position of adult population, 1973–2007

Note: Question: 'In politics, people sometimes talk about parties and politicians as being on the left or right. Using the 0 to 10 scale on this card, where the end marked 0 means left and the end marked 10 means right, where would you place yourself on this scale?'

Source: Eurobarometer.

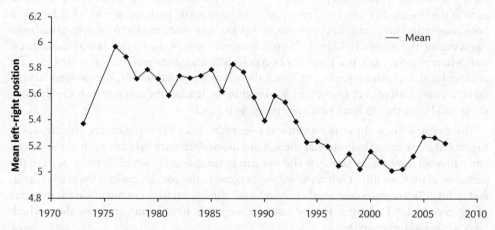

Figure 14.5 Left–right self-placement in the UK–mean position of adult population, 1973–2007

Source: Eurobarometer.

Choosing which measure of central tendency to report depends upon the kind of information you want to convey. The mode is appropriate if you are talking about data measured at the nominal level, or if you are simply interested in what is the most common value or the largest group. The median is appropriate if there are extreme outliers, which may distort the mean. Most government publications use the median rather than the mean to report average household income for just this reason. Otherwise, the mean is generally appropriate. The mean is the only measure that is mathematically based. It uses all of the information in the distribution, and is one of the main building blocks for more advanced analysis.

Measures of dispersion

Measures of central tendency provide a powerful way of summarizing large amounts of data. They are useful for summarizing what is the average or typical person or value. But it is also useful to get an idea of how individuals or objects in the distribution differ from one another. Sometimes two different distributions can have the same mean (or median) but be very different from one another in terms of the variability or spread within the distribution. An example illustrates this. Suppose students taking introduction to quantitative methods are randomly assigned to one of three classes. Each class has 12 students, and at the end of the course the students are given a test that is marked out of 10. The marks for each student in each class are shown below:

Mark out of 10
Class 1: 6 6 6 6 6 6 6 6 6 6 6 6
Class 2: 4 4 5 5 5 6 6 7 7 7 8 8
Class 3: 1 2 2 3 4 4 8 9 9 10 10 10

For each class, the measures of central tendency based on the mean and the median are the same—6—which represents a pass mark. However, the variation in the marks is different in each of the classes. In Class 1, everyone gets the same mark, perhaps because they have just been taught the bare minimum to pass, and this has been drummed into them over and over again during the course. In Class 2, there is more variation in the marks—some students do well whereas others fail, but there is not much difference between the top marks that are achieved and the bottom marks. In Class 3, there is more variation still. The students tend to do either very well or very badly, perhaps because the teacher focuses more on the able students and leaves the students who are struggling behind.

This example shows how important it is to examine both the variation and the mean. On the face of it, we might assume that there is not much difference between each of the classes since they all have the same mean and median exam mark. However, from inspecting the variation of marks within each class, we might come to the conclusion that the classes are in fact quite different from one another. And, depending upon how confident we felt in terms of our own ability to do quantitative research, we might have strong opinions about which class we would rather go in.

This example clearly illustrates the intuition behind calculating measures of dispersion. As with the measures of central tendency, variation—or dispersion—can be measured in a number of ways that vary in statistical complexity. The three most commonly used measures of dispersion are: the range; the interquartile range, and the standard deviation. These are discussed below.

The **range** is the most straightforward measure of dispersion. It simply calculates the difference between the smallest and the largest values. So with reference to the above example, the range for Class 1 is zero (6–6 = 0), the range for Class 2 is 4 (8–4 = 4), and the range for Class 3 is 9 (10–1 = 9). Even this simple measure gives us a better feel for the data than we would have from considering just the mean alone. We know that there is a lot of variability in the marks of students in Class 3, and none at all in Class 1. So if we were a student who was particularly apprehensive about taking a quantitative methods course, we might feel more confident if we had the teacher for Class 1.

However, one drawback of the range is that, since it depends on the extreme values of the distribution, it is very sensitive to outliers. One or both of these values might be atypical, so the range is not always a particularly trustworthy measure. The **interquartile range** (IQR) avoids this problem by ignoring the tails of the distribution, and only examines the dispersion within the middle 50% of the distribution. It thus divides the distribution into quartiles and compares the value of the first quartile (the value which divides the ordered set of observations into the smallest 25% and the largest 75%) and the third quartile (the value which divides the ordered set of observations into the smallest 75% and the largest 25%). This can be thought of as a related technique to the median, which divides the data into the smallest 50% and the largest 50%.

Table 14.3 provides a worked example with data from Class 3. We can see that all the students in the bottom quartile got less than 3 out of 10 on their test, and that all the students in the top quartile got full marks of 10 out of 10. The interquartile range (the middle 50%) therefore stretches from marks of 3 out of 10 to 9 out of 10, giving a range of 6.

The standard deviation is related to the mean, and is by far the most widely used measure of dispersion. Rather than just considering the difference between two points of the distribution (as with the range and IQR), it utilizes all the values in the distribution and describes how far on average each value deviates from the mean. When all the values in the distribution are the same (as in the example from Class 1), the difference between each value and the mean will be zero. However, when the values are very different from the mean (as in Class 3), the standard deviation will be relatively large.

The standard deviation is calculated with the following formula,

$$s = \sqrt{\frac{\sum(x_i - \bar{x})^2}{N-1}}$$

Table 14.3 Calculating the interquartile range

Student	X_i (Test score)	
1	1	
2	2	Lower quartile
3	2	
4	3	
5	4	
6	4	Interquartile range
7	8	
8	9	
9	9	
10	10	
11	10	Upper quartile
12	10	

where

   s = the standard deviation of the sample;

   x_i = the value for each observation in the distribution;

   $\overline{X}$ = the sample mean;

   N = the number of observations (sample size).

In other words, the standard deviation is the square root of the sum of the squared differences between each value in the distribution and the mean, divided by the sample size minus one. This sounds a bit of a mouthful, but is actually fairly straightforward if we consider each step in turn. Table 14.4 provides a worked example for calculating the standard deviation, using the distribution of test scores from Class 3, discussed above. We have 12 students in our sample, and for each student we have recorded their test score. These test scores are the values for xi, and are listed in column 2 for each student. For example, we can see that student 1 got just 1 out of 10 on the test. We are interested in how far these scores deviate from the mean. We already know that the mean is 6, so for each student we calculate how far away their score is from 6. This is done by subtracting the mean from each individual score. This is shown in column 3.

For student 1 this comes out as –5 (1–6 =–5). The problem is that some of these deviations are positive and some are negative, so if we summed them all up, the positives and negatives would cancel each other out and we would be left with zero. To get rid of the different signs, we therefore square the deviations. This is presented in column 4. Next we add up these values. This comes to 144. This value is known as the sum of the squares. We then divide this value by our sample size minus one (11) which gives us 13.09. This value is known as the **variance**. The last step involves taking the square root of this number, which gives us the standard deviation. This is 3.62. Some students got scores which were close to the mean, other students got scores which were far away from the mean, but what the standard deviation tells us is that, on average, the deviation from the mean was 3.62 points.

Table 14.4 Calculating the standard deviation

Student	X_i (Test score)	$(X_i - \overline{X})$	$(X_i - \overline{X})^2$
1	1	-5	25
2	2	-4	16
3	2	-4	16
4	3	-3	9
5	4	-2	4
6	4	-2	4
7	8	2	4
8	9	3	9
9	9	3	9
10	10	4	16
11	10	4	16
12	10	4	16
Sum (Total)			144
Sum/N–1			144/11 = 13.09
Square root			3.62

Like the mean, the standard deviation is one of the cornerstones of quantitative analysis. It can be used to summarize the dispersion of a single variable within our sample. It can also be used to compare the dispersion among two or more samples. This is often of more analytical interest. It can be hard to know how to interpret the size of a standard deviation when there is only one value. Is it big or is it small? But when we have repeated values, we can look at whether the standard deviation changes, and if so, whether it gets bigger or smaller. This is often of considerable analytical interest. Measures of variation have many practical applications in political research, and can be used to tell us about extremism, polarization, and inequality. For example, suppose we are interested in ideological extremism. There is a great deal of talk these days about ideological convergence, meaning that voters have moved towards the middle ground. One way of examining this is just to look at the mean, as we did earlier in Figure 14.5. From this figure, we can see that the centre has shifted, but that it appears to shift in a cyclical fashion. However, it doesn't tell us whether voters have converged or not. Another way of examining this is to look at the standard deviation of left–right scores. This tells us how clustered or spread out the scores are. Figure 14.6 plots the standard deviation of left–right self-placement. There doesn't appear to have been a great deal of change over time. The first value in the series appears to be a bit of an outlier, and since then, there have been some jumps up and down, with perhaps a slight downward tendency, suggesting that some ideological convergence has taken place. However, we should perhaps be wary of drawing strong conclusions.

Descriptive inference

So far we have considered ways in which we can describe our sample. But we are also interested in making inferences about the population from which the sample was drawn. This allows us to make generalizations, and it is this ability to make robust generalizations about the wider population that is one of the key strengths of quantitative analysis. In order to make generalizations, we use the data from our sample to tell us something—or make inferences—about the wider world. Inferential statistics allow us to build upon what we have

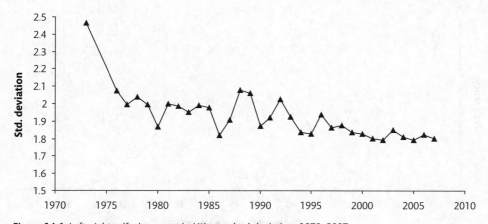

Figure 14.6 Left–right self-placement in UK, standard deviation, 1970–2007

Source: Eurobarometer trendfile.

covered so far and to make estimates about population values. These estimates often take the form of a **confidence interval**, which is a range of values within which we are fairly sure the 'real' population value is contained. This idea of the confidence interval is particularly useful when we are interested in comparing values over time or between countries, and helps us to decide whether changes or differences are 'meaningful' or not.

Before outlining how inferential statistics work in practice, it is worth discussing a little of the theory behind the approach. We do not go into great detail here, since our focus is on the analysis and interpretation of these statistics rather than how they work, but useful summaries can be found in Agresti and Finlay (2009). Our sample is interesting. We hope it is reliable, and we hope that it is representative so that we can make inferences about the population from which it was drawn. But how exactly can we do this? The **central limit theorem** is what allows us to link our sample to the population. The central limit theorem is perhaps the most important theorem in statistical theory. It states that if repeated random samples are drawn from a population, the **sampling distribution** of the sample estimate (for example, Conservative vote share) will approach normality. An example helps to illustrate this.

Suppose we interview 100 people and find that 45 said they would vote Conservative if there were an election tomorrow. We can think of this as our sample estimate. We hope that our sample estimate is a good approximation of the true population value, and that in the real world somewhere around 45% of the population would indeed vote Conservative. But if we interviewed a different 100 people, we might find that only 44 people said they would vote Conservative, and if we interviewed a different 100 people again, we might find that only 40 people said they would vote Conservative, and so on. This might sound like a potential problem, but the beauty of the central limit theorem is that it isn't. We know that each of our samples is likely to produce a slightly different estimate, and we also know that if we take a large number of random samples (of sufficient sample size), most will come up with a percentage estimate close to the true population value. In only a few samples will the sample estimate be way off the mark. In fact, the distribution of the sample estimates (known as the sampling distribution) would approximate a 'normal' distribution (see Figure 14.7).

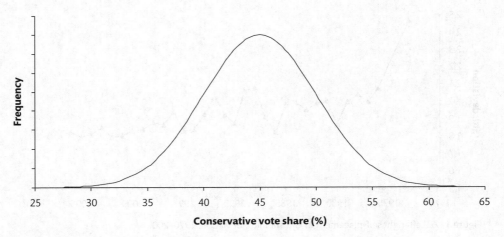

Figure 14.7 The normal distribution

We can think of the sampling distribution as being a distribution of all the possible sample estimates that we could draw from a population using the same sample size. If we were to take all these possible sample estimates, sum them and divide by the number of samples, we would have the exact value of the population. The elegance of the sampling distribution is that even if the population is not normally distributed, repeated samples will generate estimates that are approximately normally distributed. And, as with all distributions, the sampling distribution will have a mean, and this mean will be the true population value. The peak of the sampling distribution therefore corresponds to the true population value for Conservative share of the vote (45%).

Now, we hope that our sample estimate is exactly the same as the population value or at least pretty close to it, but in truth we do not know where it is. Our sample estimate could potentially be one of the extreme estimates right off in the tails of the distribution, a long way away from the true value of the population. However, if it was, we could console ourselves that we must have been pretty unlucky to have drawn such a duff sample if we had done everything right in the sampling phase of the research (see Chapter 10). Crucially, it is this idea of how lucky or not we would have to be to draw a duff sample that underpins inferential statistics. So how do we decide whether the sample we have drawn is one of the samples that is close to the true population value or one that is far away?

To answer this question we need to know about something called the standard error. This can be used to tell us how likely it is that our sample estimate is close to the true population value. As with all distributions, the sampling distribution has a standard deviation. Whereas the mean of the sampling distribution is the same as the population value, the standard deviation of the sampling distribution is smaller than the population standard deviation. This is because there tends to be more variation between values for individuals than there does between statistics summarized for samples. This makes intuitive sense. The mean income in Britain is around £20,000 per year. Individuals earning £50,000 per year or more are uncommon, though not unheard of (approximately 5% in 2007). However, a random sample of 1000 people with a mean income of £50,000 per year would be exceptionally rare.

The standard deviation of the sampling distribution has a special name: the **standard error.** Probability theory tells us that in 95% of samples that we draw, the population value will be within two (actually 1.96) standard errors of the sample estimate. With nominal variables, we can estimate the standard error of a proportion. With interval (and at a stretch ordinal) variables we can estimate the standard error of a mean. The way in which we do this is slightly different, but in both cases the size of the standard error is partly a function of sample size. These points are not only of statistical interest, but are of great practical use as well. We can utilize the idea of the sampling distribution and the standard error to make inferences about populations. This is discussed below.

Population estimates

As soon as we move into the realm of inferential statistics, there are a whole host of things we can do. The first, most basic application it that we can make guesses about the true population value that we are interested in. We can do this for nominal, ordinal, and interval data. For nominal variables, we can make a guess about the population proportion, such as what is the proportion of the population that will vote Conservative. For ordinal and interval variables, we can also make a guess about the population mean, such as what is the mean position on the left–right scale of the population as a whole.

Confidence intervals for proportions

One common use of surveys and opinion polls is to track likely voting intentions in the general election. This is something we frequently read about in the newspapers. For example, a survey may report that if there were a general election tomorrow, 44% of the sample say they would vote Conservative. This is interesting to know, but more interesting is what it tells us about our estimate of what the true level of support for the Conservative party is in the population as a whole. We think it is probably around 44%, but we would be unwise to state that it is exactly 44%. What we have is an estimate.

It is common to accompany this estimate with a margin of error. Survey companies often say that the margin of error is plus or minus 3 percentage points. This means that the best guess is 44%, but the expected true value could be between 41 and 47% (44% plus or minus 3 percentage points). This is quite a big range. During election campaigns, commentators can get quite excited about small changes in the polls, but most of the time, when a party's share of the vote appears to go up or down by a few percentage points, it is still well within the margin of error. It does not mean that the underlying level of support for the party in the population has changed, but rather just reflects what is known as sampling variation.

The technical term for this margin of error is a confidence interval. This section describes the calculation behind a confidence interval, though in practice it is not something that you need to know how to calculate, since most statistical software programmes will do it for you. To calculate a confidence interval we draw on probability theory, and the ideas of the sampling distribution and the standard error discussed above. Since we know that 95% of the time the population value will fall within 1.96 standard errors of the sample estimate, we can calculate the range within which we think the true population value lies. To estimate this we need to calculate the standard error. Because we are dealing with a nominal variable, we calculate the standard error for a proportion. But the procedure is much the same as that for calculating the standard error for the mean.

The formula for the standard error of a proportion is:

$$SE_p = \sqrt{\frac{(P_s)(1 - P_s)}{N}}$$

where

SE_p = the standard error of the proportion;
P_s = the sample proportion;
N = the sample size.

Having calculated that standard error, we can now estimate the range within which the population value is likely to be. This is our confidence interval. If we specify a 95% confidence interval, it means that we think our range will correctly contain the true population value 95% of the time. This is expressed below:

$$ci = P_s \pm 1.96 \sqrt{\frac{(P_s)(1-P_s)}{N}}.$$

If we assume our sample size is 1,000, and the percentage who say they will vote Conservative is 44%, then we can plug in the numbers as follows.

$$ci = 0.44 \pm 1.96 \sqrt{\frac{(0.44)(0.56)}{1000}}$$

$$ci = 0.44 \pm 0.03.$$

The 95% confidence interval is therefore the sample proportion (0.44) plus or minus 0.03. So in percentage terms we can say that we think the true level of Conservative support lies somewhere between 41% and 47% (44% plus or minus 3 percentage points). This is our best guess. Of course, we don't know whether our guess is correct or not. We may be wrong. But we can say that most of the time our guess will be correct. In fact, we can say that 95% of the time our guess will be right. This, of course, leaves us with the possibility of being wrong 5% of the time, which will happen when we draw one of those dodgy samples right off in the tails of the sampling distribution. This is known as **sampling error,** which is the culprit frequently blamed when surprising one-off polls are recorded which seem out of step with what else has been recorded.

There is thus a trade-off between precision and confidence. If we were not happy to be correct 95% of the time, we could extend our confidence interval. Probability theory tells us that 99% of the time the population value will be within 2.58 standard errors of the mean. This will give us a confidence interval for the true level of Conservative support of between 40% and 48% (44% plus or minus 4 percentage points). Now we have more confidence that our estimate will contain the true population value, but our estimate is wider and less precise. For this reason, the 95% confidence interval is generally accepted as the default position.

Having established a confidence interval for one proportion, we can then use this to make a comparison with the confidence interval of another proportion, to see if the difference, say between the Labour and Conservative share of the vote, could just be down to sampling variation or whether it represents a real 'statistical difference'. So, for example, if just before an election we carry out a survey and find that the Conservatives are on 44% and Labour are on 41%, how confident can we be that this represents a 'real' difference in public opinion?

Our sample estimate for Labour may be 41%, which is somewhat lower than our estimate of the Conservative vote share, but before rushing to any conclusion, the important thing is to inspect the confidence interval for Labour's vote share. The 95% confidence interval for Labour vote is between 38% and 44% (41% plus or minus 3 percentage points). There is thus some overlap between our two estimates. It could be that the true population value is at the top end of the Labour estimate and the bottom end of the

Conservative estimate, in which case there may be no real difference in their respective shares of the vote.

This leads us to a slightly different question that we want to answer. Rather than trying to find out what the true level of support for each party is in the population, we now want to know whether there is a real difference between their vote shares. Do we have enough evidence to reject the idea that they have equal support? This introduces us to the idea of hypothesis testing and the null hypothesis (which we examine in more detail in Chapter 15). Our null hypothesis is that in the population there is no difference between the Labour share of the vote and the Conservative share of the vote.

Confidence intervals for the difference between two proportions

Although it can be interesting to make estimates about the true level—or proportion—of a particular variable in the population, it is often more interesting to know about change or comparison. For example, we might be interested to see if Labour support changed when Brown took over from Blair. Alternatively, we might be interested to see if trust in politicians changed after the 2009 expenses scandal. Or we may want to know if public support for democracy is higher in Afghanistan or Iraq.

Obviously, when we make these sorts of comparisons, we have to rely on survey data that has been asked in exactly the same way, since even small changes in question wording can influence the response (see Chapter 10). However, there are now a number of surveys that have been carried out in the same way over time and between countries. One such survey series is the Audit of Political Engagement, carried out by the Hansard Society, which tracks British public attitudes towards politics over time. In the wake of the parliamentary expenses scandal of May 2009, when there were widespread allegations that many MPs were misusing or abusing their official allowances, there were widespread concerns that the reputation of MPs in general had been dealt a severe blow. However, others argued that MPs had never been held in particularly high regard, and so the scandal just reinforced what the public thought they already knew, rather than changed their opinion. To help us look at these different hypotheses, we can compare public attitudes towards MPs from before the scandal broke with attitudes after. Table 14.5 presents data collected in 2006 and 2009.

Comparing the two columns, for November 2006 and November 2009, we can see there is not much change in the percentage of people who are very or fairly satisfied with the way in which MPs do their job. There has been a slight decline in the percentage who are neither satisfied nor dissatisfied, and a slight increase in the percentage of those that are fairly or very dissatisfied. Overall, the percentage who said they were dissatisfied (either fairly or very) with the ways in which MPs in general are doing their job increased from 36% to 44%.

From this it looks like there may have been a slight change. But is this change real, or could it just be the result of sampling variation? Maybe the true level of dissatisfaction in the population is 40%, and the first sample underestimated it a little bit, and the second sample overestimated a little bit. This is a distinct possibility, and one that we would want to rule out before inferring that any real change had taken place in public perceptions about how well (or how badly) British MPs are doing their job. To try and distinguish between sampling variation and 'real' variation we use tests of statistical significance. This draws on the idea of

Table 14.5 Are you satisfied or dissatisfied with the way MPs in general are doing their job?

	November 2006	November 2009
Very satisfied	2	1
Fairly satisfied	29	28
Neither satisfied nor dissatisfied	27	24
Fairly dissatisfied	26	30
Very dissatisfied	10	14
Don't know	6	3
Dissatisfied (fairly + very)	36	44
N	1282	1156

Source: Hansard Society, Audit of Political Engagement 7.

confidence intervals discussed above. We can estimate a confidence interval for dissatisfaction with MPs for each of the surveys. This is done below.

Confidence interval for first survey in 2006:

$$= 36 \pm 1.96 \sqrt{\frac{36*(100 - 36)}{1282}}$$

$$= 36 \pm 2.63$$

$$= \{33.4, 38.6\}.$$

Confidence interval for second survey in 2009:

$$= 44 \pm 1.96 \sqrt{\frac{44*(100 - 44)}{1156}}$$

$$= 44 \pm 2.86$$

$$= \{41.1, 46.9\}.$$

Note that we can express the confidence intervals in terms of percentages or proportions. This time we express them in terms of percentages. We can see that the two confidence intervals do not overlap. The top band of the interval in 2006 is lower than the lowest band of the interval in 2009. This suggests that there has been some real change. However, we can go one step further than this, and make an estimate about how much change we think has taken place. In our two surveys, we observed an increase in levels of dissatisfaction of 8 percentage points. What we want to know is that if there had been no real increase in the population, how likely is it that we would have drawn two samples in which we observed an increase of 8 percentage points?

The way we do this is to create a confidence interval for the difference between our two proportions. Our sampling distribution is now the difference between the two sample proportions. This difference, as per the central limit theorem, will be normally distributed. We know that 95% of the time the 'true' difference in the population will lie within 1.96 standard errors of the sample difference, and what we want to know is the likelihood of this range including 0, meaning that there has been no change. We can calculate this in much the same way as we did before, but the only slight difference is in how we calculate the standard error of the sampling distribution. To do this we take into account both samples (S1 and S2). The formula for the standard error of the difference between two proportions is:

$$SE_d = \sqrt{\frac{P_{s1}(1 - P_{s1})}{n_1} + \frac{P_{s2}(1 - P_{s2})}{n_2}}$$

$$SE_d = \sqrt{\frac{(36*64)+(44*56)}{1282 + 1156}}$$

$$SE_d = \sqrt{\frac{4768}{2438}}$$

$$SE_d = \sqrt{1.96}$$

$$= 1.40.$$

Having obtained an estimate of the standard error of the distribution, we can now calculate the confidence interval in the same way:

$$ci = 8 \pm 1.96*1.40$$
$$= 8 \pm 2.74$$
$$= \{5.3, 10.7\}.$$

We can see our confidence interval ranges from 5.3 to 10.7. This is how much change we think there has been in the level of dissatisfaction with MPs between our two surveys. We can see that 0 is not contained within this confidence interval. Our estimate is that there has been change of somewhere between 5.3 percentage points and 10.7 percentage points. We are confident that this represents real change. And we will be correct in this estimate 95% of the time.

Confidence intervals for means

With ordinal and interval data, we can estimate the margin of error associated with our sample means using the same general logic. To do this we calculate a statistic called the standard error of the mean. This is based on the standard deviation of the sample. As before, we can say that 95% of the time the true value of the population will fall within plus or minus 1.96 standard errors of the sample mean.

The formula for the standard error of a mean is:

$$SE_{\bar{X}} = \sqrt{\frac{s}{N}}$$

where

$SE_{\bar{X}}$ = the standard error of the mean;
s = the sample standard deviation;
N = the sample size.

The 95% confidence interval can then be calculated in the same way.

$$ci = \bar{X} \pm 1.96 \sqrt{\frac{s}{N}}.$$

These confidence intervals are particularly useful if we are interested in whether things have changed over time or not. Suppose we are interested in the ideology of the electorate in Britain (as we discussed previously), and whether there has been any real movement over time. Using Eurobarometer, which has asked the same question since 1973, we can calculate the confidence interval for each sample estimate and compare them to each other. This is shown in Figure 14.8. The circles indicate the mean and the 'whiskers' indicate the 95% confidence interval for the mean.

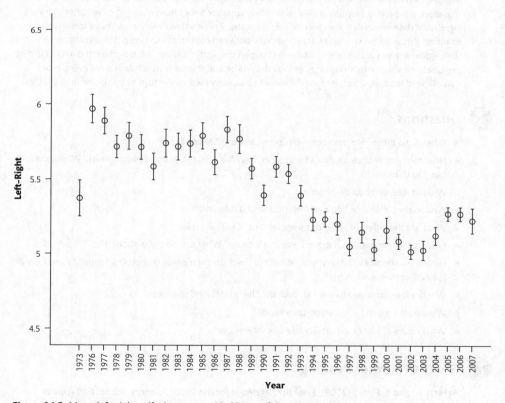

Figure 14.8 Mean left–right self-placement with 95% confidence intervals

The first thing to notice is that the first point in the time series appears to be something of an outlier. It may be that between 1973 and 1976 the electorate underwent a dramatic shift to the right, but it is probably more plausible to put the anomalous estimate of 1973 down to sampling error. Since then, we can see that there have been some fluctuations up and down. By and large, the confidence intervals for two adjacent estimates tend to overlap, indicating little short-term change, but over the long run we can see that, for example, the electorate is significantly more to the left in the mid-1990s than it was in the late 1980s. The advantage of utilizing confidence intervals is that we are less likely to over-interpret small changes, and so have a more robust basis for assessing differences. Analysis of these differences over time can be more fully explored using time series analysis.

 ## Conclusions

This chapter has provided an introduction to the first steps in analysing quantitative data. In doing so, we have encountered some of the building blocks of quantitative analysis: the mean, the standard deviation, and the central limit theorem. The latter provides the link between samples and populations which allows us to make inferences. Description is an important part of political research. It enables us to set the scene and describe the nature of the problem that we may then seek to go on to explain. Descriptive inference allows us to link the sample to the population. It not only enables us to make generalizations, but also allows us to assess whether things have changed or whether there are significant differences between two sample estimates. This is valuable when we move towards examining how things change over time or vary between countries. However, this univariate descriptive analysis is also often just the first step in the analysis. Often we are interested in developing explanations about why things vary or why they differ and this takes us towards developing more complicated models, which include different explanatory factors. We turn to this in the next chapter.

 ## Questions

- What is the difference between description and explanation?
- How can quantitative methods be used to describe different political phenomena? What examples can you think of?
- What makes for good description?
- What is the difference between description and inference?
- What are the different levels of measurement? Give examples.
- What is missing data? What problems can it cause? What can be done about it?
- How do we decide what is typical? What are the different measures of central tendency and how do they differ from each other?
- When is it appropriate to use the median? The mode? And the mean?
- What do we mean by a confidence interval?
- What issues influence our ability to make inferences?

 ## Guide to Further Reading

Agresti, A. and B. Finlay (2009), *Statistical Methods for the Social Sciences*, 4th edition (Upper Saddle River, NJ: Pearson–Prentice Hall).

Covers the basics of statistical description and inference, as well as more advanced topics on regression methods, including multiple regression, analysis of covariance, logistic regression, and generalized linear models.

Johnson, Janet Buttolph, Henry Reynolds, and Jason Mycoff (2007), *Political Science Research Methods*, **6th edition (Washington, DC: CQ Press).**
Provides an introduction to quantitative analysis and covers some more advanced topics, with lots of examples from political research.

Carlson, James and Mark Hyde (2002), *Doing Empirical Political Research* **(Boston, MA: Houghton Mifflin).**
Provides an introduction to quantitative analysis and covers some more advanced topics, with lots of examples from political research.

de Vaus, David (2002), *Surveys in Social Research* **(London: Routledge).**
A detailed and accessible introduction to quantitative methods, with easy-to-read chapters on how to carry out analysis and interpret the results.

Field, A. (2009), *Discovering Statistics Using SPSS: (And Sex and Drugs and Rock 'n' Roll)* **(London: Sage Publications).**
Provides an easy-to-follow introduction to quantitative analysis and step-by-step instructions on how to use the SPSS statistical software package to do your own analysis.

Rowntree, Derek (2000), *Statistics without Tears: An Introduction for Non-Mathematicians* **(Harmondsworth: Penguin).**
An easy-to-read introduction to statistical methods.

 # References

Agresti, A. and B. Finlay (2009), *Statistical Methods for the Social Sciences*, 4th edition (Upper Saddle River, NJ: Pearson–Prentice Hall).

Bartle, John, Sebastion Dellepiane, and James A. Stimson (2011), 'The Moving Centre: Preferences for Government Activity in Britain: 1950–2005.' *British Journal of Political Science* 41: 259–85.

Clarke, Harold, D. Sanders, M. Stewart, and P. Whiteley (2004), *Political Choice in Britain* (Oxford: Oxford University Press).

—— (2009), *Performance Politics and the British Voter* (Oxford: Oxford University Press).

Franklin, M. (2004), *Voter Turnout and the Dynamics of Electoral Competition in Established Democracies since 1945* (Cambridge: Cambridge University Press).

Gleditsch, Kristian Skrede (2007), 'Transnational Dimensions of Civil War', *Journal of Peace Research* 44(3): 293–309.

—— and Michael D. Ward (2006), 'Diffusion and the International Context of Democratization', *International Organization* 60(4): 911–33.

King, Gary, Robert Keohane, and Sidney Verba (1994), *Designing Social Inquiry: Scientific Inference in Qualitative Research* (Princeton: Princeton University Press).

Przeworski, A., M. Alvarez, J. Cheibub, and F. Limongi (2000), *Democracy and Development: Political Institutions and Well-Being in the World, 1950-1990* (Cambridge: Cambridge University Press).

Wilkinson, S. (2004), *Votes and Violence: Electoral Competition and Ethnic Riots in India* (Cambridge: Cambridge University Press).

Wlezien, Christopher (1995), 'The Public as Thermostat: Dynamics of Preferences for Spending', *American Journal of Political Science* 39(4): 981-1000.

Patterns of Association: Bivariate Analysis

 Chapter Summary

This chapter examines the association between two variables, and builds upon the previous chapter by introducing ideas about association and causality. In doing so, it provides a link between description and explanation. In particular, we focus on hypothesis testing and significance tests; and how we can describe the pattern of association between two variables. We introduce two of the most widely used statistical analysis techniques in political research, ordinary least squares (OLS) regression and cross-tabulation. The chapter considers:

● bivariate analysis;

● cross-tabulation;

● significance testing;

● null hypothesis;

● chi square;

● correlation.

Introduction

In Chapter 14 we examined the different ways in which we can describe the distribution of one variable using **univariate statistics**. This chapter builds on these ideas. It is one thing to show that people vary in terms of their left–right ideology or environmental awareness, or that some countries are more democratic or more prone to war than others, it is quite another thing to try and explain or account for these variations. Why are some people more concerned about the environment than others? Is it because of their age? Their class? Their education? Why are some people more left wing than others? If we find that working-class people are more left wing than middle-class people, we might say that there is an association between class and left–right attitudes. If we are interested in explaining the causes of ideology, then we might hypothesize that class is an important factor. But we might also be interested in exploring why this is the case, and unpicking the causal mechanisms. Why are working-class people more left wing? Is it because of their location in the labour market? Is it because of their socialization experiences? Or is it simply a function of political mobilization and persuasion by the parties that they support?

Bivariate analysis allows us to explore these issues, and examine how two variables are related. Bivariate analysis includes a number of different methods. The type of method that is appropriate depends upon the **level of measurement** of our variables. As we discussed in

Chapter 14, we use different methods for examining the relationship between categorical variables (nominal or ordinal) and continuous variables (interval). When both our variables are interval level, we can use OLS regression (or correlation); and when both our variables are categorical, we can use cross-tabulations. When our dependent variable is interval and our independent variable is categorical, we can do a comparison of means, as discussed in Chapter 14. Although the methods used are somewhat different, they serve the same basic purpose. They allow us to answer the following questions: Is there a relationship between two variables? And if so, what form does the relationship take? How can we describe it?

The chapter is divided into three main sections. The first section provides an introduction to the logic of bivariate analysis and discusses the difference between association and causality. The next section examines the association between two interval-level variables using correlation and regression, and the final section examines the relationship between two categorical variables using cross-tabulations.

The principles of bivariate analysis

Bivariate analysis is an essential tool for getting to know your data, and helping you to identify patterns of association between two variables. The variable that refers to the phenomenon that we are trying to explain is often known as the **dependent variable** (or **response variable**). The variable that we think is important for explaining the dependent variable is known as the **independent variable**, or **explanatory variable** (see Chapter 6). So, for example, if we are interested in ethnic conflict in India, our dependent variable may be whether a particular region experienced a violent clash between Hindus and Muslims (or not) within a certain period of time (say five years). This is the thing that we want to explain. Why are some regions more prone to conflict than others? Our independent variable refers to a factor that we think may be important for explaining this. According to Ashutosh Varshney's (2002) work on the subject, one important factor refers to the structure of civil society and, he argues, regions where there are dense intra-ethnic social networks that link different communities together are less prone to conflict than regions where the two communities are more socially segregated. We can specify this hypothesized relationship as a diagram:

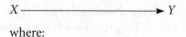

where:

Y is level of ethnic conflict in a region (our dependent variable); and
X is level of intra-ethnic civil society in a region (our independent or explanatory variable).

Bivariate analysis is a way of establishing whether or not there is indeed a relationship between two variables, as the theory predicts. It allows us to compare our theoretical expectations against evidence from the real world to see if the theory is supported by what we observe or not. In its simplest bivariate form, we have one dependent variable (which we are interested in trying to explain), such as ethnic conflict, and one independent variable (which we think influences, or causes, or helps to explain in some way our dependent variable), such as the structure of intra-ethnic civil society. When we have more than one independent variable (i.e. more than one explanatory factor), we move from bivariate analysis to multivariate analysis (which we deal with in the next chapter), but many of the analytic principles are much the same.

The hard work in quantitative analysis is not to be found in carrying out the analysis itself. This is relatively straightforward, and once a few general techniques have been acquired, they can be applied in a wide variety of ways. Rather the hard work is theoretical, developing hypotheses and interesting research questions that engage with prior research but also take it in new directions (see Chapter 5).

Regardless of which technique we use (cross-tabs or regression), the principles of bivariate analysis are much the same. Indeed, the principles of quantitative methods in general are much the same. We start off with a research question—or idea. That is, we seek to describe, or explain or predict, some social or political phenomenon (our dependent variables), and we have certain theoretical expectations about what factor (or factors) may be important in helping us do this (our independent variables) (see Chapters 5 and 6). We then collect data and develop indicators to measure our different concepts (see Chapters 7 and 10). Then, finally, we analyse the data in order to establish whether our theoretical expectations are supported by what we observe in the real world or not. This last part is relatively straightforward, and involves obtaining answers to three basic questions.

Is there a relationship between the variables?

The first question that we want to answer is whether the variables are related to, or associated with, each other or not. Two variables are associated if knowing something about one variable helps us to know something about the other variable. In formal terms, we can say that variables are associated if the conditional distribution of one variable varies across the levels of the other. For example, if economically underdeveloped countries tend to be authoritarian and economically developed countries tend to be democratic, we could say that economic development and democracy are associated; that is, the level of democracy varies across levels of economic development. In other words, we first want to assess whether the sample associations that we observe are statistically significant, or not.

Underpinning significance testing is the idea of hypothesis testing, and the **null hypothesis**. The null hypothesis is the hypothesis that we empirically test, and is normally the opposite of what we theoretically expect to observe. In this sense, it has parallels with Karl Popper's 'falsificationist thesis', which we discussed in Chapters 2 and 3. This principle of falsification lies at the heart of hypothesis testing in quantitative methods. We do not therefore test to see if there is a relationship between two variables, but rather test to see if we can reject (or falsify) the hypothesis that there is no relationship. So, for example, if we are interested in the relationship between economic development and democracy, we may think that rich countries tend to be more democratic than poorer countries. We do not directly test this though. Rather, our null hypothesis is that there is no association between economic development and democracy. If we find evidence to reject the null hypothesis, then we can reject the idea that there is no relationship, and infer that there probably is a relationship. Whether we reject (or fail to reject) the null hypothesis is incredibly easy to decide. We will discuss this in more detail later in the chapter, but the standard practice is simply to reject the null hypothesis if something called the p value is less than 0.05. The p value refers to the probability that the null hypothesis is true. So a p value of 0.05 tells us that there is a 5% chance that the null hypothesis is true. If the probability of it being true is very low (by convention less than 5%), then we assume that it is probably false.

How can we describe the relationship between the variables?

If we find evidence to suggest that two variables are statistically associated, we could then go on to describe the pattern of this association. Principally, we are interested in whether the pattern of the relationship conforms to our theoretical expectations or not (i.e. that richer countries are more democratic). How we describe this association varies according to the method that we use (cross-tabs or regression). With cross-tabs we describe the association with reference to percentages, and with regression we describe the association with reference to something called the **line of best fit**. But in either case we are principally concerned with whether the pattern that we observe is in the expected direction predicted by our theory.

How good is our explanation?

Finally the third question that we need to bear in mind is to do with how good—or how robust—we think our findings are. Put simply, are they convincing? On what grounds could they be challenged? Invariably, with bivariate analysis our explanation will be partial since we are considering the impact of only one variable on the dependent variable. We then need to think about what other variables or factors may be important, and whether our results still stand up when we take these into account. This we deal with in the next chapter.

Association and causality

In many cases, identifying patterns of association between two variables helps us to make claims about causality. We can think about this in deterministic terms, or in probabilistic terms (see Chapter 6). However, it must be remembered that just because two variables are associated with each other, it does not mean that the relationship is causal. And trying to demonstrate that a relationship is causal is not straightforward. A causal relationship can be thought of as one where X—our independent variable—causes Y—our dependent variable. For example, does economic development influence (or cause) democracy? Does ethnic diversity influence (or cause) civil war? For a relationship to be considered causal, we need to establish three conditions. First, there must be statistical association. If two variables are not associated with each other, then there cannot be a causal relationship. However, association by itself is not enough to suggest causality. It is a necessary but not sufficient condition. Second, there must be the correct temporal ordering. For variable X to cause variable Y, X must be temporally prior to Y. Sometimes this is easy to establish. It is clear, for example, that a person's age is temporally prior to their decision to go out to vote. We could not argue that abstaining makes you younger. But at other times, it is less clear cut, and it is more difficult to disentangle the temporal ordering, or direction of causality. For example, does economic development make a country more democratic? Or could it be the other way round? Does being democratic make a country richer? The theory may be uncertain, and questions of this type bedevil empirical research. Does *a* cause *b* or does *b* cause *a*? Or indeed is there a reciprocal relationship?

Third, we must rule out alternative explanations. We will return to this point in the next chapter when we consider multivariate analysis. However, even when these requirements are all met, we can still only make tentative claims about causality, and perhaps what we have achieved can better be described as 'robust association'. Ultimately, then, even if we develop theoretical hypotheses that are causal in nature, when we come to analysing the data, all we can do is see whether the pattern of association is consistent with our expectations or not.

Data considerations for bivariate analysis

Bivariate analysis includes a number of different methods. The type of method that is appropriate depends upon the level of measurement of our variables. In the following sections, we examine the association between two interval-level variables using OLS regression, and then consider the association between two categorical-level variables using cross-tabulations.

Bivariate analysis for interval data

There are a number of ways in which we can examine the relationship between two interval-level variables. The most common technique is simple linear regression (OLS regression), and Pearson's correlation. Both techniques are closely related, and we discuss them in detail below. The workhorse for both techniques is the scatter plot. Bivariate analysis with interval-level data can best be depicted through the use of figures (at least when there is a small amount of cases), as this creates a clear visual representation of how the two variables are related (or not). The pattern of this relationship can then be summarized using statistics. This section focuses on simple linear regression, which is one of the most widely used statistical techniques in political research, and which can be used both for bivariate and multivariate analysis. The first part of this section examines how scatter plots can be used to depict the relationship between two interval-level variables. The second part then looks at how we can summarize this relationship using the line of best fit—otherwise known as the **regression line**. The third part then moves on to questions of significance, and discusses how we can make inferences about whether the sample association exists in the wider population.

Bivariate analysis using scatter plots: describing the relationship

Figures provide an intuitive way of examining the relationship between two interval-level variables when we have relatively few cases. They visually represent the important characteristics of the relationship, and just by eye-balling the scatter plot, we can immediately get a rough idea of whether there is a relationship or not, and if there is, whether it is positive or negative and whether it is weak or strong. In this section, we examine how figures can be used to depict the association between two interval-level variables, and how this association can be summarized using the line of best fit. The line of best fit is also known as the regression line, which forms the basis of simple linear regression analysis, which we will examine in more detail.

To illustrate these techniques let us consider the relationship between the level of economic development of a country and its level of democracy. A great deal of research has examined this topic, and the research has gone in many different and sophisticated directions, but the starting point for much of the analysis is the simple observation that rich countries tend to be more democratic than poor countries. To examine this relationship we need to develop empirical indicators for each of our variables. To measure economic development is fairly straightforward. There are a number of measures we could use, but perhaps the most straight-forward is simply GDP per capita. To measure a country's level of democracy is slightly more problematic (see Chapter 6 on conceptual definitions). Democracy is a difficult concept to define, and wherever there is definitional ambiguity, there is also likely to be controversy over measurement. There are a number of widely used indicators to measure democracy, from simple dichotomies of whether a country is democratic or not, based on whether it holds free and fair elections (Przeworski et al. 2000), to more extensive scales based on political rights (Polity IV; Marshall and Jaggers 2010) and civil rights (Freedom House 2010). For this exam-ple we opt for Polity IV, since it distinguishes between different levels of democracy (from very authoritarian to fully democratic) on a scale of 0 to 10 (where 10 is the most democratic).

The next step is to collect information for different countries for each of these variables. Each country therefore represents a case, and for each case we collect information on its level of democracy (measured as its Polity IV score) and its level of economic development (meas-ured as GDP per capita in US dollars). To simplify this example we start by considering just ten countries. The data for these ten countries are shown below in a data matrix, similar to how data are stored in most statistical software packages. Each row represents a case, and each column represents a variable.

Country	X—GDP per capita	Y—Level of democracy
Chad	$871	1
Cambodia	$1,446	3
Georgia	$2,664	5
Ecuador	$3,203	6
Paraguay	$4,426	7
Bulgaria	$5,710	8
Venezuela	$5,794	7
Brazil	$7,625	8
Costa Rica	$8,650	10
Mexico	$9,023	8

From the raw data, it is difficult to ascertain whether there is much of an association between a country's score on each of the variables. But this becomes much clearer if we represent the data graphically. Our expectation is that those countries with low levels of economic development will also have low levels of democracy, and that those countries with high levels of economic development will have high levels of democracy. To see if this expectation is fulfilled we can simply plot the values for each variable against each other on a scatter plot. These values can be thought of as the coordinates for each country, which form the basis of correlation and regression. This is done in Figure 15.1, where the horizontal axis (the x-axis) refers to a country's level of economic development and the vertical axis (the y-axis) refers to a country's level of democracy. Each dot represents a country, and its position on the scatter plot relates to its score on each of the variables. Just from eye-balling the results, we can see that our expectation appears to be confirmed. The countries with relatively high levels of economic development, like Costa Rica and Mexico, also tend to have relatively high levels of democracy, and the countries with relatively low levels of economic development, like Chad and Cambodia, tend to have relatively low levels of democracy.

We can phrase this in a slightly different way, and say that there appears to be a positive relationship between the level of economic development of a country and its level of democracy. That is, countries with *higher* levels of economic development tend to have *higher* levels of democracy. We can see this quite clearly from the scatter plot, but we can also provide a summary measure of this relationship by fitting to the data something commonly known as the line of best fit, or the regression line (see Figure 15.2).

The regression line gives a neutral, impartial way of identifying the best fitting line to a scatter of dots in a two-dimensional space. This method involves identifying a line that minimizes the sum of squared vertical deviations from itself. The deviations are the distance between the line of best fit and each observation. The regression line cuts through the middle of all the observations. Some of the observations are above the line, like Bulgaria, some of the observations are below the line, like Chad, but the best fitting line minimizes the distance shown by the arrow between the line and the observations (also known as the residuals). This procedure is called least squares and is often called 'ordinary least squares' or OLS for short. The calculation of the line of best fit is not particularly interesting from a substantive point of view, and there is no need to go into it in detail, since practically all software packages will fit the line for you. But the general principle is simple enough. The important thing is to be able to interpret the line once it has been fitted.

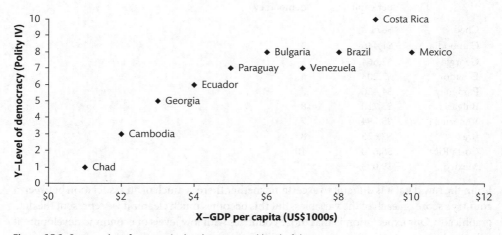

Figure 15.1 Scatter plot of economic development and level of democracy

The regression line can be represented with the following equation:

$$Y = a + bX$$

where

- Y is the dependent variable (the one on the vertical axis);
- X is the independent variable (the one on the horizontal axis);
- a is the intercept;
- b is the slope.

Sometimes this equation is written with a 'hat' over the Y to indicate that the dependent variable is not an exact function of X, and is a predicted value for which there is associated error (meaning that not all of the observations fit perfectly onto the line of best fit). Either way, the main points of interest are the values for the intercept (sometimes called the constant) and the slope coefficient and how these can be interpreted.

From the above example, the values that we obtain for our line of best fit can be expressed as follows:

$$Y = 1.93 + 0.79X.$$

The **intercept**, or the constant as it sometimes known, is the point where the line of best fit crosses the y-axis. It thus refers to the value of Y when X is zero. Here, the intercept of 1.93 refers to the predicted level of democracy for a country with a GDP per capita of zero. In most cases, this value is not of much analytical interest, since a value of zero on the independent variable does not make much theoretical or empirical sense. We are therefore rarely interested in discussing the size of the constant, but it is important if we are interested in prediction, and making a guess about Y for some given value of X, which we will return to later.

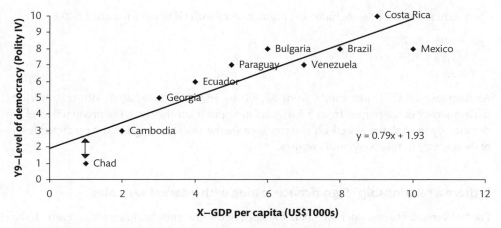

Figure 15.2 Scatter plot of economic development and level of democracy, with line of best fit

Of far more substantive interest is the *slope* of the line, which describes the functional relationship between x and y, and is sometimes known as the **slope coefficient** or **regression coefficient,** depicted by the letter b. The **slope coefficient** can tell us a number of things. First, if the slope coefficient is zero, then the slope of the line is flat, parallel to the x-axis, and there is no relationship between the two variables. In other words, an increase in the value of our independent variable has no impact on the value of the dependent variable. Second, the slope coefficient can also tell us whether the relationship is positive or negative: a positive value for the slope coefficient indicates that as values of X increase, values of Y also tend to increase, whereas a negative value for the slope coefficient indicates that as values of X increase, values of Y tend to decrease. And third, it also allows us to quantify the magnitude of this increase (or decrease) and specifically it tells us the number of units that Y changes for each unit change in X. So, in this example, a slope coefficient of 0.79 tells us that for every unit increase in X of $1,000 (since GDP per capita is measured in thousands of dollars), the predicted or estimated level of democracy in a country increases by 0.79 points on the Polity IV scale (which ranges from 0 to 10).

The value of the regression coefficient might appear small, but its size is partly a function of the scale on which the independent variable (and dependent variable) is measured. For example, if GDP per capita were measured in dollars rather than thousands of dollars, the size of the coefficient would be 1,000 times smaller. It is often helpful therefore to illustrate the substantive impact of the independent variable by calculating the predicted value of Y for different values of X. So we might want to compare the predicted level of democracy for a relatively well-off country, say one with a GDP per capita of $8,000 and for a relatively poor country, say one with a GDP per capita of $2,000. We can then plug the relevant numbers into our equation (remembering to take into account the value of the intercept) as follows:

$$Y = 1.93 + 0.79X.$$

The predicted level of democracy for a well-off country with GDP per capita of $8,000:

$$Y = 1.93 + 0.79*8$$
$$Y = 1.93 + 6.32$$
$$Y = 8.25.$$

The predicted level of democracy for a poor country with GDP per capita of $2,000:

$$Y = 1.93 + 0. 79*2$$
$$Y = 1.93 + 1.58$$
$$Y = 3.51.$$

An increase in GDP per capita from $2,000 to $8,000 is associated with an increase in democracy of 4.8 points, from 3.5 to 8.3. Or, to put it another way, the predicted level of democracy in a relatively well-off country is more than twice as high as the predicted level of democracy in relatively poor country.

Is there a relationship? Significance testing with interval variables

For two variables to be associated, then, the slope of the line must be different from zero. If the slope is positive, then we observe an upward-sloping line, as shown in Figure 15.3(a), indicating

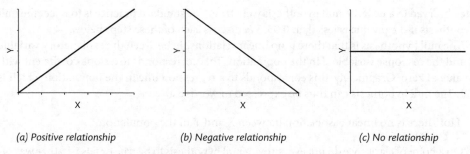

(a) Positive relationship   *(b) Negative relationship*   *(c) No relationship*

Figure 15.3 Different types of linear relationship

that as the value of the independent variable increases, the predicted value of the dependent variable also tends to increase. If the slope is negative, then we observe a downward-sloping line as shown in Figure 15.3(b), indicating that as the independent variable increases, the predicted value of the dependent variable decreases. If the slope coefficient is zero, however, then the line of best fit is flat, as shown in Figure 15.3(c), indicating that as the independent variable increases, there is no linear change in the predicted value of the dependent variable.

This raises the question of what counts as a slope coefficient that is different from zero. How big does the coefficient need to be? If our slope coefficient is, say, 0.2, can we infer that there is a real relationship? To have confidence that the relationship really exists, we have to establish how likely it is that the slope also exists in the population. To help us do this we draw on the principle of significance testing, which builds directly on what we discussed in Chapter 14.

So far we have used simple linear regression as a descriptive tool to describe the pattern of the relationship between two variables in our sample. But linear regression modelling is more powerful as a tool of inference: it allows us to make estimates of the parameters for the model *in the population.* We use inferential statistics because we want to say something about the population from which our sample is drawn. That is, in the world at large, do rich countries tend to be more democratic than poorer countries?

In order to answer this question we carry out a significance test. The method we use to test for significance in regression is called the **t test** . The t test (or t ratio) enables us to assess how likely it is that the sample association we observe could just be the result of sampling variation. Even if we had data on all the countries in the world, we would still treat this as a sample, since what we are really interested in is the relationship between the variables, and the countries in the world are in a sense a sample of the values these variables can take. The only parameter of the simple linear regression model for which we will describe methods of statistical inference is the slope coefficient *b*. Tests and confidence intervals for population values of the intercept *a* are almost never substantively interesting, so they will not be considered here. Significance testing involves a number of steps. The first step is to clarify exactly what it is that is to be tested. This is known as stating the null hypothesis. The second step involves making a decision on whether the null hypothesis can be rejected or not. To do this we refer to something that is known as the test statistic (or t ratio), which provides a summary measure of the difference between what we observe and what we would expect to observe if there was no relationship. Finally, we make a decision on whether this difference is statistically significant or not, with reference to the p value, which refers to the probability of obtaining the observed t value if the null hypothesis were true. The standard practice is to reject the null hypothesis if the p value is less than 0.05. We discuss each of these steps below.

The null hypothesis is that there is no linear relationship between the explanatory variable X and the response variable Y in the population. This corresponds to a slope coefficient with a value of zero. Graphically, this corresponds to a regression line in the population which is flat. The null hypothesis can thus be expressed in words as:

Ho: There is no linear association between X and Y in the population.

On a point of clarity, we do not ever prove a null hypothesis to be true or false. Rather we collect evidence to make an informed decision based on the balance of probability. Because we are dealing with probabilities rather than absolutes, there is always a risk that we make an error. In particular, there are two main types of error that we can make. These are known as the **Type I error** and the **Type II error**. A Type I error is when we incorrectly reject a null hypothesis that is actually true. The way to reduce these errors is just to raise the threshold for failing to reject the null hypothesis, from the 0.05 level to the 0.01 level. The problem with this approach though is that it risks introducing what is known as the Type II error, which is failing to reject a null hypothesis that is actually false. Type I errors are conventionally considered more serious than Type II errors, so what we most want to avoid is rejecting the null hypothesis unnecessarily. This implies that we will maintain the null hypothesis unless data provide strong enough evidence to justify rejecting it, a principle which is somewhat similar to Popper's injunction to 'keep a theory until falsified', discussed in Chapter 3, or even the 'innocent until proven guilty' principle of law.

Despite our dislike of Type I errors, we never try to avoid them completely. The only way to guarantee that the null hypothesis is never incorrectly rejected is never to reject it at all, whatever the evidence, which is obviously not a sensible decision rule for empirical research. Instead, we decide in advance how high a probability of Type I error we are willing to tolerate, and then use a test procedure with that probability. The convention is that we are prepared (if not happy) to be wrong 5% of the time, and so we use a 5% level of significance to make decisions from a test. The null hypothesis is then rejected if the sample yields a test statistic for which the p value is less than 0.05. This is our critical value.

The test statistic

To make some sensible statement about whether the slope in the population is flat or not, we need to rely upon statistical and probability theory. From our sample, we have an estimate of the population slope, but it is only that: an estimate. What we want to know is whether there is enough evidence to suggest that our estimate is significantly different from zero. If there is, we can reject the null hypothesis and infer that in the population there probably is a relationship between the two variables. But if we do not have enough evidence to do this, we fail to reject the null hypothesis. The logic underpinning the t test is quite intuitive. We have an estimate of the slope coefficient in the population. We want to know if this is significantly different from zero, but our coefficient is only an estimate. The true value may be a little higher or a little lower. To see whether it is significantly higher or lower than zero we utilize something called **standard error,** and from this we can calculate a confidence interval in much the same way as we did in Chapter 14. The 95% confidence interval for the slope coefficient is calculated as the coefficient plus or minus 1.96 multiplied by its standard error. So, for example, if the slope coefficient is 3; and the standard error is 2, our 95% confidence interval is between 6.92 and –0.92 (3 plus or minus 3.92). Since 0 is contained within that confidence interval, we cannot rule out the possibility that the real population parameter is zero, and so we would fail to reject the null hypothesis. Thus, as a shorthand, when the slope coefficient is less than twice the size of its standard error, we fail to reject the null hypothesis (this is why it is important always to report the standard errors of the regression estimates).

The test statistic is simply the slope coefficient divided by its standard error. The formula is shown below:

$$t = \frac{\hat{\beta}}{s\hat{e}(\hat{\beta})}$$

where

β is the estimated coefficient; and
$s\hat{e}(\beta)$ is the estimated standard error of the coefficient.

The t statistic can be thought of as is a measure of the difference between what we would expect to see if the null were true (e.g. the slope would be zero), and what we actually observe. Larger values of t therefore indicate that our sample does not conform to the expected pattern of no association. Using probability theory, we can establish how likely it is that we would observe a t of the given value if the null hypothesis were actually true. The p value gives us the exact probability of drawing a sample with a test statistic of the observed value or greater from a population in which there is no association between the two variables (e.g. slope is zero). By convention, if the probability is lower than 0.05, we reject the null hypothesis. What we are saying is that the probability of obtaining a t value of this size if the null hypothesis is true is so small that we are confident that it must therefore be false. But this is somewhat different to proving that it is false. The key word here is confidence. We can never know for sure whether the null hypothesis is true or not. We know that 95 times out of a 100 it will be the correct decision to reject the null hypothesis, but we also know that five times out of a 100 we will reject a null hypothesis that is actually true.

The strength of the relationship: a question of fit

So far we have examined whether (or not) we think there is a relationship between two interval-level variables, using significance tests, and how we can describe the form of that relationship, with reference to the direction of the relationship and the magnitude of the coefficient. There is, however, a third aspect of the relationship that it is often helpful to consider. This is sometimes known as the strength of the relationship, but is perhaps better described as the fit. If we were to say that there was a strong relationship between two variables, we could understand this in two different ways. First, we could think of a strong relationship as being one where our independent variable has a 'big' impact on our dependent variable, that is, one where the slope of the regression line is very steep. But we could also think of a strong relationship as being one where our line of best fit produces very little error, that is, when all the observations are clustered very tightly around the line.

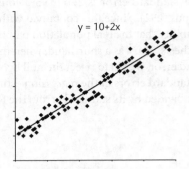 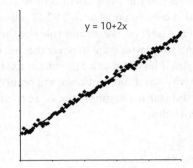

Figure 15.4 The 'fit' of the regression line

The line of best fit allows us to predict values of Y for given values of X. However, we almost always make some errors in our prediction of Y. The errors are called the residuals, and are the distance between the line of best fit and the actual observations that the line passes through. The more accurate the guesses of $\hat{Y}$, the smaller the residuals, and the better we can say the line *fits the data*. This is illustrated in Figure 15.4, which shows two graphs with exactly the same values for the intercept and slope coefficient. In the first graph, we can see that the observations are quite spread out around the regression line, whereas in the second graph, all the data points are very close to the regression line. We can describe the difference between these two regression lines in terms of which one provides the better 'fit' to the data. Both Pearson's correlation and R-square are measures for summarizing this fit.

R-square (R2) is one of the most commonly reported statistics in quantitative political research. One way to think about it is that it provides a summary measure of how much better off we are in our predictions of Y using the regression line than some other estimation technique (basically, guessing). It describes the proportion of the variation in the dependent variable that our model is able to 'explain'. If we had no information about how X is related to Y, then our best guess of Y would simply be its mean value, $\overline{Y}$. As Figure 15.5 shows, for a given value of X, the value of $\overline{Y}$ may be quite a long way away from the observed value of Y_i. We can summarize this error from guessing by adding up the squared distance between each value of Y_i and the mean value of Y $(Y - \overline{Y})$. This is known as the total sum of squares (TSS), and can be regarded as a measure of the total variation in our dependent variable:

$$TSS = \sum (Y_i - \overline{Y})^2.$$

Out of this total variation, we want to know how much our model explains. Using the regression line, we make predictions of Y, denoted $\hat{Y}$. Sometimes our predictions will be good and $\hat{Y}$ will be close to the observed values of Y; sometimes our predictions will be bad and $\hat{Y}$ will be a long way away from the observed values of Y. We can break this down into what our model explains—the explained variation, and what it does not—the unexplained variation. The explained part of the model can be thought of as the difference between our predicted value of Y and the mean value of Y. This is known as the 'Model sum of squares', denoted SSM, or the 'Regression sum of squares', RegSS:

$$SSM = \sum(\hat{Y} - \bar{Y})^2.$$

The unexplained part of the model (or the error) can be thought of as the difference between our predicted value of Y and the observed value of Y. This is known as the 'Error sum of squares', denoted SSE, or the 'Residual sum of squares', denoted ResSS:

$$SSE = \sum(Y_i - \hat{Y})^2.$$

These sources of variation are related to each other so that:

Total variation of Y = Variation explained + Unexplained variation by regression

TSS   = SSM   + SSE.

The R-square statistic is simply defined as the proportion of the total variation that the model explains. It can thus be expressed as follows:

R-square = SSM/TSS.

This is known as a PRE measure (Proportional reduction in error). It is the proportion of the total variation of Y explained by the regression model. R-square ranges between 0, when the regression explains nothing (the slope coefficient is 0), and 1, when there is perfect association (all the observed values of Y fall exactly on the line of best fit). The formal interpretation of the R-square is: 'The proportion of variance in Y that can be explained by the variance in X'. So if we obtain an R-square of 0.50, we can say that 50% of the variance in Y can be explained by the variance in X. Or, that our model explains 50% of the variation in the dependent variable.

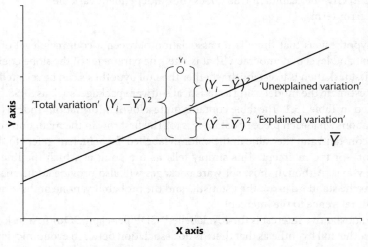

Figure 15.5 Explained and unexplained variation

This can also be put in a slightly different way, and we could say that we make 50% fewer errors when guessing Y while knowing X, as compared to guessing Y when not knowing X.

Pearson's correlation

Closely related to R-square is Pearson's correlation coefficient, or Pearson's r as it is often known. When Pearson's r is squared, it becomes R-square, and can be interpreted as a PRE measure, as discussed above. But unlike R-square, Pearson's r can also take negative values and ranges from −1 to +1. This means it can provide a useful summary about the direction of the relationship between two variables (whether it is positive or negative), as well as about the strength of the relationship (in terms of its fit to the data). When there is perfect negative association between two variables, Pearson's r is −1; when there is perfect positive association between two variables, Pearson's r is +1; and when there is no linear association between two variables, Pearson's r is 0.

Example 1: democracy and development

To illustrate how all these steps fit together, we can return to the example of the relationship between democracy and economic development that we introduced earlier, and examine the association with real data. Does democracy vary by a country's level of economic development? If so, how? The data set that we use to answer this question is the cross-national democracy data set compiled by Pippa Norris, which contains valid information on 145 countries. Each country therefore represents a case, and for each case we have information on the level of democracy (measured as Polity IV score) and level of economic development (measured as GDP per capita). We can specify the model that we estimate algebraically:

$$Y = a + b_1 X_1 + \epsilon$$

where:

Y   refers to level of democracy measured by Polity IV (our dependent variable);
X   refers to GDP per capita in US$1,000s (our independent variable);
ϵ is the error term.

Our null hypothesis is that there is no association between a country's level of economic development and level of democracy. That is, the true parameter of the slope coefficient b is zero. Our first task then is to establish whether the null hypothesis can be rejected or not. To do this, we estimate the model using a statistical software package, such as SPSS. The results are presented in Table 15.1. The table contains quite a lot of information, and it is important to be clear about what each piece of data refers to. The first row in the main body of the table is labelled 'constant', and the value in the column labelled 'b coefficient' refers to the value of the constant—or the intercept. This simply tells us the point at which the line of best fit crosses the y-axis. Although most software packages will also provide additional information, such as the standard error, the t statistic, and the probability, none of these are of much interest with reference to the intercept.

   Of more substantive interest is the row labelled 'GDP per capita'. Our first task is to establish whether the null hypothesis that there is no association between economic development and democracy can be rejected or not. To make a decision on this we inspect the associated t statistic and the p value. The t statistic is 4.15, and the p value is <0.0005. The p value tells us the probability of observing a t statistic of 4.15 or greater if the null hypothesis were true. In this instance, the probability of the null being true is very small indeed, and more importantly, is much less than our critical cut-off point of 0.05. We can therefore confidently reject the null hypothesis of no association, and infer that there probably is an association between the two variables.

Having established that there is a significant relationship, we next turn our attention to describing the pattern of this relationship. We do this with reference to the slope coefficient, which is sometimes reported as the unstandardized beta coefficient. The slope coefficient of 0.23 tells us that there is a positive association between economic development and democracy, and, more precisely, that the predicted level of democracy in a country increases by 0.23 points on the Polity IV scale for every US $1,000 increase in a country's GDP per capita. This is consistent with our prior expectations, and the evidence does suggest that on average rich countries tend to be more democratic than poor countries.

Finally, we can assess how well this model fits the data by considering the R-square, which is reported in the note to the table. The R-square is 0.11, which tells us that 11% of the variance in democracy scores can be explained by the variance in GDP per capita. On the face of it, this might not seem very much. In terms of explaining why some countries are more democratic than others, we have only scratched the surface, and there may be many other reasons apart from economic development for why some countries are more democratic than others. To gain a fuller understanding of the sources of this variation we may therefore want to explore the impact of other factors, which leads us to multivariate analysis, which we will deal with in the next chapter.

Of course, we have to bear in mind that what we have established is a statistical association between the two variables, and this is very different from establishing a causal relationship between economic development and democracy, even if that is what the theory suggests. Statistical association is, of course, the first condition of establishing causality, but we might have serious questions about whether the other two conditions of correct temporal ordering and elimination of alternative explanations have been satisfactorily dealt with. We do not know that if a country were to become richer, it it would also become more democratic (to investigate that, we would need to look at changes over time) or even why rich countries are more democratic than poorer ones. Bivariate analysis thus often leads to more questions than it can answer, and constitutes the first step in a more involved investigation. We will return to some of these points in the next chapter.

Table 15.1 Democracy and development, OLS regression, parameter estimates

	Un-standardized beta coefficient	Std error	t	p value
Constant	1.96	0.61	3.20	0.002
GDP per capita	0.23	0.06	4.15	0.000

Notes: Dependent variable: Polity democracy 10-pt score, 2000. N = 145; R-square = 0.11.
Source: Pippa Norris, Cross-national democracy project.

Bivariate analysis for categorical data: cross-tabulation

So far we have examined the bivariate association between two interval-level variables. However, many of the social and political phenomena that we are interested in exploring are not measured on an interval scale. Research on voting behaviour, political protest, democratic breakdown, and civil war often deal with dependent variables that are **nominal**, and focus on whether someone votes for one particular political party or another, or whether a country has experienced democratic breakdown or civil war, or not. Indeed, democracy can also be thought of in nominal terms: either a country is democratic or it is not. To examine these types of variables, then, we need to use a different technique. Cross-tabulations (or cross-tabs) are the appropriate method of bivariate analysis when you are interested in the association between two categorical (nominal or ordinal) variables. Cross-tabs work best when the variables have a limited number of categories. Too many categories make the tables unwieldy and difficult to analyse, and also run the risk of introducing sparse or empty cells (see Chapter 14). But even if variables do have a lot of categories, such as interval-level variables like age, it can often be helpful initially to split them into categories, such as age groups, and look at the cross-tabs. Although cross-tabs involve analysing the relationship between two variables in a slightly different way from the method of simple linear regression discussed above, the analytic principles are very similar. It enables the researcher to answer two main questions. Is there a relationship between the two variables? And if so, what does that relationship look like? How can we describe it?

Bivariate analysis using tables: describing the relationship

The essence of cross-tabs is to compare the frequency distributions (see Chapter 14) for two or more categories. These are sometimes known as conditional distributions. They are conditional because the distribution of the dependent variable depends upon the level of the explanatory variable. To illustrate the logic of cross-tabs we can think about the relationship between age and turnout. In recent years, there has been a great deal of academic research on the relatively low levels of electoral participation among young people, and what, if anything, accounts for this. To examine this relationship we can look at survey data collected by the British Election Study in 2005. Since age is an interval-level variable we need to recode it into different age bands, transforming it into an ordinal variable. By contrast, turnout is a nominal variable. People either voted or they didn't. When a variable is binary—that is, when it contains only two categories (voted/didn't vote)—it is often referred to as a **dummy variable**. We can then proceed to see whether (and how) patterns of turnout vary by age group.

Since we are interested in trying to explain turnout, this is our dependent variable. Our independent variable, or explanatory variable, is age. It is convention that the dependent variable goes along the rows, and the independent variable goes down the columns. Turnout is therefore the row variable; and age is the column variable (see Table 15.2). The intersection of a row and a column is the cell of a table. The frequencies in the internal cells describe the joint distribution: they show how many cases have each possible combination of the row and column variables. The first step is just to aggregate the cell counts for each different combination of responses. For example, the 2005 BES interviewed 3,154 people. We can see that overall 2,459 people voted and 695 people did not vote (see column labelled 'Total'). In

Table 15.2 Age and turnout in 2005 British General Election, cell counts

	18–39 years old	40–59 years old	60 years old and over	Total
Did not vote	350	224	121	695
Voted	652	947	860	2459
Total	1002	1171	981	3154

Source: British Election Study 2005.

addition, we can see that 652 of the youngest age group voted, compared with 947 of the middle age group and 860 of the oldest age group.

Tables organized in this way are not very easy to interpret, and it is difficult to tell which age groups are the most likely to vote, since the size of the different age groups varies. To help us make these comparisons more easily we therefore convert the cell counts into percentages, just as we did in the previous chapter. There is a number of ways in which we can calculate percentages, and it is important to be clear about whether we are calculating (or interpreting) row percentages or column percentages. Each type of percentage refers to something slightly different, so it is important not to get confused. Column percentages are the standard practice. These are read down the table in columns. These are reported in Table 15.3. So, for example, we can see that 65% of 18–39-year-olds voted in the election. When interpreting the table, it is useful to draw comparisons between the different cells. For example, with reference to Table 15.3, we can see that turnout appears to increase with age. Whereas only 65% of 18–39-year-olds reported having voted, 81% of 40–59-year-olds and 88% of the over 60s reported having done so. Reported turnout among the 40–59 age group was therefore 16 percentage points higher than it was among the younger age group. This difference appears to be quite substantial.

Row percentages are somewhat different. These are not reported in the table, but can easily be calculated from the cell counts in Table 15.2. In this example, a row percentage would refer to the percentage of voters who fall into each age group. So, for example, we can see that 2,459 people voted in the election. Of these 2,459, 652 were aged 18–39, which equates to 27%. By contrast, 39% of voters were aged 40–59, and 35% of voters were aged 60 or over. We have to be careful what substantive conclusions we can draw from these percentages. We can see that the largest number of voters are in the 40–59-year-old age group, but this is not because people in this age group are the most likely to vote (which they are not, as we saw in Table 15.3), but because this age group is simply the largest in terms of size, and so constitutes the biggest proportion of voters.

Table 15.3 Age and turnout in 2005 British General Election, column percentages

	18–39 years old	40–59 years old	60 years old and over	All
Did not vote	35	19	12	22
Voted	65	81	88	78
N	1002	1171	981	3154

Source: British Election Study 2005,

We can also use cross-tabs to look at the association between two ordinal variables in much the same way. Table 15.4 reports the column percentages for a cross-tab between educational attainment and support for the death penalty. Respondents were asked whether they agreed or disagreed with the statement that the death penalty is never justified. Overall, more people disagreed with this statement than agreed with it (47% vs 38%), suggesting that, on balance, public opinion in Britain is in favour of the death penalty. However, there was considerable variation in responses by education level. We can see that 57% of highly educated people agreed that the death penalty was never justified, compared with just 29% of people with lower educational qualifications. Since both variables are ordinal, we can say that support for the death penalty appears to decrease as level of education increases.

Is there a relationship? Statistical significance for cross-tabs

So far we have used cross-tabs as a descriptive tool to describe the observed pattern of association between two variables in our sample. In some instances, we may observe a clear pattern, where it is obvious (or at least appears so) that the distribution of responses varies by sub-group. But, in other instances, the observed pattern may be less clear-cut, and there may be only small differences between the sub-groups, or hardly any difference at all. Under these circumstances, it is not so obvious whether there is a 'real' relationship or not. Do the differences that we observe reflect real differences that exist within the population, or could they just be the result of sampling error?

To answer these questions we need to carry out tests of significance, based on something called chi square. As we discussed above with reference to regression, there are different ways of carrying out these statistical tests and the test that we employ depends upon the type of variable we are examining and the type of analysis that we are carrying out. However, all significance tests serve the same underlying purpose, which is to provide us with the information to make a decision based on probability as to whether or not we think the relationship we observe in our sample reflects a real relationship that exists in the population.

To illustrate these points, Table 15.5 shows two hypothetical examples. Example 1 depicts what it would look like if there were a perfect relationship between a person's social class (measured in terms of whether they are working class or middle class) and which party they reported voting for at the last election (just focusing on whether they voted for Labour or Conservatives). By contrast, Example 2 depicts what it would look like if there were no relationship. From Example 1 we can see that all the working-class respondents voted for Labour and none voted for the Conservatives, whereas all the middle classes voted for the Conservatives and none

Table 15.4 Attitudes towards the death penalty by level of education, column percentages

	Education			
	High	Intermediate	Lower	Total
Agree	57	38	29	38
Neither agree nor disagree	10	15	16	14
Disagree	33	47	55	47
N	575	695	1063	2333

Notes: Question wording: The death penalty is never justified.

Table 15.5 Association, hypothetical example, column percentages

	Example 1: Perfect association		Example 2: No association	
	Working class (%)	Middle class (%)	Working class (%)	Middle class (%)
Labour	100	0	55	55
Conservative	0	100	45	45
Total	100	100	100	100

voted for Labour. This is an example of perfect association. If we know somebody's class—that is, whether they are middle class or working class—we can perfectly predict which party they will vote for. By contrast, Example 2 depicts an example of (perfect) no association. We can see that exactly the same proportion of middle-class and working-class voters support each party. Knowing someone's class does not therefore help us at all in predicting which party they vote for. The conditional distributions of each class are exactly the same, and there is thus no association between the two variables. These two examples provide extreme scenarios. In practice, we are never likely to find the first example in the real world, but what we want to know is whether our sample is similar or not to the second example. If we think that it is similar, then we conclude that there is probably not a relationship between the two variables, but if we think that it is different from Example 2, then we can conclude that there probably is a relationship.

As before, to establish whether our sample is different or not from what we would expect to see if there was no relationship between the two variables, we carry out a significance test. The method we use to test for significance in cross-tabs is called chi square, often denoted as χ^2. Chi square enables us to assess how likely it is that the sample association we observe could just be the result of sampling variation. Although the Chi-square statistic that we use to test for significance in cross-tabs is different from the t test that we discussed with reference to bivariate analysis with interval data, the analytical principles are much the same and we go through the same basic series of steps.

- State null hypothesis.
- Calculate statistic and interpret.
- Accept or reject null hypothesis.

The null hypothesis is stated in exactly the same way as we discussed earlier. Using the example discussed above, the null hypothesis would be:

H_0: In the population, there is no association between someone's class and which party they vote.

If we can find sufficient evidence to reject the null hypothesis (at the 0.05 level), then we can infer that in the population there probably is an association between the two variables. The logic underpinning chi square is quite intuitive. It allows us to compare what we observe with what we would expect to observe if there was no association. We compare the table that we observe in our sample with a theoretical table of what we would expect to observe if there was no relationship between the variables (as shown in Example 2 of Table 15.5). To do this, we compare something called the observed frequencies and the expected frequencies.

Starting with a table with just the cell frequencies, we compare the observed frequencies (O) that we observe in our sample, with the ones that would be expected under the null hypothesis of no association (E). The chi-square test is an excellent workhorse for testing whether the differences between O and E are statistically significant or not.

Table 15.6 shows the observed distribution of frequencies for a cross-tab of class by vote choice. The cell counts refer to the observed frequencies. The expected frequencies are calculated for the middle class and working class, assuming that the distribution of responses is exactly the same as for the sample overall. Since the total proportion of Labour voters in the sample is 0.396, we would therefore expect (if the null were true) 40% of the working class to vote Labour and 40% of the middle class to vote Labour. Therefore the expected frequency of working-class Labour voters would be 1,078 (the total number of working class in the sample) multiplied by 0.3958 (the total proportion of Labour voters in the sample), which gives 427. This can be calculated in a similar way for each cell in the table.

Chi square compares the difference between these expected and observed values. The formula for calculating chi square is written below.

$$\chi^2 = \sum \frac{\left(f_o - f_e\right)^2}{f_e}$$

where:

f_o is observed frequencies; and
f_e is expected frequencies.

Although you will never need to, because computer programs will do it for you, it is very easy to calculate chi square. We can go through each of the steps with reference to Table 15.7. The column labelled f_o (observed frequencies) is what we observe in our sample. The column labelled f_e (expected frequencies) is the frequency distribution we would expect if the null hypothesis was true. The next column is simply the difference between these two values, and the column after that is the difference squared, so we get rid of the negative numbers (which would otherwise cancel themselves out when we add them all together). The final column divides the squared difference by the expected frequencies and then we simply add up these values for each cell and the total is chi square.

Table 15.6 Class and vote, observed frequencies

| | Class | | |
	Middle	Working	Total
Labour	634	528	1162
Conservative	695	238	933
Liberal	429	228	657
Other	100	84	184
Total	1858	1078	2936

Source: British Election Study 2005.

Table 15.7 Calculating chi square

	f_o	f_e	$f_o\text{-}f_e$	$(f_o\text{-}f_e)^2$	$(f_o\text{-}f_e)^2/f_e$
Middle Labour	634	735	-101	10201	13.87
Working Labour	528	427	101	10201	23.88
Middle Conservative	695	590	105	11025	18.68
Working Conservative	238	343	-105	11025	32.14
Middle Liberal	429	415	14	196	0.47
Working Liberal	228	242	-14	169	0.70
Middle other	100	116	-16	256	2.20
Working other	84	68	16	256	3.76
Σ	2936	2936	0	43329	$\chi^2 = 95.7$

Clearly, a small chi square suggests that there probably isn't a relationship, since this means that the observed pattern is quite similar to the expected pattern assuming no association, and a large chi square suggests that there probably is a relationship between the two variables, but how do we decide what value of chi- square constitutes large and what small? This is where probability theory comes to the rescue. Chi square has a known distribution, although the shape of this distribution varies according to how many cells we have in our table (known as degrees of freedom). We can thus compare our obtained chi-square statistic against the chi-square distribution for the appropriate number of degrees of freedom. If the probability of getting our obtained value of chi square is very small (typically below 0.05), then we can reject the null hypothesis. In this sense, the logic of significance testing is the same as discussed previously with reference to the t test, only we are using a different instrument (chi square), which has a different type of distribution.

We should note, however, that chi-square tests provide an overall measure of whether or not there is a statistical association between our two variables. It thus provides a global test for the table as a whole. If we are interested in whether a particular cell within the table is significantly different from what we expect, then we need to look at something else. The adjusted residuals enable us to see in which particular cell of the table the Observed and Expected frequencies significantly differ (at the 5% level). Adjusted residuals greater than plus or minus 1.96 thus indicate a significant difference.

Example 2: Ethnic diversity and civil war

As before, we can put all these different steps of analysis together to examine a real-world problem. Research on the causes of civil war has received a great deal of attention in PIR. The causes are hotly contested. Whereas Fearon and Laitin (2003) insist there is no link between ethnic heterogeneity and conflict, others find evidence that ethnic cleavages may increase the risk of conflict (Ellingsen 2000; Cederman and Girardin 2007). Part of the reason for the controversy is that different scholars use different data sets, and different operational definitions of key variables. However, the fact that these different measures tend to produce different results should give pause for thought, and raise concerns about the **reliability** and **validity** (see Chapter 10) of the different indicators.

To examine this association, we use data on civil war from the Uppsala/PRIO armed conflict data project (Gleditsch et al. 2002), supplemented with additional data from Gleditsch (2007). The data set provides information on 177 countries across every year from 1946 to 2002, detailing the incidence of armed conflict involving more than 25 casualties. To measure the ethnic composition of the different countries, we follow Gleditsch (2007) and examine the share of the population which is not in the dominant ethnic group. The ethnic dispersion measure is therefore 100 minus the percentage share of the dominant ethnic group, based on data provided by Vanhanen (2001), recoded into four equal categories ranging from societies which are very ethnically homogeneous (coded 1) to very ethnically diverse (coded 4).

Using this data, we examine the relationship between ethnic diversity and civil war. The results are presented in Table 15.8. Our null hypothesis is therefore that there is no association between the level of ethnic diversity in a country and whether or not it experienced civil war. Our first task its to establish whether or not we can reject the null hypothesis. To do this, we inspect the chi-square statistics. The value of the Pearson chi square is 330 on 3 degrees of freedom. The probability of obtaining a chi square of this size or greater if the null hypothesis were true is less than 0.0005 (SPSS actually says it is 0.000, but it is not technically zero, so we just say $p \leq 0.0005$). This is clearly very small, and well below the conventional cut-off mark of 0.05. We can therefore confidently reject the null hypothesis and infer that there does appear to be a significant relationship between ethnic diversity and civil war.

Having established that we think a relationship does exist between the two variables, our next task is to describe the pattern of the relationship to see if it conforms to our expectations. To this end, we discuss the percentages in the table. First. we can see that in very homogeneous societies there does not appear to be a very high likelihood of civil war taking place. In very homogeneous societies, only 2.6% of the cases experienced an incident of civil war. By contrast, in more ethnically mixed societies, the incidence of civil war appears to be higher. Among quite homogeneous societies, 20% have experienced civil war; in quite diverse societies, 18% have experienced civil war; and in very diverse societies 21% have experienced civil war. These percentages are all substantially higher than what we observed for very homogeneous societies, lending some support to our initial theoretical hypothesis that civil war tends to be higher in ethnically diverse countries.

But interestingly, there does not appear to be a great deal of difference in levels of civil war between countries that are quite homogeneous (20%) and countries that are quite diverse (18%) or very diverse (21%). This suggests that the relationship is not linear. It doesn't appear to matter how big the dominant ethnic group is, it just matters whether or not there is a dominant ethnic group.

Table 15.8 Civil war and ethnic diversity, column percentages

	Very homogeneous societies	Quite homogeneous societies	Quite diverse societies	Very diverse societies	Total
No civil war	97.4	80.5	81.9	79.3	85.0
Civil war	2.6	19.5	18.1	20.7	15.0
N	2003	1879	1806	1869	7557

These results appear to confirm our expectations. Ethnic diversity, or more specifically, the presence of a dominant ethnic group, does appear to increase the likelihood of civil war. However, it is also important not to over-interpret these results. To be sure, diverse countries tend to experience more civil war than homogeneous countries, but even among diverse countries the vast majority (around 80%) do not experience civil war, so the relationship is far from deterministic. We may therefore want to investigate further why some ethnically diverse countries descend into civil war, whereas others do not. What other factors are important? How does ethnic morphology interact with economic conditions, institutional structures, and security relations with neighbouring countries? To answer these questions, we need to examine other factors, and it is this aim of developing multi-causal explanations that leads us to multivariate analysis, which we consider in the next chapter.

 ## Conclusions

This chapter has provided an introduction to statistical analysis using bivariate analysis. We have introduced the key concept of hypothesis testing, which enables us to see whether two variables are statistically associated and if so, how, using simple linear regression and cross-tabs. Bivariate analysis provides a useful starting point for examining how variables are related, and is an important building block for developing explanations and causal statements about why things happen. But it does not tell us the full story. Inevitably, bivariate analysis leads us to ask more questions. In the real world, social and political phenomena are rarely mono-causal. If we are interested in why things happen, or why certain factors are influential in some conditions rather than others, the picture rapidly becomes more complicated and we are compelled to look for additional explanations, which brings us to multivariate analysis, which we will discuss in the next chapter.

 ## Questions

- Draw an arrow diagram depicting the relationship between two variables.
- Write a brief note to accompany the arrow diagram, and state clearly which is the dependent variable and which is the independent variable, and why you think they may be related.
- What is the null hypothesis? How is it tested?
- Why should we treat the results from bivariate analysis with caution?
- What is the difference between causality and association?
- How do we know whether a relationship between two variables is causal or not?
- In cross-tabs, when might it be useful to report the row percentages and when might it be useful to report the column percentages?
- In simple linear regression, what is more substantively interesting: the magnitude of the slope coefficient or the value of R-square? What does each tell us?

 ## Guide to Further Reading

Agresti, A. and B. Finlay (2009), *Statistical Methods for the Social Sciences*, 4th edition (Upper Saddle River, NJ: Pearson–Prentice Hall).
Covers the basics of statistical description and inference, as well as more advanced topics on regression methods, including multiple regression, ANOVA and repeated measures ANOVA, analysis of covariance, logistic regression, and generalized linear models.

Johnson, Janet Buttolph, Henry Reynolds, and Jason Mycoff (2007), *Political Science Research Methods***, 6th edition (Washington, DC: CQ Press).**
Provides an introduction to quantitative analysis and covers some more advanced topics, with lots of examples from political research.

Carlson, James and Mark Hyde (2002), *Doing Empirical Political Research* **(Boston, MA: Houghton Mifflin).**
Provides an introduction to quantitative analysis and covers some more advanced topics, with lots of examples from political research.

de Vaus, David (2002), *Surveys in Social Research* **(London: Routledge).**
A detailed and accessible introduction to quantitative methods, with easy-to-read chapters on how to carry out analysis and interpret the results.

Field, A. (2009), *Discovering Statistics using SPSS (and Sex and Drugs and Rock 'n' Roll)* **(London: Sage Publications).**
Provides an easy-to-follow introduction to quantitative analysis and step-by-step instructions on how to use the SPSS statistical software package to do your own analysis.

Rowntree, Derek (2000), *Statistics without Tears: An Introduction for Non-Mathematicians* **(Harmonsdsworth: Penguin).**
An easy-to-read introduction to statistical methods.

 # References

Cederman, L. and L. Girardin (2007), 'Beyond Fractionalization: Mapping Ethnicity onto Nationalist Insurgencies', *American Political Science Review* 101: 173–85.

Ellingsen, T.(2000), 'Colorful Community or Ethnic Witches' Brew? Multiethnicity and Domestic Conflict during and after the Cold War', *Journal of Conflict Resolution* 44(2): 228–49.

Fearon, J. and D. Laitin (2003), 'Ethnicity, Insurgency, and Civil War', *American Political Science Review* 91(1): 75–90.

Freedom House (2010), *Freedom in the World*, 2010 edn., available at http://www.freedomhouse.org.

Gleditsch, Kristian Skrede (2007), 'Transnational Dimensions of Civil War', *Journal of Peace Research* 44(3): 293–309.

Gleditsch, N., P. Wallensteen, M. Erikson, M. Sollenberg, and H. Strand (2002), 'Armed

Conflict, 1945–99: A New Dataset', *Journal of Peace Research* 39(5): 615–37.

Marshall, Monty G. and Keith Jaggers (2010), *Polity IV Project: Political Regime Characteristics and Transitions, 1800–2010*, Center for Systemic Peace, available at http://www.systemicpeace.org/polity/polity4.htm.

Przeworski, A., M. Alvarez, J. Cheibub, and F. Limongi (2000), *Democracy and Development: Political Institutions and Well-Being in the World, 1950–1990* (Cambridge: Cambridge University Press).

Vanhanen, T. (2001), 'Domestic Ethnic Conflict and Ethnic Nepotism: A Comparative Analysis', *Journal of Peace Research* 36(1): 55–73.

Varshney, A. (2002), *Ethnic Conflict and Civic Life: Hindus and Muslims in India* (New Haven, CT: Yale University Press).

16

A Guide to Multivariate Analysis

Chapter Summary

This chapter examines how we can develop and test multi-causal explanations of political phenomena. It builds on the previous chapter by extending the principles of bivariate analysis to take into account more than one independent variable. In doing so, we examine two of the most widely used statistical analysis techniques in political research, OLS regression and logistic regression. This chapter includes:

- causality and association;
- statistical control;
- spurious relationships;
- indirect causality;
- interaction effects;
- linear regression;
- logistic regression.

Introduction

This chapter examines multivariate analysis, which builds directly on many of the principles discussed in Chapter 15. Multivariate analysis involves examining the pattern of associations between more than one independent variable and the dependent variable. Political phenomena are rarely mono-causal. If we are interested in trying to explain 'why' things happen, then more often than not we need to develop explanations that take into account more than one explanatory factor. Bivariate analysis allows us to get an initial sense about the structure of the relationship between two variables. However, this may not accurately reflect the 'true' nature of the relationship for a variety of reasons. Undertaking multivariate analysis allows us to examine the impact of multiple factors on our dependent variable of interest, and to compare the explanatory power of rival hypotheses. It also allows us to examine whether the association between one independent variable and the dependent variable still holds up when we control for—or take into account—other factors, and to explore whether the impact of one variable also depends upon the level of another variable. Investigating these issues helps us to develop fuller explanations for why different political phenomena occur, and provides a rigorous test of our explanations to see if they still stand up in the face of close scrutiny.

As we have seen in previous chapters, the way in which we carry out quantitative analysis depends upon the types of variables that we are interested in examining. The same applies to multivariate analysis. In this chapter we consider two different methods: OLS regression (which is an extension of what we discussed in the previous chapter for interval-level dependent variables) and logistic regression (which is appropriate when our dependent variable is categorical, specifically a dichotomy). These methods of analysis are among the most widely used quantitative techniques in political research, and understanding how they can be used and interpreted provides a strong foundation for critically evaluating much of the research that is published in leading academic journals. The first part of this chapter examines the principles of multivariate analysis, and the different types of analytical question to which they can be applied. The second part examines multivariate analysis when our dependent variable is interval level, using OLS regression that builds directly upon the topics covered in Chapter 15. The third part then considers multivariate analysis when our dependent variable is categorical, using logistic regression, which builds on cross-tabs.

The principles of multivariate analysis: statistical control

Most social and political phenomena are multi-causal, which means that insights garnered from bivariate analysis, where only one causal variable is considered, are going to be partial, at best. Multivariate analysis allows us to examine the impact of multiple causal factors on our dependent variable of interest in order to see which factors matter or which matter most. It thus provides a useful tool for developing a more complete understanding of the topic of enquiry. Multivariate analysis also allows us to have confidence in our results, and to assess whether or not they are robust. Do our results still stand up when we include other potentially important factors?

Bivariate analysis provides a good starting point for examining the structure of relationships between variables. It allows us to develop causal explanations and provide tentative answers to our research questions. But establishing causation is notoriously difficult, and we are probably never able to do it completely. At best, we therefore aim for 'robust association'. This requires three conditions. The first is statistical association. The second is appropriate time ordering. And the third is the elimination of other possibilities. From bivariate analysis, we can establish the first two conditions, but not the third. This last point is very important. To have confidence in our findings we have to subject them to rigorous testing. We have to be sceptical. If we observe a bivariate relationship, we always have to think about whether that relationship is real, or whether there are potentially other factors that could account for it. This is where multivariate analysis comes to the fore.

Suppose we are interested in exploring social trust. A great deal of research has examined the benefits of living in a community with high levels of social trust, and the factors that are associated with it. We might have three different hypotheses. Our first hypothesis might be that social trust tends to be lower in ethnically diverse communities, since people are more likely to trust those who are like them. When there are many people from different ethnic backgrounds, the level of social trust in the community therefore tends to be lower, since, in the words of Robert Putnam, people 'hunker down' (Putnam 2007). Our second hypothesis might be that social trust tends to be lower in economically deprived areas, since neighbourhoods with economic problems are more likely to be run down and lack the nice civic spaces that foster social trust, and so people may become socially withdrawn. And finally our third hypothesis might be that social trust tends to be lower in areas with high levels of crime, since crime and the fear of crime stop people going out on to the street and interacting with each other, and therefore fosters social isolation. From a bivariate analysis, we might find support for each of these hypotheses: that ethnically diverse areas tend to have lower levels of social trust than ethnically homogeneous areas, that economically deprived areas tend to have lower levels of social trust than economically prosperous areas, and that neighbourhoods with high levels of crime have lower levels of trust than neighbourhoods with low levels of crime.

A multivariate model allows us to examine the relative impact of all these variables on social trust when we examine them simultaneously. That is, when we control for—or take into account—a neighbourhood's level of economic deprivation and crime level, does its level of ethnic diversity still influence social trust? Another way of thinking about this is, supposing we are comparing two neighbourhoods with exactly the same level of economic deprivation and crime, but one neighbourhood has high levels of ethnic diversity and the other has low levels of ethnic diversity, would their respective levels of social trust vary? If their levels of social trust did vary, then we could say that controlling for economic deprivation and crime, there is an association between ethnic diversity and trust. We can express the multivariate model that we want to test symbolically, using arrow diagrams, as shown in Figure 16.1.

Multivariate analysis allows us to compare the importance of these factors against each other, and to examine their independent impact on the dependent variable. For example, we might say that ethnic diversity and economic deprivation have no independent impact on levels of social trust, once we take into account levels of crime. Ethnically diverse neighbourhoods might tend to be relatively poor, and poor areas might have higher levels of crime, but it is only crime that is directly associated with levels of trust. That is, among neighbourhoods with high levels of crime, the level of trust does not vary by ethnic diversity or economic deprivation. Diverse, poor, safe communities have the same level of trust as homogeneous, rich, safe communities. The key thing is whether the communities are safe or not, not how rich or diverse they are. In this scenario, ethnic diversity and economic deprivation have no independent effect on social trust when we control for, or take into account, levels of crime.

The idea of statistical control is one of the most important ideas in quantitative analysis. The driving force behind statistical control is to rule out theoretically plausible alternative explanations for the association between two variables to see if the association still stands up when we take into account—or control for—other variables. If we can rule out the alternative

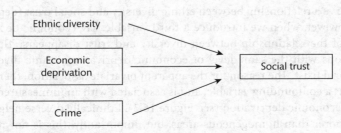

Figure 16.1 Multivariate model: predicting social trust

explanations, then this gives us more confidence that the way we have specified the relationship is the correct one. We can therefore have confidence that our results are robust, which ultimately is what we strive for. We want to be sure that they stand up. And the only way we can do this is to see if we can knock them down. This is a key strength of quantitative analysis. We are not interested in cherry-picking evidence to support our argument, but are interested in finding evidence that might contradict our argument. So if we think that the level of crime is really important for predicting a neighbourhood's level of trust, we have to think about all the reasons why it might not be. Is it crime, or the fear of crime, that drives social trust? What factors could account for the apparent association between levels of crime and social trust? If we can find other factors that can account for this statistical association, then we know our initial explanation is not very convincing. But if we can't, then we can have confidence that it might be reasonable.

Specifying different types of relationship

As the above example illustrates, when we move from bivariate analysis to multivariate analysis, we can sometimes uncover a different pattern of associations from what we initially observed. Multivariate analysis can help to knock down spurious relationships or even uncover real relationships that are hidden when we only examine two variables. But it can also allow us to examine how variables are related to each other, and distinguish between direct and indirect causal influences, and uncover how the impact of one variable is contingent on the presence (or absence) of another variable. Below we discuss each of these in turn.

Confounding variables and spurious relationships

Confounding variables are ones that might obscure the 'true' relationship between two variables. Confounding variables are associated with both the probable cause and the outcome of a specific political phenomenon, but have no direct causal influence themselves. A real-life example of this is the classic study of student admissions to the University of California. Overall, it appeared that women had a less favourable chance of being accepted to the University than men, but this proved to be spurious once the subject they applied for was taken into account: women applied for more competitive subjects than men, but within each subject, their acceptance rates were at least as good as men's. Thus the original association between sex and acceptance was spurious, and sex can be regarded as a confounding variable.

We can further illustrate the logic of a spurious relationship with reference to the example discussed earlier between a neighbourhood's ethnic diversity and level of social trust. We may observe a relationship between ethnic diversity and social trust (depicted in Figure 16.2). However, when we introduce a third variable, say economic deprivation, the significance of the relationship between diversity and trust disappears. That is, among neighbourhoods with the same level of economic deprivation, ethnic diversity has no impact on social trust. The reason for the apparent bivariate association, then, is that ethnic diversity is a confounding variable, and is associated with an unmeasured third variable, which is economic deprivation (see Figure 16.3). Ethnically diverse neighbourhoods tend to be poorer than homogeneous areas, but, importantly, this is not regarded as a causal relationship.

Figure 16.2 Bivariate relationship between diversity and trust

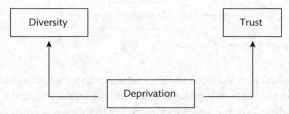

Figure 16.3 Diversity as a confounding variable

Spurious relationships can also work the other way round, and there can be a spurious 'lack of association'. This is when a 'real relationship' between two variables is masked by a third variable. Obviously, to get a true idea of how variables are causally related we want to knock down any spurious relationships. This is why we have to think carefully about our **model specification**, and whether or not our explanation includes all the theoretically relevant causal factors that we can think of. Failure to control for a theoretically important variable can mean that we attribute undue causal importance to other variables. This is also known as **omitted variable bias**.

Intervening variables and indirect causality

Intervening (or mediating) variables have a rather different role—they attempt to model the mechanisms through which, say, social class affects support for a particular political party. Possible intervening variables might be income or left–right values. For example, we might find from a bivariate analysis that there is a strong association between class and party support (see Figure 16.4), but that this association weakens (or even disappears) when we control for ideology. It might be tempting to think that the association between class and vote is spurious, as discussed above, and that class doesn't matter causally. But the key point that differentiates an indirect association from a spurious association is that we can plausibly postulate a causal sequence whereby different classes hold different ideological positions, which in turn affects one's propensity to vote for a particular party (see Figure 16.5). To be sure, these causal sequences are largely a matter of theory, but no theory could possibly suggest that, say, left–right attitudes determine one's class, although working-class people may well be disproportionately left wing.

Figure 16.4 Bivariate relationship between class and vote

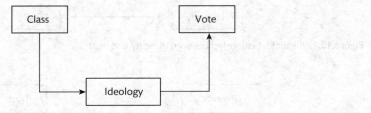

Figure 16.5 Ideology as an intervening variable

Although the distinction between indirect relationships and spurious relationships can look very similar on the surface, they have different theoretical implications. To distinguish between a confounding variable and a moderating variable we need to establish the temporal order of what comes causally prior. So if we think diversity causes deprivation, we might think that there is an indirect relationship between ethnic diversity and trust, and that economic deprivation is therefore a mediating variable. However, if we think that economic deprivation is causally prior to ethnic diversity, and that poor areas tend to be more ethnically diverse because immigrants are more likely to only be able to afford to live in poor areas (or are more likely to be allocated housing in poor areas), then we would regard ethnic diversity as a confounding variable and say that the apparent relationship between ethnic diversity and trust is spurious.

Moderator variables and interaction effects

So far we have assumed that the introduction of a third variable works in much the same way for everyone. That is, we are dealing with uniform effects. But it is also often theoretically plausible that some factors have greater influence on some groups of people (or cases) than others. An **interaction effect** is when the impact of an independent variable is conditional on the presence of another independent variable, or moderator variable. So, for example, suppose we want to investigate the relationship between someone's policy preferences and their vote choice. We might think that those who hold left-wing preferences are more likely to vote Labour and those who hold right-wing preferences are more likely to vote Conservative. There is thus a bivariate relationship between ideology and vote (see Figure 16.6). But we might also think that the form of this relationship varies across different groups. In particular, we might think that the relationship between ideology and vote choice is stronger for people who have high levels of political knowledge (since perhaps they are more aware of the ideological differences between the parties), and weaker among people with low levels of political knowledge (since perhaps they are less aware of the ideological differences between the parties). The impact of ideology on vote choice is therefore contingent upon political knowledge, which can be regarded as a moderator variable. We can summarize this type of relationship symbolically, as shown in Figure 15.7, which shows that it is the combination of ideology and knowledge together (the interaction) that is important for predicting vote choice.

Figure 16.6 Bivariate relationship between ideology and vote

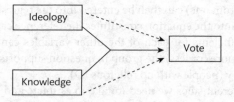

Figure 16.7 Knowledge as a moderating variable

We now turn to how these different types of relationships can be examined in practice, and discuss the principles of multivariate analysis using OLS regression and logistic regression.

Multivariate analysis using OLS regression

When our dependent variable (the thing that we are trying to explain) is interval level (or ordinal if the variable approximates a normal distribution), the appropriate method of analysis is OLS regression, as discussed in Chapter 15. Multivariate analysis using OLS is just a simple extension of the simple linear regression model, and doesn't involve any new major concepts or techniques. We specify and estimate the model in much the same way (only with more independent variables) and interpret the results with reference to the significance, direction, and magnitude of the different parameter estimates. In this section we examine how we can specify a multivariate model and interpret the results from multiple regression, with reference to the significance and direction of the parameter estimates, and the fit with the data. We also show how the results can be presented, using figures to plot the predicted values of the dependent variable for different combinations of the independent variables.

In Chapter 15 we examined the association between two interval-level variables, but we can also use OLS when one (or more) of our independent variables is measured at the nominal level. To do this, though, it is necessary to transform the nominal variable into what are known as **dummy variables**. These are binary variables. Even if the nominal variable contains more than two categories, we can break it down into a series of 'dummies'. An example of a nominal-level variable is an individual's religious identity. The variable may contain seven categories: Protestant, Catholic, Muslim, Hindu, Jewish, Other religion, and None. To estimate the association between religious identity and, say, support for the Iraq War using OLS regression, we need to recode the religious ID variable into seven different dichotomous variables, where each variable is coded 1 for the category of interest and 0 for everyone else. See below:

PROT: (1) Protestant (0) Everyone else

CATH: (1) Catholic (0) Everyone else

MUS: (1) Muslim (0) Everyone else

HIND: (1) Hindu (0) Everyone else

JEW: (1) Jewish (0) Everyone else

OTH: (1) Other religion (0) Everyone else

NONE: (1) No religious ID (0) Everyone else.

These variables (apart from one) can then be entered into the regression equation. The variable that is not entered into the equation constitutes the reference category (for example 'No religious ID'). The coefficients for each of the other variables can then be interpreted as describing how much more (or less) the group in question supports the Iraq war compared to the reference category (people with no religious ID).

To illustrate the different steps we need to take to estimate and interpret a multivariate model using OLS regression, we build on the example we considered in Chapter 15 to do with the factors that are associated with a country's level of democracy.

Example 1: democracy

A great deal of research has examined the factors that are associated with the level of democracy in a country, and there are three common explanations for why some countries are more democratic than others. These refer to economic development, ethnic diversity, and state formation. The classic (1959) study by Seymour Lipset, suggested that rich countries tend to be more democratic than poorer ones since economic development generates the wealth, social conditions, and cultural values which are conducive to liberal democracy. More recently, it has also been argued that ethnically diverse countries tend to be less democratic than more homogeneous countries, since ethnic differences can divide society and make compromise and consensus more difficult. Finally, it has also been argued that countries that have only recently gained independence may be less democratic than countries that have been independent a long time, since the institutions of the state may be weaker and less organizationally developed.

Before carrying out a multivariate analysis, it is always a good idea to look at how the independent variables are related to each other. The assumption is that they are independent—that is, they measure different things, both conceptually and empirically. If this assumption is violated, then there could be a problem of **multicolinearity**. This occurs when two independent variables are so highly correlated that they do not meaningfully measure different things. For example, if we had two independent variables, such as GDP per capita and the percentage of the population with a high-speed internet connection at home, we might find that the two variables are very highly correlated. That is, rich countries all have a high degree of internet penetration, and all countries with high levels of internet connection are rich. Under these circumstances, it becomes almost impossible to estimate the independent effect of each factor (since they are not really empirically different from one another). It is therefore advisable to either drop one of the variables from the analysis, or to combine the two variables together to form one composite measure, say of economic and technological development. There is no fixed cut-off point for how correlated is too correlated, but generally when the correlation coefficient between two independent variables is more than plus or minus 0.7, there is a problem.

Table 16.1 reports the Pearson's correlation coefficient (see Chapter 15) between each pair of variables used in the analysis. The asterisk denotes whether the bivariate relationship is significant at the 0.05 level. We can see that, at the bivariate level, each of the independent variables is significantly associated with the level of democracy. The correlation coefficient between GDP per capita and democracy is 0.4, which is significant and positive, indicating that richer countries tend to be *more* democratic than poorer countries. The correlation coefficient between

Table 16.1 Factors associated with democracy, bivariate correlation, Pearson's r

	GDP per capita	Ethnic diversity	Year of Independence	Polity IV democracy
GDP per capita	—	−0.46*	−0.33*	0.39*
Ethnic diversity	−0.46*	—	0.14	−0.27*
Year of independence	−0.33*	0.14	—	−0.24*
Polity IV democracy	0.39*	−0.27*	−0.24*	—

Notes: *Significant at $p = 0.05$ level.

ethnic diversity and democracy is –0.27, which is also significant, but this time negative, indicating that ethnically diverse countries tend to be *less* democratic than ethnically homogeneous countries. Third, the correlation coefficient between year of independence and democracy is –0.24, which is significant and negative, indicating that countries which have become independent recently are *less* democratic than countries which became independent a long time ago.

Turning to the correlations between the independent variables, we can see that there is a significant negative correlation between GDP per capita and ethnic diversity (Pearson's r = –0.46). This indicates that rich countries tend to be *less* ethnically diverse than poor countries. Similarly, there is a significant negative relationship between GDP per capita and year of independence (Pearson's r = –0.33), indicating that richer countries tend to have achieved independence earlier than poorer countries. Finally, there is not a significant correlation between year of independence and ethnic diversity (Pearson's r = 0.14). Importantly, though, none of these correlations is sufficiently large to indicate that there may be a problem with multicolinearity. Note, with correlation (unlike regression), the relationship is symmetrical. This means that its value does not depend upon which variable is considered the independent variable and which is considered the dependent variable. Thus, we can see that the correlation between GDP per capita and ethnic diversity is exactly the same as the correlation between ethnic diversity and GDP per capita.

From the bivariate analysis reported above, we can see that there is a significant negative association between ethnic diversity and level of democracy. That is, more ethnically diverse countries tend to have lower levels of democracy. But how much can we infer from this bivariate association? Would we be justified in concluding that ethnic diversity inhibits democracy in some way? We may have theoretical arguments why it might, and the data might be consistent with these expectations, but to have confidence in the result, we need to rule out the possibility that other factors are responsible for the apparent correlation.

For example, we may suspect that there is in fact no direct causal relationship between ethnic diversity and democracy. Rather, it may be the case that ethnically diverse countries tend to be rather poorer than more homogeneous countries (as we have also seen from the correlations reported above) and that it is this correlation that is driving the apparent association between ethnic diversity and democracy. Accordingly, when we control for economic development, we may find that the association between ethnic diversity and democracy disappears. To examine these possibilities, we can use OLS regression to examine the impact on democracy of all three independent variables. We can specify the model symbolically (as shown in Figure 16.8) and algebraically as follows:

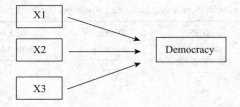

Figure 16.8   Multivariate model predicting democracy

$$Y = a + b_1 X_1 + b_2 X_2 + b_3 X_3$$

where

X1 refers to ethnic diversity on a fractionalization scale (ranging from 0 to 1, where 0 is homogeneous and 1 is diverse);

X2 refers to period of independence (where 0 = Pre-WW2 and 1 = Post-WW2);

X3 refers to GDP per capita in US$1,000s.

Now, rather than just having one slope coefficient b to estimate (as we did with simple linear regression in Chapter 15), we have three slope coefficients to estimate. These are labelled *b1, b2,* etc. These coefficients are known as **partial regression coefficients**. They are partial because their magnitude depends upon the other independent variables in the equation. That is, they indicate how much the dependent variable changes for a one-unit increase in the independent variable, holding all the other variables in the model constant. To give a clear idea of how the independent variables are related to each other and to democracy, we will not estimate the full model all in one go, but will gradually build it up by introducing each independent variable into the model one at a time. We thus estimate three models. The first model just contains ethnic diversity as an independent variable, the second model contains ethnic diversity and period when gained independence; and the third model contains all three independent variables of ethnic diversity, period when gained independence, and GDP per capita. The results are presented in Table 16.2.

Interpreting tables using OLS regression is relatively straightforward. The key things to look for are whether the independent variables are significant or not (usually at the 0.05 level) and whether the impact of the variable is in the expected direction (positive or negative). We can also inspect the magnitude of the coefficient to see if it is substantively interesting.

Model 1 reports the effect of ethnic diversity when it is the only explanatory variable in the model. We can see that the coefficient is significant at the 0.05 level (indicated by an asterisk) and the sign of the coefficient is negative, which is in the expected direction. That is, more ethnically diverse countries tend to be less democratic. The magnitude of the coefficient is $b = -7.67$. This tells us that, for every one point increase on the fractionalization scale (which ranges from 0 to 1), the expected level of democracy in a country declines by 7.67 points on the Polity IV scale (which ranges from 0 to 10). Taken on its own like this, the magnitude of the coefficient refers to the total effect of ethnic diversity on democracy. When we include additional variables, part of this effect may be accounted for by other factors, and so what we

Table 16.2   Predicting the level of democracy: OLS regression, unstandardized beta coefficients

	Model 1		Model 2		Model 3	
	B coefficient	Standard error	B coefficient	Standard error	B coefficient	Standard error
Constant	6.90*	1.10	12.49*	1.92	3.06	4.50
Diversity	-7.67*	2.11	-5.31*	2.14	-3.31	2.28
Independence			-3.99*	1.15	-2.91*	1.22
GDP					0.89*	0.39
R-square	0.09		0.16		0.19	
Adjusted R-square	0.08		0.15		0.18	

Notes: * significant at <0.05 level, N = 145.
Source: Pippa Norris, Democracy data set.

will be left with is the partial effect; that is, the impact of ethnic diversity controlling for the impact of the other variables in the model.

The last rows of the table report the R-square (see Chapter 15) and the adjusted R-square. As we add extra independent variables to the model, the adjusted R-square will only increase if the new term improves the model more than would be expected by chance. The adjusted R-square is therefore usually somewhat lower than the R-square. The interpretation of the adjusted R-square is also somewhat different from that of R-square, and no longer refers to the 'explained' variance, since this has been adjusted by the number of variables in the model. It therefore takes into account the parsimony of the model, and is higher for a model which explains a given amount of variation in the dependent variable using only a few independent variables than for one that explains the same amount of variation but uses more independent variables. It is therefore often a good idea to report both measures. The R-square of 0.09 indicates that ethnic diversity explains 9% of the variation in levels of democracy.

In Model 2, we now have two independent variables—ethnic fractionalization, and whether the country achieved independence after World War II or not. We can see that both terms are significant and in the expected direction. That is, ethnically diverse countries still tend to be less democratic than ethnically homogeneous countries, even when we take into account when they achieved independence. That is, the relationship between ethnic diversity and democracy holds both for countries that achieved independence before World War II and for countries that achieved independence after World War II. In addition, we can see that countries that achieved independence after World War II tend to be less democratic than countries which achieved independence before it (b =-3.99), controlling for ethnic diversity.

However, interestingly, we also note some change in the magnitude of the coefficient for the ethnic diversity term. It decreases from b =-7.67, when it is the only variable in the model, to b =-5.31, when we control for the effect of independence. This tells us that part of the apparent association between ethnic diversity and democracy is really a function of independence, and when we take into account when the country achieved independence, ethnic diversity does not appear to be quite so important. This is because those countries which achieved independence after World War II tend to be more ethnically diverse than those countries which achieved independence before.

Finally, in Model 3, we examine the relative impact of all three independent variables simultaneously. This is our final model. We now see that, controlling for when a country achieved independence and its level of GDP per capita, the ethnic diversity of a country has no significant impact on its level of democracy. By contrast, the effects of independence and GDP per capita are both significant and in the expected direction. Countries which became independent after World War II tend to be less democratic than countries which became independent before it (controlling for the other variables in the model), and rich countries tend to be more democratic than poor countries (controlling for the other variables in the model). Controlling for GDP therefore completely wipes out the effect of ethnic diversity. When we know how rich a country is and when it achieved independence, it doesn't make any difference to our prediction of how democratic a country is if we know how ethnically diverse it is.

How then do we account for the apparent association between ethnic diversity and democracy at the bivariate level? Well, on the face of it, this appears to be a case of spurious correlation. Although ethnically diverse countries are less democratic than homogeneous ones, this isn't really anything to do with their level of ethnic diversity, and is more to do with their level of economic development. It just so happens that ethnically diverse countries tend to be poorer than ethnically homogeneous countries, and it is this correlation that drives the apparent association between ethnic diversity and democracy. Of course, if we could think of some theoretically plausible reason for why the ethnic heterogeneity of a country might influence its level of economic development, then we could make a case for ethnic diversity having an indirect effect on levels of democracy. But, in the absence of this theory (which appears unlikely), the association is probably more likely to be spurious.

Measures of fit

The R-square for the final model is 0.19. We can interpret this in a number of ways. First, we can say that our model explains 19% of the variation in levels of democracy between the countries. Or, to put it another way, we can say that if we are interested in predicting a country's level of democracy, we will make 19% fewer errors if we know their scores on the independent variables than if we just guess based on the mean. We might not think this is very good. To be sure, there are numerous other factors that we could include in our model that might improve its predictive power. But at the same time the importance of R-square should not be exaggerated. R-square is rarely the most important part of the model's results. We may be particularly interested in R-square if the regression model is fitted solely for the purpose of predicting future observations of the dependent variable. More often, however, we are at least as, or more, interested in examining the nature and strength of the associations between the dependent variable and the explanatory variables and testing specific hypotheses, in which case the regression coefficients are the main parameters of interest.

As discussed above, we can interpret the regression coefficients in terms of their significance and their sign, and whether or not they support our theoretical expectations. Entering the variables in a step-wise fashion also allows us to inspect how the patterns of association change when we control for additional variables, which can shed light on direct and indirect causal mechanisms, as well as uncovering spurious associations. But we may also be interested in making some statement about which variable appears to be the most important. What factor has the biggest impact on the dependent variable? What matters most for a country's level of democracy? Its economic development? Its length of time as an independent state? Its ethnic diversity?

Interpreting the magnitude of the coefficients

We cannot make direct comparisons between the regression coefficients for the different independent variables because each variable is measured on a different scale. Since the regression coefficient tells us how much the dependent variable changes for each unit increase in the independent variable, the magnitude of the coefficients are all based on different scales, making direct comparison difficult. For example, independence is measured as a dummy variable, GDP per capita is measured in US$1,000s, and ethnic diversity is measured in terms of fractionalization. We cannot say that each of these units is equivalent, and so direct comparison between the sizes of the coefficients is essentially meaningless.

However, it is often useful to be able to discuss the relative impact of different variables. Even if we cannot directly compare which variables 'matter the most', there are a number of techniques that we can use to try and do this indirectly. We could just enter the variables in the model one by one in step-wise fashion and look at which variables lead to the largest increase in R-square. However, the problem with this approach is that how much each variable appears to 'explain' will partly depend upon the order in which it is entered into the model, and variables which are entered early will more easily be able to explain a lot of variation than variables entered towards the end.

Alternatively, we could just compare how much difference it makes to the dependent variable when we increase each independent variable from its minimum value to its maximum value. So, for example, controlling for all the other factors in the model, what is the expected difference in levels of democracy between the poorest country and the richest country compared with the expected difference between the most ethnically homogeneous country and the most ethnically diverse country? The problem with this approach, though, is similar to the problems associated with looking at the **range**, which we discussed in Chapter 14 with reference to measures of variation. Accordingly, since how much each variable appears to matter depends upon the extreme values of the distribution, this approach is very sensitive to outliers. One or both of these values might be atypical, giving a misleading impression of how much the independent variable really matters.

One way we can get round this problem is to base our comparisons on the standard deviation instead (see Chapter 14). From probability theory we know that a given proportion of cases fall within one standard deviation of the mean. If we then compare the amount our dependent variable changes in relation to a one standard deviation increase for each of our independent variables, then we are comparing the change in the dependent variable in relation to broadly equivalent changes in the distribution of our explanatory variables.

This 'broad equivalence' is often discussed in terms of what are known as standardized beta coefficients, or standardized regression coefficients, often denoted (capital) B. Most statistical software programs routinely include these measures as part of the output. 'Standardizing' a variable involves subtracting its mean from each individual value, and dividing by the standard deviation. The metric for a standardized regression coefficient is therefore standard deviation units. We can therefore draw comparisons between the change in Y for a broadly equivalent change in the distribution of X (measured in standard deviation units).

The final model is reproduced in Table 16.3, with information on the unstandardized beta coefficient, the standard error, the standardized beta coefficient, the t value, and the p value for each of the independent variables. We can see that the only terms for which the p value is below 0.05 are independence and GDP per capita. (Recall that the p value provides the probability of obtaining a test statistic of the observed size or greater if the null hypothesis is true.) From the standardized beta coefficients, we can get an idea of the relative importance of each variable in explaining variation in democracy. Given that the ethnic diversity term is not significant, there is no need to discuss it further. However, we can see that the standardized regression coefficient for the independence term (B =-0.21) is of almost the same magnitude as the coefficient for the GDP per capita term (B = 0.22). Both terms therefore appear to have much the same relative impact.

Presenting the results

Finally, it is often helpful to present results graphically, as this can illustrate the impact of certain key variables, and provide a clear visual representation of the results for people who may shy away from looking at tables filled with numbers and asterisks. We can do this in

Table 16.3 Predicting the level of democracy: OLS regression, parameter estimates

	b coefficient	Standard error	Standardized B coefficient	t value	p value
Constant	3.06	4.50			
Ethnic diversity	–3.31	2.28	–0.13	–1.45	0.15
Independence	–2.91*	1.22	–0.21	–2.38	0.02
GDP per capita	0.89*	0.39	0.22	2.31	0.02
N	145				
R-square	0.19				
Adjusted R-square	0.18				

Notes: * significant at 0.05 level.
Source: Pippa Norris, Democracy data set.

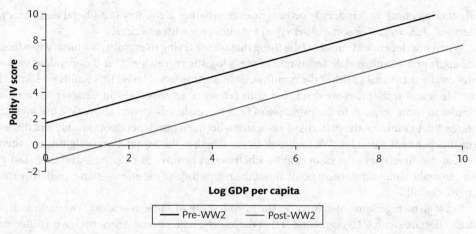

Figure 16.9 Estimated impact of GDP and period of independence on level of democracy

much the same way as we did for bivariate regression (see Chapter 15), and use the regression equation to predict values of Y, depicted algebraically as follows:

$$Y = a + b_1 X_1 + b_2 X_2 + b_3 X_3.$$

From our analysis, we have estimates for each of the different parameters, and so can substitute the values of each unstandardized regression coefficient into the equation as follows:

$$Y = 3.1 - 3.3\, X_1 - 2.9\, X_2 + 0.9\, X_3.$$

The last step is simply to plug in different values for X. We can then predict values of Y for countries that gained independence after World War II (when $X_2 = 1$) at different levels of GDP per capita, and do the same for countries that experienced independence before World War II (when $X_2 = 0$) in the same way. The predicted values of Y can then be illustrated graphically, as shown in Figure 16.9.

Multivariate analysis using logistic regression

So far we have considered multivariate analysis for when our dependent variable is measured at the interval level. However, many political phenomena that we are interested in are not measured in this way. For example, those doing research on voting behaviour are often interested in which party people vote for (Labour, Conservative, Lib Dem, or other), or even whether people vote at all in the first place (vote or not vote). Similarly, we may be interested in whether or not a country has experienced civil war or ethnic conflict or terrorism in a given period of time (measured in terms of whether they have or have not). Indeed, research on democracy often treats democracy as a categorical variable, and distinguishes between whether a county is democratic or not, or even whether a country is a liberal democracy, electoral democracy, or some other type of 'democracy with adjective'.

When our dependent variable (the thing that we are trying to explain) is a binary variable, the appropriate multivariate technique to use is logistic regression. Our independent variables can be measured at either the nominal, ordinal, or interval level. This builds on some of the ideas and techniques we discussed with reference to cross-tabs in Chapter 15, and is similar in some respects to the principle of OLS regression discussed above. We use logistic regression to examine the patterns of association between our dependent variable and different independent variables. We first look to see whether the association is significant, then look at the direction of the association—whether it is positive or negative—and then, lastly, we can make some substantive point about the magnitude of the effect—that is, whether it is large or small.

But logistic regression also involves the introduction of some new ideas. The main analytical difference with OLS regression is that the logistic regression coefficients have a different numerical interpretation. This is because they refer to odds and probabilities of change in the dependent variable, rather than simple increases or decreases in the dependent variable. Whereas the coefficient in OLS refers to the *amount of probable change* in the dependent variable—that is, how much we expect the dependent variable to change for a one-unit increase in the independent variable, the coefficient in logistic regression refers to the *probability of change* in the dependent variable.

With OLS regression, the coefficients refer to the impact that a one-unit increase of the independent variable has on the value of the dependent variable. With logistic regression, the coefficients do not refer to the value of the dependent variable—because it can only be two values—either zero or one. Instead, the coefficient refers to the **odds** or probability of the dependent variable taking one value rather than the other. So, for example, if our dependent variable is whether a country experienced civil war (coded 1) or not (coded 0), the coefficient for an interval-level variable tells us whether the probability of a country experiencing this outcome (or the odds of them having a civil war) increase or decrease for every unit change in the independent variable. By contrast, the coefficient for a categorical-level variable tells us whether the odds of experiencing civil war are higher or lower for the category in question in relation to the reference category.

If it were simply a question of dealing with changes in the probability of the dependent variable taking one value over the other, then the output from logistic regression would be quite intuitive and easy to understand. But this is not the case. For technical reasons, logistic regression involves transforming probabilities into something called **odds ratios** and **log odds ratios**. The statistics behind how these are calculated, and how the parameters are estimated, are quite complicated, and are beyond the scope of this chapter (but see Agresti 2002 for a detailed introduction). We therefore focus on how they can be interpreted, which is far more straightforward.

The workhorses of logistic regression are odds and odds ratios. The idea behind odds is fairly straightforward, and is closely linked to probabilities and percentages. So for example, if a survey reveals that 78% of the population voted in an election, we can convert this percentage into a probability that someone plucked at random would have voted. This probability is expressed as 0.78. We can phrase this in a different way, and ask what are the odds that a person plucked at random voted? The odds are calculated as the probability of having voted against the probability of not having done so. This can be expressed as: p(v)/p(1-v) = 0.78/0.22 = 3.55:1. The odds of voting of 3.55:1 tell us that for every one person who did not vote, there were 3.55 people who did vote.

Odds ratios extend this type of analysis by simply comparing the odds of two different groups. There are many different ways in which we can do this, but one comparison that we might be interested in is the odds of young people voting compared to old people. From Table 16.4 we can calculate the odds of voting for each of these age groups in the same way as above. The odds of voting among young people can therefore be calculated as: 0.651/0.349 = 1.865. And the odds of voting among old people are: 0.877/0.123 = 7.130. From these odds we can see that the odds of voting are higher among old people (7.13: 1) than they are among young people (1.86: 1). The odds ratio simply tells us how much higher (or lower) the first set of odds are compared to the last set (our reference category). So, the ratio between the odds of voting for old people compared to the odds of voting for young people (our reference category) can be calculated as: 7.130/1.865 = 3.82 (see Table 16.5). This odds ratio tells us that the odds of voting among old people are nearly four times higher than the odds of voting among young people.

Odds ratios can take values between 0 and infinity, but they are always positive numbers. If the odds ratio is 1, then odds of voting are the same for both groups. If the odds ratio is less than 1, then the odds of voting among old people is less than the odds of voting among young people (which is our reference category). And if the odds ratio is greater than 1, the odds of voting for old people are greater than the odds of voting for young people. Odds ratios are therefore not symmetrical. For example, if our reference category is young people, then an odds ratio of 4 tells us that the odds of voting are four times higher among old people than among young people. However, if our reference is old people, then an odds ratio of 0.25 tells us that the odds of voting are four times less (one-quarter) among young people than among old people.

Odds ratios are a very useful way of describing the association between two variables. They also form the basis for interpreting logistic regression coefficients. Although the output from most statistical software packages does report the odds ratios, something

Table 16.4 Voting by age group, column percentages

	18–39 yrs	40–59 yrs	60+ yrs	All
Did not vote	35	19	12	28
Voted	65	81	88	78

Source: British Election Study, 2005.

Table 16.5 Voting by age group, odds ratios

	18–39 yrs	40–59 yrs	60+ yrs
Voted	(REF)	2.29	3.82

Source: British Election Study, 2005.

called the log odds ratios are usually reported when writing up the results in tables. These are based on the odds ratios, but are transformed using something called the log function, so they are centred on zero. Log odds with positive values therefore indicate that the likelihood of voting is higher among the group in question than it is among the reference category, whereas log odds with negative values indicate that the likelihood of voting is lower among the group in question than it is among the reference category. It is therefore important always to be clear whether you are reporting (or interpreting) log odds or odds ratios.

Although the interpretation of these coefficients might lack the intuitive simplicity of the OLS regression coefficients, logistic regression is really no more complicated to use or understand than OLS regression. The principles of statistical control are much the same; as are the principles of hypothesis testing. As with OLS regression, we are primarily interested in whether our independent variable has a significant association with the dependent variable (at the 0.05 level or above) and, if so, whether the direction of the relationship is positive (indicated by positive log odds) or negative (indicated by negative log odds). We can then make some substantive interpretation about the magnitude of the effect, but this is often most easily done by transforming the log odds back into probabilities (which we will do later in this chapter).

Example 2: turnout

In recent years, there has been a great deal of concern about declining levels of turnout in Britain and many other advanced democracies. In particular there has been concern about the low participation rates of young people. Various different explanations have been proposed in order to try and explain why people vote or do not vote, and how this relates to their age. In this section, we focus on three different sets of factors that are widely thought to be associated with whether or not people vote. The first set of factors focuses on the social characteristics of voters, such as their age, sex, and education. There is a large body of research that examines participatory equality, and the extent to which people from different social backgrounds participate in politics. It is of descriptive interest to know whether participation rates vary by social background, but it is also of analytical interest to know whether those people with high levels of 'civic resources' such as education are more likely to vote, and whether people acquire the 'habit' of voting as they get older. The second factor relates to how attached people feel to political parties. If people have a strong attachment to a particular political party and feel that it 'represents' them in some way, then we may expect that they will be more likely to vote. Third, we can also look at factors related to the structure of political competition, such as whether the election is competitive and the race is expected to be close, and whether there is much policy difference at stake in terms of how different the parties are viewed as being from each other.

By examining which of these factors influence turnout, and which factors influence turnout the most, we can try and get a sense of what is most important. Is turnout something about voters? Something about parties? Or something about competition? How do these different factors relate to and interact with each other? To what extent can the answers to these questions shed light on turnout decline, and why young people have become increasingly unlikely to vote? The following analysis attempts to provide some answer to these questions.

To examine how these factors are related to a person's likelihood of voting, we analyse the combined British election surveys, from 1964 to 2005, which gives us data on individuals' social characteristics and strength of attachment to political parties, and data on elections to do with the expected closeness of the race. We can specify the model algebraically as:

$$Logit = a + b_1 X_1 + b_2 X_2 + b_3 X_3 + b_4 X_4 + b_5 X_5 + b_6 X_6,$$

where our dependent variable is the log odds of someone voting, and:

$X1$ refers to an individual's sex (1 = male; 0 = female);
$X2$ refers to an individual's age (1 = under 30 years old; 0 = 30 years old and over);
$X3$ refers to an individual's level of education (1 = university educated; 0 = school);
$X4$ refers to an individual's strength of party identification: from 0 (no attachment) to 4 (strong attachment);
$X5$ refers to an individual's perception of the policy difference between the parties: from 0 (no difference) to 1 (some difference) to 2 (big difference);
$X6$ refers to the average gap in the opinion polls between the two main parties' share of the vote (measured in percentage points).

This model can be interpreted in much the same way as the multiple linear regression model as long as we remember that the dependent variable refers to the log odds of voting, not Y or probabilities. We are not trying to predict the value of the dependent variable, but the likelihood (in terms of log odds) of the dependent variable taking one value (voting) rather than another (not voting).

Having specified our model, we state the null hypothesis for each independent variable, make a decision on whether we reject (or fail to reject) the null hypothesis, and then if we reject, discuss the pattern of the association between the independent and dependent variable and whether or not it conforms with our theoretical expectations. These steps are exactly the same as for OLS regression, though the way we carry them out is slightly different.

The **null hypothesis** is that, for example, controlling for the other variables in the model, there is no association between a person's age and whether or not they voted. If the null hypothesis is true, then the partial regression coefficient (the log odds) for the age term will be zero. The significance test for this hypothesis is much the same as the other significance tests we have described earlier. We look to see if the coefficient is significantly different from zero by comparing the magnitude of the coefficient with its standard error. However, the way we do this in logistic regression is slightly different from how we did it in linear regression. Rather than calculate the test statistic, we calculate something called the z statistic, where:

$$z = \frac{\hat{\beta}}{s\hat{e}(\hat{\beta})}$$

and $\hat{\beta}$ is the estimated coefficient and $s\hat{e}(\hat{\beta})$ is the estimated standard error of the coefficient. The square of the z statistic is often known as the Wald statistic (reported in most statistical software packages), which has a chi-square distribution. The associated p value therefore indicates the probability of obtaining a Wald statistic of the observed size or greater if the null hypothesis were true. If the p value is less than 0.05, we can reject the null hypothesis at the 5% level and go on to describe the pattern of the association. Recall that in a logistic regression we are in effect investigating how the likelihood of voting varies according to the range of predictors included in the model.

The results from this model are presented in Table 16.6. For the time being we will just focus on the significance of the parameter estimates and whether the association is positive or negative. Table 16.6 reports both the log odds ratios and the odds ratios. It is usual practice to report the findings in terms of the log odds ratios, which have the statistical advantage of being centred on zero, making the direction of the association clearly evident (positive or negative). We find support for our expectation that social characteristics, such as sex, age, and education, matter for whether an individual will vote or not, even when we control for all the other variables in the model. For each of the social characteristic variables, we can reject the null hypothesis of no association, since the associated p values are all below 0.05. We indicate which coefficients are significant by an asterisk. From the direction of the coefficients, we can see that men tend to be less likely than women to vote ($b = -0.11$); people under 30 tend to be less likely than people over 30 to vote ($b = -0.55$); and people who have been educated to degree level or above tend to be more likely to vote than those who have not ($b = 0.46$).

There is also a significant and positive association between turnout and strength of party attachment. We have treated strength of party attachment as an interval-level variable, and so the coefficient tells us that for every unit increase in the strength of attachment (on a 0 to 4 scale), the log odds of someone voting increase ($b = 0.63$). People with a

Table 16.6 Predicting turnout (logistic regression, parameter estimates)

	Log odds ratios	Standard error	Wald	Df	P-value	Odds ratios
Sex: Female (REF)						
Male	-0.11*	0.048	6.46	1	0.011	0.91
Age: Over 30 yrs old (REF)						
Under 30 yrs old	-0.55*	0.040	192.66	1	0.000	0.58
Education: No degree (REF)						
Degree	0.46*	0.071	43.10	1	0.000	1.59
Strength of party ID	0.63*	0.022	833.91	1	0.000	1.88
Policy difference	0.33*	0.026	164.55	1	0.000	1.39
Poll gap between parties	-0.02*	0.003	33.10	1	0.000	0.98
Constant	0.63	0.058			0.000	1.87

Notes: N = 21,279; chi square: 1,540; degrees of freedom: 6; *p* value ≤0.0005;-2LL: 17613; Nagelkerke R Square: 0.12.
Source: British Election Study, 1964–2005, cumulative data set.

strong party attachment therefore tend to be more likely to vote than people with only a weak attachment, or no attachment at all. There is also evidence to support our hypothesis that the political context matters. There is a significant and positive association between turnout and perceptions of policy difference between the main parties ($b = 0.33$). Since the policy difference variable is also measured on an interval scale, this indicates that for every unit increase in the perception of policy difference, the log odds of someone voting become higher ($b = 0.33$). People who think that there is a great deal of policy difference between the parties are therefore more likely to vote than people who only think there is a small difference, or no difference at all. Finally, there is a significant and negative association between the gap between the main two parties' share of the vote in the opinion polls and turnout ($b = -0.02$). For every one percentage point difference between the Conservative and Labour share of the vote in opinion polls, the log odds of someone voting decrease by 0.02. This indicates that people are less likely to vote when a landslide victory is predicted for one party than when the race is expected to be very close.

Measures of fit

We are often interested in trying to establish 'how well' we have managed to explain our phenomenon of interest. Does our model of turnout provide a comprehensive explanation for why people vote or not. To try and answer this question, we often refer to what are known as measures of fit. As with OLS regression, there is a number of measures that can be used to describe how well the logistic regression model fits the data—or explains the observed variation in the data. However, they lack the intuitive appeal of R-square, are somewhat more cumbersome to interpret, and there are disagreements about which measure is best. The logistic regression equivalent of R-square is known as pseudo R-square. The fact that it is prefaced with the word 'pseudo' indicates that it is not really the same as normal R-square, as it does not represent 'explained variation'. Rather, it refers to the proportional improvement in the fit to the data. To calculate the pseudo R-square we compare the model's fit to the data with the null model's fit to the data (when we only include the constant and do not include any independent variables), using something called the log likelihood (LL) or -2 Log likelihood ($-2LL$), as it is often reported. There are different ways of doing this, and different measures of pseudo R-square are based on slightly different calculations, so it is always important to be clear about which measure is being used. The above example reports the Nagelkerke R-Square. This is 0.12, indicating that the model improves the fit to the data by 12%.

Interpreting the magnitude of coefficients

As already mentioned, it is difficult to meaningfully interpret the magnitude of the coefficients, and to compare which factors matter more than others. Although there is no direct equivalent to the standardized beta coefficient that we discussed with reference to OLS, we can get an idea about the relative magnitude of the different parameter estimates by comparing the size of the log odds ratio to its standard error. But a more intuitive way to illustrate the relative importance of different variables is to convert the log odds back into predicted probabilities, which are much easier to interpret.

From the results of our analysis, the predicted log odds of someone voting can be expressed by plugging the values of the different parameter estimates into our equation for the model, as follows:

$$Logit = 0.63 - 0.11 * X_1 - 0.55 * X_2 + 0.46 * X_3 + 0.63 * X_4 + 0.33 * X_5 - 0.02 * X_6.$$

We can then use this equation to predict the log odds of someone voting, based on different values for each of the independent variables. The most straightforward way of doing this is simply to hold each value of X at its sample mean. Then, one by one, we can calculate the predicted log odds of voting for a one standard deviation increase in the value of each independent variable (remembering to return its value back to the mean once the calculation has been performed). For each variable, then, we have calculated the predicted log odds when all variables are held at their mean, and the predicted log odds when the variable in question has increased by one standard deviation. We can transform the predicted log odds into probabilities using the following function:

$$\check{P} = \frac{1}{1 + \exp(-(a + b_1 X_1 + \dots\dots b_6 X_6)}},$$

where exp is the inverse log function (or exponentiated function as it is often called).

Although this looks like a bit of a fiddle, it is relatively straightforward to do in packages such as Excel, and some statistical software packages such as STATA will even do it for you. The change in predicted probability of voting (or change in predicted percentage) can then be neatly depicted in a graph, as shown in Figure 16.10.

From Figure 16.10 we can clearly see that party ID—the strength of someone's attachment to a political party—has the largest impact on the predicted probability of voting. Holding all other variables at their mean, the predicted level of turnout increases by 5.5 percentage points for a one-standard-deviation increase in a person's strength of party attachment. The

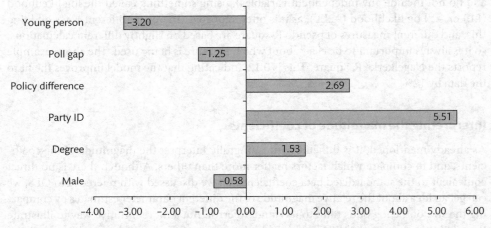

Figure 16.10 Change in predicted turnout for a one-standard-deviation change in the independent variables

next most important variable is age, and then perceptions of policy difference. By contrast, the impact of sex is relatively weak (even though it is significant). From this we can see that how attached people are to political parties, and how much difference they think there is between them in policy terms is strongly related to how likely someone is to vote. By contrast, civic resources, measured in terms of whether someone has been to university or not, is more weakly associated with turnout. This suggests that factors to do with parties and policy (at least in terms of how they are perceived) may be rather more important than factors to do with voters (in terms of their civic resources). People interested in increasing the level of turnout may therefore want to think about what parties stand for, and how this is communicated to the electorate.

Interaction effects

Up to now we have assumed that each independent variable has the same impact on the dependent variable, regardless of the other factors, such as a person's age. So, for example, that both old and young people respond to the policy difference between the parties in the same way; that is, that the impact of policy difference on turnout is the same for both groups. But we might think that the picture is more complicated than that. For example, we might think that young people are more likely to be influenced by the political context than older people, since they have not acquired the 'habit of voting'. This suggests that different groups of people respond to different factors in different ways. When we have strong theoretical reasons for suspecting this, we can fit an interaction term, which tests to see whether the impact of one variable significantly varies across levels of another variable.

   Interaction terms can be difficult to interpret correctly, but they are frequently used in quantitative research and so are well worth understanding. When done appropriately, interaction terms can also be used in an incredibly revealing way to help shed light on complex empirical problems. They help us to examine heterogeneity, and don't impose a one-size-fits all explanation on political phenomenon. Implicitly, we make arguments that involve interaction terms all the time. For example, Geddes (1999) states that no theory of democratic transition explains all real world variation. This is clearly true, but it does not mean that we have to throw up our hands and give up trying to explain transitions. Rather, we can try to develop explanations that take into account this diversity, so, for example, we can recognize that popular pressure from below does not influence transitions to democracy in all cases, but it tends to be of much stronger influence in single-party authoritarian regimes than military regimes. There is thus an interaction between the impact of civil society on democratic transition and prior regime type.

   We can illustrate the principles of how to specify and interpret interaction effects with the following example of electoral turnout. Various scholars have suggested that people's early political experiences have important long-term effects (e.g. Franklin 2004). Accordingly, it is often said that voting is a habit that is either acquired (or not) at a relatively young age. People's early experiences with elections shape their future behaviour. When there is plenty at stake, young people go out to vote and acquire the 'habit' of voting, which lasts later into life. However, when there is not much difference between the parties, and they are viewed as being all the same, they do not go out to vote, and thus acquire the habit of not voting. The key point here, then, is that once the habit of voting (or not voting) has been acquired, older people should be relatively immune to the short-term vagaries of the political context. If they have acquired the habit of voting, they will turn out to vote more or less regardless of whether there are substantial differences between the parties or not. By contrast, younger people, who have not acquired the habit of voting, will be far more responsive to the perception of how different the political parties are. We can test this expectation by fitting an interaction term between age and policy difference. The interaction is illustrated in Figure 16.11, and shows that we estimate an additional parameter for the interaction between a person's age and their perception of policy difference. Here age is a moderator variable, and we examine whether the association between perception of policy difference and turnout varies according to whether someone is under 30 years old or not.

We can also specify the model algebraically, where the interaction term is defined as a multiplicative term between age and policy difference:

$$Logit = a + b_1 X_1 + b_2 X_2 + b_3 X_3 + b_4 X_4 + b_5 X_5 + b_6 X_6 + b_7 X_2 X_5,$$

where our dependent variable is the log odds of someone voting, and:

- $X1$ refers to an individual's sex (1 = male; 0 = female);
- $X2$ refers to an individual's age (1 = under 30 years old; 0 = 30 years old and over);
- $X3$ refers to an individual's level of education (1 = university educated; 0 = school);
- $X4$ refers to an individual's strength of party identification: from 0 (no attachment) to 4 (strong attachment);
- $X5$ refers to an individual's perception of the policy difference between the parties: from 0 (no difference) to 1 (some difference) to 2 (big difference);
- $X6$ refers to the average gap in the opinion polls between two main parties' share of the vote (measured in percentage points).

The results of this model are reported in Table 16.7. We can see that all the independent variables which are entered by themselves are significant and in the same direction as before. We will therefore limit our focus to the discussion of the interaction effect. Great care needs to be exercised when interpreting interaction effects, since they can often cause confusion. There are three parameters of interest. We have what are known as two parent terms—these are the variables that appear in the model on their own, and an interaction term—which is when these variables appear in combination with each other. We can see that each of the parent terms is significant and in the same direction as before (see Table 16.7). We can also see that the interaction term is significant ($p < 0.05$). This tells us that there is evidence that the association between policy difference and turnout is somewhat different for young people and older people.

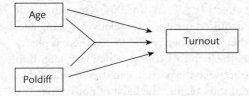

Figure 16.11 Multivariate model predicting turnout, with an interaction term

Table 16.7 Predicting turnout with an interaction term between age and policy difference (logistic regression, parameter estimates)

	Log odds	Standard error	Wald	df	P value	Odds ratios
Male	-0.10*	0.04	6.34	1	0.012	0.91
Degree	0.46*	0.07	42.08	1	0.000	1.58
Strength of party ID	0.63*	0.02	836.46	1	0.000	1.88
Policy difference	0.27*	0.03	70.34	1	0.000	1.31
Gap in opinion polls	-0.02*	0.00	34.28	1	0.000	0.98
Young person	-0.79*	0.08	100.23	1	0.000	0.46
Young person by Policy difference	0.19*	0.05	11.97	1	0.001	1.21
Constant	0.71	0.06	127.89	1	0.000	2.03

Note: N = 21,279.
Source: British Election Studies, 1964–2005.

Since old people are the reference category, the interaction terms denote how much bigger (or smaller) the magnitude of the policy difference coefficient is for young people. The interaction term between age and policy difference therefore tells us whether the association between policy difference and turnout is the same for young people (in which case the coefficient for the interaction term would be zero), stronger (in which case it would be positive), or weaker (in which case it would be negative). Since the interaction term is positive, we can conclude that the association between policy difference and turnout is stronger for young people than it is for old people. The estimated size of the policy difference coefficient for young people is therefore the size of the parent term coefficient ($b = 0.27$) plus the size of the interaction term coefficient ($b = 0.19$), which gives $b = 0.46$, whereas the estimated size of the policy difference coefficient for old people is just the size of the parent term coefficient ($b = 0.27$).

We can illustrate what this means more clearly by using this information to predict levels of turnout for young people and older people at different levels of policy difference. We do this in the same way as before, and hold all the other variables at their mean. We then calculate the predicted probability of voting for a young person when there is the perception of no difference between the parties (coded 0) and when there is the perception of big differences between the parties (coded 2). We do the same for older people. The results are presented in Table 16.8.

Table 16.8 shows that when there is a perception of big policy differences between the parties, people over 30 years old are just slightly more likely to vote (0.91) than people under 30 (0.86). Or, put a different way, holding all other factors constant, the predicted difference in their turnout rates is just 5 percentage points. However, when there is a perception of no difference between the parties, the predicted probability of voting is much higher for old people (0.84) than it is for young people (0.71), even if both groups are less likely to vote than

Table 16.8 Predicted probabilities

	Parties are all the same (0)	Big differences between the parties (2)
Under 30 years old	0.71	0.86
30 years old and over	0.84	0.91

when there are big policy differences. In this instance, holding all other factors constant, the predicted difference in their turnout rates is now 13 percentage points.

We can also see that, for old people, the predicted level of turnout is 7 percentage points higher when they think there are big differences between the parties compared with when they think there aren't any differences at all. By contrast, for young people, the predicted level of turnout is 15 percentage points higher. From this we can infer that whether the parties are all the same or not does not matter so much to older people—they are quite likely to vote in any event, perhaps because they have been socialized into voting from an earlier age when there was more at stake during elections. However, for young people, it makes more difference how different the parties are perceived to be—when they are very different, young people are almost as likely as old people to vote, but when they are much the same, then young people are far less likely to vote and are also much less likely to vote than older people.

The results from this simple model shed some light on recent discussions about turnout decline. First, we can see that important factors in deciding whether people vote or not are to do with their level of party identification, and the structure of the political context. Over the past few years party identification has declined, the difference between the parties has narrowed, and we have had a number of elections that were landslides (but notably not the one in 2010). All other things being equal, this can lead to a substantial decline in levels of turnout. However, more interestingly perhaps, we can think that these changes have had a disproportionate effect on young people. Since young people are more influenced by the political context, the policy convergence under New Labour between the two major parties had a greater impact on them than it had on older people, and so they are correspondingly less likely to vote. Part of the reason, then, why turnout among young people has been so low over the past few elections may be because the parties have become more similar to each other. It is not that young people have changed per se—they have always paid close attention to the contest—but because the parties have changed. And as they have become more similar, there is less incentive to vote.

Presenting and reporting data

Whatever the type of analysis that is being undertaken, it is important to present and report the information in a clear and accessible way. Tables must contain all the relevant information and be clear and easy to understand for the reader. In particular, it is important that they:

- have a clear title, with clear information about the dependent variable and the type of analysis used (logistic regression, OLS regression, etc.);

- indicate clearly the coefficient (unstandardized and/or standardized beta coefficients for OLS; log odds ratios and/or odds ratios for logistic regression);

- have clear labels for the independent variables (always give a self-explanatory label);

- indicate what the 'reference category' is for categorical variables;

- give information that enables the reader to judge the level of significance of the parameter estimates (asterisks and/or standard errors);

- report all parameter estimates (including non-significant ones);

- provide some indication of goodness of fit (R-square for OLS; pseudo R-square, chi square for logistic regression;

- report the source of the data;

- report the base (sample size) for the actual analysis.

When writing up the analysis, it is good practice to avoid causal language of 'effects', 'drivers', and so on and use language simply as if you were reporting patterns of association. Concentrate on whether the results confirm or refute your prior theoretical expectations, with reference to the direction of the parameter estimate as well as on the level of significance. We have compared the sizes of the parameter estimates only in the vaguest and most general terms. If we want to provide a meaningful interpretation, we can calculate and present the predicted probabilities (for logistic regression) or the predicted values of y (for OLS regression).

 Conclusions

Multivariate analysis is a powerful tool for exploring the relationship between different variables. It allows us to develop fuller accounts of why things happen, and to see whether these accounts are robust or not. Multivariate analysis also allows us to examine different types of relationship. We can use multivariate analysis to debunk spurious relationships, or to illustrate indirect causal mechanisms. We can also use it to specify interaction effects, and to examine how the impact of one variable depends upon the level of another. These techniques are incredibly powerful, and can be used to good effect to explore a wide range of political phenomena. But, at the same time, the results from multivariate analysis should always be analysed with caution. Do the results really support the argument that the author is using them for? Is there a strong link between the theoretical expectations, and how this theory has been operationalized and tested? Have any potentially important variables been left out? How might the inclusion of these variables change the results? Have the variables been measured in a satisfactory way? These questions dominate all quantitative studies, and it is up to the researcher to demonstrate that they have taken steps to answer them as best they can.

 Questions

- What is the difference between a confounding variable and a mediating variable? Illustrate your answer with examples.

- Why should we treat the results from bivariate analysis with caution? Why might the findings not stand up in a multivariate analysis?

- What is the difference between causality and association?

- How do we know if a relationship between two variables is causal or not?

Guide to Further Reading

Agresti, A (2007), *An Introduction to Categorical Data Analysis* **(New York: John Wiley & Sons).**
Presents a non-technical introduction to topics on categorical data analysis, such as odds ratios and logistic regression.

—. and B. Finlay (2009), *Statistical Methods for the Social Sciences*, **4th edition (Upper Saddle River, NJ: Pearson–Prentice Hall).**
Covers the basics of statistical description and inference, as well as more advanced topics on regression methods, including multiple regression, ANOVA and repeated measures ANOVA, analysis of covariance, logistic regression, and generalized linear models.

Carlson, James and Mark Hyde (2002), *Doing Empirical Political Research* **(Boston, MA: Houghton Mifflin).**
Provides an introduction to quantitative analysis and covers some more advanced topics, with lots of examples from political research.

de Vaus, David (2002), *Surveys in Social Research* **(London: Routledge).**
A detailed and accessible introduction to quantitative methods, with easy-to-read chapters on how to carry out analysis and interpret the results.

Field, A. (2009), *Discovering Statistics using SPSS (and Sex and Drugs and Rock 'n' Roll)* **(London: Sage Publications).**
Provides an easy-to-follow introduction to quantitative analysis and step-by-step instructions on how to use the SPSS statistical software package to do your own analysis.

Johnson, Janet Buttolph, Henry Reynolds, and Jason Mycoff (2007), *Political Science Research Methods*, **6th edition (Washington, DC: CQ Press).**
Provides an introduction to quantitative analysis and covers some more advanced topics, with lots of examples from political research.

Rowntree, Derek (2000), *Statistics without Tears: An Introduction for Non-Mathematicians* **(Harmondsworth: Penguin).**
An easy-to-read introduction to statistical methods.

 References

Agresti, A. (2002), *Categorical Data Analysis* (New York: John Wiley & Sons).

Franklin, M. (2004), *Voter Turnout and the Dynamics of Electoral Competition in Established Democracies since 1945* (Cambridge: Cambridge University Press).

Geddes, Barbara (1999), 'What Do We Know about Democratization after Twenty Years?' *Annual Review of Political Science* 2: 115–44.

Lipset, Seymour Martin (1959), 'Some Social Requisites of Democracy: Economic Development and Political Legitimacy', *American Political Science Review* 53: 69–105.

Putnam, Robert D. (2007), '*E Pluribus Unum*: Diversity and Community in the Twenty-First Century: The 2006 Johan Skytte Prize Lecture', *Scandinavian Political Studies* 30(2): 137–74.

APPENDIX

Finding and Citing Sources for Political Research

I. Types of Sources

Print Materials

Many of these materials can now be accessed online.

Bibliographic and Reference Materials

Social Sciences Citation Index (SSCI) An index to works cited in current social and behavioural science literature. The SSCI provides access to current information and retrospective data from 1956 onwards. Fields covered include anthropology, history, library science, law, linguistics, philosophy, psychology, political science, public health, sociology, urban studies, and women's studies. The SSCI adds approximately 60,000 new cited references per week.

Arts & Humanities Citation Index (*A&HCI*) Provides access to current information and retrospective data from 1975 onwards. Fields covered include archaeology, architecture, art, Asian studies, folklore, history, language, linguistics, philosophy, radio/television/film, religion, and theatre. A&HCI adds approximately 15,250 new cited references per week. http://science.thomsonreuters.com/mjl/scope/scope_ssci/.

WorldCat The world's most comprehensive bibliography. It covers virtually all the material catalogued by any of several thousand member libraries, including books, serials, archival materials, maps, visual materials, computer files, and internet resources. http://www.worldcat.org.

Library of Congress Catalog (LC) The LC is arguably the world's most comprehensive library. Its web page includes links to the catalogues of several hundred other research libraries, primarily in North America, the UK, and Australia. Available at http://catalog.loc.gov/.

Library of Congress Classification Outline Useful for identifying the LC call numbers that you should use to browse to find a particular kind of material. Available at http://lcweb.loc.gov/catdir/cpso/lcco/lcco.html.

Guide to Historical Literature (American Historical Association) The basic principle of organization is geographic, with some reliance on topical and chronological subdivisions. The geographic sections include brief overviews of scholarly trends, and helpful annotations; some also include guides to reference works and bibliographies. http://www.worldcat.org/search?qt=worldcat_org_all&q=historical+literature.

Book Review Digest Indexes reviews appearing in about 100 periodicals; includes brief excerpts. http://www.ebscohost.com/public/book-review-digest/.

Books in Print The online version includes full text reviews from *Choice*, *Library Journal*, *New York Times*, and other review sources. http://www.booksinprint2.com.

International Bibliography of the Social Sciences Contains bibliographic information from over 2,600 journals published in 100 countries and over 6,000 books per year, in the fields of anthropology, economics, political science, and sociology. Coverage is from 1951 to the present, with quarterly updates. http://www.ibss.ac.uk.

Dissertation Abstracts Online Subject, title, and author guide to virtually every American dissertation accepted at an accredited institution since 1861; selected Master's theses have been included since 1962. In addition, since 1988, the database has included citations for dissertations from 50 British universities; and citations and abstracts from Section C, Worldwide Dissertations (formerly European Dissertations). http://library.dialog.com/bluesheets/html/bl0035.html.

ProQuest Dissertations and Theses Database Citations to dissertation and theses from around the world from 1861 to the present day, together with 1.2 million full text dissertations that are available for download in PDF format. The database offers full text for most of the dissertations added since 1997 and strong retrospective full text coverage for older graduate works. http://www.proquest.com/.

The Statesman's Yearbook Information on every country in the world, covering key historical events, politics, economics, trade, and infrastructure. http://www.statesmans-yearbook.com/.

Handbooks, Yearbooks, and Encyclopaedias that provide information on various facets of the political world

Political Handbook of the World An overview of the political system and situation in countries around the world.

Europa World Yearbook Snapshots of the political, economic, and social conditions of countries worldwide.

World Encyclopaedia of Political Systems and Parties Explanation of executive, legislative, and judicial systems, political parties, and electoral systems around the world.

Public Opinion and Polling Around the World: A Historical Encyclopedia

World Encyclopaedia of Parliaments and Legislatures Country-by-country analysis of politics, parties, elections, and parliaments around the world.

The Encyclopaedia of Democracy Articles on the concepts of democracy, important figures, and country and regional assessments of the state of democracy in the world.

Encyclopaedia of World Political Systems A country-by-country survey of the political environment of a country and how that has affected governments.

Encyclopaedia of Nationalism The role of nationalist movements in politics, with entries for specific countries.

International Encyclopaedia of Elections Forms of elections and election processes.

Newspapers, News Services, News Digests, and News Magazines
Some of the sources, below, provide news summaries. Others are indexes to newspapers or to periodicals which report or analyse current events. Others tap various sources of current opinion and comment, or contain references to more general sources.

Newseum Allows you to find daily newspaper front pages from 68 countries across the globe. http://www.newseum.org.

World News Connection Provides English-language translations of material from thousands of media sources. Included are political speeches, television and radio broadcasts, and articles from newspapers, periodicals, and books. Online coverage: 1996 to the present. http://wnc.dialog.com/. For earlier coverage, see the *Foreign Broadcast Information Service. Daily Report*. Transcripts of foreign radio broadcasts, including news and comment.

Facts on File A weekly news digest (since 1941), indexed annually and with an attached atlas. http://www.fofweb.com.

Keesing's Contemporary Archives A monthly record of world events (since 1931) with indexes. http://www.keesings.com.

Annual Register of World Events http://annualregister.chadwyck.com.

Newspaper Indexes A good index to a major newspaper provides an annual register of events. See, for instance, *The New York Times Index*, or *The Times* (London) Index.

Reader's Guide to Periodical Literature Indexes general periodicals (magazines, including newsmagazines, but not scholarly journals). http://www.hwwilson.com/databases/Readersg.htm.

Africa Digest Weekly record of African events (since 1961), with index.

Africa Research Bulletin (Political and Cultural Series) Indexed monthly summary of African political developments (since 1964).

Asian Recorder A weekly digest of Asian events (since 1955), with index.

The Middle East and North Africa. A survey and directory of the countries of the Middle East (since 1948) and North Africa (since 1964), with a listing of events.

BBC Worldwide Monitoring: International Reports The BBC's Monitoring Service systematically tracks broadcasts from 120 countries in 50 languages. The Summary of World Broadcasts (SWB) was a separate part of the service until the end of March 2001, when it was discontinued. After that date, the information previously carried in the SWB became part of the International Reports. Accessible through LexisNexis: http://www.lexisnexis.com.

Academic and Trade Journals
JSTOR Reproduces the full image of over 117 scholarly journals, starting in each case with volume 1. The purpose is to provide an archival collection of core scholarly journals, not current access; most articles are at least two years old. Full text searching is available. Runs of additional titles are gradually being added to the database. http://www.jstor.org.

Project MUSE Includes the full image of all articles in over 100 scholarly journals, including all Johns Hopkins University Press journals. Full text searching, as well as subject searching, is available. http://muse.jhu.edu/.

Web of Knowledge This source includes five databases covering virtually all fields of knowledge. Two of the most useful are the *Social Sciences Citation Index* (*SSCI*) and the *Arts & Humanities Citation Index* (*A&HCI*). With these databases, you can discover networks of scholarly articles relevant to your particular research interests. Beginning with any article that you have found valuable, you can locate all subsequent journal articles that cite it. Registering for *Current Contents Connect*, which is part of the Web of Knowledge, allows you to set up a personal alerting profile for journals that you select. This profile automatically emails you the latest tables of contents for your chosen journals as they appear. Registering also enables you to set up citation alerts that notify you when future articles cite key articles you have found to be of special interest. *Current Contents Connect* includes a personal home page that displays all your selected titles and allows you to see the latest table of contents by clicking on a title. http://wokinfo.com/products_tools/products/.

Social Sciences Full Text An index to English-language periodical articles. Subjects include anthropology, area studies, economics, international relations, law, political science, and sociology. Online coverage from February 1983, with abstracts from January 1994, and some full text articles. http://www.ebscohost.com/academic/social-sciences-full-test/

Ulrich's Periodicals Directory on the Web Provides detailed information on more than 300,000 periodicals of all types: academic and scholarly journals, e-journals, peer-reviewed titles, popular magazines, newspapers, newsletters, and more. http://ulrichsweb.serialssolutions.com/.

Public Affairs Information Service Bulletin Indexes numerous periodicals in the field of public affairs and public policy: journals, pamphlets, government documents, some books. http://www.csa.com/factsheets/pais-set-c.php.

Columbia International Affairs Online (CIAO) Allows search engine access to working papers from a wide range of think tanks and to tables of contents and article abstracts from the most recent issues of about 35 international affairs journals. Also contains information on forthcoming scholarly conferences in international affairs. http://www.ciaonet.org/.

Fulltext Sources Online A systematic list of periodicals available online in full text, along with the names of the databases that contain them. Includes foreign- as well as English-language periodicals. http://www.fso-online.com.

Historical Abstracts Selectively indexes over 2,000 journals in the field of history, with abstracts. Also indexes selected books. Online coverage from 1955. http://www.ebscohost.com/public/historical-abstracts.

Humanities Full Text An index of English-language periodicals. Subjects include history, area studies, language and literature, philosophy, and religion. Online coverage: index from February 1984, abstracts from March 1994, and some full text from 1995.

International Political Science Abstracts Provides citations and abstracts for a worldwide selection of journal and yearbook articles in the fields of international relations, political science, and public administration. Online coverage: 1989 to present.

Social Sciences Index Indexes social science periodicals (scholarly journals).

Historical Abstracts Notes and abstracts of historical articles on the twentieth century. This journal began in 1955; in 1971, it spun off a second annual volume, *Twentieth-Century Abstracts*. Search it by country name.

International Political Science Abstracts Bimonthly abstracts of political science journals and yearbook articles.

Find the name of the country you are researching in the index to be directed to abstracts of articles on that country.

Education Resources information Center (ERIC) Provides access to more than 1.3 million bibliographic records of journal articles, books, research syntheses, conference papers, technical reports, policy papers, and other education-related materials, with hundreds of new records added multiple times per week. If available, links to full text are included. http://www.eric.ed.gov/.

EServer Journals Collection Provides links to popular journals. Organized by subject. http://journals.eserver.org/.

Government Reports and Legal Documents

PolicyFile: Public Policy Research and Analysis Indexes and abstracts of publications, covering a complete range of public policy research from such organizations as the American Enterprise Institute, Brookings Institution, Carnegie Endowment for International Peace, IMF, World Bank, CSIS, Rand Corporation, and many others. Where available, access to home pages and full text is provided. http://www.policyfile.com/.

Public Affairs Information Service (PAIS) A selective listing, with abstracts, of journal articles, books, and documents. Subjects include economics, business, political science, sociology, demography, and international law and relations, with an emphasis on public-policy-orientated literature. Includes titles published in six languages. http://www.csa.com/factsheets/pais-set-c.php.

LexisNexis Provides the full text of hundreds of publications, including law journals, wire services, country economic reports, government publications, magazines, newspapers, news digests, and industry newsletters and periodicals. http://www.lexisnexis.com.

Internet-only Sources

Annotated List of Reference Websites (Library of Congress) Covers many fields of the social sciences and humanities. http://lcweb.loc.gov/rr/main/alcove9.

Internet Scout Project Tracks useful websites and assesses their intellectual reliability. The Scout Report Archives is a searchable and browseable database of over seven years' worth of the Scout Report and subject-specific Scout Reports. It contains about 12,000 critical annotations of carefully selected internet sites and mailing lists. Each annotation analyses the site's general content, attribution (authors, etc.), currency, availability, accessibility, and presentation. http://scout.wisc.edu.

Social Science Information Gateway A guide to a large number of online scholarly sites, screened by experts. Includes breakdowns by anthropology, economics, geography, politics, sociology, and other fields. Orientated primarily towards British scholarship. http://www.ariadne.ac.uk/issue2/sosig/.

Weblogs/Blogs A type of interactive journal where writers post and readers respond. They vary widely in quality of information and validity of sources. Prestigious journalists and public figures may have blogs, which may be more credible than most.

Message boards, discussion lists, and chat rooms Some are useful and well researched, others are not.

Multimedia The internet has a multitude of multimedia resources, including online broadcasts and news, radio, and television broadcasts, interactive talks, public meetings, images, audio files, and interactive websites.

Internet Data and Archive Resources

Data sets When you investigate a data set and its codebooks, consider the following questions: Who collected the data? What is the unit of analysis? How many cases are there in the data set? What was the sampling method? For how many variables was data collected in each case? What (dependent or independent) variables does it contain that are of particular interest to you? Can this data help to answer the question(s) you are addressing?

Websites with links to lots of data sets

http://garnet.acns.fsu.edu/~phensel/data.html#index
http://www.psr.keele.ac.uk/data.htm
http://www.paulhensel.org/data.html

Political Resources on the Net Listings of political sites available on the internet, sorted by country, with links to parties, organizations, governments, media, and more from all around the world. http://www.politicalresources. net.

Intute Social Sciences A selective catalogue of thousands of websites in the social sciences, hosted in the United Kingdom. Users can browse by topic and region or search by keyword. Each entry has been reviewed and annotated. The focus is on high-quality sites that provide information directly rather than just linking to other sites. A good resource for international social sciences data. http://www. intute.ac.uk/socialsciences.

Internet Crossroads in Social Science Data http://www. disc.wisc.edu/newcrossroads/index.asp. Offers hundreds of annotated links to online data sources. Searchable by keyword or browsable by category, the site includes links to government and non-government sites concerned with domestic and international economics and labour, health, education, geography, history, politics, sociology, and demography. The site is maintained by the Data and Program Library Service at the University of Wisconsin, Madison.

Inter-University Consortium for Political and Social Research (ICPSR, University of Michigan) A publicly available archive of datasets constructed by political scientists. http://www.icpsr.umich.edu/icpsrweb/ICPSR/.

Data from official statistical agencies

These data are published on a yearly or quarterly basis by national and international statistical agencies.

National Statistical Offices and Data Archives such as the Council for European Social Science Data Archives (Cessda). http://www.cessda.org/.

Official Statistics in Europe: web guide to socio-economic surveys http://www.mzes.uni-mannheim.de/projekte/ mikrodaten/drafts/index.html.

Statistical yearbooks published by independent agencies and organizations, such as the statistical yearbooks from the *Encyclopaedia Britannica,* which provide data on governments, elections, economics, and demography; the yearbooks from SIPRI (Stockholm International Peace Research Institute) provide, among other things, data on military expenditures and warfare; the *World Handbook of Political and Social Indicators* (Yale University).

International statistical agencies such as the IMF, the IBRD (International Bank for Reconstruction and Development), and the OECD (Organisation for Economic Co-operation and Development). The IMF provides international financial statistics, and trade statistics; the OECD provides historical statistics, employment statistics, and also economic surveys for individual countries; and the ILO (International Labour Organization) is a source of labour force statistics.

Websites of Policy-Making Organizations There are many policy organizations, think tanks, private research institutes, and NGOs that produce relevant papers and data.

Bank for International Settlements http://www.bis.org.

Bretton Woods http://www.brettonwoods.org.

International Labour Organization (ILO) http://www.ilo. org/global/lang--en/index.htm.

International Monetary Fund (IMF) http://www.imf. org. *International Financial Statistics Online (IFS Online)* is the principal statistical publication of the International Monetary Fund. Tables for each Fund member country include data on the country's exchange rates, Fund position, international liquidity, money and banking accounts, interest rates, prices, production, international transactions, government accounts, national accounts, and population. Selected series are published in area and world tables. Data may be downloaded as HTML, MS Excel, comma-delimited, or tab-delimited files. Some series begin with 1945. Updated monthly.

Organisation for Economic Co-operation and Development (OECD) Includes many of the data sets available from the OECD. This is primarily useful for wealthy, developed countries, though comparison with other countries is sometimes included. http://www.oecd.org.

Third World Network http://www.twnside.org.sg.

United Nations (UN) http://www.un.org. United Nations Common Database (UNCDB): a broad-based statistical resource, it draws data from a wide variety of UN and UN-related (e.g. FAO, ILO, WHO) organizations. UN Commission on International Trade Law **http://www.un.or.at/uncitral.**UN Conference on Trade and Development (UNCTAD) http://www.unctad.org.

World Bank http://www.worldbank.org. GDF Online (Global Development Finance Online): Global Development Finance (GDF) is the World Bank's annual report on external financing prospects for developing and transition countries. It tracks the yearly movement of international capital flows to developing countries, and analyses policy issues for developing countries. GDF provides statistical data for 137 countries. Data may be displayed as charts or maps and exported. *World Development Indicators*: World Development Indicators includes nearly 800 statistical indicators related to social and economic development. It is organized in six sections: World View, People, Environment, Economy, States and Markets, and Global Links. The tables cover 152 economies and 14 country groups—with basic indicators for a further 55 economies. Data can be downloaded for further manipulation. http://data.worldbank.org/data-catalog/world-development-indicators.

World Economic Forum/Davos http://www.wef.org.

World Trade Organization (WTO) http://www.wto.org.

Information on National Institutions

Web Sites of National Parliaments (provided by the Inter-Parliamentary Union), http://www.ipu.org/english/parlweb.htm.

Websites for National Banks (provided by Bank for International Settlements), http://www.bis.org/cbanks.htm.

Governments on the WWW Comprehensive database of governmental institutions on the World Wide Web: parliaments, ministries, offices, law courts, embassies, city councils, public broadcasting corporations, central banks, multi-governmental institutions, etc. Includes also political parties. http://www.gksoft.com/govt/.

The World Factbook (from the CIA) https://www.cia.gov/library/publications/the-world-factbook.

The ESRC Data Archive The ESRC Data Archive is a resource centre whose holdings consist mainly of the data from past surveys. It holds almost 4,000 data sets, including those from many large and important government-produced surveys and censuses, as well as academic research and historical materials. http://www.esds.ac.uk/.

II. Citing Sources

Cite While You Write (Cite While You Write™) is a feature of EndNote, a software package that facilitates proper citation.

The Internet Public Library's Style and Writing Guide Section Resources by subject, style, and writing guides available at http://www.ipl.org/.

Modern Language Association (MLA) has a brief overview of what MLA style is. The *MLA Style Crib Sheet* provides extensive descriptions of general MLA style notes, text, and block quotations, page formatting, MLA text citations, and the MLA works cited. http://www.mla.org/.

The Online Writing Center (OWL) at Purdue An excellent overview, with information, example papers, and individual work; cited examples. http://owl.english.purdue.edu/owl/resource/747/08.

College of DuPage Library, Citing Sources http://www.cod.edu/library/research/Citenet.htm.

The Chicago Manual of Style Online: Chicago-Style Citation Quick Guide http://www.chicagomanualofstyle.org/tools_citationguide.html.

Online! Citation Styles by A. Harnack and E. Kleppinger http://www.bedfordstmartins.com/online/citex.html.

Learning APA Style http://www.apastyle.org/learn.

Glossary

Abduction: a process of inference that involves selecting from among competing explanations the one that best explains a particular event or phenomenon, given all the available evidence. Abduction produces a hypothesis that can then be affirmed through either induction or deduction.

Access: refers to how the researcher enters the chosen field site and starts to do fieldwork.

Acquiescence bias: the tendency of some respondents to automatically agree with every question they are asked.

Aggregate data: describes data referring to aggregates or collectivities rather than individuals.

Association: two variables are associated when values of one variable vary systematically with values of the other variable.

Bandwagon: Bandwagon effects are said to occur when people say they did something (for example, vote for a particular party), not because they necessarily did, but because they want to go along with the majority position.

Bar chart: a way of graphically displaying nominal or ordinal data.

Behaviouralism: the application of positivism and empiricism to the study and explanation of outcomes in politics and international relations.

Bivariate analysis: analysis of the relationship between two variables.

Case: refers to the unit of analysis.

Case selection: refers to issues to do with how and why a particular field site or case is chosen for study.

Case study: the intensive study of one case.

Causality: a relationship between two variables in which changes in one variable *bring about* changes in another.

Central limit theorem: states that when samples are large (above about 30), the sampling distribution will take the shape of a normal distribution.

Central tendency: a measure of central tendency is a way of summarizing the central value in a frequency distribution. See also **mean**, **median**, and **mode**.

Ceteris paribus: 'all else being equal'.

Chi-square test: a statistical test used to test the null hypothesis that there is no relationship between two variables. Often used in conjunction with cross-tabs.

Closed question: a question employed in a structured interview or questionnaire in which respondents are asked to select their answers from a limited range of options. Also called a 'fixed choice' question.

Closed setting: research settings with restricted access or which require permission to access.

Code: a short alphanumeric term that refers to the category of a variable and often the location of a text passage.

Coding: marking a text segment with a code.

Comprehension problems: occurs when, for a variety of reasons, the respondent does not fully understand the question that is being asked of them.

Concept-stretching: has to do with defining concepts in very broad terms in order to ensure that competing definitions or interpretations of the concept overlap with each other.

Confidence interval: range of values in which the true population value is thought to lie.

Confirmatory research: a type of research that involves 'confirming' an existing assumption or theory.

Confound: A variable that is associated with both the probable cause and outcome of a phenomenon, but has no direct causal influence.

Constant: see **intercept**.

Construct validity: an approach used for assessing the validity of a measure which is based on the extent to which the measure is associated with other theoretically relevant factors.

Constructivism: an approach which maintains that reality does not exist as something independent of us, but is socially, and actively, *constructed*.

Content analysis: analysis of the content of a text in order to uncover its meanings and intentions.

Content validity: an approach used for assessing the validity of a measure which is based on the extent to which the measure covers the full range of the concept, covering each of its different aspects.

Continuous: a continuous variable is measured on a continuous scale to varying degrees of precision, where within the range of the variable any value is possible, such as distance in metres or weight in kilos.

Control group: in experimental research, subjects in the control group do not receive the intervention and so are used as a point of comparison in order to gauge the effect of the intervention on the outcome of interest.

Correlation: the term refers to whether there is a linear relationship between two variables.

Co-variance: a relationship between two variables such that one varies with the other.

Coverage error: occurs when the sampling frame from which the sample is drawn does not completely match the population of interest.

Covert research: when the researcher does not reveal his or her identity to the informants.

Covering law: an explanatory model that holds that something is explained when it is shown to be a member of a more general class of things: when the particular case is deduced from a more general law or set of laws. See **deductive-nomological model.**

Covert participation: see *Covert research.*

Crisp set: refers to dichotomous variables that are used in Qualitative Comparative Analysis. In a crisp set analysis, a case is either in or out of a particular set.

Criterion validity: An approach used for assessing the validity of a measure which is based on how well the new measure of the concept relates to existing measures of the concept, or related concepts.

Critical realism: a position that holds that perception is a function of the human mind, and that we can therefore only acquire knowledge of the external world by critically reflecting on perception.

Cross-sectional designs: involve making observations of a sample, or cross-section, of a population or phenomenon at a single point in time and analyzing it carefully.

Cross-tabulation: a table that can be used to depict the relationship between two variables.

Crucial case: a type of case study which is based on the analysis of a case which is thought to be crucial for the confirmation or disconfirmation of a theory.

Data analysis: the processing, interpretation, and analysis of findings.

Data collection: how information is gathered.

Deduction: reasoning from a general or logical proposition to a specific or particular outcome.

Deductive-nomological model: an explanatory model, also known as the 'covering law model', which holds that explanations of individual events or actions are derived from laws that express universal empirical associations.

Dependent variable: refers to the outcome or phenomenon we are trying to explain. Often denoted as Y.

Deviant case: a type of case study which is based on the analysis of a case which is known to deviate from established generalizations and does not fit the existing theory.

Discrete: a discrete variable can only take on certain fixed values within its range and cannot be subdivided.

Dispersion: refers to the extent to which data values are clustered together or spread out. See also **standard deviation.**

Discourse analysis: a qualitative type of analysis that explores the ways in which discourses give legitimacy and meaning to social practices and institutions.

Double-barrelled question: a question that is really two questions in one.

Dummy variable: a dichotomous variable which can take one of two values (0 or 1).

Ecological fallacy: the assumption that relationships between variables at the aggregate level imply the same relationships at the individual level.

Ecological validity: the extent to which the conditions simulated in the laboratory reflect real-life conditions.

Empirical: refers to things that can be experienced through the five senses (of seeing, hearing, touching, etc.). Empirical research means research based on finding things out by experience or the sense organs: hearing, seeing new primary data (newspaper items or people's words in interviews or questionnaires).

Empiricism: the view that knowledge of the world is limited to what can be observed. Concepts apply to or derive from an experience. Empiricism believes that all knowledge originates in empirical observation.

Epistemology: a branch of philosophy which studies the nature, sources, and limits of knowledge.

Equivalence of meaning: has to do with whether the concept under investigation means the same thing to people in different contexts.

Experimental group: subjects in the experimental group do receive the intervention.

Explanatory variable: See **independent variable.**

Exploratory research: a type of research typically performed when the researcher does not have a hypothesis or does not have specific assumptions concerning the problem or question.

External validity: the extent to which findings can be generalized to other similar situations.

Falsifiability: a concept in philosophy of science, popularized by Karl Popper, that for a proposition to be scientific, it must be logically possible to show, through observation or experiment, that it is false.

Face validity: an approach used for assessing the validity of a measure which is based on whether or not the measure intuitively seems like a good measure of the concept.

Faulty presupposition: see **presuming questions**.

Field: the place where research is carried out.

Field experiments: experiments which take place in real-world settings.

Fieldnotes: how the ethnographer records the data that they observe in the field.

Filter: a filter question is used in surveys to filter out respondents for whom more detailed questions may not apply and who therefore should not be asked.

Focus group: a form of group interview organized to address a specific phenomenon of interest, a specific theme or topic, involving a group of people selected because they are related to, have experience of, or beliefs about the topic or theme in question.

Foreshadowed problems: refers to the questions or issues that the researcher intends to explore during their fieldwork.

Frequency distribution: displays the number of times each value of a variable occurs in a given sample.

Fuzzy set: refers to multi-value variables that are used in qualitative comparative analysis. In a fuzzy set analysis, a case can be either fully in or fully out of a particular set, or somewhere in between.

Gatekeeper: someone who controls access to closed settings.

Going native: when the researcher loses objective distance from the people that they are studying.

Grand theory: an attempt to construct a total theoretical system covering all aspects of social life, rather than an explanation of particular instances, societies, or phenomena.

Grounded theory: an inductive research strategy in which theory is produced through, and *grounded* in, data.

Histogram: a way of graphically displaying data for interval or continuous data.

Historicism: the idea that a society is impelled along a pre-determined route by historical laws which cannot be resisted.

Holism: the claim that the whole of something is distinct from and not directly explicable in terms of its parts. Social facts have to have social causes that are irreducible to facts about individuals.

Hypothesis: a proposition put forward for empirical testing.

Hypothetico-deductive method: this 'is an application of two operations: the formation of *hypotheses* and the *deduction* of consequences from them in order to arrive at beliefs which—although they are hypothetical— are well supported, through the way their deductive consequences fit in with our experiences and with our other well-supported beliefs (Føllesdal 1994: 234).

Independent variable: refers to a factor we think may influence or cause the dependent variable. Often denoted as X.

Indicator: empirical measure of an abstract concept.

Individualism: the claim that the basic units of society are individuals. Social phenomena are the combined results of individual actions.

Induction: reasoning from particular facts or observations to a general conclusion.

Interaction effect: when the impact of one independent variable on the dependent variable varies according to the level of another independent variable.

Intercept: the point at which the line of best fit crosses the y-axis.

Inference: the process of drawing logical conclusions on the basis of premises assumed to be true.

Informants: refers to the people who are being studied. Although this sounds a bit conspiratorial, the term implies something more than just respondent, since whether unwittingly or not informants provide information about the topic under study.

Informed consent: the principle that researchers must obtain consent to carry out research from the people they are studying.

Intentionalism: the methodological precept that explanation of social phenomena must give an account of the intentional states—the aims, beliefs, attitudes, and expectations—that motivate individual action.

Intercoder reliability: the degree of coding consistency between two or more coders.

Internal validity: has to do with whether or not we are confident that a causal relationship really exists between two variables.

Interpretivism: maintains that knowledge of the social world cannot be gained by testing hypotheses and developing 'science'; and that interpretation should be the basis of inquiry.

Interquartile range: refers to the range of values of a variable within the middle 50% of the distribution.

Interval: a variable where the values of the variable can be rank ordered, and the differences between two values are important and can be quantified and directly compared.

Intervening variable: a variable that helps to explain or account for the relationship between two other variables.

Intervention: intervention in the data-gathering process occurs when the researcher manipulates or alters a variable of causal interest (such as what the subject is exposed to).

Interviewer effects: are said to happen in survey research when respondents answer identical questions in different ways depending upon the characteristics or identity of the person who asked them.

Interviews: a method of data collection in which a researcher asks questions of participants.

Interview schedule: a list of questions to be asked of all interviewees.

Item non-response: occurs in survey research when the respondent does not provide a valid answer to a particular question.

Key informant: an informant that the ethnographer comes to rely upon as a valuable source of information and knowledge.

Laboratory experiments: experiments conducted in a facility that provides controlled conditions.

Large-N: study of a large number of cases through statistical analysis.

Latent content: meanings that do not reside on the surface of communication and are therefore not easily observable.

Law: a statement of relationship (e.g. 'A leads to B'), which is accepted as having been universally verified by observation.

Leading question: a question that encourages a specific response.

Level of measurement: refers to how a variable is measured, and how the different values of the variable relate to each other. See also **nominal, ordinal, interval.**

Line graph: a way of graphically displaying data for repeated measures of the same variable over time.

Line of best fit: a straight line representing the best linear relationship between two variables. See also **regression line.**

listserv: a list management tool consisting of a set of email addresses for a group in which the sender can send one email and it will reach a variety of people.

Logical positivism: a movement that sought to apply logic and mathematics to the discovery of empirically verifiable causal laws.

Log odds ratios: a statistical transformation of the odds ratios.

Longitudinal designs: explore changes or discern trends over time.

Manifest content: meanings that reside on the surface of communication and are therefore easily observable.

Mean: a measure of central tendency that is computed by adding the values for all the cases and dividing by the number of cases.

Measurement error: occurs when, for a variety of reasons, a respondent's answer to a question does not represent their true answer.

Median: a measure of central tendency that refers to the middle value in a rank-ordered set of cases.

Methodological holism: the claim that properties of a system as a whole cannot be deduced by the properties of its components alone. The system as a whole determines how the parts behave.

Methodological individualism: the methodological precept that explanations of social phenomena— classes, power, nations, or other social phenomena—must be reducible to the characteristics of individuals.

Methodology: the principles and procedures of inquiry used by researchers in a particular discipline.

Missing data: where a variable does not have a valid value the data is said to be missing.

Mode: a measure of central tendency that refers to the most common value of a variable.

Model specification: refers to the way in which a hypothesis is tested and what variables are included in the analysis.

Most Different Systems Design: method of comparison based on analysing cases which are very different from each other with respect to theoretically relevant independent variables.

Most Similar Systems Design: method of comparison based on analysing cases which are very similar to each other with respect to theoretically relevant independent variables.

Multicolinearity: occurs in multiple regression when two independent variables are highly correlated with each other, making it difficult to disentangle the independent impact of either variable.

Multivariate analysis: analysis of the relationship between three or more variables.

N: denotes the number of cases in the analysis. Also referred to as sample size.

Natural experiments: experiments in conditions which occur naturally, in so far as the researcher is not active in the data-gathering process.

Naturalism: the view that the social and behavioural sciences should have the same structure and logical characteristics as the natural sciences; that the primary goal of the social sciences—like that of the natural sciences—is to explain and predict social phenomena by means of laws; and that only that which exists can, at least in principle, be investigated scientifically (contrary to 'scientific realism'—see below).

Nominal: a variable where the values or categories of the variable cannot be ranked or the differences between the categories quantified.

Non-probability sampling: refers to sampling methods which do not use random selection.

Non-response bias: is introduced into a sample when people who do not complete the survey are systematically different in some respect from those people who do answer.

Normal distribution: is a probability distribution. The graph of the distribution is symmetrical and bell shaped. Sometimes known as the bell curve.

Normative theory: theory concerned with questions about what is right and wrong, desirable or undesirable, just or unjust in society.

Null hypothesis: that in the population there is no association between two variables.

Objective: objectivity means striving as far as possible to reduce or eliminate bias in the conduct of research.

Odds: refers to the likelihood of one outcome occurring compared to the likelihood of an alternative outcome occurring.

Odds ratios: compare the odds of an event occurring in one group compared with another. An odds ratio of 1 indicates that the odds of a particular outcome are equal in both groups.

Omitted variable bias: occurs when the causal significance of variables is exaggerated because important factors have been omitted from the analysis and not taken into account.

Ontology: the study of what exists and the nature of what exists.

Open-ended question: a question where respondents are free to give their own answer and no response alternatives are provided.

Open question: a question employed in a structured interview or questionnaire which allows respondents to respond by expressing themselves in an open-ended, detailed manner.

Open setting: research settings with public access which do not require permission to enter.

Operationalization: process of turning abstract ideas into empirical indicators.

Ordinal: a variable where the values or categories of the variable can be ranked, but the differences between the categories cannot be quantified or directly compared.

Outlier: refers to a value that is markedly different to the other values in the distribution.

Overt research: when the researcher reveals his or her identity to the informants.

Partial regression coefficients: a measure of the relationship between two variables controlling for the effect of other variables.

Participant observation: type of fieldwork in which the researcher becomes a regular participant in the day-to-day activities of the people whom they are studying.

Population: refers to the collection of units from which the sample is drawn and to which findings can be generalized.

Positivism: the view that advocates pursuing knowledge of the social world through the discovery of universal laws and the falsification of theories. Positivists treat the social world *as if* it were the world of *natural phenomena*. They assume that all that we know of the world is given to us in experience. Experience concerns events and happenings. Positivists systematically investigate these events and happenings so as to reveal their underlying regularities.

Presuming questions: is a survey question which assumes something that is not necessarily true.

Process tracing: a method of within-case analysis to evaluate causal processes.

Proposition: a statement which links two or more variables.

Purposive sampling: is a non-probability sampling method which involves investigators using their own 'expert' judgement to select respondents whom they consider to be typical or representative of the population of interest.

Qualitative: research that tends to be based on the discursive analysis of more loosely coded information for just a few cases.

Quantitative: research that tends to be based on the statistical analysis of carefully coded information for many cases or observations.

Questionnaire: pre-designed lists of closed questions designed to collect data from a large sample of respondents and to be completed by respondents themselves.

Questionnaire design: the way in which the survey questions are constructed and put together.

Question order effects: occurs when the order in which questions are asked influences the answers that are given to them.

Question wording effects: occurs in survey research when slight variations in the way in which questions are worded can have a significant impact on how people respond.

Quota sampling: is a non-probability sampling method which involves investigators selecting a certain number or quota of respondents to interview, according to the personal characteristics of the respondent, such as their age group, sex, and income group.

Random assignment: the experimental method for deciding which subject goes in which group.

Random digit dialling: is a sampling method for selecting people to take part in telephone surveys by generating telephone numbers at random.

Random sample: sampling method in which all units in the sampling frame have a known non-zero probability of being selected.

Range: the range of scores is the value of the smallest score subtracted from the largest score.

Reactivity: has to do with whether subjects are conscious of being studied and alter their behaviour accordingly.

Recall problems: refers to error in survey research to do with memory failure, where respondents cannot remember whether or not they have done something or when they did it.

Regression: a statistical technique for describing the relationship between two or more variables where the dependent variable is interval-level.

Regression coefficient: see **slope coefficient**.

Regression line: see **line of best fit**.

Replicability: the replicability of a study refers to whether or not it can be carried out in more or less the same way with a fresh group of subjects in another sample at a different point in time to check the validity and reliability of research.

Research design: a logical structure of inquiry that specifies the sort of test or evidence that will convincingly confirm or disconfirm a hypothesis.

Reliability: the 'repeatability' or 'consistency' of research findings.

Response rate: the response rate of a survey refers to the percentage of people who completed the survey out of the total number of people selected for the survey.

Response variable: see **dependent variable**.

Sample: refers to the cases which have been selected for analysis. A sample is a smaller subset of the population of interest. The way in which a sample is drawn affects the extent to which the sample can be used to make valid inferences about the population of interest.

Sampling distribution: refers to the distribution of possible values for a statistic that we would expect to get if we drew repeated samples from a population.

Sampling error: the extent to which the sample estimate differs from the true population value.

Sampling frame: the list of units in the population from which the sample will be drawn.

Sampling variation: the extent to which the value of a variable varies in samples taken from the same population.

Scientific realism: the view that scientific research is based, not only on evidence that is visible in the world, but on unobservable facts, objects, or properties that exist independently of our direct knowledge of them, and that the goal of scientific inquiry is to describe and explain both observable and unobservable aspects of the world.

Selection bias: occurs when our findings are not very reliable and may owe more to the cases we have selected than any real relationship between the variables we are examining.

Simple random sampling: is a probability sampling method where each member of the population has the same chance of being selected.

Single-N: in-depth study of a single case.

Slope coefficient: derived from the line of best fit. Describes the amount the Y variable increases for a one-unit increase in the X variable. Also called the b coefficient or the regression coefficient.

Small-N: in-depth study of a small number of cases.

Snowball sampling: is a non-probability sampling method where respondents who have already taken part in the survey put forward their friends or acquaintances to also take part in the study.

Social desirability bias: occurs when a respondent provides an answer to a question which they think will present them in a good light, rather than one which reflects their true feelings.

Sparse categories: occurs when a table cell only contains a few cases. Can produce unstable results.

Speech act theory: an approach to the explanation of language premised on the idea that language is a medium orientated towards action and function.

Spurious association: occurs when an apparent association between two variables is caused by an unmeasured third variable. Spurious associations are not causal.

Standard deviation: a measure of dispersion of data points around the mean.

Standard error: the standard deviation of the sampling distribution.

Structuralism: an approach that privileges the role of structures over that of agency in explanations of social phenomena.

Structurationism: the view that agents and structures are not ontologically distinct entities; they co-exist and co-determine each other.

Structured interviews: these consist of a standardized set of closed and shorter or simpler questions that are asked in a standardized manner and sequence.

Subject: refers to the participant in the study.

Surveys: a method of data collection whose goal is to gain specific information about either a specific group or a representative sample of a particular group, and that includes at least one question which is either open-ended or close-ended and employs an oral or written method for asking these questions.

Tails: the tails of a distribution refer to those values which lie at the extreme ends of the distribution.

Telescoping: occurs in survey research when respondents think that things that happened a long time ago happened more recently than they really did.

Theories of the middle-range: theories that, while they may involve abstractions, are constructed with reference to phenomena that are observable.

Theory: a proposition which has been elaborated and/or withstood repeated testing.

Thick description: combines description and interpretation, and attempts to describe the meaning of an event and the motivations of the people involved.

Treatment: see **intervention**.

Truth table: is used in QCA to display all the logical possible combinations of conditions and the outcome associated with each combination.

T test: a statistical test used to test the null hypothesis that there is no relationship between two variables.

Type I error: is said to occur when we reject a null hypothesis that is actually true.

Type II error: is said to occur when we fail to reject a null hypothesis that is actually false.

Unit of analysis: refers to the entity that you are studying (such as individuals or countries).

Univariate statistics: refer to statistical measures used to summarize some characteristic of a single variable.

Unstructured interviews: these use open, and perhaps lengthier and more complex questions that might vary in the way and order in which they are asked.

Validity: whether a question measures the concept that it is supposed to measure.

Variable: a property of an object that can take on different values.

Variance: refers to the average amount of variability (spread) of a set of data.

Verifiability: the principle that a proposition can be true either by definition, or by empirical verification.

Volunteer sample: is a self-selecting sample.

Weighting the data: is a technique that is often used in survey research, which corrects for non-response or unequal selection probabilities to try to make the sample more representative of the population.

Index